T0332497

Cases on Progressions and Challenges in ICT Utilization for Citizen-Centric Governance

Hakikur Rahman
SchoolNet Foundation, Bangladesh

Information Science
REFERENCE

Managing Director:	Lindsay Johnston
Editorial Director:	Joel Gamon
Book Production Manager:	Jennifer Romanchak
Publishing Systems Analyst:	Adrienne Freeland
Assistant Acquisitions Editor:	Kayla Wolfe
Typesetter:	Nicole Sparano
Cover Design:	Nick Newcomer

Published in the United States of America by
  Information Science Reference (an imprint of IGI Global)
  701 E. Chocolate Avenue
  Hershey PA 17033
  Tel: 717-533-8845
  Fax: 717-533-8661
  E-mail: cust@igi-global.com
  Web site: http://www.igi-global.com

Library of Congress Cataloging-in-Publication Data

Cases on progressions and challenges in ICT utilization for citizen-centric governance / Hakikur Rahman, editor.
     p. cm.
  Includes bibliographical references and index.
  Summary: "This book is a collection of case studies on the advancements and challenges of information technology in the involvements of citizens with the government"--Provided by publisher.
  ISBN 978-1-4666-2071-1 (hardcover) -- ISBN 978-1-4666-2072-8 (ebook) -- ISBN 978-1-4666-2073-5 (print & perpetual access) 1. Internet in public administration--Case studies. 2. Public administration--Citizen participation--Technological innovations--Case studies. I. Rahman, Hakikur, 1957-
  JF1525.A8C366 2012
  352.3'802854678--dc23
                                        2012019884

British Cataloguing in Publication Data
A Cataloguing in Publication record for this book is available from the British Library.

The views expressed in this book are those of the authors, but not necessarily of the publisher.

Table of Contents

Detailed Table of Contents

Chapter 1

Nicholas Maynard, RAND Corporation, USA

A country's national technology strategies can be an important contributor to economic development through its support of technology adoption and by advancing the national technology capacity. The development of a domestic information and communications technology (ICT) sector within a developing country requires the creation of specialized institutions that carefully coordinate their initiatives with the private sector. This case study research of Thai and Malaysian science and technology (S&T) institutions shows that this institutional and policy reform process is directly influenced by regional activities, as countries seek to match their regional peers for technology development. This effort to support ICT utilization requires governments to rapidly alter their policy goals and initiatives in response to shifts in technologies, global market demand, international investment, and local workforce capabilities.

Chapter 2

Sandeep Bhaskar, Temple University, USA

This chapter presents evidence of using information and communication technologies (ICTs) towards the goal of sustainable community development. It argues that the biggest impediment to the growth of communities in the developing world is a lack of information and a fair incentive system, both of which can be addressed through ICTs. A three pronged action plan comprising of a development strategy, an information strategy, and a technology strategy is proposed towards this effect. The paper also showcases how a for-profit business, ITC Limited, transformed the face of agriculture in some parts of India, and how this model can be replicated in other parts of the world. It concludes with a description of the agricultural sector in Bangladesh and show how lessons drawn from the Indian case can be applied to Bangladesh and other developing countries.

Governments the world over are increasingly implementing e-government systems as part of public sector reforms to enhance good governance and service delivery. This chapter reviews successful e-government projects in South Africa. E-governance is seen as a panacea to country's several challenges of service delivery, poverty, inequality, democracy, respect for human rights, and corruption. The South African government understands the urgency of addressing poverty and improving service delivery to majority of citizens who were marginalized during white majority rule. Most of South Africa's black majority, for example, lives in poverty compared to their white counterparts. To address these imbalances projects are guided by the principle of public service for all under the brand Batho Pele (meaning people first). Some e-government projects in South Africa have borne fruits; they empowered people to overcome development obstacles, have helped fight poverty and uplift the socio-economic and living standards of citizens. The challenges facing the e-government projects include high costs of broadband access, diversity of languages that need to be converted to the language of the Internet, red tape and bureaucratic system, as well as financial sustainability and the use of top down design approaches in projects with little or no initial user involvement.

The world has seen the unprecedented development of information and communications technologies (ICTs) and adoption of their diversified methods in elevating all forms of human endeavors. Even a few years back, it was fashionable to speak about the global village. In recent years, many countries have taken leading role in implementing innovative ICT products to accelerate their national developments, enhance their livelihoods, strengthened their national economies and improve their governance systems. This has been observed that those countries could reap the most benefits out of ICT strategies, which could penetrate at the lowest tier of their governance system. In this context, human development is an element of importance. This research emphasizes that cumulative human development through community approach would be the next level of knowledge dynamics across the world. It also argues that as much the country provides thrust on capacity development initiatives at the grass roots, it has more opportunity to reach at greater context of governance system. This chapter would like to focus on two cases, which penetrated the grass roots reaching out to the community level, act as catalyst to strengthen their national economy and government. Some features and perspectives of e-Sri Lanka and e-Korea are being discussed here to provide insight into these cases, so that researchers in developing and transitional economies could gain knowledge.

E-governance systems in India have witnessed prolific advancement over the years. India has strategically adopted e-governance as a part of its policy. In recent times each state has its own e-governance plan to deliver services as planned. National policy also aims to provide formalized services across the nation while recognizing the importance of state specific services. This approach includes various mission mode projects under national e-governance plan (NeGP). Manifestation of such approach has resulted in 100,000 common service centers (CSC) in rural areas. It is expected that rural citizens would find them useful and it may contribute for effective governance. In this chapter it is argued that such an initiative would be successful if rural citizens find these CSCs useful for their livelihood security. Various dimensions of this phenomenon are also examined through some cases in this chapter to understand their contributions to successful CSCs in India.

Chapter 6

Wide use of information technologies has lead governments across the globe to adopt the new nature of governance system for their citizens, businesses and within the government structure. Governance systems nowadays do not only enclave simply the dissemination of government regulations and directives to their stakeholders, but also target to improve their knowledge and capacity. At the threshold, by putting the information technologies as a thrust sector for many years and with well adopted e-governance framework, several countries have achieved remarkable success. However, many of them despite diversified efforts could not put into the track mainstreaming electronic format of the governance system. This research feel that to improve the governance system, inclusion of grass roots participants are necessary and nurturing of community practices targeting to raise their knowledge and skills through an adoptive e-governance framework would enhance the process. As a case study, it put forwards a case from UNDP, including hints on similar other cases.

This case describes field research investigations that were conducted in Tanzania from June 2008 to June 2009 to examine access to, and use of cell phones by women residing in rural villages and in a nearby urban center. Rural villages were considered critical in this study as key players in the wellbeing of traditional rural families.

Chapter 8

O. I. Oladele, North-West University, South Africa

This paper examines the applications of information communication technologies in agro-based livelihoods in Nigeria. A multipurpose community information access point was established at a pilot level in Ago-Are, Oyo State, Nigeria. The center equipped with basic ICT infrastructures including Internet connectivity made available through a VSAT, provided timely solutions to the basic problems of farmers' lack of information on agriculture, lack of access to inputs and output markets, and lack of access to some basic but relatively expensive equipment. The services include the Answering Farmer's Needs-a private-public collaborative project involving several organizations. There is also the Fantsuam Foundation, a not-for-profit organization that works with farmers in rural communities in Northern Nigeria with an on-going micro-credit project aimed at alleviating poverty among rural women. The paper highlights the synergistic use and challenges for each of these projects and proffers suggestions for the adoption and adaptation in different parts of the world.

Chapter 9

Tutaleni I. Asino, Penn State University, USA
Hilary Wilder, William Paterson University, USA
Sharmila Pixy Ferris, William Paterson University, USA

Namibia was under colonizing and apartheid rule for more than a century. In 1990, the country declared its independence, and since that time, great strides have been made in linking its rural communities into a national communications Grid that was previously inaccessible to them, often leapfrogging traditional landline telephone technologies with universal cell phone service. In addition, one newspaper, The Namibian, has been innovatively using newer communications technologies to maintain its historic role of nation-building. This chapter showcases how SMS via cell phone and a traditional national newspaper has a sense of national identity that transcends geographic distances and a legacy of economic/political barriers. The cell phone messages made it possible for the rural communities who have been left out of discussion relating to issues of development to be included. Although the study unveiled 11% of their participation as opposed to 30% of the rural populace, this is a step forward bearing in mind that the rural areas have a history of being passively involved in everything that is being done. They have been, and continue to some great extent to be content to receive decisions made for them by outsiders including political leaders. Mobile phones have come as empowerment for them. Like the old slogan, "information is power," this chapter illustrates that the lives of some rural area dwellers have improved a result of a technological gadget, the mobile phone.

The rural communities in South Korea have faced serious challenges as the country has gradually opened the agricultural market and extended the conclusion of Free Trade Agreement with more and more countries. Moreover, due to the national socio-economic and political structures, South Korea has been undergoing the technological imbalance between rural and urban areas. In order to cope with these vital social challenges, the South Korean government has exerted considerable investment and effort in establishing ICT knowledge and skills as well as infrastructure in rural areas. Thus, conceptualizing ICT in the context of adult education, this chapter addresses three ICT-supported adult education programs oriented toward developing ICT skills and competencies of people in agricultural areas of South Korea. The South Korean cases of agricultural ICT education represent the vast and concentrated national efforts in integrating ICT across rural areas in this fast changing global situation.

In Botswana the use of Information and Communication Technology (ICT) smart switch card system, an offshoot of the Universal Electronic Payment System (UEPS), was recently introduced. It is a worldwide communication device that is digital in providing information to the users. In Botswana, it serves to administer food and basic needs offered to the vulnerable people as one of the pillars of development in terms of catering for the needy. Furthermore, it is used to empower orphans, destitute, and HIV/AIDS home-based patients in the Social Safety Nets programs, replacing all the other strategies that were used previously. The previous program was a manual system whereby beneficiaries were getting their social grants through lining up at their district councils' office doorstep for attendants to use the roll call. The old system demanded commercial businesses to tender for supply of items to the vulnerable population, but it posed some challenges and frustrations to beneficiaries and the government.

The use of Information Communication Technologies (ICTs) in agriculture is fundamental to rural development especially in the 21st century (Rashid, et al., 2007). This chapter thus illustrates the use of an indigenous technology using the case of Madila production in a Dairy House Farm at Molapowabojang, a rural village in

Southern District of Botswana. The Dairy House Farm started production in 2002 with the aim of producing both fresh and sour or curdled milk (Madila). Although traditionally madila was for subsistence family consumption, the use of community-compatible ICT, namely, sieve like plastic bag, natural sun beam and cooling system made from a wooden shelter, combined with modern machines such as milking machines, milk tubes attached to the cow's udder have enabled the Dintwa family to convert the practice into commercial industry.

Chapter 13

Francesco Molinari, ALTEC S.A., Greece
Christopher Wills, Kingston University, UK
Adamantios Koumpis, ALTEC S.A., Greece
Vasiliki Moumtzi, ALTEC S.A., Greece

This chapter describes experiences acquired during the research work conducted as part of the European Project Tell Me (www.tellmeproject.eu). The project envisaged to support the pan-European creation of Living Labs as new forms of cooperation between government, enterprises, citizens and academia for a successful transfer of e-Government, e-Democracy and e-Services state-of-the art applications, solutions, know-how and best practices. In this chapter the authors explore the potential of providing an existing system (DEMOS) allowing moderated and goal-oriented discourses between citizens and policy makers to become parts of open-ended ventures on the creation of collaborative networks for Electronic Democracy. This work would also recommend that this form of support network elevates e-Democracy of a country and thus improves e-governance systems at the grass roots.

Chapter 14

Raija Järvinen, Aalto University School of Economics, Finland
Jarno Salonen, VTT Technical Research Centre of Finland, Finland
Aki Ahonen, OP-Pohjola Group, Finland
Jouni Kivistö-Rahnasto, Tampere University of Technology, Finland

This case study covers two R&D projects called eInsurance 1 and eInsurance 2, which are concerned with electronic insurance. This case emphasizes project organization, its activities and roles, together with the results of the projects. In addition, the structure and innovation level of the projects are analyzed and the challenges involved in launching the concepts into insurance markets are presented. The most important outcomes of the projects are novel service concepts, and valuable information of consumer expectations that corporate partners utilized in their R&D activities. For research partners, the projects brought ideas, how to organize future projects in new ways, and how to combine academic and business expertise successfully.

Chapter 15

Roman Boutellier, ETH Zurich, Switzerland

Mareike Heinzen, ETH Zurich, Switzerland

Marta Raus, ETH Zurich, Switzerland

This chapter explores the concept of paradigms, science, and technology in the context of information technology (IT). Therefore, the linear model of Francis Bacon and Thomas Kuhn's notion of scientific paradigms are reviewed. This review reveals that the linear model has to be advanced, and supports the adoption of Kuhnian ideas from science to technology. As IT paradigms transform business processes, a five-level concept is introduced for deriving managerial implications and guidelines. Within the case of e-customs, a European-funded project tries to ease border security and control by adopting a common standardized e-customs solution across the public sector in Europe. The rise of the IT paradigm within customs and its effect on business operations will be explained. This chapter contributes to the research in diffusion and adoption of innovation using science progress and the interplay of science and technology as dominant concepts.

Chapter 16

Elena Bianchini, "lAma Mater Studiorum," University of Bologna, Italy

Sandra Sicurella, "lAma Mater Studiorum," University of Bologna, Italy

The advent of the GIS technology has revolutionized the traditional field of information and cartographic production. The GIS, indeed, enables the management of much more numerous and more complex data and it is able to overcome the static and the traditional two-dimensional cartography. The Geographic Information Systems (GIS), that is used in various fields and disciplines, represent, also, in the university research, a valuable tool for investigation. In criminology, in particular, it has facilitated, regarding the city of Bologna, on the one hand, a kind of crime mapping on the nature of the so called "petty crimes" within the jurisdiction of the criminal Justice of the Peace, and the creation of a city's map on which have been identified support centers for victims operating in them. The use of GIS software is the basis in order to realize and put into practice not only operational measures designed to combat and to prevent crime, but it is also of help to social control measures, to public policy and to security. To the end of ensuring public safety, nowadays, it is essential, to have a clear, spatial and graphics representation, of the high concentrations of crime areas and of the degraded ones, in which there is a greater likelihood that some type of crime is committed.

Santhanamery Thominathan, Universiti Teknologi MARA Malaysia, Malaysia
Ramayah Thurasamy, Universiti Sains Malaysia, Malaysia

Information Communication Technology (ICT) has played an important role in today's global economy. Many countries have gained successful growth due to the implementation of ICT. In Malaysia, increased utilization of ICT has contributed significantly to the total factor productivity. One of the main contributing factors is the e-commerce and Internet based services. Therefore, this case study aims to examine the contribution of the newly introduced E-government application, namely E-filing system. E-filing system is a newly developed online tax submission services offered by the government to the tax payers in the country where they are able to easily, quickly and safely file their tax returns. The primary discussion in this case study concerns Malaysia's ICT revolution, followed by the introduction of E-Filing system, the challenges and barriers faced by the government, and the chapter concludes with future trends in the implementation of this system.

Dieter Fink, Edith Cowan University, Australia

The aim of this case study is first, to determine the extent to which web 2.0 can be the technology that would enable a strong relationship between government and its citizens to develop in managing road safety and second, to examine the endeavours of the WA Office of Road Safety (ORS) in fostering the relationship. It shows that in ORS' road safety strategy for 2008-2020, community engagement is strongly advocated for the successful development and execution of its road safety plan but the potential of web 2.0 approaches in achieving it is not recognised. This would involve the use of blogs and RSS as suitable push strategies to get road safety information to the public. Online civic engagement would harness collective intelligence ('the wisdom of crowds') and, by enabling the public to annotate information on wikis, layers of value could be added so that the public become co-developers of road safety strategy and policy. The case identifies three major challenges confronting the ORS to become Road Safety 2.0 ready: how to gain the publics' attention in competition with other government agencies, how to respond internally to online citizen engagement, and how to manage governmental politics.

Sherif Kamel, The American University in Cairo, Egypt

Over the last 20 years, the international postal sector has changed drastically due to several forces, including globalization, changing technology, greater demands for efficient services and market liberalization. For Egypt, keeping up with the changing atmosphere in the global market meant investing in information and communication technology. The Ministry of Communication and Information Technology (MCIT), as part of its efforts to transforming government performance using ICT, chose the Egyptian National Post Organization (ENPO) as a model for ICT integrated government portal. The selection was due to ENPO's extensive network, the public's confidence and its trust in the organization. The case of ENPO, capitalizing on public-private partnership models, proved successful when reflecting ICT deployment for organizational transformation within the context of an emerging economy. In addition to its importance in providing eGovernment services to citizens, ENPO is evolving as a critical medium for effectively developing Egypt's eCommerce. This case study takes an in-depth look at how ICT has improved the quality and range of services offered by ENPO, while asserting the magnitude of its impact on the country's emergence as a competitor in today's global postal market.

Chapter 20

The visually-impaired are in a distinctive disadvantage when using computer screens based on visual presentation of data. Their situation becomes increasingly critical, as most society services, including issues such as e-Commerce, e Business, e-Health, and e-Government go on-line. Yet modern technologies can too offer solutions to their problems, both at hardware and software level, and often with reasonable cost. Effective ICT can open up new communication channels and functionalities for say totally blind people, which would not have been available for them otherwise. General sensitivity for this issue, and especially, sensitivity among designers of governmental e-services must be developed. E-Government is an especially demanding activity area as it comes to all sorts of imparities (not just vision impairment), as governmental services are often in a monopoly service delivery situation: citizen have to use them, and there is often no other alternative. The issue binds it to the wider discussion on digital divide, where vision impairment is one cause for digital divide, and often very devastating, especially if still combined with other sources of digital divide.

Preface

PREAMBLE

One may need to understand in detail about the format of the government and form of governance to make it accessible to the citizen. With the advent of the information and communication technologies (ICTs), this has made it possible to reach the stakeholders through various tools and techniques. Utilizing effective methods, models, and frameworks, government around the world has implemented various forms of government models based on electronically depended communication tools, in a way popularly known as the electronic government or e-government. Along the route to enhanced and effective governance, ICT dependency has increased the awareness, availability, and accessibility to the end user, which can be seen as electronic governance or e-governance.

Electronic government is habitually heralded as the pioneering way forward for the public sector in both developed and developing countries. There are success cases around the globe on how this form of government leads to increased rates of development and allows for greater democracy, and how it can be successfully implemented in countries across the world (Krishna and Walshan, 2005; Bhatnagar, 2002).

In simple terms, e-government has been seen as "the use of information technology to support government operations, engage citizens, and provide government services." (Center for Technology in Government, 2012). Broadly defined, "e-government can include virtually all information and communication technology (ICT) platforms and applications in use by the public sector." (UN, 2002:8).

Another definition of e-government was presented by United Nation's website referring e-government as the use of ICTs, such as Wide Area Networks, the Internet, and mobile computing, by government agencies (Almarabeh and AbuAli, 2010). While, OECD recorded e-government as the use of ICTs, especially the Internet as a tool to accomplish better government (OECD, 2003: 23).

According to the World Bank website (2012), "E-Government refers to the use by government agencies of information technologies (such as Wide Area Networks, the Internet, and mobile computing) that have the ability to transform relations with citizens, businesses, and other arms of government. These technologies can serve a variety of different ends: better delivery of government services to citizens, improved interactions with business and industry, citizen empowerment through access to information, or more efficient government management. The resulting benefits can be less corruption, increased transparency, greater convenience, revenue growth, and/or cost reductions."

Given the aforementioned definitions, it is apparent that e-government is not simply the computerization of a government system, but credibility in the ability of technology to achieve high levels of improvement in various areas of government, thus transforming the nature of policies and politics, including the relations between governments and citizens (Dada, 2006).

Furthermore, following those observations and definitions, one can refer e-government as the delivery of national, state/regional, or local government information and services via the web based Internet, or intranet, or other digital mediated means to citizens, businesses, civil societies, non-governmental agencies or other governmental agencies. E-government can be seen as a one-stop Internet based gateway to major government services. With the progressions of ICTs, e-government turns to facilitate the provision of providing relevant government information in electronic form in a timely manner; offer better service delivery with improved quality; empower the grass roots population of the society or people at large through ease of access to information without any bureaucracy or restriction; improve the productivity, efficiency and cost savings in doing business with suppliers and customers of government; improve the relationships among the stakeholders, and foremost actively participate in public policy decision-making and democratic processes (Fang, 2002; Palvia and Sharma, 2006; Rahman, 2010; 2011) While definitions of e-government may vary widely, there is a common theme in terms of the utilization. E-government entails utilization of ICTs, and especially the Internet, to improve the delivery of government services to its stakeholders. E-government thus enables citizens to act, interact and receive services from the federal, state, division, region, district or local governments twenty four hours a day, seven days a week.

As mentioned above, one of the most important and prerequisite aspect of e-government is to bring citizens and businesses closer to their governments thus breaking any boundaries or barriers. This way, the government can be seen as transparent, responsive, trustworthy and accountable. Literatures outline more or less eight different potential types or models in an e-government system that is useful to define scope of e-government studies, such as interactions among Government-to-Citizen (G2C); Citizen-to-Government (C2G); Government-to-Business (G2B); Business-to-Government (B2G); Government-to-Government (G2G); Government-to-Nonprofit (G2N); Nonprofit-to-Government (N2G); and Government-to-Employee (G2E) (Fang, 2002). For sake of the progressive relationship among its stakeholders, these eight models may seem sufficient for the time being, but another emerging potential section of the society is teaming up, namely the civil society, and acting as advocate or enabler or catalyst in various government policies and legislations in relation to e-government and thus e-governance.

Towards the aspect of being citizen-centric e-government, which has been anticipated as one of the solution to improve the governance system of a country, and further "refers to the delivery of [government] information and services online via the Internet or other digital means " (West, 2000:2), and need to include opportunities for online involvement in political nation building dialogues (Mossberger, Tolbert and Stansbury, 2003). Furthermore, e-government holds pledge for enhanced delivery of many types of public services, including online transactions, and for disseminating information about the operation of the government. It can increase communication between citizens and government through e-mail and other forms of computerized communications by enabling more direct participation in government decision making processes (Thomas and Streib, 2003).

Thus, a citizen-centric e-government encompasses all government roles and activities, shaped by ICTs. Similar to the analogies to e-commerce in business, it encompasses all the domains of governance and public administration, such as the state's economic and social programs (can be termed as, e-society); its relationships with the citizen and the rule of law (can be termed as, e-democracy); its internal operations and its relationship with the international environment (can be termed as, e-governance). E-government builds on the following evolving forces: technology, management concepts and the government itself. However, it has given rise to several phenomena that are redefining the public sector environment. To reinforce the e-government at the grass roots, government structures need to be redefined as per the demand at the end users' level. Furthermore, it is observed that the following aspects of e-government have lasting impacts on public administration, such as citizen-centered service, information to be taken as a public resource, new skills and working relationships among its stakeholders, and accountability and trust (Brown, 2005).

On the other hand, E-governance refers to how managers, supervisors and facilitators utilize ICTs and the Internet to execute their functions of supervising, planning, organizing, coordinating, supporting and staffing effectively (Palvia and Sharma, 2006). E-governance, meaning 'electronic form of governance' is utilizing ICTs at all the levels of the government and the public sectors and beyond, for the purpose of enhancing overall governance (Okot-Uma, 2000; Bedi, Singh and Srivastava, 2001; Holmes, 2001). According to Keohane and Nye (2000:12), "Governance implies the processes and institutions, both formal and informal, that guide and restrain the collective activities of a group. Government is the subset that acts with authority and creates formal obligations. Governance need not necessarily be conducted exclusively by governments. Private firms, associations of firms, nongovernmental organizations (NGOs), and associations of NGOs all engage in it, often in association with governmental bodies, to create governance; sometimes without governmental authority." Evidently, this definition suggests that e-governance is not only limited to the public sector, but also implied to manage, support, facilitate and administer policies and procedures in the private sector as well (Palvia and Sharma, 2006).

E-governance is a broader term that includes transformation of the government at various levels. Firstly, it involves the transformation of the businesses of the government (e-government, as mentioned above). Secondly, it entails a transformation in the operational definitions of the principles upon which governance is founded, thus shifting towards increased participation, openness, transparency, and communication (Schiavo-Ocampo & Sundaram, 2001). Thirdly, it incorporates a transformation in the interactions between government and its (internal and external) clients, classified as government-to-citizen (G2C), government-to-business (G2B), government to its internal employee clients (G2E), government to other government institutional clients (G2G), citizen-to-citizen (C2C), and other stakeholders (Csetenyi, 2000; Stiglitz, Orszag and Orszag, 2000; Heeks, 2001). Fourthly, it accelerates the interactions among its stakeholders through effective and interactive communication channels (Rahman, 2011). Finally, it involves a transformation of the society itself, through the emergence e-societies, made up of networks of relationships like citizen-to-citizen connections, as well as relations among NGOs and other agencies, built and sustained through utilization of electronic means (Dinsdale, Chhabra & Rath-Wilson, 2002; Pablo and Pan, 2002)

In applications, e-governance comprises the utilization of ICTs to support public services, government administration, democratic processes, and relationships among citizens, civil society, the private sector, and the state. Developed over more than two decades of technology innovation and policy rejoinders, the evolution of e-governance can be examined in terms of the following interrelated objectives, such as a policy framework, enhanced public services, high-quality and cost-effective government operations, citizen engagement in democratic processes, and administrative and institutional reform (Dawes, 2008).

Moreover, included within the perception of e-governance is an emerging conception, such as e-democracy, which deals with how the citizen interacts with the government and influence the legislative or public sector process. It strives to engage the citizen with governments and their legislatures through the use of the new ICTs. It is this new dynamic that is developing between the citizen and the government that concurrent researches explore, and evaluate what impact, if any, the new ICTs are having on citizen participation in the government decision-making processes (Riley, 2003).

E-governance differs from e-government in many aspects. The latter constitutes the way public sector institutions use technology to apply public administration principles and conduct the business of government. It is the government using new tools to enhance the delivery of its existing services (Okot-Uma, 2000). E-governance is more than just a government website on the Internet. The strategic objective of e-governance is to sustain and abridge governance for all parties; government, citizens, and businesses. The utilization of ICTs can connect all three parties and support processes and activities. In other words, in e-governance electronic means reinforce and stimulate good governance. Therefore, the objectives of e-governance are analogous to the objectives of good governance. Good governance can be seen as an exercise of economic, political, and administrative authority to better administer affairs of a country at all levels (Basu, 2004).

In order to examine the risk of implementing e-governance solutions, Basu (2004) identified the following factors as pre-requisites of a country:

- Political stability;
- Adequate legal frame work;
- Level of trust in government;
- The importance of government identity;
- Socio-economic structure;
- Government structure;
- Different levels of maturity in governance; and
- Demand at the ground.

In this aspect, an effective and citizen-centric e-governance system can be seen as the focus and centricity model, as shown in Table 1, where emphasis has been given towards achieving citizen-centric government and citizen-centric governance.

However, e-government and e-governance cannot be used interchangeably. Of the two, e-government is a narrower term, referring to the transformation of the

Table 1. Focus and centricity model (adopted from Marche, 2003)

Centricity dimension	Government/Governance dimension	
	Quadrant-1 E-government (administrative) Citizen-Centric	Quadrant-2 E-governance (policy, legislation and power) Citizen-Centric
	Quadrant-3 E-government (administrative) Organization-Centric	Quadrant-4 E-governance (policy, legislation and power) Organization-Centric

businesses of a government (processes, operations, and transactions) driven primarily by ICTs. Aiming towards a citizen-centric e-governance, the transformation could be both external (through simplified, enhanced government-client interactions via online services, no longer limited to the traditional boundary of fixed office hours and physical office space) and internal (through streamlined government administration processes for greater efficiency and effectiveness) (Backus, 2001; Dinsdale, Chhabra & Rath-Wilson, 2002). Therefore, a citizen-centric e-governance needs to focus on a defined framework blending available means of interactions from the perspective of inside or outside approaches, which has been shown in Table 2.

From the above discussions, it is evident that e-government and e-governance have emerged as specialized subject of research and to achieve their effective success, much attention need to be taken at the national level in each country of their implementation. Ranging from mere transformation of the government processes, these paradigms incorporate each and every aspect of a society, community and nation. Thus, e-government applications vary from country to country, society to society and culture to culture.

This book has tried to accommodate a few cases in this aspect illustrating e-government practices, projects and researches following a generally-applicable citizen centric focus contemplating various issues and challenges in e-government applications design, development, deployment, and dissemination. As evident from the cases, emerging with e-government, theories and practices of public administration have stepped into a new digital era. This casebook has put forward cases in relation to contemporary issues that are related to e-government in public administration, rural entrepreneurship development, grass roots human development and foremost sustainable development to promote citizen centric e-governance. The book has been divided into three sections and altogether comprised of twenty illustrated cases from around the world.

Table-2. Palvia and Sharma (2006) Framework for e-government versus e-governance (modified)

		Focus	
		Outside	*Inside*
Type of organization	Public sector- Government agencies	e-government (extranet and Internet)	e-governance (intranet)
	Private sector- SMEs, MNCs	Inter-organizational systems- (extranet and Internet)	e-governance (intranet)
	Civil society- NGOs, other agencies	Intra-and-inter-organizational- (extranet and Internet)	e-governance (intranet and Internet)

ORGANIZATION OF THE BOOK

The casebook has been divided into three sections, namely policies, strategies and grass-roots human development; entrepreneurships, collaborations and empowerment of citizens; and adoption, transformation and innovation. The first section has six chapters and it is talking about policies, strategies and grass-roots human development utilizing ICTs. Chapter 1 is a case study on the evolution of ICT institutions in Malaysia and Thailand. It refers that a country's national technology strategies can be an imperative contributor to economic development through its support of technology adoption and advancement of the national technology capacity. The development of a national ICT sector within a developing country requires the creation of specialized institutions that vigilantly coordinate their initiatives with the private sector. This case study based on research of Malaysian and Thai science and technology (S/T) institutions shows that this institutional and policy reform process is directly influenced by regional activities, as countries seek to match their regional peers for technology development. Furthermore, the research has also finds that to support ICT utilization requires governments to rapidly adjust their policy goals and initiatives in response to shifts in technologies, global market demand, international investment, and local workforce capabilities.

Chapter 2 presents evidence of using ICTs towards the goal of sustainable community development. The study argues that the biggest impediment to the growth of communities in the developing world is a lack of information and a fair incentive system, both of which can be addressed through ICTs. The case study proposed a three pronged action plan comprising of a development strategy, an information strategy, and a technology strategy. It emphasizes on solving challenges on these three strategies to promote ICT based model of development. Showcasing two cases from Bangladesh and India about the transformation in agriculture sector, it indicates about replicating this model in other parts of the world, especially in developing countries.

Illustrating e-government's role in poverty alleviation, Chapter 3 put forwards a case study of South Africa. Supporting e-governance as a panacea to country's challenges of service delivery, poverty, inequality, democracy, respect for human rights, and corruption this chapter reviews successful e-government projects in South Africa. It argues that governments across the world are increasingly implementing e-government systems as part of public sector reforms to enhance good governance and service delivery. Understanding the urgency of addressing poverty and improving service delivery to majority of citizens who were marginalized, the South African government has also taken several initiatives to eradicate poverty. As the society has been divided into segments through poverty, to address these imbalances various projects have been taken by the principle of public service for all under the brand Batho Pele (meaning people first). The case study indicates that some of the e-government projects in South Africa have borne fruits as they empowered people to overcome development obstacles, have helped fight poverty and uplift the socio-economic and living standards of citizens. It also emphasizes on challenges facing the e-government projects that include high costs of broadband access, diversity of languages, red tape and bureaucratic system, as well as financial sustainability. The case study refutes the use of top down design approaches in projects with little or no initial user involvement.

Supporting the role of ICTs in promoting e-governance and grass-roots human development, Chapter 4 talks about two cases on the capacity development initiatives in South Korea and Sri Lanka. The case study mentions that the world has seen an unprecedented development of ICTs and adoption of diversified methods of ICTs in elevating all forms of human endeavors. It further mentions that even a few years back, it was fashionable to speak about the global village. However, with the emergence of the Internet technologies, many countries have taken leading role in implementing innovative ICT products to accelerate their national developments, enhance their livelihoods, strengthened their national economies and improve their governance systems. The study supports that those countries could reap the most benefits out of ICT policies and strategies, which could penetrate at the lowest tier of their governance system. In this context, human development needs to be treated as an essential element. This research emphasizes that cumulative human development through community approach would be the next level of knowledge dynamics across the world. It also argues that as much the country provides thrust on capacity development initiatives at the grass roots, it has more opportunity to reach at greater perspective of the governance system. This chapter focuses on two cases (one from Sri Lanka, namely the e-Sri Lanka and the other one from South Korea, namely the e-Korea), which penetrated the grass roots communities acting as catalyst to strengthen their national economy and government.

Evaluating the citizen-centric service dimensions of Indian rural e-governance systems, Chapter 5 describes about various e-governance systems in India. The study mentions that, in recent years India has strategically adopted e-governance as a part of its national policy and in this consequence, each state has developed its own e-governance plan to deliver services as planned. The national policy also aims to provide formalized services across the nation while recognizing the importance of state specific localized services. Furthermore, this sort of approach includes various mission mode projects under the national e-governance plan (NeGP). The study observes that manifestation of such approach has resulted in about 100,000 common service centers (CSC) in rural areas across the country and expects that rural citizens would find them useful towards the contribution for effective governance. In this chapter it is further argued that such an initiative would be effective if rural citizens find these CSCs useful for their livelihood improvement.

Chapter 6 discusses about community practices to improve e-governance at the grass roots through human development. The study refers to the widespread use of ICTs that has lead governments across the globe to adopt the new nature of governance system for their citizens, businesses and within the government structure. As a case study, this chapter put forwards a pioneering program of the United Nations Development Programme (UNDP) that acted as catalytic agents of e-government and thus e-governance in many countries since 1992. Among many of the projects within this program, the sustainable development networking programme (SDNP) lead the country´s ICT sector and eventually acted as a positive contributor towards improvement in information infrastructure, policy initiations and governance issues. The study supports that the governance systems nowadays do not only enclave simply the dissemination of government regulations and directives to their stakeholders, but also target to improve their knowledge and capacity. It further mentions that, by putting the information technologies as a thrust sector for many years and with well adopted e-governance framework, several countries have achieved remarkable success. This research suggests that to improve the governance system, inclusion of grass roots participants is necessary and nurturing of community practices is essential to raise their knowledge and skills through an adoptive e-governance framework.

The casebook incorporates various cases on advancements and challenges in utilizing ICTs for citizen-centric governance and in doing so; the second section includes seven chapters on entrepreneurships, collaborations and empowerment of citizens. In the quest for economic empowerment through rural women entrepreneurship and reduce the digital divide, Chapter 7 discusses about the application of communication tools to empower women community and develop micro entrepreneurships at the rural level. This chapter describes about a case based on field research investigations that were conducted in Tanzania from June 2008 to June 2009 to examine access to, and use of cell phones by women residing in rural villages and in a nearby urban center. The case refers that micro-business decision of marketing food crops depend on critical information in a rapidly changing supply chain environment. Also, as the rural women deal with mostly perishable goods, the uses of cell phones have emerged as important communication tools in the supply chain particularly in decision-making and managing risk-taking. The case suggests that cell phones have leapfrogged the technology and seem to overcome transport deficits that were for centuries endemic to rural and remote areas which have been poor and underdeveloped. However, the study argues that cell phones provide opportunities, but at the same time face challenges, and very little is known about ICTs and the role Cell-phone Mediated Communication (CMC) that play in the context of high demand of information that is critical to small-scale marketing of perishable goods. The case further argues that, what may happen in this precarious business environment when women are confronted with risk-taking and decision-making? The case has tried to look into detail of these challenges and find out relevant solutions.

Chapter **8** provides a synopsis of ICT applications in agro-based livelihoods in Nigeria. The case examines the applications of ICTs through multipurpose community information access points, which were established at a pilot level in Ago-Are, Oyo State, Nigeria. The centers are equipped with basic ICT infrastructures with Internet connectivity through a VSAT. The study mentions that the access point has provided timely solutions to the basic problems of farmers' that were in lack of information on agriculture, and lack of access to inputs and output markets. The services of the access point include answering of farmer's needs through a private-public collaborative project involving several organizations. The case highlights the synergistic use and challenges for each of these projects and extends suggestions for the adoption and adaptation of these strategies in other parts of the world.

Through the innovative use of ICT, as mentioned by a case from Namibia, Chapter 9 describes how cell phones are being used to empower the rural communities and bring them in nation-building activities. The study explores the use of SMS via cell phone and a traditional national newspaper in creating a sense of national identity that transcends geographic distances and an inheritance of economic/political barriers. The study suggests that the cell phone messages made it possible to include the rural communities in the dialogue of national development, who have been left out of discussion earlier. Upholding the slogan of "information is power", this case illustrates that the lives of some rural area dwellers have improved as a result of this technological gadget, the mobile phone.

Chapter 10 is a case from South Korea and it describes about ICT supported education for sustainable development in South Korean rural communities. The case indicates that the rural communities in South Korea have faced serious challenges as the country has gradually opened the agricultural market and extended the conclusion of Free Trade Agreement with more and more countries. The case further added that, due to the national socio-economic and political structures, South Korea has been undergoing the technological imbalance between rural and urban areas. Hence, in order to cope with these vital social challenges, the South Korean government has exerted considerable investments and efforts in establishing ICT knowledge and skills as well as infrastructure in rural areas. Thus, conceptualizing ICT in the context of sustainable development, this case addresses three ICT supported adult education programs oriented toward developing ICT skills and competencies of people in agricultural areas.

Utilizing ICTs for improved service delivery, Chapter 11 describes about case from Botswana that use smart switch card in the social safety nets programs. The case study mentions that, in Botswana the use of smart switch card system has been recently introduced as an offshoot of the universal electronic payment system (UEPS), and it serves to administer food and basic needs offered to the vulnerable people as one of the pillars of development in terms of catering for the needy. Furthermore, the system is used to empower orphans, destitute, and HIV/AIDS home-based patients in the social safety net (SSN) programs replacing the traditional manual system. The preceding program was a manual system where beneficiaries were getting their social grants through queuing up at their district councils' office doorstep for attendants for the roll call. The earlier system also demanded commercial businesses to tender for supply of items to the vulnerable population, and posed challenges and frustrations to beneficiaries and the government.

Illustrating the functionality of indigenous ICTs on community development, Chapter 12 describes a case of farm house dairy product from a rural village in Southern District of Botswana. The study is based on the dairy house farm that has started production in 2002 with the aim of producing both fresh and sour or curdled milk (locally known as madila). Before the utilization of ICT the product was for subsistence family consumption, but with the use of community-compatible ICT (this case argues), the effort has been converted from traditional practice into a commercial industry. The case mentions that with the use of modern equipment, milk is produced in large quantities and through quantitative and computer skills the farm output is managed well. The sales of fresh milk and madila (sour milk) are being tracked through the use of an ICT gadget, the computer. This effort is a family based one and incorporates skill input from local villagers, uses the Internet and media such as Farmers' Digest to identify cows that can produce more milk. The study argues that benefits of this farm to the community are multifold. About 80% of workers in the farm project come from the village in which this farm is located and this farm contributes to the wellbeing of its employees. The project also contributes directly to community members who are not working in the farm.

Chapter 13 is describing about a case from Europe, where ICTs have been utilized to create a citizen-centric platform to support networking and improve electronic democracy (e-democracy). The case describes experiences acquired during a research work conducted as part of the European Project Tell Me (www.tellmeproject.eu). The project envisaged to uphold the pan-European creation of Living Labs as new forms of cooperation between government, enterprises, citizens and academia for the successful transfer of e-government, e-democracy and e-services as state-of-the art applications, solutions, know-how and best practices. The case explores the potential of providing an existing system (namely, DEMOS) allowing moderated and goal-oriented discourses between citizens and policy makers to become parts of open-ended ventures on the creation of collaborative networks for electronic democracy. The case recommends that this form of support network elevates e-democracy of a country and thus improves e-governance systems at the grass roots.

Chapter 14 is the first case of the third section of this case book that incorporates cases about adoption, transformation and innovation of ICT utilization to achieve citizen centric governance. This case describes about an electronic based insurance project, e-insurance as a novel electronic service with the cooperation between academics and practitioners. The case study covers two R&D projects from Finland, which are dealing with electronic insurance. The case emphasizes on the project organization, its activities and roles, along with the results of the projects. Furthermore, the structure and innovation level of the projects are analyzed and the challenges involved in launching the concepts into insurance markets are presented. The study argues that the most important outcomes of the projects are novel service concepts, and valuable information of consumer expectations that corporate partners utilized in their R&D activities. The study further argues that, the projects brought ideas for other research partners on, how to organize future projects in new ways, and how to combine academic and business expertise successfully.

Similar to e-insurance, Chapter 15 describes about a European case based on electronic form of customs, e-customs. This case explores the concept of paradigms, science, and technology in the context of information technology (IT) in providing support for solving problems related to customs. Within the case of e-customs, a European funded project tries to ease border security and control by adopting a common and standardized e-customs solution across the public sector in Europe. In doing so, the case has explained the rise of the IT paradigm within customs and its effect on business operations and reviewed the linear model of Francis Bacon and Thomas Kuhn's notion of scientific paradigms. The study reveals that the linear model has to be advanced, and supports the adoption of Kuhnian ideas from science to technology. The study thus contributes to the research in diffusion and adoption of innovation using science progress and the interplay of science and technology as dominant concepts.

Utilizing the Geographic Information Systems (GIS) as another new form of ICTs, Chapter 16 describes its use as a tool for Criminology and Victimology's Studies in Italy. It is evident that the advent of the GIS technology has revolutionized the traditional field of information and cartographic production by enabling the management of much more numerous and more complex data, and overcoming the static and the traditional two-dimensional cartography. The GIS is used in various fields and disciplines, and this case includes a university research that use GIS as a valuable tool for investigation. The study mentions that, GIS can be used to develop a kind of crime mapping on the nature of the so called "petty crimes" within the jurisdiction, and the creation of a city's map on which there could be identified support centers for victims operating in them. The case also support the idea of using GIS in order to realize and put into practice not only operational measures designed to combat and to prevent crime, but also to help to take social control measures for public policy and security. The study argues that to ensure public safety, it is essential to have a clear, spatial and graphics representation of the area, where there are high concentrations crimes and among the degraded ones, there is greater likelihood that some type of crime will be committed. Hence, by keeping track of those areas through GIS mapping and placing support centres will improve the livelihood of the citizen.

With the notion of providing citizen centric e-government application, Malaysia has adopted an electronic form of tax return system, namely e-filing. Chapter 17 aims to examine the contribution of the newly introduced e-filing system, as a newly developed online tax submission services that has been offered by the government to the tax payers in the country to enable them to easily, quickly and safely file their tax returns. The study suggests that the electronic filing of income tax returns is an invaluable application that assists tax filers with the process of collecting their personal tax related information and provides them the ability to electronically submit their returns. The primary discussion of this case concerns on the Malaysian's ICT revolution, followed by the introduction of the e-filing system and discusses about challenges and barriers faced by the system.

Road safety is an essential element of citizen's livelihood in this dynamic world. Chapter 18 is showcasing a case from Australia on the transformation of government's approach to road safety by engaging citizens through utilization of ICTs. The aim of this case study is to determine the extent to which web 2.0 can be applied as the technology that would enable a strong relationship between government and its citizens to develop and manage road safety. It further examinee the endeavors of the Western Australia Office of Road Safety (ORS) in promoting the relationship. The case observes that in ORS' road safety strategy for 2008-2020, community engagement is strongly advocated for the successful development and execution of its road safety plan, but the potential of web 2.0 approaches in achieving the goal has not been recognized. The study suggests that, the use of blogs and really simple syndication (RSS, originally resource description framework, RDF), can be used as suitable push strategies to get road safety information to the public. The study further suggests that online civic engagement would harness collective intelligence (the wisdom of crowds), and by enabling the citizen to annotate information on wikis, layers of value could be added so that the citizen become co-developers of road safety strategy and policy. However, the case identifies three major challenges confronting the ORS to become Road Safety 2.0 ready, as how to gain the publics' attention in competition with other government agencies, how to respond internally to online citizen engagement, and how to administer governmental politics.

Chapter 19 is a case study on the Egyptian National Post Organization (ENPO), showing the transformational process using ICT. The study observes that, over the last 20 years, the international postal sector has changed radically due to several forces, including globalization, changing of technology, greater demands for efficient services and market liberalization. It further observes that, for Egypt, keeping up with the changing atmosphere in the global market meant investing in

ICTs. The Ministry of Communication and Information Technology (ICT), as part of its efforts to transform government performance using ICT, chose the ENPO as a model for ICT integrated government portal. The selection was due to ENPO's extensive network, and the public's confidence and trust in the organization. This case argues that capitalizing on public-private partnership models ENPO has proved to be successful through ICT deployment for organizational transformation within the context of an emerging economy. The case further argues that, in addition to its importance in providing e-government services to the citizens, ENPO is evolving as a critical medium for effectively developing Egypt's e-commerce sector. The case study takes an in-depth look at how ICT has improved the quality and range of services offered by the ENPO, while supporting the magnitude of its impact on the country's emergence as a competitor in the contemporary global postal market.

Along the context of citizen-centric e-governance, one of the essential elements is to include each and every person of the community, able or disable. Henceforth, there is the need to improve the capacity of each individual through various capacity development initiatives for effective e-governance. As a case of incorporating vision impaired people in e-government, Chapter 20 argues that the vision impaired are in a distinctive disadvantage when using computer screens based on visual presentation of data. Furthermore, their situation becomes increasingly serious, as most society services, such as e-Commerce, e-Business, e-Health, and e-Government go online. But, the study mentions that the modern technologies can offer solutions to their problems, both at hardware and software level, and at reasonable cost. Effective utilization of ICTs can open up new communication channels and functionalities for even totally blind people that would not have been available for them otherwise. In this aspect, the study suggests that general awareness among the policy makers, the developers and the implementers of e-services must be developed.

CONCLUSION

In a knowledge based socio-economy driven by technological transformation and innovation, new challenges are emerging. Two sets of forces have tended to bring forth the present explosion of interest in smart communities and e-governance, such as the importance of city-regions as a result of globalization, and the potentialities of citizen engagement made possible by new information and communication technology (NICT). With respect to the rise of urbanization, globalization and the rapid development and diffusion of NICT are said to be eliminating borders. Moreover, this process of international integration is paralleled by one of national disintegration. Sub-national units are forced to adapt to their specific environments and have demonstrated the greatest adaptive capacities in this turbulent environment. Naisbitt

(1994) has characterized these forces as the "global paradox," and they assist explain why interest has grown around the smart communities movement. Globally, there is a flourishing of literature on systems of innovation from a local perspective. Terms such as industrial and technology clusters, local industrial systems, and local systems of innovation have been used to denote sub-national entities, their patterns of coordination and learning, including their main determinants of socioeconomic development. This growing body of literature has informed much of the recent thinking on digital or smart communities (Coe, Paquet, and Roy, 2001) and restructuring of government system (Rahman, 2011).

The restructuring of government administration and the stipulation of improved services to citizens have long been acknowledged as major criteria for the overall development of a country and today´s drive towards e-governance in many parts of the world can be considered part of this wider developmental goal. Although the term e-governance is predominantly used to refer to the usage of ICTs to improve administrative efficiency, but it is argued to generate other effects that would give rise to increased transparency and accountability of government processes, reflect on the relationship between government and citizens, and help build new spaces for citizens to participate in the overall development (Gasco, 2003; Madon, 2004).

However, before implementing e-government in various economies, there were concerns about its outcome, and raises several questions, such as does e-government improve citizens´ attitude toward government?; can it cure the problem of declining public trust and confidence in government that has been apparent in many countries? According to Norris (2001: 113); " There is widespread concern that the public has lost faith in the performance of the core institutions of representative government, and it is hoped that more open and transparent government and more efficient service delivery could help restore that trust ".

In this aspect, with the aspiration of finding progressions and challenges towards establishing citizen-centric governance through effective utilization of ICTs, this case book has tried to compile various success cases, projects and researches from around the world to illustrate the effectiveness of ICT utilization and be a guideline for future research. From these cases, one may conclude that, time has come to utilize the innovative ICTs for the betterment of the people at large. Furthermore, nations and communities have realized that the government is for the people, and thus the governance. Hence, increased inclusion of the citizen of a nation in the transformed form of government, which is e-government should lead into improved e-governance and thus tend towards citizen centric governance.

Hakikur Rahman
SchoolNet Foundation, Bangladesh

REFERENCES

Almarabeh, T., & AbuAli, A. (2010). A general framework for e-government: Definition, maturity challenges, opportunities, and success. *European Journal of Scientific Research, 39*(1), 29–42.

Backus, M. (2001). E-governance in developing countries. *IICD Research Brief*, Vol. 1, March 2001 Issue.

Basu, S. (2004). E-government and developing countries: An overview. *International Review of Law Computers & Technology, 18*(1), 109–132. doi:10.1080/136 00860410001674779

Bedi, K., Singh, P. J., & Srivastava, S. (2001). *Government Net: New governance opportunities for India*. New Delhi, India: Sage.

Bhatnagar, S. (2002). Egovernment: Lessons from implementation in developing countries. *Regional Development Dialogue, 24*, 164–174.

Brown, D. (2005). Electronic government and public administration. *International Review of Administrative Sciences, 71*(2), 241–254. doi:10.1177/0020852305053883

Center for Technology in Government. (2012). *Definition of e-government*. Retrieved March 12, 2012, from http://www.ctg.albany.edu/publications/reports/future_of_egov?chapter=2

Coe, A., Paquet, G., & Roy, J. (2001). E-governance and smart communities: A social learning challenge. *Social Science Computer Review, 19*(1), 80–93. doi:10.1177/089443930101900107

Csetenyi, A. (2000). Electronic government: Perspectives from e-commerce. *Proceedings of the 11th International Workshop on Database and Expert Systems Applications* (DEXA'00), IEEE Press.

Dada, D. (2006). The failure of e-government in developing countries: A literature review. *Electronic Journal of Information Systems in Developing Countries, 26*(7), 1–10.

Dawes, S. S. (2008). The evolution and continuing challenges of e-governance. *Public Administration Review, December Special Issue,* 86-102.

Dinsdale, G., Chhabra, S., & Rath-Wilson, J. (2002). *A toolkit for e-government: Issues, impacts and insights*. Canada: Canadian Centre for Management Development.

Fang, Z. (2002). E-government in digital era: Concept, practice, and development. *International Journal of The Computer . The Internet and Management, 10*(2), 1–22.

Gasco, M. (2003). New technologies and institutional change and public administration. *Social Science Computer Division, 21*(1), 6–14. doi:10.1177/0894439302238967

Heeks, R. (2001). *Understanding e-governance for development.* I-Government Working Paper Series. Retrieved March 12, 2012, from http://www.sed.manchester. ac.uk/idpm/research/publications/wp/igovernment/igov_wp11.htm

Holmes, D. (2001) *eGov: eBusiness strategies for government.* London, UK: Nicholas Brealey.

Keohane, R. O., & Nye, J. S. Jr. (2000). Introduction . In Nye, J. S., Nye, J. S. Jr, & Donahue, J. D. (Eds.), *Governance in a globalization world.* Washington, DC: Brookings Institution Press.

Krishna, S., & Wlashan, G. (2005). Implementing public information systems in developing countries: Learning from a success story. *Information Technology for Development, 11*(2), 123–140. doi:10.1002/itdj.20007

Madon, S. (2004). Evaluating the developmental impact of e-governance initiatives: An exploratory framework. *The Electronic Journal on Information Systems in Developing Countries, 20*(5), 1–13.

Marche, S. (2003). E-government and e-governance: The future isn't what it used to be. *Canadian Journal of Administrative Sciences, 20*(1), 74–86. doi:10.1111/j.1936-4490.2003.tb00306.x

Mossberger, K., Tolbert, C., & Stansbury, M. (2003). *Virtual inequality: Beyond the digital divide.* Washington, DC: Georgetown University Press.

Naisbitt, J. (1994). *Global paradox.* New York, NY: William Morrow.

Norris, P. (2001). *Digital divide: Civic engagement, information poverty, and the internet worldwide.* New York, NY: Cambridge University Press. doi:10.1017/ CBO9781139164887

OECD. (2003). *The e-government imperative* (p. 23). Paris, France: OECD.

Okot-Uma, R. W. O. (2000). *Electronic governance: Re-inventing good governance.* London, UK: Commonwealth Secretariat.

Pablo, Z. D., & Pan, S. L. (2002, September 2-4). A multi-disciplinary analysis of e-overnance: Why do we start? *Proceedings of the 6th Pacific Conference on Information Systems* (PACIS 2002), Tokyo, Japan.

Palvia, S. C. J., & Sharma, S. S. (2006). *E-government and e-governance: Definitions/domain framework and status around the world, foundations of e-government.* Computer Society of India.

Rahman, H. (2010). *Developing successful ICT strategies: Competitive advantages in a global knowledge-driven society. Hershey, PA*. USA: Idea Group Inc.

Rahman, H. (2011). *E-governance framework at the local government level: Empowerment of community people and improvement of e-governance at the grass roots*. PhD Thesis, Empresarial University of Costa Rica, Costa Rica.

Riley, C. G. (2003). *The changing role of the citizen in the e-governance & e-democracy equation*. Commonwealth Center for E-governance.

Schiavo-Ocampo, S., & Sundaram, P. (2001). *To serve and preserve: Improving public administration in a competitive world*. Manila, Philippines: Asian Development Bank.

Stiglitz, J., Orszag, P., & Orszag, J. (2000). *The role of government in a digital age*. Retrieved April 16, 2002, from http://www.ccianet.org/digital_age/report.pdf

Thomas, J. C., & Streib, G. (2003). The new face of government: Citizen-initiated contacts in the era of e-government. *Journal of Public Administration: Research and Theory, 13*(1), 83–102. doi:10.1093/jpart/mug010

Tolbert, C. J., & Mossberger, K. (2006). The effects of e-government on trust and confidence in government. *Public Administration Review*, (May/June): 354–369. doi:10.1111/j.1540-6210.2006.00594.x

UN. (2002). *Benchmarking e-government: A global perspective - Assessing the UN member states*. New York, NY: United Nations Division for Public Economics and Public Administration.

West, D. M. (2000). *Assessing e-government: The internet, democracy, and service delivery by state and federal governments*. Washington, DC: World Bank.

World Bank web site. (2012). *Full definition of e-government*. Retrieved March 12, 2012, from http://web.worldbank.org/wbsite/external/topics/extinformationandcommunicationandtechnologies/extegovernment/0,contentmdk:20507153~menupk:6226295~pagepk:210058~pipk:210062~thesitepk:702586~iscurl:y,00.html

Chapter 1
The Evolution of ICT Institutions in Thailand and Malaysia

Nicholas Maynard
RAND Corporation, USA

EXECUTIVE SUMMARY

A country's national technology strategies can be an important contributor to economic development through its support of technology adoption and by advancing the national technology capacity. The development of a domestic information and communications technology (ICT) sector within a developing country requires the creation of specialized institutions that carefully coordinate their initiatives with the private sector. This case study research of Thai and Malaysian science and technology (S&T) institutions shows that this institutional and policy reform process is directly influenced by regional activities, as countries seek to match their regional peers for technology development. This effort to support ICT utilization requires governments to rapidly alter their policy goals and initiatives in response to shifts in technologies, global market demand, international investment, and local workforce capabilities.

DOI: 10.4018/978-1-4666-2071-1.ch001

INTRODUCTION

National public support for increased technology innovation and utilization can take many forms, including government-supported technology training; aggregating demand and serving as an anchor tenant; fostering e-government, e-health, and other services; universal service funds; and governmental safeguards for services such as e-commerce (Frieden, 2005). The communications technologies also need to be adapted to the needs of the local economic, political, and cultural environment, particularly if these services are originally introduced by an international entity. To meet local requirements, these national efforts require public-private-university coordination to successfully adapt information and communications technology (ICT) technologies transferred internationally and to enhance services created indigenously (Feinson, 2003; Balaji & Keniston, 2005).

The chapter offers a detailed look at both Thai and Malaysian ministries of ICT and S&T, including a discussion of the evolution of these institutions, the cross-border influence between the two countries, and the organizational challenges facing these agencies as they seek to implement their national technology strategies.

LITERATURE REVIEW

To understand the ICT policy choices of national governments, it is first important to note three major trends identified by the literature within the telecommunications sector. The first is the development of mobile and Internet technologies in addition to fixed line telephony (Baliamoune-Lutz, 2003). The second shift is the global trend away from monopoly operators to competitive carriers across these fixed, mobile, and Internet technologies (Wilson & Wong, 2003). The third shift under way is from governmental control to private ownership, or a mix of public and private with independent regulatory agencies (Levy & Spiller, 1994). Steinmuller suggests that ICTs, which can lower transaction costs, may be able to offer developing countries a conduit for avoiding stages that require high levels of capital and fixed asset concentration, as defined by Rostow's "stages of development" (Rostow, 1960), and moving directly to a knowledge-based economy (Steinmueller, 2001). As a result, many developing countries now view these technologies as an important conduit to fostering both productivity gains (McGuckin & Stiroh, 1998; Baumol & Solow, 1998) and economic development (Saunders, 1994).

Developing countries have accelerated their efforts to deliver affordable ICT access and improved utilization rates among their residents through a range of ICT policy initiatives (Graham, 2000). The two goals of increased access and utilization are important in enhancing a developing country's ability to compete globally for jobs and investment. Although these goals are touted frequently, they are not always tailored for a given country (Cohen-Blankshtain & Nijkamp, 2003). Policymakers must ask themselves how they define affordable access and improved utilization within the geographic, competitive, and political environment of the country (Javary & Mansell, 2002). Once these goals are defined, a set of policies can be implemented and a decision on the optimal ICT solutions can be made.

ICT infrastructure and applications will be adopted by a developing country in stages, with policymakers shifting their goals from supporting increased access, to developing a robust private sector, and finally to creating a globally competitive ICT industry (Grubesic & Murray, 2004). Although these goals are not mutually exclusive, there is a progression in policy and technological complexity as countries move away from directly supporting access infrastructure through a state-owned enterprise, to directing market competition through a regulatory agency, and then to indirectly supporting access through a ministry of ICT. In countries that support a domestic ICT industry, the government's role shifts to becoming a coordinator and advisor to the private sector. To overcome these changing priorities and governmental roles, countries are forced to reevaluate their goals on a regular basis, adjusting their policies and technology choices accordingly. As a result, ICT goals within a developing country will not be static; in fact, they must be flexible enough to adapt to the changing technological and economic conditions to achieve an optimum outcome (Strover & Berquist, 1999).

Institutional structure is defined as the level of institutional, legal, and regulatory structures put in place to support the creation of a national ICT strategy. Depending on the focus of the national policy, there can be a wide range of institutional structures across developing countries. For policies focused on indirect support to the market, such as financial subsidies to the private ICT sector, there are few institutional or regulatory hurdles for sustaining the effort. However, to fund and operate an ICT research park and the requisite infrastructure, similar to Malaysia's Multimedia Super Corridor (MSC), a governmental institution or other organization may need to be created that has the necessary authority to fund and coordinate these policies (Shari, 2003).

This institutional structure requires significant governance capabilities on the part of the new organization as well as a sustained financial commitment. Institutional structure is also linked to market and infrastructure requirements. For ICT strategies that are truly national in scope, rather than a regional effort, this may add a layer of bureaucracy for the ICT institution to coordinate. An increase in the complexity of the infrastructure for the strategy – for a national network, for example – will increase the institutional and regulatory hurdles for the ICT policy.

RESEARCH METHODOLOGY

Current ICT research focuses heavily on economic and market factors behind ICT adoption and utilization, and its impact on economic growth. Many of these studies have found significant benefits to developed countries of the Organization of Economic Co-operation and Development (OECD) and Newly Industrialized Economies (NIEs), but have not been able to conclusively demonstrate a correlation between ICT investment and economic growth in developing countries (Bassanini, 2002; Storm & Naastepad, 2005; Wilson & Wong, 2003). Rather than working to quantify the impact ICTs have on macroeconomic conditions, this research focuses on the process through which policies to support ICT adoption are successfully implemented across a range of emerging economies.

This case study approach outlines the economic, political, and technological environments of Thailand and Malaysia, highlighting the key policy and institutional choices that have resulted in their respective technological utilization rates. This case study analysis focuses on the growing gap between the two countries, where Thailand has not been able to keep pace with Malaysia, which has accelerated its ICT utilization rate and sector development. Malaysia has achieved this by successfully completing a series of ICT institutional and policy reforms that have created a competitive ICT market while directly supporting the local ICT industry. This research was completed using primary sources within the Thai and Malaysian governments, including the ministries of Finance, science and technology policy, and the national regulator. Interviews also include private sector service providers as well as non-profit and think tank organizations. This ICT institution study is driven by the following research questions:

- Are institutional reforms necessary to sustain the growth in the local ICT sector?
- How is development of a domestic ICT sector influenced by regional market and institutional factors?
- What lessons for other developing countries can be drawn from the challenges faced by Malaysia and Thailand in their institutional reform process?

INTERNATIONAL INVESTMENT AND TECHNOLOGY TRANSFER IN THAILAND AND MALAYSIA

The section below discusses foreign direct investment (FDI), multinational corporations (MNCs), and the role of technology transfer because these issues are vitally important to the creation and expansion of a developing county's ICT sector.

4

FDI in Thailand

An important component to the development of local industries and the acceleration of technology adoption is the foreign investment and technology transfer from global corporations located in Thailand (Jansen, 1995; Blomstrom & Kokko, 1998). Like other developing countries, Thailand's high-tech industries in particular must rely on international investment and technology transfers (Kohpaiboon, 2006). Through technology and knowledge transfer from these MNCs to local branches and suppliers, a developing country can rapidly expand the capabilities of local industry to adopt and utilize technologies. Thailand has attracted significant amounts of FDI into its economy, reaching over 6 percent of gross domestic product (GDP) before the financial crisis in 1997. However, the country has not been able to expand this investment since the technology collapse in 2001 (World Bank, 2008). In addition, successful diffusion requires government intervention as well as coordination with the private sector to ensure that these technologies diffuse throughout the economy rather than concentrate within a single industry or region (David, 1997). Thailand has not been able to address this issue. In addition, the government has failed to directly link its approach to foreign direct investment with its efforts to enhance local technological capabilities. This is in contrast with Malaysia and Singapore, which were able to utilize FDI to expand local technology capabilities and accelerate adoption (Wong, 1999).

According to interviews that I completed with the Ministries of ICT, Finance, and others, there are increasing concerns within Thailand about losing investment from multinational corporations to neighboring countries. Although FDI incentive efforts are run by the Office of the Board of Investment, Thailand does not have the high levels of governmental coordination incentives, or marketing that other Southeast Asian economies use to increase their foreign investment. Several government officials each commented that Thailand is currently competing with low-cost countries, such as China and Vietnam, with which it cannot compete on price, and countries such as Malaysia and Singapore that have a much higher level of available talent for ICT and S&T. This situation makes it particularly difficult for Thailand to attract investment in technology sectors, which are deemed strategically important to the long-term growth of the economy.

A major component to enhancing local ICT industry development is the creation of a venture capital industry that invests in startups that are either commercializing local research or adapting international technology to the local market (Ramasamy, Chakrabarty, & Cheah, 2004). The local Thai venture capital (VC) community organized itself into the Thai Venture Capital Association in 1994, with members from the financial, accounting, legal, and advisory services industries. The VC community focuses its investments on firms that have reached their expansion stage.

5

As a result, Thailand faces significant hurdles supporting early round startups with adequate financial backing due to the high levels of risk – a common problem for many developing countries. The Thai government has supported the expansion of the small venture capital community through tax incentives and a number of government-backed funds (Intarakumnerd, 2004). These VC funds target both small business development and areas affected by the financial crisis, seeking to fill in gaps left by the private sector.

FDI in Malaysia

Malaysia has long been successful at attracting FDI and MNCs in the manufacturing and IT sectors, reaching a level few developing countries can match (Jomo et al., 1997). Hundreds of MNCs and billions of dollars in FDI have flowed into the country, particularly into the free trade zones (FTZ) and technology parks set up near the regional manufacturing and technology centers. This includes over 1,700 technology companies – both domestic and international – in Malaysia's Multimedia Super Corridor (MSC), according to the MSC's online reporting. Government officials interviewed for this research suggest that there is close coordination across government ministries as well as between the private and public sectors to promote targeted ICT sectors. The public and private sectors also develop FDI incentive programs, creating packages tailored to specific firms and sectors.

Fueled by these foreign corporations, Malaysia has become an IT equipment exporter, boosting economic growth and local incomes. The government has been able to attract a wide range of software and IT MNCs, and meet its internal targets for relocating firms within the technology parks, even after the global technology downturn in the early part of the decade. This resilience despite downturns at home and abroad is a testament to the coordinated efforts of the public and private sectors to attract technology transfer, investment, and employment opportunities.

Few Association of Southeast Asian Nations (ASEAN) countries approach the high rate of FDI that Malaysia has maintained during the past 10 years, reaching 9 percent of GDP. In contrast, both Korea and Japan averaged around 2 percent of FDI during their development phases, preferring instead to use licensing agreements with MNCs to foster technology transfer rather than direct investments (Ismail & Yussof, 2003). This policy choice within Korea and Japan proved to be very beneficial in developing indigenous innovation capacity, where Malaysian policy is now focused (Hsiao & Hsaio, 2003). Jomo et al. (1997) argues that one of the main political reasons for allowing such a high influx of FDI into the country was to balance the economic power between the ethnic Malays and the minority ethnic Chinese, which have a disproportionate influence within the economy. The FDI was encouraged by the Malaysian government as a way to lower the Chinese minority's economic

6

influence while supporting the growth of Malay-owned firms (Jomo, 2003). This has allowed the country to rapidly expand its global presence within the ICT sectors. However, it has also increased the country's dependency on MNCs and FDI. In addition, several sectors such as the electronics industry have not significantly expanded their roles and are limited to providing low-skill assembling within the global supply chain (Wah & Narayanan, 1999).

This predominance of foreign investment has created a gap in funding available to start-up technology firms in Malaysia and has led the government to develop entrepreneurial financing options for local firms. This has prompted the Malaysian Industry-Government Group for High Technology (MIGHT) to support the development of a financing corporation that coordinates with private sector financial institutions to lower the barriers for investment, according to officials within the organization. The finance corporation's activities include completing due diligence on prospective firms for investment while helping to foster relationships between start-up firms and private sector investment houses. These activities are vital to jump-starting local technology start-ups since the venture capital industry in the country is very small and relatively new. This government entity also identifies global technology niches – such as biotechnology, photonics, and advanced manufacturing – where Malaysian firms will have a competitive advantage due to the large base of local technology expertise.

TECHNOLOGY INSTITUTIONS

The efforts of the Malaysian and Thai technology institutions can be divided into three basic categories. The first includes network infrastructure deployment plans that have been based on South Korea's very successful government initiatives to support ICT network expansion (Frieden, 2005). These plans focus on increasing access, deploying fiber networks, and expanding universal service obligations. Some of these efforts have been successful, depending on the demand for ICT services that already exists within each country.

The second key area includes workforce skill development to assist in ICT knowledge transfers from MNCs while increasing local technology innovation capabilities. Thailand has moved to support training and skills development through its Ministry of Education and Ministry of Industry. However, Malaysia has made it a primary focus for its national development strategy.

The third area, IT industry development, was the primary area of focus for the private sector and the two national ICT strategies. In 2003, Thailand created Software Park and the Software Industry Promotion Agency to bolster its fledgling industry. In Malaysia, the IT sector has grown rapidly through the involvement of foreign capital and MNCs, both of which are coordinated through the Multimedia Super Corridor. Through the MSC, the government was able to attract a range of software and IT MNCs. The country is now focused on increasing the technology transfer and training from these global IT firms into its local ICT industries.

This section provides a background on the ICT and technology institutions of Thailand and Malaysia; examining the institutional development of science and technology Ministries in both countries as well as a discussion of the hurdles both countries must overcome to improve the design of their ICT institutions.

EVOLUTION OF THAILAND'S SCIENCE AND TECHNOLOGY INSTITUTIONS

Thailand watches its neighbors very closely to benchmark its own ICT policies and institutional structure. Thailand was implementing its first structural reform when Malaysia was undertaking a similar effort. As a result, Thailand mirrored its restructuring after its neighbor. Now that Thailand is working on a second reform, it has looked to Malaysia again to see how that country has evolved its ICT structure. Both countries' science ministries were previously the permanent secretary to their respective National IT Councils. In addition to Malaysia, Thailand's ICT agencies have looked to other countries in Asia to develop its ICT policies and institutions, including Singapore, Japan, Korea, and other ASEAN countries (Koh, 2006). Singapore has been widely viewed has having a successful ICT sector as well as an institutional and regulatory reform process (Painter & Wong, 2007).

The administrative organization charged with coordinating the design and implementation of Thailand's national ICT policies and initiatives is the National IT Committee (NITC). When NITC was created in the early 1990s, its efforts were directly supported by NECTEC, which worked with the committee to draft a national ICT policy. The Committee is officially headed by the prime minister and includes members of IT, telecommunications, banking, and other industry trade groups. A former official with the NITC stated that a deputy PM is typically assigned to run the Committee, in addition to other duties and obligations. As a result, the Committee's ability to develop and implement ICT policies would vary widely depending on the personal interests of the deputy assigned. According to government officials interviewed for this case study, those deputy ministers with a strong interest would inject their vision into the Committee, where it would cascade through the other ministries, accelerating efforts and improving initiative outcomes. In contrast, ICT policy design and implementation would suffer a significant slowdown under deputies who were not as interested in this NITC leadership position.

Thailand's National Electronics and Computer Technology Center

The national innovation agency, the National Electronics and Computer Technology Center (NECTEC), was created through the National Science and Technology Development Act by Parliament as an independent agency to focus on research and development (R&D) efforts within the electronics, information technology, and communications technology industries (Intarakumnerd, 2004; Hobday & Howard, 2007). NECTEC was placed under National Science and Technology Development Agency (NSTDA), which is part of the Ministry of Science and Technology and was created as part of the same act. Officials interviewed for this research stated that NSTDA is focused on developing and supporting S&T policy within the Thai industry through four key divisions: nanotechnology, biotechnology, material sciences, and NECTEC.

The development agency works with major universities to develop and commercialize technology innovations and has recently set up a Technology Licensing Office to work with universities to license and commercialize their research. The Ministry of Science and Technology completed its own master plan for science and technology policy (NECTEC, 2003). This plan identified several industrial sectors to target for support by NSTDA and the other agencies within the ministry, including food processing, automotive, garment, and others. According to NSTDA officials, prior to this plan, university and government researchers had applied for funding based on their own disparate interests, which left R&D efforts uncoordinated within these sectors. To receive funding under the science master plan, researchers and ministries must demonstrate how their funding and policy support the government's S&T goals.

Officials at NECTEC stated that the agency focuses much of its work on applied R&D efforts, commercialization efforts, and technology transfer. Its agenda is tailored to ensure that there is commercial demand for the R&D activities currently being funded by public and private sources. In addition, the agency runs its own labs, staffed by researchers that complete university training through NECTEC scholarships both in Thailand and abroad. These researchers are contracted to the government for twice the length of their schooling. However, NECTEC loses many non-scholarship researchers to the private sector due to uncompetitive compensation packages. Similar to the National Science Foundation in the US, NECTEC provides grant funding to university researchers in addition to its own labs, particularly in areas where the agency is lacking in expert personnel (Liefner & Schiller, 2008).

The national innovation policies aimed at developing the ICT sector are designed by NECTEC and the Ministry of ICT (MICT) for implementation across the other ministries. Interviews with officials at NECTEC and the MICT confirmed that once

NECTEC develops the policy, the Ministry of Science and Technology presents it to the cabinet for approval. If the policy is approved, it is set as a national policy for all of the ministries and departments to follow. Although NECTEC and MICT are responsible for the ICT policies within the country, both of these government organizations are short on funding and manpower. This is due to the lack of large-scale projects, which tend to receive the most funding and political attention. NECTEC, the MICT, and the Ministry of Science and Technology have very limited authority, political influence, and budget while the Ministries of Finance, Commerce, and Transport all have high levels of political power due to their budgeting authority for large infrastructure projects.

Software Industry Promotion Agency of Thailand

Formerly a part of the MICT, the Software Industry Promotion Agency (SIPA) is a public organization similar to NECTEC, with flexible regulations and employment contracts. According to discussions with a former executive of SIPA, the agency has focused on deploying several pilot programs aimed at improving government services. One pilot was completed using local software developers to build an online interface for the immigration service. Another example included the development of an online portal to promote Thai regions for business investment and job creation. This is similar to the efforts of local US chambers of commerce, aggregating key economic, demographic, and quality of life indicators for prospective investors and businesses. Although this is an easy step for a US region, in Thailand the data is spread across many disparate agencies and databases, making integration difficult. SIPA also tracks and provides information on available ICT experts and upcoming graduates to attract investment in the software sector.

The Thai government has set a target of creating an indigenous IT sector, but even with this public sector support, the private sector has made little headway. The government has been working on a series of IT bills to support the sector, but in the last nine years has only passed two. As a result, there is no master plan or policy strategy for developing this IT sector – although it is outlined in IT2010. There have been some successes by the Software Industry Promotion Agency and within the Software Park, a national technology park devoted to the industry. However, the Software Park has done little outside of training individuals and SMEs (Mephokee & Rvengsrighaiya, 2005; Gray & Sanzogni, 2004).

In addition, a Software Park was developed by the NSTDA as part of an industry support policy designed for the National IT Committee. The Software Park has the same independent agency status as NECTEC and offers office space and shared computer facilities to small software entrepreneurs. The park also offers a firm matching program, linking small software companies to larger Thai and international partners. Both SIPA and the Software Park have similar goals and there is overlap between the two efforts due to a lack of institutional coordination.

EVOLUTION OF MALAYSIA'S SCIENCE AND TECHNOLOGY INSTITUTIONS

Malaysia's Ministry of Science, Technology and Innovation (MOSTI) identifies target sectors for national technology policies for the next 10 years, focusing on areas where the Malaysian government can support private sector competitive advantages. Its activities include risk assurance for private sector development, and monitoring and evaluation of policy implementation. MOSTI was previously the permanent secretary for the National Information Technology Council (NITC), which is similar to Thailand's NITC; is also chaired by the prime minister; and is coordinated across the private sector and several ministries for ICT policy implementation in Malaysia, including education and energy, water, and communications (Lall, 1999).

In interviews, ministry officials described additional initiatives including technology development and innovation, as well as best practice development for R&D within the local S&T industries including the ICT sectors. MOSTI also supports improved coordination across private and public research centers through strong leadership directed by the prime minister's office. MOSTI views its role as an ICT enabler through increased investment, expanded R&D activities, and enhanced innovation capacity. MOSTI also is responsible for regulating and enforcing the Communications and Multimedia Act. This regulation is in coordination with the national regulatory commission.

Through the NITC, MOSTI conducted an assessment of national ICT needs in 2006 to revise the national ICT policies and initiatives. The Malaysian government is currently in its 2006-2010 economic plan and ministerial budgets have already been set. But MOSTI will utilize the 2007 budget to launch its initiatives and then move to revise the 2008 budgets during the mid-plan review. This flexibility of funding is key to Malaysia's ability to respond to the rapidly changing landscape within the ICT sectors. From the NITC planned report on ICT needs, focus areas on the ICT road map include sector development, infrastructure deployment, R&D, and community development.

Malaysian Industry-Government Group for High Technology

Malaysian Industry-Government Group for High Technology (MIGHT) is a non-profit, quasi-governmental organization that operates under the oversight of MOSTI, Malaysia's innovation and science agency. The organization is charged with sup-

11

porting and operationalizing "Malaysia Incorporated," which is modeled after Japan and Singapore's public, private, and academic coordination to innovate and compete in the global marketplace. This coordinated initiative, called the "triple helix," to build innovation capacity is driven by the stakeholders in these three sectors across the country. MIGHT is made up of 15 to 20 business, government, and academic leaders and is co-chaired by the PM's science adviser. All policy proposals, once accepted by MIGHT, flow through the science adviser to the PM's office and then to the cabinet for approval and funding. MIGHT has successfully bridged the gaps across these three sectors and coordinated with competitive firms within the private sector to support globally competitive industry development.

In the early 1990s, there was little coordination within Malaysia's private sector let alone across the public or academic sectors, according to interview officials. In 1993, the organization was under the prime minister's office when it was moved to MOSTI (Kam, 1999). The decision was made to place the organization under the prime minister to bolster its ability to draw political support from the PM as well as the other executive agencies. Aside from these political considerations, this move was also necessary due to MIGHT's focus on specific privatized industries that cut across multiple agencies and as a result had previously not received the necessary governmental support to bolster their development. One example outside the ICT sector is the aerospace industry, which had previously fallen under the communications, transport, and finance ministries. With no single ministry leading the effort to support this industry within Malaysia, and no single ministry able to coordinate across the overlapping efforts, there was a lack of support and coordination. Under MIGHT's direction, a national aerospace blueprint was developed through 12 months of policy meetings by a technical committee that included the airlines and manufacturers, and a steering committee that was chaired by the prime minister's science adviser. Once presented to the prime minister, the government funded a multi-year effort that was coordinated by a purpose-built policy vehicle chaired by the prime minister – the Malaysian Aerospace Council – that evaluates the progress of the national aerospace blueprint every six months.

According to interviewed officials, MIGHT's process of governmental support is to use successful interventions, whether they are within the aerospace or ICT industries, as pilot programs for launching efforts across a range of technology sectors. For MIGHT to target a given sector, it must fall within the portfolio of several ministries, have already undergone the privatization process, and cannot have a private sector organization already operating to support sector development. This last requirement prevents the government from duplicating private sector efforts or reducing the incentive within the private sector to establish these coordinating bodies on their own. MIGHT also looks to see where Malaysia can find global technology niches, where it is feasible for the country's existing technical expertise to compete internationally while driving national exports and innovation. It also looks to leverage the existing industrial and technological base within the country. The other areas of focus for MIGHT include entrepreneurial development financing, pharmaceuticals, and radio frequency identification (RFID) tags.

Malaysia's National RFID Program

There is a clearly defined process for evaluating the technology niches that will receive support through the ICT road map. This includes an assessment of the market demand for a given information technology, the viability of this technology, Malaysia's ability to compete in this market, and the global competition within this sector. Once this technology for global export is chosen, a road map will be created for governmental support that will include key performance indicators (KPIs) developed and monitored by MOSTI.

According to interviewed officials at MIGHT, the goal of the national RFID program is to develop a cluster of firms capable of supporting the development, innovation, and marketing of this emerging technology. RFID tags are inexpensive chips that can be used to track inventory by a range of industries, most notably retail and logistics. The program's larger goal is to support the revival of the national semiconductor industry, which has seen its market share and margins shrink due to global competition and the global technology slowdown in the early 2000s (Rasiah, 2003). Although Malaysia is third in the world for semiconductor manufacturing, the country's design houses for hardware, software, and middleware had begun to whither and lose their attractiveness to top engineering talent during this downturn. Malaysian wafer facilities, built with government funding, were very competitive but had lost out to global companies with combined chip design and application capabilities. In response to this situation, the government decided that it could not rely on manufacturing capabilities alone and began working to support the development of chip applications along with the revival of the country's chip design houses. The government support for the revival of the national semiconductor industry included MIGHT negotiating a technology license from Japan for an RFID chip and then leasing this technology to a newly created private company, Senstech.

To build a sustainable level of supply and demand, the government has created a multistage plan for development and deployment. The first phase includes using the government as a test bed and to have the government act as a coordinator across the key private sector players to begin the transition away from bar codes. The government is offering these government agencies the right to use these RFID chips if they are suitable to the program. The government has also agreed to act as the anchor tenant for the technology once it is produced, purchasing the chips for governmental applications to jump-start the industry. These governmental purchases will be used for government programs as well as by state-owned enterprises in sectors such as cattle tagging, logging, and auto manufacturing. However, if agency or SOE testing demonstrates that these chips are not suitable, end users can transition to other available RFID sources. The second phase includes extending the program to wholesale and retail logistical support within Malaysia. To serve the needs of these sectors, the program will expand production to benefit from the economies of scale that are essential in lowering the costs of individual RFID chips. The final step will focus on the international markets and competing against global firms for exports. This phase's approach is key to developing a financially viable sector while positioning Malaysia's semiconductor at the forefront of this growing ICT sector.

Malaysia's Multimedia Super Corridor

The Multimedia Super Corridor is a large technology park devoted to ICT sector development and is the cornerstone of the government's efforts for supporting the development of ICT industries within Malaysia (Bunnell, 2002). The MSC is run by the Multimedia Development Corporation (MDeC), which has representation within Malaysia's National IT Council. Another key institution supporting the MSC is the MSC Implementation Council, which focuses on technology sector investment and development. The MSC Implementation Council is chaired by the prime minister and the MDeC acts as the permanent secretary. Other ministries provide oversight for these efforts, with MOSTI approving MDeC policies and programs, and the Ministry of Finance approving budgets and five-year development plans. MDeC's focus on the MSC is complementary to MIGHT, which has a broader portfolio of expanded technology industries nationwide.

The MDeC is also working to bolster the development of these SMEs through a program that targets these firms at each stage of development (Ramasamy, Chakrabarty, & Cheah, 2004). Starting with support for idea creation, seed capital, first stage, and all the way up to IPO, there is a tailored program within the MSC to support the investment, training, supplies, and industry connections of these firms (Jomo, 2003). There is also significant funding and expertise available to support R&D efforts. The MDeC is also working to improve commercialization efforts of university research by matching faculty and students with MSC companies as well as providing incubators for university-based start-ups.

The MDeC is currently implementing plans to expand the MSC to additional population centers around Malaysia (Bunnell, 2002). This effort is championed by each state within Malaysia, with the MDeC coordinating the development of the regional technology parks. To avoid duplicated efforts and state-level competition, each of the new MSCs must differentiate their economic and innovation goals to win approval to develop a park. One example is the MSC in Penang, which is focused on the electronics industry and leverages the state's robust semi-conductor industry (Wah & Narayanan, 1999). As of 2006, four additional MSCs had begun development with the support of government tax breaks, no labor restrictions, no hurdles for fund transfers, and government guarantees on communications services.

An important point, noted by MDeC officials interviewed, is that the MSC effort is driven by KPIs, which are benchmarked annually with goals for exports, employment by function, and investment, among others. To help ensure these targets are met, there is regular communication between MOSTI and MDeC as well as monthly dialogue between MDeC and its MSC tenants. MDeC also reviews the operations and tax status of each business and has revoked the licenses of both MNCs and local SMEs for breach of contract. A majority of the companies with revoked licenses have been local; these SMEs have difficulty maintaining their efforts to compete within ICT sectors.

CHALLENGES FACING NATIONAL ICT INSTITUTIONS

Institutional Challenges in Thailand

Within Thailand, leadership issues and conflicts of interest have both been major impediments to policy implementation. The country's National Information Technology Committee is officially headed by the prime minister, but this position was typically delegated to a deputy minister. As a result, the ability of the Committee to develop and implement ICT policies would vary widely depending on the personal interests of the deputy assigned. Policy implementation would suffer a slowdown under deputies who were not interested, according to participants who were later interviewed. More recently, the prime minister headed the NITC himself, but was also found to have a conflict of interest — potentially steering the Committee to benefit his personal business interests.

Another major hurdle for ICT institutions and agencies in Thailand is the lack of program evaluation. ICT programs are developed by ministerial chief information officers (CIOs). They are evaluated only at the project level and this limited monitoring is completed in a vacuum. The focus of the evaluation work is on gathering quantitative data on hardware deployment, not on qualitative data on ICT utilization and the economic benefit of the ICT initiative. Most important, there is no overall benchmarking or evaluation effort by the government against its own master plan – an essential component to ICT strategy success (Docktor, 2004).

Although there is no overarching benchmarking or evaluation effort by the government, one avenue for monitoring and evaluation is the submission of ministry-level ICT Master Plans to the MICT and the Budget Bureau (Banerjee & Chau, 2004).

These Master Plans are developed by the ministries and mapped back to the national ICT plan for justification. However, there are no set criteria for doing this. Plans may be rejected due to political considerations or may be rubberstamped to avoid bureaucratic confrontation. When plans are reviewed, they are only completed at the project level with little connection to the government's larger efforts.

Another key component missing from the MICT's efforts is the establishment of public-private partnerships (PPPs) aimed at harnessing the expertise of the private sector and the financial support of the government to spur ICT sector development. This has been a key focus of discussion and is recognized as crucial within the ministry – particularly because neighbors such as Malaysia have successfully implemented public-private partnerships across several technology sectors (Shapira, et al., 2005). However, there is little activity or implementation around fostering partnerships, particularly in ICT applications. Currently, when the government implements a partnership for its e-governance programs, there is a tendency to become overly reliant on the vendor for customization or changes downstream, according to officials. This leaves government ministries vulnerable to high additional costs for these programs as their IT requirements change over time.

Institutional Challenges in Malaysia

By housing ICT infrastructure programs within the Ministry of Energy, Communications and Multimedia (KTAK), Malaysia can emphasize ICT infrastructure deployments while concentrating the necessary budget and authority on implementing those policies within a single agency (MCMC, 2006). However, officials with KTAK and the ministry both reported that this new institutional structure does not have the critical mass of ICT expertise that was within the original Ministry of ICT and is now spread out among separate agencies.

Although there have been many successful efforts to launch government technology initiatives, this has not been the case across all potential sectors (Wee, 2001). Interviewed officials with MIGHT suggested that in areas falling under the purview of a traditional sector ministry, such as agriculture, there have been fewer new initiatives to support private sector development and little institutional reform to be more responsive to market changes. MOSTI works in conjunction with the Economic Planning Unit, a civil service agency, to develop institutional restructuring plans for each of the other ministries. There is a review and restructuring process for reducing agency overlap, which has restructured and dismantled several agencies, most recently in 2004, to make the government more responsive to market changes. These changes were deemed necessary and supported by the prime minister to enhance governmental efforts to bolster national competitiveness. However, there is still a significant tendency for traditional sector agencies to strongly resist any governmental restructuring and revitalization effort.

CONCLUSION

ICTs can help accelerate the development process by reducing transaction costs, increasing transparency, and enhancing links across sectors and with neighboring countries. These national efforts then bolster research and knowledge transfer, which accelerates productivity growth and helps to diffuse economic benefits. To capture these benefits of ICT adoption, countries like Malaysia and Thailand need a strong state intervention that supports and regulates the private sector in delivering affordable access across the country.

In addition, national governments must also focus on spreading the economic benefits beyond capital while ensuring that technology and expertise from MNCs are transferred to local firms across the economy – as Malaysia is currently striving to achieve. Governments must carefully craft incentives for local and international businesses to invest in local ICT industries while demonstrating their willingness to withdraw these incentives from local and international firms that no longer meet the standards for support.

REFERENCES

Balaji, P., & Keniston, K. (2005, July). Tentative conclusions. *Information and communications technologies for development: A comparative analysis of impacts and costs*. Department of Information Technology, Government of India. Retrieved from http://www.iiitb.ac.in/Complete_report.pdf.

Baliamoune-Lutz, M. (2003). An analysis of the determinants and effects of ICT diffusion in developing countries. *Information Technology for Development*, *10*, 151–169. doi:10.1002/itdj.1590100303

Banerjee, P., & Chau, P. Y. K. (2004). An evaluative framework for analyzing e-government convergence capability in developing countries. *Electronic Government*, *1*, 29–48. doi:10.1504/EG.2004.004135

Bassanini, A. (2002). Growth, technology change, and ICT diffusion: Recent evidence from OECD countries. *Oxford Review of Economic Policy*, *18*(3), 324–344. doi:10.1093/oxrep/18.3.324

Baumol, W. J., & Solow, R. (1998, Fall). Comments. *Issues in Science and Technology*, *15*(1), 8–10.

Blomstrom, M., & Kokko, A. (1998). In G. B. Navaretti Foreign investment as a vehicle for international technology transfer. In G. Barba Navaretti, P. Dasgupta, K-G. Maler, & D. Siniscalco (Eds.), *Creation and transfer of knowledge: Institutions and incentives*. New York, NY: Springer Verlag.

Bunnell, T. (2002, March). Multimedia utopia? A geographical critique of high-tech development in Malaysia's multimedia super corridor. *Antipode, 34*(2), 265. doi:10.1111/1467-8330.00238

Cohen-Blankshtain, G., & Nijkamp, P. (2003, August). Still not there, but on our way: Thinking of urban ICT policies in European cities. *Tijdschrift voor Economische en Sociale Geografie, 94*(3), 390–400. doi:10.1111/1467-9663.00265

David, P. A. (1997). Rethinking technology transfers: Incentives, institutions and knowledge-based industrial development. In Feinstein, C., & Howe, C. (Eds.), *Chinese technology transfer in the 1990s: Current experience, historical problems and international perspectives*. Cheltenham, UK: Elgar.

Docktor, R. (2004). *Successful global ICT initiatives: Measuring results through an analysis of achieved goals, planning and readiness efforts, and stakeholder involvement*. Presentation to the Council for Excellence in Government.

Feinson, S. (2003, June). National innovation systems overview and country cases. Knowledge flows and knowledge collectives: Understanding the role of science and technology policies in development. In Bozeman, B. (Eds.), *Synthesis report on the findings of a project for the global inclusion program of the Rockefeller Foundation*.

Frieden, R. (2005). Lessons from broadband development in Canada, Japan, Korea and the United States. *Telecommunications Policy, 29*, 595–613. doi:10.1016/j.telpol.2005.06.002

Graham, S. (2000, March). Symposium on cities and infrastructure networks: Constructing premium network spaces: Reflections on infrastructure networks and contemporary urban development. *International Journal of Urban and Regional Research, 24*(1), 183. doi:10.1111/1468-2427.00242

Gray, H., & Sanzogni, L. (2004). Technology leapfrogging in Thailand: Issues for the support of ecommerce infrastructure. *Electronic Journal on Information Systems in Developing Countries, 16*(3), 1–26.

Grubesic, T. H., & Murray, A. T. (2004, Spring). Waiting for broadband: Local competition and the spatial distribution of advanced telecommunication services in the United States. *Growth and Change, 35*(2), 139–165. doi:10.1111/j.0017-4815.2004.00243.x

Hobday, M., & Howard, R. (2007). Upgrading the technological capabilities of foreign transnational subsidiaries in developing countries: The case of electronics in Thailand. *Research Policy, 36*(9), 1335–1356. doi:10.1016/j.respol.2007.05.004

Hsiao, F. S. T., & Hsiao, M.-Ch. W. (2003, February). Miracle growth in the twentieth century – International comparisons of East Asian development. *World Development*, 227–257. doi:10.1016/S0305-750X(02)00188-2

Intarakumnerd, P. (2004, April). Thailand's national innovation system in transition. *First ASIALICS International Conference on Innovation Systems and Clusters in Asia: Challenges and Regional Integration.* National Science and Technology Development Agency, Bangkok Thailand.

Ismail, R., & Yussof, I. (2003). Labour market competitiveness and foreign direct investment: The case of Malaysia, Thailand and the Philippines. *Papers in Regional Science, 82*, 389–402. doi:10.1007/s10110-003-0170-2

Jansen, K. (1995). The macroeconomic effects of direct foreign investment: The case of Thailand. *World Development, 23*(2), 193–210. doi:10.1016/0305-750X(94)00125-I

Javary, M., & Mansell, R. (2002). Emerging internet oligopolies: A political economy analysis. In Miller, E. S., & Samuels, W. J. (Eds.), *An institutionalist approach to public utilities regulation* (pp. 162–201). East Lansing, MI: Michigan State University Press.

Jomo, K. S. (2003). Growth and vulnerability before and after the Asian crisis: The fallacy of the universal model. In Martin, A., & Gunnarsson, C. (Eds.), *Development and structural change in Asia-Pacific: Globalising miracles or end of a model?* (pp. 171–197). London, UK: RoutledgeCurzon.

Jomo, K. S., Chung, C. Y., Folk, B. C., Ul-Haque, I., Phongpaichit, P., Simatupang, B., & Tateishi, M. (1997). *Southeast Asia's misunderstood miracle: Industrial policy and economic development in Thailand, Malaysia, and Indonesia.* Boulder, CO: Westview.

Jomo, K. S., Rasiah, R., Alavi, R., & Gopal, J. (2003). Industrial policy and the emergence of internationally competitive manufacturing firms in Malaysia. In Jomo, K. S. (Ed.), *Manufacturing competitiveness in Asia: How international competitive national firms and industries developed in East Asia* (pp. 106–172). London, UK: RoutledgeCurzon.

Kam, W. P. (1999). Technological capability development by firms from East Asian NIEs: Possible lessons for Malaysia. In Jomo, K. S., & Felker, G. (Eds.), *Technology, competitiveness, and the state: Malaysia's industrial technology policies* (pp. 53–64). London, UK: Routledge. doi:10.4324/9780203031179.ch3

Koh, W. T. H. (2006). Singapore's transition to innovation-based economic growth: Infrastructure, institutions and government's role. *R & D Management, 36*(2), 143–160. doi:10.1111/j.1467-9310.2006.00422.x

Kohpaiboon, A. (2006). Foreign direct investment and technology spillover: A cross-industry analysis of Thai manufacturing. *World Development, 34*(3), 541–556. doi:10.1016/j.worlddev.2005.08.006

Lall, S. (1999). Technology policy and competitiveness in Malaysia. In Jomo, K. S., & Felker, G. (Eds.), *Technology, competitiveness, and the state: Malaysia's industrial technology policies* (pp. 148–179). London, UK: Routledge. doi:10.4324/9780203031179.ch6

Levy, B., & Spiller, P. T. (1994). The institutional foundations of regulatory commitment: A comparative analysis of telecommunications regulation. *Journal of Law Economics and Organization, 10*(2), 201–246.

Liefner, I., & Schiller, D. (2008). Academic capabilities in developing countries – A conceptual framework with empirical illustrations from Thailand. *Research Policy, 37*, 276–293. doi:10.1016/j.respol.2007.08.007

Malaysian Communications and Multimedia Commission and Ministry of Energy, Water and Communications. (2006). *The national broadband plan: Enabling high speed broadband under MyICMS 886.* Cyberjaya, Malaysia: Malaysian Communications and Multimedia Commission. Retrieved from http://www.mcmc.gov.my

McGuckin, R., & Stiroh, K. (1998, Summer). Computers can accelerate productivity growth. *Issues in Science and Technology, 14*(4), 41–48.

Mephokee, C., & Ruengsrichaiya, K. (2005, December). *Information and communication technology (ICT) for development of small and medium-sized exporters in East Asia: Thailand.* United Nations Publication, Comisión Económica para América Latina y el Caribe (CEPAL), Project Document.

NECTEC. (2003). *Thailand: Information and communication technology master plan (2002-2006).* Bangkok, Malaysia: National Electronics and Computer Technology Center.

Painter, M., & Wong, S.-F. (2007). The telecommunications regulatory regimes in Hong Kong and Singapore: When direct state intervention meets indirect policy instruments. *The Pacific Review, 20*(2), 173–195. doi:10.1080/09512740701306832

Ramasamy, B., Chakrabarty, A., & Cheah, M. (2004). Malaysia's leap into the future: An evaluation of the multimedia super corridor. *Technovation, 24*, 871–883. doi:10.1016/S0166-4972(03)00049-X

Rasiah, R. (2003). Foreign ownership, technology and electronics exports from Malaysia and Thailand. *Journal of Asian Economics, 14*, 785–811. doi:10.1016/j.asieco.2003.10.006

Rostow, W. W. (1960). *The stages of economic growth.* Cambridge, UK: Cambridge University Press.

Saunders, R. J., Warford, J. J., & Wellenius, B. (1994). *Telecommunications and economic development* (2nd ed.). Baltimore, MD: Published for the World Bank by the Johns Hopkins University Press.

Shapira, P., Youtie, J., Yogeesvaran, K., & Zakiah J. (2005, May). *Knowledge economy measurement: Methods, results and insights from the Malaysian knowledge content study.* Triple Helix 5 Conference - Panel Session on New Indicators for the Knowledge Economy, Turin, Italy.

Shari, I. (2003). Economic growth and social development in Malaysia, 1971-98: Does the state still matter in an era of economic globalisation? In Andersson, M., & Gunnarsson, C. (Eds.), *Development and structural change in Asia-Pacific: globalising miracles or end of a model?* (pp. 109–124). London, UK: RoutledgeCurzon.

Steinmueller, W. E. (2001). ICTs and the possibilities for leapfrogging by developing countries. *International Labour Review, 120*(2), 193–210. doi:10.1111/j.1564-913X.2001.tb00220.x

Storm, S., & Naastepad, C. W. M. (2005). Strategic factors in economic development: East Asian industrialization 1950–2003. *Development and Change, 36*(6), 1059–1094. doi:10.1111/j.0012-155X.2005.00450.x

Strover, S., & Berquist, L. (1999, November 22-24). *Telecommunications infrastructure development: The evolving state and city role in the United States.* Cities in the Global Information Society Conference, Newcastle upon Tyne.

Wah, L. Y., & Narayanan, S. (1999). Technology utilization level and choice: The electronics and electrical sector in Penang, Malaysia. In Jomo, K. S., Felker, G., & Rasiah, R. (Eds.), *Industrial technology development in Malaysia* (pp. 107–124). London, UK: Routledge.

Wee, V. (2001, June). Imperatives for the k-economy: Challenges ahead. *InfoSoc Malaysia Conference,* Penang, Malaysia.

Wilson, E. J. III, & Wong, K. (2003). African information revolution: A balance sheet. *Telecommunications Policy, 27*, 155–177. doi:10.1016/S0308-5961(02)00097-6

Wong, P. (1999). *National innovation systems for rapid technological catch-up: An analytical framework and a comparative analysis of Korea, Taiwan, and Singapore.* Paper presented at the DRUID's Summer Conference, Rebild, Denmark.

World Bank. (2008). *World Bank development indicators data base 2006.* Washington, DC: World Bank.

Chapter 2
Moving with Time and Strategy:
India and Bangladesh's Development in the Era of ICTs

Sandeep Bhaskar
Temple University, USA

EXECUTIVE SUMMARY

This chapter presents evidence of using information and communication technologies (ICTs) towards the goal of sustainable community development. It argues that the biggest impediment to the growth of communities in the developing world is a lack of information and a fair incentive system, both of which can be addressed through ICTs. A three pronged action plan comprising of a development strategy, an information strategy, and a technology strategy is proposed towards this effect. The chapter also showcases how a for-profit business, ITC Limited, transformed the face of agriculture in some parts of India, and how this model can be replicated in other parts of the world. It concludes with a description of the agricultural sector in Bangladesh and show how lessons drawn from the Indian case can be applied to Bangladesh and other developing countries.

DOI: 10.4018/978-1-4666-2071-1.ch002

INTRODUCTION

Development is a term that comes with multiple connotations, the most common one being that of growth in income. But many argue that this does not accommodate all dimensions of the development. Sen (1999) understands development as a process of expanding the real freedom that people enjoy. Growth in income can, of course, be an important driver to expanding the freedom enjoyed by the members of the society, but real freedom is complex to define. It is multifaceted. It is shaped by the social and economic arrangements or practices, as well as political and civil rights one enjoys. Though it may be useful to have a broader understanding and conceptualization of this term, development, in this paper, a more narrow definition of development as income growth is applied. Income growth is a tool that is easier to construe, and once made is a very formidable means to achieve other goals.

Lonergan (1971), Prahalad (2005), and Wankel (2008) argue that a major reason for the under-achievement of grand social engineering and development projects is that they provide an exalted role to social goods and not actual production, conveniently ignoring the fact that capitalism has been the most effective weapon against poverty. Most development projects are based on the premise that the poor lack resources, and that private, for-profit business, cannot help alleviate poverty. They refuse to go beyond the familiar, or to modify abstract ideas in light of emerging realities. They also ignore the fact that incentives play a major role in individual decision making and unless these incentives and incentive mechanisms are addressed the lofty goals will remain unattainable.

The chapter posits one possible way in which the emerging information and communication technologies can be used to address the issues of incentives, particularly those in the primary sector. It is important to focus on the agricultural sector since most developing countries are overwhelmingly dependent on agriculture. Even in the cases where agriculture's contribution to gross domestic product (GDP) has become very small, it still supports the biggest chunk of country's population. Therefore, it is imperative that any sustainable development program should involve agriculture, either directly or indirectly, and also work around the incentives of the primary stake-holder: the farmer. Information and communication technologies can help design, support, and sustain such mechanisms.

The chapter is organized as follows. Section 2 explains the working of agricultural markets in the Indian subcontinent. This is followed by a model of using ICT for direct marketing of agricultural products in Section 3. The section explains the structure and technology that can help create this direct marketing network, and argues that while ICTs offer a lot of promise one should remember that ICTs are a means and not and end unto themselves. In Section 4 I provide an example of how an Indian conglomerate, ITC Limited, set up a direct marketing initiative, e-Choupal, and the successes that the initiative has achieved. Section 5 then presents the case of Bangladesh and the need of a similar model there. I conclude in Section 6.

Agricultural Markets in South Asia

Agricultural marketing in the Indian subcontinent is still based on the colonial Agriculture Produce (Grading and Marketing) Act of 1937. The act prohibited procurement of grains outside government designated markets called "mandi." The Great Bengal Famine of 1943 that claimed more than 1.5 million lives and the socialist programs adopted by the governments of the region after independence meant that this act was never revoked, and the governments continued to have very tight control of food-grain production, supply, and distribution. The shadows of those policies still haunt food policy in the subcontinent. The little agricultural liberalization that countries saw in the 1990s dealt with input markets, and not with the produce market. In the meanwhile a small group of individuals ended up monopolizing agricultural trade in the government designated markets killing all competition and incentive mechanisms.

In traditional economics, a market's efficiency and development outcomes are taken to be axiomatic and underdevelopment is then characterized by an incomplete correspondence of markets with productive activity. Various studies including Bharadwaj (1974), Bharadwaj (1985), Bhaduri (1983), Chowdhury (1992), Chowdhury (1994), Crow (2001), and Rudra (1984) also point out that these axioms may not be entirely true in these markets. Some authors argue that large traders control the market subtly through an intricate network of credit to the local traders and farmers, and that though the markets look competitive superficially, the actual story is not so rosy.

In the absence of an institutional source of cheap and easy information about a supplier's ability to supply the product on time, the traders have to come up with new ways to conduct business. Due to unreliable trading partners, poor quality grains, and with poor and costly facilities for enforcing contracts, the traders develop a person equation of trust amongst themselves (Annamalai and Rao 2003, Chowdhury 1992, Chowdhury 1994, Chowdhury, Farid and Roy 2006). Although it is difficult to conclusively decide if these relations are exploited, one certainty is that these relations do present a barrier of entry into the market.

Related studies (Sarkar 1979, Bhaduri 1983, Rudra 1984, Crow 2001) conclude that prices in agricultural markets are created by the speculative exchange activities of large farmers with smaller farmers playing a marginal role. The dominance of the marketed surplus by large farmers also influences the way in which different farmers respond to price changes. The small indebted farmers are completely price-unresponsive and sell their produce as soon as they can, without observing price trends. The middle income farmers are more inclined towards a fixed income and gradually release the produce in the market. The third group is one of the richest farmers who have holding capacity and usually release the product when the prices are at their highest. Table 1 tracks the harvest time price and the average price of some agricultural products over the last 10 years in Bangladesh. These numbers seem to support the idea that the markets may be inefficient. Macro level studies cannot explain this market structure, and are hence not able to explain poverty even with increased productivity in the farming sector. One source of problem might be that traditional models assume that commodity markets in developing countries are static, when in fact they are very dynamic. The data suggests that assuming agricultural markets in developing countries to be efficient and competitive may not be correct.

The studies mentioned above also suggest a possible alley where changes might have an intermediate impact on the welfare of people: reducing information inefficiency. Rest of the paper argues how this inefficiency can be minimized in agricultural markets through the use of information and communication technologies.

Table 1. Harvest time and average food crop prices in Bangladesh, BDT per ton, 1995-96 to 2005-06

Year	Rice		Wheat		Potato		Garlic		Ginger	
	Harvest	Aver-age	Harvest	Average	Harvest	Average	Harvest	Average	Har-vest	Average
1995-1996	6560	12060	7420	8500	4640	6750	17590	27050	22770	28420
1996-1997	5430	10790	7340	8650	4720	6860	14880	22150	14950	21780
1997-1998	5740	11830	7624	8740	4835	5650	15950	26230	20600	24600
1998-1999	7380	14040	8500	8640	5500	7400	26950	37400	20900	37700
1999-2000	6460	12570	8060	8860	6230	8610	21930	36240	16430	38550
2000-2001	6120	11990	8190	8580	4870	5030	17250	28070	22350	30190
2001-2002	6770	12560	8420	8595	5030	5960	22760	35190	19010	27280
2002-2003	7810	13550	9630	9010	8500	8980	34500	35530	24710	24070
2003-2004	7030	12920	9380	10860	7710	8610	22180	28840	27430	40630
2004-2005	9010	14680	11850	12020	5250	7160	20110	28610	44640	58370

Source: Ministry of Agriculture, Government of Bangladesh.

ICT Based Model for Development

The role of ICTs in development and poverty alleviation has been suggested for a long time, with education being the area of focus. There is a substantial support for this idea both amongst development theoreticians and the political class. Most, if not all, theorists believed that poverty in developing countries might be explained, at least in parts, by the knowledge and skill deficits in the local populations, and education was the tool to overcome that deficit. The wide spread use of radio in the post World War II era made it possible to impart this knowledge from a distance. It suited the period's optimism and political goals.

The success of the Marshall Plans gave further credence to the idea. The problem was that the initiation of programs, and not their success, took center-stage (Hornik 1988). Most such programs were tailored to suit the views of the donors and not those of the benefactors. This resulted in programs that were geared towards the views of the donors, assuming away ways in which different societies react to different situations. Theologist Lonergan (Lonergan 1971) aptly said that the programs were stunted by the bias of conceptualism (the refusal to modify abstract concepts in the presence of new information), and the bias of common sense (the refusal to go beyond the familiar), and these deficiencies hurt the programs and their benefactors.

A second stream of development communication projects started emerging in the 1980s in the wake of the failure of older programs that tried to do things locally (called participatory development) and achieved more success than their predecessors. These participatory development programs were again primarily targeted towards social goods, and it was assumed that economic aspects will take care of themselves once the social aspects were in place. Another common theme to emerge from the programs was that poverty was primarily a political issue, and to make things work political reforms were needed. In case of democracies this requires the participation of the masses, and the incentive mechanisms as they exist in most developing countries do not provide the means to bring such reform. All this suggests that for any poverty reduction plan to succeed the primary stake-holders have to play a major role. This means involving the agriculture sector in the decision making process, which in turn requires that the farmers trust the system and understand that their welfare lies in the success of the system, again emphasizing the idea of a proper incentive mechanism. ICTs can help introduce, support, and sustain this incentive mechanism.

When arguing about the role of ICTs in agriculture it is important to note that like in other businesses access to information, capital, and insurance against risk play an important role in determining the extent of profits. The use of ICTs makes information sharing more efficient, connects producers to global markets, and satiates the animal spirits in each one of us. Besides providing information on good agricultural practices ICTs can help in connecting the sector to global markets and creating a sustainable sense of involvement, dignity, and confidence: very primal feelings, but perhaps the most important ones in the decision making process of every individual (Akerlof & Shiller 2009).

An ICT based system can be viewed as a three stage process with bidirectional interaction between each stage. The first stage is to identify the problem and work on possible solutions (the development strategy), then decide what information is required to solve that problem (the information strategy), and finally determining how to provide that information (the technology strategy). The whole process for the case of agricultural markets in South Asia is depicted in Figure 1.

The system mentioned here requires substantial initial investment and that can only be done either by a major aid agency (which is unlikely in the present context as we shall see), or a for-profit company. The company will need to have interest in agricultural marketing, and have the potential to make that investment. Hopefully, there are firms willing to take the plunge and make the investment required.

The Development Strategy

Development has to take into account both short-term and long-term goals. In the short run there is a need to reduce inefficiencies in the system, and ensure that the smallest farmers get their due. In the long-run the system should make it possible

Figure 1. A three level design of the relation between information & development

for farmers to access and utilize advanced farming practices, and should help alter the production portfolio to help move it up the value chain.

To reduce existing inefficiencies in any system it is necessary that people understand how it works. The general business principle is to scrap off the system that does not work, and create a new system from scratch. Such a solution is based on the idea that if something does not work then it points towards an intrinsic problem in the system, but the costs involved in creating a new system from scratch are way too high. A better way is to take the best practices from the existing system and work on improving it. This will serve two complementary purposes, (1), lowering costs and (2), creating a sense of belonging, of ownership, in the mind of the benefactors.

Some common inefficiencies that can be targeted are skewed patterns of cropping and production, lack of quality standards, and inefficient agricultural markets.

The Information Strategy

The most important aspect of an information system is the ease and simplicity with which it can provide the requisite information. In the present case the system should provide three levels of information. One is it has to provide commodity prices in various markets, and with the assumption that the company that set up the network actually wants to buy the product, also provide the offer price that the company is willing to pay for the produce. Besides this it makes sense to provide other information, since even when the fixed cost of establishing an information network is high, incremental information can be provided virtually free.

It should also provide weather information on a local basis. For most farmers in the region the timing of sowing, transplantation, and reaping, can define whether the farmer's family gets its share of food for the year or not. Reliable, local weather information can help optimize these timings.

Finally, it should provide a reliable explanation of quality standards. Distrust of businesses runs deep in the psyche of the poor in the region, and any measure that hints towards information hiding can unravel the whole system. For example, in case of rice, explaining the role of the length of grain, and the presence of foreign matter can be simple, but the firm has to come up with a way to explain the importance of moisture content and how it is determined. The traditional method of biting into a sample of the grains is both unscientific, and infeasible, on a commercial scale. Therefore one has to come up with a ready determinant of measuring moisture content. Over a longer time frame the system can provide information about advanced farming practices including, but not limited to, ways to deal with weeds and pest, and the role and importance of the water table.

The Technology Strategy

The model is centered on a network of information kiosks that are equipped with a computer and are connected to the Internet. We have to consider both the hardware and software aspects of the system, and how to minimize the cost while retaining efficiency. The hardware needs to support two applications, web browsing and word processing. The biggest problem is getting the system on the Internet. Given the state of telecommunications in most developing countries traditional dial-up models will not work. Electricity is still not available to a lot of people. These are serious constraints and will push up the initial cost of setting up the system, but do not inhibit the feasibility of establishing a network. The question of Internet connection can be solved using VSAT Stations. Electricity problems can be taken care of by using any of the different portable electric generation systems. Small diesel engines are being used to run tube wells in many developing countries. The same diesel engines can supply enough power to run a computer and a VSAT system.

The front-end (client-side) software system needs three components: an operating system, a web browser, and a word processor. The use of any version of Linux and any Netscape based web browser like Mozilla Firefox, will eliminate the cost of these since they are all open source systems available for free. The system interface has to be in a language that people understand. Linux based systems offer support for most major languages. A version of Linux, *Ubuntu*, supports 89 languages in all its applications including word processing (through Open Office). At the back-end (server-side) we need a web server, and a database system that will provide information about prices and also gather information from the villages. We can utilize some implementation of Apache as the web-server and use MySQL or SQLite for the database system. The kiosk coordinators can be provided writing privileges in some fields of the database using the web-browser. They can provide information about expected production and procurement from villages under each kiosk, information about farmers, and about rural demand of goods and services.

The system will need a group of people to man and manage it. This is where one part of the existing system can become useful. The presence of traders provides a ready pool of 'experts' on agriculture who can handle the systems with little training. The traders will need to be trained in using a computer based information network: the use and purpose of the computers, switching it on and off, using the web browser, word processor, and the database system. The network will also need a small group of technicians to troubleshoot when the coordinators cannot rectify a problem. Each district can have one technician to support the kiosks in that district.

System Organization

As stated earlier, the model is centered on a network of information kiosks that are equipped with a computer and are connected to the Internet. Figure 2 provides a schematic representation of the system.

The information kiosk will provide the market price as well as serve as a sales point. When the crop is ready, the farmer can bring a sample of the produce to the information kiosk where the coordinator will inspect the produce and offer a conditional quote based on the offer price of the company. The farmer can then decide whether to sell the produce to the company or not. If the farmer decides to sell the produce to the company, the coordinator of the kiosk will provide the farmer with a note stating the particulars of the sample and the quoted price. The farmers will then take the produce to the nearest procurement hub, get the assessment of the produce verified, get it weighed, and collect the payment. In case the procurement hub believes that the conditional quote is not appropriate it can alter the price, but the farmer will be provided an explanation of the change. If the farmer is not satisfied with the offered price or the explanation of change the farmer can retract from selling the produce to the company. To avoid problems to the farmer, and more importantly to generate trust amongst them, the procurement hubs can be located close to the conventional markets, so that if the farmer decides not to sell it to the

Figure 2. Organization of the information network

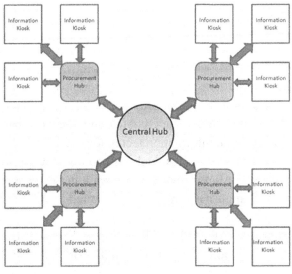

(Bi-directional arrows indicate bi-directional information flows)

company he/she can move to the other markets without incurring high costs. Though it will not influence the margins of the company it can generate trust amongst the farmers who have traditionally been exploited by the traders.

Coordinators' incentive mechanism can be so designed that their pay will depend on the amount of sales they generate. The coordinators cannot quote a very low price since that may drive away farmers, and neither can they quote a very high price since in that case the offer price may differ from the final price offered at the hub and again drive away the farmers. The coordinator then has an incentive to provide a reasonably correct estimation of the final price.

The kiosks can also serve as a center of risk and insurance management. The coordinators can recommend farmers for loans to the company and the quality of loans can influence the payment of the coordinators. If the recommendations of the coordinator lead to good quality loans, that are loans that are repaid promptly, then the coordinator can get a share of the margin/premium that the company generates. The coordinators then have an incentive to recommend actively, and also pursue recovery in an active manner.

Internet can also be used to provide other information to the villagers like weather, news, job postings, and even government and private tender information. It can also be used to provide a service like e-Post wherein the farmers can send information to their relatives and friends in other villages through the Internet where the coordinators at the recipients village can deliver the message in return of some payment. Together these three aspects, the development strategy, the information strategy, and the technology strategy, have the potential to alter the incentive mechanism in the agricultural sector and bring the benefits of productivity gains to the agents of change: the farmers.

ITC e-Choupal

ITC Limited is one of India's largest private sector companies with a market capitalization of INR 764 billion, and sales of INR 219 billion in 2008. It has diversified presence in cigarettes, hotels, paperboards and specialty paper, packaging, agri-business, packaged food, information technology, and other FMCG products. It is one of India's best known brands, and has had a visible presence across the country for a long period of time. Owing to its origin in the tobacco business ITC built an enviable distribution network that it exploited to the hilt when entering other businesses.

ITC was incorporated on August 24, 1910 as Imperial Tobacco Company of India Limited in Calcutta (now Kolkata), the then capital of British India. The company's ownership progressively 'Indianized' and today its parent, British American Tobacco, owns less than one-third of the common equity, with government sponsored financial companies holding a much bigger share. Though the first foray outside tobacco was way back in 1925 when it started making paperboards for the cigarette business, it started large-scale diversification only in the 1970s.

Owing its presence in the tobacco business ITC decided to utilize its agri-sourcing competencies and the Agri-Business Division (ABD) was set up in 1990 for the export of agricultural commodities, starting with soy and shrimps. Today it is one of the largest exporter of agricultural and aqua products from India and exports soya meal, rapeseed meal, rice, lentils, coffee, black pepper, sesame seed, ground nuts, castor oil, shrimps and prawns. ITC-ABD came out with the idea of an internet based direct marketing program in 1998 when the division faced innovation or closure. The initiative was called e-Choupal. Today e-Choupal is one of the most successful IT-driven solutions for rural growth.

e-Choupal

e-Choupal is the name of ITC's IT-led system of direct marketing of agricultural products. From the time of conception in 1998, roll out in 2000, and the first center in 2001 it has scaled some unimaginable peaks. In the ten years since the first node opened the initiative has grown to more than 6200 centers, covering 10 states, 40000 villages, and more than 4 million farmers! The same period has seen ITC's revenue grow more than three-fold, and the agri-business division led by e-Choupal was one of the prime drivers of this growth.

The system is based on a network of nodal centers connected to a central hub. The centers are located in villages and are connected to the Internet through VSAT or conventional phone line depending on the location of the village and availability of infrastructure. The computer is located in the home of the coordinator, called the *sanchalak*. Thus, ITC does not have to bear the cost of setting up an office for the center.

ITC gathers and provides information about the prevailing prices across markets on agricultural products through its portal where all coordinators have logins. Farmers can go to the coordinator at the time of harvest and inquire about the price of the produce in different markets, as well as the price that ITC is offering each day for the produce. Thereafter the farmer can decide if he wants to sell the produce in any particular market, or to ITC. What was perhaps most relevant here was that ITC decided to provide real time information that fulfilled the complete spectrum of farmer needs and this information was provided independent of transactions, so the farmers could take all information they need and still sell to someone else and not ITC. The company recognized that IT based systems are like utilities, the initial set up cost is large, but incremental information can be provided at negligible costs.

To ensure that the coordinators can operate the computers they are called for an initial training that the company pays for, and then a subsequent refresher course once the coordinators have used the system for some time. They also serve as the first point of contact between the farmer and the company by quoting a price to the farmer if the farmer wants to sell the product to ITC.

If the farmer is happy with the quote he/she takes the produce to the procurement hub. In some cases ITC also arranges for the produce to be procured straight from the farmers' village. At the procurement center the product is again sampled and the farmer is paid in full for the produce. ITC also sets aside a sample for laboratory testing and if the quality exceeds the acceptable level the farmer is rewarded with bonus points that can be redeemed for farm equipment, insurance premium etc. The coordinator is awarded a commission on all sales that he/she generates, and thus he/she has an incentive to ensure quick and good service for the farmers in his/her area.

Though it is difficult to quantify the gains to the company from some of the steps the company has taken, the progress has helped sustain the primary stake-holders' interest. When ITC started the initiative the Agriculture Produce (Grading and Marketing) Act 1937 prohibited procurement outside the government designated markets. The company had to convince the government that its initiative was in the spirit of the act and it will continue to operate with that spirit. It also convinced that their procurement process was in line with the goals of the act, and that they will continue to pay the *mandi*-tax even if they were buying products outside the market. This earned them the permission to start their business, and today, in just ten years since the first e-Choupal opened, most states have passed their own acts permitting direct marketing of agricultural produce.

e-Choupal offers the farmers a fair price, hassle free trading, and most importantly it is respectful and transparent. An early example of the kind of support the initiative has garnered was evident in Bhopal in December 2004. The state was contemplating passing agricultural reforms that would have allowed a blanket approval for direct marketing of grains, and the traders who controlled the *mandis* came out strongly against the provision that allowed companies to completely bypass the *mandis*. Farmers came out in support of the bill from all over the state to stage a rally in Bhopal on December 16, 2004 and the groundswell pushed the bill through the legislature. It is important to look at the event in light of the fact that traders are one of the strongest political lobbyists in the rural hinterlands of the subcontinent and a regular source of campaign funds for the political class. Even with their political clout they could not prevent the bill from becoming a law: a prime example of political empowerment of the farming sector.

None of this would have happened if the farmers did not have faith in the working of the new system, and belief about their own gains from the new law. It was a big moment in the history of the relation between farmers and industrialists in the subcontinent where the marginal farmers have long been exploited by the moneyed class.

What Was Different?

The question that naturally arises is what was different in this project? What is it that the project provided that was missing in earlier efforts? I believe that the most important aspect was that the project was driven by a motive of profit: both for the company, and the farmers, the two most important spokes in this wheel. It is difficult to explain an under-educated person the gains from sanitation, but even the most illiterate person understands that more money means it will be easier to make ends meet. ITC offered nothing less and nothing more than this.

They offered a price that was based on the price in the market on each day, and not on the government minimum support prices and the market prices were inevitably higher than the minimum support prices. In some cases the difference was as high as 60%! The company provided the price they were willing to offer through the e-Choupal portal. Unlike earlier the farmer knew beforehand the price they will get, thus they did not have to go to the *mandi* and accept the price prevalent on that day. An average *mandi* serves an area of about 700 square kilometers (Annamalai & Rao 2003), so the transport costs for most farmers are very high, making it almost impossible for the small farmer to go back with the produce in hope of a better price later. Last, but not the least, the farmers were paid in full, unlike the case of *mandi* where they had to wait to get the full payment. These might seem like small steps, but in some districts it led to more than 90% of the farmers switching over to crops that ITC bought (Annamalai & Rao 2003).

Another aspect that was given due weight was that ITC did not go about reinventing the wheel. Even with all its deficiencies Indian agriculture has attained self-sufficiency in all major grains, and when you can feed more than a billion people with most areas still dependent on rain for crops something must be right about the system. In the zeal to modify things ITC did not go about dismantling the whole system. For example, they tried to make the traders in every area their coordinator. This move served many goals. One, the coordinators knew the working of the local markets well, and two, hiring them meant at least some of the traders were not going to oppose the project. They also act as a source of credit worthiness of the farmers in case the farmers wanted to borrow from ITC, since they know the people in the area well. Though not covering all traders this move probably provided ITC with long run support and strength. The company also initiated a performance related bonus scheme for the coordinators, thus providing them an incentive to work hard.

These efforts to bring together all stake-holders on the same plane and making them a partner in the success of the project have meant that the initiative has gone from strength to strength. All stake-holders have an incentive to work towards its success, and given the impact on ITC's bottom-line: the only quantitative parameter we have, it has worked.

Beyond e-Choupal

After the success of the e-Choupal system ITC decided to take the initiative one further step: that of taking products and services into rural India. Rather than the supply chain being a one way road of produce from farmers to ITC they decided to make it a two way transaction. In this regard they started setting up rural hyper-marts, called Choupal Saagar, with the first one coming up in 2004. As of 2008 there were 24 such hyper-marts in business, with another 76 in the pipeline. Unlike the traditional urban shopping mall, these stores carry products that are in demand in the rural hinterlands. One can get anything from a needle to tractor parts and more in these stores. They also provide services like soil testing, clinics, banking, cafeterias etc. A Google™ search of Choupal Saagar popped up a page describing a south Indian meal in the Hindi heartland of the country!

ITC has further plans of setting up a complete supply chain that works with equal efficiency in both ways. What they have done through this project, while serving their bottom line, is they have opened a way to access what Prahalad calls the fortune at the bottom of the pyramid (Prahalad 2005).

The question then is whether this model can be replicated elsewhere? I think it is possible. In the next section I present the case of Bangladesh, another heir to the British Indian laws, with similar agricultural system where some aspects are so arcane that they shout out for reform.

THE CASE OF BANGLADESH

A history of thirty-seven years as a modern nation-state does not do justice to a nation where remnants of civilization date back more than four thousand years. When Bangladesh gained independence from Pakistan in 1971 many observers questioned the economic viability of the new nation. The country was grappling with pervasive poverty, poor endowment of physical resources, loss of infrastructure in the war for freedom, and thin margins for generation of surplus for investment. People from Pakistan, who dominated the industrial sector, banking, insurance, transport, and foreign and domestic trade, had fled the country leaving behind a vacuum. A "geographical accident" that left the country prone to natural disasters, particularly severe cyclones and floods, along with the above-mentioned factors meant that in 1973 more than 80% of the population was living under the poverty line (Ahmed, Haggblade and Elahi Chowdhury 2000).

Bangladesh continues to be one of the most impoverished countries in the world with per capita GDP of just about $445. Even though the economy grew at an impressive 7% in 2007, the state of an average citizen in the country is dismal. The country is overwhelmingly dependent on agriculture, and more than 75% of the population still lives in the rural areas. Though agriculture's share in the country's GDP has declined below 25% it continues to employ more than 50% of the labor force.

The country is home to the largest delta in the world, and lies in the basin of two mighty rivers: the Brahmaputra, and the Ganges (which bifurcates into Padma, and Meghna). The rivers give rise to one of the most fertile regions in the world, but also bring devastating floods. The catchment areas of both rivers lie far away from Bangladesh and expose the country to the specter of droughts. Bangladesh has suffered from repeated famines in the twentieth century, and memories of these famines still haunt the country. The first, Great Bengal Famine of 1943, claimed more than 1.5 million lives, and along with the Second World War set the background for very tight government control of food-grain production, supply, and distribution whose shadows still haunt the food policy of the Indian subcontinent. The second, in 1974, soon after the country gained independence proved equally devastating with some estimates claiming a loss of more than a million lives! These historical facts underline the most important aspect of Bangladesh's government policy: food. At its zenith in 1990 Bangladesh's public food distribution system consumed US$300 million, or over 17 percent of total government expenditure (Ahmed et al. 2000).

Bangladesh is still struggling to come to terms with its vast rising population and the means to feed it. Even though the country has grown at nearly 5% per year since independence, the rising population has mitigated the impact of this growth. Table 2 provides some select development indicators from three census surveys that have been carried out since independence. Growth in almost all indicators has been rather modest. Literacy level across regions is fairly uniform; though the gains from the recent initiatives in improving the rates are expected to show some major changes in the next census.

The disturbing aspect though is not captured in Table 2: that of stagnation of the income of the bottom two-thirds of the population. Table 3 examines the income of the bottom sixty percent of the population in the decade from 1986-1996. The figures for 2003, the last year for which data is available, do not show any changes

Table 2. Select indicators of development, 1981-2001

Series	2001	1991	1981
Geographical Units			
Zila	64	64	21
Villages	87362	86038	83666
Households	25490822	19397992	15075887
Population	124355263	106314992	87119965
Population Growth Rate	1.59	2.17	2.35
Adult Literacy Rate	47.9	35.3	29.2
Rural	42.2	30.1	25.4
Dwelling Structure (in %)			
Jhupri	8.80	N/A	N/A
Kutcha	74.40	N/A	N/A
Semi-Pucka	10.12	N/A	N/A
Pucka	6.68	N/A	N/A
Source of Drinking Water (in %)			
Tap	6.18	4.30	3.61
Tube-well/Deep Tube-well	84.60	85.20	53.12
Pond/Dighi	3.32	7.88	37.50
Others	5.90	2.62	5.77
Toilet Facilities (in %)			
Sanitary	37.38	12.46	N/A
Others	41.17	53.34	N/A
None	21.45	34.20	N/A
Electricity Connection (in %)	31.70	14.29	N/A
Ownership of Agricultural Land (in %)	55.58	55.51	N/A

Source: Ministry of Finance, Government of Bangladesh, Various Census Surveys.

Table 3. Income distribution, 1986-1996

Series	1996	1986
Income of Bottom 20% of Population (% of Total) 10 9	9	10
Income of Second 20% of Population (% of Total) 14 12	12	14
Income of Third 20% of Population (% of Total) 17 16	16	17
Total Income of Bottom 60% of Population (in Billions of USD)	14.142	10.489
Per Capita Income of Bottom 60% of Population (in USD)	182.82	169.76

Source: World Bank, World Development Indicators Online and Author's Calculations

from 1996. The table illustrates that for the bottom 60% of the population the per-capita income has gone up by a miserly 0.7% per year during the period while the economy was growing at 5% per annum.

What we see from here are two points: one is that Bangladesh is very poor, and two that the bottom two-thirds of the population is not reaping the benefits of the 5% growth that the country has seen over the last couple of decades. Given that most of the country still resides in small villages it will not be far-fetched to assume that most of the bottom two-third population of the country lives in the rural areas and is primarily involved in farming. Therefore, any effort to improve the situation in Bangladesh will have to look at the agricultural sector, and more importantly the rice market.

Role of Rice and Rice Markets

Rice has an unusually important place in the Bangladeshi diet, and this is reflected in the cropping pattern and agricultural output. It accounts for about 80% of total agricultural output. Three quarters of total gross cropped area in Bangladesh is used for rice production. This number rises to more than eighty percent in case of irrigated land. Rice accounted for 94% of national food-grain production in the late 1990s (Chowdhury & Haggblade 2000). No other country has such skewed cropping pattern.

The most important crop has traditionally been the Aman crop that is sown at the beginning of the rainy season and harvested in early Fall but over the last decade Boro output has exceeded that of Aman. Plots are usually used to grow more than one crop, and sometimes grow three crops in one year, though rice is not grown more than twice on any plot in any given year. Aus crop is harvested in the summer just before Aman crop is sown, and Boro is sown after Aman has been harvested. The country grows more than 500 varieties of paddy, but no generally agreed-upon quality standard exists in rice and paddy trade other than the director general of food's (DGF) single, long standing grade, Fair Average Quality (FAQ) (Chowdhury & Haggblade 2000), the single standard applied to government procurement. Even with so many different varieties farmers get one standard price from the trader. Lack of good information and transportation networks limit the choice that a farmer has. International measures of quality such as moisture content, presence of foreign matter, length of grain, etc. do not play a role in the Bangladesh rice market. 90% of all sales take place by visual inspection in both paddy and rice markets (Harriss-White 2007).

There are about 88000 villages in Bangladesh with an average of more than 200 households per village. The number of small rice traders in the country is about 50000, or about one trader for every two villages. Traders are the major buyer of the crop from the farmers, and with more than 50% of the total crop being marketed; their role in the economy is substantial. The traders buy the produce from the farmers, and in turn sell it to the wholesalers, or the rice mills. The traders do not have an incentive to work on the quality of produce since in the absence of any standardized measure of quality the price they get is fixed. This is passed down to the farmers, who in turn do not have an incentive to improvise or work on the betterment of the production process.

A quality scale needs to be introduced in the market. Table 4 details the average price of rice in various markets in the state of West Bengal, India, which lies on the western border of Bangladesh and those in Bangladesh. The harvest time average price of rice in Bangladesh is about 40-50% lower than that in West Bengal. Like Bangladesh, West Bengal produces various types of rice, but unlike Bangladesh, the rice markets in West Bengal offer differential prices. Hence there are some varieties which command a lower price, while there are others that command a higher price. This provides the farmers in West Bengal an incentive to innovate and invest in higher quality seeds, and better farming practices to improve the quality of output: something that is lacking in Bangladesh. With the government adopting a hands-off approach to quality standards, a private business has the opportunity to define new rules for the game and gain in the process.

In case of Bangladesh, there is one company which has the reach and the potential to do this: Grameen Group. They have everything that a company running the information network will need: Grameen Bank has more than 2500 branches which are accessible to 80000 of the 88000 villages; they have interests in telecom and information industries; and most importantly they share their dream of profit with the dream of inclusive growth of Bangladesh's poor people. There can be no better candidate there. One can find similar candidates elsewhere.

The prices for West Bengal are from Department of Agriculture & Cooperation, Ministry of Agriculture, Government of India.

Table 4. Price of rice in West Bengal (select markets) and Bangladesh, 1996-2001

Year	West Bengal			Bangladesh	
	Contai (INR)	Siliguri (INR)	Balurghat (INR)	Bangladesh (BDT)	Bangladesh (INR)
1996-97	905	940	870	543	458
1997-98	955	1069	1065	574	478
1998-99	1207	1273	1275	738	655
1999-2000	1050	1200	1146	646	565
2000-01	958	1098	1045	612	530
2001-02	936	1093	1093	677	583

The prices for Bangladesh have been calculated as the weighted average of the harvest prices of all three crops of Aus, Aman, and Boro, as reported by Ministry of Agriculture, Government of Bangladesh. The equivalent price in Indian Rupees has been estimated using the annual average exchange rate for each of the years. Data for exchange rates is from http://www.oanda.com/convert/fxhistory

CONCLUSION

The idea that private profit can drive a development project has not found many supporters, but ITC e-Choupal has probably initiated a change in that perception. The biggest strength of the project is that it is a simple solution that targets the most fundamental aspect of human lives: the betterment of one's own life and addresses this in simply terms for everyone to understand. The new system gives due respect to the existing one, and adds on to what was already good about the old system, rather than creating something from scratch. This reduces the cost of operations and makes transitions easier for all stakeholders. In addition, this system provides an excellent, sustainable, incentive mechanism that benefits everyone concerned. These are lessons that can be drawn from this case to be applied in different contexts.

The biggest problem with a mechanism like this is that the costs are still very high for most developing countries. Any person or institution wanting to implement something similar needs to have two things: a reach into the hinterlands, and the money needed to get the system going. According to some estimates, each center has upwards cost of $1000 to set up, though the cost to sustain it later will be much lower. This money has to be in place for preparation purposes. Scalability should not be an issue since the technical requirements of such a system are very basic. Malaysia, for example, has a similar project on smaller scale run by Malaysian Institute of Microelectronic Systems (MIMOS). A similar agricultural marketing initiative has taken root in China. If India, Malaysia, and China can do this, so can the others.

The model provides the opportunity of sustained growth to the farmers, whose produce has been compromised by a number of aspects including the colonial legacy of downplaying the importance of agriculture, inefficient agricultural markets, and others factors. It introduces an incentive mechanism for the farmers, and makes them a partner in the success of the whole system. By introducing competition, they take away the opportunities of rent seeking that is prevalent in most developing countries' agricultural markets. Political power will follow economic power as growth in almost every country has shown.

The biggest threats to the model are the political and social unrests that may be created as a result of a new system. Traders, though not a large portion of the populace, still wield very strong influence in the day-to-day social and political activities, and they are the group that might be hit the most in the process of creating a new system. Another issue might be the possibility of the coordinators taking the role of rent seekers as their number increases. In case of e-Choupal ITC recognizes this risk, and has therefore made every effort to introduce competition amongst the coordinators. There is the possibility of the evolving computing environment altering the complete scene, but the possibility of that happening in the rural parts of developing countries in the near future are very miniscule.

The model also has the potential to pass on the benefits of productivity increases to the farmers. Even with all the challenges and threats that the project may face, the benefits justify taking the big leap forward, but if only some company realizes the fortune at the bottom of this pyramid!

REFERENCES

Ahmed, R., Haggblade, S., & Elahi Chowdhury, T. (Eds.). (2000). *Out of the shadow of famine: Evolving food markets and food policy in Bangladesh*. Baltimore, MD: John Hopkins University Press.

Akerlof, G. A., & Shiller, R. J. (2009). *Animal spirits: How human psychology drives the economy, and why it matters for global capitalism*. Princeton, NJ: Princeton University Press.

Annamalai, K., & Rao, S. (2003). *ITC's e-Choupal and profitable rural transformation: Web-based information and procurement tools for Indian farmers*. Technical report, World Resource Institute Case Study.

Bhaduri, A. (1983). *The economic structure of backward agriculture*. London, UK: Academic Press.

Bharadwaj, K. (1974). *Production conditions in Indian agriculture*. Cambridge, UK: Cambridge University Press.

Bharadwaj, K. (1985). Agricultural market reforms in South Asia. *A View on Commercialization in Indian Agriculture and the Development of Capitalism, 13*, 82-89.

Chowdhury, N. (1992). *Rice markets in Bangladesh: A study in structure, conduct and performance. Bangladesh Food Policy Project Manuscript 22*. Washington, DC: International Food Policy Research Institute.

Chowdhury, N. (1994). *Credit and Bangladesh's food grain market: New evidence on commercialization, credit relations, and effect of credit access. Bangladesh Food Policy Project Manuscript 64*. Dhaka: International Food Policy Research Institute.

Chowdhury, N., Farid, N., & Roy, D. (2006). *Food policy liberalization in Bangladesh: How the governments and the markets delivered*. MTID Discussion Paper No. 92. Washington, DC: International Food Policy Research Institute

Chowdhury, N., & Haggblade, S. (2000). Evolving rice and wheat markets. In Ahmed, R., Haggblade, S., & Elahi Chowdhury, T. E. (Eds.), *Out of the shadow of famine: Evolving food markets and food policy in Bangladesh*. Baltimore, MD: John Hopkins University Press.

Crow, B. (2001). *Markets, class and rural change in Bangladesh*. London, UK: Palgrave.

Harriss-White, B. (2007). *Rural commercial capital: Agricultural markets in West Bengal*. New Delhi, India: Oxford University Press.

Hornik, R. C. (1988). *Development communication: Information, agriculture, and nutrition in the third world*. White Plains, NY: Longman Inc.

Lonergan, B. (1971). *Method in theology*. Toronto, ON: University of Toronto Press.

Prahalad, C. K. (2005). *The fortune at the bottom of the pyramid*. Upper Saddle River, NJ: Pearson Education, Inc.

Rudra, A. (1984). Local power and farm level decision making. In Desai, R., & Rudra, A. (Eds.), *Agrarian power and agricultural productivity in South Asia*. New Delhi, India: Oxford University Press.

Sarkar, S. (1979). *Marketing of foodgrains and patterns of exploitation*. Department of Economics, Occasional Paper No.1, Visva Bharti, Santiniketan, WB, India.

Sen, A. (1999). *Development as freedom*. New York, NY: Alfred P. Knopf.

Servaes, J. (Ed.). (2008). *Communication for development and social change*. New Delhi, India: Sage Publications.

Sorel, E., & Padoan, P. C. (Eds.). (2008). *The Marshall Plan: Lessons learned for the 21st century*. OECD Publishing.

Wankel, C. (Ed.). (2008). *Alleviating poverty through business strategy*. London, UK: Palgrave Macmillan. doi:10.1057/9780230612068

This work was previously published in Cases on Developing Countries and ICT Integration: Rural Community Development, edited by Rebecca Nthogo Lekoko and Ladislaus M. Semali, pp. 146-161, copyright 2012 by Information Science Reference (an imprint of IGI Global).

Chapter 3
E–Government's Role in Poverty Alleviation:
Case Study of South Africa

Stephen M. Mutula
University of Botswana, Botswana

EXECUTIVE SUMMARY

Governments the world over are increasingly implementing e-government systems as part of public sector reforms to enhance good governance and service delivery. This chapter reviews successful e-government projects in South Africa. E-governance is seen as a panacea to country's several challenges of service delivery, poverty, inequality, democracy, respect for human rights, and corruption. The South African government understands the urgency of addressing poverty and improving service delivery to majority of citizens who were marginalized during white majority rule. Most of South Africa's black majority, for example, lives in poverty compared to their white counterparts. To address these imbalances, projects are guided by the principle of public service for all under the brand Batho Pele (meaning people first). Some e-government projects in South Africa have borne fruits; they empowered people to overcome development obstacles, have helped fight poverty, and uplift the socio-economic and living standards of citizens. The challenges facing the e-government projects include high costs of broadband access, diversity of languages that need to be converted to the language of the Internet, red tape and bureaucratic system, as well as financial sustainability and the use of top down design approaches in projects with little or no initial user involvement.

DOI: 10.4018/978-1-4666-2071-1.ch003

INTRODUCTION

E-government is the use of information and communication technologies (ICTs) to improve the activities of public sector organizations (Heeks, 2002). It is aimed at enabling public administration to optimize its internal and external functions, facilitate social governance processes or objectives, such as information for political participation, consultation and consensus-seeking among governments, public servants, politicians and citizens (Sheridan and Riley, 2006). On the other hand, the term e-governance, is simply not a noun of e-government, but is used to describe an advanced form of e-government where instead of citizens being merely the recipient of government services, there is some engagement between the government and its people (Sheridan and Riley, 2006). Whether one uses the term e-government or e-governance as some people do, the focus is on enhancing service delivery by simplifying bureaucratic procedures, promoting efficiency, facilitating transparency, improving information sharing, innovation of service, and greater citizen empowerment.

There are different levels of government. Government-to-Citizens (G2C) is a form of government that includes all the interactions between a government and its citizens that can take place electronically with the aim of offering citizens faster, more responsive, more convenient and less complicated means to public services. Government-to-Business (G2B) refers to e-commerce in which government sells to businesses or provides them with services, as well as businesses selling products and services to government. The objective of G2B is to enable businesses to interact, transact and communicate with government online, with greater speed and convenience. Government-to-Employees (G2E) includes activities and services between government units and their employees aimed at developing and cultivating IT capabilities among government employees to deliver efficient and cost-effective services. Finally, Government-to-Government (G2G) interaction refers to activities between government ministries and/or departments. G2G may also involve government dealing with governments in other jurisdictions (Abissath, 2007).

Governments the world over, are increasingly implementing e-government systems as part of public sector reforms aimed at enhancing good governance and service delivery. Traditional-based government systems are characterized by transactions that involve manual physical filing systems which are burdened by enormous movements of correspondence, duplication of files, wastage of paper, difficulty in accessing information in files, and loss of data and general inefficiency of operations. Through e-government, governments want to provide efficient service delivery by integrating services and reduction of red-tape. Beck, Wigand and König (2003) observe that governments are implementing e-government systems, to obtain efficiency gains, improve service delivery to citizens and force governments to become more transparent and accountable in the way they carry out their businesses. Holmes (2001) adds that the purpose of e-government is to realize delivery of public services in a much more convenient, customer-oriented, cost-effective, and better way. E-government is also aimed at cutting costs, meeting citizen expectations and facilitating economic development. E-government systems also aim to bring about electronic delivery of high-quality and easily accessible administrative services to citizens and business.

However, implementation of e-government is not without challenges especially in developing countries. Gerhan & Mutula (2005) in a study of bandwidths problems in Botswana found that shortage of computers and poor connectivity were major factors hampering effective access. Lenhart, Horrigan, Rainie, Allen, Boyce, Madden, & O'Grady (2003) commenting on challenges of bridging the digital divide noted that not all "have nots" necessarily want to be "haves" and neither do they view engagement in ICTs as a positive force that would transform the quality of their life. Research work in the area of digital government in the US has revealed how the lack of appropriate access points amongst communities hinders the provision of social services by forcing individuals, often the poor, to travel long distances between offices (Bouguettaya, Ouzzani, Medjahead, & Cameron, 2001). African countries face even more challenges as testified by the Executive Secretary of the South African Development Community (SADC) who in 2003, observed that while efforts had been channeled towards the development of ICTs in the region (southern Africa), many challenges still prevailed such as low proportion of electrified households in most member states. Moreover, telecommunications facilities were generally poor and fixed line teledensity was low, with less than five percent of the population in the majority of SADC countries (SADC E-readiness Task Force, 2002).

The United Nations (2008) points out that in some instances, governments have spent vast amounts of money building online systems and products only to observe that their citizens do not fully utilize them. This challenge is in part occasioned by the multiple aspects of ICT implementations that have to be dealt with or people simply not willing to use it. Ngulube (2007) says that in sub-Saharan Africa, the ICT infrastructure is not widely available to rural populations, and in most cases, both government officials and the people who may want to use government services online lack basic skills. The World Bank in a report on 'African Region Communications Infrastructure Programme' released in early April 2007 (Nyasato & Kathuri, 2007) observed that east and southern African region suffers bandwidth deficiency as it accounts for less than one per cent of the world's international bandwidth capacity. Furthermore, telecommunication users face some of the highest costs in the world. The international wholesale bandwidth prices in the east and southern Africa region are 20 to 40 times higher than in the United States, and international calls are on average 10 to 20 times more costly than in other developing countries (Nyasato & Kathuri, 2007).

Despite challenges facing e-government implementation some efforts are being made to address them in different jurisdictions across the world. Countries in the developed world have in particular, enhanced e-readiness environment to enhance uptake of ICTs in most sectors of their economies. E-readiness refers to a community that has high-speed access; constant access and application of ICTs in government offices, businesses, healthcare facilities and homes; user privacy and online security; and government policies which are favorable in terms of promoting connectedness and the use of the network (Bridges.org, 2001). The e-readiness status of the nation should also be accompanied by education and training of the people, use of appropriate technologies (e.g. radio and television), private public partnerships for resource mobilization, research and development and creating relevant content accessible and useable to all citizens.

A policy framework that ensures universal access is a necessary precondition for enhanced digital inclusion and trust-building of citizens in e-government. As part of universal access strategies, diversity of choices of accessing content should be encouraged by allowing users to use a variety of technologies with which to gain access, such as the telephone, fax, e-mail, kiosks, face-to-face interaction, etc. Universal access should be accompanied by freedom of access to information through constitutional guarantees that enhance sharing of information (Farelo and Morris, 2006). The European Union member states (European Commission, 2005) have undertaken measures to ban the sale of inaccessible technology products while enhancing the growth of assistive technology as one way of promoting universal access. Moreover, national strategies of member states emphasize interoperability of products, universal service policies for electronic communications, affordable pricing of network, and interactive content. The European Commission through the eEurope initiative recognizes accessibility for disabled users such as the blind, deaf people or people with learning impairments. Elsewhere, the Singaporean government portal provides information services on culture, recreation, sports, defence and security, education, employment, family, community development, health and environment that are at the heart of day to day needs of the people. The portal also includes user-centric hot links such as 'give us your feedback on national issues and policies' (Government of Singapore, 2004). The Canadian e-government portal on the other hand, enables public participation that allows individuals to share their opinions on specified subjects, or to participate in various activities (Government of Canada, 2006).

A legal oriented framework is also necessary in e-government implementation to cater for cyber laws, consumer protection, and the security of transactions online (Department of IT eTechnology Group -India, 2003). Content providers must also promote cultural and linguistic diversity online with regard to identity, traditions and religions. Sensitivity to cultural values can be buttressed by local content development, providing local content that is relevant to the people and in languages they understand. Efforts in addressing e-government challenges should also include providing useful and beneficial content to the customers if they have to be motivated to use it (Baeza-Yates and Ribeiro-Neto, 1999). Holzer and Kim (2005) outline other areas of e-government where attention is needed to include: security online, usability of government portal, IT spending as a percentage of GDP, PC penetration, and improved broadband households and wireless subscribers,

This chapter draws from international practice and experience then, reviews successful e-government projects in South Africa and discusses the challenges facing the country in its e-government implementation. The lessons learned include the critical success factors such as improving access, creating of awareness among people, having a clear vision shared and communicated, setting achievable targets, investing enough resources in the projects, political support, developing private-public partnership, enabling infrastructure, branding and marketing. The chapter concludes with tangible questions and suggested solutions.

BACKGROUND

South Africa's population was estimated at 50 000 000 million in 2008 (Department of Communications 2008). About 45 percent of this population live in rural areas (Geness, 2004) spread in nine provinces of the country whose dynamics are shown in Table 1.

The country has eleven official languages of which Afrikaans, English, Nguni, Sotho, Tswana, Zulu, and Xhosa are most widely spoken. The human poverty index (HPI) in 2004 was estimated at 20 percent. The high HPI was attributed mainly to challenges related to poverty eradication, job creation, security, housing, health, education, water and electricity, and a bureaucratic system of government (Geness, 2004).

The Republic of South Africa (RSA) is a constitutional democracy consisting of three structures of government, namely: national, provincial and local governments. Each of the country's nine provinces has its own provincial legislature. The National Assembly is the supreme law-making body. Laws made by the National Assembly are applicable throughout the RSA. The same is true of policies made by the Cabinet of the National Government. While there are areas of exclusive legislative competence for the National Assembly, it shares its legislative authority with provincial legislatures. Parliament consists of two Houses: the National Assembly and the National Council of Provinces (NCOP). The National Assembly is elected for a term of five years and consists of up to 400 Members. Members are elected in accordance with an electoral system, based on a common voters' roll with a minimum

Table 1. South Africa population demographics (Source: SITA 2002b)

Province Name	% of Rural Population	% of Population Urban
Eastern Cape	63.4	36.6
Free state	68.6	31.4
Northern Cape	70.1	29.9
Kwazulu Natal	57.9	42.1
Northwest	65.1	34.9
Limpopo	89.0	11.0
Mpumalanga	60.1	39.9
Gauteng	97.0	3.0
Western cape	88.9	11.1

age of 18 years, resulting in a system of proportional representation. The provincial governments are bound by laws and policies passed at national level, but can develop their own laws and policies within this framework to suit their specific needs. Provincial legislatures may pass their own constitutions subject to the provisions of the Constitution of the RSA. Finally, Local governments consist of municipalities which are responsible for providing democratic and accountable government for local communities, ensuring the provision of services to communities and promoting social and economic development (Department of Communications, 2008).

Most of South Africa's black majority lives in poverty compared to their white counterparts. This disparity is the result of several years of apartheid white government that marginalized the blacks from mainstream economic activities. The Democratic Government has put in place various poverty alleviation programmes and is using e-government as part of the interventions in an attempt to improve service delivery. The Government's commitment to using e-government is reflected in policy/regulatory framework and ICT infrastructure development aimed at fighting poverty and uplifting the socio-economic and living standards of all citizens. ICT has the potential to empower people to overcome development obstacles, address social problems, and strengthen democratic institutions. Some of the e-government projects in South Africa have borne fruits but others have faced significant challenges. Government has also improved telecommunication infrastructure including radio and television access, broadband internet connectivity, cell phone and fixed line penetration as part of its efforts to enhance service delivery in order to improve the living standards of its people...

The challenges facing the e-government projects in South Africa include: higher costs of broadband access, diversity of languages that need to be converted to the language of the Internet, red tape and bureaucratic system of government, several agencies' involvement in e-government implementation without central coordination mechanism, shortage of electricity supply, lack of a comprehensive and easily accessible evidence base to support strategic policy decision-making, limited focus on corruption, serious shortage of ICT personnel, rural-urban digital divide, financial sustainability and the use of top down design approaches in projects with little or no initial user involvement.

Setting the Stage

E-government has been adopted by the World Bank and the United Nations as a developmental instrument (Cloate, 2007) because it makes easier for business and individuals to deal with government directly and timeously; enables government to offer services and information through new media like the Internet; improves communications between different parts of government so that people do not have to be asked repeatedly for the same information by different service providers. E-government also gives staff in offices better access to information so that they can deal with members of the public more efficiently and more helpfully; and makes it easier for different parts of government to work in partnership with central government. E-government encourages citizen participation in the decision-making process and makes government more accountable, transparent and efficient (UNESCO, 2004).

E-government is perceived as a panacea to the deficiencies of the traditional form of government where, citizens physically go to government offices to seek services, such as applying for a passport, birth certificate, death certificate or filing tax returns with the consequent delays arising out of long queues, lost files or the absence of relevant officials. Developed and transitional economies have made remarkable strides in electronic government while, African states' performance remains poor. The leading e-government countries in the world according to 2005 statistics are shown in Table 2.

Regionally, Europe provided leadership in e-government, followed by North America, while South Asia, Central Asia and Africa were ranked last in that descending order respectively. The 2006 global e-government readiness rankings by the Economist Intelligence Unit (2006) showed that of the 68 countries ranked, Denmark retained its top position from the previous year, followed by the US, Switzerland, and Sweden. The next five countries, in order of e-government readiness, were the UK, Netherlands, Finland, Australia, Canada and Hong Kong. Overall, Europe remained the dominant region worldwide as far as e-government was concerned. In Africa, the only countries that made it to the list of those that were ranked well included South Africa (35th), Egypt (55th), Nigeria (60th) and Algeria (63rd). The governments that are leaders in e-government have relatively high service/product quality compared to traditional form of government where there is unnecessary

Table 2. Global e-government readiness index

Country	E-government Readiness Index	Rank
United States	(0.9062	1st
Denmark	0.9058),	2nd
Sweden	0.8983	3rd
United Kingdom	(0.8777	4th
South Korea	0.8727	5th
Singapore	(0.8503	6th
Estonia	0.7347	7th
Malta	0.7012	8th
Chile	0.6963	9th

(Source: United Nations, 2005)

level of red-tape, bureaucracy and restrictive procedures and processes. Moreover e-government enabled jurisdictions have advanced government systems with regard to efficient delivery of public services; digital democracy and citizen participation in government (Holzer and Kim, 2005)

E-government ensures that government processes and services observe the law and maintain their integrity in satisfying citizen needs through the delivery of relevant, value-added and high-quality services. Moreover, e-government is expected to enhance accountability and integrity in government. It also offers the prospect of cheaper and more effective management and processing of information; facilitates free flow of information between departments; enhances transparency especially with regard to procurement of services; provides opportunities to work in partnership with the private sector, and enables citizens to participate directly in governance especially in influencing policy decision. Moreover, e-government improves internal operations of government to reduce cost and time of service delivery; increase accessibility of information about public services in order to empower citizens; enhance accountability and provide specific services electronically.

The importance of e-government in enhancing service delivery through cutting bureaucracy and making government more accountable and transparent to the citizens cannot be over emphasized. E-government also plays an important role in improving the lives of the people by enabling access to opportunities available on government portals. United Nations Department of Economic and Social Affairs, UNDESA (2005) observes that the application of information and communication technology within public administration optimises its internal and external functions, (thereby providing) government, the citizen and business with a set of tools that can potentially transform the way in which interactions take place, services are delivered, knowledge is utilized, policy is developed and implemented, the way citizens participate in governance and public administration reform; and the way good governance goals are met. The application of ICTs on all sectors of the economies is perceived in the context of leap-frogging development, information societies and host of other electronic age applications for the previously excluded communities (The Economist Newspaper and The Economist Group, 2005). This view is shared by the World Summit on Information Society which in its declaration of principles after the Geneva Summit noted that digital revolution fired by the engines of the information and communication technologies had fundamentally brought new ways of running government, providing speedy delivery of healthcare, and improving the living standards for millions of people around the world (World Summit on Information Society, 2003).

E-Government in South Africa

The government of South Africa has expressed intention and commitment in rolling out ICTs throughout the country to enhance universal access and universal service in order to bridge the digital divide and achieve digital inclusion for all in the country. Through various national ICT initiatives including e-government, the government expects to leverage the needed resources to realize the Millennium Development Goals (MDGs), Vision 2014 (the nation's development blue print) aspirations, and the World Summit on Information Society Declaration of Principles to bridge the digital divide and enhance digital inclusion for all South Africans in order to promote socio-economic development of the citizens. There are various players in the South African e-government environment the major ones being: Department of Communications, State Information Technology Agency (SITA), Government Information Technology Organising Committee (GITOC), Meraka Africa Institute, Presidential National Commission on Information Society & Development (PNC-ISAD 2005; Cloate, 2007).

E-government is seen by South African government as a panacea to country's several challenges of service delivery, poverty, inequality, democracy, respect for human rights and corruption. Meyer (2007) in a study of the use of Internet at provincial and local level found that majority of them was unhappy with the level of success in using the Internet to seek services. Consequently, the South African government understands the urgency of addressing poverty and improving service delivery to majority of citizens who were marginalized during white majority rule for more than three decades. To address these imbalances the government is implementing e-government projects guided by the principle of public service for all under the brand '*Batho Pele*' (translated to mean people first)'. The eight Batho Pele principles serve as acceptable policy and legislative framework regarding service quality in the public service. These principles include (Department of Public Service and Administration, 1996): consultation (engaging with customers in terms of what they want, etc), service standards (continually improving services, etc); access (enabling disadvantaged persons to access services, speaking in understandable language, etc); courtesy (being polite, courteous and friendly to customers, etc); information (reaching all customers to make sure they are well informed about the services government departments provide, etc); openness and transparency (being open and honest about every aspect of work by publishing annual reports to tell citizens how resources were used, how much everything cost, including costs for staff, equipment delivery, services, etc); redress / dealing with complaints (providing a mechanism for customers to tell when they are unhappy with service, etc); and best value (giving customers the best service using all the resources, eliminating waste, fraud and corruption, and finding new ways of improving services at little or no cost, etc).

E-Government Supporting Infrastructure in South Africa

The government of South Africa is using ICT or e-government generally and specifically to implement various poverty alleviation programmes. The Reconstruction and Development Programme (RDP) is a government's commitment to meet basic needs of the citizens in addition to the provision of safe portable water to all by 2008 and universal access to energy by 2012. The Municipal Public-Private Partnership Pilot Programme (MPPP) is geared towards encouraging and supporting municipal public/private partnerships. Growth Employment and Reconstruction (GEAR) advocates for reducing state spending also for the deficit and the size of the public sector. Besides, the Reconstruction and Development Programme (the RDP) is concerned with bringing the private sector into a programme of service extensions. Black Economic Empowerment aims at enhancing the socio-economic status especially of the South African blacks (Burger, 2005; Mail and Guardian Online, 2008). To ensure speedy implementation of the poverty alleviation strategies, the government of South Africa at all levels has prioritised in regulatory and policy reform. The most significant policy reforms have included citizen-centred and multi-channel delivery of services with a particular emphasis on online delivery; making use of public-private partnerships to realize integrated and citizen-centred outcomes, efficiency - cost reductions; service - better quality, easier access (i.e. 24/7), new services; democracy -participation and interactive dialogue (Remmen, 2003).

Policy and regulatory framework is a necessary precondition for enhancing digital inclusion to achieve an information society (Commonwealth Telecommunications Organization, 2004). The country's freedom of information (FOI) act stipulates the constitutional right of access to information by its citizens (Farelo and Morris,

2006). The act enables the sharing of information between the public and all levels of government departments. The ICT policy on the other hand, focuses on transforming interaction between government and society; improving e-government, e-services and e-business; improving service delivery, productivity and cost effectiveness. The policy has been responsible for the enhanced telecommunication environment through the liberalization of telecom sector. The universal service and access policy a component of the ICT policy aims at achieving universal service for all South Africans. The universal service and access policy has created an enabling environment for stimulating public awareness of the benefits of ICT services and also for building capacity to access these services.

The South African government has also put in place an e-government vision which addresses three main domains: electronic services across government departments (G2G); e-service to citizens (G2C); and electronic services with business sector (G2B) among others (Farelo and Morris, 2006). The Government Communication and Information System (GCIS) - a government information service, ensures the public is informed of the e-government implementation through direct dialogue, with people in disadvantaged areas. The State Information Technology Agency SITA co-ordinates IT resources in government in order to increase delivery capabilities of services and enhance interoperability. The Government enacted Broadband Infraco Act in 2007 which establishes the new state owned enterprise with the aim of increasing bandwidth capacity and ultimately reducing the cost of telecommunication for South African public. Broadband Infraco is responsible for expanding the availability and affordability of access to electronic communications networks and services, including but not limited to underdeveloped and under-serviced areas; national long-distance backbone network; metro and access networks (other licensed operators); and international connectivity network (Government Gazette, 2008). South African government through its major telecommunication operator Telkom operates both fixed line and mobile communications services throughout the country with broadband footprint of ADSL and WiMAX covering the whole country (Telkom, 2007). Moreover, South Africa has a network that is exclusively digital and includes the latest in fixed-line, wireless and satellite communications. The country has also an expansive cell phone infrastructure consisting of four mobile phone operators, namely Vodacom, MTN, Cell C and Virgin Mobile. The 2007 estimates of cell phone penetration were close to 90 percent. The FIFA soccer world cup held in South Africa from 11 June-11 July 2010 s caused government to set aside between 2-5 billion Rands (US$ 312.5 billion) for ICT infrastructure development (Telkom, 2007) which s accelerated the provision of powerful, state-of-the-art ICT infrastructure in the country.

South African government in partnership with other African countries such as Kenya, Botswana, Mozambique, Uganda, Rwanda, and Sudan undertook major undersea fibre optic cabling on the east coast of Africa to provide faster broadband connectivity of the continent to the rest of the world. Notable among other projects included: SEACOM an undersea fibre optic cable system which was completed (in July 2009) to connect South and East Africa to the global networks in India, the Middle East and Europe. In particular, SEACOM connects South Africa, Mozambique, Madagascar, Tanzania and Kenya to India and Italy, where other international cables currently exist (Free Daily Newsletter, 2007). South Africa is already connected to Europe through SAT-3/WASC or South Atlantic 3/West Africa Submarine Cable linking Portugal and Spain to South Africa, with connections to several West African countries along the route. In addition, the Eastern African Submarine Cable System (Eassy) project that has been completed links South Africa from Mtunzini to Sudan and provides landing stations in countries along the coast of east Africa. The government of South Africa is also involved in building a West Coast marine cable to link South Africa to Europe and another cable to the Americas. Known as UhuruNet, this west coast of Africa undersea broadband fibre optic cable will piggyback on a two-fibre link from Nigeria to Portugal (Hamlyn, 2008). This cable is intended to upgrade the SAT-3-WASC which was installed several years ago. These fibre optic undersea infrastructure projects are expected to enhance communication in South Africa with the rest of Africa and the entire world.

Department of Communications (2008) points out that South Africa has also expansive infrastructure in terms of radio broadcasting. For example, South African Broadcasting Corporation, SABC is the country's public broadcaster. Established in 1950, it broadcasts in 11 languages that include among others English, Afrikaans, Zulu, Xhosa and Sesotho. The SABC's national radio network comprises 15 public broadcast-service radio stations, and three commercial radio stations reaching an audience of 19 million. Moreover, apart from radio broadcasting, SABC has three full-spectrum free-to-air channels and one satellite pay-TV channel aimed at audiences in Africa. A daily adult audience of almost 20 million people is reached daily via the terrestrial signal distribution network and a satellite signal. Four million licensed television households are available in South Africa. Besides, the public broadcaster SABC, there are private broadcasters such as E.tv, South Africa's second-largest television channel with a viewership of 10 665 000. There is also M-Net, South Africa's subscription television service. With regard to connectivity, the Internet connectivity is also expanding in South Africa among the people. In 2007, some 3.9 million active unique browsers were registered, representing a 121 percent increase on the number in May 2005 (Department of Communications, 2008).

The expansive cell phone infrastructure in South Africa is facilitating community development. Some of the cellular phone providers are involved in promoting access in rural communities. For example, Vodacom deployed more than 90 000 community-service telephones to South Africa's underserviced areas where they provide invaluable sources of entrepreneurial activity for hundreds of community phone-shop operators. Since its launch in 1994, the Community Phone Shop concept has expanded into communication centres in which entrepreneurs, job seekers and schoolchildren access essential business communication services, such as faxes, e-mails and the Internet daily (Department of Communications, 2008). The government has also rolled out Multi-purpose Community Centres (MPCC), public places where people can access computers, the Internet, and other digital technologies that enable them to gather information, create, learn, and communicate with others while they develop essential digital skills (Benjamin, 2000). Similarly, the South African Post Office with the policy to provide a universal service at an affordable price for all citizens in partnership with the Department of Communications installed public information terminals in about 800 post offices throughout the country especially in settlements without internet cafes or other form of access to the internet (Department of Communications, 2008).

Government has been involved in deploying wireless broadband to 500 Dinaledi schools (model schools of excellence) and target clinics, hospitals, libraries, post offices, and Thusong Centres to help increase uptake and usage of ICTs and help deliver inclusivity in building an information society. Government is also undertaking G2G initiatives that include automation of department of justice processes for state attorneys, common databases for citizens, wireless internet labs for distance education, and computer centres in informal settlements using converted containers to provide training (SITA, 2002).

Case Description: E-Government Experience in South Africa

Each of South Africa's nine provinces has a website providing provincial information (SITA, 2002). Two provinces (Western Cape and Gauteng) are ahead of the others. Both Gauteng and Western Cape provinces have an information portal about the provincial government. The provincial government also provides each school with a computer for students to access internet and have e-mail addresses. Gauteng province has a GIS – information about the geography of the province. Both Western Cape and Gauteng provinces have automated library services. In addition, they have a document warehousing which enables information sharing for ministers. The national government of South Africa has made progress in implementing e-government including implementation of a video and audio streaming solution to enable virtual collaboration for management; management information system for collecting data and information. The Department of Public Service and Administration implemented a document, information, knowledge sharing and virtual collaboration system in a secure environment for the cabinet members. The Department of Home Affairs has implemented a network information system consisting of an integrated data base of citizen. In addition, the government has implemented wireless internet labs for distance education and computer centers in informal settlements using converted containers to provide training. The South African Revenue Services has implemented a call centre for tax queries, personal tax e-filing and electronic delivery of tax certificates. The government portal provides information about services offered by government. The portal provides a seamless access to information and services of the government (SITA, 2002).

The South African government successfully implemented a National Traffic Information System (eNATIS) in 2007. During the first six months of 2008 more than 75 million transactions were performed on the National Traffic Information System (eNaTIS). With the exception of routine maintenance outside of business hours, downtime was virtually non-existent in the first half of the year and phenomenal system processing time was experienced. The eNaTIS processed 96 percent of all transactions in less than two seconds, 99.8 percent in less than 10 seconds and 99.95 percent in less than 60 seconds. The eNATIS is an e-government application that is used for processing driving license; registration and licensing of motor vehicle; notification of change of ownership/sale of motor vehicle; and application for learner's license. The transactions and services carried through this application can be provided by most transport offices across all the provinces in the country (National Traffic Information System, 2008). Before e-NATIS was launched on April 12, 2007, its predecessor (Natis) maintained an average of 300 000 transactions a day. But the average daily transaction rose to 600 000 a year later (Segar, 2008).

The other land mark of an e-government project in South Africa is the Independent Electoral Commission (IEC's) e-procurement system that allows for open and transparent bidding of government tenders aimed at preventing corruption. Through this project, the IEC leverages tools of multi-access to promote free and fair elections. In 2004 for example, IEC in partnership with cell phone service providers, enabled voters to short message service their identity number and in return receive messages back indicating their eligibility to vote and voting stations details. Moreover, a satellite-enabled network made it possible for the commission to register voters, relay, collect and verify ballots, and relay results across the country. During the 2004 elections results, custom-designed handheld scanners captured information from bar-coded ID books and greatly streamlined the process of voter registration (Farelo and Morris, 2006).

The government of South Africa has enabled 355 multipurpose community centres (including cyber labs in schools) to provide villages access to ICT. Moreover, all universities in the country and about 6000 schools are ICT enabled and about 800 public information terminals (PITs) have been established. Additionally, over 80 percent of health centres are connected with ICTs and all provincial and national government departments and many local governments have websites and e-mail addresses. The educational portal Thusong has been established to help educators and learners to access curriculum related information and a language portal using all official languages has been established. Furthermore, an open source software desktop application has been translated into South African Official Languages (Farelo and Morris, 2006). The other remarkable achievements have been in the horizontal integration of e-government across agencies and departments within the same level of government. Moreover, integration of transversal systems in government in particular the case management system used by police, pensions and unemployment insurance systems and the subsidy management system used by housing; integrated financial management systems (IFMS) are in place. The automation of finger prints; development of an electronic population registry; home affairs national information system (HANIS) through which citizens can access birth and death registration forms online are established. Finally, the pensions and unemployment insurance systems used respectively by Welfare and Labour; and the subsidy management system used by Housing (Farelo and Morris, 2006) have been put in place.

The UN Global E-government Readiness Survey for 2008 (United Nations, 2008) observes that South Africa had a strong online presence. In particular, the website of the Department of Labour was an excellent example of a public agency portal that was well tailored to the needs of its stakeholders. The website was commented for being attractive and simple in design allowing users to easily find information they were looking for. In addition, there were various online filings/registrations and the posting of online vacancies. Perry (2008) noted that the Department of Labour website was a full featured site that was a one stop-shop for Labour issues. Meyer (2007) in his study of use of internet for e-governance in South Africa found that 38 percent of respondents participated in opinion polls, 36 percent commented on white papers, 34 percent participated in policy making and 37 percent engaged political leaders through e-mails. He concluded that there was high usage of e-governance services by citizens.

Kekana and Heeks (2008) found that the introduction of IT into the national Welfare Agency which administers social security funds including national pension fund (NPF) paid to those who retired normally from work and a Workers' Compensation Fund (WCF) paid to those forced to retire because of various reasons had some success. The purpose of the project was to integrate and decentralize previously separate manual based centralized operations of NFP and WCF. The computerized system was expected to address problems associated with payments delays, incorrect recordings of figures, and lack of communication between the two agencies. The project was partly successful because, lead times were reduced. For example, the processing of funeral grants which used to take three months now takes 30 minutes; monthly bills are now accurate and timely making debt chasing faster; the number of complaints has been reduced, and timely status reporting is available to managers. Key success factors in this project were attributed to consultants who were hired to fill gaps of in-house and in-country shortage of skills; organization-wide user training exercise that was undertaken, and the fact that the project was taken in an incremental way first through pilots.

Local government is South Africa has demonstrated successful implementation of e-government projects. For example, local authorities in the cities of Cape Town, Johannesburg, Pretoria and Durban are cases in point. The city of Cape Town has successfully integrated GIS applications that are considered best practices in Africa (Cloete, 2007). Moreover, Leo van den Berg, Andre van der Meer, Willem van Winden and Paulus Woets (2006) compared globally eight cities – Barcelona, Cape Town, Eindhoven, Johannesburg, Manchester, Tampere, the Hague and Venice on a range of innovative urban e-governance strategies with regard to access policies (for improving access to ICTs for all citizens), content policies (directed at improving the use of ICTs in the city administration and semi-public domains) and infrastructure policies (for improving the provision of broadband infrastructure). These cities were selected for their best practices in e-government. For each of the cities, e-strategies and policies were critically reviewed and compared. In another, study in 2005 of global digital government of 98 municipalities, the city of Cape Town (South Africa) was the only one selected from Africa. It was ranked at 31st position (Holzer and Kim, 2005). The evaluation focused on current practices in government with regard to digital governance (delivery of public services), digital democracy (citizen participation in government), security, usability, content of websites, type of online services offered, and citizens' participation in governance.

Current Challenges of E-Government in South Africa

South Africa amid its efforts to enhance e-government services faces several service delivery challenges. A study by the Business Leadership Group on 15 well performing economies worldwide found that ADSL (broadband) costs in South Africa were 139 percent higher than the average rate in the nations surveyed. The study noted that local calls at peak hours were 199 percent more expensive (Naidoo, 2007). The Minister for Communications of South African on 3 June 2008 told Parliament that with regard to uptake as well as access and the cost to communicate…'we face great challenges… our goal in making these services universally affordable is yet to be achieved…the costs still remain high (Matsepe-Casaburri, 2008). President Thabo Mbeki in the 2005 state of national address (Mbeki, 2005) noted we [have] unacceptable situation in which some of our fixed line rates are 10 times lower than those of developed in the OECD.

Geness (2004) pointed out that the 45 percent of the population living in rural areas in South Africa suffers from least developed ICT infrastructure compared to the urban areas coupled with low PC penetration. South Africa has also diversity of languages with 11 official ones that need to be converted to the language of the Internet. Excessive red tape and bureaucratic system of government does not favour speedy service delivery. For example, longer delays characterized the introduction of second network operator (SNO) and VOIP for over ten years. There was also conflict between Telkom the official telecom provider and government on pricing regimes of bandwidth. Moreover, there is incessant state interference with telecommunication regulatory agencies contributing to poor service delivery. During the better part of 2008 South Africa experienced shortage of electricity supply needed to power the ICT infrastructure for service delivery and socio-economic development. The March 2007 NEPAD Support Unit of Economic Commission for Africa (ECA) publication noted that without access to sufficient, quality and reliable energy, every social and development activity was critically constrained (Economic Commission for Africa, 2006). President Thabo Mbeki the then South African President in the 2008 state of the nation address noted that the national emergency presented by the power outages posed the challenge to the entirety of the [South African] nation. In essence the significant rise in electricity demand outstripped the new capacity that was brought on stream. The resultant tight supply situation made the overall system vulnerable to any incident affecting the availability of energy. This situation precipitated the inevitable realization that the era of very cheap and abundant electricity had come to an end.

Farelo and Morris (2006) point out that South Africa lacks a comprehensive and easily accessible evidence base to support strategic policy decision-making and programme design to leverage ICTs for Information Society development. This negatively affects timeous detection of service delivery challenges for the purpose of effecting corrective action, thereby impinging on the ability of the state to deliver effectively and efficiently in terms of the ICT for development agenda. Moreover, although the e-government vision is articulated in various policy documents, reference to corruption is notably absent. Besides, until recently, the e-government strategy did not include G2E (government to employee) component yet, this is crucial for successful e-government implementation programmes.

Department of Communications (2008) points out that the central challenge to the implementation of Information Society Development Plan (ISAD) in South Africa is the serious shortage of ICT skills and the state's limited capacity to deliver these critical skills. This skills shortage is exacerbated by brain drain of skilled ICT personnel and professionals to developed countries and from public to private sector. Education and training is unable to produce the essential and technical management skills that most employees seek. The School Register of Needs Survey in 2000 reveals that schools that used computers for teaching and learning in South Africa was 12.3 percent and those that had access to e-mail and Internet was 6.9 percent. The 2003 Human Resource Development review showed that over the last ten years only 12 percent of graduates in 1999 obtained postgraduate qualifications in ICT. UNDP (2003:57) observes that the Government of South Africa has not yet succeeded in building the human resource base at local government level. Instead, efforts were directed at national and provincial level. The government business and administration processes have also been dogged with several problems related to lack of a central accessible information pool for important personal details on citizens and this has resulted in unnecessary duplication and wastage of manpower. Former President Thabo Mbeki noted that it was clear that more work needed to be done to raise the skills levels of the people of South Africa. The reasons for the delay in implementing some of the programmes included the subjective capacity of the implementing agents where at least financial resources were made available (Mbeki, 2005) and the fact that many of [the] people, including the youth, lacked the education and skills that [the] economy and society needed.

Geness (2004) writing in the context of South African e-government initiatives noted that delivery of services was largely hampered by unequal access to all citizens to national resources. Meyer (2007) in a study of the utilization of multipurpose community centres identified among other constraints, long distance travelled by users to nearest centre (on average they travelled up to 7 kilometres); lack of skills to use the Internet, read or understand the content; long waiting times to use the internet and high costs of access. These challenges were exacerbated by the fact that there was a growing theft of copper cables that undermined the implementation of the local loop unbundling policy in South Africa (Matsepe-Casaburri, 2008).

During 2005, SADC member states were assessed for digital opportunity index (DOI) – a tool used to measure and evaluate the opportunity, infrastructure and utilization of ICTs by government and its people. It monitors recent technologies such as broadband and mobile Internet access, falling price of broadband, and increasing broadband speeds (World Information Society Report, 2006). The DOI ranking of SADC member states in general showed that though great opportunities existed for most countries to partake in e-government, little was being done in terms of taking advantage of such opportunities. South Africa did not fare well either as it was ranked 91st in the world behind Seychelles and Mauritius in SADC region out of 180 countries that were surveyed. Benjamin (1999) in the context of post-apartheid South Africa has shown how community-based ICT projects have failed due to non-participatory approaches being used. The Golaganang (coming together), a joint initiative between South African government on one hand, and the private sector on the other in 2002 which was conceived to provide public service employees with affordable computer bundle (multimedia PC, operating systems, application software, modem and internet connectivity, a printer, three year extended warranty and interactive tutorial software) did not achieve desired outcome. Each school in the Golaganang community was to receive a computer each. It was expected that through this project, inequitable access to technology would in part be addressed, improve digital literacy among public servants, improve utilization of ICT in their work, and bring benefits of employment. The project was premised on shared risks and benefits but the project failed to take off when HP (private sector partners in the project) asked government to give guarantees to the value of (US$ 73m) to allow the project to go ahead (Levin, 2008).

Kekana and Heeks (2008) found that the introduction of IT into the national Welfare Agency which administers social security funds including national pension fund (NPF) paid to those who retired normally from work and a Workers' Compensation Fund (WCF) paid to those forced to retire because of various reasons in part failed. The initial plan was to computerize 100 of the system in three years, but six years down the line, only 40 percent of the system was computerized. Cost cutting did not happen because of hiring consultants and costs moved from US$43million to US$60million.

For e-government to be effectively implemented in South Africa, a number of interventions or improvements are needed. A national information infrastructure with foot prints across the country would help achieve universal access to the entire population especially the disadvantaged rural folk. Physical Infrastructure that consists of Internet access points in convenient places such as public libraries, shopping malls, government offices, hospitals, subway stations and clubs and relevant public places for the citizens to use free of charge is imperative. Technology infrastructure made up of computers, servers, networks (broadband and wireless), mobile devices, smart cards as well as technology standards that are open and scalable such as Java, XML, Web services would facilitate transversality and portability. It is also important that government considers private public partnerships to help finance costly infrastructure development across the country. Government priorities for e-government should espouse accessibility, affordability, and appropriate citizen content. It is imperative for the South African government to ensure that citizens are aware about the potential of e-government and should be trained to make use e-government services. Authentication infrastructure that consists of e-government id and password for all its citizens would help instill a sense of security while online. Services that consist of portal which enables citizens to ask questions and receive answers on for example, payment of taxes and fines; issuance and renewal of driver's licenses; employment opportunities; social services such health and education are needed if e-government has to play its rightful role in poverty reduction in South Africa.

REFERENCES

Abissath, M. K. A. (2007). *E-government: The Singapore experience.* Retrieved November 26, 2007, from http://abissathfeatures-mawu.blogspot.com/2007/10/e-government-singapore-experience2.html

Beck, R., Wigand, R. T., & König, W. (2003). Beyond the electronic commerce diffusion race: Efficiency prevails. *Proceedings of the 11th European Conference on Information Systems (ECIS) on ICT standardization,* 14 December 2003. Sheraton Seattle WA.

Benjamin, P. (1999). Community development and democratization through Information Technology: Building the new South Africa. In Heeks, R. (Ed.), *Reinventing government in the information age. International practice in ICT-enabled public sector reform* (pp. 194–210). London, UK: Rutledge.

Benjamin, P. (2000). *Telecentres in South Africa.* Retrieved August 13, 2009, from http://ip.cais.cornell.edu/commdev/documents/jdc-benjamin.doc/

Bouguettaya, A., Ouzzani, M., Medjahead, B., & Cameron, J. (2001). Helping citizens of Indiana: Ontological approach to managing state and local government databases. *IEEE Computer,* February.

Bridges.org. (2001). *Comparison of e-readiness assessment models: Final draft.* Retrieved July 16, 2003, from http://www.bridges.org/eredainess/tools.html

Burger, R. (2005). What we have learnt from post-1994 innovations in pro-poor service delivery in South Africa: A case study-based analysis. *Development Southern Africa, 22*(4), 483–500. doi:10.1080/03768350500322966

Cloate, F. (2007). *Knowledge management and trust in government: Lessons from South Africa.* Global Forum on Reinventing Government: Building Trust in Government, 26 – 29 June 2007 Vienna, Austria.

Commonwealth Telecommunications Organisation. (2004). *Regional round-up: Libraries help bridge the digital divide.* IFLA Submission to WSIS Process. Retrieved July 22, 2009, from http://www.ictdevagenda.org/frame.php?dir=07&sd=10&sid=1&id=441

Department of Communications. (2008). *South African yearbook*. Retrieved July 30, 2009, from http://www.gcis.gov.za/docs/publications/yearbook/2008/chapter5.pdf

Department of IT e-technology Group (India). (2003). *Assessment of central ministries and departments: E-governance readiness assessment 2003*. Draft Report 48.

Department of Public Service and Administration. (1996). *Green paper transforming public service delivery*. Pretoria, South Africa: GCIS.

Economic Commission for Africa. (2006). *Per capita electricity use in Africa is less than 2 percent, says new report by ECA's NEPAD Unit*. Retrieved April 2, 2007, from http://www.uneca.org/nepad/Story070326.htm

Economist Intelligence Unit. (2006). Digital divide narrows. *The Economist*. Retrieved May 28, 2007, from http://www.ibm.com/news/be/en/2006/04/2601.html

European Commission. (2005). *Transforming public services*. Report of the Ministerial eGovernment Conference, Manchester, UK. Retrieved December 12, 2008, from http://www.egov2005conference.gov.uk/documents/pdfs/eGovConference05_Summary.pdf

Farelo, M., & Morris, C. (2006). *The working group on e-government in the developing world: Roadmap for e-government in the developing world, 10 questions e-government leaders should ask themselves*. Retrieved December 24, 2008, from http://researchspace.csir.co.za/dspace/bitstream/10204/1060/1/Morris_2006_D.pdf

Free Daily Newsletter. (2007). Is SEACOM racing past EASSy? *MyBroadband*. Retrieved September 12, 2008, from http://mybroadband.co.za/news/Telecoms/563.html

Geness, S. (2004). *E-government, the South African experience*. Paper presented at SADC E-government Workshop, Gaborone 14-16 April 2004.

Gerhan, D., & Mutula, S. M. (2005). Bandwidth bottlenecks at the University of Botswana: Complications for library, campus, and national development. *Library Hi Tech, 23*(1), 102–117. doi:10.1108/07378830510586748

Government Gazette. (2008). *Broadband Infraco Act 2007*. Retrieved June 14, 2009, from http://llnw.creamermedia.co.za/articles/attachments/10610_broadinfraact33.pdf

Government of Canada. (2006). *Online forms and services*. Retrieved May 13, 2007, from http://canada.gc.ca/form/e-services_e.html

Government of Singapore. (2004). *E-citizen: Your gateway to all government services*. Retrieved May 14, 2007, from http://www.ecitizen.gov.sg/

Hamlyn, M. (2008, September 4). *UhuruNet broadband cable, INet-Bridge.* Retrieved July 12, 2009, from http://mybroadband.co.za/news/Telecoms/5094.html

Heeks, R. (2002). *E-government in Africa: Promise and practice.* Manchester, UK: Institute for Development Policy and Management University of Manchester.

Holmes, D. (2001). *E-gov: E-business strategies for government.* London, UK: Nicholas Brealey.

Holzer, M., & Kim, S. T. (2005). *Digital governance in municipalities worldwide: A longitudinal assessment of municipal websites across the world.* Retrieved February 15, 2007, from http://unpan1.un.org/intradoc/groups/public/documents/ASPA/UNPAN022839.pdf

Kekana, M., & Heeks, R. (2008). *Design-reality gap case no. 3: Computerised integration of two pension funds in Southern Africa.* Retrieved August 20, 2009, from http://www.egov4dev.org/success/case/twinpension.shtml

Lenhart, A., Horrigan, J., Rainie, L., Allen, K., Boyce, A., Madden, M., & O'Grady, E. (2003). *The ever–shifting Internet population: A new look at internet access and the digital divide.* Retrieved May 11, 2003, from http://www.Pewinternet.org/

Levin, A. (2008). *E-government for development: Success and failure in e-government projects.* Retrieved August 21, 2009, from http://www.egov4dev.org/success/case/golaganang.shtm

Mail and Guardian Online. (2008, August 20). DA points to service-delivery problems. *Mail and Guardian.* Retrieved August 18, 2009, from http://www.mg.co.za/

Matsepe-Casaburri, I. (2008). *Budget vote speech by minister of communications Dr. Ivy Matsepe-Casaburri.* Cape Town, South Africa: National Assembly.

Mbeki, T. (2005). *Address of the President of South Africa. Second Joint Sitting of the Third Democratic Parliament, Cape Town 11 February 2005.* Cape Town, South Africa: The Presidency.

Meyer, J. A. (2007). *E-governance in South Africa: Making the populace aware: An Eastern Cape perspective, communities and action.* Johannesburg, South Africa: Prato CIRN Conference.

Naidoo, S. (2007, April 8). Telkom has lost its head. *Business Times.* Retrieved April 18, 2008, from http://www.mybroadband.co.za/nephp/?m=show&id=6099

National Traffic Information System. (2008). *eNATIS.* Retrieved August 12, 2009, from http://www.enatis.com/

Ngulube, P. (2007). The nature and accessibility of e-government in sub Saharan Africa. *International Review of Information Ethics, 7*. Retrieved November 25, 2007, from http://www.i-r-i-e.net/inhalt/007/16-ngulube.pdf

Nyasato, R., & Kathuri, B. (2007). High phone charges hamper region's growth, says W Bank. *The Standard*. Retrieved April 10, 2007, from http://www.eastandard.net/hm_news/news.php?articleid=1143967136

Perry, S. (2008, June 8). E-governance in Africa goes backwards. *ITweb*. Johannesburg.

PNC-ISAD. (2005). *Towards an inclusive information society for South Africa*. A country report to Government, November 2005.

Remmen, A. (2003). *Images of e-government – Experiences from the digital north*. Aaolborg, Denmark: Department of Development and Planning, Aalborg University.

SADC E-readiness Task Force. (2002). *SADC e-readiness review and strategy*. Johannesburg, South Africa: SADC.

Segar, S. (2008, June 11). eNATIS working well now. *The Witness*. Retrieved August 12, 2009, from http://www.enatis.com/Media-coverage-2008/eNaTIS-working-well-now-The-Witness-11-June-2008.html

Sheridan, W., & Riley, T. B. (2006). *Comparing e-government and e-governance*. Retrieved December 12, 2008, from http://www.electronicgov.net/pubs/research_papers/SheridanRileyComparEgov.d

SITA. (2002). *Government to government initiatives*. Retrieved July 26, 2009, from http://www.sita.co.za

SITA. (2002b). *E-government experience in South Africa*. Retrieved May 21, 2007, from http://www.sita.co.za

Southwood, R. (2005). E-government special – Does it exist in Africa and what can it do? *Balancing Act, 93*.

Telkom. (2007). *Telkom corporate profile*. Pretoria, South Africa: Corporate Communications.

The Economist Newspaper and the Economist Group. (2005). *Behind the digital divide*. Retrieved April 10, 2009, from http://www.economist.com/printedition/PrinterFriendly.cfm?Story_ID=3714058

UNDESA. (2006). *E-government readiness assessment methodology*. Retrieved July 14, 2009, from http://www.unpan.org/dpepa-kmb-eg-egovranda-ready.asp

UNDP. (2003). *South Africa human development report (2003): The challenges of sustainable development- Unlocking people's creativity.* Pretoria, South Africa: Oxford University Press.

UNESCO. (2004). *E-governance.* Retrieved June 15, 2008, from http://portal.unesco. org/ci/en/ev.php-url_id=3038&url_do=do_topic&url_sec

United Nations. (2005). *Global e-government readiness report: From e-government to e-inclusion.* Retrieved November 16, 2006, from http://unpan1.un.org/intradoc/ groups/public/documents/un/unpan021888.pdf

United Nations. (2008). *UN e-government survey 2008: From e-government to connected government.* Retrieved June 29, 2009, from http://unpan1.un.org/intradoc/ groups/public/documents/UN/UNPAN028607.pdf

van den Berg, L., van der Meer, A., van Winden, W., & Woets, P. (2006). *E-governance in European and South African cities: The cases of Barcelona, Cape Town, Eindhoven, Johannesburg, Manchester, Tampere, The Hague and Venice.* Rotterdam, The Netherlands: Ashgate.

World Information Society Report. (2006). *Digital opportunity index 2005.* Retrieved February 13, 2007, from http://www.itu.int/osg/spu/publications/worldinformation-society/2006/World.pf

World Summit on Information Society. (2003). *Document WSIS-03/GENEVA/ DOC5-E, December 2003.* Geneva, Switzerland: WSIS.

ADDITIONAL READING

Annan, K. (2001). Information and communications technologies? *Tools for development cooperation: Federal Ministry for Economic Cooperation and Development.* Retrieved November 11, 2008, from http://www.bmz.de/en/issues/Cooperation/ germany/Information_technologies/index.html

Buitendag, A., & Van Der Walt, P. (2008). *Creating knowledge objects for knowledge support in a virtual web-based environment.* Paper presented at the 10th Annual Conference on the World Wide Web Applications, 3-5 September 2008, Cape Town, University of cape Town Campus Leslie Social Sciences Building.

Fillip, B., & Foote, D. (2007). *Making the connection: Scaling telecentres for development.* Washington, DC: Information application Centre. Retrieved July 30, 2008, from http://connection.aed.org/pages/MakingConnections.pdf

Gronlund, A., Andersson, A., & Hedstrom, K. (2005). *Next Step e-government in developing countries: Report D.* Orebro; Orebro University [Informatics], Sweden, May 15, 2005.

ITIL. (n.d). *Service delivery.* Retrieved August 23, 2008, from http://www.knowledgetransfer.net/dictionary/ITIL/en/Service_Delivery.htm

Niekerk, S. (1998). Private gain, public loss? Service delivery in the new S.A. *Southern Africa Report, 12*(4), 3.

Chapter 4
Capacity Development Initiatives for Grass Roots Communities:
Two Cases

Hakikur Rahman
ICMS, Bangladesh

EXECUTIVE SUMMARY

The world has seen the unprecedented development of information and communications technologies (ICTs) and adoption of their diversified methods in elevating all forms of human endeavors. Even a few years back, it was fashionable to speak about the global village. In recent years, many countries have taken leading role in implementing innovative ICT products to accelerate their national developments, enhance their livelihoods, strengthened their national economies, and improve their governance systems. This has been observed that those countries could reap the most benefits out of ICT strategies, which could penetrate at the lowest tier of their governance system. In this context, human development is an element of importance. This research emphasizes that cumulative human development through community approach would be the next level of knowledge dynamics across the world. It also argues that as much the country provides thrust on capacity development initiatives at the grass roots, it has more opportunity to reach at greater context of governance system. This chapter would like to focus on two cases, which penetrated the grass roots reaching out to the community level, act as catalyst to strengthen their national economy and government. Some features and perspectives of e-Sri Lanka and e-Korea are being discussed here to provide insight into these cases, so that researchers in developing and transitional economies could gain knowledge.

DOI: 10.4018/978-1-4666-2071-1.ch004

ORGANIZATION BACKGROUND

The twenty-first century predominately constitutes a information and knowledge-based society, where every country aspires to achieve its goal of social and economic development, including education, food security, health, environment, gender equity and cultural pluralism. However, the most important problem would remain as attaining and sustaining those goals. Therefore, every continent is concentrating in building its own Information Society, until a global village is formed.

However, in contrast to the developed countries that have been steadily capitalizing the rapid pace of information and communications technologies (ICTs), a large number of developing countries, particularly low-income countries are lagging behind in adapting these technologies and contributing to the information-divide or digital-divide, or more appropriately knowledge-divide (GITR, 2006; 2007). This is also true in case of rural villages where modern technologies are struggling to reach. The majority of people living in rural areas has neither access nor the means to obtain modern ICT because of their low economic position (Gunatunge & Karunanayake, 2004; Escudero-Pascual, 2008). They aggravate further when other hindrance parameters such as policies or politics, cultures or societies, regulations or regulators, promotions or motivations, and economic gain or status gain mingle up altogether.

The term 'global village' perhaps, coined by the United Nations Development Programme (UNDP) in 1998 (UNDP, 1998) with aspiration that everyone will be a full member of this village. With support from UN, ITU and others, IGF (IGF, 2008) coined another term, 'Internet for All', which could bring everyone on the planet under this future umbrella. But, author argues that both of these terms are over ambitious, despite their importance, and need to be nourished with total subsidized support from all corners to establish at least the information backbone in all countries, which is the most basic pre-requisite for carrying out those two slogans. Furthermore, he argues that with the shifting of focus of international organizations and donor agencies towards the development of information base knowledge society may lead to another form of divide within or among the country's in need. He would like to give one example from the Internet Governance Forum, which is the most effective and dynamic forum providing all out issue support for the development of the Internet. Focus of IGF has even shifted from openness, security, diversity, access (emphasizes the openness) (IGF, 2006); access, diversity, openness, security (emphasizes the access) (IGF, 2007); Reaching the Next Billion, Promoting Cyber-Security and Trust, Managing Critical Internet Resources, Emerging Issues: The Internet of Tomorrow- Innovation and the Evolution of the Internet (more pragmatic approach in reaching out for the grass roots, emphasizing perhaps the access) (IGF, 2008);

Managing Critical Internet Resources, Security, Openness and Privacy, Access and Diversity, Internet Governance in the Light of WSIS Principles (emphasizes more on technology issues; access is there, but in diluted form (IGF, 2009).

The shift of focus or emphasizing of efforts or re-direction of resources are inevitable for any development programme, especially who are dealing with human development utilizing the novel techniques of ICTs. But, there remain several forms of gaps or laggings, in those countries who are not among the forerunners. Hence, in spite of putting all out painstaking efforts and resources, and even dedicated willingness, many set apart from being among the mainstream. There could be many failed projects, programmes or strategies, but this research scope would like to focus on two success cases of ICT strategies in two countries, who have taken lead in terms of providing e-government services at the grass roots.

This chapter as a continuation of research work in the perspective to reach the people at large, especially the marginalized and disadvantaged through utilization of ICT (for previous work, see the case portion of e-Srilanka from Islam, Murelli, Noronha & Rahman, 2006:338-351), would like to revisit a case, the e-Srilanka who has proved itself as a success case in South Asia, and in addition being familiar with the other project, e-Korea (through three consecutive visits to various project area in 2001, First Asia Internet Right Conference, Organized by Jinbonet and the Association for Progressive Communications, Seoul, South Korea; participant of a World Bank and S. Korean Government e-government programme, 2002 and a visit under the Sustainable Development Networking Programme of Bangladesh, 2005), author would like to discuss a few policy issues of e-Korea. Main purpose is to follow up the e-Srilanka that was initiated in 2001 and officially launched in 2002 (Rainford, 2006), on the other hand, e-Korea project has been finalized in 2006-2007, and now it has been taken as a role model in many countries to roll out their e-governance systems.

SETTING THE STAGE

ICT undoubtedly brings profound changes to every community. It influences how the community knows and understands the world. It also changes working methods and the ways in which they communicate. At the same time, it affects how the community accesses and shares it with others and establishes information as an important source of power. But, despite advances in many aspects, yet pro-poor or for the grass roots people as per se, glitches are there (Heeks, 1999; 2002; 2009; Rahman, 2006; 2007; 2009). It has been broadly recognized, by acquiring the equipment and necessary skills to use information effectively, the poor and marginalized population can gain access to power, and the Internet can act as the tool to raise their skills and share knowledge based information among them. However, to avail the aggregated benefit from the information society, manifestation is not good enough, but to act rigorously in achieving the result. Two cases in this chapter are good examples in this regard.

Even though there have been increased global initiations to reduce digital divides, technology gap is expanding at the periphery. Digital Access Index (DAE), the ITU launched new index[1] which measures the overall ability of individuals in a country to access and use new ICTs. It has Sweden with the highest ranking of .85 (in a score of 1.00)[2] (with high competition at the top), while the bottom ranked ten countries could not achieve over 0.01 or 0.02 in this ranking[3]. The picture is not so gloomy in recent years, due to the innovation of cellular phones across the globe, but while comparing in contrast to the developed countries the margin is there. Economist Intelligence Unit (EIU, 2009) is carrying out another benchmarking index, called e-readiness ranking for many years. If one looks at the ranking for 2009, Denmark is at the top with 8.67 (ranked first in 2008 with score of 8.83, thus increasing the level of competition), while bottom 5 countries of 70 countries in the study could not score over 3.5[4].

One may argue about citation of those two indices, but author would reason that it will provide similar picture in other indices. However, as a manuscript in a casebook on e-governance issues, author would like to put forward the e-government readiness ranking that has been carried out by the UN (2008) for many years. Sweden is at the top with ranking of 0.9157 (shows tremendous competition among the top ranked countries with Denmark scoring 0.9134), with lowest scoring of 0.2110 in West African region. The promising fact is that bottom 35 countries among the top chosen 70 countries have ranked almost 0.5 (in a score of 1.0), which provides sufficient confidence and prospects of e-governance across the globe.

A NUA survey conducted in 2002 (NUA Internet Surveys, 2004) found that the number of users connected to the Net was about 605.60 million: World Total 605.60 million, Africa 6.31 million, Asia/Pacific 187.24 million, Europe 190.91 million, Middle East 5.12 million, Canada & USA 182.67 million, Latin America 33.35 million; and these figures raises to (Internet World Stats, 2009): World Total 1,733.99 million, Africa 67.37 million, Asia 738.25 million, Europe 418.03 million, Middle East 57.42 million, North America 252.91 million, Latin America/Caribbean 179.03 million, and Oceania/Australia 20.97 million.

There was a clear indication that Internet subscribers were rapidly increasing in Asia, Africa and pacific regions. Thereby, by taking pragmatic steps, many countries have brought their grass roots communities under ICT based development umbrella. Currently, with the highest growth rate on Internet in the Middle-East (2000-2009)

1,648.2%; followed by Africa 1,392.4%; Latin America/Caribbean 890.8%, Asia has the highest number of Internet users (42.6% of the world Internet user) (InternetWorldStats, 2009).

It is now proven fact that ICT can accelerate economic development through better manipulation of information usage at appropriate way, at appropriate form and at appropriate time. Availing this opportunity, many developing countries have made economic management their prime agenda and trying to overcome the problems of rural poverty, inequality, and environmental degradation (Bhatnagar, 2000). In those countries, it is observed that management of information system, such as on-line/off-line document management, electronic data exchange, file sharing, electronics groups, groupwares, blogs, moodles, mashups, open source software, and the Internet are leading to innovative planning and thereby becoming a means of empowering the communities through raising their knowledge (Bhatnagar, 2000; Kiangi & Tjipangandjara, 1996; Traunmuller & Lank, 1996; Gunatunge & Karunanayake, 2004; Rahman, 2006; 2008). Both the countries, in these two cases have adopted ICTs methods to promote their governance system and at the same time to gain economic benefit for their communities.

CASE DESCRIPTION

Sri Lanka

By definition of a person with age of 15 and over who can read and write, Sri Lanka´s 90.7% of the total population are literate[5]. In 2008, the country had 246,000 Internet users, which gives 5.8% Internet penetration[6]. In 2008, Sri Lanka´s position in the e-governance readiness index (UN, 2008) is 101 among 189 countries with index value of 0.4244 (in a score of unity), and in 2009, the country has the e-readiness ranking (EIU, 2009) of 63 among 70 countries with score of 3.85 (in the total score of 10). In comparison to the world leaders, these figures are low, but in comparison to the other countries in the South Asian region, they are significant (India scored 4.17 and Pakistan scored 3.50 in e-readiness ranking (EIU, 2009), while in terms of e-government readiness index, except Maldives- 0.4491, other countries are struggling to achieve a better ranking; India-0.3814, Pakistan-0.3164, Bangladesh-0.2936, Nepal-0.2725) (UN, 2008).

To achieve success in terms of promoting e-government services, three constituents are essential. They are Government, Citizens and Businesses (Davidrajuh, 2004). e-Sri Lanka enclave all three of them with clear vision, defined objectives, and transparent strategies, which help the country to achieve those rankings. Apparently, all those stakeholders also have the benefit out of the project, which has been described next.

E-Srilanka

Earlier version of this research (Islam, Murelli, Noronha & Rahman, 2006:pp. 338-351) provided the rationale, project description, selection process, implementation of pilot projects and programmes, including the vision and objectives of the project. To obtain an overview on strategic ICT implementations and analytical issues in a few other countries, readers may follow another consecutive research (Rahman, 2008). This research, as a continuation of the earlier versions, will try to provide new insight into the vision, objectives and strategies with critical assessments on e-Sri Lanka project.

The Vision: Use ICT to enhance education at the school and tertiary level, to increase the number and quality of high-level ICT professionals and to develop a computer-literate citizenry.

Note: The high literacy rate of Sri Lanka acted as an added catalyst to material-ize this project including educated mass at the school and tertiary level. The former group raised the basic stronghold of ICT base in that country, and the later group carried out it further in terms of applying it for the benefit of the community through applied research.

Objectives:

- To establish a multi-layered and multi-skilled pool of ICT trained staff at workforce, professional and managerial levels;
- To provide ICT education to students in schools throughout the country;
- To increase the number of undergraduates at university courses in ICT and provide higher-level training to university staff;
- To enhance the opportunities and incentives for improving English and ICT literacy, and
- To increase the supply of ICT professionals to the rest of the world and to encourage foreign ICT professionals to set up training institutes in Sri Lanka.

Note: To achieve national success in ICT projects, a multi-layered and multi-skilled pool of ICT professionals are pre-requisite. e-Sri Lanka intelligently could pinpoint that area and targeted to attain the same. Furthermore, emphasis was given to promote English skill and raise the local ICT professional's to global standard.

To achieve these, the three-pronged strategy adopted:

Firstly, in building an ICT skilled workforce and increasing the employability of school leavers with the help of the government, the private sector and academia to:

- Facilitate the establishment of quality, affordable ICT skills enhancement programmes and recognized ICT qualifications, both at a foundation and a diploma level;
- Facilitate the upgrading of the skills of trainers at IT training institutes, especially in the outstations; and
- Improve the quality and availability of text books and course materials for IT training.

Secondly, strengthening teaching in primary and secondary schools, tertiary education and universities, so that:

- All school children would obtain basic ICT training and user-level skills through e-learning programmes;
    ◦ The management of school IT centres be strengthened;
    ◦ ICT could be introduced into national curricula; and
    ◦ Schools could be connected to the Internet.

Thirdly, strengthening management and professional skills in ICT industry by:

- Organizational scholarship programmes for postgraduate/specialist qualifications;
- Providing grants for short courses;
- Assisting national conferences, seminars and study tours; and
- Empowering the ICT industry to attain excellence by strengthening HR and promoting innovation (Islam, Murelli, Noronha & Rahman, 2006:pp. 338-351).

As benefits, e- Sri Lanka provided support to;

A. The government:
    1. To empower civil servants with information and communication tools, to facilitate coordination across government agencies and increase competition and transparency in public procurement
    2. To integrate marginalized regions and communities within an equitable resource distribution framework,
    3. To facilitate effective decentralization and broadening of public participation in development policy formulation and program implementation,
    4. To transform government services to become cost-effective and citizen-centred;

B.   The entrepreneurs:
1.   To revitalise Sri Lanka's main and traditional industries, like agriculture, tourism and apparel, so that the share of value-addition to the end product is increased, and to penetrate into new markets via internet-based sales channels
2.   To emerge as a major transportation hub for air and sea cargo, by modernizing ports and by developing a modern trade net that dramatically reduces transaction costs for importers and exporters; and
C.   The citizens:
1.   To improve the delivery of public services and knowledge and education to all, and to make government (services, information, and overall government structure) accessible and accountable to the average citizen
2.   To create a communication environment that allows optimal opportunities for all Sri Lankan citizens to participate fully in the global information economy, and for all citizens to support their economic, learning and personal needs
3.   To facilitate inexpensive contact with families abroad via e-mail and voice over the Internet via Cyber Cafes in all towns (Davidrajuh, 2004).

South Korea

With the same definition of literacy given above, South Korea's 97.9% of the total population are literate[7]. ITU's 2008 (ITU ICT EYE[8]) statistics states that the country's Internet penetration rate is 76.5%, based on the number of Internet users. E-readiness ranking (EIU, 2009) is 19 among 70 countries with a score of 7.81(out of 10.00); and e-government readiness ranking (UNDP, 2008) is 6 among 189 countries with score of 0.8317 (index score is 1.00).

Having the same notion of incorporating the government, businesses and citizens, e-Korea played a successful role and the country progressed further as a key player in the global market through providing robust information infrastructure, promoting relevant industries, providing cyber-security, and establishing international cooperation (see Figure 1). A few features of e-Korea Vision 2006 is being described next.

E-Korea Vision 2006

Rationale

The Korean government enacted the Framework Act on Informatization Promotion in August, 1995 (Framework); established the first Master Plan for Informatization Promotion in June, 1996 (Action Plan); and established a national organization for

Figure 1. Framework for e-Korea Vision 2006 (Adopted from Govt. of Korea, 2002)

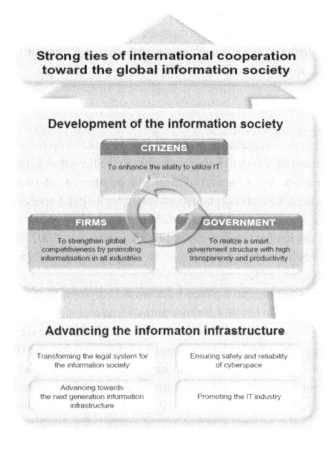

planning and implementation of the goals outlined in the Master Plan (Institution-alization). The plan presented 10 key projects for the realization of an advanced information society by the year 2010 (Definite deadline and specific tasks). In March, 1999, the government established Cyber Korea 21 as the blueprint for the new information society of the 21st century in order to overcome the Asian economic crisis and to transform the Korean economy into a knowledge-based one (dynamic adjustment of action plans according to nature and demand of the situation) utilizing an advanced information infrastructure.

Main aims and objectives were to:

• Reform legal and institutional systems and increase the capacity to utilize information technologies in all areas of society including the government, private companies and individuals in order to increase the positive effects of informatization

- Strengthen the ability to respond rapidly to changes in the social environment caused by the rapid developments of information technologies; and
- Stimulate national development through informatization efforts in order to resolve the national agenda such as strengthening our competitiveness in the global economy (Govt. of Korea, 2002).

Technology Concerns

High-speed telecommunications networks were constructed up to the village level to enable the citizens of Korea to have fast access to the broadband Internet services throughout the nation. As of the end of 2001, the number of Internet users totaled 24.38 million, where 7.81 million households had high-speed access to broadband Internet services. In addition to this, mobile telephony has become a basic tele-communication device for the general public. As of March, 2002, the number of mobile subscribers has reached 30.31 million, surpassing the 22.95 million fixed line subscribers (Govt. of Korea, 2002).

ICTs are extensively being utilized in economic or social activities including financial transactions and health administration. Financial institutions are utilizing ICTs to provide 24 hour electronic banking services. In 2002, there were about 11.31 million customers subscribed to Internet-based banking services, and the popularity of online financial transactions has risen dramatically. For example, 66.6% of the total monetary value of stock trades was handled on the Internet as of December 2001. As of December 2001, approximately 40,400 health care facilities have in-troduced EDI to health insurance to improve the efficiency in the health insurance administrative process (Govt. of Korea, 2002).

The IT industry has become an industry which increases the competitiveness of other industries and leads the growth of the Korean economy. Establishment of numerous IT ventures helped to create numerous professional jobs in the past few years. In addition, the industrialized sectors have benefited with an increase in productivity from the employment of the IT experts and specialists. As of December, 2001, the number of IT ventures reached 5,073 companies (44.5% of the total ventures). The number of IT workers increased from 1.01 million in 1997 to 1.16 million in 2001 (Govt. of Korea, 2002; 2003).

A Few Major Applications and Benefits

Informatization of the overall administrative processes in the government increased not only the administrative efficiency, but also established a solid foundation for the e-Government, such as:

- **Informatization of Customs Services:** Has shortened the processing time (for exports processing and services, from more than a day to less than 2 minutes; for imports processing and services, from more than 2 days to less than 2 and half hours), and has reduced logistic costs by at least 500 billion won a year; UNI-PASS of the Korea Customs Service (KCS, http://portal.customs.go.kr) is the world's first 100 percent electronic clearance portal system, which provides a one-stop PASS service by unifying all customs clearance procedures, including export/ import clearance, duty drawback, inbound/outbound passenger control, and tracking of bonded cargo;
- **Establishment of The Electronic Employment Information System:** Has assisted 1.9 million people obtain jobs between 1999 and 2001 by providing comprehensive employment information regarding job openings, vocational training programs, and other related information;
- **Informatization of Government Procurement Services:** Through the introduction of online services enhanced the productivity and transparency by reducing the time to process documents (from more than 2 days to less than 30 minutes) (Govt. of Korea, 2002; 2007).

E-Korea, also embraced the three prong approach which contained; promotion of national informatization, advancing the information infrastructure, and strengthening international cooperation for the Global Information Society. For easy reading and obtain a glimpse of the action plans along with the objectives in this aspect, a detail notes up to three levels of segregation are being provided in Appendix 1. However, the dynamic characteristics of the initiation are worth noted:

The government will establish and implement a yearly operational plan based on the Master Plan, e-Korea Vision 2006 each year. The Master Plan will be revised in response to the rapid environmental changes and technological developments of each year. The government will develop a detailed action plan in order to evaluate achievements semi-annually and report annually to the Informatization Promotion Committee. The realization of the global leader, e-Korea will be promoted through the systematic management of all issues and outcomes from each area, and cooperation will be strengthened between relevant government ministries and departments for the promotion of related businesses through the coordination of the Informatization Promotion Committee (Govt. of Korea, 2002:88).

Utilizing the benefits of ICTs on national economies on the ROK is fourfold; they have created:

- New industries and economic sectors or sub-sectors (e.g. the software industry, cellular phones, computers and peripherals),
- New ways of doing business (e.g. electronic commerce, globally distributed organizations, integrated supply chains),
- New tasks and opportunities for government (e.g. electronic government, privacy policy legislation, ICT industrial policy, security), and
- New issues in economic and political development (e.g. availability of information access, computer literacy, the digital divide) (Chadwick, 2005).

Thus, one can observe that the consequences of ICTs and the digital revolution on economic growth, social capital, and political development in a country goes far beyond the contribution of the ICT sector to national GDP. ICTs influence the efficiency and productivity of other economic processes as well, including the distribution of economic gains and basic services, and foremost, the transparency and accountability of the government (Chadwick, 2005). This research would like to thank the unnamed author(s) who has minutely compiled many aspects, issues, developments and policy formations of South Korea and preserved it in the APNG (Asia Pacific Networking Group) server. Some major aspects are being included in this research as Appendix-2, with intention that they will be extremely beneficial to new comers (even as a refreshment of doing things for others), who are looking forward to establish grass roots e-governance in their economies.

CURRENT CHALLENGES FACING THE ORGANIZATION

Overcoming the barriers toward empowering grass roots communities through information networking vary over places, localities, regions and times, which need to be addressed both horizontally and vertically. Literatures reviewed during earlier research with respect to policy formulation (Accascina, 1999; Gurstein, 2003; Keniston & Kumar, 2004; UNDP, 2001; World Bank, 2000; Bridges, 2004; OECD, 2004; G8DOT Force, 2001; DFID, 2001; ITU, 2003), found that contemporary trends tend to be biased against marginal populations. Literature review during the current research (Pascual, 2003; DRAP, 2003-2004; 2005-2006; 2007-2008; 2009-2010; NCA, 2003; UNDP, 2005; 2007), poise much better scenario in many countries, but still, there is a need for broad-based and equitable access to ICTs in areas consistent to the processes of decentralization, democratization, and mobilization of targeted population through policy reforms to achieve grass roots governance.

At the beginning of the information technology revolution governments in many of the developing countries, were not only slowly catching up with the new communication technologies, but also in a few cases adopted a negative view on the expansion of electronic network to the community level. At the same time, networking at the civil society level found to be increasingly challenging to national governments on many issues (Slim & Thompson, 1993). However, as NGO networking within and among countries of common peripheries, as well as, in many outreach programmes related to marginal people increased over time – mostly through the use of e-mail, e-groups, blogs, private sector TV, community radio and cell phones, their leverage vis-à-vis at the national government levels has also increased.

Generic challenges that e-government projects faces are how to expand the coverage to more agencies and regions; how to provide essential services in the rural areas; how to design projects to deliver economic value; how to enhance their impacts on increase in transparency and reduction of corruption; and foremost how to make those projects self-sustainable in the longer run.

Apart from the low awareness on ICT based programmes and their acceptance by the general community people, there were several challenges e-Sri Lanka project faced. One of them was the unstable and constantly changing political environment. In terms of implementation, ICTA faced various challenges to take the e-Sri Lanka Roadmap from what was essentially a comprehensive vision document and programme strategy, to a detailed plan of implementation, with actionable and fundable programmes and projects. Other challenges include, the process of ensuring ownership, role of key stakeholders and beneficiaries in the design and planning stages, to ensure equal opportunities for all to benefit, and to ensure that the introduction of ICT does not in any way diminish the social fabric, history and strong cultural traditions prevalent in the communities, but instead serve as a complement (Rainford, 2006; ICTA, 2005; 2009).

Despite high motivation and high absorptive capability of S. Korean people, e-Korea project had weakness of the resources gap and the institutional gap. In addition to these, there were disputes over the digitization initiatives, such as national electronic ID card, e-procurement, or electronic education system. The government in Korea as in other countries has also faced opposition from citizens and suffered setbacks in pursuing its ICT projects (UN, 2006; Suh & Chen, 2007).

SOLUTIONS AND RECOMMENDATIONS

The basic objective of human capacity development is to widen the range of people's choice and make development more participatory and democratic (UNDP, 1991). ICT can improve the knowledge and awareness of people by providing information about social and economic programmes, markets, employment opportunities, health, agriculture, education and learning, weather and disaster warning. These can be achieved only by being able to reach out at the lowest tier of the society or the governance level, and global agenda has accepted several ways of reaching out to them, such as establishing integrated knowledge centres/ information centres within the communities and integrating them to the nearest communication centre/ local centre/ regional centre to form comprehensive knowledge networks (Barton & Bear, 1999; Gunatunge & Karunanayake, 2004; Rahman, 2004).

ICT offers opportunities for individuals and communities in two ways; one as the information consumers and the other as the information generators. Through media convergence, ICTs can also build on and integrate the capacities of other media (e.g. cell phone, radio and television) to cover the people at large. These facilitate low-cost infrastructure development, easy access and fast distribution of information, which requires a distributed approach rather than a centralized one (Stillitoe, 1998). Moreover, there is a need for peoples' centered ICT institutions in the public and non-profit sectors to avail these opportunities. With that objective in mind this chapter recognized that key to the impact of ICTs is not the technology itself, but the networking and information exchange with particular emphasis on the information those grass roots people needs. This research while synthesizing those two projects implementing ICT strategies through various programmes and activities found that they eventually cover all the eight broad areas of MDG, including community mobilization, capacity building, information networking, ICT policy issues, sustainability, and ICT applications and research.

At the outset it is always felt about the necessity to promote a culture of information management and inclusion of new skills. Moreover, human and social capacity development through ICT aiming at empowering grass roots communities involve establishment of targeted, goal-oriented, horizontal and vertical linkages. Firstly, capacity development should be achieved through development at the individual level; secondly, bringing the individuals under a network; and finally, through congenial national, as well as, international policy support the whole initiative can be turned towards a result based outcome.

At the horizontal level, each individual should be brought under network of multi-faceted information blanket for creating a positive change in the marginal society as a whole. At the vertical level, adequate awareness raising programmes need to be initiated for decision makers, practitioners, researchers, academics and stakeholders on the investment assessment in ICT capacity building through formal and non-formal methods. This may include training of development workers incorporating ICTs in their activities with emphasis on training of rural women, youth, and deprived groups. With respect to content and its applications, it is observed that currently available and practiced networks have limited scope of empowering marginal communities as well as rural uplift. To make it applicable to the community beyond physical access to information, it has to be made timely, retrievable and easily applicable to a broad range of users, accessible in their own languages and consistent with their need and at the same time, demand driven. Top down approach of S. Korea in this aspect is worth mentioning.

To improvise these processes further, needs assessment for information flow in various network layers should be carried out periodically to enable feedback and widen participation in developing these information resources with user-specific, locally sensitive content and applications. This calls for piloting, monitoring, evaluating and documenting successful and unsuccessful applications of ICTs for the people at large. From these applications, models may be developed by providing guidelines for future strategic investments and replication of similar programmes in other places of the country. Both the cases adopted this form of localization and extended their networks at the horizontal level.

Adequate ICT education and capacity building programmes facilitate to form a coalition of stakeholders and organizational partners, in conjunction with national agencies, to develop policies for supporting the application of ICTs to empower peoples at large. Evidently, both the projects have taken such initiatives to reach out their entire population in various phases and trajectories.

To achieve the long-term benefit of ICT integration, ICT initiatives have to be self reliant and financially sustainable. However, this type of development process should proceed within a social accountability context and specific demand from deprived populations. A portion of revenue from telecommunications sector can be used to support the expansion of ICTs for marginal community as well as in rural areas. In turn, there is a need for integration of policies and extended investments to stimulate initial demand for reducing investment risks for rural ICTs. This could include, for example, enabling the potentiality of e-commerce for rural producers. S. Korea, by providing information infrastructure to the village level, has ensured e-commerce at the community level.

At the national level of ICT design, there is a need to develop strategies and action plans for rural areas by taking care of the differences in languages, culture, socio-economic conditions and infrastructure. This should be reflected in participatory need assessment and development of the technology itself. The forms of information content, including linkages to more conventional communication media such as rural radio can be thought of as development media. There is also a need to move away from centrally managed hub of information towards distributed repository system, which should not assume ownership of information resources that are generated by variety of providers. Both of the projects have adopted various strategies and plans to reach the entire population through education, learning, skill development initiatives, policy development, and mostly incorporation of various other agencies taking on a unified platform.

In this cyberspace context of developing countries, thanks to a mixture of adoption of innovations and of the national cultural values, as well as the co-operation among all the nations, which are creating a positive atmosphere for providing easy access to information and knowledge that can be used for the development of the country and eliminate the gap between the information rich and the information poor. However, this demands integration of available lower level information networks to form larger networks covering wider areas and regions opting updated locally generated contents. In this way, they create not only positive aspiration among the participants, but also, enhance their responsibilities and participation. Eventually these networks of network emerge as knowledge hubs for the entire community, region and country.

In conclusion it is imperative to recommend a coordinated network of access centres (efforts are there to establish village centres or knowledge centres in both the cases) acting as delivery nodes for community empowerment which in turn act as powerful resources at the national context (Robinson, 1998; Fouche, 1999). These access centres support grass roots communities and at the same time have their sustainability by providing accurate information about local needs, and facilitating cooperation and interaction among organizations, institutions and communities distributed throughout the country. They may be termed as information centres or knowledge centres or village centres whatever appropriate. But their rationale lies in shared-access models that allow provision of a wide range of services to more users at lower cost than commercial entities which are often out of financial reach of common people (Digital Dividend, 2003). Widespread rollout of these access centres, however, can be achieved only by mobilizing private sector entrepreneurship and investment (Wellenius, 2003), through appropriate national policies and favorable regulatory reforms. On the top, government subsidies for the period of survival act as catalytic agent to involve commercial entities and civil societies in establishing similar ventures.

Finally, looking into causes and effects along these cases it can be derived that, to address policy issues related to information management and access for need based information at community level, it is essential to improve not only the capacities of the out reach communities, but also, capacities of decision-makers and professionals.

REFERENCES

G8DOT Force. (2001). *Digital opportunities for all*. Meeting the Challenge Report of the Digital Opportunity Task Force (DOT Force) including a proposal for a Genoa Plan of Action, May 2001.

Accascina, G. (1999). *Keynote presentation, APDIP Regional Information technology Conference*. March 24-27, 1999, Kuala Lumpur, Malaysia.

Barton, C., & Bear, M. (1999). *Information and communication technologies: Are they the key to viable business development services for micro and small enterprises?* Report for USAID as part of the Micro enterprises Best Practices Project. March 1999 by Development Alternatives Inc, MD, USA.

Bhatnagar, S. (2000). Social implications of information and communication technology in developing countries: Lessons from Asian success stories. *The Electronic Journal on Information Systems in Developing Countries* [Electronic version]. Retrieved from http://www.unimas.my/fit/roger/EJISDC/EJISDC.htm

Bridges. (2004). *The real access / real impact framework for improving the way that ICT is used in development*, November 2004.

Chadwick, B. P. (2005). Information technology revolution in the Republic of Korea: Socio-economic development issues and policymaking challenges. In Mansourov, A. Y. (Ed.), *Bytes and bullets: Information technology revolution and national security on the Korean peninsula* (pp. 52–69). Honolulu, Hawaii: Asia-Pacific Center for Security Studies.

Davidrajuh, R. (2004). Planning e-government start-up: A case study on e-Sri Lanka. *Electronic Government, 1*(1), 92–106. doi:10.1504/EG.2004.004139

DFID. (2001). *Sustainable livelihoods guidance sheets*. Department for Informational Development, 2001.

Digital Dividend. (2003). Retrieved June 08, 2003 from www.digitaldividend.org.

DRAP. (2003-2004). *Digital review of Asia Pacific 2003/2004*. Orbicom, IDRC, UNDP-APDIP.

DRAP. (2005-2006). *Digital review of Asia Pacific 2005/2006*. Orbicom, IDRC, UNDP-APDIP.

DRAP. (2007-2008). *Digital review of Asia Pacific 2007-2008*. Orbicom and the International Development Research Centre. SAGE Publications India Pvt., Ltd.

DRAP. (2009-2010). *Digital review of Asia Pacific 2009-2010*. Orbicom and the International Development Research Centre. SAGE Publications India Pvt Ltd.

EIU. (2009). *E-readiness ranking 2009: The usage imperative*. A report from the Economist Intelligent Unit, The Economist Intelligence Unit Limited, UK.

Escudero-Pascual, A. (2008). *Tools and technologies for equitable access.* Association for Progressive Communication (APC) issue paper. Retrieved from www.apc.org

Fouche, B. (1999). *A Web-based agricultural system for South Africa. Feasibility study - Part 1.* National Department of Agriculture March 1999. Unpublished document.

GITR. (2005). *Global information technology report* (2004-2005). World Economic Forum. Retrieved March 12, 2005, from www.weforum.org

GITR. (2006). *Global information technology report* (2005-2006). World Economic Forum. Retrieved January 12, 2009, from www.weforum.org

GITR. (2007). *Global information technology report* (2006-2007). World Economic Forum. Retrieved January 12, 2009, from www.weforum.org

Govt. of Korea. (2002). *e-Korea Vision 2006: The third master plan for informatization promotion* (2002-2006). Ministry of Information and Communication, Government of the Republic of Korea Govt. of Korea. (2003). *To enhance efficiency and transparency in the public procurement sector by utilizing the government electronic procurement system (GePS).* Government Procurement Experts Group, Phuket, Thailand, 15- 16 August 2003, 2003/SOMIII/GPEG/009 Agenda Item:7a, Asia-Pacific Economic Cooperation (APEC).

Govt. of Korea, (2007). The best practice, UNI-PASS Korea customs service. *Korea e-Government Webzine, 6.* Ministry of Government Administration and Home Affairs (MOGAHA), Government of the Republic of Korea. Retrieved September 30, 2009, from http://www.idrc.ca/en/ev-140957-201-1-DO_TOPIC.html

Gunatunge, R. S., & Karunanayake, M. M. (2004). *Information and communication technologies for enhancing socio-economic development at the local level in Sri Lanka: Issues, challenges and strategies* A research report for Sida/SAREC Research Cooperation Project on Overcoming Regional Imbalances and Poverty, 2004.

Gunawardana, N., & Wattegama, C. (2004). Sri Lanka. In *Digital Review of Asia Pacific.* GKP.

Gurstein, M. (2003). Effective use: A community informatics strategy beyond the digital divide. *First Monday, 8*(12).

Heeks, R. (1999). *Information and communication technologies, poverty and development.* Development Informatics: Working paper Series. Paper No 5, June 1995 Institute of Development Policy and Management. Retrieved from www: http://www.man.ac.uk/idpm

Heeks, R. (2002). Information systems and developing countries: Failure, success and local improvisations. *The Information Society, 18*(2), 101–112. doi:10.1080/01972240290075039

Heeks, R. (2009). *The ICT4D 2.0 manifesto: Where next for ICTs and international development?* Working Paper Series for Development Informatics Group, Institute for Development Policy and Management. University of Manchester, Manchester, UK

ICTA. (2005). *Draft ICT policy for the government.* Colombo, Sri Lanka: Information and Communication Technology Agency of Sri Lanka (ICTA).

ICTA. (2009). *Information and Communication Technology Agency of Sri Lanka.* Retrieved November 05, 2009 from http://www.icta.lk/index.php/en/icta/739-e-sri-lanka-transforming-a-nation-through-ict

IGF. (2006). *First IGF Meeting,* Athens, Greece. Retrieved December 5, 2009, from http://www.intgovforum.org/cms/index.php/athensmeeting

IGF. (2007). *Second IGF Meeting,* Rio de Janeiro, Brazil. Retrieved December 5, 2009, from http://www.intgovforum.org/cms/index.php/secondmeeting

IGF. (2008). *3rd Annual Internet Governance Forum (IGF),* Hyderabad, India. Retrieved December 5, 2009, from http://www.intgovforum.org/cms/index.php/2008-igf-hyderabad

IGF. (2009). *Fourth Annual IGF Meeting,* in Sharm El Sheikh, Egypt. Retrieved December 5, 2009, from http://www.intgovforum.org/cms/index.php/the-meeting

International Telecommunication Union. (2003). *ITU report,* 2003.

Internet World Stats. (2009). *World internet users and population stats.* Miniwatts Marketing Group. Retrieved from http://internetworldstats.com/

Islam, M. A., Murelli, E., Noronha, F., & Rahman, H. (2006). Capacity development initiatives for marginal communities: A few case studies. In Rahman, H. (Ed.), *Empowering marginal communities with information networking* (pp. 318–353). Hershey, PA: Idea Group Inc. doi:10.4018/978-1-59140-699-0.ch013

Keniston, K., & Kumar, D. (Eds.). (2004). *Bridging the digital divide: Experience in India.* London, UK: Sage Publications.

Kiangi, G. E., & Tjipangandjara. (1996). Opportunities for information technology in enhancing socio-economic development of a developing country. In M. Odedra-Straub (Ed.), *global information technology and socio-economic development,* (pp. 73-81). Nashua, NH: Ivy League Publishing.

NCA. (2003). *Informatization: White paper*. Seoul, Rep. of Korea: National Computerization Agency (NCA).

NUA. (2004). *Internet surveys*. Retrieved from http://www.nua.ie/surveys/how_many_online

OECD. (2004). *Organisation for Economic Co-operation and Development annual report*, 2004.

Pascual, P. J. (2003). *e-Government*. e-ASEAN Task Force, UNDP-APDIP, Malaysia.

Rahman, H. (2004). *Empowering marginal communities with interactive education systems, Commonwealth Open Learning* (COL). 3rd Pan-Commonwealth Forum on Open Learning (PCF3), Dunedin, New Zealand, July 4-8, 2004.

Rahman, H. (2006). Empowerment of marginal communities through information driven learning. In Rahman, H. (Ed.), *Empowering marginal communities with information networking* (pp. 16–43). Hershey, PA: IDEA Group Publishing. doi:10.4018/978-1-59140-699-0.ch002

Rahman, H. (2007). Role of ICTs in socioeconomic development and poverty reduction. In *Information and communication technologies for economic and regional developments* (pp. 180–219). Hershey, PA: Idea Group Inc. doi:10.4018/978-1-59904-186-5.ch010

Rahman, H. (2008). An overview on strategic ICT implementations toward developing knowledge societies. In *Developing successful ICT strategies: Competitive advantages in a global knowledge-driven society* (pp. 1–39). Hershey, PA: Information Science Reference.

Rahman, H. (2009). Local e-government management: A wider window of e-governance. In *Handbook of research on e-government readiness for information and service exchange: Utilizing progressive information communication technologies* (pp. 295–323). Hershey, PA: Information Science Reference. doi:10.4018/978-1-60566-671-6.ch015

Rainford, S. (2006). *e-Sri Lanka: An integrated approach to e-government case study*. Bangkok, Thailand: Asia Pacific Development Information Programme (APDIP).

Robinson, S. (1998). *Telecentres in Mexico: The first phase*. Paper presented to the UNRISD Conference.

Slim, H., & Thompson, P. (1993). *Listening for a change: Oral history and development*. London, UK: Panos Publications.

Stillitoe, P. (1998). The development of indigenous knowledge: A new applied anthropology. *Current Anthropology, 49*(2), 223–253. doi:10.1086/204722

Suh, J., & Chen, D. H. C. (Eds.). (2007). *Korea as a knowledge economy: Evolutionary process and lessons learned.* Washington, DC: The World Bank. doi:10.1596/978-0-8213-7201-2

Traunmuller, R., & Lenk, K. (1996). *New public management and enabling technologies: Advanced IT tools.* London, UK: Chapman and Hall.

UN. (2006). *E-procurement, a joint publication of Economic and Social Commission for Asia and the Pacific* (UNESCAP). Asian Development Bank (ADB) Institute, and Public Procurement Service of the Republic of Korea, United Nations publication.

UN. (2008). *United Nations e-government survey 2008: From e-government to connected governance.* New York, NY: UN.

UNDP. (1991). *Human development report. United Nations Development Programme (UNDP).* Oxford University Press.

UNDP. (1998). *Human development report.* UNDP, Rosemberg & Seller.

UNDP. (2001). *Human development report: Making new technologies work for human development.* UNDP.

UNDP. (2005). *Promoting ICT for human development in Asia: Realizing the millennium development goals. Regional Human Development Report.* Elsevier.

UNDP. (2007). *E-government interoperability: Guide.* Bangkok, Thailand: UNDP.

Wellenius, B. (2003). *Sustainable telecenters: Private sector and infrastructure network.* World Bank, Note number 251, January 2003.

World Bank. (2000). *World development report 1999/2000.* Washington, DC: World Bank.

ADDITIONAL READING

Asgarkhani, M. (2003). *A strategic framework for electronic government.* Paper presented at 22nd IT Conference, Colombo, Sri Lanka. Retrieved from http://www.cssl.lk/conferences/A%20Strategic%20Framework%20for%20Electronic%20Government_medi%20asgarkani%20letter%20size.doc

Backus, M. (2001). *E-governance and developing countries: Research report – No 3*. Retrieved from http://www.ftpiicd.org/files/research/reports/report3.pdf

Bhatnagar, S. (2004). *Enabling e-government in developing countries: From vision to-implementation*. Retrieved from www.worldbank.org/publicsector/egov/lweek/Bhatnagar.pdf

Carlos, A. P. B. (2003). *Government in the information age*. Colombo, Sri Lanka: National E-Government Conference.

Choudrie, J., & Weerakkody, V. (2004). Evaluating global e-government initiatives: An exploratory study. In Gupta, M. P. (Ed.), *Towards e-government –Management challenge*. Tata McGraw Hill Publishing Company Ltd.

Davidrajhu, R. (2004). Planning e-government start-up: A case study on e-Sri Lanka. *Electronic Government, 1*(1).

Deok-Hyun, K. (2002). *Telecom industry undergoes revolutionary change in two decades*. Seoul: Korea Times.

Government of Sri Lanka. (2003). *Policy on e-government*. May, Sri Lanka: Government of Sri Lanka.

Govt. of Korea (1999). *Cyber Korea 21: Korea's vision for a knowledge based information society.* Seoul, ROK: Ministry of Information and Communications.

Govt. of Korea. (2002a). *Broadband in Korea: Korea information infrastructure.* Seoul, ROK: National Computerization Agency, Ministry of Information and Communication.

Govt. of Korea. (2002b). *E-Government in Korea.* Seoul, ROK: National Computerization Agency, MIC

Govt. of Korea. (2003). *White paper: Internet Korea 2003.* Seoul, ROK: National Computerization Agency, Ministry of Information and Communication.

Govt. of Korea. (2004a). *The realities of informationization in the first quarter of 2004.* Public opinion survey, Ministry of Information and Communication and Korea Network Information Center, Seoul, ROK.

Govt. of Korea. (2004b). *The road to US$20,000 GDP/capita: IT 8-3-9 strategy.* Seoul, ROK: Ministry of Information and Communication.

KAIT. (2001). *Research on the trend of major information and communication items*. Seoul, ROK: Korea Association of Information and Telecommunication.

KAIT. (2002). *Survey on current trends in the IT industry.* Seoul, ROK: Korea Association of Information and Telecommunication.

KAIT. (2003). *Information and communication industry statistics reports for 2000, 2001, 2002, and 2003.* Seoul, ROK: Korea Association of Information and Telecommunication.

Kelly, T., Grey, V., & Minges, M. (2003). *Broadband Korea: Internet case study.* Geneva, Switzerland: International Telecommunication Union.

Ki-Seok, H. (2004). *Korea wireless services 2004-2008 forecast and analysis: 2003 year-end review.* IDC Korea. Retrieved from http://www.idckorea.com/

KISDI. (2002). *IT industry outlook of Korea 2002.* Seoul, ROK: Korea Information Society Development Institute.

KISDI. (2003). *IT industry outlook of Korea 2003.* Seoul, ROK: Korea Information Society Development Institute.

KISDI. (2004). *IT industry outlook of Korea 2004.* Seoul, ROK: Korea Information Strategy Development Institute.

Kumarawadu, P. (2003). *Assessing and benchmarking our digital readiness for e-government: Moving towards e-Sri Lanka.* Paper presented at 22nd IT Conference, Colombo, Sri Lanka. Retrieved from http://www.cssl.lk/conferences/360,1,Slide1

Madan, S. (2004). Evaluating the development impact of e-government initiatives: An exploratory framework. In Gupta, M. P. (Ed.), *Towards e-government – Management challenges.* Tata McGraw Hill Publishing Company Ltd.

KEY TERMS AND DEFINITIONS

E-Governance: E-Governance is a network of organizations to include government, for-profit, not-for-profit, non-profit, civil societies, practitioners and private-sector entities.

E-Government: E-Government refers to the utilization of innovative information and communication technologies (ICTs) by governments as applied to the full range of government functionalities.

Grass Roots E-Governance: Effective utilization of local e-government structures and capacity in establishing a reliable, efficient and transparent governance system reaching out to the grass roots communities leading to economic, social, political, cultural and technology gains.

Local E-Government: Local e-government could be seen as the improvement, effectiveness and efficiency of local government in leading and delivering services to people at large through the use of ICTs with a vision of central and local government working in partnership to deliver better outcomes for people and places, including real challenges for local government in terms of political and managerial leadership, thus enhancing citizen engagement and participation for better service delivery.

Local Government: The lowest level of formal state institutions, such as district-level officials or local, publicly accountable decision-making and service-delivery organizations constituted in accordance with national laws (such as in local elections). It is a city, county, parish, township, municipality, ward, borough, board, district, or other general purpose political (and or administrative) subdivision of a state.

ENDNOTES

[1]   http://www.itu.int/ITU-D/ict/dai/index.html

[2]   http://www.itu.int/ITU-D/ict/dai/high.html

[3]   http://www.itu.int/ITU-D/ict/dai/low.html

[4]   http://www.eiu.com/site_info.asp?info_name=ereadiness&page=noads&rf=0

[5]   https://www.cia.gov/library/publications/the-world-factbook/geos/ce.html

[6]   http://www.itu.int/ITU-D/icteye/Indicators/Indicators.aspx#

[7]   https://www.cia.gov/library/publications/the-world-factbook/geos/ks.html

[8]   http://www.itu.int/ITU-D/ICTEYE/Indicators/Indicators.aspx

APPENDIX 1

Three prong approach of e-Korea Vision 2006, included objectives and policy plans for;

A. Promoting national informatization, which firstly, targeted to enhance the capacity by expanding opportunities brought by ICTs, with objectives to:
    1. Expand Internet usage to 90% of the overall population
    2. Connect schools to a world-class information infrastructure
    3. Raise the participation rate of the life-long learning system to the level of OECD member nations; and policy plans included, to:
    4. Enhance the ability of utilizing information and communication technologies by all citizens, by
        a. Strengthening IT education
        b. Creating a more accessible information environment
        c. Creating an "Information Welfare" system
    5. Establish a lifelong learning system, by
        a. Creating an environment for online learning
        b. Expanding opportunities for online lifelong learning
    6. Establish the e-work system, by
        a. Promoting online and mobile working
        b. Strengthening IT job training for the unemployed
B. Secondly, targeted to promote industrial informatization by leading economic growth through the realization of a digital economy, with objectives to:
    1. Enhance productivity and competitiveness of the existing manufacturing and service industries through informatization
    2. Develop and upgrade B2B e-commerce
    3. Create a reliable online business environment; and policy plan included, to:
    4. Expand the reach of information and communication technology to all industries, by
        a. Promoting informatization across industries
        b. Promoting informatization of SMEs
        c. Setting standards for efficient informatization of industries
    5. Advance B2B e-commerce, through
        a. Enhancing productivity and transparency through informatization of all business activities
        b. Expanding B2B networks
        c. Improving logistics and payments systems for promoting B2B e-commerce

      d.   Establishing an infrastructure for international e-trade

6.   Provide a safe and reliable online business environment, by

      a.   Establishing an online trust management system

      b.   Protecting e-consumers

      c.   Protecting personal information involved in e-commerce; and

C.   Thirdly, aimed to promote informatization in the public sector by realizing a productive and transparent smart government, with objectives to:

1.   Expand online services to all the civil affairs

2.   Enhance speed and transparency of the public administration on a "mobile government" infrastructure

3.   Upgrade digital public services; and policy plans included, to:

4.   Expand and upgrade online civil services, by

      a.   Expanding online civil services

      b.   Introducing customized digital civil services

      c.   Constructing a mobile government infrastructure

      d.   Establishing an electronic authentication system

5.   Continue innovation in the public administration through informatization, through

      a.   Strengthening the linkage between informatization and public administration reforms

      b.   Encouraging greater electronic participation by the general public

      c.   Promoting joint utilization of public information

6.   Expand informatization efforts in the administration of public finance, and science and technology, by

      a.   Promoting informatization in the public finance field

      b.   Promoting informatization in the industry, energy, science and technology fields

      c.   Promoting informatization of social overhead capital

7.   Promote informatization of public services for social welfare and the environment, through

      a.   Establishing an e-medical system

      b.   Diversifying information services on social welfare

      c.   Improving employment information services in response to the flexible labor market

      d.   Expanding information services for a clean and healthy environment

8.   Upgrade information services in education and culture, by

      a.   Improving administrative services in education

      b.   Expanding cultural information services to enhance quality of life

      c.   Strengthening national competitiveness through continuous expansion of knowledge and information resources

9.   Enhance efficiency in the administration of foreign affairs, justice and social security through informatization, by
   a.   Raising efficiency of foreign affairs and trade administration through informatization
   b.   Raising efficiency in the legal and criminal justice system
   c.   Building and managing an integrated information system for public safety

Advancing the information infrastructure, which:

A.   Firstly, targeted to transform the legal system to establish the information society by adjusting the legal framework, with objectives to:
   1.   Create the legal foundation which reflects the characteristics of the information society
   2.   Redesign institutional mechanisms in accordance with technological progress; and
   3.   Policy plans included, to:
      a.   Adjust basic laws and institutional mechanisms to the information society
      b.   Revise laws for the information society
B.   Secondly, to ensure Safety and Reliability of Cyberspace by Strengthening the security of the information infrastructure with private and public sector cooperation, with objectives to:
   1.   Establish a partnership between the private and public sectors against acts of cyber terrorism
   2.   Ensure the systematic protection of the national information infrastructure; and
   3.   Policy plans included, to:
   4.   Implement preventative measures and establishing a response system against acts of cyber terrorism, by
      a.   Establishing a cooperative partnership to prevent acts of cyber terrorism
      b.   Protecting critical government information
   5.   Develop information security technology and training new information security experts, through
      a.   Developing information security technology in response to new technological trends
      b.   Promoting public awareness of information security and training new experts in information security technologies
   6.   Create a sound cyberspace

C. Thirdly, to advance towards the next generation telecommunications infra-structure by constructing a world-class next generation telecommunications infrastructure, with objectives to:
    1. expand the broadband telecommunications networks for the realization of universal access to the broadband internet with a minimum transmission speed of 1 Mbps by 2005
    2. distribute digital televisions to more than 50% of the total households in Korea until 2006; and
    3. policy plans included, to:
    4. Upgrade high-speed telecommunications networks, by
        a. Upgrading backbone networks
        b. Upgrading broadband subscriber networks
        c. Upgrading KOREN (KOrea advanced REsearch Network)
        d. Introducing QoS to broadband internet services
    5. Advance the construction of the Next Generation Internet, through
        a. Promoting the Next Generation Internet and its applications
        b. Improving user environment for wireless internet
        c. Developing a next generation management system for IP addresses
        d. Preparing for the convergence of fixed line and wireless telecom-munications; and
D. Fourthly, for strategic promotion of the IT industry by advancing them as a source of economic growth, with objectives to:
    1. Develop core information technologies which enhance the competency of the Korean IT industry and become a source for job opportunities and future economic growth
    2. Foster advanced IT experts and specialists with global competitiveness
    3. Promote technology-intensive ventures as a driving force for all industries; and
    4. Policy plans included, to:
    5. Strengthen the core competency of the IT industry by developing strategic products
    6. Promote R&D for next generation IT, by
        a. Promoting research and development for a new leap
        b. Upgrading the information infrastructure for R&D of next genera-tion strategic technologies
        c. Promoting interdisciplinary research in response to the convergence of technologies
        d. Improving the R&D planning and evaluation system
        e. Promoting standardization of IT for market initiatives
    7. Foster IT experts and professionals, through

        a.   Fostering IT experts

        b.   Supporting studying abroad programs and employing foreign experts and specialists

        c.   Strengthening applied education programs

        d.   Conducting institutional amendments for fostering IT experts

        e.   Fostering researchers in basic science and interdisciplinary fields

   8.   Foster technology intensive ventures, by

        a.   Enhancing the efficiency of venture policies

        b.   Creating a favorable environment to stimulate growth of IT ventures

        c.   Providing a favorable business environment for the survival of venture companies

   9.   Conduct institutional amendments for the software and digital contents industries, through

        a.   Providing an institutional foundation for the competitiveness of the software industry

        b.   Conducting institutional reforms for the development of the digital contents industry; and in the third sector

Strengthening international cooperation for the Global Information Society, which:

A.   Firstly, targeted to establish a business hub in the East Asian region by building an IT hub in East Asia, with objectives to:

   1.   Take a leading role in the world market by facilitating e-business in East Asia

   2.   Promote information culture as a mediator of cultural exchange; and

   3.   Policy plans included, to:

   4.   Lead the world market through cooperation in East Asia, by

        a.   Establishing a system of economic cooperation in IT

        b.   Establishing CDMA coalition in East Asia

        c.   Strengthening cooperation to stimulate e-commerce activities in East Asia

        d.   Strengthening cooperation for facilitating software industries in East Asia

   5.   Globalize information culture in East Asia, through

        a.   Building cooperative frameworks for information culture in East Asia

        b.   Promoting exchanges in information culture in East Asia

B.   Secondly, targeted to take the initiative in international cooperation by emerging as a leader in global informatization, with objectives to:

1. Lead global informatization efforts through the expansion of the IT infrastructure at a global level
2. Lead the establishment of global governance and standard-setting in the global arena; and
3. Policy plans included, to:
4. Play a leading role in international organizations
5. Bridge the global digital divide
6. Expand the international information infrastructure; and

C. Thirdly, to facilitate the advancement of IT companies to enter into the world market by attaining international competitiveness, with objectives to:
   1. Attain IT export levels of $350 billion, a trade balance of $110 billion in the period beginning in 2002 to 2006
   2. Promote 30 key IT items as world-class products; and
   3. Policy plans included, to:
   4. Promote leading sectors for advancing into the world market, by
      a. Promoting key IT products
      b. Advancing the software and contents industries into the overseas markets
   5. Establish support systems for the advance into overseas markets, through
      a. Creating a foundation for advancement into the overseas market
      b. Providing financial support for the advance into world markets
      c. Diversifying IT Export Markets
      d. Building an information system to facilitate IT exports

APPENDIX 2

Table A1. Internet Chronological Table of Korea

Year	
▶ 1981	
Jan	- Main subjects of communication part for the 5th 5-year economic and social development plan for modernization of telecommunication (1982~1986): Fulfillment of communication demand, call automation, support of semi-conductor industry and promotion of radio waves utilization - Korea Institute of Science and Technology (KIST) and Korea Advanced Institute of Science (KAIS) merged into Korea Advanced Institute of Science and Technology (KAIST), integrating research and education (Divided again in June, 1989)
▶ 1982	
Mar	- Korea Data Communication Co. Ltd. was established as a private company handling data communication
Jul	- SDN (Sustainable Development Network), the first computer network and also the first Internet in Korea, was implemented via TCP/IP connection between the computers in Seoul National University and Institute of Electronics Technology
▶ 1983	
Jan	- The year of information industry's was proclaimed
Mar	- Comprehensive information industry promotion plan for semi-conductor industry and information industry (including training for experts and expansion of education on computer)
May	- Ministry of Science and Technology, established the plan for computerization of administration - Korea Information Industries Association was established (changed to Federation of Korea Information Industries)
Aug	- Framework Act on Telecommunications and Telecommunications Business Act established
Dec	- Information Industries Promotion Committee, reported the State Backbone Network Plan to the President
▶ 1984	
Mar	-Information Industries Promotion Committee was reorganized to State Backbone Network Coordination Committee
Nov	Information Telecommunications Training Center (ITTC) was established, reorganized to Information Cultural Center (ICC) in 1988 and Korea Agency for Digital Opportunity and Promotion (KADO) in 2003
▶ 1985	
Mar	- Institute of Electronics Technology and Korea Institute of Telecommunications Technology were merged into Institute of Electronics and Telecommunications, which was reorganized into Electronics and Telecommunications Research Institute (ETRI) in 1997.
▶ 1986	
Mar	- Education and research network committee was established
Jul	- .kr domain was first registered

continued on following page

Table A1. Continued

Year	
Dec	- Act on Computer Network Promotion established - Computer Programs Protection Act established
▶ 1987	
Jan	- National Computerization Agency founded
Feb	- Administrative computer network basic plan established
Jul	- Free import of personal computer
Nov	- National Computerization Agency, established the State Backbone Network Standardization Plan
▶ 1988	
Jan	- Korea Information Society Development Institute (formerly, Telecommunications Policy Institute) was established
Apr	- The first agricultural and fisher area computer training class was opened in Goheung, Jeonranam-do - The 1st Information Cultural Month event organized
Jun	- Korea Software Industry Association was established
	- Education and research network out of State Backbone Network were separated as education network (KREN) and research network (KREONet) - National Defense Computer Network Committee, established the national defense computer network basic plan
▶ 1989	
Jan	- Information Cultural Center (ICC) opened Information Cultural Promotion Center
Feb	- Federation of Korea Information Industries proclaimed 'Declaration of Information Society'
Jun	- Ministry of Education, decided the training program for computer with 16bit computers
Jul	- Selected as ITU management executive country Ministry of Communications, opened communication lines
▶ 1990	
Jan	- home banking service started
May	- Research network (KREONet) implemented experimentally in Daedeok complex
Aug	- Seoul National University launched campus integrated network SUNNET
▶ 1991	
Jan	- Ministry of Home Affairs started resident registration computerization service - Ministry of Commerce and Industry released DB promotion plan
Mar	- Ministry of Communications announced draft for regulation on computer network technology standard
Apr	- Korea PC Telecommunication founded
May	- International packet exchange based data communication started
▶ 1992	
Feb	- ANC, established Korea Network Information Center (KNIC)
Dec	- 2nd stage State Backbone Network Plan established - Subscriber line optical cable first launched; Pacific ocean submarine cable launched
▶ 1993	
Jan	- KAIST, started operating KNIC

continued on following page

Table A1. Continued

Year	
Apr	- National Computerization Agency, installed KOSInet
Jun	- Ministry of Government Administration, opened administration information network
▶ 1994	
Jan	- Act on the Protection of Personal Information Maintained by Public Agency was established
Mar	- Ministry of Communications announced basic plan for information super highway
May	- Information super highway committee was organized
Sep	- National Computerization Agency started KRNIC (formerly, KNIC) service
Dec	- Ministry of Communications is reorganized into Ministry of Information and Communication (absorbed the information related functions of Ministry of Science and Technology, Ministry of Commerce and Industry, and Bureau of Public Information)
▶ 1995	
Feb	- National Computerization Agency, opened Korea Internet Exchange Center (KIX), and started education network and research network interoperation centering on KRNIC - Established information super highway infrastructure implementation plan (by 2015)
Mar	- First Internet newspaper was published
Aug	- Information Communication Ethics Committee was organized
Sep	- Framework Act on Informationalization Promotion was established
Nov	- First Internet café 'Netscape' was opened - Computer technology lab in Daegu Univ. developed the first search engine "Kachine", which provided free search service
▶ 1996	
Jan	- Ministry of Information and Communication, implemented the first web site among the government authorities
Apr	- KT deployed information super-highway model network in Daedeok - Korea Information Security Center organized (reorganized to Korea Information Security Agency in July, 2001)
May	- The first internet shopping mall 'Interpark" and "Lotte Internet Department Store" were opened in Korea
Jun	- The world first cyber expo "Information Expo 96"
Jul	- LAN opened in Government Offices
Sep	- I-net published the first webzine 'Image (im@ge)'
Nov	- Consortium of CERT (CONCERT) founded
▶1997	
Jan	- Korea Internet Association (KRIA) founded
Feb	- Ministry of Information and Communication and Ministry of Labor, opened the remote occupational training system
May	- First Internet home trading service (HTS) started
Aug	- Korea Information Security Center, started online security check service
Oct	- Federation of Korea Information Industries, held the first presidential candidates' forum on information policy
Nov	- Ministry of Information and Communication, announced information security industry development plan

continued on following page

Table A1. Continued

Year	
▶ **1998**	
Jan	- Office for Government Policy Coordination, established comprehensive measures against Y2K problem - Seoul University Hospital started remote diagnosis service - Information and Communications University was opened
Apr	- National Computerization Agency, started the Y2K Support Center - 2nd stage Information Super Highway Infrastructure Plan
May	- Ministry of Government Administration and Home Affairs opened the government representative homepage
Jun	- Korea Information Security Industry Association founded
Jul	- Internet based government's civil petition service was started
Oct	- Korea IT Industry Promotion Agency was founded
Dec	- Ministry of Information and Communication, announced the plan for content class system in PC communication and Internet (introduced in May 1999)
▶ **1999**	
Jan	- Institute of Information Technology Assessment was founded
Feb	- Ministry of Information and Communication, started paid Internet address registration system - Digital Signature Act was established
Mar	- Framework Act on Electronic Commerce was established
May	- Cyber Korea 21 Vision was established - Korea Education & Research Information Service was opened
Jul	- Online community service launched - Korea Information Security Center, opened digital signature authentication center
Aug	- IPv6 based Internet implementation technology was developed - KRNIC was opened
Oct	- KOREN, secured IPv6 addresses
▶ **2000**	
Jan	- Recorded 10 million Internet users - KRNIC, established the domain name registration rules
Mar	- Recorded 1 million Information super highway subscribers - KRNIC, hold APNIC Conference in Seoul
Jun	- Ministry of Information and Communication, established 10 million people information education plan
Aug	- IPv6 forum Korea workshop
Nov	- KRNIC, announced Korean domain model service plan
Dec	- Korea Personal Information Security Association was founded - Recorded 19 million Internet users - Recorded 4 million Information super-highway users - KRNIC established agreement on wireless domain search service
▶ **2001**	
Jan	- Information Communication Infrastructure Protection Act was established - KRNIC hold the AT LARGE workshop of ICANN - First paid community portal service started

continued on following page

Table A1. Continued

Year	
Feb	- Next generation Internet infrastructure implementation plan was announced - 5-year plan for information security technology development - Ministry of Education and Human Resources Development, started Internet ethics education
Mar	- PC room associations integrated into Internet PC Culture Association - Ministry of Information and Communication, established Internet broadcasting promotion plan - Korea recorded 1st place out of OECD member states in broadband Internet propagation rate - Ministry of Commerce, Industry and Energy, opened online intelligent education information network 'Edunet'
Apr	- KRNIC, started receiving plural application of personal domains, and started 2 letter service - Korea Wireless Internet Standardization Forum was founded - KRNIC, established the agreement with Korea Women's Development Institute for joint research to solve 'digital divide' of women - Korea Information Cultural Center, dispatched 1st overseas internet young men service group - KRNIC made agreement with Vietnam NIC for cooperation on internet
May	- Designated the cyber terror protection day (15th of each month)
Jul	- OECD announced that Korea took the 1st place in Information Super Highway propagation rate
Aug	- Recorded 24 million Internet users
Oct	- Korea Knowledge Portal service was started
Nov	- Information Communication Ethics Committee, established the Cyber Defamation and Sexual Violence Mediation
Dec	- Personal Information Dispute Mediation Committee was founded - Recorded 10 million Internet banking subscribers
▶ 2002	
Jan	- kr Domain Mediation Committee was established - State URI basic plan for implementation of next generation infrastructure - KT started NESPOT commercial service
Feb	- Act on Consumer Protection for Electronic Commerce was established
Mar	- Ministry of Information and Communication founded CONCERT - On-line stamp system service started - e-Korea Vision 2006 plan was fixed
Apr	- Korea Information Cultural Center, opened Center for Internet Addiction Prevention and Counseling - KRNIC, started Wireless Internet Access Number System (WINC) service.
Jul	- .kr domain name registration agent was selected - KRNIC and 3 mobile service providers, started real-time registration of WINC
Aug	- The world first next generation network access gateway was opened - Korea's IPv4/IPv6 conversion technology was registered as the official document (RFC) of IETR
Sep	- Recorded 10 million information super highway subscribers
Oct	- World first commercialization of information superhighway media based home media service
Nov	- KISA started the first wireless authentication service

continued on following page

Table A1. Continued

Year	
Dec	- Korea e-Government was opened - National Education Information System (NEIS) was launched - Wireless Internet promotion plan was started - Online 3D game engine was developed in Korea - KRNIC reserved word domain name deregistration and registration - KRNIC provides free WINC supplementary service
▶ 2003	
Jan	- Korea Information Cultural Center (ICC) was reorganized to Korea Agency for Digital Opportunity and Promotion (KADO)
Feb	- Internet based national tax notification system was started - Medium-small sized enterprise informationalization adverse effect prevention center was opened
Mar	- Registered seal impression computerization was started
May	- mil.kr domain registration for military defense authorities KRNIC detained route DNS in Korea
▶ 2003	
Jun	- KRNIC started WINC based mobile brand service
Jul	- Yonsei University implemented the world first 'u-Campus'
Aug	- KRNIC received registration for Korean .kr domain name
Oct	- KRNIC started e number (ENUM) test service
▶ 2004	
Jan	- Act on Internet Address Resources was established
Jun	- Recorded 30 million Internet users
Jul	- KRNIC was reorganized into National Internet Development Agency of Korea (NIDA) - KR domain, registered the world first IPv6 name server address in the route DNS zone - Internet Address Policy Deliberation Committee was founded - Domain Name Mediation Committee was reorganized into Internet Address Dispute Resolution Committee
Sep	Gyeongbuk Univ., operated the first Internet Control Center in Korea

http://www.apng.org/museum/ppt/20050510-Internet_Chronological_Table_of_Korea.doc, Retrieved November 20, 2009

Chapter 5

Citizen–Centric Service Dimensions of Indian Rural E–Governance Systems:
An Evaluation

Harekrishna Misra
Institute of Rural Management Anand, India

EXECUTIVE SUMMARY

E-governance systems in India have witnessed prolific advancement over the years. India has strategically adopted e-governance as a part of its policy. In recent times each state has its own e-governance plan to deliver services as planned. National policy also aims to provide formalized services across the nation while recognizing the importance of state specific services. This approach includes various mission mode projects under national e-governance plan (NeGP). Manifestation of such approach has resulted in 100,000 common service centers (CSC) in rural areas. It is expected that rural citizens would find them useful and it may contribute for effective governance. In this chapter it is argued that such an initiative would be successful if rural citizens find these CSCs useful for their livelihood security. Various dimensions of this phenomenon are also examined through some cases in this chapter to understand their contributions to successful CSCs in India.

DOI: 10.4018/978-1-4666-2071-1.ch005

BACKGROUND

E-governance initiatives, despite acceptance to an extent in the form of e-government systems, have so far remained hype in many parts of the world. Failure stories abundantly reflect that such initiatives with development perspectives have not yielded encouraging results. Estimates indicate that 35 per cent are total failures, 50 per cent are partial failures, and 15 per cent are successes in developing and transitional countries. It is argued that e-governance initiatives are often on project mode and each project forms island for deliveries creating an overwhelming gap between project design and on-the-ground reality (known as design-reality gaps). This gap contributes to failures (Heeks 2003). Despite such discouraging outcomes, e-government initiatives in developing countries have evolved to a level of acceptance among government agencies and backend service provisioning organisations. Most countries are now in the phase of assessing the "impact" on issues related to "efficiency," "effectiveness," and "equity" since they have gone beyond the initial phases of addressing primary challenges of "digital divide," "setting up infrastructure," and "spreading awareness" for ICT use and delivering citizen-centric e-governance services. Most of the countries are now able to showcase their e-governance services and declare the "availability" of these services uninterrupted crossing the spatial challenges (Figure 1). E-governance systems in many countries have evolved to the level of maturity. However, usage of such services has been a challenge. E-governance systems have so far remained supply-driven in most countries and their actual use largely depends on the type of services rendered. E-government services

Figure 1. Changing e-government issues over time

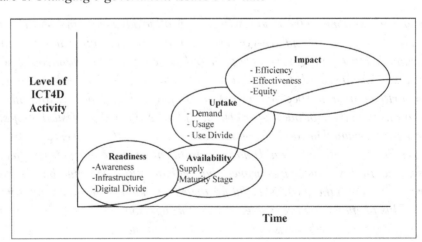

Adopted from (Heeks, 2006; Heeks & Molla, 2009)

are "mandatory" in nature and citizens are expected to use them. However, usage of many services which have development perspectives like income generation, health and education depends largely on the success of these services related to citizen needs. Though it is argued that readiness, availability, and uptake phases of e-governance systems are not contemporary anymore for evaluation of success in managing such projects, most of the developing countries still grapple with this phenomenon. There is still use divide, low latent demand, and sub-optimal usage of e-governance services (Misra & Hiremath 2009; Misra 2009).

Discussion on global e-governance systems suggests a clear direction to policy makers and implementers which calls for provisioning of converged and value added services to citizens with least cost, time, and effort. It is also evident that e-governance systems need to evolve to connected governance through establishment of robust infrastructure, backend integration with all stakeholders, and transforming the government itself through innovation and value addition (UN, 2008). Information indicates that connected governance is possible through phases (Heeks, 2006; Heeks & Molla, 2009; Archmann,2008). It needs a concerted effort to graduate any e-government effort to connected governance.

As shown in Figure 1 and Box 1, it is mandatory for any country to ensure its readiness in each stage before going to the next higher stage. In the context of Indian e-governance efforts, the situation is not different when compared to global e-governance scenarios, experiences, and trends. In India, foundation of e-governance was laid during 1954 when the Planning Commission introduced computers followed by setting up of the Department of Electronics (DOE) in 1970 and establishment of the National Informatics Centre in 1970 as a national agency to make available necessary infrastructure across all states to provide required connectivity with the central government (Mishra 2007; Prabhu 2004; Planning Commission, 2001). The government's policies to encourage digital empowerment are presented in Table 1.

Box 1. Three critical considerations for establishment of connected governance (UN, 2008)

In order to establish ICT enabled connected governance, UN recognizes following three areas:
A. Infrastructure: Creating an information infrastructure both within the public sector and across society at large, one based upon reliable and affordable Internet connectivity for citizens, businesses and all stakeholders in a given jurisdiction;
B. Integration: Leveraging this new infrastructure within the public sector in order to better share information (internally and externally) and bundle, integrate, and deliver services through more efficient and citizen-centric governance models encompassing multiple delivery channels; and
C. Transformation: Pursuing service innovation and e-government across a broader prism of community and democratic development through more networked governance patterns within government, across various government levels and amongst all sectors in a particular jurisdiction.

Table 1. Indian e-governance genesis

Year	Mile-stones for E-Governance Efforts	Goal
1984	New Computer Policy	Spread of Computer Use
1986	Policy on Software Export, Development and Training	To promote Sectoral growth in ITeS, Business Process Outsourcing
1987	Setting up of NICNET, DISNIC	Setting up of IT infrastructure in Government Sector
1994	Policy on National Telecommunication (NTP 94)	To ensure better Tele-density, focus on Rural Tele-phony
1995	Launching of Internet; Spectrum Alloca-tion and Release	Web Access and bandwidth allocation for use
1997	Establishment of Telecom. Regulatory Authority (TRAI)	To unbundle telecommunication services (last mile)
1998	National Task Force on IT	To formulate an IT policy document
1999	Creation of Ministry of IT	To oversee implementation of IT policy
1999	Policy on National Telecommunication (NTP 99)	To accelerate tele-density
2000	Formulation of IT Act	To provide legal status to use of IT in business, government, and governance systems
2000	Formulation of Communication Conver-gence Bill	Convergence of content, convergence of carriage, and convergence of Terminal
2000	Telecom Disputes Settlement and Appel-late Tribunal (TDSAT)	Fair and transparent telecom. services
2000	Corporatization of DoT (formation of BSNL)	Unbundling of the telecommunication sector, private sector investments and managing USO
2004	Formulation of Broadband Policy	To implement broadband services in the last mile
2006	National E-Governance Plan (NeGP)	To formulate, plan, design, and deploy e-government solutions and establish citizen interfaces
2007	Mission 2007	To consider each village a knowledge centre

Adopted from (Misra & Hiremath, 2009).

E-governance efforts globally have been challenged by plethora of socio-technical, cultural and economic issues (Riga Declaration,2006). In India, theses challenges are enormous because of the diverse nature of the issues concerning not only the socio-technical, cultural and economic dimensions but the rural citizens who constitute an integral part to contribute to the success of the e-governance efforts. Despite e-governance policies formulated and directed towards rural citizens, voluntary participation of rural citizens is yet to gain momentum. However, sporadic efforts are visible through pilot projects directed towards collaboration of rural citizens. Therefore, there is a considerable need to examine the influencing factors for ensuring participation of rural citizens in the national level effort for development. In this chapter, various dimensions influencing rural citizen participation are discussed aimed at fruitful delivery of e-governance services. In this chapter it is posited that demand driven information infrastructure needs to be developed for successful implementation of e-governance systems and especially demands of rural citizens need to be reflected adequately in the e-governance systems. In order to provide demand driven rural information infrastructure in India, it is argued that livelihood security based assessment of such information infrastructure would be beneficial. This chapter verifies the dimensions of such demands and assesses the status of e-governance efforts undertaken in one of the districts in Gujarat state, India.

The organization of the chapter is as follows. The chapter provides a global perspective of e-governance initiatives, their rationale to adopt such strategies, challenges and opportunities faced during implementations of e-governance projects. It includes underpinnings of current global e-governance initiatives. It then presents the e-governance scenario and initiatives taken up in India and discusses the challenges faced for its effective implementation. Subsequently, focus on rural e-governance scenario, role ICT for development in the context of rural India are examined through a model. The model is aimed at interfacing demand and supply characteristics of information infrastructure and relating them to e-governance models deployed nationally. The chapter also examines the of a village information system (VIS) with livelihood perspectives which needs to be established before any ICT infrastructure is deployed. It is argued that VIS should aim to provide information and "services" on demand through "stakeholder-ownership oriented development" initiatives. In order to appreciate the applicability of the proposed framework, results obtained through a survey undertaken in a sample district in Gujarat are discussed. Finally, the chapter discusses observations and elaborates on the direction for further research.

E-GOVERNANCE ASSESSMENT IN INDIA: THE NEED

As discussed in Figure 1 (Heeks 2006) and as recognized by UN (UN 2008), infrastructure is a critical contributor to the success of "connected governance." E-governance efforts in a country strongly reflect the role and contributions of infrastructure in their policies, projects and implementation strategies. Infrastructural readiness is one of the concurrent evaluation criteria which have been set for the countries globally. There are various agencies involved in assessment exercises globally. In Table 2, a list of such agencies are presented. E-governance assessment frameworks have evolved with the intention to benchmark the e-government strategies, policies and provide an environment of learning from these ever dynamic processes. It is largely recognized that e-governance efforts are country specific, related to national level

Table 2. Profile of e-readiness assessment agencies (global)

Study	Focus
APEC (Asia Pacific Economic Cooperation)	E-Commerce Readiness
CIDIF (Centre International pour le Development de l'Inforoute en Francais)	Internet Service Market
EIU (Economist Intelligence Unit) with IBM	E-Business Readiness
IDC	Infrastructure
World Bank (KAM)	K-Economy
McConnell International (MI)	Infrastructure, Digital Economy, Education, and Government
MN (Metric Net)	E-Economy
MQ (Mosaic Group)	Internet
NRI (CID, Harvard)	Infrastructure, E-Society, Policies, Digital Economy, Education, and Government
CID (Centre for International Development)	Society
CIDCM (University of Maryland)	Qualitative Assessment based on past performance and current internet pervasiveness
World Telecommunication/ ICT Development Report; International Telecommunication Union (ITU)	Telecommunication; Measuring ICT for Social and Economic Development; Measuring ICT availability in Villages and Rural Areas (ITU, 2006a; ITU,2007b)
SIDA (Swedish International Development Cooperation Agency)	Mainly Strength, Weakness, Opportunity and Threat (SWOT) analysis of a Nation
USAID (US Agency for International Development)	Access, Government,
World Economic Forum; Global IT Report	E-Readiness
United Nations Development Programme	E-Governance
World Economic Forum	Global Competitiveness Report
Measurement of Information Society, ITU	ICT Opportunity Index
Economic and Social Commission for Asia and The Pacific (ESCAP), UN	Regulations, Polices, Legal Framework Related to ICT; UN's Global E-Government Survey
United Nations Development Programme (UNDP)	ICT Indicators for Human Development; Democratic Governance Indicators

Compiled from (Budhiraja & Sachdeva,2009; Misra & Hiremath, 2009)

policies, socio-cultural systems and government systems. Though it is not easy to map all the success factors of e-governance efforts made in other countries to the Indian scenario, overall learning from them would help the country to improve upon.

While the number of agencies involved in the assessment process is not important, their approaches lead to the conclusion that the e-readiness exercises have their importance in any phase of deployment of e-governance. E-governance efforts are continuous and these efforts require concurrent evaluation to add value progressively. In the Indian context, the global e-readiness exercises provide an insight to various challenges that the country faces to set up and use infrastructure. India, being a developing country, experiences harsh realities of e-readiness attributes explained in Figure 1. However, in recent times last mile dimensions of digital divide is increasingly being addressed through various policies like tele-density increase, broadband penetration, establishment of common service centers, and state and centre sponsored content management through state- wide area network backbones (SWAN) under NeGP. A close look at the global IT report indicates that India needs to improve upon many other dimensions of e-governance including digital divide (Misra & Hiremath, 2009).

E-readiness assessment exercise is an implicit phenomenon for all nations and there is a mechanism to display the status of e-readiness of each country in order to examine the progress and identify the areas of improvement. There are various components of e-readiness exercise and important among them are "infrastructure readiness," "individual readiness," "government readiness," and "political and regulatory readiness." In Figure 2 the e-readiness components in India vis-à-vis other countries are shown in a time line. It may be observed that infrastructure readiness needs considerable attention in India to achieve better e-governance service utilization. Other readiness indicators have shown appreciable improvements in global standards, despite diverse socio-economic ambience. Individual readiness, government readiness, and political and regulatory readiness indicators support the fact

Figure 2. E-readiness indices of India

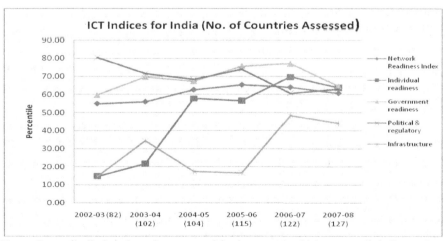

Note: Percentile displays the rank among participating countries; higher percentile indicates better status; Adopted from (Misra, 2009)

that awareness among stakeholders to accept ICT enabled services has increased. But as a nation, India has to traverse a long path to achieve all inclusive readiness in order to bring in overall development and appreciable use of e-governance services.

Availability of Integrated E-Governance Infrastructure and Services

Availability of integrated infrastructure in a nation is reflection of its sound policy and implementation strategy. In India ICT initiatives and their convergence are integral parts of its policies. Various policies and Five Year Plans have elaborated the role of connectivity and possible road maps for converged approaches. The tenth and eleventh five year plan documents (Planning Commission 2001) provide a comprehensive approach towards achieving convergence in ICT infrastructure and content management with special emphasis on rural development. Some among them are convergence bill, broadband policy, NeGP with MMPs, and universal service obligation (USO).

As a strategic move, spread of basic telephony to all citizens has been part of India's sound infrastructure policy. Telephony has been a powerful mode of establishing the required connectivity among citizens. It has catalyzed the convergence of other stakeholders in the governance system which is involved in provisioning of user services. Telephony has also been instrumental in spread of Internet services and the Internet is the backbone of e-governance infrastructure today. Tele-density has been a globally accepted metric for understanding the spread of telephony because of such critical contribution. A comparative assessment of urban-rural tele-density in India is provided in Figure 3. However, the picture is far from satisfactory and there is a huge disparity in urban-rural tele-density despite policy level support.

Internet and telephone users in India are way below world figures. From Figure 4, it is evident that there is tremendous scope to improve upon the infrastructure as India's rank ranges between 87 and 107 among 127 countries assessed. As regards Internet users in India, it is estimated that 12 per cent of urban population are using the Internet whereas only 1.2 per cent of rural population is using the Internet (JuxtConsultIndia Online 2008).

Availability of services is another important dimension of e-governance systems. Conceptualization, design, development, and deployment of electronic services online are major responsibilities of content management. The Convergence Bill of India calls for convergence of content and convergence of carriage as national initiatives (Planning Commission 2001). Convergence of carriage calls for major changes in structures of the computer industry and more comprehensively the telecommunication and networking industry that are responsible for data communication and broadcasting of multi-media applications.

Figure 3. Tele density in India

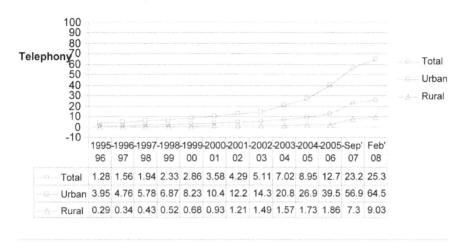

(No. of Telephones per 100 Persons)

	1995-96	1996-97	1997-98	1998-99	1999-00	2000-01	2001-02	2002-03	2003-04	2004-05	2005-06	Sep' 07	Feb' 08
Total	1.28	1.56	1.94	2.33	2.86	3.58	4.29	5.11	7.02	8.95	12.7	23.2	25.3
Urban	3.95	4.76	5.78	6.87	8.23	10.4	12.2	14.3	20.8	26.9	39.5	56.9	64.5
Rural	0.29	0.34	0.43	0.52	0.68	0.93	1.21	1.49	1.57	1.73	1.86	7.3	9.03

Source: www.Indiastat.com, accessed on 2 March, 2009

Figure 4. Status of internet and telephony in India

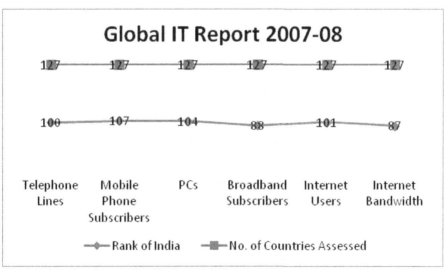

Note: Lower the rank better the status; (Misra, 2009, Dutta et al., 2008)

The National Task Force on IT and Software Development recommended in 1998 in addressing the last-mile connectivity problem. Convergence of content calls for efforts in e-government and e-governance, and provision of a single window service to the citizen. Another issue is to address the convergence of terminal in order to provide multilingual services on multimedia applications anywhere and anytime in India. Today there are various attempts made to provide the content in local languages including the operating system initiative of C-DAC named as the Bharat Operating System Solutions (BOSS). As regards service oriented contents, NeGP recognizes the scope for large-scale implementation of application under mission mode projects (MMPs) with emphasis on integrated services. Under NeGP, national level MMPs and state level MMPs are identified for implementation on scale-up mode as presented in Figure 5 (Ministry of Information Technology [MoIT] 2009a).

Every interested state government is now under a state wide area network (SWAN). Each state is now in the process of having state data centres under the NeGP policy. This endeavour is part of state readiness exercise which is adapted

Figure 5. MMPs under NeGP

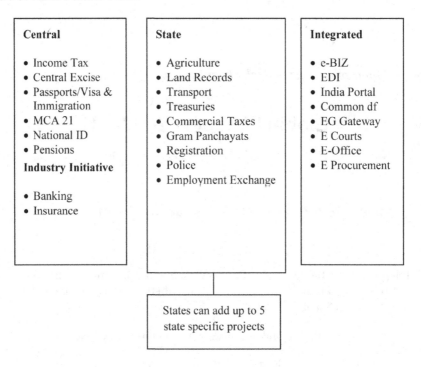

Source: Adopted from (MoIT, 2009).

mostly from the global information technology report framework published annually by the World Economic Forum. This assessment commencing in 2003 has provided insight to the performance of states which are placed in six categories: Least Achievers (L1), Below Average Achievers (L2), Average Achievers (L3), Expectants (L4), Aspiring Leaders (L5), and Leaders (L6). The latest rankings of the participating states are given in Figure 6.

E-readiness for districts has been on the agenda of the e-governance policy in India. This readiness is essential to implement e-district services which are parts of the state level mission mode projects under NeGP. It envisages provisioning of services through CSCs planned to be made available in every sixth village across the country and these services include district administration and citizen- centric government services (MoIT 2009).

Uptake of E-Governance Services in India

It is quite evident that Indian efforts are in line with global e-governance scenarios and the Indian government is making all possible efforts to establish the e-governance infrastructure and provide converged services for the citizens. This supply mode of services has long lasting effect on the readiness of government systems and integration of backend services. As regards mission mode projects at the state and national levels, most of them are related to government systems and citizens would have no option but to accept them as made available to them. The real challenge, however, lies in assessing the net uptake of the services which largely depends on demand;

Figure 6. State e-readiness pyramid of the states

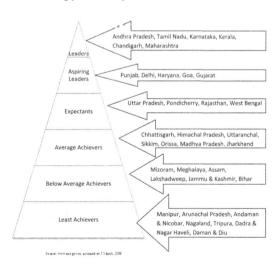

usage and usage divide as shown in Figure 1. In the Indian context, these three dimensions of demand are quite relevant because of the digital divide. It is largely felt that the digital divide has now been converted to digital opportunities because of various policies/acts such as the Broadband Policy, NeGP, and RTI Act. There are many well documented challenges in India to maximize the uptake of services because of the diversity and disparities in the needs of rural-urban citizens. Despite many efforts, e-government services are yet to render the desired pro-citizen services and are mostly targeted towards internal efficiency (Bhatnagar 2006). Pro-poor services may be available through state and national MMPs in due course since the projects are in the phases of transition.

Impact of E-Governance Services in India

The current scenario e-governance efforts has provided the right platform to render effective services at the national and state levels through organized backbones, data centers, and MMPs. NeGP caters to the 100,000 CSCs and provides the platform for convergence of various services through the private-public-partnership (PPP) mode. There is a significant change in the way government systems are working now because of the impact of the information technology Act, and the RTI Act. MMPs alike NCA-21, Income Tax, and Railways have added the right impetus to citizen-acceptance of IT enabled services. Penetration of telephony (wire and wireless) has been phenomenal, triggering the right ambience for m-government (mobile government) applications. But the real challenges to improve upon the impacts are many. It is argued that mere provisioning personal computers, connectivity, and content do not correlate with actual use of services (Heeks et al. 2009). This situation is prevalent especially in rural areas.

NATIONAL E-GOVERNANCE PLAN IN INDIA: THE CASE

In the previous sections, e-governance efforts supporting the development process in developing countries are discussed. E-inclusion has been a critical consideration for global apex bodies such as UN, EU, UNDP, and ITU in provisioning of e-governance services to citizens (EU,2007). MDG efforts include ICT enabled services as one of the most critical indicators for understanding the success of goals set. It is also recognised that global e-governance efforts face challenges of infrastructure, integration, and transformation. There are many failures in implementing e-governance projects and some of the attributes leading to unsuccessful results are design-reality gaps, digital divides, supply-driven services and scanty usage of services.

In India, e-governance services have gone beyond the phases of incubation, prototyping and showcasing of standard software engineering processes. Despite sincere efforts, the services have remained supply driven and need to be transformed to a level of high use through creation of latent demand at village level. Along these lines, National e-Governance Plan (NeGP), has laid emphasis on deploying MMPs at state and central government levels and has provided the desired attention to integrate them so as to generate citizen-centric services on demand and to increase the latent demand. In Figure 7, the approach to integrate various services is presented.

In this integrated approach NeGP intends to provide a service grid through adequate connectivity, increased influx of capital with focused deliveries, increase in the capacity and capabilities of service provisioning agencies in the government, providing adequate content in local languages, establishing required policies and legal frameworks to encourage convergence of services and service providers, establish security standards, and channel the grid based services to citizens through an established channel of interface.

The citizen interface is the most critical element in the grid which largely influences the success of e-governance services. In this chapter, it is hypothesized that services supplied would meet their desired level of success through sustained use

Figure 7. NeGP approach for integration

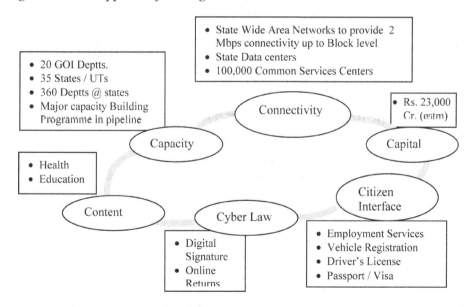

Source: www.mit.gov.in , accessed on 5 March, 2009, MoIT (2009).

by end users. The study discusses the interface of NeGP services being planned, designed, and deployed with that of the latent demand and its influencing factors. The objective is to understand user-divides prevalent in rural areas in India since the success of e-governance efforts largely depends on their contributions to rural development indicators nationally and as per MDG imperatives. This study is largely a continuation of our work in the sample district in Gujarat in India (Misra & Hiremath, 2006). The study also posits that user-divides in rural India is intensely influenced by livelihood security metrics of the households. In this chapter, an attempt is made to explore the effects of livelihood metrics on the latent demand of the information and services network being deployed.

NeGP, in its phase of implementation and scale up recognizes the fact that CSCs should work on sustainable basis with public-private-partnerships (PPP). This approach calls for a sustainable demand from the rural citizens and this demand largely depends on usability, usefulness and usability of services. User interfaces and user orientation of services have still remained a challenge for ICT planners, developers and implementers (Heeks et al., 2009; Misra, 2009). The situation is more complex in the Indian context where information infrastructure for ICT enabled governance systems grapple with development challenges. The challenges are not limited to "technology," but the "people" and the "processes." Specifically rural ICT enabled governance initiative face daunting task, not because it involves the rural infrastructure, but the complex process of involving the rural masses. These masses (the rural citizens), who lack access to basic livelihood opportunities, are oblivious of ICT initiatives. They continue to remain so because of poor reflections of their interests in such projects. Such apathy has contributed immensely to "poor user interfaces" which is termed as "citizen interfaces."

FRAMEWORK FOR ANALYSIS OF THE CASE

Considering the challenges in implementing e-governance services in Indian context, a framework is presented to reflect the contributors to the success of such endeavor (see Figure 8).

The framework suggests that success of e-governance services is dependent on the "demand" created locally in rural ambience in India (Misra, 2009). As discussed earlier, various agencies are engaged in extending services to rural citizens in villages/ Panchayats through entrepreneurship models. Thus there is a strong need for assessment of demand in the village/ Panchayat so that entrepreneurs engaged in providing the services earn their livelihood, make the service provisioning centre as an income generating avenue and establish the right linkage between service providing agencies and rural citizens.

Figure 8. The framework to reflect demand influencers (adopted from Misra & Hiremath, 2009; Misra, 2009)

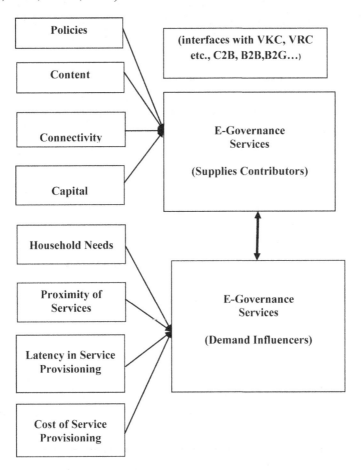

The Influencers of Supply-Demand

The framework recognizes the need for a strong collaborative interface between "e-governance service- information supplies" and "e-governance service- Information demands." It is considered that e-governance centered information supplies are mostly contributed by policies, infrastructure for establishing connectivity, content developed for the purpose and capital invested in the process. These are mostly incubated, piloted and implemented within the framework of policies. The framework includes influencers discussed in the first method and uses them in the second method to understand the "supply-contributors" as shown in Figure 7. Readiness, availability, uptake and impacts are essentially influenced by policies, content, connectivity and capital which remain supply-driven. The framework suggests that parameters like e-readiness, availability of content, connectivity and capital would critically influence the uptakes and impact of e-governance services. However, the framework also considers the citizens' demand to be local, household specific. It also considers that "supply-demand interface" can be successful only when service is made available on demand, with better proximity at optimized cost and low latency. Suitable interface with information demands generated at the points of services is also necessary to build a sustainable and trustworthy relationship with the citizens. The citizens in general and rural citizens in India in particular, are influenced by the quality of services that are provided for better and sustained use. These influencers are household needs, proximity of services, latency in service provisioning and cost of services. The information supply mechanisms need to consider all these influencers well in advance and incorporate them in the supplies contributors discussed in the framework. In other words, policies, infrastructure for establishing connectivity, content developed for the purpose and capital invested in the process should recognize household needs, proximity of services, latency in service provisioning and cost of services. Besides, the services to be rendered need to recognize the intentions of citizen who look for support of agencies to have better infrastructure, income generation opportunities, and increased awareness etc.

The Framework for Impact Study

The village information system assumes a critical role in contributing to the national information services plan. Diversity in social, cultural, demographic, economic and infrastructural assets in a village influences the household livelihood security options and thus generates a unique scenario. Information economics principles has a far-reaching effect on VIS which argues that information is increasingly recognised as a capital and can add to the livelihood pentagon framework which has five faces of capital to assess the livelihood of a household: financial, human, natural, physical, and social. This information capital can be used for the advantages of citizens in developing countries to support livelihood options (Heeks et al. 2009; World Bank 1986). Box 2 explains these advantages.

Box 2. Advantages of information capital for rural citizens in a developing country

---

• **Information absence:** key information that development actors need is not available.
• **Information quality:** key information that development actors need is available but of poor quality.
• **Information uncertainty:** key information that development actors need is available but its quality is uncertain.
• **Information asymmetry:** some development actors have access to key information that others lack.
• **Information cost:** key information can only be obtained at high cost (often a physical journey).
Source: (Heeks & Molla, 2009).

Availability of information capital at the household level in developing countries can immensely influence local livelihood opportunities through information management at right time, at appropriate locations, and with right language interfaces. Therefore, it is important that information availability is measured through its proximity to the source and recipient, latency in extending information and its related services, decrease in the uncertainty in provisioning of information through integration, and ability of citizens to gain access to the information at affordable cost. The proposed framework aims to establish a synergy between the information provisioning agencies and citizens in the villages and map the services through these metrics. It is posited that VIS would assume this role in establishing the required synergy.

Methodologies

There are two aspects that the framework intends to address. First, the e-governance services-supplies are assessed. This is done through examination of two cases of e-governance efforts "NeGP" and "E-Gram" which are considered for scale up at national level and state level respectively. This assessment is based on the parameters explained in Figure 7 under "e governance services, supplies contributors." The objective is to understand the rigor of the deliveries based on information supplies of the suggested framework. Second, these two cases are examined with viewpoints of interfaces with information demand influencers.

Primary surveys are conducted in seven sample villages to understand the efficacy of these influencers. These sample villages are drawn from a particular district in the state where both E-Gram and NeGP projects are co-existing. These samples are mostly homogeneous, small and therefore, there is a limitation in generalization of the findings. Research method included a sampling plan to elicit responses of rural citizens with respect to their aspirations and the limitations these endeavours attempt to meet them. There are 284 respondents who participated in the interview and participatory rural appraisal (PRA) exercises in the village. In the interview method, random sampling was adopted to avoid bias. However, seven villages provided a cluster scenario for the researcher. As regards PRA exercise, each village had one and interested villagers were encouraged to participate (Misra & Hiremath, 2009).

Readiness would relate critically to local infrastructure and local sources for information retrieval and integration among these sources in order to encourage citizens to avail such services. Availability largely depends on the readiness of infrastructure and integrated services. Besides, it is also largely influenced by the cost factor. Increase in uptake would depend on availability of integrated services and low latency with focus on livelihood-centric services because it might build trust in the system. Impact assessment is also an important stage in the evolution since it measures the net effect of e-governance services. Latency and integrated services in a sustainable manner are expected to provide a larger impact. While all stages of evolution in e-governance services are expected to be largely influenced by the integrated information infrastructure, latency in availing and providing services are the next most important metric for successful evolution. Proximity and cost of information and services are considered important metrics; they are largely critical for the readiness, availability, and uptake stages of the evolution process.

Village Information System: The Critical Interface

Village Information System (VIS) is the core issue in this study. The research propositions are as follows:

1. VIS is expected to provide the desired interface with the citizens and supplied services for supporting their livelihood prospects in local conditions.
2. VIS is treated as "atomic" in order to establish the uniqueness of the demand that the concerned village would place on the service providing agencies to meet livelihood security based challenges at the household level. It is argued that each village has uniqueness in raising demand on e-governance services. Each village is therefore, a unit of study. Each village provides an aggregated ambience based on household level demand to understand prioritised information requirements.
3. Proximity to information and service resources, latency, integrated information, and cost of services influence readiness, availability, uptake, and impact in provisioning e-governance services.

The research propositions demand a primary survey at the household level because of the premise that each household has uniqueness in placing its demand on the "orchestrated" information network available through the e-governance policy framework.

In this chapter, severity metrics are formed to support the measurements. Severity is presented as a term associated with difficulty/ importance attached to citizens' critical needs to support livelihood security. Severity metric depends on quantifiable parameters of the livelihood security profile of a household aggregated at the village level. This metric indicates the difficulty level of a household/village to get support from agencies for receiving information. In Table 3, this severity is explained for the purpose of benchmarking results that the proposed framework examines. These metrics are indicative of the perspectives of sample respondents who participated in the exercise. An assessment of these metrics indicates that rural citizens are not averse to payment for availing services provided desired services are rendered

Table 3. Information severity metrics and benchmarks

Livelihood Security Profiling	Severity Metrics			Demand on VIS
	Description	**Range**	**Metric**	
Food Security	Sufficiency of Food	0-4months	+++ (Most Severe)	Very High
		5-8 months	++ (Severe)	High
		9-12 months	+ (Less Severe)	Important
	Income Generation Opportunities (Information Asymmetry)	Proper Sale Value Realization in the Village		
		> 80 per cent said Yes	+ (Less Severe)	Important
		<80 per cent>40 per cent	++ (Severe)	High
		<40 per cent	+++ (Most Severe)	Very High
		Distance Travelled for Sale		
		< 5 Km	+ (Less Severe)	Important
		> 5 < 10 Km	++ (Severe)	High
		> 10 Km	+++ (Most Severe)	Very High
		Availability of Work Opportunity in Village		
		> 80 per cent said Yes	+ (Less Severe)	Important
		<80 per cent>40 per cent	++ (Severe)	High
		<40 per cent	+++ (Most Severe)	Very High
		Household Asset Sold for Purchase of Food		
		> 80 per cent said Yes	+++ (Most Severe)	Very High
		<80 per cent>40 per cent said Yes	++ (Less Severe)	High
		< 40 per cent said Yes	+ (Severe)	Important
Health Security	Human	Accessible to Health Infrastructure		
		< 5 Km	+ (Less Severe)	Important
		> 5 < 10 Km	++ (Severe)	High
		> 10 Km	+++ (Most Severe)	Very High
		Availability of Health Services in the Village		
		> 80 per cent said Yes	+ (Less Severe)	Important
		<80 per cent>40 per cent	++ (Severe)	High
		<40 per cent	+++ (Most Severe)	Very High
		Availability of Immunization /Health Training Services in the Village		

continued on following page

Table 3. Continued

Livelihood Security Profiling	Severity Metrics			Demand on VIS
		> 80 per cent said Yes	+ (Less Severe)	Important
		<80 per cent>40 per cent	++ (Severe)	High
		<40 per cent	+++ (Most Severe)	Very High
	Livestock	Availability of Livestock Support Services in the Village		
		> 80 per cent said Yes	+ (Less Severe)	Important
		<80 per cent>40 per cent	++ (Severe)	High
		<40 per cent	+++ (Most Severe)	Very High
Education Security	Formal Education Facility (Primary)			
	> 80 per cent said Yes	+ (Less Severe)	Important	Important
	<80 per cent>40 per cent	++ (Severe)	High	High
	<40 per cent	+++ (Most Severe)	Very High	Very High
	Access to Formal Education Facility (Primary)			
	< 5 Km	+ (Less Severe)	Important	Important
	> 5 < 10 Km	++ (Severe)	High	High
	> 10 Km	+++ (Most Severe)	Very High	Very High
	Formal Education Facility (Secondary)			
	> 80 per cent said Yes	+ (Less Severe)	Important	Important
	<80 per cent>40 per cent	++ (Severe)	High	High
	<40 per cent	+++ (Most Severe)	Very High	Very High
	Access to Formal Education Facility (Secondary)			
	< 5 Km	+ (Less Severe)	Important	Important
	> 5 < 10 Km	++ (Severe)	High	High
	> 10 Km	+++ (Most Severe)	Very High	Very High
	Formal Education Facility (Higher)			
	> 80 per cent said Yes	+ (Less Severe)	Important	Important
	<80 per cent>40 per cent	++ (Severe)	High	High
	<40 per cent	+++ (Most Severe)	Very High	Very High
	Access to Formal Education Facility (Higher)			
	< 5 Km	+ (Less Severe)	Important	Important
	> 5 < 10 Km	++ (Severe)	High	High
	> 10 Km	+++ (Most Severe)	Very High	Very High
Financial Security	Ability to meet Household Expenses			
	> 80 per cent said Yes	+ (Less Severe)	Important	Important

continued on following page

Table 3. Continued

Livelihood Security Profiling	Severity Metrics			Demand on VIS
	<80 per cent>40 per cent	++ (Severe)	High	High
	<40 per cent	+++ (Most Severe)	Very High	Very High
	Availability of Credit/ Insurance Services			
	> 80 per cent said Yes	+ (Less Severe)	Important	Important
	<80 per cent>40 per cent	++ (Severe)	High	High
	<40 per cent	+++ (Most Severe)	Very High	Very High
	Access to Credit/ Insurance Services			
	< 5 Km	+ (Less Severe)	Important	Important
	> 5 < 10 Km	++ (Severe)	High	High
	> 10 Km	+++ (Most Severe)	Very High	Very High
	Savings Activities			
	> 80 per cent said Yes	+ (Less Severe)	Important	Important
	<80 per cent>40 per cent	++ (Severe)	High	High
	<40 per cent	+++ (Most Severe)	Very High	Very High
Social Security	Activities in Groups (Social)			
	> 80 per cent said Yes	+ (Less Severe)	Important	Important
	<80 per cent>40 per cent	++ (Severe)	High	High
	<40 per cent	+++ (Most Severe)	Very High	Very High
	Activities in Groups (Religious)			
	> 80 per cent said Yes	+ (Less Severe)	Important	Important
	<80 per cent>40 per cent	++ (Severe)	High	High
	<40 per cent	+++ (Most Severe)	Very High	Very High
	Activities in Groups (Community Organisations)			
	> 80 per cent said Yes	+ (Less Severe)	Important	Important
	<80 per cent>40 per cent	++ (Severe)	High	High
	<40 per cent	+++ (Most Severe)	Very High	Very High

on demand and at a convenient place. Besides, the rural citizens are unanimous to argue that services need to be rendered as per their convenience and they also agree that service supplying agencies need to provided improved services keeping in view the rural citizen's livelihood centric requirements. It means a continuous innovation approach should be adopted for sustainability of services. Sample citizens also viewed that trust in the system would accrue if such an approach is taken in a concerted manner.

In the proposed framework, VIS metrics are posited to be the interfaces with the livelihood security oriented delivery systems for rural citizens. This delivery system needs to understand the ICT imperatives to provide livelihood-centric information. These metrics will be used to examine critically the processes and services available to citizens. In Table 4, VIS metrics are mapped to the four stages of evolution in e-governance services, readiness, availability, uptake, and impact. As per the sample respondents, influencers discussed in the framework have a varied impact in the interfaces of services that VIS could manage.

SOLUTIONS AND RECOMMENDATIONS

The framework is applied to understand two dimensions of e-governance services in India. The first one is to understand the supply contributors whereas the second addresses the demand influencers for the cases related to NeGP, and E-Gram services.

Result of the First Method

In this method e-readiness, availability, uptake and impact are examined to appreciate the efforts planned during development of information supplies and actual deliveries. In Table 5 below the status is presented. It is noted that both the e-governance initiatives are backed by state and national level polices. These two initiatives are in growth stages and their infrastructure is readily available in the Panchayat/ for a group of villages. As regards uptakes, e-gram has better uptake because of local contents, state managed and controlled by Panchayats. NeGP services, on the other hand, are driven by national policies and are based on entrepreneurship model. Business models are integrated with e-governance objectives. Maturity of the services is yet to be assessed which could have been examined during pilots. There were no

Table 4. Relationship of VIS metrics with e-governance evolution

Stages of E-Governance Evolution	VIS Metrics			
	Proximity of Source of Information/ Services	Latency in Availing Information/ Services	Requirement of Integrated Information	Cost of Services
Readiness	+++	+	+++	+
Availability	+	+++	+++	+++
Uptake	+++	+++	+++	+
Impact	+	+++	+++	+

Highly Critical: +++ Important: +

Table 5. Assessment of supplies contributors

Parameters	NeGP	E-Gram
E-Readiness	CSCs are established; Connectivity is in place; Services are through entrepreneurs; MMPs are being introduced; State level integrations are being implemented.	E-Gram centers are established and connected to state Head Quarters; Services are through Panchayats; State controlled applications are in place.
Availability	Available for every six villages	E-Gram centers are in Panchayats (a group of villages)
Uptake	Growth stage and Uptake is minimal	Growth stage and uptake is minimal
Impact	Non-availability of integrated services lead to low impact	Non-availability of integrated services lead to low impact

pilots for both these services. Digital divide issues are not visibly addressed since the uptake is minimal. Impacts are also not visible since most the citizens resort to conventional governance procedures.

In Table 6, the results obtained through primary survey are presented. These seven sample villages provide varying results in each of the assessment factors. Under e-readiness, it indicates that awareness and digital divide issues need immediate attention whereas infrastructure is adequately available in each sample village.

As regards availability, both supply and maturity issues are critically poised and they need to be addressed with due attention. Because of poor availability and moderate e-readiness, the uptake has been affected severely in terms of demand, usage and usage divides. Similarly, low impact has remained visibly dismal in terms of efficiency and effectiveness whereas equity has moderately improved. This is because of some increased inquisitiveness and acceptability among women, poor and children in the households.

Result of the Second Method

The second stage of the evaluation is to understand and capture influencers of information demands of the citizens. In Table 7 these influencers are discussed. The respondents were encouraged to contribute to the assessment based on their household needs, proximity of source or point of service, requirement of integrated services (single window service) and their cost.

Citizens' demands in Indian context are influenced by various factors. Some of them have been considered here for evaluation. It is considered important here that information on citizens' basic requirements need to be made available on demand,

Table 6. Assessment of e-governance efforts in villages

Assessment Factors	Factors	Sample Villages						
		1	2	3	4	5	6	7
E-Readiness	Awareness	++	+++	+++	+++	+++	+++	+++
	Infrastructure	+	+	+	+	+	+	+
	Digital Divide	+++	+++	+++	+++	+++	+++	+++
Availability	Supply	+++	+++	+++	+++	+++	+++	+++
	Maturity	+++	+++	+++	+++	+++	+++	+++
Uptake	Demand	+++	+++	+++	+++	+++	+++	+++
	Usage	+++	+++	+++	+++	+++	+++	+++
	Use Divide	+++	+++	+++	+++	+++	+++	+++
Impact	Efficiency	+++	+++	+++	+++	+++	+++	+++
	Effectiveness	+++	+++	+++	+++	+++	+++	+++
	Equity	++	++	++	++	++	++	++

+ -> quite adequate, ++ -> moderately adequate and +++ -> poor

Table 7. Understanding demand influencers

Demand Influencers				
Household Needs	Proximity of Source of Information / Services	Latency in Availing Information / Services	Requirement of Integrated Information	Cost of Services
Income Generating Opportunities	In the Village	In Hours	Full Integration	Free Information
Providing Information on Doctors, Interaction with Doctors, Receiving advice from Doctors	Doctor/ Agency in the vicinity of the Village	No Latency	Full Integration	May be Priced for Access to Information
Information on the Institutions and Courses	In the Village	No such Criticality	Full Integration	May be Priced for Access to Information
Information on demand on Appropriate skills	In the Village	No such Criticality	Full Integration	May be Priced for Access to Information

with least latency and at the village or nearby locations so that their opportunities to receive the desired services are adequately available at an affordable cost. Such a scenario needs appropriate integration of services, networking of service providing agency with ICT backbone.

In Table 8, results of the survey conducted on the influencers n the influencers considered for evaluation in seven sample villages are presented. In this evaluation process, information needs described in Table 3 are taken as the influencers in Table 8. This evaluation exercise indicates that in five out of seven sample villages, information needs for income generation opportunities is regarded as very critical and these services are poor. Health service related information is also poor in four out of seven sample villages which need adequate attention. As regards formal education related information, the services are adequately available in all sample villages whereas skill development related information is not adequately available.

Recommendations

The chapter intended to set an agenda to appreciate rural citizens' aspirations for sustaining their livelihoods and incorporate them in the e-governance services being rendered at the local level. It argued that a VIS needs to be developed to assess demand influencers and supply contributors at the village level so that right information and services are rendered locally. The case analysis through the framework substantiated the argument and suggested that e-gram and NeGP should provide the desired synergy by including the demand influencers.

The framework provided a tool to assess the village level demand for establishing the desired interfaces with NeGP services being supplied. Application of this framework for ample villages indicated that VIS metrics are different and are dependent on the livelihood centric demands. Such diversity in demand makes VIS more critical and dynamic. It is thus important that e-governance projects should

Table 8. Understanding demand influencers

Information Demand Influencers	Sample Villages						
	1	2	3	4	5	6	7
Income Generating Opportunities	++	+++	+++	+	+++	+++	+++
Providing Information on Doctors, Interaction with Doctors, Receiving advice from Doctors	+	++	+++	+	+++	+++	+++
Information on the Institutions and Courses	++	++	++	++	++	++	++
Information on demand on Appropriate skills and vocational courses	++	+++	+++	+	+++	+++	+++

+ -> quite adequate, ++ -> moderately adequate and +++ -> poor

capture desired demand and provide citizen centered services so as to ensure desired impact. This is more prevalent in Indian context. In this chapter, it was argued uptake and impact are influenced by several citizen needs and especially these factors critically influence the success of e-governance services in Indian context. In India, e-governance services to be successful, rural citizens' needs are to be captured adequately and interfaced with e-governance service network being designed. Rural citizens' livelihood perspectives are important contributors to organize a sustainable interface between "e-governance service- information supplies" and "e-governance service- information demands."

This chapter focused on citizen interface in general and rural citizens in particular in Indian scenario and argued in favour of an interface with backend e-governance plan through an agile VIS. This VIS arguably concluded that rural citizens' would continuously access the services rendered by e-governance services if certain dimensions like proximity, latency, quality of services are taken care of and are related to their livelihood options. It concluded that mere supply of services through e-governance network would not sustain itself in the long run. Strategic planners need to take cognizance of the demands of rural citizens if overall development is to be assured in the context of rural India,.

REFERENCES

Archmann, S., & Kudlacek, I. (2008). Interoperability and the exchange of good practice cases. *European Journal of ePractice, 2*.

Bhatnagar, S. (2006). *Paving the road towards pro poor e-governance*. UNDP, APDIP, UNCRD Workshop Report, 26-27, Bangkok.

Budhiraja, R., & Sameer, S. (2009). *E-readiness assessment (India)*. Retrieved March 2, 2009, from http://www.unpan1.un.org/intradoc/groups/public/document-sAPCITY/UNPAN014673.pdf

Dutta, S., Lopez-Claros, A., & Mia, I. (2008). *The global information technology report. INSEAD*. New York, NY: Oxford University Press.

EU. (2007). *Inclusive e-government: Survey of status and baseline activities*. European Commission, DG Information Society and Media, e-Government unit, December.

Heeks, R. (2006a). *Most e-government projects-for-development fail: How can risk be reduced?* Working Paper 14, IDPM, University of Manchester, UK.

Heeks, R., & Alemayehu, M. (2009b). *Impact assessment of ICT-for-development projects: A compendium of approaches*. Working Paper 36, IDPM, University of Manchester, UK.

ITU. (2006a). *World telecommunication/ICT development report 2006*.

ITU. (2007b). *World information society report, beyond WSIS. Ministry of Information Technology*. (2009). Retrieved March 3, 2009, from http://www.mit.gov.in/default.aspx?id=832

Mishra, D. C. (2007). *Sixty years of development of e-governance in India (1947-2007). Are there lessons for developing countries?* ICEGOV2007, December 10-13, Macao, ACM. 978-1-59593-822-0/07/12

Misra, H. K. (2009). Managing rural citizen interfaces in e-governance systems: A study in Indian context. *Proceedings of ACM ICEGOV2009*, November 10-13, 2009, Bogota, Colombia, (pp. 155-162).

Misra, H. K. (2009). *Governance of rural information and communication technology: Opportunities and challenges*. New Delhi, India: Academic Foundation.

Misra, H. K., & Hiremath, B. N. (2006). Citizen-led participatory e-governance initiatives: An architectural perspective. IIM Lucknow. *Metamorphosis, 5*(2), 133–148.

Misra, H. K., & Hiremath, B. N. (2009). *Livelihood perspective of rural information infrastructure and e-governance readiness in India: A case based study*. IRMA Working Paper Series 215, IRMA, Anand, India.

Planning Commission. (2001). *Government of India, report of The Working Group on Convergence and E-Governance for tenth five year plan* (2002-2007), (pp. 6-25). New Delhi, November.

Riga Declaration. (2006). *Internet for all: EU ministers commit to an inclusive and barrier-free information society*. Press release of June, IP/06/769.

UN. (2008). *UN e-government survey: From e-government to connected e-governance*. New York, NY: UN.

ADDITIONAL READING

Department of Information Technology. (2003). *E-readiness assessment report*. New Delhi, India: Ministry of Communication and Information Technology, Government of India.

Department of Information Technology. (2004). *E-readiness assessment report.* New Delhi, India: Ministry of Communication and Information Technology, Government of India.

Department of Information Technology. (2006). *E-readiness assessment report.* New Delhi, India: Ministry of Communication and Information Technology, Government of India.

EU. (2007). *Inclusive e-government: Survey of status and baseline activities.* European Commission. DG Information Society and Media, e-Government unit, December.

European Commission. (2005). *i2010 – A European Information Society for Growth and Employment.* SEC (2005)717, 01.06.2005 COM(2005)229 final, Brussels (BE).

Kochhar, S., & Dhanjal, G. (2005). *Skoch e-governance report card 2005: From governance to e-governance.* New Delhi, India: Skoch Consultancy Services Pvt. Ltd.

Korten, D. C. (1980). Community organisation and rural development: A learning process approach. *Public Administration Review,* (5): 480–510. doi:10.2307/3110204

Levina, N., & Vaast, E. (2005). The emergence of boundary spanning competence in practice: Implications for implementation and use of information systems. *Management Information Systems Quarterly, 29*(2), 335–363.

Luftman, J. (2000). Assessing business – IT alignment maturity. *Communications of the AIS, 4.*

Rao, T. P., Rao, V. V., Bhatnagar, S., & Satyanarayana, J. (2004). *E-governance assessment framework. EAF Ver-2.0.* New Delhi, India: Department of Information Technology, Ministry of Communication and Information Technology, Government of India.

Riley, T. B. (2003). *E-governance vs. e-government.* I4D, November, 1-4, New Delhi.

Satyanarayana, J. (2004). *E-government, the science of the possible* (pp. 8–22). New Delhi, India: Prentice-Hall of India.

Shah, T. (1997). *Design issues in catalyzing peoples institutions for sustainable development.* (IRMA, Unpublished).

Signore, O., Chesi, F., & Pallotti, M. (2005). *E-government: Challenges and opportunities.* XIX Annual Conference, CMG-Italy, 7-9 June, Florence, Italy.

Subramanian, K., & Sachdeva, S. (2003). *Quantifying and assessing e-governance.* I4D, November, 1-4, New Delhi

UN. (2008). *UN e-government survey: From e-government to connected e-governance*. New York, NY: UN.

UNDP. (2004). *ICT and human development: Towards building a composite index for Asia- Realising the millennium development goals*. Elsevier.

Venkatesh, V., Morris, M. G., Davis, G. B., & Davis, F. D. (2003). User acceptance of information technology: Toward a unified view. *Management Information Systems Quarterly*, *27*(3), 425–478.

Ward, J., & Peppard, J. (2002). *Strategic planning for information systems* (pp. 25–59). London, UK: John Wiley and Sons.

Weill, P., & Broadbent, M. (1998). *Leveraging the infrastructure: How market leaders capitalize on information technology*. Boston, MA: Harvard Business School Press.

World Bank. (1986). *Poverty and hunger: Issues and options for food security in developing countries*. Washington, DC: A World Bank Policy Study.

KEY TERMS AND DEFINITIONS

E-Governance: Electronic form of citizen interfaces and citizen service delivery.

E-Government: Electronic form of back end and formalized services for citizens that bureaucracy provides.

Governance: Participation of citizens in availing services of government.

Government: Formalized bureaucracy for provisioning of citizen services.

Information: Processed data for the benefit of users or intended recipients.

Latency: Minimum delay in a system to render services.

Livelihood: Sustaining opportunity provided for having better living conditions.

Metrics: Measurement criteria for interpreting the result.

Proximity: The distance for the citizen to travel for availing the services.

This work was previously published in Cases on Adoption, Diffusion and Evaluation of Global E-Governance Systems: Impact at the Grass Roots, edited by Hakikur Rahman, pp. 35-56, copyright 2011 by Information Science Reference (an imprint of IGI Global).

Chapter 6
Community Practices to Improve E–Governance at the Grass Roots

Hakikur Rahman
ICMS, Bangladesh

EXECUTIVE SUMMARY

Wide use of information technologies has lead governments across the globe to adopt the new nature of governance system for their citizens, businesses, and within the government structure. Governance systems nowadays do not only enclave simply the dissemination of government regulations and directives to their stakeholders, but also target to improve their knowledge and capacity. At the threshold, by putting the information technologies as a thrust sector for many years and with well adopted e-governance framework, several countries have achieved remarkable success. However, many of them, despite diversified efforts, could not put into the track mainstreaming electronic format of the governance system. This research feel that to improve the governance system, inclusion of grass roots participants are necessary and nurturing of community practices targeting to raise their knowledge and skills through an adoptive e-governance framework would enhance the process. As a case study, it put forward a case from UNDP, including hints on similar other cases.

DOI: 10.4018/978-1-4666-2071-1.ch006

BACKGROUND

This chapter, as a case study would like to put forward a pioneering programme of the United Nations Development Programme (UNDP) that acted as catalytic factor in many developing countries initiating from 1992. Many of projects under this programme, namely the sustainable development networking programme (SDNP) lead the country's information technology sector and eventually act as a positive contributor towards improvement of the government infrastructure. However, the theme of the chapter has been focused to a broader lens of community development approach that has been termed as community practice, which this chapter would like to showcase as an effective way to improve the grass roots e-governance.

In doing so, the chapter has tried to define different facets of the title focusing utilization of information and communication technologies (ICTs) at the initial part of this section. Subsequently, it tries to involve different accepted methods of community practices that are being applied to improve the e-government structure at the outer peripheries of the government structure. To support the argument, it will put forward a framework for e-governance augmenting community practices leading to local level governance improvement. Furthermore, it will try to designate products, processes or services that surround the concurrent development actors or may direct the agencies and parties involved in this process. Finally, it will illustrate the case of SDNP Bangladesh (SDNBD) that existed during 1998-2006 as a project and later on transformed into a not-for-profit entity since January 2007. However, as an enhancer of argument or justification or simple exemplification, the chapter will enlighten its readers with similar projects and programmes that existed earlier in various formats or currently running in other countries enhancing the governance systems.

According to Shaffer & Anundsen (1993:10), a community is a dynamic entity that emerges when a group of people participate in common practices, depend on each other, identify themselves as part of something larger than the sum of their individual relationships, and commit themselves for a long term relationship to improve their well-being. This relates to another pertinent term that requires commitment from the community participant to be part of the development process of a nation, which is community development. Spergel (1987) referred to community development as a premeditated intervention into the social network among people and organizations to facilitate social problem solving and improve patterns of service delivery. This definition was updated by Harrison (1995:556) as the process of working with communities to help them recognize how they can improve community life and welfare both in the present and in the future. NASW (2006a; b; c) and Petter, Byrnes & Choi (2002) further emphasizes both the achievement of specific goals and the development of less tangible qualitative aspects of social life in a community, such as the improvement of their leadership capabilities, especially the ability to take adequate decision by their own.

Author would like to redefine the term, in association with the Wiki, as a community building one should consider approaches to be applied through community practices and basic academic disciplines should incorporate knowledge and ideas (through interactive interactions) of civic leaders, civil societies, community participants, professionals and researchers to improve various aspects of local communities. Community development seeks to empower individuals and groups of people by providing with necessary skills to prompt necessary changes in their own communities. These skills could range from enhancement of civic knowledge, understanding of basic laws and governance system, validation of national identity (national consensus or voting), and knowledge on establishing small entrepreneurship to tax proclamation, land registration, vehicle registration or obtaining driving license, requesting national identity cards or certificate, birth or death certificate, loan acquisition, and so on.

In recent years, governments, and non-government agencies including development partners and research institutions are actively involved in promoting e-governance through utilization of information and communication technologies and using the diversified applications of ICTs in enhancing the livelihood activities at community level. However, in spite of placing ICT as high priority in many countries, much of the efforts to raise the magnitude of governance at the community level remain unattended. During the evolution of Internet in early nineties of the last century, many developing and under-developed countries were in high enthusiasm to include ICT in their national manifestos, and advocate about introducing ICTs in every aspect of the social process. A recent research[1] reveals that almost 840billions USD annually spent around the globe for ICT for development purpose. Despite, all these efforts, in many countries ICT for Development initiatives have been failing in larger rates.

Author argues that, instead of involving the actual beneficiaries, i.e., the community participants, often development agencies and their partners try to implement their own ideas and philosophies to the community without being improving their mental capacities or their real necessities. Of course, food and shelter are the basic part and parcel of most of the disadvantaged communities, which are major element of a developing or transitional country. But, whenever they would feel the real urgency of governance system to be an effective tool in their livelihood, either now or very near future, and most importantly could reduce some economical burden or provide some economical gain, they would certainly welcome the entire system of development. Furthermore, when they would feel themselves as a part of this important development process, they would be eager to participate, not being remained aloof or bypass the system, as it is happening nowadays in many countries. These processes require introduction of the development sequences through community practices.

Community practices evolve from very early days of socialization when human being adopted to live in socialized form of life by sharing a common geography, culture, economy, desire, objective, belief, resource, risk, and other numerous numbers of parameters affecting a common group of people living together. Social pattern transforms through evolution, demand, and availability of resources. Subsequently, community practices changes to elevate the life pattern of each community. They may comprise of human service management, community development, policy advocacy, community foresting, community learning (basic laws of the country, tax payment, and civic rules); collaborative learning (pedagogy, and non-formal), community health and sanitation; ecosystem management; disaster preparedness; and other initiations to improve the life pattern of the community participants. The essence of this form of participatory approach is to include the practitioners (development agencies, international organizations, donor agencies, etc.), participants (government, citizen, civil society including all mentioned before), and pedagogists (academics and researchers) inclusively are the part of the participation and fit into the learning curve. One of the important components of the learning curve is to translate current knowledge into community practices (Tandon, et. al., 2007), and at the same time, these community practices could be utilized on the sustainable use of natural resources, community forest and biodiversity management (Saelee, 2002), life-long learning, skill development, micro-entrepreneurship, and healthcare (Saelee, 2002; Anderson, 2004; McIntyre, 2005; McDowell, Nagel, Williams & Canepa, 2005; Michael & Margaret, 2007; Rahman, 2006; 2007).

To improve e-governance at the outer periphery of the government structure, several channels already exist in almost all countries, including the traditional government structure. In terms of e-governance, many adopted dynamically developed e-governance framework, many replicated some established framework, or many just converted the traditional government transactions into electronic formats. Consequences are that only a handful of countries could achieve sequential gain from those e-governance frameworks, and majority of them are yet to pin-point the specific demand of the society to develop the eco-system of governance as a whole, nonetheless projects or programmes in some countries have already at failed state. This research would like to argue that, to promote e-governance at the grass roots several channels of learning sequences need to be adopted focusing community practices.

Channels of Learning Sequences

Education

As a base instrument to raise the platform of knowledge ecosystem of local community, education is the best channel. However, to rapidate the process of knowledge acquisition aiming at improved e-governance, the basic education system up to at least secondary level should incorporate knowledge about common civil rules and regulations, bio-diversity and ecosystem of environment, and management of basic livelihood systems, as such agriculture, food security, consumer commodity, common laws, practices and regulatory issues of a country. Furthermore, many countries have achieved successes in adopting mandatory secondary or pre-secondary education. Under graduate syllabuses' would include curriculums not only leading to science, arts or technology, but also necessary technical skills and knowledge to be readily fit the learners to local industries and entrepreneurships. Utilization of ICTs can enhance the learning methods. Tertiary education system may be focused to specific channel of learning as per requirement of the community, or nation, or learner. At this junction, both community and learner would be synthesized according to the demand of the society (not leading to earning money, but to uplift the livelihood of the community).

In many countries, lack of a unified syllabus or curriculum has developed multiple channels of education systems, which are creating tremendous knowledge gaps among learners and this may lead to some form of uncontrollable situation from where there will no way out after 10 or 15 or 20 years of continuation of such multiple channels of education systems. Nations are losing hard earn local and foreign currencies; outcome of the education system is not directly benefiting the community or nation; like other commodities, education is also being adulterated by cheap middle men and farias; and creating enough confusion at the national level thus even creating a generation gap.

Capacity Development

To nurture and sustain local community development sequences in tune of the governance system of that country, in addition to the traditional and or technical or vocational pedagogical channels, a separate channel needs to evolve through existing information infrastructure if not too late just waiting for a new layout of infrastructure that often seem too critical to design, establish and maintain, especially in developing and transitional economies. Capacity development initiatives can target subjects like homestead horticulture, or domestic cattle breeding, or automobile mechanics, or readymade garments skills, or consumer electronics or basic ICT skills. One may wonder, already all these programs are running in their countries, but author argues that lack of creating a sustainable network among them utilizing ICTs many of them could not create necessary impact in their society instead of high class technology incorporation or abundance of funding during the establishment stage or lack of support from the highest statute in their countries.

Social Network

Large scale access of mobile phone and rapidly increasing Internet penetrations failed in many countries to target the basic necessities of their communities in terms of producing some form of social network (targeting knowledge building), or creating value added services. Lacks of proper manipulations, providers of these services are misleading the community participants, especially the younger generation. Similar to age old radio network or FM stations or community radios, Internet based social network or mobile based community network could enhance the process of knowledge development and rapidify the e-governance system in a country rather than mere late night subsidy offerings.

Local E-Governance Network

Using the services of village centers, or knowledge centers, or tele-centers, or entities closer to the communities connected with ICT facility may promote a portal or an interactive web site (one or many, depending on availability, not complicating the acceptance of the local community, but leading to value added propositions) comprising the basic social infrastructural system transformed into a virtual format. In the longer run, like basic commodities of live, community people would feel this network as an essential element of their livelihood.

Framework of Community Practices

This research argues that, a comprehensive framework is desired at the national level emphasizing development at the local level incorporating community practices. The framework of community practice should aim to improve the knowledge capacity of the community participants and enhance their knowledge dimension so that they can make independent intelligent decisions to improve their livelihood surroundings leading to improved governance system. If, ICTs could be embodied within the system intermingling the service providers and the beneficiaries at an elevated platform of value addition, the system would be effective and sustainable.

Framework of community practices may form a four-dimensional circular cycle of emancipation. They would evolve within any of the existing dimension, fitting into the framework, and create metabolism within the process (with or without external catalyst) to expedite the process of improvement. Figure 1 illustrates the grass root e-governance improvement framework. Bi-directional extended threads are indication of processes that may oscillate between two stages targeting positive achievement, and the uni-directional arrows marks the sequential development of the whole system, but should swivel at each stage of the elevated platform of the knowledge communities. The system should act as a perpetual system, desiring increased emphasis of the previous stage at each consecutive stage. Author argues that, an improved e-governance system would always demand greater input from its preceding stage, and after a sequential run of a few rotations, the entire system would act on its own and rotate itself.

Contexts of SDNP

Acting in similar framework, the Sustainable Development Networking Programme (SDNP) was a revolutionary concept to promote community practices and sustainable development in small island countries and developing economies. Initiated by the

Figure 1. E-governance framework leading to community practices

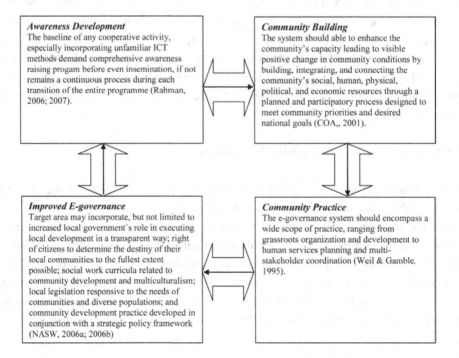

Table 1. Context of the framework.

• Awareness development activities can be carried out in partnership with government agencies, non-government organizations and civil societies;

• Community development activities should incorporate available physical and logical infrastructures (information, social, or other form of networks);

• Community practices may follow social work curricula related to community development. Social work participants should be knowledgeable about the ways in which communities and populations with socio-economic disadvantages can become more involved and competent in drawing on their strengths to solve problems and enhance the quality of their lives. Community developers should have a broad view of the community so that they can provide and develop local leadership and participate in the coordination of the multidisciplinary efforts incorporating a variety of community groups.

• The framework would promote legislation related to support the self-identified need of communities and strategies that directly engage community residents in leadership and service provision

• The framework would advocate the development and dissemination of best practices supporting open communications, intergroup dialogue, and expanded educational curricula that honor and reflect the strengths of diverse groups and encourage participation of these groups within their communities

• The framework would promote increased local government's role in executing functionaries at the local government level

• The right of citizens would determine the destiny of their local communities to the fullest extent possible

• Activities at local level should assist communities in gaining access to information and resources, develop local and participatory organizational mechanisms, and help citizens make socially responsible decisions and contributions

• Community development practice would be developed in conjunction with a strategic policy framework in which community participants may have effective contribution on both local and larger community context

• Knowledge workers can learn from their efforts in partnering with citizens from low-income, minority communities through community development activities, which address community concerns within positive and systemic strategies (NASW, 2006a; b; c).

United Nations Development Programme (UNDP) through a seed funding of around USD 4.7 millions, SDNP started establishing national hubs in about 15 countries during 1992-1996. By 2000, SDNP covers it's activities close to 80 countries to promote greater use of ICT for sustainable and human development (SDNP, 2004). There were about 14 in Africa; 7 in Asia; 9 in Eastern Europe; 2 in Middle East, 10 in Latin America; and 1 in South Pacific. This novel project was thought-provoking in those early days of information and communication technology evolution and enactment of another new concept, the sustainable development in many countries. It was a pragmatic step taken by the UNDP to promote grass root governance, and luckily the programme was taken in such a period when the whole world was thinking of promoting ICT for grass roots governance and sustainable development. As such, SDNP philosophy was nurtured at the WSSD[2] and WSIS[3]. Till date, much of those SDNP concepts are being carried out by major international forums that are involved in capacity development of the society as a whole, namely ITU[4], IGF[5].

SDNP, in most of the country of implementation, were the forerunner in terms of opening a new dimension of information dynamism in each country they started their journey. Ranging from providing simple secretarial services, information infrastructure development, skills development, and development of knowledge communities at the grass roots to advanced core information technological platforms like maintenance of root server, country code top level domain (ccTLD) servers, Internet exchange (IX), and so on.

SETTING THE STAGE

Concept of SDNP at the UNDP HQ

SDNP was launched by UNDP in May 1992, a month before the UN Conference on Environment and Development in Rio de Janeiro. The programme initiated about forty five country-level SDNP programmes and supported related feasibility studies in another thirty. It launched three sub-regional projects and provided managerial and technical support, including conceptual motivation to others. Over the years it was an advocate for the use of ICTs for sustainable development within UNDP itself and outside. Although new funding for the programme has not been secured at the global level after 2000, many SDNP projects continue to operate, and a significant legacy remains (Siochrú, 2002; SDNP, 2004).

At the United Nations Conference on Environment and Development (UNCED) in Rio de Janeiro, Brazil in June 1992, a global plan of action for sustainable development was endorsed by over 179 countries. This blueprint of action, more popularly known as AGENDA 21, emphasizes the importance of environmentally competent technologies, education, public awareness and training in achieving the goals of sustainable development. AGENDA 21 also recognizes the importance of capacity building, especially in developing countries in order that strategies for sustainable development could be implemented. Capacity building refers to cooperation among developing countries that encourages them to develop human and organizational resources to plan and implement sustainable development. At the Earth Summit, the UNDP was given the leading role within the UN development system for capacity building. CAPACITY 21, an action plan to assist developing countries formulate economic, social and environmental goals, plans, programs and policies that would lead to sustainable development became UNDP's response to this challenge (Siochrú, 2002; SDNP, 2004).

Originally called the *Sustainable Development Network* (SDN), it was later changed to *Sustainable Development Networking Programme*, reflecting the ongoing process of building consensus on the benefits of sharing information through the use of ICTs, and its design not as a single network but as many interlinked networks with gateways and linkages among them (Siochrú, 2002).

The objectives were to facilitate access to information for knowledge building leading to decision-making and encouraging the participation of various development actors such as civil society organizations (CSOs) in the development process. Originally conceived as a support mechanism for Agenda 21[6], the programme expended about USD 16 millions from a variety of sources inside and outside UNDP by 1998 (SDNP, 2004).

The focus was forward looking, in the sense that the goal is to extract lessons, and examine to what extent SDNP projects might in the future contribute to areas related to sustainable development and ICTs. As indicated earlier, the initial inspiration for the SDNP concept came during preparations for the 1992 Earth Summit, with the perception that many countries, especially poorer ones, lacking in reliable information base on sustainable development issues. However, the basic question was: How could countries take responsibility and be accountable implementing decisions at UNCED, in the absence of information needed to analyze and understand the current situation, and to monitor developments in the future? (SDNP, 2004).

Though conceptually mainstream, they were quite novel and exciting for UNDP at that time, but their combination into a single programme was a real challenge. The idea that information and access to it could play a critical role in decision-making; that networking and opening out to stakeholders to render the process and outcome of decisions on sustainable development in a more robust and effective way; and that ICTs and especially the Internet were tools that could revolutionize information and networking; were also new to many countries, developed and developing. SDNP as a programme thus came lightly (but, adequately) equipped with strategies and concepts. Neither was it overburdened with institutional infrastructure and procedures (Siochrú, 2002; SDNP, 2004)

SDNP in Other Countries

SDNP lasted in the main form during the period of 1992 to 2000 and reached close to 80 countries in efforts to promote extended use of ICTs for sustainable development and human capacity development. Presumably, the SDNP was one of the first global initiatives focused on bringing the benefits of ICTs to people in the developing world. A small team at UNDP HQ in New York managed the corporate programme, but the essence of the SDNP's activities took place in over 40 partner countries located around the world. Table 2 is compiled from a variety of sources, including documentation, interviews and Internet searches. It very briefly depicts the situation as of March 1, 2002 of all SDNP national and regional level projects (SDNP, 2004). During this research, available URLs were re-visited on June 10, 2009.

SDNP in Bangladesh

As stated in the Project Implementation Plan (PIP) of SDNP Bangladesh (SDNP, 2001), the SDNP is one of the concrete initiatives under the Global Agenda 21, specifically on Chapter 40 entitled "Information for Decision Making." In a sense, it is more than an information network. It embraces a whole spectrum of processes and events that ultimately contributes to the formulation and implementation of sustainable development strategies. In linking sources and users of information, the SDNP employs both face-to-face meetings, electronic and other means of communications. In this manner, the target population becomes more active for participating in the development processes.

The Government of Bangladesh put efforts to address these issues in collaboration with donors, policy initiators, NGOs and other advocacy groups. Among others the government approved the National Environment Management Action Plan (NEMAP) in 1996. NEMAP was in line with Agenda 21 and the Rio Earth Summit of 1992 (SDNP, 2003).

In 1997, as a follow-up to NEMAP, the Government also approved the UNDP assisted Sustainable Environment Management Programme (SEMP). There were five sub programmes under SEMP: Policy and Institutions, Participatory Eco-System Management, Community Based Environmental Sanitation, Awareness and Advocacy, and Training and Education. One of the strategies for promoting Awareness and Advocacy was enabling easy access to information and knowledge. To effectively implement such a strategy, the Sustainable Development Network (SDN) aimed to capitalize on the revolution in electronic communications technology and tried to provide a new set of tools to achieve sustainable human development through a sharing of vital information, experience and expertise both within the country and globally. The Bangladesh Institute of Development Studies (BIDS) was the Implementing agency for two of the 26 components in SEMP - The Policy Analysis Studies which falls under the Policy and Institutions Sub-Programme, and the Sustainable Development Network (SDN, later given the name SDNP Bangladesh as other SDNPs across the globe) under the Awareness and Advocacy Sub-Programme (SDNP, 2001). After the funding was over in December 2006, SDNP Bangladesh became a not-for-profit Foundation, namely Sustainable Development Networking Foundation (SDNF).

CASE DESCRIPTION

With the advent of ICTs and the Internet, community practices inclined towards more virtual form of communication, rather than physical mode of communication. This chapter remained confined among community practices that seem beneficial to the community participants through effective utilization of ICTs, with special focus on knowledge development and e-governance at community level. For sake of comparison, it will cite a few other initiatives around the globe that are or were adopting community practices through ICTs, but as a case study the chapter will put forward information about SDNP Bangladesh. Like other countries, as initiated by the UNDP, the programme was one of the pioneers in adopting community practices to raise the standard of community participants in the country. Furthermore, the chapter will try to put forward a few future research hints for researchers acting in this field around the globe. The reason for choosing this case though it has been died out in 2006, is that SDNP in Bangladesh has acted as a pioneer in leading several strategies on ICT driven activities for knowledge acquisition at the community level, of which a few could be taken as success stories and perhaps, could even be replicated in other places of the country. This case will try to generate some illustrations from various reports and studies about its dilution, despite its tremendous potential to be a unique institution of excellence.

As mentioned earlier, unusually among SDNP projects globally, SDNP in Bangladesh from the outset was conceived an integral part of a much larger $26 million UNDP-supported initiative, the Sustainable Environment Management Programme (SEMP). This provenance accounts for its exceptionally large budget as compared to other SDNPs of around USD1.5 million, but also incurs some delays and ambiguities around its objectives (Siochrú, 2002).

SEMP[7] was a Programme of twenty six components, under the Ministry of Environment and Forest (MoEF). It follows on from the National Environment Management Plan (NEMAP) which ran from 1997 until 1999 and traces its linkage to Agenda 21 and the Rio Summit. SEMP components were organized into five sub programmes (mentioned earlier). It was quite decentralized in structure, the components being implemented by selected Sub-Implementing Agencies (SIAs). Most of these were autonomous entities, including statutory agencies, several NGOs, and even the World Bank. Built into this programme was a sub-programme component 4.5, "Awareness and Advocacy and Training and Education" which constitutes the basis for SDNP in Bangladesh (Lal, 1999; Siochrú, 2002).

The SDNP in Bangladesh comprised one component of SEMP under the Sub-Programme: Awareness and Advocacy, and the SIA responsible for it was the Bangladesh Institute of Development Studies (BIDS). BIDS is a highly-respected, influential and relatively impartial policy-oriented research organization, working across many disciplines of social science and human aspects. It has a major national information dissemination function through publications, library services, regular seminars and workshops. Mainly due to its central role in research and information dissemination made it a candidate to implement SDNP.

UNDP in Bangladesh floated the idea of SDNP Bangladesh as early as mid-1996, but initially it had not been taken up. A UNDP mission's visit to SDNP in Pakistan had developed some ideas relating to ISP (Internet Service Provider) development. But by 1997 there were already about 20 ISPs operating in Bangladesh (though full internet services were available only in Dhaka and perhaps one to two other metropolitan cities) so that the Pakistan model (at that time SDNP Pakistan was the leading national ISP) would not easily slot into place. Moreover, at government level, there was also little initial interest in SDNP (Siochrú, 2002).

In early 1997, as SEMP appeared on the horizon, UNDP found a more welcoming context. It was promoted primarily as an 'internal' resource for SEMP, but always had its broader SDNP objectives alongside. Without the SDNP input, SEMP would undoubtedly have had a support component for interaction and dissemination, but it would probably have lacked the ICT dimension and the specific experience and approaches of SDNP (Siochrú, 2002; Zambrano, 2003; SDNP, 2004).

Development Goals

The objective of SDNP was to create an appropriate framework for achieving and facilitating exchange of information/knowledge, encouraging increased collaboration, communications and networking among development partners, academia, policy makers and the civil society at local, national and international level, in order to design and implement plans for sustainable development in Bangladesh (SDNP, 2001; 2003).

Immediate Objectives

As stated in the development goals, the main objective of the programme was to provide an ICT-based information, content and service network for Bangladesh that was open, inclusive and participatory so that an increasingly level playing field is created for all. Other broad objectives were to:

- Help create conditions for civil society, the government, business and individuals to work, both together and separately towards facilitating quality and transparent governance through knowledge and information sharing;
- Create an instrument for generation of public opinion on matters of developmental importance and facilitate the exchange of experiences and follow-up of civil society actions;
- Facilitate social, economic, cultural and intellectual development of individuals and groups in society;
- Facilitate the development of the private sector through e-commerce;

- • Facilitate proper development of a knowledge management system; and
- • Promote the Bengali culture and heritage (SDNP, 2003).

The programme had several specific objectives, though, as such, to achieve the broad objectives, the SDNP would:

- • Design, develop, establish and continuously improve upon the web portal and its database;
- • Provide access to information and resources through suitable means to end users for enhancing knowledge and experience;
- • Create a common platform of information bench mark for shared materials, making dialogues, problem solving sessions with easy access and faster communication speed;
- • Generate, design and disseminate data and information for utilization by the stakeholders;
- • Provide links to ideas and success stories, best practice information about development activities and trends, funding sources, and commercial and research opportunities;
- • Support the local government, community representatives and NGOs, particularly small ones in their development activities thus increasing transparency, speed of action and better governance (SDNP, 2003).

Management

The policy oversight was provided by a Steering Committee, chaired by Prof. Jamilur Reza Chowdhury (a renowned ICT expert in the country) and comprised of Secretary, Planning Division, Ministry of Planning; Secretary, Ministry of Post and Telecommunications; Resident Representative of UNDP, National Programme Director, SEMP; Director General, BIDS and representatives from NGOs, ISPs, journalists and social elites. The terms of reference of the Steering Committee is given in Box 1.

Initial Scenario

As it was conceived, the methodology for achieving those aims in a sustainable way, was to consider a model where SDNP would be a non-profit Internet service provider (ISP) having a central hub in Dhaka city at the Bangladesh Institute of Development Studies (BIDS), and five regional nodes in Chittagong, Khulna, Barisal, Sylhet, and Rajshahi involving a combination of systems including Local Area Networking, Wide Area Networking, and Microwave links. However, as both the technology

Table 2. Summary table of sustainable development networking programme projects in various countries

Country	Began	Host	Website (spin-offs and comments in brackets)	Status (2002)	Revisit (2009)
Angola	1994	National University	http://www.angonet.org/ (www.ebonet.net)	Funding ended 1998. Project merged with ANGONET; Project staff created Ebonet	Site found live; acting as a repository for information on humanitarian NGOs and projects operating in Angola
Armenia	1996	UNDP	http://www.freenet.am/	Project 1999. Armenia Freenet part of the outcome.	Site found live; acting as an ISP
Bangla-desh	1998	Research Center-BIDS/ Government	http://www.sdnbd.org/	Funding continuing. Project still active with UNDP funded	Site found live; acting as a repository for information on sustainable development, acting as a Foundation
Benin	1996	Government	www.agentic.bj	Funding ended 1999. Transformed into government supported agency for IT promotion	The name server was unable to process this query
Bolivia	1993	Government Ministry of Sustainable Development	www.coord.rds.org.bo (closed)	Project closed in 1998, absorbed by government. Undertook Y2K project and Open Source, and ICT policy, including Dot Force focal point	Site found live; acting as a directory of web sites
Bulgaria	1996	Centre for Study of Democracy (NGO)	www.online.bg	Closed 2000. Training focus. Mainly ARC funded. Website now commercial Portal.	Site found live; acting as an ISP
Camer-oon	1996	University	www.sdnp.undp.org/sdncmr	Funding ended 2001. Spun off as School-net, independent from UNDP, active.	The requested URL was not found on this server.
Chad	1994	Research Center	closed	Project closed 2000. First ISP in Chad.	No URL
China	1995	Government	www.acca21.org.cn	Funding completed 2002. Current status uncertain	Site found live; found as the site of the Administrative Centre for China's Agenda 21
Colom-bia	1996	Local NGO/ APC	www.rds.org.co	Active with UNDP CO support, new partnership with Development Gateway	The name server was unable to process this query

continued on following page

Table 2. Continued

Country	Began	Host	Website (spin-offs and comments in brackets)	Status (2002)	Revisit (2009)
Costa Rica	1995	Research Center	http://www.rds.ucr.ac.cr/ Page not updated	SDNP support ended 1999. Development Observatory continues supported by University.	The name server was unable to process this query
Dominican Rep.	1998	Local NGO	www.rds.redid.org.do (inactive)	Project closed in 2000, no clear results	The name server was unable to process this query
El Salvador	1997	National Centre for Science & Technology	www.rds.org.sv (inactive)	Project closed in 1999, no clear results	The domain name does not exist
Estonia	1994	University	www.ciesin.ee (not updated – material archived)	Closed 1997. Regional Baltics, CIESIN partnership	Site found live; acting as an archive
Gabon	1996	Library, National Archives, Government of Gabon	www.primature.gouv.go or www.primature.gov.go	Closed 1998	The domain name does not exist
Guatemala	1995	University	www.rds.org.gt (inactive)	SDNP funding ended 1998. Content and training based. Project active, now an NGO Red de Desarrollo Sostenible (RDS-GT)	The domain name does not exist
Guinea		Isoc Guinee	http://www.snu-gn.org/CD-ENV/rddgn-ndx.htm	Inactive	The domain name is free for sale
Guyana	1998	UNDP	www.sdnp.org.gy	SDNP funding ended 2002. Recently founded an NGO called DevNet, with good prospects for the future.	Site found live; acting as a non-governmental non-profit organization
Haiti	1997	Government	www.rddh.org	SDNP funding ended 2000. Project active, now an NGO with UNDP CO support.	Site found live; providing various on-line services
Honduras	1993	Various	www.rds.org.hn	SDNP funding ended 1999. Successful NGO, starting large rural telecentre with IADB	The domain is free for sale
Hungary	1997	NGO (REC)	www.omikk.hu/sdnp (inactive)	Part of HP Donation, limited SDNP activity.	The name server was unable to process this query

continued on following page

Table 2. Continued

Country	Began	Host	Website (spin-offs and comments in brackets)	Status (2002)	Revisit (2009)
India	1995	Government	www.sdnp.delhi.nic.in	SDNP funding ended 2001. Continuing, revised, with World Bank funding until mid 2003.	The domain name does not exist
Indonesia	1994	Government	www.sdn.or.id	Closed 1997. Limited results due to Government intervention. Web site now contains Open Source resources.	The domain name does not exist
Jamaica	1998	University	www.jsdnp.org.jm	SDNP funding ended 2002. Active, major activity in telecentres with some IADB funding	Site found live; acting as an NGO
Jordan	1998	University	www.sdnp.jo	Site not up to date although accessible.	Site found live; acting as an archive
Korea	1995	NGO (YMCA)	www.ksdn.or.kr (inactive 2001)	Closed 1998. Integrated into Korean APC node	The domain is free for sale
Kyrgyzstan	1997	NGO	www.ecology.elcat.kg (sporadic)	SDNP funding ended 1999; continues precariously on voluntary basis	The domain name does not exist
Latvia	1994	University	www.ciesin.ee	Regional Baltics, CIESIN partnership. Reference to the work undertaken before 1997 has been archived.	Site found live; acting as an archive
Lebanon	1996	Ministry of Env.	www.sdnp.org.lb (not updated)	Ended late 1999, active within Ministry	The name server was unable to process this query
Lithuania	1994	University	www.ciesin.ee (not accessible)	Part of regional Baltics project, CIESIN partnership	Site found live, acting as an archive
Malawi	1997	University	www.sdnp.org.mw	SDNP funding ended 2000. Active, self-sustaining ISP	Site found live; acting as a UNDP supported Malawi Government Programme

continued on following page

Table 2. Continued

Country	Began	Host	Website (spin-offs and comments in brackets)	Status (2002)	Revisit (2009)
Maurita-nia	1998	Government	www.iiardd.mr in no more	Partnership with RBA IIA (no SDNP funding). Civil Society cyber café active. http://www.pnud.mr/cyberforum/index.html is an NGO e-forum that was developed as a result of the IIA/SDNP and is still active.	The name server was unable to process this query
Mexico	1996	Ministry of Environment	www.rds.org.mx (inactive)	SDNP funding ended 1999. Active, now a national NGO.	Site found live; acting as a directory service
Morocco	1994	Ministry of Environment	www.minenv.gov.ma (inactive)	Closed in 1997. Ministry took over the operation..	Site found live; acting as the site of the Ministry
Mozam-bique	1997	Ministry of Environment	www.sdnp.org.mz	Closed in 1999	The name server was unable to process this query
Nicara-gua	1994	NGO	www.sdnnic.org.ni	Funding ended 1998. Active as national NGO, with ongoing funding difficulties.	The name server was unable to process this query
Pakistan	1993	IUCN Paki-stan	www.sdnpk.org	SDNP funding ended 2001. Active, successfully changing gear. Associated with the Pakistan Development Gateway. Although it exists as a separate entity as well.	Site found live as a Fedora test page
Philip-pines	1993	Foundation	www.psdn.org.ph	Funding ended in 1998. Active, A foundation since its inception	Site found live; acting as a Foundation
Poland	1997	University	www.ciesin.ci.uw.edu.pl	SDNP was a junior partner in CIESEN; received HP Donation, limited SDNP work	The domain name does not exist
Romania	1997	Research Centre	www.sdnp.ro	Continuing until at least December 2004 with LA 21 funding.	Site found live; acting as the National Centre for Sustainable Development
South Pacific	1994	South Pacific Comm.	Never developed.	Closed after funding ended, little impact	No URL

continued on following page

Table 2. Continued

Country	Began	Host	Website (spin-offs and comments in brackets)	Status (2002)	Revisit (2009)
Togo	1996	Chambre de Commerce, d'Agriculture et d'Industrie du Togo	www.rdd.tg (inaccessible)	Continues to be associated with the Chambre de Commerce but no further details available.	The name server was unable to process this query
Tunisia	1993	Ministry of Environment		Developed as intranet for Ministry Funded end 1997. Ministry executed.	No URL
Ukraine	1993	UNDP	freenet.kiev.ua (inactive)	FreeNet, associated with SDNP. Limited SDNP funding.	The name server was unable to process this query
SIDSNet	1996	UNDP	www.sidsnet.org	SDNP funding ended 1999. Moved to UN-DESA in 2000, active. Now funded by the GEF	Site found live; acting as an archive

Note 1: Websites were visited on January 09, 2004 (Adopted from SDNP, 2004) and re-visited on June 10, 2009

Note 2: A few of those SDNPs are still alive serving communities in various forms, varying from non-profit, not-for-profit, foundation to commercial entities (shaded in Table 1)

Box 1. Guideline for the formation of the steering committee

TERMS OF REFERENCE
OF
THE SDNP STEERING COMMITTEE
"The SDNP Steering Committee is an integral part of the overall implementation process of the project. The role of the Steering Committee is to provide advice, direction and support to the SDNP Implementing Unit (SDNPIU) on an ongoing basis. The Committee will comprise IT specialists as well as representatives of the Government, of the SEMP partners, of the media, of academic/research institutions, of the private sector, and other stakeholders. The Steering Committee thus ensures stakeholder participation in the management and operation of the SDNP, without being directly responsible for any aspects of project implementation such as financial management.

The Committee will seek consensus on decisions, and where consensus is not possible, a majority vote will carry weight with any dissenting notes recorded in the minutes if so desired.

The Chairperson of the Committee will be selected from among the members and will be appointed for a period of one year. The Secretary of the Committee will be the SDNP Administrator from within BIDS. Quorum for a meeting of the Committee is 50 percent of membership and meetings will initially take place quarterly which may later be reduced to half-yearly if SDNP progresses satisfactorily. Extra-ordinary meetings may be called as and when necessary.

The Steering Committee will advise on:
 • Plans, activities and achievements with the SDNP Coordinator;
 • Long-term planning measures;
 • Sustainable operation of the SDNP on a non-profit basis;
 • Contents of database;
 • Policy issues regarding operation of SDN;
 • Resolving conflicts between SDNP users/members;
 • Sensitizing and promoting actual and potential user groups;
 • Any other relevant issues that may arise from time to time" (SDNP, 2001:40).

and management of such network was unfamiliar in Bangladesh, and it was being established for the first time, by the suggestion of the Steering Committee, another regional node was included for Mymensingh. The reason was that by learning from the experience in running the Mymensingh regional node, operating other regional nodes that are far away from the head quarter would be easier. Moreover, there were tremendous demand of Internet based information network at the nearest periphery of the capital, Mymensingh, which is about 100Km away from the BDIS. Most importantly, the regional node was established in the largest agricultural university in the country, which obtained high appreciation from home and abroad[8]. Figure 2 shows the five regional nodes, including the Mymensingh node.

Initial concept of SDNP was like that, subscribers to the SDN would be given access to standard Internet services as well as to a database maintained by BIDS. The target subscribers would include Ministries of the Government of Bangladesh and other agencies implementing the various components of SEMP. They were allowed to contribute to the database, and/or through the SDN and have their websites, setup to disseminate information on their activities and achievements, hosted on the SDNP server. In addition the SDNP catered to other corporate users wishing to access the database and to standard Internet services, including national and regional press clubs, academic and research institutions, and public libraries (Lal, 1999).

Project implementation began in mid 1999. An inception workshop, an important step for SDNP in Bangladesh to formally begin the process of concretizing SDNP, was held on July 4th 1999. Input from the stakeholders provided information on on-going initiatives by other sectors and focused on the conditions under which the

Figure 2. Six regional nodes of SDNP Bangladesh

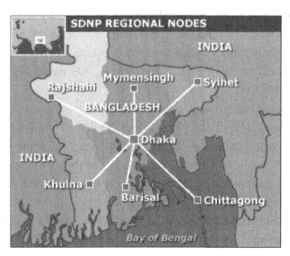

project could be sustainable, whether or not the project should offer services free of charge (which the ISPs felt could undermine their own profitability), whether given the pace at which the Internet was proceeding to penetrate Bangladesh there should be a rethinking about the formation of the project, the ways in which the project could reach out to the poorest of the poor. The first SC meeting scheduled for the week of July 12th, 1999.

As per the project implementation plan (PIP), outlined by BIDS, over the next few months, the project was expected to:

- Determine connectivity solution and contract selected ISP;
- Recruit project staff;
- Train project and other BIDS staff;
- Procure necessary hardware and software;
- Prepare BIDS site and arrange communication systems and other necessary facilities such as electricity, a stand-by generator, UPS, etc.;
- Install and operationalise central hub in BIDS, including LAN, intranet, etc.;
- Develop database;
- Develop BIDS policy for SDN´s usage by BIDS staff;
- Recast/revise budget with approval of UNDP and the Ministry of Environment;
- Operationalise desktop publication section for printing/publishing brochures/ reports for information dissemination on SDN (Lal, 1999; SDNP, 1999).

Technology Concerns

The Methodology

The methodology for developing the SDN was to establish a non-profit ISP with the central hub in Dhaka city at the BIDS and six regional nodes throughout the country. Regional nodes would be established in Barisal, Chittagong, Khulna, Mymensingh, Rajshahi, and Sylhet through a combination of systems that include Local Area Networking, Wide Area Networking, Microwave links, and Online networking using VSAT.

Stakeholders would be given access to standard Internet services, web support and database services. The primary subscribers included Ministry of Environment and Forests, Ministries and other agencies that were implementing the various components of SEMP. Those agencies were also contributed to the database through the SDN, set up websites for better information dissemination to showcase their activities and achievements.

In addition the SDN was catering to other corporate users wishing to access the database, build web sites for them and avail standard Internet services. Such users included national and regional press clubs, academic and research institutions, and public libraries. Later on to promote community practices on ICT, SDNP extended its operation through multifarious activities, such as School Programme, Telemedicine, eLearning, Online Bloodbank, accessing server using cellular phone (long before it was commercialized) for email, news update and database search. To assist in the establishment of the SDN, UNDP provided BIDS with a starter kit comprising computer hardware and software, key databases, management and training tools, decision support tools, and other resources to meet individual needs and ensure long-term compatibility with SDNs operating in other developing countries. Later on SDNP acquire adequate hardware of information infrastructure to establish the most complex Internet based information network at that period in the country.

The Steering Committee provided advisory support to BIDS. The Committee comprised of ICT specialists as well as representatives of the Government, of the

SEMP partners, of the media, of academic/research institutions, of the private sector, and other stakeholders, as depicted in Box 1 (SDNP, 1999).

Project Strategy and Institutional Arrangements

Technological

The telecommunications sector in Bangladesh was characterized by a very low level of penetration, limited capability to meet the growing demand, low level of investment and old outdated systems and technologies necessitating reactive remedial measures. In order to develop a national sound telecommunication infrastructure to support the economy and welfare of the country by providing telecommunication facilities on demand, assuring satisfactory quality of service and ensuring value to the customers, a sound National Telecommunication Policy was essential. The strategic vision of the government was to facilitate Universal Telephone Service throughout the country and where there is a demand, all those value added services such as cellular mobile telephone paging, data service, access to Internet, voice mail and video conferencing- all at an affordable cost without compromising performance (SDNP, 2001).

SDNP emerges in Bangladesh throwing a challenge to provide networking support through IT media using the available infrastructure, which could at most meet a minor demand of that contemporary period. Lack of a defined national communication backbone similar to many other developing countries remained the prime factor among numerous inclusive constraints. SDNP aimed to develop a unique tool set at the national level for establishing communications network among development partners in the country capitalizing innovative methodologies and adoptive policies. The project also contributed in the national IT policy consensus by devoting knowledge, experience, expertise and collaboration.

The strategy of SDNP depended on building information infrastructure, institutional collaborations and strategic alliances with all the stakeholders as development partners. The outreach programme included the community at large and reached through not only the digital media, but also through other available means and technologies. The essence of SDNP was to offer the services to all linked organizations and extend the linkages by assisting in setting up multi-directional interactive communications.

The Technology strategy was divided in three criteria:

1. **Base Stations:** Establishment of the information infrastructure in main node, regional node, information centres, cyber centres, Public Access Centres, Press clubs, schools, libraries and other important places;
2. **Organizational Linkage:** Efforts were given to develop at least 100 active users at each nodal point of SDN. Beside SEMP components, SDN connected environment and forestry, agricultural, science and technology, water resources and similar activity related government, non-government, UN and international agencies to establish a digital information network;
3. **Outreach Programme:** By the extension of SDN's nationwide network, activities involved offering:
    a. Information dissemination processes through egroups, web sites and BBS[9];
    b. Web site design, development and hosting;
    c. Database access;
    d. Email and Internet connectivity;
    e. UUCP connectivity;
    f. Leased line connectivity;
    g. WAP connectivity;
    h. Training facility;
    i. School Programme;
    j. E-Health Programme;
    k. Institutional Collaboration Programmes
    l. Establishment of Cyber centres and Public Access Centres and
    m. Other human resources development programmes (SDNP, 2001).

Technology Components

The Pilot Phase Project of SDNP Bangladesh comprised of the following technology components in Box 2 (to provide readers and researchers the ground view of ICT project implementation in those days, author preferred to provide the direct quote from these two documents- Lal, 1999; SDNP, 2001).

Networks of SDNP Bangladesh

As stated in earlier section, after various modifications of implementation strategies, the Barisal regional node (due to some unforeseen reasons) was shifted to Dinajpur (most North-West part of the country, agriculture rich base and predominantly more community focus). Mymensingh node (which was established at the Bangladesh Agricultural University (BAU) about 100Km from BIDS) was further penetrated to Phulpur (22Km from BAU) in partnership with a local NGO engaged in community practices, and more further to Haluaghat (28Km from Phulpur) in partnership with one of the largest privately run library in the country. Khulna regional node at the South-West was further extended to Tala (20Km away from Satkhira where the node was established), in partnership with the Bangladesh Red Crescent Society, BDRCS (which gave the opportunity to serve the remotest Bay areas through various fishermen villages and BDRCS (see Figure 3). The Tala sub-node was surprisingly run by village women providing emergency and regular health care services to the nearby communities. The astounding fact was that in 2005, the Tala node provided health care services to community women in number more than the government run institute in that area.

In the North-east, the Sylhet regional node could not be established due to the local partner's engagement with solely for-profit mode of operation, though the MoU was signed much earlier. However, experience sharing and technology sharing continued till the end of SDNP. Being a base of non-expatriate Bangladeshis', Sylhet region find various investors to establish their Internet based services in more attractive ways. SDNP's initial non-profit entity refrained the programme to take various for-profit or not-for-profit ventures, though that was necessary for its sustainability.

Along the South-East belt, Chittagong University, another renowned public university hosted the Chittagong regional node, and as Sylhet node could not be established, the hardware were utilized to established another unique interface across the Bay of Bengal, the sea-resort city, Cox's Bazar. Establishing, the Cox's Bazar regional node not only provided an interface between environment and calamity prone Bay areas, but also bought immense opportunity towards its sustenance through providing Internet based services to a private run university at Moheskhali (an isolated island,

Box 2. Technical setup of SDNBD at the initial stage of its pilot phase

---

1. Technical Setup: The Pilot Phase (PP) of the project is planned by keeping the 'Daughter nodes' of the SDNBD (with a "Mother Node" at BIDS). At a later stage, the PP will be moved to a nodal point and the setup will be duplicated there.

2. The Servers: In the PP, there will be two servers. They will act as primary and secondary servers.

3. The Primary Server: This server will perform as the database server. Since the 'Daughter nodes' will only mirror the database from the 'Central server', the database server is not going to be a single server by itself. The same server will act as the authentication server for the users, electronic mail (e-mail) server and primary Domain Name System (DNS) server as well. In addition, it will be configured for World Wide Web server and newsgroup server (which will be served by the secondary server) so that in case of a failure of the secondary server, it can resume those services to the users.

4. The Secondary Server: The Secondary server will provide World Wide Web service, File Transfer Protocol (FTP) service, News group service and also act as the secondary DNS server. But this server will have a duplicate setup of the main server, so that in case of a failure of the primary server, this will act as the primary server until the primary server restores its operation for uninterrupted services. This server will also be connected to the data backup device.

5. Other Major Hardware: The other major hardware are the Terminal server, the Modem pool and the Local Area Network (LAN) Switch. The details are provided below.

6. Terminal Server: A Terminal server acts as an answering machine for the users connecting over phone lines using modems. Since most of the users will be connecting over phone lines, a Terminal server is required. All the ports of the Terminal server will be configured for dial-in. The users will get connected to the Terminal server from outside the BIDS by dial-up method and the Terminal server will connect them to the whole network. Until further modification of the central node's setup, the PP is going to be connected to the Internet through one of the ports of the Terminal server by dial-up to the ISP.

7. The Modem Pool: The Modem pool is nothing but a group of modems in a single box or chassis for better management. The Modems in the pool will be connected to the Terminal server. The dial-in phone lines will be connected to each of the modems in the pool.

8. Local Area Network Switch: For a UTP cable based Ethernet network, a LAN Hub or a Switch is required. It's opted to use a Switch because it provides much better bandwidth utilization over a Hub by reducing collision and caching the hardware addresses of the network adapters in the servers.

9. Software: The Operating System (OS) and the various server software used for the project has to be highly reliable and stable as well as well performed. That is why Linux has been selected as the Operating System. All other various server software that are required are available under Linux, a Unix platform. The added advantage of Linux is that it is completely free of cost. The other SDN projects are also using Linux for their servers all around the world. Using Linux will give the flexibility of configuring the system better suited to the SDNP targets.

10. Network Protocol: The Network protocol is going to be the Transmission Control Protocol/Internet Protocol (TCP/IP). TCP/IP is the standard protocol for the Internet. It is also the native network protocol for the selected OS, Linux. Using TCP/P will give the PP the option of connecting to the Internet and exchanging information without any major modification to the setup.

11. Servers setup Details: The servers (Primary, Secondary server and the Terminal Server) will be connected to the Switch, thus forming the server LAN. The Hub of the Local Area Network consisting the workstations will be connected to a port of the Switch.

12. Software setup Details: Both the primary and the secondary servers will run under Linux. To make the setup robust, both servers will be configured to run all common services.

13. Database Server: The Primary server will run as the database server. At the PP stage not much have been done regarding the database and they are not been finalized yet. Rather at the primary stage, it will be acting as a dummy database server by offering accessibility through any web browser.

14. Authentication Server: When someone will try to log in over phone lines, the Terminal server will have to verify that the person is indeed a valid user with appropriate access. The Terminal server does this by contacting the authentication server. The primary server will hold all the user accounts and passwords. Therefore, the authentication service will be running on the primary server. The authentication service for dial-in will be the standard Remote Authentication Dial In User Service (RADIUS). The primary server will run the RADIUS service. The secondary server will keep a duplicated copy of the user database in case it has to serve as the Authentication server.

15. Electronic Mail Server: The email server software is going to be sendmail, the Internet standard Mail Transport Agent (MTA). All Linux distribution comes with the sendmail software. However, sendmail only acts as the transport agent, in other words, a different service is required for the user to download their mails. The standard protocol for that is POP3. Both of these services will be running on the primary server, since the user accounts are going to be on that. The secondary server will also have these services configured.

16. Domain Name System Server: In the network world based on TCP/IP, each computer (either a user or a server) is identified by a numeric address. This numeric address is known as the IP Address. But for human usability, all the machines are given a name as well. The name to IP address mapping is known as the Domain Name System (DNS). Both the primary and the secondary server will run the DNS service. The DNS server software going to be used is Berkeley internet Name Domain (BIND). BIND itself has the feature of running in primary and secondary mode, which is going to be deployed in the standard way in the servers.

17. World Wide Web Server: The protocol used for the World Wide Web is Hyper Text Transfer Protocol (HTTP). The WWW or HTTP server we are going to use is Apache, the most used http server on the Internet. The Secondary server will run this service, but the primary server will be configured for it as well.

---

continued on following page

Box 2. Continued

18. File Transfer Protocol Server: A File Transfer Protocol (FTP) server acts as a server that has many files (could be information, could be programs) which the user can transfer (known as download) to his or her computer. The Secondary server will provide this service. That means, all the downloadable files will also reside on the Secondary server. The primary server will also have this service configured.

19. Newsgroup Server: A Newsgroup is a discussion group, where any user can post an article or respond to an article posted by someone else. The Newsgroup server going to be used is InterNetNews (INN). INN is the most used Newsgroup server software on the Internet and comes with Linux as well.

20. The PP in Operation: When a user needs some information and accesses the servers over the phone line, this is what happens:

a. A user wants to access some information

b. He/She dials the PP dial-in number using his/her computer

c. The modems get connected

d. The Terminal server asks for the users credentials (i.e. login and password)

e. The Terminal server consults the Authentication server to verify that the credentials provided by the user is valid

f. If they are invalid, access is denied and the user is disconnected. If they are valid, connection to the Terminal server is allowed to establish, which makes the user connected to the whole Local Area Network.

g. The user starts the appropriate application software (a web browser or email software) to access his required information

h. The application package connects to the server and fetches the information

i. The user disconnects. The phone line is freed.

If the user is on a local workstation on the LAN, the process is different. Since the user is already on a connected computer (the workstation), it is assumed that he or she is an authenticated user. Therefore, no additional authentication is required, except in case of the service he wants to access requires it (for example, checking e-mail requires authentication in all cases).

21. Maintenance and Backup Schedule: During the normal operation of the servers, the major maintenance job is to take backup of the servers on a regular basis. We have selected to use DLT4000 tape drives, which can hold up to 2OGB of uncompressed (40GB compressed) data. Backup will be taken every other day to a new tape. The tapes will be received after 30 days, which means there are going to be 15 tapes, each holding the backup of the servers for the past 30 days at an interval of 2 days. The backup device will be connected to the secondary server. The Primary server will be backed up over the network and the secondary server will be backed up directly (Lal, 1999: Direct quote from http://www.sdnbd.org/mission_report.htm).

Figure 3. Transformed regional nodes of SDNP

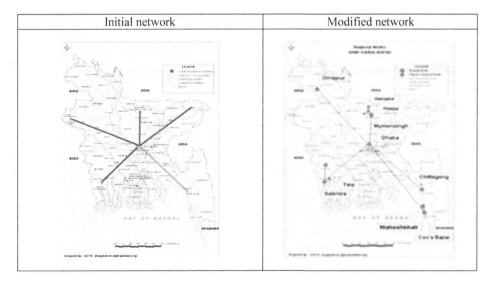

where SDNP also established one multi-purpose village information center), and sea-resorts, hotels and motels through a privately run Internet service provider. As stated, utilizing the dedicated services of BDRCS, the Southern belt of the country was taken under disaster management program (Figure 4). Even, many computers were donated to different fishermen villages under SDNP School Programme.

SDNP took the advantage of running weekly tele-medicine sessions utilizing this complex backbone of MCPC (Multi Channel Per Carrier) VSAT (see Figure 5), SCPC (Single Channel Per Carrier) VSAT, own established radio links (operating on free frequency of 2.4 and 3.6GHz), ADSL, and simple data cables. SDNP could provide its various services across the country through its multi-faceted clients and stakeholders. They varies from government high officials, to NGO workers (especially, at Phulpur and Satkhira), to journalists (at Dinajpur), to salt farmers in Moheskhali, to village women (at Tala), to students (at all stations), to patients (at all stations), and to fishermen across the Bay of Bengal. All of the community participants could obtain their respective services from all regional nodes, sub-nodes, and multi-purpose village information centers, but within parenthesis the activities at those particular areas are being emphasized.

In terms of establishing community based information center and cyber center where Internet services were be made available, SDNP was a forerunner in the country. Establishment of the first publicly available free cyber center at BIDS, and later on extension of the service to other parts of the city (see Figure 6) was a milestone for SDNP. Similarly, wherever the project went, it tried to made partnership with local communities, whether they were village women, or fishermen, or re-

Figure 4. Southern portion of the country across Bay of Bengal

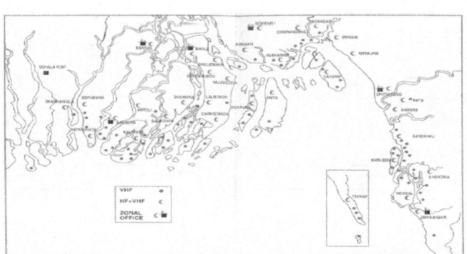

Figure 5. MCPC VSAT circuit of SDNP covering Chittagong, Dinajpur, and Satkhira regional nodes

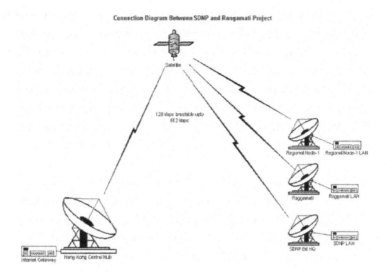

Figure 6. Several free cyber centers in Dhaka city

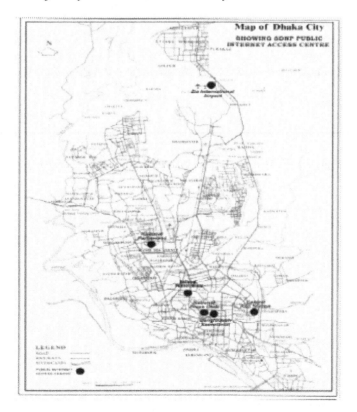

searchers or academics. While going to Mymensingh over Gazipur (a town of edu-
cation and agricultural hub, see Figure 7), SDNP made partnership with Bangladesh
Rice Research Institute (BRRI), and BIT (Bangladesh Institute of Technology)
Dhaka (later on became, Dhaka University of Engineering and Technology, DUET).
Moreover, Bangabandhu Sheikh Mujibur Rahman Agricultural University
(BSMRAU) was purposely chosen as the repeater station for the radio relay towards
Mymensingh. BSMRAU was a successful partner of SDNP Bangladesh. Further-
more, as another relay station at Bhaluka, the local rural electrification board of
Bhaluka, REB Bhaluka was selected, as they were the successful rural electricity
provider of the country, and deals with huge databases on energy distribution (see
Figure 8).

Finally, to show some more community partnership of SDNBD, connectivity
between the lone government high official training centre at Savar, namely Bangladesh Public Administrative Training Centre (BPATC); connectivity between geographically dispersed database servers of SDNBD, but sequentially updated; and
connectivity of Bangladesh Internet Exchange (BDIX), the lone Internet exchange
at that period in the country are shown in Figures 9, 10 and 11 respectively.

Figure 7. The Gazipur sub-node along the Mymensigh regional node

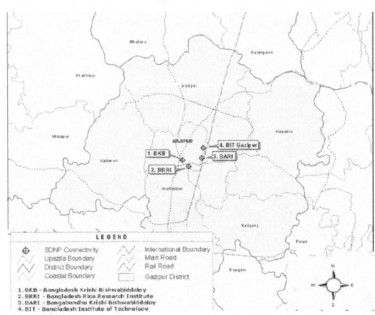

Figure 8. Radio link connectivity between BAU and SDNP at BIDS

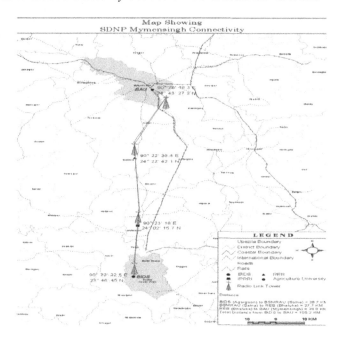

Figure 9. SDNP network connecting Bangladesh Public Administrative Training Center (BPATC) at Savar

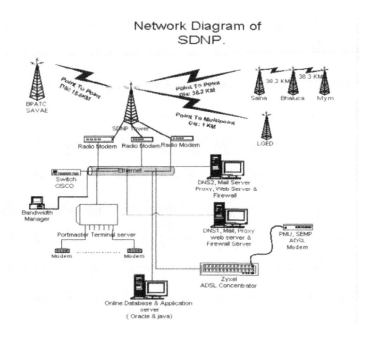

Figure 10. SDNP data bank located at various regional centers

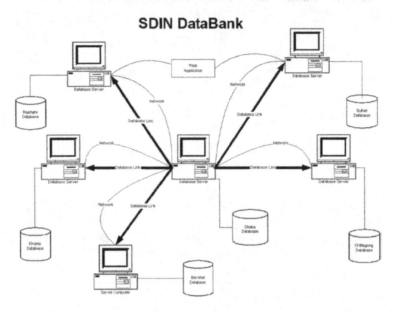

Figure 11. Bangladesh internet exchange

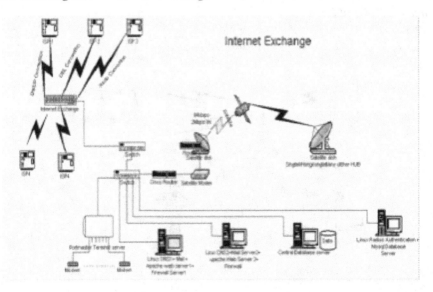

MANAGEMENT AND ORGANIZATIONAL CONCERNS

As the project has already been closed since December 2006, the author would like to draw attention of concurrent researchers on the management and organizational issues, just quoting from various reports and investigations, rather not rephrasing any words or sentences. They were taken with the intention to enlighten researchers engaged in similar researches across the globe (Box 3).

Global SDNP projects were developed in collaboration with the governments of the countries concerned, but did not always focus their operations on the government. CSOs were mainly the main beneficiaries (community participation was emphasized) along with other non-governmental stakeholders. The project in most, but not in all countries included a Steering Committee that brought together representatives of different stakeholder groups as advisors and partners with a stake in the SDNP project. A local management group was established, and a manager was sought, preferably with entrepreneurial skills and some understanding of local needs and of the potential of ICTs (SDNP, 2004). In this way, in terms of operational management, SDNP (globally and locally) established a unique pattern of community participation and community practices.

CURRENT CHALLENGES FACING THE ORGANIZATION

Challenges Faced at the SDNP HQ

Most of the projects of SDNP across countries faced various challenges, especially in terms of sustainability, after the completion of funding from UNDP. Sustainability involves a transition from the status of a donor-funded project guided by an initial set of prescribed objectives, to an entity with the capacity to support itself by attracting the necessary resources, capable of autonomous strategic thinking and flexible adaptation to a changing environment. In the best of circumstances it was a difficult transition to navigate since it demanded an inversion in approach. From being driven by concrete finite *goals*, sustainability means evolution towards a more abstract and ongoing *process*. From an initially secure (and hence ignored) resource base, it was to learn to tap into ongoing resources as a critical survival tactic. The skills required to implement a project were sometimes quite different, even contradictory to, those needed to build institutional sustainability. Thus, achieving sustainability comprised two parallel processes that sometimes came into tension. The task for project management at every level was to steer the process such that tension would be minimized, and the optimal balance was maintained during the lifetime of the project between capacities essential to effective project implementation and those essential to institution building and sustainability (SDNP, 2004).

Box 3. Management concerns for the SDNP Bangladesh

"SDNP in Bangladesh did not from the beginning have a 'natural' home, as happened in some other countries. The idea did not originate with an organisation or entity that would later become the obvious candidate in which to house it. Rather, integrated as a component in a larger programme solely on the merits of the concept, an implementing agency had to be found, and SDNP had to be incorporated into this context or beneath its umbrella. BIDS was chosen because of its national reputation and national information generation and dissemination capacity and role.

However, it did take a little time for the more or less autonomous form of SDNP, housed within but not integrated within BIDS, to emerge, and this followed a number of discussions between BIDS and UNDP. The current institutional form and management structure were secured at the end of the first year with the appointment of the Project Coordinator.

The Project Director is also the Research Director of BIDS, and devotes part-time only to the Project – though in general his time commitment goes well beyond what is expected. The Project Coordinator is the full-time manager. The two work well together. The Project Director provides high level guidance and advice, often some ideas and contacts, and ensures a smooth and productive relationship with BIDS. SDNP has benefited from BIDS' good reputation.

The role of the Steering Committee is to provide "advice, direction and support", and is intended also to provide broad stakeholder input into the Project. It has met four times in the life of the Project so far (*till the report was written in 2002*), first in mid 1999, and includes representatives of BIDS, UNDP, PMU, the Ministry of Posts and Telecommunications, IUCN Bangladesh, MoEF, IUCN, the ISP Forum, and the SDNP Coordinator (member-secretary). It has been chaired from the beginning by Professor Jamilur Choudury, the Vice Chancellor of BRAC University and a renowned ICT specialist in the country.

Though only four meetings have been held, it offers at least some link to major stakeholders including the MoEF, the PMU and UNDP. It also facilitates positive relations with non-SEMP stakeholders such as the ISP Forum (representing private ISPs) - although they have other occasions to interact. Meetings have given advice and, as far as can be ascertained, that advice has been acted upon.
The Project interacts more frequently with some individual members of the Steering
Committee on an informal basis, especially with the Chair. Professor Choudury is a highly experienced and respected professor from BRAC University, with a strong commitment to the Project and with a broad vision of its potential. His support continues to be an important element.

Overall then, the management oversight structure and functions reasonably well. It has allowed flexibility and not hindered progress. It has met and given advice which has largely been followed. And, as is often the case, it is at the personal level of commitment and caliber of individuals that the positive value has arisen, and here the Project is served well. Internal management is distinct.
SDNP has a total of 14 staff, with at present only the Project Coordinator (advised by the
Director) engaging in management activities *per se*. The SDNP team appears to be appropriately-qualified, very committed and highly motivated, and the technical quality and outputs of activities is high. The Coordinator is well-qualified and suited to the job, experienced and extremely committed. But he is personally responsible for a huge range of simultaneous tasks that are generated by the project's large, diverse and demanding portfolio.

The fact that delays resulted in the need to move concurrently on many fronts compounds the challenge. As a result, management is extremely stretched and cannot possibly handle all the demands currently upon it, no matter the level of commitment. Understandably, the highest priority is given to designing, launching and running the main activities.

This probably explains, at least in part, the relatively poor communication, in level and quality, between SDNP and the PMU and UNDP. Exacerbated by the accelerated rate of implementation, the result is that the UNDP and PMU appear to underestimate the potential and actual achievements of the SDNP Project; whilst SDNP is failing to report on its strategies and ideas and even successes.
A further contributory factor may be the dual origins of this Project. SDNP reports to the PMU on both SEMP and non-SEMP related activities; but the PMU is understandably focused on SEMP. UNDP provided the original inspiration for many of the non-SEMP SDNP activities, yet with its changing personnel and removed relationship, it cannot offer the continuity in direction. Thus the non-SEMP activities are somewhat out on a limb.

Perhaps the Steering Committee might have been expected to bring together the several objectives of SDNP into a more coherent whole. However, the first step would have been to identify the issue of the dual objectives, and the strains it causes internally within the Project and in relation to communications with major stakeholders. This was not done, but the question could be raised again now.

SDNP has not so far suffered materially from the relatively poor lines of communication.

However, as the SEMP Programme comes under review, it will be essential that all sides are communicating well and understand their challenges and achievements.

The PMU itself also seems to be under pressure in terms of its management and coordination burden. It appears to have made little effort to familiarise itself with non-SEMP activities of SDNP, or indeed to prioritise the networking and dissemination activities of SEMP to which SDNP is to act as the key partner.

This points to another area in which SDNP is not achieving as much as it might – serving the SEMP programme. This was already considered above, but the pressure on management, combined with poor communication with PMU, probably results in less creative energy on both sides being devoted to devising ways in which the SEMP programme can be better supported and disseminated through the use of ICTS and networking.

A third area receiving insufficient attention is around monitoring and evaluation of activities. This is not merely a question of learning abstract lessons. It is about feeding into the ongoing management design of the activities, reporting on successes, and building for future sustainability. It also related to formulating and reformulating objectives and resources usage" (Siochrú, 2002:24-25).

The pressure to generate income, in itself, also raised tensions within Projects, and continued to, in terms of a tradeoff between maximizing income and keeping the focus firmly on development. For some, the issue became how much the project would have to forego its original mission on the grounds, in terms of financial survival, especially where there was doubt over the development value of the income-generating activity, as such the provision of conventional ISP services. But even an apparently effortless transition, moving from a project within a Ministry to a mainstreamed activity or programme was problematic. Although funding would be secured through mainstreaming, the challenge facing an SDNP in retaining a clear identity and a focus on the principles and *modus operandi wa*s probably only just beginning. This was not helped in many countries where governments could not, for legal reasons, allow SDNP as a UNDP funded project to adopt a cost-recovery strategy that might have helped to secure its identity and character. Maintaining a responsive and flexible approach to ongoing needs, innovating in a dynamic environment, remaining transparent and inclusive, and sustaining credibility and interaction with non-governmental stakeholders was difficult while operating within a government environment and without the corrective influence and support of external donor agencies. Much depended on whether the government understood the concept, the value it has placed on it, and the benefits it believed could be derived. This in turn was likely, initially at least, to rely on a few 'champions' to take it to secure moorings within the governmental complex, and on constructing a credible internal institutional context (SDNP, 2004).

Internally (including the Steering Committee), the transition referred to above meant that basic objectives would be reformulated in the light of the experience of the project, and the requirements of sustainability. On the business side, the development of Business Plans and management information systems was essential, but not enough. A psychological transition towards maturity and self-sustainability was often a critical part of that. And management and staff would take control and responsibility for the future of the project, changing the entire culture. This could involve a combination of income-generation, donor funding, government programme support and other elements. However, even if successful in terms of income generation, those models resulted in severe strains to the development approach or policy of SDNP. It demanded a constant balancing act between the incentive to maximize revenue generation, and the need to remain true to clear development goals and address currently marginalized groups (SDNP, 2004).

There were some constraints that negatively affected management, including:

- The combination of ICT, sustainable development and entrepreneurial experience required of coordinators was not always easy to find, sometimes causing significant delays in recruitment

- The short duration and uncertainty of some projects led to a high turnover. Some coordinators and other key staff understandably accepted offers from the private sector, once technical or managerial training provided by SDNP was finalized
- Occasionally, the Ministry or other agency in charge severely constrained the activities of the Coordinator and the project, leading to disillusionment, inaction and sometimes staff departure
- Projects varied in staff numbers from two or three up to fifteen or more, which generated different levels of complexity of management tasks. It is difficult to adjudicate on management effectiveness beyond considering results and achievement, but as a general rule, projects often had some difficulty with nonoperational management tasks. Thus developing Business Plans and Strategies, communicating results, monitoring and evaluating progress and other 'secondary' matters were sometimes less well implemented than the main project actions (SDNP, 2004).

Challenges Faced by SDNP Bangladesh

The main challenge of SDNBD was to keep track of the development processes in general and monitor development indicators and activities and their consequences in particular, and make these information freely available to all stakeholders including the Government, civil society, business community, professional and other organizations, development partners and the people at large (SDNP, 2001).

The reach and effectiveness of SDNBD was critically depended upon resolution of other challenges successfully. They were:

- **Technology:** Keeping track of modifications regarding innovations in the field of information technology and adapt them for implementation within the network;
- **Social:** An overriding consideration for SDNBD was that no strata in society should be debarred from information (free flow of information down to earth to reach the terminal community, is a precondition of e-governance). However, the social challenge was to create awareness among all social elements and remove as far as possible the digital divide within the country, target the potential beneficiaries through proper techniques to improve their access to information technology;
- **Manpower:** The original project profile lacked to focus on adequate manpower provisions and hence needed to be upgraded with additional manpower both at the central node and regional nodes, including Public Access Centres (PACs), or multi-purpose village information centers (MVICs);

- **Resources:** Other than manpower, logistics and resources were also need to be upgraded for continuous technological updating. Most of the equipment needed to be upgraded at three to five years of interval; and

- **Sustainability:** The most important aspect of the project was a pragmatic plan of sustenance for its continuity in future. A sustainability plan was needed to be developed and operationalized (SDNP, 2001; SDNP, 2004).

SOLUTIONS AND RECOMMENDATIONS

Several of the SDNPs had success in bringing affordable connectivity to many stakeholders and creating adequate local capacity (through community participation) to carry the effort on a sustainable basis; and furthermore, those were coupled with awareness promotion and skill development aimed at marginalized and more rural groups. SDNP fostered the introduction of Free/Open Source Software (FOSS), provided adequate governance mechanisms for the management of national Internet domain names and numbers, helped in the creation of national and regional Cisco Academies and contributed on a substantial basis to the emergence of e-governance networks that connected citizens and governments. Moreover, many of the technologies and applications were not readily available in developing counties and this favored the SDNP as an instrument of change that introduced new technologies and ways of doing things through utilization of ICTs (SDNP, 2004).

At the same time, even during the early days of Internet revolution, global SDNP guidelines could identify essential features of national level management and the institutional context, including a multi-stakeholder Steering Committee, and an independently appointed Project Coordinator. But recognizing that no single blueprint was possible or desirable, national stakeholders could steer this model in directions most suited to the local characteristics (adopted to local demand), building in these features as appropriate and thus enhancing the national 'ownership' and maintaining UNDP as a neutral facilitator. At the outset, the flexibility of the SDNP was essential to allow for adaptation to local specificities (SDNP, 2004). That assisted SDNPs to grow locally, and at the same time adopting global level technologies to the door step of extremely marginalized communities in their own ways, advocating community practices.

The SDNP Guidelines called for external recruitment and open competition in the selection of a Project Coordinator (National Project Coordinator, in most cases, as most of the projects were being implemented at national contexts), and this was insisted upon in every case. Open and public recruitment was the norm and the local media were used the medium for communicating employment opportunities at the SDNP. Selection criteria were established in several cases and selection was undertaken on the basis of an interview involving UNDP and representatives of the Steering Committee and of others as well, depending on the circumstances. In a number of SDNP projects, candidates were scouted for during the pre-feasibility study if possible. So some candidates were being already being courted before the establishment approval of an SDNP; in others recruitment took some time. There were a few cases where the Coordinator did not perform satisfactorily, and procedures were applied to remedy this situation. In overall, however, external recruitment was a success, and yet could be one of the fair selection process of recruitment at global level. Furthermore, SDNP projects were often perceived as exciting and rewarding jobs, which attracted high quality candidates who brought enthusiasm, commitment, entrepreneurial skills, experience and ability to the job. However, the quality and commitment of SDNP staffs and the Coordinator were absolutely critical to success. The level of commitment of some was such that even where financial sustainability was not achieved, staff members continued working for much lower remuneration or on a voluntary basis. In a few projects, delays and suspensions also left staff in part-time employment for lengthy periods during which departures were surprisingly few. Conversely, a few coordinators who never extended their employment horizon beyond the duration of funding significantly reduced prospects for sustainability (SDNP, 2004).

The SDNP Legacy

Within the context of UNDP's mainstreaming on ICT4D (ICT for Development), there was clearly a role for an expanded SDNP inspired or "*SDNP like*" activity aimed at enhancing the capacity of development actors to take advantage of ICTs, to be informed and to participate in the development process and in decision making as well as in government. They acted as catalytic factor in many countries in improving grass roots e-governance, if not initiated the process of e-governance in many countries. Indeed, the importance of ICTs as enablers of many of the essential ingredients of good governance combined with the need to build the capacity of governments and of other development actors to take advantage of these technologies and management practices are reasons to seriously consider supporting an ICT for Governance (or e-Governance) initiative or activity at UNDP (SDNP, 2003; SDNP, 2004).

The SDNP created many bridges between government and NGOs as mentioned above. In some cases, the Steering Committees were useful in bringing key decision makers together, people that would otherwise not meet. SDNP's experience in many countries of working closely with the government and especially with civil society organizations is a model upon which UNDP build as a way of delivering the benefits of ICTs in support of good governance. Given the agency's strong corporate experience as a result of the SDNP and other successful ICT for development initiatives, this would seem as a logical consideration. As a result, UNDP was in a very good position, given the expertise and corporate experience that the agency has acquired through the SDNP, to support endeavors to use appropriate ICTs and community participation practices in support of more transparent, inclusive and informed decision making within the government and in general across those involved institutional bases in support of human development (SDNP, 2004).

SDNP, more than most other development agencies, has a track record that UNDP could leverage to the benefit of the countries, development actors and other partners it worked with internationally.

One of many possible future directions that UNDP could move in, would be to work closely with governments and other development actors in pushing for a model of governance for development (in effect, e-governance) that uses ICTs at the best advantage in order to encourage greater participation, access to and exchange of information and knowledge in development decision making and foster similar activities. UNDP could be involved with other partners in documenting best practices of ICT use for managing the development process in a fashion consistent with the principles of human resource development. This could form the base for activities and/or a practice area that focuses on helping countries and development actors to apply appropriate ICTs and appropriate management practices in support of good governance and human development. This practice area could draw on the extensive corporate experience of UNDP and help apply the lessons learned as a result of over 10 years and several millions of dollars of work undertaken and experience gained by the SDNP (SDNP, 2004).

Sustainability of SDNBD

This research argues that despite being a leading national project in the country, and befitting through a win-win situation from all stakeholders involved within, and despite smooth transition from the project state to the formation of an independent autonomous entity, SDNBD struggled to survive along the context of the SDNP legacy. Though the good news is that several of the partners became self-sufficient through the capacity development initiatives of SDNBD (Bangladesh Agricultural University at Mymensingh, Chittagong University at Chittagong, Bangabandhu Sheikh Mujibur Rahman Agricultural University at Salna, Bangladesh Internet Exchange at Dhaka, and the mother institute itself at Bangladesh Institute of Development Studies), many of the extremely essential components of SDNBD could not continue after the funding was exhausted. There remains, a big question of why, though along the day of inception, till the day of transition, SDNBD had all out support from all corners, including UNDP, the government and BIDS. This research feel that, a specific research may be carried out with restricted mandate to study the follow up actions, and that study will be learning instrument for many donor agencies and civil-society organizations who are still finding new ways of strategies to improve grass roots e-governance through community participation. Similar to above, this research would like to point out a few remarks from a report prepared during the final evaluation of SDNBD during 2002. The surprising fact is that majority of the text in Box-3 remained applicable to SDNBD's future existence, even after the project run for over six years from the submission of the report (The project started with a funding assurance from UNDP at around 1.4million USD, later on half way, during 2001-2002, the project budget was being reduced to around 700,000USD, however, with support from the UNDP core ICT4D team and the government, and by the recommendation of another independent evaluation carried out during 2003, final funding of SDNBD raised to around 1.9million USD). The observations of SDNP (2004) report are included in Box 4.

Finally, it may soon be an opportune time to seek work in the ICT area. In September 2002, the Government endorsed a national Information and Communication Technology Policy, which proclaims the intention of using ICTs "as the key driving element for social-economic development". It covers a huge range of topics, from infrastructure to regulation to education and training. Although it is as yet low on specifics, a number clearly could relate to SDNP.

For instance, objectives include:

- To "set up national databases that are reliable and easily accessible to all the people";
- "Special allocations for ICT project implementation in the public sector"; and~
- There are proposals around extensive ICT education in public and private educational institutions, for the creation of an Internet-exchange, 'cyber kiosks' in Post Offices; the provision of ICT facilities to NGOs; and much more. SDNP is well placed to bid for or implement many of these, if and when these aspirations are translated into an Action Plan, budget lines and concrete projects (Siochrú, 2002:26-27).

CONCLUSION

In e-government programmes, access has been considered as an essential element to reach out the citizens, but greater facilitation, broadening the gateway of knowledge,

Box 4. Sustainability of SDNBD

"The issue of SDNP Bangladesh's long-term sustainability, as in a number of other SDNPs, has been somewhat ambiguous. The original Programme Support Document (PSD) of August 1998 for SEMP talks of a 'Terminal report' to evaluate the project and draw lessons. But the first Project Implementation Plan in March 1999 proposes by Year 3 to "place major focus on making SDN financially sustainable…" and the UNDP mission there in July 1999 takes it for granted that sustainability is "a major concern for the implementing agency and UNDP" but points to the absence of plan. The July 2001 Project Implementation Plan argues that if the Project is given additional funding until the end of 2004, sustainability will be possible. A Section is devoted to the topic, under a page in length, noting that many of its activities can contribute to sustainability. It singles out services such as training, Website development, UUCP and other Internet services, and professional networking consultancy. The Steering Committee of July 23rd 2001 approved a 'sustainability plan', which it has to be said amounted to no more than a revised tariff sheet for e-mail, Web browsing, UUCP, Web hosting and leased line, and (proposed) WAP services.

At present, the project still lacks a coherent model of what sustainability might look like, what it means in terms of its development goals, and how it can be achieved. Ultimately, the prevarication and uncertainty probably comes back to a combination of having two masters, as well as the frantic level of activity imposed on the Project in an attempt to make up lost time. But some months back, both project management and the Steering Committee fully acknowledged the urgent need for a Business Plan to follow this evaluation that will address sustainability in a comprehensive manner. Here, we make merely a few comments on the potential for sustainability evident in the various activities; as well as the avenues suggested by those interviewed. In the Recommendations at the end, we suggest a few first steps that could begin even before the business Plan is developed.

The following are relevant to a future sustainability plan and emerged in discussion with the various SDNP stakeholders:

• Most believe that SDNP has a future as an autonomous entity, a registered non-profit company with development goals. SDNP management would favour this.

• BIDS, whose status is as an implementing agency of a Project, would also be satisfied with this, and might consider prolonging its close association with the continued use of the space and transmission tower, in return for the provision of services. BIDS has benefited from the SDNP project, especially in building up its LAN and general ICT capacity. At this point, however, BIDS has reached a reasonable ICT capacity, and Internet services generally are less costly and more readily available than before.

• All the income generated by SDNP has been held by BIDS for the Project. There is a general will to utilise this towards sustainability

• The not inconsiderable bank of equipment in SDNP could also go forward as an asset, and UNDP would probably be happy to see it used to development ends. This would include the Regional nodes, infrastructure links, Community Access Centres, as well as the ISP technologies. Of course, as assets, these are rapidly decreasing with the pace of technological change.

The more important assets in terms of sustainability are somewhat less tangible:

• As noted, the team at SDNP is highly skilled and motivated, and works well together. But their institutional capacity goes beyond the sum of individual staff members. There can be few groups in Bangladesh with this combination of technological, applications, and content development capability, and surely none with a development orientation. Technical skills include: IT system design and specification; Open Source software development; content sourcing, analysis and processing; advanced online database and Portal design; Domain name maintenance; Web design and maintenance; ISP service provision; and training and capacity building. Management skills in terms of identifying opportunities, building partnerships, project design and implementation are particularly strong.

• SDNP has, as far as we could ascertain, already gained a reputation for work of integrity and efficiency, among educational circles, with the press, and with some agencies and NGOs. This can be built upon.

• Partnerships entered into represent a net cost to SDNP, and are likely to continue to do so (at least overall) until the end of the funded period. Where income is generated, there is no assumption that it should match the cost, since this is a development project funded by the UN. These partnerships, as outlined-earlier, have significant potential to support a sustainability plan through the contacts made, the experience gained, the reputation earned. But in addition, a few may seamlessly evolve in the short to medium term from a net cost to a net income earner, such as Financial Information Service (BFIS10) and the JOBS11 initiatives.

• The Regional Nodes may also have significant potential for income generation, much of it as yet unrecognised and emerging when services are rolled out around the nodes.

• When SDNP is confronted with private sector competitors for some of its activities, it may retain a certain cost advantage. There is evidence that private sector consultants currently charge very high prices – SDNP as a non-profit could offer similar services for considerably less (notwithstanding issues of unfair competition, which must be guarded against.) Furthermore, government ministries and agencies may be more comfortable working with an organisation like SDNP in relation to the internal organisation, networking and dissemination of its information. Both these points were made during interviews with well-placed non-SDNP informants.

• Although income generation is bound to comprise at least part of a sustainability package, the demonstrable success of its current activities would place the project well to attract further international grant funding.

deepening the openness of the community participant, and mostly increased community participation in national dialogues would remain challenge for community participated programmes (Pacific Council on International Policy, 2002).

Community informatics is an emerging field that incorporates the utilization of ICTs for community practice in order to improve the socioeconomic well-being of a community. As mentioned by Gurstien (2000), community informatics is the application of ICTs to enable community development processes and achieve community objectives, including overcoming "digital divides" both within and among communities. Furthermore, the pervasive nature of the Internet has brought ICTs to large numbers of people who have never used them before, especially community-based telecentres in developing countries have provided access to ICTs where there is very little likelihood of individual to own a personal computer (Songan, Hamid, Yeo, Gnaniah & Zen, 2004). Recently developed community practices across many countries involve multi-dimensional aspects in terms of raising the livelihood standards through various means of ICTs, and found to be effective in elevating the basic knowledge level of community participants, which in effect has enhancing e-government structures in those countries.

However, as detailed out in this case study, it is worthwhile to mention that despite efforts from all corners towards attaining positive achievement and sustenance, many programs and, or projects across the world failed (just failed due to lack of proper attention or fund or support: total failure), or could not produce the desired outcome (failed to create sufficient community participation to remain to be part of the community: partial failure), or could not able to mainstream ICT4D within the local social domain (failed to attract interest at the national scenario, though somehow surviving at the local level providing various services: semi-failure), or could not remain within the legacy of SDNP (with which the novel project was designed at the very early stage of information revolution: a failure but need to be termed). The last terms, which has not been defined in this research and perhaps, the other terms are very fragile in terms of providing sufficient background, ethics and impetus on the entire subject matter. As mentioned before, this sort of project failures demand intricate, thorough, transparent, and inclusive research so that similar other projects may take preventive measure, and reach towards sustainability. Otherwise, many billions of dollars are being entered in this sector globally, but without much visible outcome.

Talking about this specific project of UNDP in Bangladesh, this research is quoting the concluding paragraph from the report of Siochrú (2002:28), "Overall, this Project is ambitious, dynamic, capable and could potentially make a significant contribution to sustainable development, using ICTs, in Bangladesh. As SDNP Project's go, it is very well funded, but it expends these resources in a responsible and well directed manner. If anything, it risks taking on too much, to the extent that its management can barely stay on top of developments. The solution at this point is not to scale back on activities, but to redefine and refocus them, improve the monitoring and management information systems, provide additional management support, and design and implement a meaningful and robust sustainability plan". This research would like to look beyond horizon for a successful project in a sustainable way to reach out the people at large through community practices.

REFERENCES

Anderson, R. (2004). *Removing barriers, not creating them: Submission to the senate inquiry on the progress and future direction of life-long learning.* Canberra, Australia: Adult Learning Australia.

COA. (2001). *COA's standards and self-study manual,* 7th edition, for Public Organizations. Council on Accreditation of Services for Children and Families.

Gurstein, M. (2000). *Community informatics: Enabling communities with communication technologies.* Hershey, PA: Idea Group Publishing.

Harrison, D. D. (1995). Community development. In Edwards, R. L. (Ed.), *Encyclopedia of social work* (19th ed., *Vol. 1*, pp. 555–562). Washington, DC: NASW Press.

Lal, R. (1999). *Mission report: SDNP Bangladesh.* Retrieved from http://www.sdnbd.org/mission_report.htm

McDowell, C. L., Nagel, A., Williams, S. M., & Canepa, C. (2005). Building knowledge from the practice of local communities. *Knowledge Management for Development, 1*(3), 30–40.

McIntyre, J. (2005). *Adult learning and Australia's ageing population: A policy briefing paper.* Canberra, Australia: Adult Learning Australia. Retrieved June 15, 2009, from http://www.artpages.com.au/johnmac/Age_learn_report.pdf

Michael, N., & Margaret, R. (2007). Creating older adults technology training policies: Lessons from community practices. *Australian Journal of Adult Learning, 47*(2), 308–324.

Murty, S. A. (2005). The future of rural social work. *Administration in Social Work, 6*(1), 132–144.

NASW. (2006a). *National Association of Social Workers policy statements: 2006-2009.* Washington, DC: NASW Press.

NASW. (2006b). *Social work speaks.* Washington, DC: NASW Press.

NASW. (2006c). *Community development: The community development policy statement* (pp. 56–60). Washington, DC: National Association of Social Workers.

Pacific Council on International Policy. (2002). *Roadmap for e-government in the developing world: 10 questions e-government leaders should ask themselves.* CA, USA: Pacific Council on International Policy.

Petter, J., Byrnes, P., & Choi, D. (2002). *Social work speaks: Community development* (pp. 56-60). Policy statement approved by the NASW Delegate Assembly. Washington, DC: NASW Press.

Rahman, H. (2006). Empowerment of marginal communities through information-driven learning. In *Empowering marginal communities with information networking* (pp. 16–43). Hershey, PA: Idea Group Publishing. doi:10.4018/978-1-59140-699-0.ch002

Rahman, H. (2007). Role of ICT in socioeconomic development and poverty reduction. In *Data mining applications for empowering knowledge societies* (pp. 180–219). Hershey, PA: IGI Global.

Saelee, K. (2002). *Sustainable use of biological resources: Indigenous peoples' contributions to COP-8 of the CBD,* (pp. 227-243).

SDNP. (2001). *Project implementation plan: Sustainable development networking programme, Bangladesh, Version-D, 2001.* Retrieved from www.sdnbd.org

SDNP. (2003). *Status report of sustainable development networking programme (SDNP): Bangladesh Institute of Development Studies.* September 30, 2003. Retrieved from www.sdnbd.org

SDNP. (2004) *Sustainable development networking programme: Final assessment.* Report of an independent external assessment, February, 2004. Retrieved from www.sdnbd.org

Shaffer, C. R., & Anundsen, K. (1993). *Creating community anywhere.* New York, NY: Tarcher/Perigree.

Siochrú, S. Ó. (2002*). Sustainable development networking programme, Bangladesh: Final report.* December 2002. Retrieved from www.sdnbd.org

Songan, P., Hamid, K. A., Yeo, A., Gnaniah, J., & Zen, H. (2004). Community informatics: Challenges in bridging the digital divide. In Khalid, H. M., Helander, M. G., & Yeo, A. W. (Eds.), *Work with computing systems 2004* (pp. 267–270). Kuala Lumpur, Malaysia: Damai Sciences.

Spergel, I. A. (1987). Community development. In Minahan, A. (Ed.), *Encyclopedia of social work* (18th ed., *Vol. 1*, pp. 299–308). Silver Spring, MD: NASW Press.

Tandon, S. D. (2007). *Progress in community health partnerships: Research, education, and action* (pp. 11–30). The Johns Hopkins University Press.

Weil, M. O., & Gamble, D. N. (1995). Community practice models. In Edwards, R. L. (Ed.), *Encyclopedia of social work* (19th ed., *Vol. 1*, pp. 577–594). Washington, DC: NASW Press.

Zambrano, R. (2003). *Mission report: SDNP Bangladesh*. 22 – 27 February 2003. Retrieved from www.sdnbd.org

ADDITIONAL READING

Amulya, J., & McDowell, C. (2003). *How reflection support learning in race and democracy work*. Retrieved from http://crcp.mit.edu/documents/ReflSupportsLearning.pdf

Annie E. Casey Foundation. (2007). *Making connections: A neighborhood transformation family development initiative*. Retrieved from http://aecf.org/initiatives/mc

Aspen Round Table. (1995). *Voices from the field: Learning from the early work of comprehensive community initiatives*. Retrieved from http://www.aspeninstitute.org/site/c.huLWJeMRKpH/b.612045/k.4BA8/Roundtable_on_Community_Change.htm

Bala, P., Harris, R. W., & Songan, P. (2003). E Bario project: In search of a methodology to provide access to information communication technologies for rural communities in Malaysia. In Marshall, S., Taylor, W., & Yu, X. (Eds.), *Using community informatics to transform regions* (pp. 115–131). Hershey, PA: Idea Group Publishing. doi:10.4018/978-1-59140-132-2.ch008

Bellefeuille, G., Hemingway, C., & Schmidt, G. (2004). Move to community governance fails again: Why can't the Liberals — or the NDP — get it right? *Perspectives, 26*(3), 1–3.

Bellefeuille, G., & Hemingway, D. (2004). *Transition to regional community governance: An opportunity to discover the partnership power of community*. Presented to the Circles of Influence: Building Capacity Through Partnership and Collaboration Conference, May 9-12, 2004, Prince George, BC.

Bowen, G. L., Martin, J. A., Mancini, J. A., & Nelson, J. P. (2000). Community capacity: Antecedents and consequences. *Journal of Community Practice, 8*(2), 1–21. doi:10.1300/J125v08n02_01

Castelloe, P., Watson, T., & White, C. (2001). *Participatory change: An integrative approach to community practice*. Asheville, NC: Center for Participatory Change.

Castelloe, P., Watson, T., & White, C. (2002). Participatory change: An integrative approach. *Journal of Community Practice, 10*(4), 1–32.

Chaskin, R. J. (2001). Building community capacity: a definitional framework and case studies from a comprehensive community initiative. *Urban Affairs Review, 36*(3), 291–323. doi:10.1177/10780870122184876

Coare, P., & Johnston, R. (2003). *Adult learning, citizenship and community voices: Exploring community-based practice*. Leicester, UK: National Institution of Adult Continuing Education.

Johnston, R. (2000). Community education and lifelong learning. In Field, J., & Leicester, M. (Eds.), *Life learning: Education across the lifespan* (pp. 12–28). London, UK: Routledgefalmer.

Kubisch, A. C., Auspos, P., Brown, P., Chaskin, R., Fulbright-Anderson, K., & Hamilton, R. (2002). *Voices from the field II: Reflections on comprehensive community change*. Washington, DC: The Aspen Institute.

Organisation for Economic Cooperation and Development. (2001). *Devolution and globalization: Implications for local decision makers*. Paris, France: OECD.

Rohe, W. M., Bratt, R. G., & Biswas, P. (2003). *Evolving challenges for community development corporations: The causes and impacts of failures, downsizings and mergers*. Chapel Hill, NC: University of North Carolina.

KEY TERMS AND DEFINITIONS

Capacity Development: Human skill development through community practices for community building.

Community Building: Community practices in relationship to build communities in a homogeneous way for taking intelligent decision and contribute in community livelihood development.

Community Practices: Activities, processes or performances conducted by government, academia and civil society at the local level of the government structure through collaborative approaches inclusive of the participation from the community people.

E-Governance: This research would like to define e-governance as the action of electronic form of government system to improve the overall governance system of a country.

Grass Roots E-Governance: This terms may refer to elevated electronic form of governance at the local government structure in that country, so that the basic notion of governance system reaches out to the poorest of the poor, or the disadvantaged communities.

ENDNOTES

1. http://ict4dblog.wordpress.com/
2. World Summit on Sustainable Development (WSSD), available at http://www.un.org/events/wssd/
3. World Summit on the Information Society (WSIS), available at http://www.itu.int/wsis/index.html
4. International Telecommunication Union (ITU), http://www.itu.int/en/pages/default.aspx
5. Internet Governance Forum (IGF), http://www.intgovforum.org/
6. What is Adenda 21?
7. [project: BGD/96/007/A/01/99]
8. BBC Feature- Web without wires reaches out, Wednesday, 15 January, 2003, 11:58 GMT, available at http://news.bbc.co.uk/2/hi/technology/2660715.stm; BBC Feature- Wireless net strides Bangladesh, Sunday, 6 October, 2002, 11:28 GMT 12:28 UK, available at http://news.bbc.co.uk/2/hi/technology/2303431.stm; DANIDA's Good ICT Practices Website, available at http://goodictpractices.dccd.cursum.net/client/default.aspx?CAID=218526 ; Communication Initiative Network, available at https://www.comminit.com/en/node/133700/36, e-Health & Learning Project, available at http://www.comminit.com/en/node/132650
9. Bulletin Board Services
10. A proposed Project prepared for Bangladesh Sangbad Shangstha (BSS), the state run news agency of the country.
11. A USAID funded ICT4D Project, who supported SDNBD in many ways

This work was previously published in Cases on Adoption, Diffusion and Evaluation of Global E-Governance Systems: Impact at the Grass Roots, edited by Hakikur Rahman, pp. 1-34, copyright 2011 by Information Science Reference (an imprint of IGI Global).

Chapter 7

Quest for Economic Empowerment of Rural Women Entrepreneurs in Tanzania:
ICTs Leapfrog the Digital Divide

Ladislaus Semali
Pennsylvania State University, USA

EXECUTIVE SUMMARY

Microbusiness decisions of marketing food crops depend on critical information in a rapidly changing supply chain environment. Because rural women deal with mostly perishable goods, the uses of cell phones have emerged as important communication tools in the supply chain particularly in decision-making and managing risk-taking. A variety of anecdotal evidence suggests that cell phones have leapfrogged the technology and seem to overcome transport deficits that were for centuries endemic to rural and remote areas which have been poor and underdeveloped. As with any new technology, cell phones provide opportunities as well as challenges. However, little is known about Information and Communication Technologies (ICTs) and the role Cell-phone Mediated Communication (CMC) play in the context of high demand of information that is critical to small-scale marketing of perishable goods. Consequently, what happens in this precarious business environment when women are confronted with risk-taking and decision-making? Do they use CMC to augment stakes or expedite the enterprise? This case describes field research investigations that were conducted in Tanzania from June 2008 to June 2009 to examine access to, and use of cell phones by women residing in rural villages and in a nearby urban center. Rural villages were considered critical in this study as key players in the wellbeing of traditional rural families.

DOI: 10.4018/978-1-4666-2071-1.ch007

BACKGROUND, RATIONALE, AND METHODS: CELL PHONES, THE NEW AGE TECHNOLOGIES

The digital divide is really diminishing, and it's the mobile phones doing it, not the PC (Len Waverman, London Business School, 2010, p. 3)

The principal rationale for this study was to compare the characteristics of two groups of women entrepreneurs—heavy and low users of CMC tools of phone calling, text messaging and beeping, particularly to understand how they make decisions and take risk over their purchasing habits. The data was necessary to enable researchers to determine the suitability of establishing a business enterprise in a rural village near Moshi in Northern Tanzania, targeting women as a way of addressing the U.N. Millennium Development Goals (MDGs), the internationally agreed-upon goals to reduce poverty, disease, hunger, gender inequality, and environmental degradation by the year 2015 (United Nations, 2005), and policies affecting their wellbeing.

The use of CMC technology stands out as a unique and emerging convenient mode of communication for community development. For example, at a recent presentation (March 2008) titled "Will Science Save or Destroy Africa?", the National Science Foundation's Director for International Collaboration, Wayne Patterson, identified Cell phones as a technology that is rapidly transforming the African continent. He concluded that these CMC technologies are revolutionizing the ways in which people communicate and CMC seems to change the way people do small business, particularly among historically marginalized groups like women entrepreneurs. Unlike computer access to the World Wide Web, cell phones are the single technology that is accessible to women, and can facilitate the small-scale entrepreneurial initiatives of rural, as well as urban women. However, little is known about existing opportunities to enhance the wide use of mobile phones for development and collaboration or for economic empowerment of rural women entrepreneurs. What then can be done to strengthen and facilitate the use of mobile phones as a tool for advocacy in responding to the United Nations MDGs in East Africa? How is ICT and mobile communication impacting these populations? What contribution do these tools make toward human wellbeing and rural development?

The theoretical assumption behind this study was that the ability of women in Africa to sustain the livelihoods of their households will occur largely through small, agriculture-related enterprises in which the optimal use of CMC technology may result in increased income for women. When household income is generated and managed by women, it is likely to be used for children's school fees, uniforms, books and school supplies as well as for medical care, better quality food for the family and improvements to the home environment. These quality of life improve-ments result in fewer missed days of school and more years of schooling for children

(Commission, 2005). The result of having a sustainable livelihood is to discourage early marriage and the resultant pregnancies that frequently result in poor maternal outcomes for young girls. As confirmed by many researchers, the education of girls is the best strategy for reducing infant and child mortality, a critical issue in developing countries (Bloch & Beoku-Betts, 1998). Tanzania is no exception.

The use of mobile phone technology stands out as a unique and emerging convenient mode of communication for community development across Africa. However, little is known about existing opportunities to enhance the wide use of these devices for development and collaboration. In parts of rural East Africa, for example, technology such as the beep of her cell phone has made it possible for grandmother in a remote village to receive monew from her son working hundreds of miles away. A teenager can buy groceries with a few punches of keys. Like many countries in East Africa, Tanzania boasts of a small but thriving mobile phone industry operated by Vodacom, Zain (Celtel), and Mobitel networks. More recently, other networks have joined the ranks. For example, Tigo which is based in Dar es Salaam and Zantel which is based on the island of Zanzibar.

In recent years, debates have raged around developmental issues particularly regarding poverty alleviation (Polak, 2008; Prahalad, 2006; Sachs, 2005). To a large extent, these debates have been fueled by high visibility conferences that aim to reduce poverty and to set targets for poverty reduction worldwide. But one wonders what this rhetoric can yield to make a difference to rural populaces that are often poor and underserved educationally and in many other respects. The persistent poverty widely observed in developing countries has motivated much research on poverty traps into which households may fall and have difficulty escaping. The fundamental features of most poverty trap models center on the existence of financial market imperfections that impede investment in productive assets or technology, and thus prevent households with poor initial endowments from reaching higher-level equilibriums in systems characterized by multiple equilibriums (Smith, 2005). Information and Communication Technologies (ICTs) can make tremendous contributions in these communities.

A recent study from Rwanda (Caine, Hargrove, & Sun, 2007) shows that both high domestic interaction and high cost interactional contact can benefit from the application of additional information and communication technologies (ICTs). In addition, despite having little experience using most ICTs, Rwandan farmers were eager to integrate ICTs into their everyday agricultural practices. In terms of usefulness for business, this study confirmed that coffee farmers rated cell phones most useful, followed by desktop computers and face-to-face communication. However, when coffee farmers ranked the ease of use, computers fell far below top-ranked face-to-face communications, letters, and cell phones as useful communication methods (Caine, Hargrove, & Sun, 2007).

This finding from Rwanda is yet another testimony to the case that ICTs leapfrog the digital divide. In the past century, we have witnessed an ever-accelerating revolution in the ways by which we communicate with each other, and that revolution is far from being complete. Understanding how our literacy skills and behaviors are evolving and how critical development may be fostered is arguably one of the greatest challenges of the twenty-first century. Some of the barriers to gaining a comprehensive grasp of how people understand and use contemporary ICTs lie in differential adoption of communication technologies. To the surprise of many observers, the best example that helps us to make sense of these complexities and the global explosion of interest and research in ICTs, is the mobile technology that has already revolutionized communications in the world's poorest continent, bringing phones to millions of poor and isolated people who had never before made a call.

Nowadays cell phones are serving as a bank in your pocket, providing virtual accounts for poor Africans excluded from the financial mainstream by exorbitant charges and branch networks clustered in wealthy suburbs. Open to anyone with a phone, mobile banking has proved a hit with people in Tanzania, Kenya, Uganda and South Africa's townships and villages, and is spreading quickly like wild fires throughout the rest of Africa. For example, account holders use text messages, or SMS, to pay for goods, transfer money to friends and family and top up the credit on their pay-as-you-go pre-pay phones. Bosses can pay salaries directly into cellular accounts and customers can deposit cash at Post Offices or in some bank branches or use cell phone accounts to pay for utilities (e.g., electricity) bills. Widespread banking services are seen as crucial to boosting growth in Africa's biggest economy and shrinking the huge gap between mostly well-off city dwellers and poor villagers, but banks often put off low earners with cumbersome bureaucracy and high fees. A 2003 survey by Itano estimated that only half of South African adults had a bank account, but a third of those without an account owned a mobile phone (Itano, 2005: 3).

Cell phones have spread quicker than bank accounts across the rest of Africa. It is really amazing how quickly the technology has spread regardless of age, gender, level of education, or access to capital. In Tanzania, for example, people of all ages own a cell phone, sometimes two or three sets. Since the network coverage is regionally distributed among with a different network provider dominating the coverage, it becomes necessary for users to carry a different Cell phone card as one moves through neighboring regions or sometimes parts of the country. However, this inconvenience is changing rapidly with service by bigger networks like Vodacom and Zain (Celtel) coverage crossing over the borders into Kenya and Uganda, thus eliminating the need to carry a second cell phone and doing away with roaming charges.

METHODOLOGY

The case study took place in Northern Tanzania from May to August 2008. Permission from the University Institutional Review Board was granted for this research. This study was based on social network analysis of women entrepreneurs. Social network analysis is based on an assumption that relationship ties are key and important to interacting units. Individuals engage in interactions and networking in order to produce profits. Social scientists suggest that social networks will enhance the outcomes of actions as facilitating the flow of information. In this case study, the key issues are, how information is accessed through ICTs, stored, and circulated as well as the channels used and their advantage.

The unit of analysis in network analysis is not the individual (known as "ego"), but rather an entity consisting of a collection of individuals (called "alters") and the linkages among them in the networks they belong. The decision to study ego networks was based on the ease of collection of data compared with collecting data on whole networks. Four assumptions guided the methodology of this study:

1. Actors and their actions are viewed as interdependent rather than independent, autonomous units;
2. Relational ties (linkages) between actors are channels for transfer or "flow" of resources (either material or nonmaterial);
3. Network models focusing on individuals view the network structural environment as providing opportunities for or constraints on individual action;
4. Network models conceptualize structure (social, economic, political, and so forth) as lasting patterns of relations among actors.

In this study, the information on "alters," including how they are connected, was obtained entirely from ego. Since the networks of women involved in agribusiness in Northern Tanzania were unorganized and indefinable, it was not appropriate to use the saturation sampling technique to collect data from all individuals and their relationships identified and measurements of network locations developed. Instead, for less definable networks, as was the case of the women traders, network analysts favor ego-network sampling techniques such as the "name-generator" technique (Burt, 1984; Laumann, 1966; Marsden, 1987), McCallister & Fischer, 1978; Wellman, 1979).

Sampling

Data were obtained through a stratified sample from populations of women entrepreneurs operating in several markets in Northern Tanzania. These women sold produce daily in one of three municipal markets in the town of Moshi. These markets are spread far apart around town but are regulated by the Municipality. For the purposes of the study, the markets were identified as Market A, B, and C. Market-A was located centrally in a predominantly residential area of about 80 rental and family-owned properties. It occupied an area of approximately ten thousand square feet. First, the investigator compiled a census of the marketers based on existing tables or stands at the marketplace. The assumption was that each table or stand was occupied by the same individual marketer, and prior random visits proved this to be true. To identify the tables from which to obtain the sample of women for the study, we contacted the caretaker of the market at the time of closing to allow us to stick numbers under the tables. Additional color coding was added to these tables to distinguish tables occupied by men from women. This way, we were able to have an accurate count of total marketers on a given day. Street and roadside vendors surrounding the fenced area of this market were not included in the sample. This study was interested in women sellers who lived in surrounding villages and travelled to the market daily. A total of 15 women were sampled from this market but only ten showed up on the day of the interviews.

Market-B was located in the business district of the town of Moshi. Because of its central location, the entrance to this market was often crowded with marketers, hawkers, buyers and lots of cars. Concrete stands for displaying produce were placed within the market building while additional tables were placed along its inside perimeter wall. Together, there were about 225 tables from which you would find male and female marketers selling meats, poultry, vegetables, grains, small household items and artifacts. Women were mostly selling fish, grains and vegetables. A total of 17 women were sampled from this market but seven showed up for the final interviews. They were offered refreshments.

Market-C was located on the outskirts of Moshi town. This market was similar in many ways to Market-B but the fenced area with tables was larger. However, this market attracts lots of peddlers and wholesalers. Every evening trucks delivered fruits, vegetables and other produce. Marketers from other markets including street vendors and marketers from the outskirts of Moshi town came here to buy produce from the wholesalers. Tables for women sellers at this market were identified in similar fashion like in Market-A, and 14 women were included in the sampling frame. Only nine showed up on the day of the interview. Thus, a total of 46 members of the first order zone of a sample of women entrepreneurs were identified from the three markets. Each designated participants from each of the markets was invited to a conference center in Moshi to take part in a four-hour afternoon interview session.

Data Collection and Analysis of Network Data

To examine the structure and function of social networks employed in the interactions of small-scale women agro-entrepreneurs in Northern Tanzania, the investigators focused on uncovering the pattern of women entrepreneurs' interactions by employing SPSS and UCNet software packages to analyze the data (Borgatti, Everett & Freeman, 2002). This approach was based on the intuitive notion that these patterns are important features in the lives of the individuals who display them. Network analysts believe that how an individual lives depends in large part on how that individual is tied into the large web of social connections. Many believe, moreover, that the success or failure of organizations or business enterprises depends on the patterning of the actors' internal structure (Wasserman & Faust, 1994).

To get to the internal structure, the researchers posed the following questions: (1) Do small business women have more or less weak ties in their relationships? (2) Do their networks comprise of similar or dissimilar people? (3) Is their network dense or sparse? (3) How does network density help or constrain small business? These questions reflected the three objectives that were driving the study, which were:

1. Identify and describe nodes (actors) within the social networks of African women agro-entrepreneurs who sell agricultural commodities in urban markets in Northern Tanzania
2. Measure the structural importance (centrality) of the points of intersection in their networks
3. Explore access to, and willingness to use communication (cell) technologies in their agro-businesses

This chapter focuses on the cell phone study only (i.e., objective 3 above). To implement these objectives, the research team conducted a 3-day workshop to train six women to serve as data collectors and facilitators. The workshop focused on the following activities:

1. Train data collectors in the use of the PDA survey instrument and the survey protocol.
2. Provide simulation exercises to illustrate lessons learned in Kenya regarding the importance of women's social networking in the sustainability of a nutri-business cooperative.
3. Engage interviewers in the process of pilot testing the group interview protocol and involve them in a discussion of the information obtained during a pilot interview with local women marketers.

Following the simulation activities, Tanzanian interviewers were assigned to small groups whose task was to critique and refine a set of preliminary questions for a pilot interview with ~ 10 women farmers selected at random from urban markets. The group interview lasted for about one hour. To do this, questions addressed the initiation, content, frequency, duration, usefulness and setting (face-to-face or via cell phone) of women's business-related interactions with other women, with men, with government agencies and with NGOs or other intermediaries in the women's business environment. Information was collected on various dimensions of the respondent's social network such as the number of close relatives in agricultural trade, the number of (non-family) traders that respondents know, and the number of friends and family members who can help the business stay afloat in times of trouble. Information about each of these significant others was sought from the survey respondent and this system produced ego-networks, that is, networks centered about a particular individual respondent. Network resources were also obtained from the name-generator technique. The name-generator technique elicits a list of ties from ego, and the relationships between them as well as among them are identified.

From these data, locations of ego as well as these ties, relative to one another, will be computed. The interviewers also probed to determine whether the persons identified were known to be central or peripheral to the women's business activity. The advantages of this approach included (1) the identification of specific content areas, relative to actions under investigation, as naming items, and (2) the mapping of ego-network locations and characteristics as well as social resources embedded in the ego-network. The disadvantages included: (1) the lack of frames for sampling naming items, and (2) bias toward the inclusion of stronger ties. To this end, we designed a questionnaire that consisted of 61 items which collectively included the nine types of relationship roles, described by Wasserman and Faust (1994) that can be represented through ego network data (See Table 1). These items were divided into three sections to capture the following: (1) information on ego (demographic information), (2) information on alters (relationships and attributes of alters), (3) information on groups and organizations related to ego and alters.

The focus group interviews were conducted over the course of three consecutive days. The purpose of the focus group was to identify who communicated with whom, how the communication took place, and what the communication was about whereas the purpose of the "ideal communication" portion of the focus group was to identify who the women entrepreneurs would like to be able to communicate with and what information they would like to communicate.

Each participant went through three stages of separate data collection activities in round robin manner. First, PDAs (hand-held computers) were equipped with a custom-developed application that allowed a respondent to rate the strength of

Table 1. Types of social relations that can be represented through network data

1.	Kinship	Parent, sibling, child, or fraternal connection
2.	Social Roles	Neighbor of, business contact, leader,
3.	Affective	Likes, respects, hates, dislikes, trust, respect,
4.	Cognitive	Knows, views as similar, same age, poor/richer, knows private information
5.	Actions	Talks to, gives advice, sees information, about credit, influence selling/buying, seek help to mind kiosk, attacks
6.	Flows	Lend borrow money, equipment, recent interactions
7.	Transfer of Material Resources	Business transactions, lending, social bonding, asking/giving favor
8.	Distance	Number of miles between (e.g., lives in walking distance, or lives too far to walk
9.	Co-Occurrences	Goes to the same church, belongs to cooperative, or other women's groups; sells at the same market.

Source: Wasserman & Faust, 2007, (p. 21)

her social ties to each person she had previously identified as being in her social network and to examine the respondent's cell communication use and preferences. The social ties were rated on the basis of the nine relationship roles discussed earlier (Wasserman & Faust 2007). The survey consisted of 15 static questions (including demographics) and 45 questions on the relationship roles. These 45 questions were repeated for each person the respondent had identified as being a part of her ego network.

Second, individual interviews were conducted by a trained data collector. The individual interviews consisted of nine questions and focused on the nature of the woman's business, how the business was started and conducted, how she sourced the produce she sold, her perspectives on leadership qualities of good business leaders and the kind of people with whom she would or would not do business.

Third, group interviews were conducted by the Principal Investigator. The group interviews lasted about an hour and addressed the question of how a group of women similar to theirs might initiate a value-added food processing operation. The specific questions included "Who could provide the leadership to organize the women and help them develop a business plan?" "How would they get the money they would need?" "To whom would they go for technical help?" "To whom would they sell their product?" and "What problems might such a group encounter?"

RESULTS

Results from the three data collection techniques – PDA surveys (for ego network data), individual interviews and focus group interviews are presented here. Because of space limitations, analysis of the social network data is not provided here but references are alluded to its preliminary findings (see Table 2).

Observations from Ego-Network Data

The PDA surveys were administered to 26 participants. The survey revealed that a total of 92 members were networked. The most common roles played by individuals in the social networks of these women included:

- **Wholesaler:** 21 contacts;
- **Farmer:** 10 contacts;
- **Street Restaurant Person:** 6 contacts;
- Majority of women communicate orally with other business women in day-today transaction but the Cell phone is currently used more frequently to reach distant suppliers and farmers.

Some of the demographic characteristics included:

- Almost all women who participated in the survey did not complete secondary school. Most of them completed primary school (81%). With the exception of

Table 2. Survey results

Questions	Yes %	No %	Don't K. %	Not Sure %
Responses regarding business relationships of the 26 participants considered together (N=92)				
3. Do you trust each other?	96	1	3	
4. Do you respect each other?	100	0		
5. Would you consider this person a community leader?	67	19	14	
6. Do you consider this person very much (similar) like you?	2	48	29	16
7. Is this person good at recovering from business set-backs?	84	0	16	
8. Is this individual open-minded to opinions that differ from his/her own?	90	6	4	

two women participants, the rest resided in rural areas. The participants were spit almost half and half between married and single women doing business.

- The characteristics of the women involved in the produce marketing business revealed that 91 percent of the women in the network have a business relationship and this relationship is beneficial because they have the same education. However, having the same age, religion or speaking the same ethnic language did not matter at all and was not considered beneficial to the relationship.
- Gender seemed to play a big part on business relationships. 93 percent said that gender connection was beneficial because both were women.
- Focus group interviews revealed that there is a very strong desire to own a Cell phone and women are looking for any opportunity to purchase one or replace existing one for a smarter one. To some, the Cell phone was a status symbol as well.
- When asked how the women communicate with other people in their network, about 60 percent use cell phones while 40 percent use face-to-face including travel. (See Table 3).
- Women have frequent communication and contacts with the public transport operator, immediate family, food safe keeper, stall setup, cell phone related, hired house-help, tour guide, district councilor, teacher, church leader;
- Fifty-four percent of the women used cell phones whereas 46 percent used face-to-face communication (including travel) as their primary means of communication. 70 percent of the business relationships of the women were older than one year. Other interesting observations are tabulated in Table 3.

Table 3. Crosstabulation: Own a cell phone and communicating with other people (N=92)

Count				
		How do you primarily communicate with other people?		
		Cell phone	Face to face including travel	Total
Do you own a cell phone?	Yes	30 (56.6%)	23 (43.4%)	53
	No	25 (45.5%)	14 (37.8%)	39
	Total	55 (59.8%)	37 (40.2%)	92

DISCUSSION: HOW DOES IMPROVEMENT IN INFORMATION IMPACT MARKET PERFORMANCE?

Insights from this study of women entrepreneurs gave us introspection to what is going on in the women's business relationships. The use of Cell phones was quite prevalent and it seems to us that these women are learning innovative ways of using ICTs to advantage their business. Cell phone communication is taken for granted and the women swap telephone numbers frequently. Network coverage is strong in the towns but begins to fade as one moves away from towns or metropolitan areas. *But this phenomenon is changing as some women reported that with the introduction of additional network providers has improved connectivity a great deal.* These findings are informative but further research is needed to focus on the impact of ICTs on the business culture among women entrepreneurs.

This study confirmed the value of information in these markets, particularly when dealing with perishable goods. In fact, economists have long emphasized that information is critical for the efficient functioning of markets. In reality, the information available to women is often costly or incomplete, as emphasized by Stigler (1961). In such cases, there is no reason to expect excess price differences to be dissipated or the allocation of goods across markets to be efficient. This was evident when we compared prices between the three markets we surveyed. Yet despite the fact that information is both central to economic theories but limited in reality, there are few empirical studies assessing the effects of improvements in information. Thus, questions such as how much market performance can be enhanced by improving access to information, how much society gains from such improvements, and how those gains are shared between agricultural producers and consumers remain largely unanswered. In this project, we examined these questions by exploiting the introduction of cell phones in Tanzania as a natural experiment of improvement market information.

When information is limited or costly, entrepreneurs are unable to engage in simultaneous buying and selling in different markets in order to make an immediate profit without risk. Excess price dispersion across markets can arise, and goods may not be allocated efficiently. Elsewhere, for example, in Southeast Asia, Cell phones are known to help fishermen to set prices, eliminate waste, and improve human wellbeing (Jensen, 2007). The Kerla study reported by Jensen (2007) showed that information technologies may improve market performance and increase human wellbeing. Between 1997 and 2001, mobile phone service was introduced throughout Kerala, India, with a large fishing industry. The study shows that the adoption of mobile phones by fishermen and wholesalers was associated with a dramatic reduction in price dispersion, the complete elimination of waste, and near-perfect adherence to the Law of One Price. Both consumer and producer wellbeing increased (Jensen, 2007).

Beyond its prominent place in economic theory, the effect of information on market performance and welfare is also relevant to the debate over the potential value of information and communication technologies (ICTs) for economic development. Many critics argue that investments in ICTs should not be a priority for low-income countries, given more basic needs in areas such as nutrition, health, and education. But when we assess the ubiquitous nature of Cell phone in the Moshi area, this argument becomes mute. The women see the value of this new gadget. They would tell you that this argument overlooks the fact that the functioning of output markets plays a central role in determining the incomes of the significant fraction of households engaged in agriculture, forestry, or fisheries production in low-income countries; for the most of the world's poorest, living standards are determined largely by how much they get for their output. Additionally, the functioning of these markets determines the prices and availability of food, fuel, and other important consumer goods that often times, the women have no control over. However, in most developing countries and Tanzania in particular, markets are dispersed, and the communications infrastructure is poor. Producers and traders often have only limited information, perhaps knowing only the price in a handful of nearby villages or the nearest town, so the potential for inefficiency in the allocation of goods across markets is great.

By improving access of information, ICTs may help poorly functioning markets work better and thereby increase incomes and/or lower consumer prices. In fact, it has become increasingly common to find farmers, fishermen, and other producers throughout the developing world using mobile phones, text messaging, pagers, and the internet for marketing output. However, while there is some macro level evidence that ICTs promote economic growth, the micro level evidence has been purely anecdotal. Much of what has been written about the uneven spread of ICTs and how the spread has created a "digital divide" between rich and poor countries (O'Donnel, 2000; Parker, 2000; Waverman, 2010), considerably less is known about the benefits such technologies can provide the latter.

CONCLUSION

The results of this research study will inform the design of subsequent projects intended to assist women escape the poverty trap in rural villages of Tanzania and elsewhere. The original idea underlying this study was to gather information about the business climate among women who live in rural areas and to use that information to organize these women to form a cooperative. In a meeting with these women after the completion of this study, the researchers learned that the results of this study have been helpful in making women understand their abilities and organizational challenges. The establishment of the women's cooperative to produce and market a healthful product for nutritionally-vulnerable residents in Northern Tanzania area can help prevent malnutrition among children 6-36 months of age and to enable HIV infected adults to better tolerate the Antiretroviral drugs they receive. The goal however was also to enable the women shareholders to form a cooperative venture to increase their household income through an economically sustainable business initiative.

REFERENCES

Blair's Commission for Africa. (2005). *Our common interest*. London: Blair's Commission for Africa Report.

Bloch, M., Robert, B., & Beoku-Betts, J. (1998). *Women and education in Sub-Saharan Africa: Power, opportunities, and constraints*. New York, NY: L. Reinner Publishers.

Borgatti, S. P., Everett, M. G., & Freeman, L. C. (2002). *UCINET for Windows: Software for social network analysis*. Analytic Technologies, Harvard.

Burt, R. (1984). Network items and the general social survey. *Social Networks*, *6*(4), 293–339. doi:10.1016/0378-8733(84)90007-8

Caine, K., Hargrove, W., & Sun, M. (2007). Information and communication needs of Rwandan coffee stakeholders. In Best, M. (Ed.), *Last mile initiative innovations: Research findings from Georgia Institute of Technology*. Washington, DC: AED.

Itano, N. (August, 26, 2005). Africa's cellphone boom creates a base for low-cost banking. *The Christian Monitor* (p. 2). Johannesburg, South Africa.

Jensen, R. (2007). The digital provide: Information (Technology), market performance, and welfare in the South Indian fisheries sector. *The Quarterly Journal of Economics*, *122*(3), 879–924. doi:10.1162/qjec.122.3.879

Laumann, E. O. (1966). *Prestige and association in an urban community*. Indianapolis, IN: Bobbs-Merrill.

Marsden, P. V. (1987). Core discussion networks of Americans. *American Sociological Review*, *52*, 122–131. doi:10.2307/2095397

McCallister, L., & Fischer, C. S. (1978). A procedure for surveying personal networks. *Sociological Methods & Research*, *7*, 131–148. doi:10.1177/004912417800700202

O'Donnell, S. (2000, October 9). Closing the digital divide. *The Irish Times*, (p. 8).

Parker, E. (2000). *Closing the digital divide in rural America*. Elsevier. doi:10.1016/S0308-5961(00)00018-5

Polak, P. (2008). *Out of poverty: What works when traditional approaches fail*. San Francisco, CA: Berrett Koehler.

Prahalad, C. K. (2006). *The fortune at the bottom of the pyramid: Eradicating poverty through profits*. Upper Saddle River, NJ: Wharton School Publishing.

Sachs, J. (2005). *The end of poverty: Economic possibilities of our time*. New York, NY: Penguin Books. doi:10.1111/j.1600-0579.2007.00476.x

Smith, S. (2005). *Ending global poverty*. New York, NY: Palgrave Macmillan.

Stigler, G. J. (1961). The economics of information. *The Journal of Political Economy, 69*, 213–225. doi:10.1086/258464

United Nations. (2005). *The millennium development goals report*. New York, NY: United Nations.

Wasserman, S., & Faust, F. (2007). *Social network analysis: Methods and applications*. London, UK: Cambridge University Press.

Wasserman, S., & Faust, K. (1994). *Social network analysis*. Cambridge, UK: Cambridge University Press.

Waverman, L. (2010). *Connectivity scorecard*. Calgary, Canada: University of Calgary.

Wellman, B. (1979). The community question: The intimate networks of East Yorkers. *American Journal of Sociology, 84*, 1201–1231. doi:10.1086/226906

Chapter 8

A Synopsis of Information Communication Technologies Applications in Agro-Based Livelihoods in Nigeria

O. I. Oladele
North-West University, South Africa

EXECUTIVE SUMMARY

This chapter examines the applications of information communication technologies in agro-based livelihoods in Nigeria. A multipurpose community information access point was established at a pilot level in Ago-Are, Oyo State, Nigeria. The center equipped with basic ICT infrastructures including Internet connectivity made available through a VSAT, provided timely solutions to the basic problems of farmers' lack of information on agriculture, lack of access to inputs and output markets, and lack of access to some basic but relatively expensive equipment. The services include the Answering Farmer's Needs-a private-public collaborative project involving several organizations. There is also the Fantsuam Foundation, a not-for-profit organization that works with farmers in rural communities in Northern Nigeria with an on-going micro-credit project aimed at alleviating poverty among rural women. This chapter highlights the synergistic use and challenges for each of these projects and proffers suggestions for the adoption and adaptation in different parts of the world.

DOI: 10.4018/978-1-4666-2071-1.ch008

INTRODUCTION

This paper examines the applications of information communication technologies in agro-based livelihoods in Nigeria. This is based on the fact that the overwhelming breakthrough in the information communication technology has lent use of these technologies in agriculture. Along the production chain, all crops and livestock production systems are users of the information technology. Information is widely acknowledged as one of the critical factors of production decisions and farmers' demand for information has increased in recent years due to greater market instability, more complex production technologies among others. As a means of transferring agricultural technologies to practice, several methods have been adopted in Nigeria. These practices include the Answering Farmer's Needs in Nigeria - a private-public collaborative project involving several organizations namely Commonwealth of Learning (COL), International Institute of Tropical Agriculture; (IITA), Ibadan, Total Development International Foundation (TODEV), and Oke-Ogun Community Development Network. A multipurpose community information access point was established at a pilot level in Ago-Are, Oyo State, Nigeria. The center equipped with basic ICT infrastructures including internet connectivity made available through a VSAT provided timely solutions to the basic problems of farmers' lack of information on agriculture, lack of access to inputs and output markets, and lack of access to some basic but relatively expensive equipment.

Fantsuam Foundation, a not-for-profit organization, works with farmers in rural communities in Northern Nigeria with an on-going micro-credit project aimed at alleviating poverty among rural women, Health Education, Promotion of the use of solar stoves, Promotion of Rainwater Harvesting, Literacy and Numeracy programs for adults and the Staging Post' project. The Staging Post provides relevant health information and re-training for frontline health workers in rural clinics and health centers. The internet is our most prolific source of health information at the moment, which is downloaded on discs for translation, re-phrasing and editing to adapt the information for health workers.

Mobile Phones in Sustainable Fisheries Livelihoods Programme (SFLP)

In April 2006, representatives of fishing cooperative unions on the Lake Chad basin in Nigeria contacted local mobile phone operators inviting them to visit the fishing communities with a view to providing mobile coverage to the area. Only one of the companies responded and after a field visit it has begun installing the necessary equipment in Baga to provide coverage within a radius of 34 kilometres thus benefiting 20 fishing communities. The cooperative unions trained their members in the use of the phones and set up a microcredit scheme to purchase the phones. Pilot Fishnet Initiative (FNI): A model information network that provided data on fish production techniques and methods was established by the Ilaje local government area of Ondo State in Nigeria. It aims to network all fishermen in the administrative area. Information on marketing and fish distribution was disseminated through traditional village meetings; TV; leaflets; radio; posters and etc. It was under the authority of chairmen of fisher cooperative groups.

The United States Agency for International Development (USAID), in partnership with the MTN telecommunications company, has launched Nigeria Agriculture Information Services (NAMIN) to boost commodity trade in Nigeria as the introduction of internet services would serve as a veritable tool to increase access to information on commodities. The framework would improve decision making processes and ensure smooth flow of information on trade, food products, processing and marketing of agricultural commodities. Currently NAMIN collects and disseminates information of over 25 agricultural commodities from about 80 urban and rural markets weekly to empower farmers and end users to negotiate better.

Tradenet started in 2001 through a regional market information project called MISTOWA, and is now used in ten countries in West Africa including Nigeria. Tradenet is a software platform that allows market data to be easily accessed via mobile phone (Short Message Service [SMS], fax, or via the Internet using computers including hand-held personal digital assistants [PDAs]. This allows farmers and traders to receive daily price information, download video/audio files, access research documents, post buy & sell offers to the community, and contact other market participants. A data manager reviews and provides final authorization to incoming entries (via email, SMS or on-line) to ensure that data quality is maintained. Once approved, data is entered into a database and copied to a secure server held online. Using Tradenet, users can access both current and archived data on-line. They can analyze information by commodity or by market through the online graphing tools, and data files can be downloaded for analysis with Microsoft Excel.

The paper highlights the synergistic use and challenges for each of these application and proffer suggestions for the adoption and adaptation in different parts of the world.

BACKGROUND

African economy is agriculture dependent and this practice dominates the rural landscape of the entire continent. Agriculture plays a leading role in the non-oil sector of Nigeria. It supports 63 percent of the population directly by providing about 28 percent of the gross domestic product (GDP) from the total exports and 70 percent non-oil export production (World Bank, 1988). Since 1970, however, agricultural production has stagnated, food prices have risen and import of food rose fifteen folds between 1970 and 1978 in response to sharp declines in domestic production. Many times agricultural development is often assumed to mean rural development and in some cases has implemented following this understanding.

As agriculture is the principal occupation for people in rural areas, a broader view had emerged which distinguishes rural development form agricultural development. Rural development is equated with changes in social and economic structures, institution, relationships and processes. This means that rural development is not agricultural and economic growth alone but as the creation and fair sharing of social and economic benefits resulting from this growth. Ekong, (2003) defined rural development as the transformation of rural community into a socially, economically politically, educationally, orderly and materially desirable condition with the purpose of improving the quality of life of the rural population. The number of people living in rural areas exceeds the capacity of agriculture to provide sustainable livelihood opportunities. Even with a decline in fertility rate and a slowing of population growth, this situation will not change significantly. This indicates that rural people's livelihoods are derived from diverse sources and are not as overwhelmingly dependent on agriculture. Madu (2009) reported that Nigeria is still dominantly rural based as depicted by the rural structure of Nigeria on the consideration of some indicators and internationally accepted methodology rather than just the population criterion. For Nigeria, an agrarian country, the production of foods and other raw materials is a necessary ingredient for the take-off of all other sectors of the nation's economy. Agricultural practice in Nigeria should be based on efficient information sharing and accessibility to the needed information.

There is a growing awareness of the importance of information in rural development. That is, the development can be achieved through the acquisition of adequate information needed by the people engaging in these activities. Information is recognized as an essential component of the development process to empower poor communities, informal development agencies, policy makers and linking and informing decision making process at every level. In rural areas, information provide responses to the need of people for knowledge they can use to improve their productivity, incomes and welfare and to mange the natural resources on which they depend in a sustainable way. Lack of self sufficiency in day-to-day work constitutes information need which is usually specific and generally time bound either immediate or deferred. The changing information environment calls for meeting the need of information users and professionally requires operational management of the information resources. To ensure this, there is an urgent need to understand and grasp the complex process of identifying information need which is very vital in the chain of operations from information gathering to dissemination. The effectiveness of an information system depends on the extent to which the system characteristics are in correspondence with the situation of the users and on how much the potential users are willing and able to make use of the services provided by the information system. Information needs are affected by a variety of factors such as, the range of information sources available, the uses to which the information will be put to use, the background, motivation, professional orientation and other individual characteristics of the users, the social, political, economic, legal and regulatory systems surrounding the users and the consequences of information use (Ozowa, 1995).

Setting the Stage

Answering Farmers Needs in Nigeria

Due to the recognized roles of information in agricultural decision-making, "Answering Farmers Needs in Nigeria" was implemented at a pilot scale in Ago-Are Nigeria as a private-public collaborative project involving several organizations such as Commonwealth of Learning (COL), the International Institute of Tropical Agriculture; (IITA), Ibadan, Total Development International Foundation (TODEV), and Oke-Ogun Community Development Network. This is based on the premise that the Commonwealth of Learning (COL) is the only international intergovernmental agency that focuses exclusively on using technology, placing special emphasis on open and distance learning (ODL), to expand the scope and scale of human learning due to the fact that knowledge is the key to individual freedom and to cultural, social and economic development. To achieve high impact, COL works in partnership with other international and bilateral organizations as well as with grassroots non-governmental organizations working on the Millennium Development Goals. The project provided access to information through an integrated resource center in which information and communication technologies including the internet provided communication links for farmers. Besides, the center provided some Open and Distance Learning Materials to meet the felt needs of the farmers, linked them through the internet to other useful websites providing information on agricultural production, processing and marketing and to inputs and output markets. The resource center was connected to market information services providing market prices for a number of commodities from about a hundred markets across Nigeria and corresponded directly with the "farmers support desk" established at the International Institute of Tropical Agriculture for the provision of timely responses to farmers' requests. The center was established in the last quarter of 2004 with funding that lasted for six months. Thereafter, the farmers continued to manage the center using internally generated resources. Participating farmers increased their yields per unit area, holdings, external inputs used, and productivity all leading to higher incomes with attendant evidence of graduation into commercial farming.

Internet Access for Distance Learning and Health Education in Rural Communities

Fantsuam Foundation, a not-for-profit organization, works with rural communities in Nigeria initiated Health Education, through the Staging Post project. The Staging Post provides relevant health information and re-training for frontline health workers in rural clinics and health centers based on information from the internet which are downloaded on discs and taken back to field stations for translation, re-phrasing and editing to adapt the information to health workers and environment. A similar approach is used for distance learning program. Internet access is provided affordably, through Mobile Community Telecentre in Kunyai, Nigeria, where there is no electricity or phone lines. The Mobile Community Telecentre is a van that is being rigged up to carry four computers from one rural community to the next within a 55 km radius. The program provides basic skills training for rural communities (comprising women, youths, secondary school teachers and students, and Community Health Workers) English language lessons and other subjects relevant to the secondary school curriculum as well as relevant information for frontline health workers in our rural communities. Five village Communities within the radius as of 15-20km are covered as a pilot area in which the distance learning program. These villages will also have access to email services from the Mobile Community Telecentre.

Internet and Mobile Phones Use among Coastal Fishing Communities

Since the 1960s, the fisheries sector has contributed between 1.11 to 2.4 percent of the Gross Domestic Product (GDP) or 3.0 and 6.0 percent of the Agricultural GDP. This is because fish is a major source of animal protein and has continued to grow in importance over the years, particularly, as a substitute to beef. The artisanal fisheries sub-sector constitutes a major source of employment, especially in the southern coastal maritime/riverine areas. The Nigerian coastal zone sprawls a total of nine states, out of the thirty-six states of the federation, namely: Akwa-Ibom, Bayelsa, Cross River, Delta, Edo, Lagos, Ogun, Ondo and Rivers. The coastal states are estimated to account for 25% of the national population. The major economic activity for the general and common individual in the coastal zone is fishing. The major problems of the coastal zone derive from human and natural impacts due to high populations, industrial and agricultural activities aimed at meeting food, energy, goods and other requirements of the populace. A lot of the environmental problems of the coastal zone are caused primarily by land based activities. The following problems have been identified i) overexploitation of fisheries, ii) coastal and marine pollution, iii) oil spills, iv) coastal erosion and flooding, v) physical modification and destruction of habitats, vi) climate change and sea level rise, vii) invasive species. Similarly the Lake Chad basin, located in Northern Central Africa, covers almost 8% of the continent and spreads over seven countries is home to about 20 million people. About 20% of the total area of the Lake Chad basin, or 427500 km2, is called the Conventional Basin (42% in Chad, 28% in Niger, 21% in Nigeria and 9% in Cameroon), which is under the mandate of the Lake Chad Basin Commission. In these coastal areas, the difficulty of the terrain and poor infrastructural development have often left the teeming population out of the information network which constitute the major loss to their productivity. To overcome these information problems, a project on Mobile phones in Mobile phones in Sustainable Fisheries Livelihoods Program (SFLP) was initiated. The type of ICT used is the Mobile - spoken communication. In April 2006 representatives of fishing cooperative unions on the Lake Chad basin in Nigeria contacted local mobile phone operators inviting them to visit the fishing communities with a view to providing mobile coverage to the area. Only one of the companies responded and after a field visit it has begun installing the necessary equipment in Baga to provide coverage within a radius of 34 kilometres thus benefiting 20 fishing communities. The cooperative unions trained their members in the use of the phones and are set up a microcredit scheme to help purchase the phones. In the same vein the Pilot Fishnet Initiative (FNI) was developed based on the use of various network of ICT for the fishing communities in Ondo state. A model information network that provided data on fish production techniques and methods was established by the Ilaje local government area of Ondo State in Nigeria. It networks all fishermen in the administrative area. Information on marketing and fish distribution was disseminated through traditional village meetings; TV; leaflets; radio; posters and etc. It was under the authority of chairmen of fisher cooperative groups (FAO 2009)

Nigeria Agricultural Market Information Service (NAMIS)

The United States Agency for International Development (USAID), in partnership with the MTN telecommunications company, has launched Nigeria Agriculture Information Services (NAMIN) to boost commodity trade in Nigeria as the introduction of internet services would serve as a veritable tool to increase access to information on commodities. The service market and commodity information would cover major markets at the local and international levels and helps to improve the knowledge base of private entrepreneurs to enhance their efficiency, improve decision making processes and ensure smooth flow of information on trade, food products, processing and marketing of agricultural commodities. The program serves to empower farmers and end users to negotiate better. Currently NAMIN collects and disseminates information of over 25 agricultural commodities from about 80 urban and rural markets weekly to empower farmers and end users to negotiate better.

NAMIS was established 2004 through MOU between PCU, DAIMINA & PFS and funded by the three organizations till Dec 2004. It is based at PCU, Abuja and staff members are drawn from these organizations with collaborating with PRS/ FMARD, SGR, ADPs as well as technical; staff from a cross section of stakeholders. The objective was to establish a sustainable agriculture market information service that address the needs of producer groups, Traders associations and policy makers, that would facilitate procurement of inputs, sales of raw and processed produce in the domestic, regional and international market. The products and services covered by NAMIS are currently market prices of 14 commodities based on 30 markets across the geopolitical zones of Nigeria and disseminated through fortnightly bulletin, farm broadcast on radio and Fortnightly publication in 2 newspapers (This Day & Daily Trust). The planned structure is such that NAMIS at Phase 1 April 2004 covers 10 states, Phase 2 April 2005 covers 27 states and by Phase 3 April 2006 it would have National coverage of 3 major markets in each state, covered by trained ADP enumerators. Enumerators are trained on: data collection, use of ICT for transmission, collation of prices data, dissemination of prices, sensitization of stakeholders on MIS and participation in regional meetings/consultations on MIS.

Tradenet

Tradenet started in 2001 through a regional market information project called MISTOWA, and is now used in ten countries in West Africa including Nigeria. Tradenet Is a software platform that allows market data to be easily accessed via mobile phone (Short Message Service [SMS], fax, or via the Internet using computers including hand-held personal digital assistants [PDAs]. This allows farmers and traders to receive daily price information, download video/audio files, access research documents, post buy & sell offers to the community, and contact other market participants. A data manager reviews and provides final authorization to incoming entries (via email, SMS or on-line) to ensure that data quality is maintained. Once approved, data is entered into a database and copied to a secure server held online. Using Tradenet, users can access both current and archived data on-line. They can analyze information by commodity or by market through the online graphing tools, and data files can be downloaded for analysis with Microsoft Excel.

In addition to the numerical data, Tradenet can hold both text and sound files. For radio stations, news and educational programs can be downloaded and re-broadcast to a mass audience using sound (MP3) files. Tradenet offers the opportunity to provide updatable lists of service providers, traders, and financial services. In time, this registry can also have approval ratings of good business conduct. New versions of Tradenet allow for groups to be formed so that people interested in one commodity can create their own information area and manage this part of the site. The Tradenet software platform aims to make African markets more transparent and efficient. It provide stakeholders with regular information to improve their negotiating position and support better decision-making in terms of which crops or livestock products to produce, where and when to sell produce, and when to store, in order to maximize profits. The use of a reliable information platform allows for rapid data management and plays a key role in reducing the costs of information sharing. Given this new approach based on outsourced management, we believe that future market information services will be operated by trader groups, banks, radio operators, farmers' associations and/or NGOs. This new constellation of potential operators can mean that market information will be more readily available to farmers in the future at a price that is attractive to service providers and farmers alike.

CONCLUSION

The cases presented in this chapter have shown the different areas in the use of ICT to improve the livelihoods of the populace engaged in the aforementioned agro-based activities. Central to these projects is the participation of the beneficiaries and the push for a better life and then the collaborative involvement of the project planners and the beneficiaries. It has also described the significance and pragmatic ways by which ICTs can be incorporated in these livelihood activities which can serve as cases for application in may other parts of the world.

REFERENCES

CIAT. (2007). What is Tradenet? *The Highlights Series, 38.* Retrieved from www.ciat.cgiar.org

Ekong, E. E. (2003). *Introduction to rural sociology* (2nd ed.). Uyo, Nigeria: Dove Educational Publishers.

FAO. (2009). *Mobile phones in sustainable fisheries livelihoods programme.* Retrieved from http://www.e-agriculture.org/ict_project.html?&L=tisihaiufsjqrvj&tx_ictproject_pi1[showUid]=10&cHash=d8b6dd2a31

FAO. (2009). *Pilot fishnet initiative*. Retrieved from http://www.e-agriculture.org/ict_project.html?&L=tisihaiufsjqrvj&tx_ictproject_pi1[showUid]=35&cHash=df4f74bfa2

Madu, I. A. (2009). The structure and pattern of rurality in Nigeria. *GeoJournal*, *75*(2), 175–184. doi:10.1007/s10708-009-9282-9

Ozowa, V. N. (1995). Information needs of small scale farmers in Africa: The Nigerian example. *Quarterly Bulletin of the International Association of Agricultural Information Specialists*, *40*(1).

PCU. (2009). *Nigeria agricultural market information service* (NAMIS). Retrieved from www.pcuagric.org

World Bank. (1988). *Agricultural research and extension: An evaluation of the World Bank experience*.

This work was previously published in Cases on Developing Countries and ICT Integration: Rural Community Development, edited by Rebecca Nthogo Lekoko and Ladislaus M. Semali, pp. 25-32, copyright 2012 by Information Science Reference (an imprint of IGI Global).

Chapter 9

Innovative Use of ICT in Namibia for Nationhood:
Special Emphasis on *The Namibian* Newspaper

Tutaleni I. Asino
Penn State University, USA

Hilary Wilder
William Paterson University, USA

Sharmila Pixy Ferris
William Paterson University, USA

EXECUTIVE SUMMARY

Namibia was under colonizing and apartheid rule for more than a century. In 1990, the country declared its independence, and since that time, great strides have been made in linking its rural communities into a national communications Grid that was previously inaccessible to them, often leapfrogging traditional landline telephone technologies with universal cell phone service. In addition, one newspaper, The Namibian, has been innovatively using newer communications technologies to maintain its historic role of nation-building. This chapter showcases how SMS via cell phone and a traditional national newspaper has a sense of national identity that transcends geographic distances and a legacy of economic/political barriers. The cell phone messages made it possible for the rural communities who have been left out of discussion relating to issues of development to be included. Although the study unveiled 11% of their participation as opposed to 30% of the rural populace, this is a step forward bearing in mind that the rural areas have a history of being

DOI: 10.4018/978-1-4666-2071-1.ch009

passively involved in everything that is being done. They have been, and continue to some great extent to be content to receive decisions made for them by outsiders including political leaders. Mobile phones have come as empowerment for them. Like the old slogan, "information is power," this chapter illustrates that the lives of some rural area dwellers have improved a result of a technological gadget, the mobile phone.

INTRODUCTION

In most of the developing world, where colonial footprints still linger, the uneven distribution and access to infrastructure has led to an unequal participation in national conversations. The uses of Information Communication Technologies (ICTs) are making a meaningful impact on everyday lives, even in nations without rural technological infrastructures. ICTs are mitigating the gap between urban and rural population, which are often stratified and allow for both to inform and affect national governance.

Namibia offers an instructive example of how the use of an "everyday" ICT helps empower rural populations. This paper examines the ways in which ICTs have enabled a national newspaper to be more successful in empowering rural populations. For 25 years, *The Namibian* has been the liberal voice of Namibia. Today its use of Short Message Service (SMS) from readers, both urban and rural, gives them voice in developing nationhood in Namibia. *The Namibian*'s use of SMS exemplifies the effective use of ICTS to allow local, rural populations to participate in larger collective units (Eisenstein, 1983), ensuring that their interests, concerns and propositions are given a voice.

Historically, newspapers have played a vital role in the development of the modern nation. In fact, as Finnegan (1988) observes, many of the economic, social, religious, political characteristics of the modern world are built on the foundation provided by print. One important impact of the technology of the printing press was the rise of national literatures, printed in the local language, which were a vital force in the development of nation states (Eisenstein, 1983). In developing countries such as Namibia, however, newspapers largely remained under the control of colonial powers and were used as instruments of colonialism rather than for nascent nation-alism. Furthermore, in countries with cultures strongly grounded in the oral and tribal ways of knowing, the medium of print tended to destroy the existing sense of community and social integration (Ong, 1982). The advance of ICTs changed both these factors dramatically. In the case of Namibia, ICTs allowed a geographically dispersed people to have a voice in national issues through letters to the editor of *The Namibian* newspaper; as well as a medium that drew people together.

While SMS generally serves to connect dyads and groups of friends, they also can, due to the affordability, unite people geographically removed from each other by merging geographical infrastructures and technology (Ito & Okabe, 2005). When SMS is used in conjunction with a more traditional print medium like a newspaper, it becomes an ICT that provides a vital link to people who would otherwise be disenfranchised from having a voice in nation building.

The Infrastructure, Technology, and Nationhood in Namibia

A historical context is necessary to understanding the current role played by SMS in nation building in Namibia today. Before achieving Independence in 1990, the majority of Namibians were not only unable to participate in the national dialogue, but also had limited options for receiving daily national news, particularly, for the people in rural areas. This happened due to a series of historical events. For example, the policies and laws enacted by colonial Germany and the apartheid laws of South Africa after the First World War, had irrevocable effects on the country and ensured that Namibia was segmented as a means of control. Segmentation worked hand-in-hand with exclusion from the technological infrastructure to create a population that was too dispersed and isolated to unite in nationalism. Consequently, Namibia today is a sparsely populated country with a population of 2.1 million people.

As can be seen in Table 1, the majority of the population resides in rural areas. Additionally, the ethnic groupings and population patterns continue to exist in Namibia today, further exacerbating the lack of national unity. The pre-independence Colonial authorities cordoned ethnic divisions, making interactions between ethnic/tribal groups very difficult and thereby ensuring that the country remained divided. Although the patterns are shifting, the majority of the population remains in rural areas not fully served by a technological or modern transportation (e.g. tarred roads) infrastructure.

Table 1. Namibia: population statistics, 1950-2010

Namibia - population Statistics - 1950-2010							
	1950	1960	1970	1980	1990	2000	2010
Total population (thousands)	485	599	772	993	1 417	1 879	2 157
Percentage in rural areas	86.6	82.1	77.7	74.9	72.3	67.6	62
Percentage in urban areas	13.4	17.9	22.3	25.1	27.7	32.4	38

Source: Population Division of the Department of Economic and Social Affairs of the United Nations

The country's division, and people's lack of access to a communication infrastructure, was fueled by Colonial powers who ensured that Namibia was also structured on a hierarchical racial paradigm. White Afrikaaner peoples were at the top; mixed race peoples (known as coloureds) were in the middle and native black Africans at the bottom. The South African apartheid regime instilled in people's minds that Namibia was a land for the whites, with blacks subservient to whites and incapable of self-determination and governance. Stemming from governmental policies, Namibia's national grid (roads, electricity, running water, telephone lines etc.), was not designed to benefit the indigenous peoples of Namibia or modernize the country. The infrastructures were created for administrative and economic purposes, linking military centers, mines, ports, and white farmers as a means to exploit the vast mineral wealth and agricultural assets of the country (Mbuende, 1986).

Since independence, the government and private corporations have been struggling to overcome the economic, logistical, bureaucratic and geographic barriers to include all Namibians into the national infrastructures. Today there are landline phones and Internet access in towns that historically had a critical mass of white Afrikaaners, but a comprehensive technological infrastructure has yet to extend to rural areas, leaving rural populations without quality access to media or technology. This problem is exacerbated by the fact that although Namibia is wealthier than most of its sister African nations, a majority of its population is not sharing in this prosperity. The World Bank ranks Namibia as an "upper-middle income country" (World Bank, nd) but at the same time, the country has the world's highest GINI coefficient (i.e. substantial disparities between rich and poor. (CIA, nd)).

The historical legacies highlighted above play out in the control of, and access to, news media. The printed press, prior to independence, was largely state owned, and represented the interests of political parties that supported the colonial white rule. Only two newspapers, *The Namibian* and *The Windhoek Observer*, could be considered independent (Mwilima, 2008).Of the two, *The Namibian* has a history of representing and reporting on the issues relating to black Namibia. From its inception in 1985, *The Namibian* newspaper espoused the cause of independence and promoted freedom of information. *The Namibian* was made a constant target by the South African regime that vied to suppress images and stories of oppression of Namibia (Sturges, Katjihingua & Mchombu, 2005).

The South African government's continued occupation of Namibia in the 1960s to late 1980s was based on the propaganda to the world that their occupation was just and benefited the Namibian population the most. Thus, *The Namibian's* reporting on atrocities and injustices in the country presented a direct challenge for the regime. Today, *The Namibian* continues to be involved in issues of national politics, voice of the people and nation building, often taking on the current government and holding them accountable for ensuring universal democratic rights.

In addition to lack of access to news or other media, communication across Namibia remained hampered until the advent of cheap mobile phone technologies. Although telephone lines were present in urban areas, the cost of installing telephone landlines was prohibitive. Mobile phones changed this in 1995, with the establishment of Mobile Telecommunications Limited (MTC), the country's first cell phone service provider. This was a crucial moment for Namibia because it set in motion access to ICT by every Namibian citizen including those residing in rural areas. Access was further expanded by the introduction of a second mobile operator, Cell One (currently renamed Leo), in 2007. Leo brought competition in the mobile sector and forced MTC to upgrade its services for the benefit of the population. Both MTC and Leo use a pay-as-you-go service, allowing the reasonably priced purchase of a mobile phone with a SIM card and pre-paid minutes without the requirement of in-home installation, long-term contract, or complex paperwork. A user can begin using the mobile phone as quickly as 15 minutes after purchase, especially when using the pay as you go option (Stork and Aochamub, 2003). The success of mobile phone technology is clear, and by 2003, the number of mobile phone users was already higher than the number of landline telephones, and certainly outnumbered the number of computers.

The gaps in the communication infrastructure are being bridged by the rapid adoption of mobile phone technology, which brought with it not only oral connectivity among users, but the enthusiastic use of SMS. The use of SMS by mobile phone users is the norm in many developing countries, as Ghyasi and Kushchu (2004) suggest SMS provides a "vital tool for communicating information and a precursor to Internet" (Ghyasi & Kushchu, p. 5). SMS has the advantage of not only being effective as a communication tool, but it is also a robust and cost-effective technology.

SMS and Nationhood in Namibia

The Namibian's SMS program initially started as a way for readers to respond to specific issues. This, however, quickly evolved due to readers enthusiastic responses to communicate with *The Namibian* newspaper and submitting letters to the editors in 2007. This use of SMS extended the reach of the paper and allowed any Namibian with a mobile phone to participate in the national dialogue. As Carmen Honey, *The Namibian's* sub-editor in charge of this section notes

...before long the messages were coming thick and fast on every topic under the sun, some connected to published issues, others even to international events (C. Honey, personal communication, October w04, 2010).

For the first time in Namibian history, participation from citizens through the SMS initiative program, included a real representation of all areas, rural and urban, central and dispersed. Ms. Honey captures it succinctly when she said that participation remains broadly inclusive and truly national. The newspaper hears from all, on all topics:

...from the tiniest villages in the most remote spots on a daily basis. Even the government officials on the borders, north, south and east regularly get in touch. People are participating in the national debate from far and wide with the ideas and opinions as varied as the topics at hand. There are many instances where readers have complained about things like litter, dangerous roads, noise, broken water points etc. at regional and local authority level, civic issues in general, which have been neglected and later seen to after the SMS messages appeared. Then the complainants send in thank you messages stating the problem has been solved. SMS messages have been discussed in Parliament and then reported on in other media. International news media have picked up on it too as the SMS page appears on our website every day. (C. Honey, personal communication, October 04, 2010).

METHODOLOGY

The subject of this chapter is both descriptive and explanatory in nature and as such a case study research method was utilized. What distinguishes the case study method and makes it preferable for this study was its potential to help researchers situate this case in its historical context and the three common characteristics that Yin (2009) argues are integral to its definition. Specifically, a case study is marked by its concern with the questions of "how" and "why"; the researchers lack of "control over the events"; and the researchers' interest in a "contemporary phenomenon within a real-life context."

Collection of data consisted of a secondary data analysis, conducted on the SMS available on the website of *The Namibian*. A purposive sampling was used because the focus was on messages that dealt with national as well as local issues. By intentionally selecting a time frame from which to obtain data for analysis, purposive sampling allowed the researchers to hone in on the aspects that are most critical to the research (Creswell 1998, Creswell & Plano Clark 2011). Selection was limited to messages printed for one week in November 2008, March 2009, November 2009, and March 2010 (November being an election month (the presidential election was held in 2009) and March being the independence celebration month (the 20th anniversary was celebrated in 2010). Additional information for "data triangulation"

(Yin, 1994) was gathered through the telephone and email interviews with the editor responsible for the SMS section of the newspaper, noted above.

An examination of messages sent to *The Namibian* effectively illustrated the power of citizens' participation in Namibian nationhood. The analysis of the data relied on the daily subsets that had been chosen for publication in the newspaper (and restricted to one full printed page), which were then archived on *The Namibian's* website. It should be noted that the editor of *The Namibian* made a conscious decision to give some priority to messages sent from rural areas, and most of the pages had a section entitled "In and From the Regions" as well as a section entitled "City Fathers Please" (where 'city' refers to the capitol city of Windhoek). The other constraint on the dataset was that we had to look only at the messages that were signed or implicitly identified as being sent from either a rural or an urban area, for example, these messages from March 16, 2009):

WORKERS' wages? Government must start doing research in Kunene Region. Labourers in the Outjo area and Kamanjab are struggling. We need help please! (implicitly localized)

THEY blame the victims for their action. Whereby the victim starts feeling guilty and intimidated and this becomes an ongoing process until it's too late to realize what happened. We should stand up to domestic violence because the first cut is the deepest. – Judd, Windhoek (explicitly signed)

Approximately 30% of the total printed messages contained localization information, and as expected, the majority of those (approximately 87%) focusing on local issues, since those that dealt with national issues by definition did not necessarily need to specify localization information. Local issues could either be aimed at national (e.g. government) organizations, for example:

WE from Aussenkehr don't know what clean water is, what happened to the people that we voted for? Twenty years have gone by now since Independence, diarrhoea [sic] is killing us. Please help. (Mar. 17, 2010)

WE people of Musanga area are left behind when we mean development in Caprivi. We are also part of Namibia. We don't have electricity but we are near town and also we have network problem. People higher up must do something. We also have a problem with a road, they should give us even a gravel road. Please (Nov. 26, 2008)

Some messages were directed at local organizations with the intent of bringing national attention to them, for example:

MR Naftal Andimba, Mayor of Ondangwa town, we are very tired of waiting for you and your team to relocate our Old Omashaka village. It has been eight years now promising to bring changes to our village like electricity etc. Please we need responses. (Mar. 20, 2009)

LET me air my problem to Eenhana Town Council. Please we residents have a problem with mosquitoes. We are afraid of malaria. Please do something to help our people, especially the small kids who are helpless. – Twaloloka (Nov. 23, 2009)

However, there were also messages from identifiable rural senders that focused on national issues, giving people from those areas a voice in the national debate, for example, (SPYL (SWAPO Party Youth League) and SWAPO (South West Africa People's Organization) are both national political organizations.):

SPYL, set priorities! Please SPYL leaders, leave politics for the politicians. Set priorities. Focus on educating male youths to stop abusing and killing innocent ladies in this country. Too many lives are being lost among youths and what have you done thus far to address this serious matter? – Tangi, Ongwediva (Nov. 24, 2008)

THE content of Gwen's Friday column gave me a laugh of my life. Madam, when will you submit to the fact that Swapo is still the force that it has been? The erosion of Swapo dominance is a far-fetched hallucination. Please just bear with the IPPR truthful findings that Swapo is strongly retaining its dominance in the electoral landscape. The target is a 72 seats swoop. What you say will just strengthen us. Viva Swapo! – Fikameni, Okalongo (Mar. 17, 2009)

Table 2 shows a breakdown of the SMS in terms of being identified from rural versus urban senders, and dealing with nation versus local issues.

From the data sampled above, it is obvious that through the two-year period of study, people from both rural and urban contributed to the national dialog by sending messages addressing both local and national issues. To be noted that is the possibility that the 11% recorded of message sent from the rural areas may not reflect the actual pictures as researchers were unable to categorize those messages that did not reflect the location. This observation applies to the 30% recorded for urban places. Further study which will require all necessary information from the participants is needed.

Table 2. SMS in rural vs urban senders on national vs. local issues

	Total SMSes printed that week	% of SMSes with identifiable location of sender out of total	% of identifiable location SMSes from rural sender/ local issue	% of identifiable location SMSes from rural sender/ national issue	% of identifiable location SMSes from urban sender/ local issue	% of identifiable location SMSes from urban sender/ national issue
Nov. 24-28, 2008	157	34%	68%	17%	13%	2%
Mar. 16-20, 2009	177	32%	55%	9%	34%	2%
Nov. 23-27, 2009	223	33%	62%	5%	32%	1%
Mar. 15-19, 2010	223	23%	52%	13%	27%	8%
Averaged across 2-year period	195	31%	59%	11%	27%	3%
			Total identifiable rural: 70%		Total identifiable urban: 30%	

CONCLUSION

An examination of phone messages sent to *The Namibian* shows the readiness level of residents of Namibia to adopt current and modern ICTwhether for discussion on national issues including those of the local rural communities. In Namibia the growth of mobile phone technology has far outpaced the growth of a technological infrastructure that supports landline telephones and computers. This is not surprising as the literature indicates that this is the trends in many developing nations. Both Ghyasi and Kushchu (2004) and Lallana (2004), for example, note that the widespread use of mobile phones is a phenomenon common to many developing countries where cell phone technology leapfrogs that of traditional communication technologies. The adoption of mobile phone technologies is complemented by the equally widespread use of SMS.

SMS is a unique ICT in that, while it relies on print, it extends the oral fashion. Rural, and even urban, Namibians continue to have what Ong (1982) calls a verbomotor lifestyle, that is a lifestyle that is not high technology but rather one in which "courses of action and attitudes towards issues depend significantly more on effective use of words, and thus on human interaction" (p. 68). Perhaps a different study is needed to explore themes of unity, collaboration and community.

While our research on SMS in Namibia is limited, it does show that in SMS technology, ICTs can offer an interpersonal medium that functions to draw people together while allowing them to communicate across geographical and political distances to speak to national issues. Our research also demonstrates that in cultures strongly grounded in the traditional tribal community structure, a print-based ICT can reinforce rather than destroy the existing sense of community and national integration.

REFERENCES

Central Intelligence Agency. (n.d.) *CIA - The World Factbook country comparison: Distribution of family income Gini index.* Retrieved from https://www.cia.gov/library/publications/the-world-factbook/rankorder/2172rank.html

Creswell, J. W. (1998). *Qualitative inquiry and research design: Choosing among five traditions.* Thousand Oaks, CA: Sage Publications.

Creswell, J. W., & Plano Clark, V. L. (2011). *Designing and conducting mixed methods research* (2nd ed.). Thousand Oaks, CA: Sage Publications.

Eisenstein, E. (1983). *The printing revolution in early modern Europe.* Cambridge, UK: Cambridge University Press.

Finnegan, R. (1988). *Literacy and orality: Studies in the technology of communication.* Oxford, UK: Basil Blackwell.

Ghyasi, A. F., & Kushchu, I. (2004). *M-government: Cases of developing countries.* Mobile Government lab report. Retrieved from http://www.mgovernment.org/resurces/mgovlab_afgik.pdf

Ito, M., & Okabe, D. (2005) Technosocial situations: Emergent structurings of mobile email use. In Ito, M., Okabe, D., & Matsuda, M. (Eds.), *Personal, portable, pedestrian: Mobile phones in Japanese life.* Cambridge, MA: MIT Press.

Lallana, E. (2004). *E-government for development, m-government definitions and models.* Retrieved from http://www.egov4dev.org/mgovdefn.htm

Mbuende, K. (1986). *Namibia the broken shield: Anatomy of imperialism.* Malmo, Sweden: Liber.

Mwilima, F. J. (2008). Practical reality of media freedom: An examination of the challenges facing the Namibian media. *Global Media Journal, 2*(2). Retrieved from http://sun025.sun.ac.za/portal/page/portal/Arts/Departemente1/Joernalistiek/ Global%20Media%20Journal/Global%20Media%20Journal%20-%20Files/8C985 44F010C4CCDE04400144F47F004

Ong, W. J. (1982). *Orality and literacy: The technologizing of the word.* New York, NY: Routledge. doi:10.4324/9780203328064

Population Division of the Department of Economic and Social Affairs of the United Nations Secretariat. (n.d.). *Population prospects: The 2008 revision.* Retrieved from http://esa.un.org/unpp

SMS of the Day. (2008, November 24). *The Namibian.* Retrieved from http://www.namibian.com.na/smses/full-story/archive/2008/november/article/smses-for-monday-24-nov-08/

SMS of the Day. (2008, November 26). *The Namibian.* Retrieved from http://www.namibian.com.na/smses/full-story/archive/2008/november/article/smses-for-wednesday-26-nov-08/

SMS of the Day. (2009, March 16). *The Namibian.* Retrieved from http://www.namibian.com.na/smses/full-story/archive/2009/march/article/smses-for-mon-16-mar-09/

SMS of the Day. (2009, March 17). *The Namibian.* Retrieved from http://www.namibian.com.na/smses/full-story/archive/2009/march/article/smses-for-tue-17-mar-09/

SMS of the Day. (2009, March 20). *The Namibian.* Retrieved from http://www.namibian.com.na/smses/full-story/archive/2009/march/article/sms-of-fri-20-mar-09/

SMS of the Day. (2009, November 23). *The Namibian.* Retrieved from http://www.namibian.com.na/smses/full-story/archive/2009/november/article/smses-of-monday-23-november-2009/

SMS of the Day. (2010, March 17). *The Namibian.* Retrieved from http://www.namibian.com.na/smses/full-story/archive/2010/march/article/sms-of-the-day-17-march-2010/

Stork, C., & Aocahmub, A. (2003). *Namibia in the information age.* (NEPRU Research Report No. 25). Windhoek, Namibia: Namibian Economic Policy Research Unit. Retrieved from http://www.nepru.org.na/index.php?id=159&no_cache=1&file=155&uid=227

Sturges, P., Katjihingua, M., & Mchombu, K. (2005). Information in the national liberation struggle: Modelling the case of Namibia (1966-1990). *The Journal of Documentation, 61*(6), 735–750. doi:10.1108/00220410510632068

Tellis, W. (1997). Introduction to case study. *Qualitative Report, 3*(2). Retrieved from http://www.nova.edu/ssss/QR/QR3-2/tellis1.html

World Bank. (n.d.). *Namibia data.* Retrieved from http://data.worldbank.org/country/namibia

Yin, R. (2009). *Case study research: Design and methods* (4th ed.). Thousand Oak, CA: Sage Publishing.

Chapter 10

ICT–Supported Education for Sustainable Development of South Korean Rural Communities

K. P. Joo
Penn State University, USA

EXECUTIVE SUMMARY

The rural communities in South Korea have faced serious challenges as the country has gradually opened the agricultural market and extended the conclusion of Free Trade Agreement with more and more countries. Moreover, due to the national socio-economic and political structures, South Korea has been undergoing the technological imbalance between rural and urban areas. In order to cope with these vital social challenges, the South Korean government has exerted considerable investment and effort in establishing ICT knowledge and skills as well as infrastructure in rural areas. Thus, conceptualizing ICT in the context of adult education, this chapter addresses three ICT-supported adult education programs oriented toward developing ICT skills and competencies of people in agricultural areas of South Korea. The South Korean cases of agricultural ICT education represent the vast and concentrated national efforts in integrating ICT across rural areas in this fast changing global situation.

DOI: 10.4018/978-1-4666-2071-1.ch010

INTRODUCTION

Information and communication technology (ICT) prevails worldwide. According to Rijsenbrij (1997), ICT can be viewed as technologies that enable human beings to communicate and cooperate with one another in the process of creating and exchanging knowledge. A concept, ICT, has evolved from information technology (IT) into a synthesized communication method and technique. The connotation of ICT, therefore, encompasses network systems designed for collaboration with various other systems by producing and sharing information (Herselman & Britton, 2002).

The United Nations Development Program (UNDP) built a research model that illustrates the relationship between technology and economic development in 2001. This model demonstrates that ICT plays a critical role in enhancing the capabilities of citizens in a country. Likewise, ICT has been acknowledged as a major factor in accelerating economic development (Grimes, 1992). Increased technological abilities conversely undergird the development of technological infrastructure in the society or community. In other words, technological development of a nation and skill development of the citizens contribute to each other, demonstrating a structural 'virtuous circle' (as opposed to vicious circle). However, not every part of the globe enjoys the recent technological heyday and its positive influences.

The asymmetric ICT development is observed both at the international and intra-national levels. The polarizing divide between urban and rural people, and the rich and poor, in many nations remains quite remarkable (Bridges, 2001; United Nations, 2000; World Bank, 1999). As some underdeveloped countries are undergoing worsening relative poverty, technologically undistributed areas, especially some rural communities, experience growing technological disparities in development and service. In particular, this intra-national imbalance in the realm of technology is salient in some developing countries where urbanization has accelerated in the last several decades.

In this regard, the case of South Korea adequately represents the socio-technological imbalance because its economic and structural contexts cause this societal problem to become more serious. South Korea is one of the developing countries that have experienced relatively fastest economic development in the last century. According to Statistics Korea, the gross national product (GNP) per capita of the country right after the Korean War in 1950 was merely $67. In contrast, the Bank of Korea (2008) reported that Gross National Income per capita in 2007 is $20,045.

However, this striking economic growth has also generated persistent side effects within the nation. Several major sociopolitical problems of the country can be posited as an increasingly aging population, economic inequality, severe political polarization, and developmental discrepancies among regions. As noted above, ICT advancement is considered a significant driving force for economic development in this information age, but at the same time, it has widened developmental gaps between urban and rural areas (Ministry for Food, Agriculture, Forest, and Fisheries, 2008). Particularly, the rural communities in South Korea face serious challenges as the country has gradually opened the agricultural market and extended the conclusion of Free Trade Agreement with more and more countries.

In order to cope with these vital social challenges, South Korea has put several affronting schemes such as 'The Five-year Master Plan for Rural ICT Promotion' in 2001 and 'The Countermeasure to Deal with Agricultural/ Rural Problems' in 2003. The focus of 'The Five-year Master Plan for Rural ICT Promotion' is on preparing rural people for adjusting new technological environments, including constructing agricultural database, building agricultural information networks, developing software for agricultural management, and reinforcing rural education to narrow the information discrepancy between rural and urban citizens. The government has invested ₩253,400,000,000 (about $220,000,000) for the establishment of this national plan. On the other hand, 'The Countermeasure to Deal with Agricultural/ Rural Problems' emphasizes professionalization of agricultural skills and enhancement of farming productivity. Therefore, these two distinctive national initiatives for rural ICT development are mutually and closely interconnected.

South Korea has witnessed fast-changing agricultural circumstances in the millennium, and thus acknowledged the increasing needs for high technologies, innovative knowledge and skills in the realm of agricultural business. ICT in rural areas is considered a key to successful development of these two national enterprises. In an attempt to bridge the ICT gap among regions, the government, along with various stakeholders (e.g., local governments, civic groups, education and research institutions etc), has so far put sustainable investments and concerted efforts into ICT infrastructure and services nationwide.

Among such interventions imposed by the government, there are educational enterprises driven by ICT. These are intended to develop rural people and communities' capacities and skills in ICT. Given the potential roles and functions of education, these national enterprises are significant areas for investigation. Initiatives based on sound educational principles play a critical role in accomplishing the goal of ICT establishment for rural development by serving as remedial methods for resolving problems embedded in rural communities, which have been generated in the context of political and social complication. The South Korean government anticipates that ICT-supported adult education for rural development will result in disseminating innovative agricultural knowledge. In addition, this type of education will lead to the advancement of agricultural competitiveness and help bring the rural populace together by means of electronic communication channels (e.g., farming web-pages, blogs, online communities, etc).

To this end, this chapter addresses ICT related skills and competencies for developing South Korean rural regions, especially agricultural areas. It presents ICT-supported adult education programs in several agricultural areas to illustrate how those enterprises have been structured and managed. These empirical cases are delineated on the basis of a legitimate conceptualization of adult ICT education for rural development by reviewing relevant literature. In so doing, the cases of South Korea illuminate the ways in which a national government's efforts and investments in exploiting ICT for rural development can be effectively deployed in a developing country as well as challenges and implications for further ICT integration.

Conceptualization of ICT in the Context of Adult Education for Rural Development

There are extraordinary opportunities for ICT to generate significant change for adults, especially for those who are less likely to be blessed with technological development. As a part of national efforts to respond to this change and its associated challenges, the South Korean government has set a rural ICT education plan and established attendant policies (The Ministry for Food, Agriculture, Forest, and Fisheries, 2008). The government has continually implemented this national initiative in collaboration with localized administrative units and other related institutions (e.g., universities, research institutions, civic groups etc.).

ICT education for rural populations in South Korea is based on the assumption that human capital and the power of knowledge have significant impacts on national development. According to the 1998/99 World Development Report announced by the World Bank (1999), the "recognition of the importance of knowledge has gained momentum, and there is a renewed impetus to integrate knowledge into countries' development strategy" (p. 21). The emphasis on ICT education for rural development by the South Korean government reflects the orientation of a national economic development strategy, more specifically its rural reinvigoration, derived from the human capital principle.

In order to draw a legitimate illustration of adult education initiatives with regard to application of ICT for rural development, it is necessary to examine literature pertinent to ICT education for adults as a notional intersection between ICT and adult education in order to construct a sound conceptual framework of the study. A host of recent ICT studies have paid more and more attention to the theories of learning and how learners can be supported by ICT (Watson, 2006). In those studies, ICT is viewed as more than a tool to develop individual capacities. Rather, ICT is referred to as a 'mindtool' (Jonassen, 2000). This metaphor is underpinned by a variety of contemporary adult learning theories such as situated learning theory (Lave & Wenger, 1991), transformational learning theory (Mezirow, 1991), and activity theory (Engeström, 1995), whose foci are on situatedness and mindfulness of human activity, providing a rationale to illuminate the relationship between ICT and adult education. Some of these learning theories have been internationally discussed over decades, highlighting aspects of human-technology relationships, human learning and development under ICT conditions, and so forth. As Watson (2006) maintains, even though some people argue that the ICT studies employing such learning theories do not provide sound evidence of effective learning outcomes, these theories have increasingly entered the discourse to support the use of ICT for adult learning.

Based on the preceding discussion of ICT for adult learning, one sees adult education as a mediating tool to develop capacities of the rural South Korean communities to resolve their persistent struggles. To maximize the potential of adult education, rural people, especially those with few learning opportunities and little motivation, should be guided to discover their potentials to develop in skills and knowledge through adequate education practice. In this way, all community members may be willing to embark in education for their development. Insofar as organizational context is concerned, adult education can only make an effective impact if it is viewed as learning that continues throughout life and especially if recognized as a prerequisite to the development and sustainability of knowledge economics (Swelyn, 2006). When the potential of adult education in imbuing people with skills and competencies to use ICT for their development is well appreciated, as in communities and workplaces, then those who have been capacitated should be in a good position to resolve persistent struggles of their development.

A definition of adult education adapted for use in this chapter is all educational activities that benefit the adult population. Forms of adult education or learning vary, and the nature of educational programs is dependent on the educational level and needs of target participants. Thus, adult education attains different meaning shaped by the context in which it is practiced. Despite the difficulties of making a generalized definition of adult education that encompasses all of these volatile and flexible features of education for/by/of adults, organizations such as United Nations Educational Scientific and Cultural Organization (UNESCO) have attempted to come up with a common definition. UNESCO's (1976) comprehensive definition of 'adult education' over the past thirty years bolstered the necessity for the extended use of ICT in adult education (Kwapong, 2007). Innovative learning methods which encompass science and technology have been recommended as a way to attain sustainability (UNESCO, 1976).

In the similar vein, The Food and Agricultural Organization (FAO)/ World Bank (2000) affirm ICT's roles within the context of adult education. Their research asserts that new ICT and a multi-technological approach can accommodate rural peoples' needs for increasing social, economic, and political participation. Therefore, ICT becomes an effective tool for empowering rural and peripheral people by providing them more extensive accessibility to advantageous information. Likewise, when educational activities are focused on promoting competencies and skills for using ICTs, the outcomes can move beyond merely active learning to technology-based development. Nevertheless, the research also illuminates that ICT education has its challenges that include a variety of social, political, and cultural effects on rural development, such as empowerment or enfranchisement of people, innovation of political systems, and development of local and regional cultures. These aspects have to be attended if the use of ICT is to be promoted and appreciated by all.

Studies on ICTs in the context of adult education are not confined to some internationally eminent organizations only. Several individual studies also highlight the significance of ICT in adult education. Holmes (2004), for example, views ICT as a tool to share information and foster communication, acknowledging that the notion of ICT involves not only new and innovative technological devices (e.g., World Wide Web, mobile phone, and satellites) but also conventional technologies (e.g., telephone, radio, television, and print media). The implication of Holmes' view of ICT for adult education is that both old and new technologies have to be considered. Adult education programs would thus become important in helping learners who are also responsible citizens to embrace both traditional and modern ICT methods. Namely, ICT gives a better chance to extend adult education practice and to enhance its quality.

In reality, educating the rural population for ICT-development demands a concerted effort of various stakeholders and interest groups. The success of such an education relies heavily on how well program providers combine, and often compromise, contrasting needs of a variety of stakeholders and interest groups. Tenywa et al. (2008) noted that ICT can significantly contribute to strengthening linkages among stakeholders in the agricultural sector. The authors underline expanding ICT needs for overcoming constraints by proposing a model for integrating ICT in agricultural education, research, and outreach. The 'value chain' to consolidate pre-existing mechanisms resolves the lack of information about agricultural markets and the loose interlink with education and research institutions. This model explicates the complexities and relationships among stakeholders.

Case studies from some developing countries specify the factors that affect ICT integration in rural areas. Beyene et al. (2007) discuss ICT-supported education for sustainable rural development in Ethiopia. They analyze interactive influences of technology, organization and society by examining technological infrastructures and educational organizations in the country. Consequently, they explicate how different levels of ICT integration take place in the process of ICT education. This study maintains that various e-learning related factors (e.g., system specification, modeling, simulation, knowledge-acquisition, problem-oriented learning strategies, workflow, and modern means of communication) should be integrated within an organizational and technological system. That is, ICT in adult education also demands a vital step in implementing each level of associated systems.

Unwin (2004) briefly provides an overview of one of the recent initiatives taken by British government to support ICT-based activities to help deliver the Millennium Development Goals of education in Africa. He argues that the project, *Imfundo*, still remains underdeveloped and it is not feasible to fully assess its contributions for several other years. However, the educational orientations articulated in the study give us a critical sense of how ICT-based educational activities can effectively work in developing countries. The most fruitful message from this study is that ICT-related educational projects can be successfully accomplished by incorporating multi-interests of stakeholders and balancing diverse subsystems.

Grimes (1992) explores ICT strategies of several countries for rural development, focusing on some policy issues with respect to ICT-driven rural development. He acknowledges that educational needs of the local community should be catered in deploying ICT initiatives. It is worth noting that policy-makers have to focus on the need for reducing both cost and skill barriers, so that people can enhance their competitiveness by exploiting ICT. He also points out the positive function of ICT for networking among people. Given various functions and potentials of education, this study implies that adult education can play a significant role in crushing these barriers ultimately for rural development.

ICT-related activities are a fundamental element of any rural development activity (Chapman & Slaymaker, 2002). Many rural areas are more often than not characterized as information-poor so that ICT provision has been a central constituent of rural development initiatives. The potential of ICT to improve currently inadequate educational services, and to ensure the access of rural people to reliable information about agricultural technologies and markets, illuminates the vital as well as urgent need for adult ICT education.

As the series of relevant studies verify, education has a crucial role in providing skills to rural communities or people for using ICT. Through appropriate education, rural people are able not only to acquire useful knowledge for their livelihood strategies, but also to strengthen their capacities for approaching higher-level knowledge that represents more sophisticated structures such as high-technical business knowledge, e-communication knowledge, etc. As a result of ICT education for adults, ICT manifests itself in its positive impacts in developing rural societies.

Likewise, ICT plays extensive as well as critical roles in adult education practice. Additionally, adult education that draws from ICTs has meaningful implications for South Korean rural development in terms of agricultural life, work, communication, and empowerment. Agricultural ICT education is geared toward enhancing effectiveness and quality of the agricultural works of rural people. Losing competitiveness in productivity has been recognized as a serious problem in rural areas; therefore, the South Korean government has chosen agricultural ICT education for rural innovation as an effective alternative to improving agricultural work and life for farmers.

Another important role that agricultural ICT education plays is facilitating communication and networking capabilities in both learning and work among rural people who have had relatively few opportunities to encounter ICT and realize its productive usage. As rural people develop communication and networking capacities, they are more easily empowered. Hence, widening educational participation via ICT automatically entails empowerment issues in rural communities. People will be able to have a better understanding of their communities and political agenda around the communities. Consequently, they will more extensively and conveniently assemble and combine their collective voices in regard to those social and political issues through ICT educational activities.

However, the success of educational ICT activities is heavily influenced by the ways in which program providers harness ICT through existing systems in rural communities. In other words, innovative ICT will be only successful as long as it is tailored to form an integrated knowledge system. Effective development of adult ICT education necessarily requires a primary focus on improving the professional development and contemplating circumstantial factors of farmers' livelihood. In this regard, the role and responsibility of ICT education should be underscored again. The fundamental goal of any educational practice is to bring about positive changes among people and organizations. For the purpose of successful ICT integration for rural development, education is the key (1) to incorporating pre-existing systems in which complexities with various cultures and interests are intertwined, and (2) eventually creating an effective and viable integrated rural community. From this point of view, exploring a variety of cases of ICT integration through education practice worldwide is productive both academically and practically.

Before elaborating ICT-supported adult education and its functional impacts on rural development, it is necessary to note that there is a conceptual ambiguity in positioning ICT in the context of adult education. When we attempt to adapt contingent roles or meanings of ICT within the context of reality and adult education, ICT can be considered as either merely an innovative method for delivering knowledge and building communication channels among participants, or a substantive topic of adult education programs such as e-business programs. To elaborate further, on the one hand, given the fact that ICT enables us to use a variety of electronic pedagogical tools such as diverse instructional software and programs, ICT in adult education can be regarded as an instrument as compared to other traditional instructional methods. On the other hand, a host of ICT education programs for adults in rural communities are designed along with ICT-centered topics. That is, the deliverables of these programs refer to increased knowledge and skills of participants in ICT-centered educational subjects. For instance, software utilization and e-business competencies are the themes and contents of these adult education programs. This notional distinction leads us to conceptualize ICT education within two differentiated epistemic ranges: a method and a topic. Since this study concerns adult education for rural development, literature and cases in this chapter will focus on not merely instrumental uses of ICT, but ICT-oriented educational programs that regard ICTs or ICT-centered subjects as their substantive topics in adult education.

AGRICULTURAL ICT EDUCATION INITIATED BY THE KOREAN GOVERNMENT

South Korea has faced complicated historical and sociopolitical dilemmas, which has led the South Korean government to adopt an economically development-oriented strategy. After the Korean War in 1950, both South and North Koreas experienced extreme poverty across most of their industries. In the beginning of armistice, North Korea was in better economic condition than South Korea because it had more useful natural resources. However, South Korea's national economic development strategy based on democracy and capitalism has gained an upper hand in GDP over North Korea's socialist economy.

However, drastic economic development of South Korea has caused the alienation of agricultural communities and rural people from balanced development across industries and regions. Alongside the rapid urbanization, many young people left rural areas for cities in order to seek high-paying jobs and to enjoy modern conveniences. See Figure 1.

More seriously, South Korea's economic development has been primarily driven by an export-oriented model since 1960s (Kang, 2002), and this economic situation made diverse industrialization strategies unavailable. The transformation of South Korea from an agricultural to an industrial society has resulted in the excessive influx of agricultural resources from abroad. Moreover, the recent diplomatic policy that supports the Free Trade Agreement (FTA) has also accelerated the alienation of rural communities from the balanced advancement. Because of the struggle with price and productivity competitiveness, rural communities have come to face a serious challenge in terms of agricultural livelihood. The agricultural income in rural communities has dramatically decreased as the structure of agricultural industry has been debilitated. In addition, along with the huge migration of workforce from rural to urban areas, the agricultural population has become older. This inner-communities' and intra-national transformation has generated a severe adversity for rural communities and people, and consequently has threatened rural livelihood.

Figure 1. The rural population of South Korea (thousands)

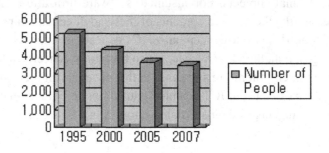

Source: Adapted from Rural ICT Education
(Korean Ministry for Food, Agriculture, Forestry, and Fisheries, 2008)

However, despite the consistent decreasing population in rural areas, the number of large-scale agricultural lands is paradoxically increasing. This increase is attributed to a lower population in rural areas and the introduction of innovative tillage techniques, whereas this phenomenon runs opposite to the one observed in the 1990s. However, obvious resistance to new technology, especially among old people, has been observed across most rural areas in the country. Hence, it is imperative for the South Korean government to seek an adequate rural development strategy to cope with these challenges. Therefore, developing a professional agricultural workforce has been conceived of as central to resolving the aforementioned disoriented dilemmas in South Korean rural areas.

In dealing with rural problems, the government chose to promote ICT for rural communities. In 2001 'The Bridging Information Disparity Act' was legislated, and 'The Five-year Master Plan for Rural ICT Promotion' was established. Due to concentrated governmental efforts, the information disparity between rural and urban areas has gradually narrowed. Nevertheless, the informational gap of farmers and fishermen still remains more considerable than those of the other groups in exclusion. Such information disparity persists as an obstacle to the success of rural development. See Table 1.

The government has made arduous efforts to bridge the informational disparity by initiating institutional interventions. These efforts have been executed on the basis of several associated laws and policies. A series of governmental initiatives aim to promote ICT education in rural areas, and to assimilate the informational gap by facilitating more rural people to participate in educational activities such as using internet and making documents by computer. In addition, the government

Table 1. The disparity of information in South Korean communities

Groups	2004		2006		2007		Compare to last year (point)
	Gap index (point)	Compared level (%)	Gap index (point))	Compared level (%)	Gap index (point)	Compared level (%)	
The disabled	42.5	57.5	26.1	73.9	24.0	76.0	2.1↓
The low-income bracket	44.4	55.6	27.0	73.0	24.5	75.5	2.5↓
Farmers and fishermen	66.2	33.8	50.2	49.8	45.4	54.6	4.8↓
The old	59.1	40.9	41.6	58.4	37.4	62.6	4.2↓
Average	55.0	45.0	38.0	62.0	34.1	65.9	3.9↓

Source: Korea National Information Association (2008)

provides specialized programs for growing ICT farmers who can utilize the digital information for agricultural business, manage the history of productions, control electronic commercial transactions, and making own home (web) pages. Also, this enterprise intends to extend online communication channels in rural communities. Many relevant local organizations (e.g., local agricultural associations, agricultural colleges, regional agricultural centers, special agencies for ICT education, etc.) support these national efforts.

As a result, ICT education has become more and more prevalent in many South Korean rural regions. A plethora of rural people have participated in ICT education programs in the nation. Table 2 shows that according to Ministry for Food, Agriculture, Forestry, and Fisheries (2008), the number of those who have experienced ICT education marks 17.6%. Among rural people who have experienced ICT education programs, 70.8% intend to register other ICT programs. On the contrary, only 39.0% of those who haven't experienced the program answered they will. These statistics reveal that the governmental efforts have motivated people to participate in ICT educational activities.

These governmental attempts produce both successful outcomes and future challenges for the national enterprises in terms of ICT infrastructure and utilization for rural development. On the one hand, they have contributed to improving life quality of agricultural people and assimilating the informational discrepancy between rural and urban areas. Also, educational activities sparks rural people's learning needs for developing ICT capacities. Through participating in these activities, a lot

Table 2. Actual information gap between urban and rural areas in 2007

	Persons experienced		Persons not-experienced	
	Rate	Intention to re-register	Rate	Intention to re-register
Percentage (%)	17.6	70.8	82.4	39.0

Source: Adapted from Korea Agency for Digital Opportunity and Promotion (2008)

of rural people have experienced the benefits of ICT in their agricultural lives, and this has consequently resulted in more productive agricultural workforce who can continuously develop their ICT capacities and produce additional values from the increased abilities. Also the Figure 2 indicates the informational disparity between the rural and urban has actually assimilated.

On the other hand, this centralized model has failed to diversify programs in which more people can engage in. Therefore, Ministry for Food, Agriculture, Forestry, and Fisheries (2008) announced three future challenges in regard to ICT education for rural development.

Firstly, educational programs for developing ICT capacities among rural peoples disregard various levels of learners. ICT in educational activities have a variety of meanings as discussed above, and adult learners have diverse needs for joining ICT education programs. Thus, needs analysis should be emphasized as a prerequisite to designing those education programs. However, current ICT education programs are chiefly designed and driven by the government, and this top-down model has largely excluded learners' voices in constructing the ICT education system. To be more inclusive, and consequently effective, ICT education should reflect more

Figure 2. Information disparity rates (%)

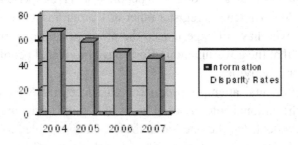

Source: Adapted from Rural ICT Education
(Korean Ministry for Food, Agriculture, Forestry, and Fisheries, 2008)

individual needs that can be characterized as grass-root and pragmatic participation in addition to national needs for revitalizing rural communities and growing productive agricultural workforce.

Secondly, in a line with the contents of the program, instructional methods should also become more sensitive to rural people's needs. A vast of resistance among old, peripheral people arises when they first encounter ICT-driven or -focused programs. Therefore, it is imperative to cope with this resistance by optimizing pedagogical methods. Few ICT education program-providers in South Korea have attempted to take this resistance into consideration so as not to fail to achieve the best performance. To this end, face-to-face programs and blended (online and offline) programs are recommendable to reduce the resistance, and subsequently to obtain the best results from agricultural ICT education programs.

Thirdly, some people problematize the practicality of program outcomes. In the case of South Korean rural ICT education, most of participants do not have enough motives to participate in the programs by themselves. This passive participation results from the lack of connection between a series of programs. That is, most programs apply a uniform standard to participants, neglecting various learners' levels. This negative aspect of the programs directly or indirectly affects the mechanism of processes and outcomes within the programs. Therefore, in developing ICT programs, this mechanism should be seriously revisited by program providers.

How to evaluate or assess processes and outcomes of programs is always of significant interest to stakeholders. Clearly, it is continuous evaluations such as monitoring programs and policy analysis that enable the government and related institutions to make adequate decisions about rural ICT education. Both formative and summative evaluation models should be tailored with respect to cultural and sociopolitical particularities of a region. Also, these institutions have to collaborate with each other in building own evaluation system.

Cases of Agricultural ICT Education Programs in Three Rural Areas

Since 1998, the Korean Ministry for Food, Agriculture, Forest, and Fisheries in collaboration with the Korean Information Centers for Agriculture and Fisheries (AFFIC) have engaged in various types of educational enterprises geared toward narrowing the informational gap between rural and urban areas. They expect that, through this project, rural people can have more opportunities to access useful information, and effectively utilize it to establish their competiveness in agricultural productivity, which can eventually lead them to create high-value products. This section concretely illustrates several ICT education programs in some rural regions of South Korea, highlighting the distinctive features of each program and its conspicuous process or outcome.

The Blended ICT Education Program in Jinju

The Jinju city, located in the south coast, has developed various agricultural ICT education programs for its citizens. These programs, mostly funded by the national and local government, are designed for the pursuit of improving farmers' motivation for engaging in ICT activities. The themes of these agricultural ICT education programs are categorized by their foci: living-focused and farming-focused. The contents of programs include not only practical farming skills, but also knowledge relevant to indigenous culture and communication for lively agricultural life.

Farmers in Jinju also have opportunities to develop their knowledge and skills in relation to scientific agricultural business by attending these programs. Such programs are designed for farmers to diagnose and identify their own problems and educational needs, and subsequently to find adequate resolutions for themselves. Furthermore, those who have limited or even no knowledge about ICT can improve their ICT abilities by practicing basic computer skills through a series of introductory courses. Among those who possess relatively development ICT skills, the technological level of some higher-level ICT programs such as the Good Agricultural Products, Farm-to-Table, and Standardized Account Management programs is nearly tantamount to the programs in agriculturally advanced countries.

Among various types of instructional design for ICT education, Jinju has adapted a blended (combining online and offline strategies for the instruction) education program, entitled 'the Product History Management program.' Participants in this program are selected as leading farmers whose primary products are strawberries and rice. Its blended strategy aims at advancing the program by reducing learners' resistance to ICT. On the one hand, online courses provide rural people more chances to participate in educational activities, namely more availability, since learners do not always want to participate in on-site education programs due to their busy farming business. Through this online course, learners can also get used to computer use. Along with online instructions, it is also necessary to offer adequate offline educational services in order to improve their motivation and commitment to the ICT education. Particularly, for those who are not familiar with online educational environments, it is critical to facilitate their engagement in this ICT education by providing on-time and direct interventions, such as visiting homes, collective classes and individual counseling.

This blended ICT education program is constructed on the basis of users' customization balancing the online instructions and offline, on-site educational activities. Interestingly, the roles of on-site educational activities vary according to knowledge and skill levels of participants. These activities play a role in instilling courage and motivation into learners as well as enforcing learners to carry on educational activities through this ICT program. ICT education programs designed solely with online methods cause high drop-out rates, especially among ICT strangers such as most of old rural people in Jinju. Therefore, the city has strived to reduce drop-out rates by means of blending online and offline strategies for this ICT program.

The city has two main foci on implementing this ICT education program. First, blended strategy consists of collective, on-site education, and subsequently complementary online instruction. In the beginning, people attend the on-site Standardized Account Management program for twenty hours. The actual practice for using computer is a part of this collective education activity. Ten-hour online instructions involve the Good Agricultural Products and Farm-to-Table programs designed on the emphasis of developing learners' expertise in tracing and managing farm products history.

Second, the local government collaborates with agricultural information centers located in each district for achieving the goal of this program. The local agricultural information centers have been established across rural areas of South Korea for the purpose of developing rural people's ICT capabilities. Therefore, the collaboration between local governments and individual information centers is imperative for the success of every ICT education program. In the case of the Jinju's blended program, each informational center significantly functions as an agency to promote or implement ICT education programs by advertising the positive effects of program, choosing participants, providing instructors, and developing ICT education programs.

However, this program also entails several practical problems. First of all, the wide range of participants' ages hinders program providers from efficiently implementing the program due to a big gap among learners' technological skills. Those who have less ICT capabilities are more likely to dropout during the program. This problem raises the need for developing diversified programs in line with different levels of learners' technological skills. Second of all, even though much investment has been put in the Korean rural areas by the national government, obsolete infrastructure on the education site prevents the program from being successful.

Recent technological development has been faster than ever so that it has produced a lot of new knowledge and skills accompanying with innovative techniques. Even if up-to-date information is delivered through ICT education program, most computers and other technological equipments in South Korean rural areas have become superannuated. Consequently, people cannot successfully practice to develop expected knowledge and skills. Likewise, this problem reveals again that technological infrastructure is a critical precondition of, and has a significant part in deploying national ICT education strategies. The last problem arises due to the lack of capable ICT instructors who have trained for rural ICT education. In every class, there is only one assistant instructor available for about fifteen participants, and most of them have expertise in neither adult education nor community development, but in ICT techniques. Therefore, programs are not managed in a competent manner due to the lack of their experiences in adult ICT education and agricultural situations of the region.

The ultimate goal of the Jinju's Product History Management program is to procure customers' reliability by means of enhancing farmers' capabilities to effectively utilize the product history management system. This expectedly sparks reinvigoration of the community through improving price and quality competitiveness of farming products. The blended approach to the ICT education has enhanced learners' satisfaction, but the program fails to lead people to join grass-roots and self-motivated educational activities whereby they can adeptly exploit ICT.

The Creating-Farming-Webpage Program in Kyungsan

In 2009, Kyungsan, a city in North Kyongsang province (the southeast part of the Korean peninsula), has developed several ICT education programs for its citizens such as the e-business program, ubiquitous ICT program, and creating-farming-webpage program. These programs are designed and built based on the educational needs analysis of the community, which has been conducted during several years. Among those ICT education programs, the creating-farming-webpage education program, whose goal is to develop the citizens' ICT abilities to create and manage their own farming-webpage for product promotion and electronic transactions, is one the most people gave preference to. This program targets farmers who are willing to develop individual farming webpage so as to reduce unnecessary mediating transactional processes. Since this program deals with high-leveled knowledge and skills, it demands at least a certain level of basic skills of participants in using computer.

Differently put, unlike the other ICT education programs that accommodate various levels of participants, this program specifies the minimum level of ICT ability to apply for participation. Therefore, target participants are limited as those who possess more than basic computer skills and have already taken basic ICT courses. At the same time, participants should be highly encouraged to improve their skills to create their own webpage. Applicants can register for the program by phone or visit, and this program accommodates fifteen people in the order of arrival. This program goes on for six days (thirty one hours in total).

The structure of farming transaction in South Korea has enormously transformed alongside the technological development. Many farmers are now directly selling their products to customers by using online transaction. In this regard, the expected outcomes of this program are to develop participants' skills for creating and managing their effective farming webpage, and thus they can promote high quality agricultural products online and utilize electronic transaction. Farming webpage contributes to enhancing agricultural price competitiveness by reducing the accruing costs caused by multiple transactions throughout many middlemen.

However, a practical problem can be pointed out in terms of the deficit of instrumental availability. For constructing an attractive webpage, various innovative computer programs and software are needed. Even if up-to-date hardware was provided for this ICT education program, learners could not help but depend on instructors to get the latest software needed to create farming webpage. Due to the high price of software, program providers are not able to cater with all newest software and computer programs people need. Therefore, they need to hit on a clever idea to meet this need such as cooperating with the regional agricultural information centers or other relevant institutions that possess innovative devices and software.

The program consists of a series of instructions for delivering useful skills and knowledge about farming webpage. For example, there are some fundamental functions of farming webpage in order to promote products and use electronic transaction. Therefore, in the beginning of the program, participants learn such fundamental factors that characterize farming webpage. And then they practice with computers in a step-by-step way, from planning through designing to developing a webpage. A series of these steps should entail systematic and organized approaches. Once people have clear and creative schemes, they practice to use Hyper Text Markup Language (HTML). They also learn how to employ graphic designing software such as the Photoshop during this program.

The noticeable feature of the Kyungsan's Creating-Farming-Webpage program is ascribed to its evaluation system. The local agricultural information center takes responsibility to assess the effectiveness of the program in terms of learners' satisfaction and following performance. At the end of the program, participants are asked to complete brief questionnaires for measuring their satisfaction. Even though the small size of the sample hardly represents statistical significance of the result, learners' satisfaction with the 2009 program (See Table 3) presents the high satisfaction of participants.

The information center also counts the number of web pages that actually used for their farming business after the program, which reveals overall performance of the program participants. Moreover, some of the web pages are put up on the program blog to represent productive outcomes of the program. However, the only summative form of evaluation for this program scarcely devotes to enhancing the

Table 3. Learners' satisfaction on the Creating-Farming-Webpage education program

Evaluation Items	Excellent	Good	Fair	Not good	Poor
Instructor qualification	9	9	3	0	0
Program management pattern	9	8	4	1	0
Service of the institution and staffs	11	7	3	0	0
Educational environments & equipments	16	4	1	0	0
The number of class times and duration	10	6	2	3	0
The number of participants	12	9	0	0	0

Source: Adapted from the information provided by the Kyungsan Agricultural Information Center (2009)

quality of the program. How to effectively conduct formative evaluation remains as a challenge of this ICT education program. By adapting various formative evaluation models such as monitoring and process evaluation models, the effects before, during, and after the program are comprehensively measured and analyzed.

The Kyungsan's Creating-Farming-Webpage program manifests itself in its follow-up activities. After people complete the program, the program provider guides people to manipulate what they have learned through the program. In addition, some participants have opportunities to collaborate with local universities for further improving their ICT knowledge and skills. Most participants are also continually encouraged to participate in further related ICT education programs by online promotion materials.

The Female Web Account Management Program in Yesan

Yesan, a city in South Chungcheng (the Middle West of South Korea), has developed several ICT education programs for corresponding with various farmers' needs. Such programs encompass not only basic computer skills but also knowledge and techniques for electronic farming business. A notable effort that Yesan has exerted is in establishing a female ICT education program, the web-account management program. The more do female population run farming business in Yesan, the more has the city witnessed the needs for adult ICT education for this population. As the overall female population in rural areas of South Korea increases, it is considered significant to raise competitive female workforce in rural areas. Accordingly, the Yesan's female education program represents how gender issues are dealt with in agricultural ICT education in South Korea.

Yesan provides female farmers the web-account management program for the purpose of establishing capable female workforce in the region. The recent transformation of women's social roles in South Korea has impacted rural areas. Given the modern Korean history largely influenced by Confucian that had emphasized the traditional role of women as being households, this social transformation appears salient. Female workforce is now considered a driver of economic growth of the country. However, in contrast to urban women, the social role of rural women had been underdeveloped in terms of their potentials as being more active and productive workforce beyond households until a recent date. However, fast growing female population in rural areas has transformed the social role of rural women, and thus many female farmers have recently engaged in their own farming business. Under this circumstance, the needs for developing farming business skills among female farmers naturally become prominent in most rural areas.

The web-account management program of Yesan intends to develop farming business knowledge and skills of female farmers. The ultimate goal of this program is to advance female farming business by the effective management of web-account. In order to be skillful at utilizing web-account, participants exercise several statistics programs such as the Microsoft Excel 2007. This program accommodates every level of female farmers, from ICT beginners to adepts. Throughout the program, participants experience a standardized agricultural account management program and well-executed samples whereby they can get familiar with various electronic accounting programs. Yesan expects this program will make an important contribution to the income of farm households. Also, female participants have more chance to build network among community members by joining this educational practice.

The most distinctive need of female farmers in Yesan has been identified as creating and managing their own blogs to promote their products. Therefore, instructors in this program relate the web-account management skills to managing farming blogs. Also, instructors give adequate assignments to participants in every class to enhance their commitment to the program. As a result, participants reveal more interests and deeply engaged in this program. A lot of productive outcomes from the program advance participants' ICT attitudes, and thus contribute to reinforcing the agricultural competitiveness in the region (see Figure 3).

However, several practical problems have also emerged from the program. Since most participants prefer evening classes to day classes to avoid losing working time, it appears difficult to provide quality program instructors. This problem can be diagnosed as a conflict of different groups of stakeholders' needs. The Yesan city needs to establish a quality instructor pool for readily allocating adequate instructors. The varying levels of participants' readiness can also be pointed out as a problem. Lower-leveled participants demand complementary programs such as face-to-face tutoring.

After the completion of the program, the program providing institution opens an online blog to facilitate networking among participants. Also, it offered further opportunities to participate in other subsequent programs. The interconnection among a series of ICT education programs is crucial to accomplish the expected outcomes of the Yesan's educational enterprise.

Figure 3. The female Web-management program in Yesan

* This picture was obtained with permission from Yesan agricultural information center in Sep, 2009.

IMPLICATIONS OF KOREAN CASES FOR RURAL ICT INTEGRATION AND DEVELOPMENT

As global economy has advanced, ICT dramatically diverts a host of resources into networking and digital economy. In this globalized world, it is a worldwide phenomenon that more and more countries take the ICT-based strategy for national economic development. However, we have witnessed that ICT has been unsuccessfully integrated to pre-existing systems for various reasons in some rural areas. Such struggles are due to not only characters of agricultural industry that rarely fit into ICT but also preset circumstances or systems in rural areas that preclude harmonious ICT integration into rural community and people. The potential of educational enterprises for ICT integration, in this respect, draws significant attention to the policy makers.

Contemporary trends of adult ICT education in rural areas are concerned with indigenous and people-centered approaches as opposed to exogenous and institution-centered approaches of the past. However, in some developing countries, the governmental endeavors in ICT establishment for rural development necessarily require a centralized model to ameliorate pre-existing barriers such as resistance of adult population to ICT learning and lack of ICT infrastructures. A diverse of benefits from ICT integration into rural industry appears to be less possible unless these obstacles are adequately dealt with at the national level.

The South Korean cases of agricultural ICT education represent the vast and concentrated national efforts in integrating ICT across rural areas in this fast changing global situation. As the rural alienation was pointed out as a serious problem for economic development within the nation, the South Korean government has been deploying centralized initiatives for ICT development in rural areas since the end of the twenty century. And the educational enterprises are central in this South Korea's rural development strategy. The roles and functions of adult education, therefore, are salient in rural development strategies in terms of advancing people's skills and knowledge as well as constructing quality agricultural system. In this respect, the South Korea's cases reveal systematic national initiatives in order to demonstrate important roles of adult ICT education.

The seriousness of the informational discrepancy between rural and urban areas should be bold because it worsens the economic gap across regions at the intra-national level, which consequently has negative impacts on the whole and sound national development as well as social integration. The balance of developmental levels within a country, especially some developing countries, requires contemplating considerations of policy makers. Particularly in this knowledge- and information-based society, narrowing information gaps between rural and urban regions remains a persistent problem in many countries. Without timely proper and effective interventions by governments, this gap must be worsening rather than narrowing. To this end, the potentials of education are seriously conceived of and adequately reflected in national rural development tactics between politicians. Otherwise, ICT deteriorates the alienation of rural communities and people. However, if the ICT education system is well-established in rural communities, the agricultural competitiveness would be enhanced so that the nation would be able to achieve balanced national development.

REFERENCES

Ashley, C., & Maxwell, S. (2001). Rethinking rural development. *Development Policy Review, 19*(4), 395–425. doi:10.1111/1467-7679.00141

Beyene, B., Möller, P. F., & Wittmann, J. (2007). *Introducing ICT supported education for sustainable rural development in Ethiopia.* 2007 Summer Computer Simulation International Conference. San Diego, CA: International Society for Computer Simulation.

Chapman, R., & Slaymaker, T. (2002). *ICTs and rural development: Review of the literature, current interventions and opportunities for action.* Overseas Development Institute, Working Paper No. 192.

Engström, Y. (1995). Innovative organisational learning in medical and legal settings. In Martin, L., Nelson, K., & Tobach, E. (Eds.), *Theory and practice of doing and knowing*. Cambridge, UK: Cambridge University Press. doi:10.1017/CBO9780511896828.016

European Commission. (2005). *EU report on millennium development goals 2000-2004*. Brussels, Belgium: Directorate-General Development.

Food and Agricultural Organization/ World Bank. (2000). *Agricultural knowledge and information systems: Strategic vision and principles*. Rome, Italy: FAO/ World Bank.

Grimes, S. (1992). Exploiting information and communication technologies for rural development. *Journal of Rural Studies*, *8*(3), 269–278. doi:10.1016/0743-0167(92)90004-P

Herselman, M., & Britton, K. (2002). Analyzing the role of ICT in bridging the digital divide amongst learners. *South African Journal of Education*, *22*(4), 270–274.

Holmes, R. (2004). *Advancing rural women's empowerment: Information and communication technologies (ICTs) in the service of good governance, democratic practice and development for rural women in Africa*. Women's Net Resource Paper. Retrieved from http://womensnet.org.za/dimitra_conference/papers.shtml

Jonassen, D. H. (2000). *Computers as mindtools for schools: Engaging critical thinking*. Ohio: Prentice Hall.

Kang, K. J. (2002). A study on the status and the direction of agricultural information technology workforce development in Korea. *Journal of Korean Agricultural Education*, *34*(2), 87–98.

Kwapong, O. A. (2007). Problems of policy formulation and implementation: The case of ICT use in rural women's empowerment in Ghana. *International Journal of Educational Development*, *3*(2). Retrieved from http://ijedict.dec.uwi.edu/view-article.php?id=324&layout=html

Lave, J., & Wenger, E. (1991). *Situated learning: Legitimate peripheral participation*. Cambridge, UK: Cambridge University Press. doi:10.1017/CBO9780511815355

Mezirow, J. (1991). *Transformative dimensions of adult learning*. San Francisco, CA: Jossy-Bass.

Ministry for Food. Agriculture, Forest, and Fisheries. (2008). *The 2009 master plan for agricultural ICT education*. Retrieved from http://jinlae.com/Jinlae/area_04.php?ptype=view&code=area_04&idx=1254

Rijsenbrij, D. B. B. (1997). *The design, development and deployment of ICT systems in the 21st century.* Retrieved from http://www.cs.vu.nl/~daan/progx/eng/contents.htm

Swelyn, N. (2006). ICT in adult education: Defining the territory. In OECD (Ed.), *ICT and learning: Supporting out-of-school youth and adults* (pp. 13–42). Paris, France: OECD.

Tenywa, M. T., Fungo, B., Tumusiime, F., Bekunda, M., Niuitengeka, M., Nakanyike-Musisi, B., et al. (2008). *ICT in agricultural education, research, and outreach in Uganda.* Presented at World Conference on Agricultural Information and IT, Tokyo University of Agriculture, Tokyo, Japan.

The Bank of Korea. (2008). *Quarterly national accounts.* Retrieved on November, 2009 from http://www.kosis.kr/search/totalSearch2.jsp

The Bridges Network. (2001). *Spanning the digital divide: Understanding and tackling the issues.* Retrieved from www.bridges.org/spanning/report.html

United Nations. (2000). *Report of the high-level panel on information and communication technology.* New York, 17-20 April, 2000, United Nations.

United Nations Development Program. (2001). *Making technologies work for human development. Human Development Report 2001.* Washington, DC: Author.

United Nations Development Program, and UNESCO. (1976). *The experimental world literacy program: A critical assessment.* Paris, France: UNESCO Press.

Unwin, T. (2004). ICT & education in Africa: Partnership, practice & knowledge sharing. *Review of African Political Economy, 31*(99), 150–160.

Watson, D. (2006). Understanding the relationship between ICT and education means exploring innovation and change. *Education and Information Technologies, 11*(3), 199–216. doi:10.1007/s10639-006-9016-2

World Bank. (1999). *Knowledge for development: World Development Report 1998-99.* Oxford, UK: Oxford University Press.

Chapter 11

ICTs for Improved Service Delivery:
A Case of Smart Switch Card of the Social Safety Nets Programs in Botswana

Keba Hulela
Bostwana College of Agriculture, Botswana

EXECUTIVE SUMMARY

In Botswana the use of Information and Communication Technology (ICT) smart switch card system, an offshoot of the Universal Electronic Payment System (UEPS), was recently introduced. It is a worldwide communication device that is digital in providing information to the users. In Botswana, it serves to administer food and basic needs offered to the vulnerable people as one of the pillars of development in terms of catering for the needy. Furthermore, it is used to empower orphans, destitute, and HIV/AIDS home-based patients in the Social Safety Nets programs, replacing all the other strategies that were used previously. The previous program was a manual system whereby beneficiaries were getting their social grants through lining up at their district councils' office doorstep for attendants to use the roll call. The old system demanded commercial businesses to tender for supply of items to the vulnerable population, but it posed some challenges and frustrations to beneficiaries and the government.

DOI: 10.4018/978-1-4666-2071-1.ch011

BACKGROUND

The administration of SSN using ICT by the government of Botswana is a deliberate plan towards achieving the goals aligned to social justice and poverty reduction for social and economic development. The UEPS developed by NET 1 Technologies Inc. is used internationally to enhance the management and administration of Social Safety Nets (SSN). This form of ICT was explicitly selected for Botswana's program to counterbalance the challenges and further empower beneficiaries to access their basic needs baskets through the card. The card works equally and more like the banking system, sparing patients long drives and walking to obtain their social needs and medication. It also facilitates narrowing of the gap between the poor and the rich thus promoting equity in the society.

The adoption of ICT smart switch cards in Botswana as a new strategy is to offset the socio-economic constraints experienced by the vulnerable people in the society. This chapter provides background of UEPS ICT smart switch card, setting-the-stage, project overview, challenges, and further readings on similar themes related to ICT usage in the social programmes.

The Universal Electronic Payment system (UEPS) is an Information and Communication Technology (ICT) that was developed by NET 1 Technologies Inc International. Smart switch card is an offshoot of UEPS technology. The card is now used in several countries worldwide particularly developing nations. For example, the technology can be found in South Africa, Nigeria, Tanzania, Namibia, Vietnam, Columbia, the Netherlands, Luxembourg, and the USA.

In Botswana, the NET 1 technologies an international organization has made a joint venture with Capricorn Investment Holdings (PTY) Limited to form a company named Smart Switch Card Botswana in 2006. The goal of the new company is to provide citizens with information and communication technology (ICT), namely, smart card. The technology is to help people access financial services, enable the purchasing of basic needs by the less privileged people. Its top management structure comprises of the director and the managing directors who are citizens of Botswana.

The smart switch card technology was introduced in Botswana in 2008 as a piloting project by the government through the Ministry of Local Government, Department of Social Services. The government saw the need to enhance the administration of social safety nets to the vulnerable people through the use of electronic card. According to the Department of Social Services of the Ministry of Local Government, currently, there are 96,000 poor people nationwide, approximately 5.6 percent of Botswana's 1.7 millions people who are categorized as destitute, orphans and home-based patients. These are the "marginalized" people who exist due to several social factors in the society including the scourge of HIV/AIDS. The ICT smart switch card provides these vulnerable people with the means to access their basic needs through a quicker means like any other person in the society. The card also provides the government with means to obtain relevant data about distribution of basic needs to beneficiaries.

Smart Switch Card Botswana (2007) is suitable for use in different programs including healthcare, banking, pension programs, micro-finance, insurance and transportation programs. Smart switch Card Botswana (2007) further stated that, this form of technology is used to provide affordable banking solutions for the underprivileged population in the society. It provides technologies that are within the means (inexpensive), helpful and effective as well as user-friendly to the poor.

Setting the Stage

The prevailing circumstances of the HIV/AIDS epidemic, the incessant droughts and the consequent poverty and poor livelihoods in Botswana stress the need for digital technology intervention in order to sustain the welfare of the populace in the country. HIV/AIDS is a universal social problem taking its turn as the most dreadful disease that has adverse effect on social welfare of many people worldwide (World Health Organization, 2009; Mawar, Sahay, Pandit & Mahajan (2005).). As a result of HIV/AIDS problems, at the end of 2007, an estimated 22 million adults and children were living with HIV in sub-Saharan Africa (Global facts and Figures, 2008). During the same year, the HIV statistic for sub-Saharan Africa revealed that approximately 1.5 million Africans died from AIDS. The epidemic has left behind some 116 million orphans in the continent. In Botswana, the impact of the HIV is felt as people living with HIV/AIDS are estimated at 300,000; Adults of 15-49 olds; rate 23.9%; Women with HIV/AIDS 170,000; Children with HIV/AIDS 15,000; AIDS deaths 11,000 and orphans due to AIDS, 95,000 (Nicodim Liliana and Utureanu Simona Luize, 2009).

According to Reynolds (2007), According to Casale & Whiteside. (March 2006), HIV/AIDS leads to destruction of social capital, weakening of the socio-economic institutions and deepening poverty among the people in a society. Many farmers appear to be experiencing reduction in labour quality and quantity as a direct result of HIV/AIDS pandemic. A compounding factor is that infection rates are higher among women, who account for as much as 70 percent of the agricultural labour force and 80 percentage food productions in some developing countries (FAO, 1997). Actually, FAO (2006; 2008) revealed that increased morbidity and mortality due to HIV/AIDS often lead to medical and funeral costs. As morbidity increases, an increasing number of labour is diverted to care for the sick member of the family and AIDS related matters, including care of the patients and funeral duties. Additional contact hours are lost due to staff attrition and time spent attending funerals. The foregoing sets the stage for the introduction of the ICT smart switch card on social safety nets programs to cater for the orphans, destitute, as well as HIV/AIDS infected home-based patients. The Smart switch card system replaces the manual programmes whereby beneficiaries were getting their social grants through lining up at the council's office.

PROCESSES IN IMPLEMENTING THE ICT CARD

Three processes were followed in the implementation of the electronic smart card; identification of beneficiaries, electronic registration and the actual usage of the smart switch card. The processes are discussed in the subsequent sub headings.

Identification of Beneficiaries

The first process involves identification of beneficiaries (Figure 1). Several steps are followed to identify beneficiaries. In Figure 1, several stakeholders play one or more roles in making the electronic card system works. The government in this case plays the leadership role in the program. It occupies the highest position as mandated to address the policy on poverty reduction and social justice. It also plays the supervisory role of stipulating principles and criteria adopted by the district councils. On the other hand, the district councils are directly involved through identification of the beneficiaries, assessing their social, economic, health status, lifestyle and other demographic characteristic. They make recommendations as per the criteria set by the government through ministries of Local Government and Finance Development and Planning. The district councils, located in different parts of the country are given the mandate by the central government to form committees that work on the processes of adopting smart switch card in social safety nets programmes.

Figure 1 also shows the formal organizational chart on how the key players interact in the process of identifying beneficiaries. It helps illustrate that the district Councils are directly involved to ensure that the applicants are registered and benefit from the program. Stakeholders such as parent/guardian, chiefs, and village development committees, health centres serve important roles as they are mandated to ensure that beneficiaries are identified and listed accordingly. Close relatives, friends and others in the community are deemed the first people to notice the needy and marginalized people. Local authorities are informed of the existence of marginalized people. The list is obtained from each village to the local district council office where it is further assessed using the criteria available in the office. The list is then submitted to the council authority to undergo a similar scrutiny at a district council committee which will recommend to the local government Social Service department for inclusion in the final list of beneficiaries.

Figure 1. Process of identifying beneficiaries

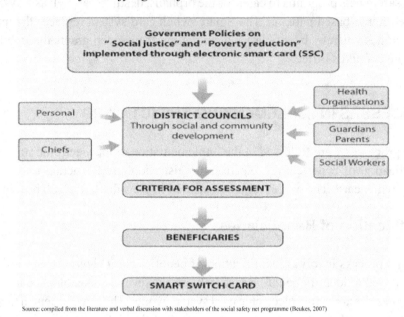

Source: compiled from the literature and verbal discussion with stakeholders of the social safety net programme (Beukes, 2007)

Electronic Registration

The second process in the implementation of the electronic card in the Botswana's social safety nets (SSN) programmes involves entering stakeholders' names into the computer database software to be managed electronically. Figure 2 shows steps followed to enter names of both beneficiaries and officials of Social Services Department of the Ministry of Local Government. These stakeholders are given pin numbers for operation purposes. All stakeholders in the project will have their names included in the system.

Usage of the ICT by Beneficiaries

Upon arrival at the Point of Sale (POS), the beneficiaries report to the management and hand over the Smart card indicating their wish to purchase items from the merchant. Figure 3 shows the steps followed to obtain the goods and services purchased from the merchant (Beukes 2007).

Figure 2. Steps in electronic registration

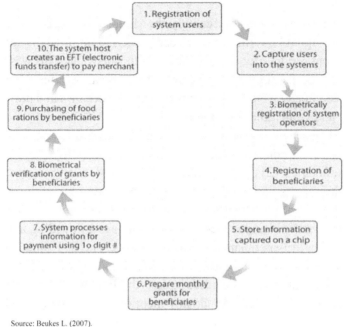

Source: Beukes L.. (2007).

Figure 3. Steps

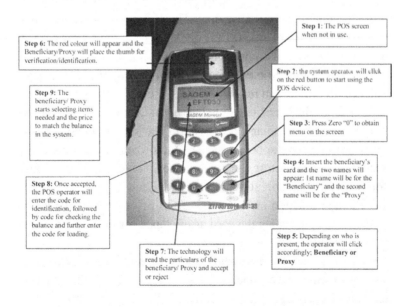

DESCRIPTION OF THE SMART SWITCH CARD

At the beginning of the twenty-first century, the Ministry of Local Government found it fit to use the digital ICT Smart Switch card (SSC) to improve the administration and management services for social safety nets in Botswana. This was a deliberate plan to improve service delivery and the lives of beneficiaries. Smart Card Botswana, a local based company won the government tender to perform and provide services to the needy and vulnerable community.

The use of smart card system was triggered by several factors which included among others; (1) the congestion of serving points during delivery of food and basic needs to beneficiaries, (2) the distribution of unhygienic food by some local retailers, (3) regular reports on unavailability of products by some of the suppliers, (4) inconsistency and poor distribution of food to the beneficiaries. Other challenges of the manual system included lack of proper database, travelling long distances, and long queuing of beneficiaries at serving points. The ICT Smart Switch Card (SSC) is critical to counteract the above mentioned challenges and further empower beneficiaries to access their basic needs baskets through the ATM card which works more like the banking system. As already mentioned, the smart switch card is an offshoot of the Universal Electronic Payment System (UEPS).

The Universal Electronic Payment system (UEPS) is used to describe the hardware and software that enable card users to effect financial and none monetary transactions in the system. It does that through loading, spending and settlement. As stated in the Capricorn (2006) presentation, the UEPS is built around set of hardware and software that work simultaneously to offer a secure payment transaction among consumers, merchants and financial service providers. The ICT digitized system is complete when it has the card, point-of-sale (POS) digital device, the server or system host, and the supporting bank. The components of the ICT system are described below.

The card known as the "Smart Switch Card" is a chip driven tag which offers access to finance off-line and in real time, looks like a normal bank ATM card, storing information about the beneficiary such as grant details, amount per month, and personal details of the beneficiary. It uses a biometric identification system and it requires the finger print of the beneficiary to authorize a transaction at a point-of-sale in selected merchants (stores). Figure 4 shows an example of a smart switch card for Botswana with specifications as labelled. Each beneficiary owns his or her card bearing the name. Upon arrival at the point-of-sale (POS) device located in a store, the beneficiary presents the card as evidence for purchase and payment of the items to be bought.

The Merchants are retailers and wholesalers whose function is to install a point of sale device or a form of ATM machine. To be eligible for a Point of service (POS) device, merchants have to apply to the Ministry of Local government which admin-

Figure 4. Smart switch card. (Adapted from Net 1 UEPS presentation, 2007)

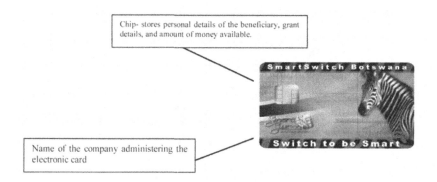

isters the government social grants. The merchants have to satisfy criteria set by the government which include security, availability of at least 80% of the prescribed food basket stock and have connections to Mascom and Orange cellular networks. The POS is used by beneficiaries to purchase food rations, balance enquiries and provide account statements. The POS device requires the finger print of the beneficiary to authorize the transaction. Figure 5 shows the POS technology device as installed at a merchant. Figure 6 shows the beneficiary's thumb placed on the POS device at a merchant to verify the particulars of the individual.

The System Host: This is a server based central processing information technology system that stores and manages the database for the beneficiaries in the program (Figure 7). It integrates the point-of-sale (POS) device, smart switch card, the trust accounts, and links with the government (Ministry of Local Government) which coordinates the administration and management of the social grant programmes through specialized software. The system also helps process transactions from other stakeholders and transfers the data to the trust account for payments of beneficiaries. It also keeps data for employees of the district councils who operate the system.

The Trust Account: This is coordinated by the bank which received funds from the government and administers them for beneficiaries. Currently the programmes use the Bank Gaborone as the underwriting bank. The bank processes payment received from merchants following any transactions performed by the beneficiaries at POS countrywide.

Figure 5. POS device. (Adapted from Net 1 UEPS presentation, 2007)

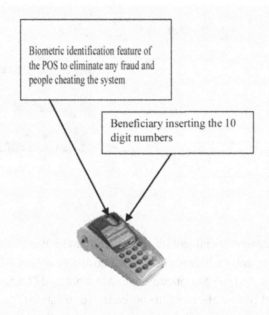

Figure 6. Beneficiary entering her particulars at a merchant (Photo taken in Tlok-weng, Botswana)

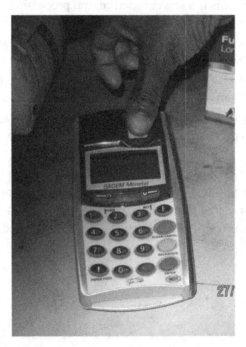

Figure 7. Server-based central processing systems. (Adapted from Net 1 UEPS presentation, 2007)

THE IMPACT OF ICT

A study conducted by Tella et.al. (2007) reported that generally the use ICT is growing but cautioned the lack of adequate information with regard to how ICT is used particularly in countries that are developing. The authors suggested the inclusion of ICT in the educational curriculum since teachers perceive technology as a useful aspect of education. The Universal Electronic Payment system (UEPS), an information and communication technology (ICT) is one technology with great potential to change people's ways of living as well as their perceptions of the world. It is rapidly becoming a modern device for empowering different groups in the society when they access their food baskets and social grants.

The use of ICT allows people of all categories be it young, old, poor, and rich to use advanced smart switch card to manage their social grants, access food baskets and other basic needs. The literature documents success stories of how technologies are impacting and will continue to impact social safety nets programmes in developing countries. The chapter too adds to this literature.

The digital ICT Smart Card has several advantages. These include but are not limited to the following; safe and secure distribution of social grants and payments; having access to cash while in remote areas; enabling people to access their payments at any service point; reducing distances travelled by beneficiaries; saving clients costs of travelling and reduce the risks of transporting cash from one place to the other. ICT smart switch card also helps to facilitate easy transfer of money between individuals at affordable costs, embedded value adds, insurance microfinance and the ability to transfer value via bank where necessary, and also ensures availability of cell phone banking (Beukes, 2007).

Challenges in Using ICT Smart Switch Card

The use and application of ICT smart switch card system (SSC) has become a need to improve the socio-economic status of the rural and urban communities. ICT smart switch card helps to create equity and reduce poverty among the people in the society. However as indicated by Dede (2000) technology adoption is full of challenges. The challenges that the government as the implementers is faced with include less education of the beneficiaries. The beneficiaries who are orphans, destitute and HIV/ AIDS home based patients need to be educated about the goal of the whole exercise, importance of adopting the technology, and the need to change their attitudes to accept getting their social safety net services through electronic means. Thus, a major challenge that the government is faced with is preparation of beneficiaries to use the technology. Majority of the vulnerable communities in remote areas are young and like the old people, some may lack adequate education to use the card.

Another major challenge is the availability of resources to implement electronic technology in all parts of the country. Resources in terms of money, skilled human resources are never adequate especially for experiments such as this one in a developing country. The government is expected to bear the impact of what is required to make the policy work and not see the returns from the project in the near future as the numbers of beneficiaries continue to increase. Thus, education on the importance of using this card is very important particularly for the young ones (orphans). It is important to educate the society about the government's wish to see them becoming responsible and accountable citizens graduating from the social safety nets programs and participating positively in the development of their country.

Psycho-social challenge is perhaps another challenge for using technology by vulnerable people. The introduction of some technology-based devices such as smart switch cards demand that people's attitude should be welcoming. This is needed to promote the desired performance and the goal to see beneficiaries making use of that which is meant for them especially the vulnerable groups targeted by this card in Botswana.

The vulnerable people have minimum education. The agents or implementers need to provide education to bring them to a certain level in order to understand security involved in working with technology devices. Like any other technology, people's readiness to accept developments is also important. The willingness of a person to change may be coupled with fear to accept the change, literacy level, and lack of electricity in remote areas may affect the desired changes.

Other challenges faced by the implementers include theft, vandalism and negative attitudes by the society which tend to jeopardize efforts to improve people's conditions of living.

CONCLUSION

This chapter presented a case of an ICT, Smart Switch Card of the Social Safety Nets Programs in Botswana. It is as advanced communication device that provides information to the users. In Botswana, it serves to manage and administer food and basic needs for the social safety nets to cater for the needy. The ICT digitized system has four components; the card, point-of-sale (POS) digital device, the server or system host, and the supporting bank The system which uses biometric information to verify the beneficiaries and the system attendants makes the process safe and secure for the vulnerable society. The service delivery has since improved as beneficiaries believe that they can now get their needs conveniently.

REFERENCES

Beukes, L. (2007). *Managing director, Capricorn Investment holdings: Botswana Financial service conference presentation slides*. Wednesday 8ᵗʰ May 2007. Retrieved 15 June, 2011, from http://www.google.co.bw/search?q=Beukes+L.+(2007).+Man aging+Director.+Capricorn+HOLDINGS&hl=tn&ei=KB7iTITeDJHzsgaq24XwC w&start=20&sa=N

Casale, M., & Whiteside, A. (March 2006). *IDRC working papers on globalization, growth and poverty. The impact of HIV/AIDS on poverty: Inequality and economic growth*. Health Economics and HIV/AIDS Research Division (HEARD) University of KwaZulu Natal, South Africa. Retrieved 15 June, 2011, from http://www.idrc.ca/uploads/user-S/122157487911438239471GGPWP3-AIDS.pdf

Chademana- Munodawafa. K. E. (2009). *An analysis of livelihood strategies of HIV/AIDS affected households receiving support from Catholic Relief Services (CRS) in Chegutu, Zimbabwe*. Unpublished dissertation, University of Kwazulu-Natal.

(n.d.). curriculum. *Journal of Curriculum Studies*, *32*(2), 281–303.

Dede, C. (2000). Emerging influences of information technology on school

FAO. (1997). *FAO and socio-economic impact of HIV/AIDS on agriculture. World Food Summit Report*. Rome, Italy: Food and Agriculture Organisation.

FAO. (2008). *Expert meeting on climate-related transboundary pests and diseases*

Global facts and figures. (2008). *UNAIDS: Report on the global AIDS epidemic 2008*. Retrieved 15 November, 2010, from http://data.unaids.org/pub/globalreport/2008/20080715_fs_global_en.pdf

including relevant aquatic species. Food and Agriculture Organization of the United Nations, 25-27 February 2008, Options for Decision Makers.

Mawar, N., Sahay, S., Pandit, A., & Mahajan, U. (2005). The third phase of HIV pandemic: Social consequences of HIV/AIDS stigma & discrimination & future needs. *The Indian Journal of Medical Research, 122,* 471–484.

Net 1 U.E.P.S presentation. (2007). *Smartcard to smartcard: Distribution of social*

Smartswitch Botswna. (2007). Special report on e-banking. Smartswitch Nigeria— E-payment for all Nigerians. *Smartswitch, 12*(4500). Retrieved from http://www. smartswitch.co.bw/news/release070817 retrieved on 2009/08/07

Suarez, P., Givah, P., Storey, K., & Lotsch, A. (2009). *HIV/AIDS, climate change and disaster management: Challenges for institutions in Malawi.* The World Bank Development Research Group Sustainable Rural and Urban Development Team (May 2008) WPS4634.

Tella, A. (2007). An assessment of secondary school teachers uses of ICTs: Implications for the further development of ICT's use in Nigerian secondary schools. [Disclosur]. *The Turkish Online Journal of Educational Technology, 6*(3), lic.

UNICEF. (May 2007). *Rapid assessment of cell phones for development.* Women's Net,

UNICEF. Retrieved 16 November, 2010, from http://www.unicef.org/southafrica/ SAF_resources_cellphones4dev.pdf

welfare grants through smart card food coupons for destitute persons, orphans and community home based care patients.

World Health Organization. (2009) *WHO, UNODC, UNAIDS technical guide for countries to set targets for universal access to HIV prevention, treatment and care for injecting drug users.* Retrieved 16 November, 2010, from http://www.unodc. org/documents/hiv-aids/idu_target_setting_guide.pdf

World Summit of the Information Society. (2003). *Background note. High-level panel on women in the information society: Building a gender balanced knowledge-based economy.*

Chapter 12

Experiencing the Functionality of Mathematical Indigenous ICTs on Community Development:
A Case of Farm House Dairy Product

Kgomotso G. Garegae
University of Botswana, Botswana

EXECUTIVE SUMMARY

The use of Information Communication Technologies (ICTs) in agriculture is fundamental to rural development especially in the 21ˢᵗ century (Rashid, et al., 2007). This chapter thus illustrates the use of an indigenous technology using the case of Madila production in a Dairy House Farm at Molapowabojang, a rural village in Southern District of Botswana. The Dairy House Farm started production in 2002 with the aim of producing both fresh and sour or curdled milk (Madila). Although traditionally madila was for subsistence family consumption, the use of community-compatible ICT, namely, sieve like plastic bag, natural sun beam and cooling system made from a wooden shelter, combined with modern machines such as milking machines (milk tubes attached to the cow's udder) have enabled the Dintwa family to convert the practice into commercial industry.

DOI: 10.4018/978-1-4666-2071-1.ch012

INTRODUCTION

From manual to usage of machines, milk is produced in large quantities and through quantitative and computer skills, the farm output is managed well. The sales of fresh milk and *madila (sour milk)* are tracked through the use of an ICT gadget, the computer. This family uses internet and media such as *Farmers' Digest* to identify cows that can produce more milk. In the future, the Dintwa family plans embark on another project, that of the production of food for the cows as a strategy to reduce costs for buying from others and maximize profits. Currently, the Dairy House Farm is negotiating the possibility of engaging in the cross border trading with farmers in South Africa because of customer demand in that country.

The benefits of the farm to the community are multifold. About 80% of workers in the Dairy House Farm project come from Molapowabojang, a rural village in which this farm is located. There is no doubt that this farm contributes to the wellbeing of its employees. This project also contributes directly to community members not working in the farm. They are given liquid whey for free and the product is useful in a number of ways. It can be used to cook sour meal (sorghum or porridge). Overall, the *madila* product is highly nutritious making the farm contribute to development of the village by reducing the rate of malnutrition among people especially, children who benefit from it.

Ownership of cattle has been part of the Botswana culture time immemorial. It was a sign of social significance in that poverty was measured by the number of beasts a family had. The head of the family with fewer cattle attracted less dignity from the community members. However, farming practices were not motivated by profit making as is it recently. ICTs have played a role in this new direction. For instance, a modern farmer obtains information from various sources including ICT gadgets like computers and internet for a successful profiting making business. Such information includes topics on disease management, modern animal feeds, cross-breeding techniques, etc. Moreover, the farmer is now able to predict his production from the quantity and the quality of the animal feeds he or she buys. However, the use of technology in animal agriculture is not new. The need to improve animals especially cows, necessitated the use of artificial insemination and the freezing of semen, which became successful because of research and the generation of information through experimentation. Thus, ICTs have been and continue to be used to enhance agriculture, which is a cornerstone of rural developments in villages such as Molapowabojang. The purpose of this study was to explore how modern technology is integrated into the cultural techniques of dairy farming to commercialize the production and how such initiative contribute to community development.

BACKGROUND

The Dairy House Farm (Figure 1) showcased in this chapter belongs to a family, Mr Batshwari Dintwa and his wife Lucy. They embarked on this project in January 2002 through the help of Citizen Entrepreneurial Development Agency (CEDA).

CEDA is a government initiative grant scheme to help Botswana engage in entrepreneurship with the goal of diversifying the country's economy (Republic of Botswana, 2007). The Farm is located in Molapowabojang, and it occupies 25 hectares of land. It houses about 100 herds of cattle, of which 50 were being milked at the time of the research.

Molapowabojang is one of the villages in the Ngwaketste Sub-district with a population of about 5 000 and 19 associated localities with 2 600 people. It is a typical rural area in the sense that both arable and pastoral farming are practiced. Although it experiences lack of rain like some parts of the country, pastoral and subsistence farming are a norm. It is, for example, the culture among Batswana to rear cattle for meat, fresh milk, *madila* and skin but not for commercial purposes. Recently, cattle industry has now grown to be commercialized and this industry has attracted many who otherwise could be concerned about white collar jobs. This turn of events has come with the extensive use of ICT in the sector, example of which is the Dairy House Farm which belongs to Mr and Mrs Dintwa and is located at Molapowabojang, about 4 km from the center of the village.

The Dintwas use mainly two types of breeds: the jerseys and Brown Swiss. They made an informed choice of breeds considering factors of costs and profits. These farmers used computations to calculate the feed and pasture needed per beast on daily, monthly and yearly basis and compared it with the output. This led them to choose Jersey because it consumes about 15-20 kg per day and produces at least 40

Figure 1. Part of entrance to Dairy House Farm

liters of milk daily. Other breeds, e.g. Friesian, consume more than 30 kg of feed each day and that makes it not cost effective to rear them. There are 30 workers in the Dairy House Farm project, 13 of which are at the farm while others are at the packaging house in Pitsane, head quarters in Lobatse and Gaborone *madila* kiosk. The dairy is located 85 km from the city of Gaborone.

INTUITIVE/INDIGENOUS MATHEMATICAL KNOWLEDGE AND ICT

Man has developed a notably great and variety of techniques and artifacts in order to survive and to satisfy the many material wants he has developed; and in the course of doing so he has utilized a great deal of practical intelligence. ... Given the mobility of human hand, the flexibility of human mind, and the variety of natural materials, it is not difficult to understand the variety and ingenuity of human technology (Taylor, 1969:65).

The term technology has since been associated with modernization or civilization such as radios, televisions, and typewriter, yet technology is as old as the existence of human being. According to Taylor (1969:52), technology encompasses all "techniques of manipulating raw materials to produce artifacts, ways of handling or modifying artifacts, and means of manipulating animal and human bodies". As depicted from the above quotation, these techniques have been culturally constructed since they came into being as a way of meeting the physical demands of national or ethnic groups in particular contexts, and thus vary accordingly. Through the mobility of human hand and the flexibility of human mind, the techniques varied and were for the creation of shelter, clothing, bags and utensils. In Botswana, for instance, our forefathers used animal skins to make clothes, felt ropes *(dikgole)* for spanning cows, bottles to carry water or milk, and a rhombus-shaped bag to ferment milk into *madila*. Before the hide is used to make these products, it is treated by applying urine, brain substance and tannin from a certain tree bark (Taylor, 1969) and thereafter it is kneaded to make it soft and manageable. The hair is scrapped off using an adze before the application of the mixture. However, methods of kneading vary according to different cultures and ethnicity. In most cases, the goat, steenbok or a cow's skin is treated for constructing sour milk container called *lekuka* in the Tswana language.

Indigenously, quantitative and technological knowledge are intertwined (Garegae, 2005; Scope, 1973). People observed phenomenon to come up with experiential guesses to explain them. The amount of heat needed to produce a quality clay pots, for instance, is derived from several observations; the kind of grass that makes a good basketry is also found through experimentation. These quantitative techniques permeate day to day activities such as estimations of amounts in mixing food stuff, right temperatures, and in the case of *madila* production, the amount of water to seep out as liquid whey. The proportion of dye ingredients in cloth, body and leather coloring, or the ratio of mud to cow-dung in the case of floor maintenance (Garegae, 2005), and the reckoning of time using phenomenon calendars through the aid of moon phases (Lekoko and Garegae, 2006) are a few examples of how indigenous technology is inseparable to intuitive mathematical concepts in practical life experiences. This chapter illustrates how these indigenous technologies and intuitive mathematical knowledge are integrated with modern information communication technologies (ICT) to expand the usually small scale family based *madila* production into a commercial public phenomenon.

Decision to Integrate ICT

The decision to use ICT at the Dairy House Farm was incorporated at the initial stage of its conception in 2002 because the family wanted to expand the trade from subsistence to commercial. ICT can be integrated into animal health management, milk and *madila* production, storage, cow feed production, as well as management of records (Segrave, 2004; Rashid, et al., 2007). Initially, milk was harvested manually, but of late, machines are used instead. It is through the use of these machines that a bulk collection of milk is affordable. In the olden days, milk was harvested and stored in relatively small containers such as a 20 liter buckets and needed to be managed by one or two persons. The big containers and refrigerators installed in the farm to cool and store the milk are also part of the ICTs compatible gadgets. They are used instead of treated hides and natural tree shades. Therefore, the integration of ICT to this project was not only to transform dairy farming but also to create jobs for more people, especially the locals.

For the farm to progress well, the managing director needs to make continuous decision. These decisions, however, depend on the evaluation of data from the farm informed by latest research on issues at hand (Ohanga, 2005). ICTs make it possible to obtain and store data with ease as opposed to much paper work. Thus Mr. Dintwa asserts that he reads '*Farmer's Weekly Magazine*' and informs his manager of the latest news of *madila* production. *Farmer's Weekly Magazine*' is the South Africa's magazine that informs farms about farming business especially concerning global trends and development. The farm manager insisted that 'if you don't go around and look for new information, your farm may not prosper'. He regards communication technologies as essential for a healthy dairy business. He, therefore, uses ICTs for various things such as milk tests, tracking individual cow details, feed mixing and distribution, an area where quantitative skills become fitting since the mixture should be at the right proportions. Below we describe one of the technology used, that is, the machine for harvesting milk. Cows are parraded in a parralle formation; the milk tubes are attached to cows' udder and the milk flows through the milking machine into the gathering tank.

Machines provide simultenous milking and quick service as opposed to human hand or fingers (Figure 2).

Madila Production Using Community-Compatible ICT

When you arrive at the Gaborone kiosk you met by the placard shown in Figure 3 informing a customer about the name of the farm, the products produced at the farm, the prices of fresh milk and madila and giving the contact information. (The contact information and the prices are not shown here for lack of space)

Madila (curdle coagulated milk) is seasonal and is plenty in the months of January to May, where grass is plenty because of rains. In the winter months, it is not possible to make it because of lack of food for cows. In the olden days, a 5 liter rhombus-shaped bag made out of tanned animal skin was used to ferment, curdle or coagulate the milk. Every day fresh milk was added into this bag, and thus layer upon layer of thick curdles which was basically milk fat, was formed. This bag was kept at a normal temperature and in the process liquid whey and fat get separated. This whey was drained through a small hole at the bottom of the bag, thus separating whey from milk fat. Every day more milk was added to this bag until it becomes full with the mass (curd). As more milk is added, more and more whey is drawn

Figure 2. Milking stall

Figure 3. A placard at Gaborone kiosk

and the product becomes thicker. The taste of this product is unique from other sour milk products found in retails such as *inkomazi*, a South African product.

When making *madila*, fermenting milk is natural; that is, chemicals are not used to coagulate the milk as it is the case in the western practice. After milking, the milk is put into tanks of 200 litres to start fermenting. As it starts coagulating, the curd is transferred into sieve-like plastic bags for four day (see Figure 4). Each day, liquid whey (about 68% of milk is water) gets strained through the small holes of the sack. The duration of the brewing period, makes the product expensive when compared with fresh milk. For instance, one cup (250 ml) of fresh is sold at half price of the *madila* product.

Figure 4. Madila in the bag ready for harvest

After milk has become thick and creamy, the curd is transferred from the containers into the sieve like plastic bags for four days at the 'right' temperature estimated to be the same as that of a natural tree shadow. The liquid whey is sieved and drops onto the flow as seen in the opposite picture, and seeps into a furrow that leads outside the shelter into a deep hole. Liquid whey can also be obtained by containers for other uses including animal consumption.

Madila is a delicacy dish for an ordinary Motswana. Traditionally, it was expected that each family (or home) had its own portion of *madila* according to the number of the cows one owns. However, as time went by and life styles changed, the product became scarce and whenever it is found, it sells quickly and with a good price.

One mug (approximately 250ml) of madila costs P7. 00 (~$US 1.00). Shopping plastic bags are used to improvise (Figure 5). In the olden days madila was not sold for cash but rather for exchange of other food stuff. For example, a basin of madila exchanged with a basin of sorghum or sorghum flour

Madila can be used for various dishes. For instance, in most cases it is used as an ingredient in making soft porridge. This dish was common among Batswana and it is still enjoyed even today. In modern days, *madila* can be used in baking to give scorns a sour flavor. Madila can also be used as an accompaniment to other dishes especially maize meal *(phaletshe)* or sorghum *(mabêlê)* porridge. It can also be eaten as the main dish, especially in homes where it is plenty. Also, madila can be used to boost fermentation in bread (dough) and sorghum flours. It is rich in Vitamin B Complex and is highly recommended for people with weak immune system.

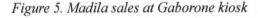

Figure 5. Madila sales at Gaborone kiosk

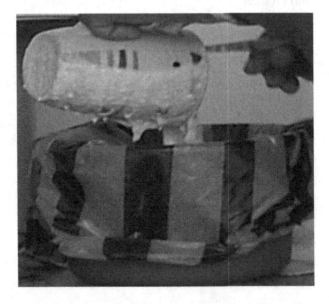

As stated earlier, *madila* is delicacy in Setswana culture and it is in high demand such that the farm is unable to satisfy its customers from various part of the country. Although it is too dear, individuals buy it in bulk and sell it at bus stations and along the streets. This does not only improve peoples' economic status especially the unemployed women who run kiosks and street vendors but also helps in distributing the product widely, hence helping the majority to eat healthy and nutritious soft porridge, the staple food of Batswana. For instance, since the farm is in Molapowabojang, it supplies local residents, Lobatse and Gaborone. At the time of research, the farm was visited by some customers from the Northern part of the country looking for some business partnership in buying and selling yoghurt.

As already stated, by the time of this research, there was no cross-border trading but Dintwa reported that he was engaged in negotiations with farmers outside Botswana. He said those farmers would like to buy the Botswana *madila* because in their country, no one knows how to make it the way Batswana do. He hopes that from next year (2011), his farm will be supplying farmers outside Botswana.

CHALLENGES RELATED TO THE INTEGRATION OF ICT IN THE FARM AND THE WAY FORWARD

The literature corroborates challenges and problems faced by the *madila* farm presented in this chapter. (Berman, undated), for example, observes several challenges associated with the use of ICTs in dairy farming. One such challenge is the lack of comprehensive software that can capture data concerning production and dairy related issues and other issues such as births, deaths, sales, purchases of animals, feed production, etc. Mr Dintwa, the farm managing director explained that the dairy package software that he used was limited to management issues and by the time of the first interview, he was in the process to install better software called PASTE2. His wish is to buy software that handles dairy farm industry with efficiency but the price is prohibitive. For example, FarmWizard software which has the potential to maximize profits by improving herd fertility may not be accessible to Farm Dairy because of the high price.

Another challenge related to use of ICTs is the lack of or little expertise on how to use computer and software technology. Mr. Dintwa, like some farmers in Botswana, is not fully conversant with the advanced software and has since hired someone to meet ICT needs in his farm. However, this issue may be a handicap especially when the expertise is needed immediately and the expert is nowhere nearer. The participants of WITFOR 2005 had long identified this problem and in their Gaborone

Declaration, they proposed that relevant technology should be in place "to address the managerial and financial skills of traditional livestock farmers with a system based on the principles proposed in the Cattle Management System" (Gaborone Declaration, 2005:7).

Yet another challenge that the Dairy House Farm encounters concerns milk and *madila* sales in the months of December and January. This is because milk and *madila* are now scarce due to lack of rains that provide both green grass and animal feed for animal feed. Thus, the production of milk and *madila* slow down making the farm incur large losses. Finally, the Dairy House Farm like most of the small business in developing countries is faced with financial constraints. Cow feed, housing, water, and storage devises need a lot of money for continual maintenance. Mr Dintwa reported that the Jersey cows are unable to survive the harsh climate of Botswana such that during the dry seasons, the farm lost most of the cows through dehydration and malnutrition. In the future, it is likely that Mr Dintwa and other dairy farmers will use artificial insemination to improve Tswana breed to produce a lot of milk so that he owns more of the cows that can stand the harsh weather.

CONCLUSION

Despite the challenges that engulf the Farm House dairy, it has the potential to flourish and improve the livelihood of a number of Batswana. The sales are promising since recently, the farm attracted tenders from three of the largest government institutions in Botswana including Botswana Defense Force (BDF). The Dintwa family is hoping that they will win additional tenders in the future. However, to prosper a number of factors including incentives and high production should be planned for. Currently, the product being made (*madila*) serve only a small portion of the population and much production is needed to service a reasonable population proportion. The farm manager is hoping to increase the production and quality through the use of bigger cowhides and larger shelters. They plan to extend their buying territory beyond the southern part of the country. This will increase the use of other ICTs gadgets such as more packaging machine, yoghurt making machines, etc. The expansion of the farm would also provide more jobs and hence more developments in the community where the farm is located. Accelerated uses of ICTs is necessary for the improvement of animal breeds to cope under difficult weather. This trend would transform farming in Botswana such that the objectives of Vision 2016 are likely to be observed.

As stated earlier, interest from farmers outside the country put the farm in an advantageous side. The sour milk produced in this farm is unique to products produces in South Africa and elsewhere, therefore, the demand for this product is likely to increase tremendously over time. The use of intuitive mathematics in estimation and measuring will continue to enhance the farm production because the product would not be over priced or underpriced.

REFERENCES

Berman, A. (n.d.). *ICT in the dairy farming system.* Retrieved on June 6, 2009, from http://departments.agri.huji.ac.il/economics/gelb-farming-6.pdf

Garegae, K. G. (2005). Mathematics in different cultures and societies: The case of Botswana. In Sica, G. (Ed.), *What mathematics from Africa?* Monza, Italy: Polimentrica International Scientific Publisher.

Garegae, K. G., & Moalosi, S. S. (2010). Botswana ICT policy and curriculum concerns: Does school connectivity guarantee technology integration into mathematics curriculum? In Adomi, E. E. (Ed.), *Handbook of research on information communication technology: Trends, issues and advancements* (*Vol. 1*, pp. 15–32). Hershey, PA: IGI Global. doi:10.4018/978-1-61520-847-0.ch002

Gaspereni, L., & Mclean, S. (2001). *Education for agriculture and rural development in low-income countries: Implications of the digital divide.* A paper presented at the Global Junior Challenge, Rome, Italy, December 3-4.

Lekoko, R. N., & Garegae, K. G. (2006). Intuitive mathematical knowledge as an essential aspect of contemporary adult learning: A case of women street vendors in the city of Gaborone. *Literacy & Numeracy Studies, 15*(1), 61–77.

Ohanga, M. (2005). *Ministry of Economic Development.* Retrieved on June 6, 2009, from http://www.med.govt.nz/templates/Multipage DocumentPage_1085.aspx

Republic of Botswana. (1997). *Vision 2016: Towards prosperity for all.* Gaborone, Botswana: Government Printers.

Republic of Botswana. (2007). *Maitlamo: Botswana ICT policy.* Gaborone, Botswana: Government Printers.

Rushid, M. M., Roy, B. C., Asaduzzaman, M., & Alam, M. M. (2007). Study of the dairy cattle management systems at farmer's level in Jessore District of Bangladesh. *Pakistan Journal of Nutrition, 6*(2), 155–158. doi:10.3923/pjn.2007.155.158

Scopes, P. G. (1973). *Mathematics in secondary schools: A teaching approach.* New York, NY: Cambridge University Press.

Segrave, R. (2004). Communication technologies and knowledge building in agriculture. *Australian Journal of Adult Learning, 44*(1), 27–43.

Tamang, N. B., & Perkins, J. M. (2005). Cattle management systems in humid subtropical areas of Western Bhutan. *Journal of Bhutan Studies, 13*, 105–117.

Taylor, R. T. (1969). *Cultural ways: A compact introduction to cultural anthropology.* Boston, MA: Allyn and Bacon, Inc.

Chapter 13

A Citizen–Centric Platform to Support Networking in the Area of E–Democracy

Francesco Molinari
ALTEC S.A., Greece

Christopher Wills
Kingston University, UK

Adamantios Koumpis
ALTEC S.A., Greece

Vasiliki Moumtzi
ALTEC S.A., Greece

EXECUTIVE SUMMARY

This chapter describes experiences acquired during the research work conducted as part of the European Project Tell Me (www.tellmeproject.eu). The project envisaged to support the pan-European creation of Living Labs as new forms of cooperation between government, enterprises, citizens and academia for a successful transfer of e-Government, e-Democracy, and e-Services state-of-the art applications, solutions, know-how, and best practices. In this chapter, authors explore the potential of providing an existing system (DEMOS) allowing moderated and goal-oriented discourses between the citizens and the policy makers to become parts of open-ended ventures to allow the creation of collaborative networks for Electronic Democracy. This work also recommends that this form of support network elevates e-Democracy of a country and thus improves e-governance systems at the grass roots.

DOI: 10.4018/978-1-4666-2071-1.ch013

ORGANIZATION AND TECHNOLOGICAL BACKGROUND

After the "Helsinki Manifesto" (2006) put the "human-centric way" at the very centre of the measures needed "for turning the Lisbon Strategy (2000) into a living reality", the topic of competitiveness and innovation in Europe has been enriched of a further dimension, namely, co-creative collaboration with the forthcoming users of the developing products and services. This is especially useful in the field of (private and Government) e-Services, where the people can be considered as "twice" beneficiaries, namely of public services as such – impacting per se on their lives and businesses – and of ICT based or supported services, where the question becomes to which extent this novel user-centric approach can improve customization (if not "tailoring") to individual needs and requirements.

Some "champions" of this new dimension of innovation belong to the so-called ENoLL – European Network of Living Labs. In a purely business perspective, a Living Lab can be seen as a service providing organization in the topic of R&D and innovation, based on the "co-creation" concept, which focuses on people in their daily living environments as active, if not decisive, contributors to products and services design, development and testing.

In spite of a limited evidence on the known experiences – most of which could count on a significant external funding - it can be affirmed that the cost of building up and maintaining a Living Lab from scratch (i.e. deploying the communication and collaboration infrastructure, gathering and orchestrating the community of users, carrying out the requested evaluation services) can be substantial, thus preventing a long-term impact into the regional innovation systems.

Here is where the Tell Me project initiative starts up. Through the adaptation of a service already operational in Germany and other European Countries, originally thought for the animation of democratic discussions and participative public opinion formation at local and regional level, establishes a solution for the networking and interaction of Living Lab trials participants during the development and implementation of innovative projects. More specifically, Tell Me objectives were to investigate the administrative viability of the service on a European scale and to identify the conditions for future, pan-European deployment of the service under a juridical and a financial perspective.

The service is based on an existing infrastructure for moderated and goal-oriented discourses involving citizens and political institutions as well as project developers and investors, at national and European level.

The users who tested the service during the pilot phase of the Tell Me project falls into two categories:

A. Living Lab 'Owners' (as their staff validated the services from the technical and administrative point of view and assess their viability and usability);
B. Living Lab 'Members' (Public Administrations, Citizens, Enterprises, Non Profit Organisations, who are the ultimate beneficiaries of these services), mostly operating in the same territorial areas, but also coming from different cities/countries. After each trial/pilot, the results were analysed with a view to mapping the most relevant application areas and to replicating the service in one or more additional Living Labs in order to align the service to the national regulations (if any) and activate cross-fertilisation among the Living Labs through the exchange of best practices at European level.

In the light of the above, main purpose of this work is to provide a Trans-European service integrated with a proven methodology that can enable a co-creative user driven e-Democracy service development. The most important is the fact that the service can "link together" the different stakeholders in order to let them work more efficiently establishing an intimate communication channel between participants in a region. Besides, what is crucial is to increase the availability of easier-to-use eGovernment applications that have been validated in advance through online interaction with the potential users. This will potentially enlarge the scope for public sector innovation in Europe.

The aim is to establish what users (the local public) expect from e-Government, e-Democracy and e-Services applications and to explore the cross-fertilization advantages of a "co-design/co-creation approach" using e-Democracy-like tools to plan, communicate and evaluate technologies, ideas, solutions and applications by moderated discourses. This implies the adaptation of a service already operational in Germany and other European Countries, originally thought for the animation of democratic discussions and participative public opinion formation at local and regional level.

In order to enhance the added value of the service deployment our target user fall into two categories, those who validate the services from the technical and administrative point of view and those mostly operating in the same territorial areas, but also coming from different cities/countries. This relates to align the service according to the national regulations (if any) and exchange of best practices at European level.

Information and communication technologies and the Internet have great significance in a service-based economy. Just as service is not clearly defined in the literature, so too is the term e-service. Rust & Lemon (2001) consider that the term is used in general to denote transactions in which information is the primary value exchanged. Gronroos et al. (2000) claim that e-service is any product or service that is exchanged over the Internet. Others restrict their scope on services that are delivered electronically (Javalgi et al. 2004) or over electronic networks (Rust & Kannan, 2003). In Tell Me, the focus is on any type of (web) service that can be found or exchanged via the Internet.

The Internet tends to shift bargaining power to end consumers in their transactions with businesses (Porter, 2001) because it allows the end consumer to get in contact directly with a great number of producers. On the other hand, the concepts of "mass customisation" (Gilmore & Pine 2000), "one-to-one marketing" (Peppers et al., 1999) and "long tail economics" (Anderson, 2006) are based on the premise that, with the support of information technologies, business firms are able to target each consumer separately, personalise their services and disseminate them efficiently.

This is taken into account in the Tell Me Framework. The Framework supports both 'one-to-one' and 'many-to-many' marketing and dialogues within a social network which enable the consumer to communicate with providers and other consumers able and willing to meet a need.

In order to design this network of consumers and providers ideas can be gleaned from current business networks and ecosystems. In the literature we can find different kinds of business networks, such as business constellations (Normann & Ramirez, 1993), extended enterprises (Prahalad & Ramaswamy, 2003), value nets (Bovet & Martha, 2000), virtual enterprises (Sawhney & Parikh, 2001; Walters & Lancaster, 1999), strategic networks (Jarillo, 1988) and business ecosystems (Moore, 1996; Iansity & Levien, 2004). The concept of business ecosystem is a metaphor that steps forward the movement towards symbiotic and co-evolutionary business networks.

Although Tell Me allows user-defined services as well, in the case of business services, the Tell Me Framework's network takes the form of a business and consumer ecosystem. Here, the role of the customer is of prime importance. Therefore, the network is crafted to respond to his/her special needs and where these needs cannot be met the social network would rise to fill this gap. This would also be of use in cases where the services sought are not related to business services, but rather of a voluntary nature.

The OASIS Group defines Service Oriented Architecture (SOA) as a powerful framework for matching needs and capabilities and for combining capabilities to address those needs (OASIS, 2006). Services in SOA are defined in a similar way to the definition of service in the business world that is as deeds performed by the service provider for the benefit of the service client. Consequently, from a conceptual point of view, SOA could be used to provide the technological foundations that are required for the empowerment of consumers in the selection, composition and consumption of products or services in electronic markets.

The services' world is discussing issues more closely related to providing Software as a Service (SaaS) components and how we can handle issues relating to security and transactions in web services. Security, the first of these issues, allows for secure usage of services regardless of the underlying platform and provides specifications (like WS-Security - Rosenberg & Remy (2004)) and languages (SAML – OASIS (2009)) for secure services. Additionally proposals for supporting transactions in web services have already been implemented, like the WS-AtomicTransaction - OASIS (2009)). Finally, the Software as a Service (SaaS) model promises to deliver "all" existing software that we use daily on our computers as services in the near future – this idea is now slowly emerging and it's being exploited in this project.

From an operational point of view, a SOA can be implemented with the use of Web Services. The basic Web Services model endorses three roles (service requestor, service provider and service registry) and three operations (publish, find and bind). Web Services follow the "find, bind and invoke" paradigm, where a service requestor performs dynamic service search by querying the service registry for a service; if the service exists, the registry provides the requestor with contact details for the service.

Such an operational model is clearly consumer-oriented and could support consumer-oriented value creation. The service requestor recognizes some need, searches for solutions, makes the selection, invokes the service and composes it with other services in his own context, in order to create value for him. Through a social network, other users can assist the service requestor in the composition and provide feedback.

Composition can be implemented with the use of mash-up technologies. Mash-ups are a new kind of data intensive and data integration applications which are based on the fusion of heterogeneous data sources that provide a public set of APIs. Depending on the API either a more traditional server based content generation process is followed or a client side scripting language or applet is used to mash-up the content. Most of the available mash-ups rely on the first solution and use the browser side technologies to produce an aesthetically pleasing result for the user. A technology or better an application model that characterizes mash-ups is AJAX (Asynchronous Javascript and XML) Lauriat (2007). AJAX has revolutionized the way web applications behave and provide a more robust and fulfilling user experience.

Other technologies involved in developing and supporting mash-ups include web services related protocols like SOAP (W3C, 2009) and REST Tyagi (2006). SOAP is the basic message exchange protocol used by services (including of course services used in the mash-ups) to communicate with each other. On the other hand REST provides a simple protocol for web services that supports only basic functions (like POST, PUT, DELETE, etc) but its simplicity makes it a prime candidate for mash-ups since it allows the easy fusion of different data sources.

An important issue in the mash-ups is the interoperability among the different data sources. This is addressed by the use of semantic web technologies like RDF/S based ontologies and RDFa (W3C, 2009) based annotations. That way data and their meaning can be seamlessly exchanged among the different sources and can carry their real meaning along. Mash-ups can be used as the main integration point for semantically described data bringing closer the concepts of Semantic Web and Web 2.0 by providing the best of both worlds.

Composition of services through mash-ups is also a consumer-oriented approach, as the consumer decides which services to mash-up and in which way in order to create value for him/herself and the community at large.

It must also be mentioned however that most existing research on Service-Oriented Architectures focuses on software services which are seen as software components providing access to "real" services (for example a software service for travel booking provides access to the actually service for travelling) (Pistore et al., 2009). In addition, software services are used, but not necessarily owned (in the sense of being able to customize them according to needs) by consumers (NESSI, 2006). This leads to the needs to define Service Level Agreements where appropriate (e.g. in chargeback mechanisms) as software services are not used exclusively by their producers.

In this project, authors recognize the importance of technical considerations (e.g. Service Level Agreements) for business services. However, we also aim to provide a more user-friendly approach to services, trying to contribute towards viewing the Internet as an enabler of "real" services aimed towards the end consumer, instead of pure "software" services created by the provider of these services.

As has been mentioned, there are two levels of users in the system, and for each of those different requirements (to be confirmed during the project) are foreseen to be essential:

- For the citizens (plain users), they may want to access services, and therefore issues such as Service Level Agreements, Quality of Service, chargeback according to different service models are still important. These considerations point to looking at the technical aspects of web services, therefore we are still looking at services from a "software" point of view.
- For institutional / public users, "real-world" considerations of services are of importance. It is for these reasons that some key assets relating to services must be defined with which the user (citizen) is able to construct / mash-up / configure services. Following the paradigm by Pistore et al. (2009), these assets (which can be enablers or constraints) are:
  - Time, representing the temporal relation of the activities of the user, as well as conflicts and overlaps between these activities.

- ○ Location, representing the (current and perspective) location of the user, the availability of (real-world) services in these locations, as well as the necessity of moving or travelling to use these services.
- ○ Social relations (representing other parties such as family, friends, colleagues) involved in the user activities.
- ○ Money and other values, representing costs and assets involved in the user activities.

NEEDS FOR E-DEMOCRACY AND CITIZEN PARTICIPATION

As indicated in the (OECD, 2001a) report: "A key challenge will be to make the transition from area wide (metropolitan) technical structures to area wide (metropolitan) political structures which empower citizens by addressing the 'democratic deficit' and thereby improve the effectiveness of policies at the local level. This implies central government building community policy frameworks, but leaving policy content largely in the hands of local actors".

"Achieving such a transition will involve a cultural change towards a people centre local democracy, not imposed from above, but achieved through strong community policy frameworks in which citizens are empowered to decide the changes they want to see.

This will require a more transparent and accountable decision-making process in which citizens are more fully informed and involved. Key elements of cultural change and improving the policy framework include: modernizing voting procedures, developing new leadership skills among the local political elites, encouraging new forms of participation, and ensuring that area-based approaches are linked to mainstream policy, are properly evaluated, and involve a long-term commitment by local government."

Identifying the "right" structures for local actors to participate may, however, present several difficulties. Municipalities are often both too big and too small to perform democratically. On the one hand, the gigantism of some contemporary metropolises tends to "alienate" the citizen who is far from decision-making centers. On the other hand, sub-national government may be too small to solve some problems that extend beyond its administrative boundaries, such as air pollution and traffic congestion.

Combined with the difficulty of encouraging a new sense of belonging and people's identification with topics of mutual concern is the additional problem of ensuring that the solutions allowing greater participation are not achieved at the cost of the socially and economically excluded. Making a transition to more effective forms of governance is, thus, not just a question of changing institutions, but crucially of moving to a political culture that is centered on the interests of people.

As indicated in another report (OECD, 2001b): "Engaging citizens is a sound investment in public policy-making. As these new relationships have evolved and matured, local governments have increasingly recognized their reliance upon the active contribution of citizens in making better decisions and achieving policy objectives. In this perspective, strengthening government relations with citizens may be seen as a sound investment in tapping new sources of policy-relevant ideas, information and resources for implementation".

Among the driving forces that have led governments to strengthen their relations with citizens, are the needs to:

- Improve the quality of policy, by allowing governments to tap wider sources of information, perspectives, and potential solutions in order to meet the challenges of policy-making under conditions of increasing complexity, policy interdependence and time pressures.
- Meet the challenges of the emerging information society, to prepare for greater and faster interactions with citizens and ensure better knowledge management.
- Integrate public input into the policy-making process, in order to meet citizens' expectations that their voices be heard, and their views be considered, in decision-making by government.
- Respond to calls for greater government transparency and accountability, as public and media scrutiny of government actions increases and standards in public life are codified and raised.
- Strengthen public trust in government and reverse the steady erosion of voter turnout in elections, falling membership in political parties and surveys showing declining confidence in key public institutions.

Three types of local Government-Citizen interaction might be present all along the policy life cycle, see Table 1 (adopted from OECD, 2001b).

The major contribution of the citizens' involvement into the public action is to make better decisions and achieve in a consensual way policy objectives. In this perspective a local government has to adjust public action by a continuous evaluation of objective and results along the policy life cycle. The Table 2 (adopted from QUALEG, 2004) includes the dynamically adjusted actions along the policy life cycle.

The "ideal" process of designing, implementing and evaluating public (e-)Services should come as a specific instance of the above scheme. However, what hap-

Table 1. Types of local government-citizen interaction

Stage of policy making	Information	Consultation	Active participation
Formulation (Agenda Setting)	• White Papers, policy documents • Legislative programmes • Draft laws and regulations	• Large-scale opinion surveys • Use of discussion groups or citizens' panels • Invitation of comments on draft legislation	• Submission of alternative draft laws or policy proposals • Public dialogue on policy issues and options
Implementation	• New policy or regulations and their provisions	• Use of focus groups to develop secondary legislation	• Partnership with Civil Society Organisations to disseminate information on compliance with new laws
Evaluation	• Public notice of evaluation exercises and opportunities to participate	• Inclusion of stakeholders in reviews of government evaluation programmes and results	• Independent evaluation conducted by Civil Society Organisations

Table 2. Dynamically adjusted actions along the policy life cycle

Stage of policy making	Continuous objectives evaluation	Continuous results evaluation	Continuous actions readjustment
Formulation (Agenda setting)	Understand the citizen needs	Proposal or action plan presentation to the citizens	Change of objectives formulation and key indicators
Implementation	Continuous actions adaptation to the citizen's solicited or unsolicited feed back	Continuous measurement of quantitative or qualitative action's results	Continuous change of the qualitative indicators in order to action evaluation
Evaluation	Collect the qualitative and quantitative citizen feedback and reconfigure the objectives	Collect the qualitative and quantitative results and reconfigure the means	Reformulate a new action plan for the next cycle

pens in reality – as noted, among others, by Følstad et al. (2007) – is that an insufficient care is given to users' involvement, in three respects:

A. To introduce and gain experience with resource-effective methods from the multitude of user groups and stakeholders relevant in the development of e-Government systems and services;

B. To manage evolving goal structures for public e-Services, where the goals of different users are reflected;

C. To give proper attention to the administrative and/or legislative reforms needed to align the new services to the underlying institutional and organizational framework.

DESCRIPTION OF THE SERVICE

Currently the DEMOS.2 platform facilitates large-scale e-participation and on-line deliberation projects. This flexible framework supports integration of nearly every discourse process model currently used by on-line moderators. The DEMOS.2 platform transcends the common approach of structuring user contributions (e.g. articles) in hierarchical and inflexible "threads". Instead, every contribution is deemed as equal; its position in e.g. listings of articles depends on meta information attributed to each article, for example the number of votes, hits, or comments. The moderators (as well as the users) may choose and combine these pieces of meta information to generate specific "views" (i.e. filtered and sorted lists of articles).

Together with innovative capabilities to structure discourses on a time-line and to integrate a huge variety of voting and rating mechanisms, the DEMOS.2 system fosters goal-oriented on-line deliberations. Most features of the system are easily switched on and off by the moderators in the administration backend, for example the option to comment on any contribution may be turned off for the whole system but turned on for one specific view.

However, the main strength of the system emerges from the user interaction; e.g. users are allowed to create links between articles or assign articles to a specific position on a map which results in visually stunning cluster effects. Furthermore, the content is effortlessly available, due to compliance with the relevant accessibility and syndication standards.

DEMOS.2 goes beyond the usual Internet chat or discussion forums to provide a powerful and integrated toolset with the following, configurable and customizable state-of-the-art features for supporting large-scale public participation in political discourses on the Web:

*   Support for a wide range of types of discourses, from not moderated, ad hoc discussions and to complex moderated, structured and goal-directed deliberations differentiated user roles and access rights
*   Modes for communication and feedback (direct/indirect, public/protected) supporting a variety of types of user interaction
*   Support for analysing and visualizing the results of surveys, including sorting and aggregating quantitative data and qualitative semantic content (free answers, comments and statements)

- Participative "bottom up" specification of issues, construction of questionnaires, and selection of experts
- Conflict resolution strategies allowing differentiated outcomes (convergence, consensus, divergence, "rational dissent")
- Support for self-organization and subgroup formation, with different levels of aggregation and distribution
- These features have presented various technical challenges to the software developers, including:
- Assuring scalability, to maintain process coherence and coordination in the face of a large numbers of participants
- Providing powerful and convenient administration features for moderators and mediators, especially for structuring and dynamically restructuring large scale participative discourses
- Using surveying, rating and voting to help discussions progress and to enhance conclusiveness of debates
- Supporting procedures, similar to "rules of order", for essential parts of the participation process.
- Apart from Living Labs the DEMOS.2 system has been adapted and specialized either to the needs and demands of informal and formal processes especially public administrations are promoting themselves or even obliged to perform as well as several e- services.

Tell Me services have been identified and built upon the DEMOS.2 system and shifted to solution-oriented services in order to include a focused potential final users' analysis.

METHODOLOGY

Within this research, it builds and populates the targeted experiential service according to the following steps of a Living Lab configuration process:

Contextualization

Contextualization means a prior exploration of the technological and social challenges implied by the technology or service under investigation. Applicable methods are, consequently:

- A technological scan, giving an overview of current and future technologies but also to map the specific functionalities and characteristics related to them;

- A (state-of-the-art) study in order to determine the socio-economic implications of the research focus (framework as well as topic).

The contextualization phase is the starting point for the preparation of a Tell Me Living Lab process. Within this phase all important decisions on topic selection, process structure, user to be involved and evaluation issues have to be made.

Tell Me Living Labs can be adapted to the following application fields:

- Urban and regional planning (UP)
- E-Services (E-S)
- Product innovation / product development (PI)
- Participative decisions on policies, projects or budget planning (BP)
- Idea development (ID)

These fields require using different tools and the adaptation of different evaluation criteria. For this reason it is important to draw a clear picture of the test application / service / technology and to focus on the crucial research question.

To achieve this, so-called technological scans can be performed to provide an overview of current and future technologies but also to map the specific functionalities and related characteristics. State-of-the-art studies can additionally determine the socio-economic implications of the topic under consideration.

The selection of topics to be discussed and processed in the context of the Tell Me Living Lab process have to be defined carefully and the particular context should be explored in detail. All following phases and activities and the configuration of the DEMOS 2 system are depending on this first decision about the issue to be debated.

It is left to the individual testbeds of the Tell Me project to clarify these aspects in more detail. Within the Contextualization Phase, five different tasks are specified:

A. Development of goals, quality standards and evaluation methods
B. Adaptation of DEMOS process and technology
C. Preparation of background information
D. User selection
E. Administration and moderation

Selection

Selection phase includes the identification of potential users or user groups, by means of non probabilistic or purposeful sampling. Useful criteria are, for instance:

- The maximum variation of underlying phenomenon (e.g. education or age);
- The search for a significant variation of observations (e.g. selective or criterion sampling)
- The theoretical variation of relevant concepts (according to some preexisting study).

The scope of participation has to be clarified in advance in order to avoid disappointments. The topic must be specified as well as the groups of people that have to be involved. It is recommended to write a list of daily activities to monitor the progress in this area.

The following issues have to be solved:

- Exploration of the user groups to be involved, e.g. experts, interest groups, members of authority etc.
- Investigation of already existing networks which can be directly addressed by the discussion
- Invitation of users to participate
- Preparation of a strategy and local activities in order to make people aware of the Tell Me Living Lab and motivate them to participate in advance and during the ongoing process.

The following Concretisation Phase is based on the assumptions made here.

Concretization

Concretization phase means a thorough description of the current characteristics, everyday behavior and perceptions of the selected test users regarding the research focus. In this initial measurement authors looked at specific user characteristics (sociodemographic and economic) as well their relation towards the introduced technology or service. The methodology used depends on the size of the test panel: for instance, a quantitative survey can be integrated, depending on the sample scale, by qualitative interviews. The initial measurement of the sample is made before a technology or service is introduced or before the test panel becomes active in the Living Lab; it then enables to perform a second measurement and a full evaluation at the end of the project.

This phase is intended to mainly cope with the user registration. DEMOS 2 offers a registration mode that is adaptable to the needs of the trails. The registration process and the underlying threshold (low/high) have to be defined. It must be made clear which data are requested for the registration process, which information is

Table 3. Checklist registration

Tasks	Specification
Define set of registration information	• Necessary for all Tell Me Living Labs • More and specialised questions for target group related issues like UP, E-S
Distinguish between mandatory and optional information	• Necessary for all Tell Me Living Labs
Define registration threshold	• Necessary for all Tell Me Living Labs • Lower for ID

mandatory or optional for registration. The Table 3 includes an example of registration ckecklist. Examples for optional data:

- Full name
- Gender
- Age
- Town
- District
- Education
- Occupation

Examples for different thresholds are:

- **Very low:** Within the registration process the user has to choose a login name and a password. No information else is mandatory or proved.
- **Medium:** Within the registration process, the user has to choose a login name and a valid email address. The mail is sent to the given address to validate the request.
- **High:** Just pre-invited users are able to register to the process.

User Rights are related to forum access, writing / reading and change documents, upload content etc. Typically three different types of users are to be distinguished:

- Moderators and administrators have all rights (read / write, access to all forums / wikis /documents etc., can change the content on the platform DEMOS 2)
- Normal users have restricted rights (access to public forums, right to read and write, access to wikis)

- Special or expert users have restricted rights (access to public and expert forums, right to read and write)

In the following, in order to gather information about current characteristics and every day life behavior of the users and their perceptions regarding the research focus, an initial online-survey has to be conducted. The participants who have registered to the platform should actively be motivated to take part in that survey.

Implementation

Implementation is actually the behavioral validation and operationally running test phase of the Living Lab. From a user-oriented and ethnographic viewpoint. Authors distinguish two major research methods:

- Direct analysis, using remote data collection techniques and strategies (like technological monitoring) and software logging tools (if applicable) on the device level (e.g. pda, mobile phone or digital television) as well as on the platform/network level;
- Indirect analysis, based on (thematically organized) focus groups, in-depth interviews and self-reporting techniques like diaries, all being applied to investigate the meaning and motivation for behavior.

The following description specifies the 3 different stages of the DEMOS 2 process with respect to their outcome and the moderator's intervention strategies. Due to the specification made within the Contextualization Phase, closed forums, polls, user diaries have to be put in place.

Stage 1

The purpose of the first phase is to initiate and facilitate the discussion, to generate different viewpoints and collect a widespread collection of opinions and statements and finally to identify the central and most important (sub) topics of the general subject matter. The phase concludes splitting up the main forum into different thematic sub forums dedicated to the most central issues in stage 2.

The moderators have to analyze and cluster the free text contributions in order to find out the issues most participants seem to be interested in. Additionally, the moderators will have to summarize the discussion during the course of the first stage following a specific procedure. These summaries consist of content and progress related parts and highlight and profile emerging lines of conflict. The first stage finally results in a set of proposed sub topics that can be more intensively discussed in separate discussion forums in the next phase. Since this procedure is relying on interpretations of the individual postings as well as of the entire discussion, the result may not exactly meet the preferences of the participants. At this point the survey method might come into play in order to evaluate whether or not the proposed sub forums meet the demands of the community and, if necessary, to generate ideas on how to revise the list of sub topics.

Stage 2

In the second stage a limited number (~3) of sub forums will be offered on the basis of the poll results. This phase is meant to intensively discuss the chosen topics among smaller discussion groups in thematic sub forums and to work out ascertained and feasible solution strategies.

In this stage specific aspects can intensively be discussed in smaller groups of interested participants, while the main forum still catches those participants who want to discuss the topic on a more general level. Again the moderators will summarise the developing debate on a regular basis and at the same time try to tease out and manage emerging conflicts. They clarify how and to what extent people are agreeing or disagreeing and at the same time try to reduce the distance between diverging positions by deliberation.

In order to generate concrete results or possible solution strategies the moderators invite the participants to fix their ideas in so called "wikis". Wikis are documents that can be developed collaboratively by different participants on the Internet. If the moderators foresee that a concrete idea is emerging, they will open a wiki that the participants can jointly work out or adapt to the discussion going on in the forum. At the end of this phase the sub forums and the wiki documents will be closed again. The participants can still read the content but not revise it any more. Finally, the moderators will close this phase with a summary of what was discussed so far and an outlook about what will happen in the last phase.

Stage 3

The third stage reintegrates the sub forums into the still existing main forum by transferring the summaries (wikis) and related survey results. Here the participants have the opportunity to see the particular sub topic as part of the general subject matter and a 'big picture' will emerge. Participants have the last chance to comment on the main topic and the assembled results of the sub forums. The community will be asked to rate the sub topics in terms of importance for the main topic that the DEMOS process was intentionally set up for. The final result will be a condensed document depicting both the results of a dynamic discussion and the importance accorded its different aspects in the view of its participants.

Stage 3 intends to open the single discussions again towards a wider perspective and the interrelations of the different aspects. The moderators have to keep track of the discussion and help the participants to finally scrutinize the results of the discussion and the wikis. By help of the rating system users can rank the different ideas (wikis) which were developed in the second phase with regard to their quality and feasibility for the underlying discussion topic.

In cooperation with the users the moderators will work out the final summary of the discourse and its detailed results.

Feedback

Feedback phase consists of two research steps:

1. An ex post measurement based on the same techniques of the initial measurement, to check if there is any evolution in the users perception and attitude towards the introduced technology or service, to assess changes over time in everyday life in relation to technology use and to detect transitions of usage over time.
2. A set of technological recommendations from the analysis of data, gathered during the previous implementation phase. This outcome of the feedback phase can be used as the starting point for a new research cycle within the Living Lab; in this way the iterative feature of our research cycle can be made operational.

At Tell Me project there are three different layers of feedback that have to be taken into account:

1. **Ex-Post Measurement:** Conduct and analyse a final online survey. At the end of the Living Lab process a final survey has to be conducted, analysed and compared with the results of initial survey. The aim is to track a change of attitudes and opinions in the course of the Living Lab process. The result of this comparison should be cross checked with the discussion.
2. **Analysis of the Contribution:** If necessary, a thematic analysis within the feedback phase of a Tell Me Living Lab should provide an in-depth analysis of the content by
    a. Analysing the argumentation process in forums
    b. Bby analysing user diaries especially for PI

  c. In-depth comparison of the different proposals UP, BP, ID especially with regard to users agreement / disagreement

  d. Analysis of change between different version of the same wiki

3. **Analysis of the Quality of the Outcome:** To assess the quality of the outcome it is important to keep in mind the goal of the Tell Me Living Lab process.

EVIDENCE FROM A PRACTICAL CASE STUDY: TUSCANY REGION LIVING LAB

Case studies are generally regarded as particularly useful in depicting a "holistic portrayal of a experiences and results" regarding the application or implementation of a new concept or program as in the case of the Tell Me services. Though case studies are used to organize a wide range of information about a case and then analyze the contents by seeking patterns and themes in the data, and by further analysis through cross comparison with other cases. The case study's unique strength is its ability to deal with a full variety of evidence such as documents, interviews and observations. The multiple perspectives, methods and observations in the studies also provide a strategy of triangulation to add rigor, breadth and depth to the investigation.

The simple fact that what people say and what people do is not necessarily the same thing is also taken into consideration through observation and cross checking with the perspectives of others involved in various transactions in different settings. Evidence from the case studies highlighted many instances of the disparity between the language used to articulate the desire to collaborate and the organizational reality of how decision-making is exercised in implementing the practice. However, sufficient evidence has been collected that supports the efficacies of using the Tell Me service as a collaboration infrastructure for carrying out processes that are communications-intensive and exhibit a high degree of complexity as the result of the involvement of many actors and shareholders.

The Regional Government of Tuscany in the late 2007 published the Law n.69 on "Rules on the promotion of participation in the development of regional and local policies" also known as 'law on participation' (See Figure 1).

That law is an innovative tool for encourage and disseminate new ways and methods of participation, through the construction of new participatory institutions, new processes and shared rules to discuss any size issues within a community and to assess possible solutions through dialogue and confrontation, within a defined time.

The trial was dedicated to evaluate the citizenship knowledge of the law and their comments and expectation about the law.

Figure 1. Home -Living-Lab.toscana.it (adopted from TELL ME project trial website http://www.living-lab.toscana.it/)

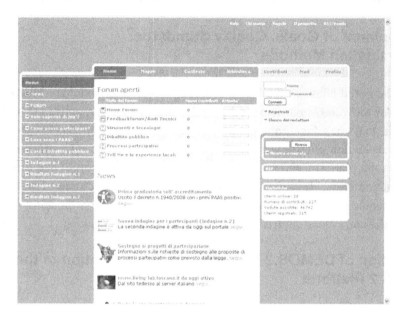

Contextualization

In the Tuscany land there is a community network whose name is PAAS (Access Points to the Services see http://www.e.toscana.it/paas/). The 270 nodes are spread across the whole Tuscany region and at present have more than 25.000 subscribers. The network is an evaluable result of an e Inclusion initiative of Regional Government of Tuscany (RGT).

The PASS-LL has been built with the focus of e Participation, c Government and e Services, but, taking in account the importance of the law, the trial addressed only the e Participation theme.

The target group of the trial are the citizens of all 10 Provinces of Tuscany, with age between 18 and 80 and therefore all the PAAS subscribers are considered in that group.

By means of a call for proposal were selected 20 PAAS nodes using criteria like geographic coverage different (2 every Province) and knowledge and experience about participation and social network of every single node manager. This choice has been taken in order to have a simpler management of the trial and to include the more motivated node-owners.

In the following the four different areas of contextualisation phase are detailed, as stated in D4.1 Operational Methodology the contextualisation phase of TELL-ME.

Development of Goals, Quality Standards, and Evaluation Methods

During the initial phase of the trial discussion subject was about the Tuscany Regional Law n.69/2007 "participation give the chance of a new active citizenship". Trial main goal was a debate about the law's effectiveness and citizen's expectations.

Trial evaluation criteria were the definition of the number of participants registered on the platform, the number of contributions in the forum and the degree of satisfaction of the Regional Government of Tuscany Directorate. The last ones are responsible of the Participation Law publishing. Based on the above Table 4 includes the corresponding trial Contextualization phase checklist.

Adaptation of DEMOS.2 Process and Configuration of the DEMOS.2 Platform

The adaptation of DEMOS.2 has been carried out in two different phases.

The first phase has been used in order to learn the platform functions and complete the Italian translation of menus and windows. During the second phase the platform has been customised and settled for the trial (see Table 5).

Selection

The new regional law on participation affected all the citizenship of Tuscany and hence all the PAAS subscribers and visitors were interested by our survey. It has to be considered also that the goal of the trial was to highlight the powerfulness of the e Participation when used within a well-organised Community Network just like a Living-Lab.

Table 4. Checklist of contextualization phase

Tasks	Specification	Checked y/n
Definition of type of TELL ME Living Lab (UP, E-S, PI, BP, ID)	• Explain the purpose of the TELL ME Living Lab	Yes
	• Explain main research focus	Yes
	• Define evaluation standards	Yes

Table 5. Checklist of DEMOS adaptation

Tasks	Specification	Checked y/n
Translation	• Translation of information material • Translation of advertising material • Translation of system and process description • Provide translation possibilities during the process	Yes
Layout specification	• Necessary for all types of TELL ME Living Labs • Logo integrated? • Typo correct? • Phrases and sentences integrated? • Wording correct? • Color scheme correct?	Yes Yes Yes Yes Yes

Therefore, all the PAAS-LL node maintainers were instructed to invite all their own subscribers over 18 years old to participate to survey. The people selected were a good sample of Tuscany citizenship because of the presence in the Living-Lab of two PAAS node for every Province. In the following figures are shown the sample composition considering age, sex, and education (see Table 6).

Concretisation

In order to give to all the participants to the trial all the tools and information to understand the innovation of the web 2.0 and social network platforms during the month before the pilot itself it was started a common discussion and insight about the different ways to support debates within a network community. As a result all the subscribers and visitors could start the trial with a full awareness of what they were going for and hence endorse their trust on the survey goals.

Table 6. Checklist of selection phase

Tasks	Specification	Checked y/n
Define user groups	• Necessary for all types of TELL ME Living Labs especially for E-S and UP	Yes
Define communication channels	• Necessary for all types of TELL ME Living Labs • Define communication channels and marketing strategies for each target group separately	Yes
Invitation to participate	• Necessary for all types of TELL ME Living Labs • Plan invitation waves for each target group during the whole process • Develop a schedule for invitations and reminders of participating	Yes Yes

Furthermore, in order to let every subscriber to take part to the initial online survey they were all registered to the DEMOS.2 platform as debate participants and therefore they get used to consider themselves as a member of the coming trial (see Table 7).

Implementation

The implementation phase duration was one month. The debates were divided in 5 different forums, two of them with the main topic of participation law and participative process, while the other topics were to support the discussion on web 2.0 tools, TELL-ME project, and user assistance. At the end of the 23 day of trial there were 215 registered subscribers that produced 227 contributions, having the amazing number of 11047 hits that means that the DEMOS.2 platform was visited by subscribers of all PAAS nodes, not by PAAS-LL only (see Table 8).

Feedback

In order to collect feedback from users two questionnaires were prepared. One questionnaire was sent to the entire registered user in order to get their feedback, while the other questionnaire was prepared for collecting qualitative feedback from the PAAS-LL maintainers and moderators. The summarized results are presented in the following sections (see Table 9).

BENEFITS AND CHALLENGES

Tell Me brings a subjective richness to bear on decision-making problems faced by Public Administrations. This research believes that Tell Me service, through more

Table 7. Checklist of concretization phase

Tasks	Specification	Checked y/n
Define user groups	• Necessary for all TELL ME Living Labs	Yes, not relevant
Define access rights for user groups	• Necessary for all TELL ME Living Labs	Yes
Define user profiles in Demos.2 for invited guests / experts	• Necessary for all TELL ME Living Labs	Yes
Conduct initial online survey	• Necessary for all TELL ME Living Labs	Yes

Table 8. Checklist of implementation phase

Tasks	Explanation	Checked y/n
Moderation	• Summarize topics • Report on rule violation • Comment on discussion process • Provide hand-over on shift change	Yes Yes Yes Yes
News announcement	• Produce daily news due current development • Report on events and summarize them • Produce news in advance • Report from the discussion	Yes Yes Yes Yes
Open wikis	• Name and implement subforums • Provide first structure for the wikis	Yes Yes
Edit final document	• Add user polls and rankings to this final document • Include results from starting / final questionnaire	Yes Yes

conscious attention and deliberate experimentation and adoption in the real world, it aims to offer the following benefits:

Improved functioning of Living Labs (public administrations)- With Tell Me, a basic infrastructure (integrated with a methodology) is provided to "link together" the different stakeholders in order to let them work more efficiently. Equally important is that Tell Me establishes an intimate communication channel between participants in a Living Lab. This communication service is the first step towards the provision of user centred and customised services.

Co-creative e-Government- Another benefit of the Tell Me service is to develop trust between the people and stakeholders in a region, this is the first step to enable a co-creative user driven e-Government service development.

Table 9. Checklist of feedback phase

Tasks	Explanation	Checked y/n
Final survey	• Conduct a final survey and compare results with initial survey	Yes
Thematic analysis (main method: content analysis)	• Argumentation process in forums, necessary for all types of TELL ME Living Labs	Yes
	• Proposal comparison, especially for UP, BP, ID	Yes
Evaluation of quality outcome (main method: content analysis, quantitative research)	• Quantitative Research to evaluate user profile (especially for UP, E-S, BP)	Yes
	• Content analysis to value the quality of the ideas, suggestions, arguments etc, necessary for all types of TELL ME Living Labs	Yes

Improved quality of public services- It should not be forgotten that the main area of public interest for the project will be related to the online service provision to citizens by European public administrations. Tell Me will enable on one hand, improved staff efficiency and on the other hand, more citizens/customers oriented and "socially accepted" e-Services.

Easily available e-Government applications- Another benefit for the community will be the availability of easier-to-use eGovernment applications that have been validated in advance through online interaction with the potential users. This will potentially enlarge the scope for public sector innovation in Europe.

Improved efficiency/effectiveness of the validation process- Outside and beyond the public sector, a number of additional benefits can be experienced by the repeated use of the Tell Me methodology in the private sector context.

SOLUTIONS AND RECOMMENDATIONS

The field of e-Democracy in Europe has been developed by different players on the European, national and local level over the course of the last years.

On the European level the different organisations (EuroParl, EC etc.) have tested and implemented a series of e-Democracy programmes and initiatives to support the development of the field: The European Commission funded ca. 20 Information Society Technology projects with more than 30 million euro and many of the sixth Framework Programme projects support the field of e-Democracy (Chrissafis, 2005). One major step forward to implementing "contribute to easing mobility of European citizens within the Internal Market, making European Citizenship a reality, supporting them as active citizens through innovative government services and through participation" (IST policy, 2004) on the European level is the Interactive Policy Making (IPM) project. The system has been put into place "to facilitate the stakeholders' consultation process by the use of easy-to-use and straightforward online questionnaires, making it easier both for respondents to participate and for policy makers to analyse the results" (Interactive Policy Making, 2007).

The Council of Europe supported the general development by the set up of the ad hoc Committee on E-Democracy of the Council of Europe (CAHDE, 2006). The goal of CAHDE is among others to "examine developments on e-democracy/e-participation at European and international level"; to "develop proposals for the Forum for the Future of Democracy as to how it could embrace issues of e-democracy". The recommendations on e-Democracy developed by CAHDE are finalized by the end of 2008 will certainly help to convince policy makers in the 47 member states to support the field of eDemocracy.

Another factor in the development of eDemocracy even thou it does not touch the four products to be marketed by the consortium is eVoting. Internet voting was assessed in the cybervote project with was "tested in 2003 during trial election that will be held in Germany, France and Sweden. These trials will involve more that 3000 voters and will allow full assessment of the system before any potential product launch". Electronic Voting machines however have been implemented in many European states on different organisational levels. eVoting in all of its forms is subject to critical discussion which is mainly focussed on security and transparency concerns. The technical and also procedural criticism related to eVoting resulted in a focus on deliberative and issue focused forms of implementing eDemocracy. In the following some projects will be described as examples to give an overlook on the wide diversity of eDemocracy projects in Europe established during the last years. The collection is manly based on the major comparative review of current practice by Prof. Ann Macintosh published in the OECD study "Promise and Problems of eDemocracy" (2003).

Summing up beyond the small list of examples given in this text there are many different eDemocracy projects beyond those given here. Various initiatives are already in place or planned on the European, national and local level and its count is still growing. This hints at a larger market potential lying ahead for electronic democracy in Europe or as Stephen Coleman puts it:

"Politicians are beginning to realise that connecting directly with the citizens they represent can lead to better policy-making and legislation, informed by public experience and expertise; a new kind of relationship between government and governed, based upon politicians' listening, learning and sharing ideas as well as steering and aggregating; and the reward of enhanced public confidence in democratic institutions and the renewed legitimacy of governance." Coleman (2003).

According to the "Helsinki Manifesto" issued on 20th November 2006, a further dimension, namely, co-creative collaboration with the forthcoming users of the developing products and services, has enhanced the issue of competitiveness and innovation in Europe. The most important impact to citizens is its usefulness in the he field of (private and Government) e-Services. As a result, the concept of e-Democracy networking can be an extremely beneficial toolset to bring together regions and industrial stakeholders with citizen academia and researchers.

Besides, it is obvious to us that citizens and community members develop a positive feeling for local authority budgets, both intuitively and through learning by playing; they also gain a better understanding of the scope and limits of budgetary planning.

Municipalities and regions acquire more information about the desires, preferences and needs of their citizens, enabling them to create opportunities for debating about future avenues for development or new projects.

Any sustainable solution would require to:

1. Communicate the scope and limits of local authority budget-setting in an intelligent and innovative way.
2. Use the tool to explain the meaning of individual budget items.
3. Let the public participate in making important decisions.
4. Identify citizens' desires and priorities at an early stage.
5. Generate acceptance for budget consolidation.
6. Create more transparency – and thus more local democracy.
7. Integrate the planner in the political process: create opportunities for discussion.

Users of the Tell Me platform learn what it means to implement political "dreams" against a background of limited resources and spending limits imposed by law. The complexity of the budget planner varies according to the degree to which the user goes deeply into the subject – from a smart game to a level verging on reality.

TELL ME is a European project, which focuses on the design of transnational public services built on ICT in e-Government related areas. We aimed at demonstrating the pilot implementation and exploring the market potential of what was originally presented as a (joint) methodology and toolset for the configuration and the pan-European deployment of Living Labs in the areas of e-Government, e-Democracy and e-Services. As a result, the existing and upcoming best practices in such domains have been considered as a first market segment for our service since the beginning of the project. This deliverable documents the steps ahead made by the TELL ME partners in the market validation of such a complex service during the 1st project year.

A Living Lab is a real-life environment, managed by a business/citizens/government partnership, which enables users to take an active part in the research, development and innovation process. Products and services are developed in a person-centric and co-creative way, based on continuous feedback from users to developers. As an open innovation platform, it creates an environment where users are confronted with ideas, concepts and prototypes or demonstrators of technology since the early stages of the research, development and innovation process, not only at its end, like in more classical field trials or product testing approaches.

The intuition behind the TELL ME project has been to replicate an existing service (DEMOS) - originally thought for the animation of democratic discussions and participative public opinion formation at local and regional level - and adapt it to the networking and repeated interaction of participants during the development and implementation of Living Lab trials. After a first phase where the TELL ME consortium focused into the preparation of five regional Living Lab trials in the domains of e-Government, e-Services and e-Participation, the second phase has been based on the most important findings derived from market analysis, project dissemination and the collection of the trials results, to build up a first draft of business plan for the consortium as a whole.

Ata higher level, our analysis has focused on the understanding of the TELL ME service "portfolio" composition i.e. what are the services making up the TELL ME suite?

In fact, a first piece of evidence has been that the DEMOS system – though very effective in allowing moderated and goal-oriented discourses between citizens and policy makers, as well as trial managers, developers and other stakeholders, at national and European level - simply adds up to a plethora of existing ICT solutions that are already operational at Living Lab level. It was then necessary to prepare an overview of the actual strengths and weaknesses of the service to lay the proper foundations for a good marketing action.

A second piece of evidence relates to the fact that, until now, very few Living Labs are actually operating in the areas of eGovernment, eParticipation and eDemocracy. This can be seen as a promising market scope, at the only condition that it should not hide the good or best practices that are already operating in these domains, though not (or not explicitly) under the Living Labs "umbrella". In that respect, what we thought was missing from our original approach is a deeper consideration of the original traits being born and brought up in the context of public administration and participatory policy making.

ACKNOWLEDGMENT

Our thanks to the European Commission for partially funding the Tell Me project and the architect of the Tell Me ideas and vision, Mr Rolf Luers. Tell Me is an eTEN Project, running as part of the European Union's Framework Programme 6 for Research in Information Society Technologies, aiming towards 'e-Government'. Official project Web site: http://www.tellmeproject.eu

REFERENCES

W3C. (2009). *RDF annotations (RDFa)*. Retrieved October 22, 2009, from http://www.w3.org/TR/xhtml-rdfa-primer/

W3C. (2009). *RDF schema (RDFS)*. Retrieved October 22, 2009, from http://www.w3.org/TR/rdf-schema/

W3C. (2009). *Resource description framework (RDF)*. Retrieved October 22, 2009, from http://www.w3.org/RDF/

W3C. (2009). *Simple object access protocol (SOAP)*. Retrieved October 22, 2009, from http://www.w3.org/TR/soap/

Ad hoc Committee on E-Democracy of the Council of Europe (CAHDE). (2006). *Introduction to the Ad Hoc Committee on E-democracy (CAHDE)*. Retrieved from http://www.coe.int/t/e/integrated_projects/democracy/02_activities/002_e-democracy/00%20Intro%20CAHDE_en.asp

Anderson, C. (2006). *The long tail: Why the future of business is selling less of more*. New York, NY: Hyperion.

Anttiroiko, A.-V. (2003). Building strong e-democracy: the role of technology in developing democracy for the information age. *Communications of the ACM, 46*(9).

Bovet, D., & Martha, J. (2000). Value nets: Reinventing the rusty supply chain for competitive advantage. *Strategy and Leadership, 28*(4), 21–26. doi:10.1108/10878570010378654

boyd, d., & Ellison, N. B. (2007). *Social network sites: Definition, history, and scholarship*.

Cardoso, J., & Sheth, A. P. (Eds.). (2006). *Semantic Web services: Processes and applications*. Springer. doi:10.1007/978-0-387-34685-4

Chrissafis, T. (2005). *eDemocracy: Challenges and actions in the EU*. TED Conference on e-Government Electronic Democracy: The Challenge Ahead, Bolzano, Italy.

Gilmore, J. H., & Pine, B. J. (2000). *Markets of one: Creating customer-unique value through mass customization*. Boston, MA: Harvard Business School Press.

Grönroos, C. (2000). Service management: A management focus for service competition. *International Journal of Service Industry Management, 1*(1), 6–14.

Iansiti, M., & Levien, R. (2004). *The keystone advantage: What the New dynamics of business ecosystems mean for strategy, innovation and sustainability*. Boston, MA: Harvard Business School Press.

Interactive Policy Making Online Consultations website. (2007). *Report on interactive policy making*. Retrieved from http://ec.europa.eu/yourvoice/ipm/index_en.htm

IST-507767 – QUALEG. (2004). *Deliverable 4.1: Marketing research*.

IST policy on the objective of ICT research for innovative Government website. (2004). Retrieved from http://cordis.europa.eu/ist/so/govt/home.html

Jarillo, J. C. (1988). On strategic networks. *Strategic Management Journal, 9*(1), 31–41. doi:10.1002/smj.4250090104

Lauriat, S. M. (2007). *AJAX- Advanced Ajax: Architecture and best practices* (1st ed.). Upper Saddle River, NJ: Prentice Hall PTR.

Lisbon Strategy. (2000). *Lisbon European Council 23 and 24 March 2000 presidency conclusions.* Retrieved from http://www.europarl.europa.eu/summits/lis1_en.htm

Maglio, P., & Spohrer, J. (2008). Fundamentals of service science. *Journal of the Academy of Marketing Science, 36*, 18–20. doi:10.1007/s11747-007-0058-9

Moore, J. F. (1996). *The death of competition: Leadership and strategy in the age of business ecosystems.* Winchester, UK: J. Wiley & Sons.

NESSI. (2006). *Strategic research agenda: Framing the future of the service,* Vol. 1.

Normann, R., & Ramirez, R. (1993). From value chain to value constellation: Designing interactive strategy. *Harvard Business Review, 71*(4), 65–77.

O'Hear, S. (2006, June 20). Web's second phase puts users in control. *The Guardian, Education.* Retrieved November 21, 2009, from http://education.guardian.co.uk/elearning/story/0,1801086,00.html

OASIS. (2006). *Reference model for service oriented architecture 1.0.* Retrieved from http://www.oasis-open.org/committees/ tc_home.php?wg_abbrev=soa-rm

OASIS. (2009). Business process execution language v 2.0. Retrieved October 22, 2009, from http://docs.oasis-open.org/wsbpel/2.0/OS/wsbpel-v2.0-OS.html

OASIS. (2009). *Security assertion markup language* (SAML). Retrieved September 22, 2009, from http://www.oasis-open.org/committees/tc_home.php?wg_abbrev=security

OASIS. (2009). *Web services atomic transaction* (WS-AtomicTransaction). Retrieved October 22, 2009, from http://docs.oasis-open.org/ws-tx/wsat/2006/06

OECD. (2001a). *Cities for citizens: Improving metropolitan governance* (pp. 39–43). Paris, France: OECD Publications.

OECD. (2001b). *Citizens as partners: Information, communication and public participation in policy making* (pp. 20–22). Paris, France: OECD Publications.

Pistore, M., Traverso, P., Paolucci, M., & Wagner, M. (2009). From software services to a future internet of services. In Tselentis, G. (Eds.), *Towards the future internet*. IOS Press.

Prahalad, C. K., & Ramaswamy, V. (2000). Co-opting customer competence. *Harvard Business Review, 78*(1), 79–87.

Prahalad, C. K., & Ramaswamy, V. (2003). The new frontier of experience innovation. In Rosenberg, J., & Remy, D. (Eds.), *Securing Web services with WS-Security: Demystifying WS-Security, WS-Policy, SAML, XML Signature, and XML Encryption*. Pearson Higher Education.

Prahalad, C. K., & Ramaswamy, V. (2004). *The future of competition: Co-creating unique value with customers*. New York, NY: Harvard Business School Press.

Rust, R. T., & Kannan, P. K. (2003). E-service: A new paradigm for business in the electronic environment. *Communications of the ACM, 46*(6), 37–42. doi:10.1145/777313.777336

Rust, R. T., & Lemon, K. N. (2001). E-service and the consumer. *International Journal of Electronic Commerce, 5*(3), 85–101.

Sawhney, M., Balasubramanian, S., & Krishnan, V. V. (2003). Creating growth with services. *Sloan Management Review, 45*(2), 34–44.

Sawhney, M., & Parikh, D. (2001). Where value lives in a networked world. *Harvard Business Review, 79*(1), 79–86.

Shirky, C. (2003). Social software: A new generation of tools. *Esther Dyson's Monthly Report, 10*.

The Helsinki Manifesto. (2006). Retrieved from http://elivinglab.org/files/Helsinki_Manifesto_201106.pdf

Tyagi, S. (2006). *RESTful Web services*. Retrieved October 22, 2009, from http://java.sun.com/developer/technicalArticles/WebServices/restful/

Walters, D., & Lancaster, G. (1999). Value and information: concepts and issues for management. *Management Decision, 37*(8), 643–656. doi:10.1108/00251749910291613

ADDITIONAL READING

Avramidis, G., Manolopoulos, C., Sofotasios, D., Spirakis, P., & Stamatiou, Y. (2009). *PNYKA e-voting system.* 3rd International Conference on e-Democracy, 23-25 September 2009, Athens, Greece.

Bouras, C., Giannaka, E., Karounos, T., Priftis, A., Poulopoulos, V., & Tsiatsos, T. (2008). A unified framework for political parties to support e-democracy practices: the case of a Greek party. *International Journal of Electronic Democracy, 1*(1), 98–117. doi:10.1504/IJED.2008.021280

Breindl, Y., & Francq, P. (2008). Can Web 2.0 applications save e-democracy? A study of how new internet applications may enhance citizen participation in the political process online. *International Journal of Electronic Democracy, 1*(1), 14–31. doi:10.1504/IJED.2008.021276

Fraunholz, B., & Unnithan, C. (2008). Anti-apathy approaches in representative democracies: e-governance and web 2.0 – Facilitating citizen involvement? *International Journal of Electronic Democracy, 1*(1), 51–84. doi:10.1504/IJED.2008.021278

Klein, H. (1999, January). Tocqueville in cyberspace: Using the internet for citizens associations. *The Information Society, 15,* 213–220. doi:10.1080/019722499128376

Manolopoulos, C., Efstathiadou, R., & Spirakis, P. (2009). The impact of the Web and political balance to e-democracy. *Proceedings of E-Democracy, 2009,* 13–28.

Meneklis, V., & Douligeris, C. (2010). *Studying the interaction of the epistemology in e-government, organization studies and information systems (Vol. 26,* p. 79). Lecture Notes of the Institute for Computer Sciences, Social Informatics, and Telecommunications Engineering. doi:10.1007/978-3-642-11631-5_7

Norris, P. (2001). *Digital divide: Civic engagement, information poverty, and the Internet worldwide.* Cambridge, UK: University Press. doi:10.1017/CBO9781139164887

Ntaliani, M., Karetsos, S., & Costopoulou, C. (2007). *Accessing e-government services via TV.*

Paganelli, F., & Giuli, D. (2010). Telep@b project: Towards a model for eParticipation and a case study in participatory budgeting. *Lecture Notes of the Institute for Computer Sciences, Social Informatics, and Telecommunications Engineering, 26,* 118–127. doi:10.1007/978-3-642-11631-5_11

Panagis, Y., Sakkopoulos, E., Tsakalidis, A., Tzimas, G., Sirmakessis, S., & Lytras, M. D. (2008). Techniques for mining the design of e-government services to enhance end-user experience. *International Journal of Electronic Democracy, 1*(1), 32–50. doi:10.1504/IJED.2008.021277

Triantafillou, V., & Kalogeras, D. (2010). *E-Democracy: The political culture of tomorrow's citizens* (*Vol. 26*, p. 99). Lecture Notes of the Institute for Computer Sciences, Social Informatics, and Telecommunications Engineering.

Xenakis, A., & Loukis, E. (2010). Using structured e-forum to support the legislation formation process. *Lecture Notes of the Institute for Computer Sciences, Social Informatics, and Telecommunications Engineering, 26*, 29–40. doi:10.1007/978-3-642-11631-5_3

KEY TERMS AND DEFINITIONS

Best Practice: One technique, method, process, activity, incentive or reward which is considered to be the most efficient and effecting in delivering a particular outcome among the other already existing solution is called best practice. Undoubtedly, the desired outcome can be achieved with fewer problems after a series of proper processes, checks, and testing. Even if the processes are continuously improved, a best practice is considered as a business buzzword used to describe the "methodology" and the standards for the development in cases of multiple organizations related to management, policy, and especially software systems.

Citizen-Centric: After the "Helsinki Manifesto" (2006) put the "human-centric way" at the very centre of the measures needed "for turning the Lisbon Strategy (2000) into a living reality", citizen-centric is meant to denote any approach related with or focused to the co-creative collaboration with the forthcoming users of products and / or services under development. This is especially useful in the field of (private and Government) e-Services, where the people can be considered as "twice" beneficiaries, namely of public services as such – impacting per se on their lives and businesses – and of ICT based or supported services, where the question becomes to which extent this novel user-centric approach can improve customization (if not "tailoring") to individual needs and requirements.

Contextualization: It is considered as the first amd most important part of the Living Lab configuration process. It builds on the exploration of both the technological and social challenges implied by a technology or a service under investigation. From a methodology point of view two alternative methods can be applied for its execution: (i) a technological scan, giving an overview of current and future technologies but also to map the specific functionalities and characteristics related to them; (ii) a (state-of-the-art) study in order to determine the socio-economic implications of the research focus (framework as well as topic).

E-Democracy: Direct democracy tries to find the solution to the democracy deficit from the quantity of direct citizen participation in decision-making. E-democracy comes for the combination of the words "electronic" and "democracy". In particular it includes the use of electronic communications technologies such as the Internet in enhancing democratic processes within a democratic republic, representative democracy or any other democratic model. It is a political development still in its infancy, as well as the subject of much debate and activity within government, civic-oriented groups and societies around the world.

Policy: Typically, the term policy is used to describe a deliberate plan of action to monitor and moderate decisions and achieve rational outcome(s). Sectors such as government, private sector organizations and groups, and individuals are using the term policy. Besides, the term policy is appropriate when it refers to the process of taking crucial decisions, including the recognition of several different alternatives such as programs or spending priorities, and finally the selection of the basic ones according to the impact they have. Policies are considered as management, political, financial, and administrative mechanisms that meet the explicit goals.

Policy Life Cycle: It includes three stages namely *formulation* (agenda setting), *implementation* and *evaluation*.

Chapter 14

E–Insurance Project:
How to Develop Novel Electronic Services with Cooperation between Academics and Practitioners

Raija Järvinen
Aalto University School of Economics, Finland

Jarno Salonen
VTT Technical Research Centre of Finland, Finland

Aki Ahonen
OP-Pohjola Group, Finland

Jouni Kivistö-Rahnasto
Tampere University of Technology, Finland

EXECUTIVE SUMMARY

This case study covers two R&D projects called eInsurance 1 and eInsurance 2, which are concerned with electronic insurance. This case emphasizes project organization, its activities and roles, together with the results of the projects. In addition, the structure and innovation level of the projects are analyzed and the challenges involved in launching the concepts into insurance markets are presented. The most important outcomes of the projects are novel service concepts, and valuable information of consumer expectations that corporate partners utilized in their R&D activities. For research partners, the projects brought ideas, how to organize future projects in new ways, and how to combine academic and business expertise successfully.

DOI: 10.4018/978-1-4666-2071-1.ch014

ORGANIZATIONAL BACKGROUND

In spring 2002 two Finnish academics, two professors who were involved in research on e-business expressed their concern regarding the lack of customer orientation in the case of electronic insurance services available on the Internet. They raised a question: "How do insurance companies get electronic services closer to their customers?" This can be considered as the starting point for a discussion about launching a research and development project with the aim of increasing the customer friendliness of the electronic insurance environment.

In autumn 2002 the discussion spread to insurance business practitioners when the above-mentioned question was raised in public seminars and at other events. Both academics and the business world realized that they share a common interest in developing electronic insurance services that better respond to customers' needs. At the same time the insurance sector was generally interested in putting more effort into adopting electronic services. Although the hype of the Internet was already over, the new communication channel still had great potential for offering services. Enthusiasm might be an appropriate expression to describe the attitude of both the business and scientific communities towards electronic services at that time. Hence, a favorable environment for creating a temporary organization assisted in designing and executing a research and development project. The academics did have no problem in persuading companies to participate and funding for the project was easily obtainable, even though, previously these kinds of development activities had been performed as in-house projects.

The co-operation between the academics and representatives of the two large insurance companies in Finland started with negotiation of relevant research questions in the area of electronic services and continued by preparing a research plan. After a year, a public research and development project titled "eInsurance - Electronic insurance business and risk management" (later referred to as "eInsurance 1") was launched. It was carried out between August 2003 and December 2004. The project also led to a follow-up project called "eInsurance – Novel electronic insurance services" (later referred as "eInsurance 2") with a similar but more extensive objective of enhancing the customer friendliness of electronic insurance services. This project was executed between June 2005 and February 2007. Both eInsurance projects received public funding from the Finnish Funding Agency for Technology and Innovation (Tekes), as well as additional funding from participating companies and research organizations. The project reports and other results are therefore publicly available. The two eInsurance projects were not only research projects, but also development projects that aimed at developing concrete electronic service concepts for the insurance industry. In fact the eInsurance projects were pioneering projects in examining and developing pilot concepts for electronic insurance services in Finland as a whole.

SETTING THE STAGE

Before starting eInsurance projects, insurance companies have globally put some effort into developing electronic insurance services. It all started in the middle of 1990s when the first insurance companies introduced their Internet sites. The very first insurance company web sites contained only company related information, for example annual reports and the latest news, but gradually the amount of information widened in scope to cover insurance brochures, terms and guidelines on how to protect life and property. In due course the pioneering companies started to sell insurance products on the Internet, even though the very first offers consisted of rather simple insurance types, such as travel and home insurance.

Järvinen et al. studied the Finnish insurance business on the Internet in 2001 and they discovered that it was impossible to purchase all the insurance types required for one household on the Internet. At that time some insurance types were available on the Internet, but the choice was somewhat limited. As a result, customers had to contact the insurance companies in person in order to take care of some of their insurance-related issues, and while they were there, they also dealt with all their other insurance affairs, that could have been taken care of using the Internet. As a result the Internet channel remained unfamiliar to customers. The fact that insurance companies did not agree on standardization of their web sites led to a situation in which some companies offered only information online, while others concentrated on selling insurance products or providing information about risk prevention. This caused confusion among customers. Despite the above problems, the importance of the Internet as a channel for business-to-consumer insurance services was growing.

In many service fields more signs of development in the direction of electronic services emerged after the millennium. Insurance companies in many advanced insurance markets, e.g. in the USA, U.K., Germany and the Nordic Countries, started to offer online purchase of insurance products. In addition, online claim applications became possible, at least in the Nordic Countries. However, the Internet is still used mainly for information acquisition purposes while the actual service transactions (e.g. purchase and claims applications) are performed face-to-face in the branch offices or by telephone (Ahonen & Salonen, 2005). The growing demand for electronic insurance services on the other hand and the obvious lack of user friendliness on the other, revealed a gap between current use and the future vision for electronic systems.

CASE DESCRIPTION

This case study aims at describing the content of the two eInsurance projects, particularly from the perspective of the project organization but also as research and development activities. The primary objective of the two projects was to make electronic insurance services more closely match the customers' mindset. The research and development activities comprised two eInsurance projects that were carried out between 2003 and 2007. As a result, the project team developed an electronic service concept that supports customers in their insurance service transactions. This case study provides an example of how the development of electronic insurance services can be performed with cooperation between several distinct organizations. The case study is thus a useful example from an organizational point of view.

Case Study Organization and Key Players

The core project organization was the same in both projects. The core of the "eInsurance" organization was developed in 2003 and comprised the University of Tampere, VTT Technical Research Centre of Finland and two leading insurance companies in Finland (later referred to as IC1 and IC2). By August 2003, after expanding the organization with additional participants, the final project consortium consisted of four business participants including two software companies. In addition the Federation of Finnish Insurance Companies also participated in the project management team. From the research point of view, the University of Tampere provided a business approach while VTT Technical Research Centre added to this by providing technical skills for the use of the research consortium.

Both IC1 and IC2 are key players in the Finnish insurance markets with approximately 2000 employees in Finland. The two other business participants were software companies. One of them (referred to as SWC1) is one of the leading software providers in the Finnish financial market, especially in the insurance business. It has approximately 100 employees in Finland, but it also has business operations in other Nordic and Baltic countries. The other software company (referred to as SWC2) is a "small business" company which was established in 2001 and specializes in identity and access management in online services.

From the operational perspective, the project organization was supervised by the project management team (11 members), consisting of executive-level members from each participant organization. In addition, an operational team was established to be responsible for concrete research and development activities conducted through the "eInsurance" project. The operational team, in which the middle management of the companies and researchers collaborated, consisted of 9 members. The project management team held 4-5 meetings a year, while the operational team had meetings

6-8 times a year. The overall director of eInsurance came from the University of Tampere. In the beginning the project was coordinated by one researcher from the University of Tampere and one from VTT (later referred to as project managers). Soon after the start of the project the coordinator at VTT was appointed professor of safety management and engineering at Tampere University of Technology and thus, he was replaced by another researcher.

The challenge for the new project organization was to motivate its members to work effectively from the beginning of the project. In many cases the efficiency of a new organization is hindered by the lack of cohesiveness in the organization as well as by established working practices. However, this was not a problem in this case as the key project members had already existing personal relationships with each other. As a result the existing core of collaboration encouraged the new members to cooperate with each other from the outset. In addition, collaborative meetings and a few "kick off" events molded the coherence of the new organization. More importantly, however, the motivation to gain new information and encouragement to design and develop something truly new in the area of electronic insurance services provided a good basis for the cohesiveness and functionality of the organization.

During the follow-up project, eInsurance 2, the basic philosophy remained the same, but the project extended to cover a total of four research themes: "service business and usability, safety and risk management, jurisprudence and technological environment." One of the two participating insurance companies, IC1, from the first eInsurance project showed clear interest and motivation to continue work in a project-based organization and therefore, it also joined in the follow-up project. Similarly, the larger of the software companies, SWC1, was interested in participation. In addition, another software company SWC2 specializing in developing IT solutions and consulting, joined the consortium for the eInsurance 2 -project. Hence, a total of three companies participated in the second eInsurance project. The research participants in the first eInsurance project (University of Tampere and VTT research Centre of Finland) formed again the core of the eInsurance 2 project. In addition, another university, Tampere University of Technology, also joined the consortium and another public research organization, National Consumer Research Centre also became part of the team. Thus, a total of four research parties participated in the second eInsurance project. Therefore, the project organization needed updating in order to fulfill the requirements of the project in terms of competence and professional knowledge.

The director of eInsurance 2 was the professor of data processing at the University of Tampere. The other key personnel were two project managers, one from the University of Tampere and one from VTT. There were two reasons for these changes in the project organization between eInsurance 1 and eInsurance 2. Firstly, some of the key personnel had moved to new positions and secondly there were more participants in eInsurance 2 project than in eInsurance 1. The overall director of the eInsurance 1 project had moved to the position of Research Director at the National Consumer Research Centre. Together with the first coordinator at VTT, who was now professor at Tampere University of Technology, she took new joint responsibility for the safety and risk management theme.

The operational functionality of the eInsurance 2 project was arranged close to the first project organization, and comprised the project management team and the operational team. In addition, four research teams worked under the operational team in order to facilitate the research activities within the research themes (service business and usability, safety and risk management, jurisprudence and technological environment).

The research organizations provided skills within the areas of business, technology, risk management, insurance and consumer research. These skills supported especially the idea-generation phase of the project. The corporate partners, on the other hand, provided general information, segmentation of target groups (e.g. customers) and a marketing perspective on the project which the research organizations lacked. In addition, the corporate partners provided resources by funding part of the project in addition to the main funding granted by the national funding agency.

It is worth to emphasize the unique and developing nature of the eInsurance organization. The corporate partners expressed their satisfaction with the appropriateness of the organizational structure of the two eInsurance projects. As one of the most fundamental benefits of this structure, the corporate partners emphasized the value of freedom to focus on creating innovative electronic service solutions. The business partners perceived the organization of the eInsurance projects creative, since it allowed even humorous and crazy ideas to be put forward by participants without having to worry about the disapproving reactions or financial pressure from the firm, which is often the case in in-house projects. Furthermore, the corporate members of the project found that the eInsurance projects enabled corporate partners temporarily to break away from their daily routines and to concentrate on being innovative. In addition, several members of the project management team recognized how surprisingly well the participating members, especially within the operational team, blended to form a cohesive and functional entity.

At this point, it is relevant to clarify that in the insurance business area, service development has mainly consisted of utilizing technology, i.e. transferring the existing traditional services to the electronic environment instead of developing completely new service concepts. Furthermore, customers often do not expect much from insurance services since they are considered to be low frequency and low interest services. From the service providers' point of view, this has often lead to a limited and somewhat restricted attitudes towards service innovations, which may cause automatic rejection of new ideas with large market potential, since such ideas would require a change in the standard processes and/or culture of the organization. This tendency might, in turn, also diminish customers' willingness to accept innovations.

During the projects, the role of the research organizations was vital as their perspective is often different from that of business life. In particular their organizational culture supported entrepreneurship and innovativeness, but they lacked the resources needed to complete a project. In addition, more advanced and science based innovations tended to require the external support of universities and research organizations (Tödtlinga et al., 2009). Hence, research organization projects often target development of some kind of preliminary service concept instead of a commercial product or service, since marketing and other business operations, aimed at commercializing the service concept, require resources that research organizations usually do not have.

Uncertainty about the results often characterizes R&D projects aimed at creating innovations. Therefore, managers must pay special attention to build psychological safety among project team (Annique Un 2010). This was also the case in the two eInsurance projects. The uncertainty at the beginning of the project caused a certain amount of stress, particularly for the insurance companies. After the participating organizations had learned to accept the working practices, the tolerance of this uncertainty increased.

The project members assumed different roles that are close to the roles in the innovation processes. O'Connor and McDermott (2004) suggest that a radical innovation requires multiple roles, such as those of *idea generator, opportunity recognizer, champion, project leader* and *project alumni*. They stress that the idea generator and opportunity recognizer are usually different persons. They also emphasize the role of the project alumni, some of whom are acting in the project team in leadership roles during the project regardless of any eventual change in their actual functions within the companies where they are employed (see also McDermott, 1999).

In the eInsurance projects, various roles of innovators can be found. Representatives from the participating universities and the public research organizations can be considered as *idea generators* since they form the ultimate core of the two eInsurance projects. Although they were not officially *project leaders,* they acted as such in practice by ensuring that everything went as intended. Furthermore, the Finnish Funding Agency for Technology and Innovations (Tekes) as well as the corporate partners and public research organizations can be considered as "opportunity recognizers; first, because they supported the idea of starting the project, and second, because of their role in funding the project." The members of the project management team in both projects can be considered as *champions*, but also act as *project alumni*. Some members participated officially in the first project, but not in the second project. Despite this, these members tended to be "unofficially available" for the second project.

To conclude, the virtual eInsurance project organization that involved different organizational cultures, information, and individuals supporting each other, provided a functional and fruitful environment for the development of electronic insurance services. Many corporate partners even commended the working methods followed in the projects, and the encouraging and open atmosphere prevailing within the organization. In this respect, it is highly recommended as a collaborative model for organizations in the process of designing and developing (electronic) service innovations. On the basis of this experience, the eInsurance projects can be considered as national, if not a global, models for organizational innovation in the insurance research and development context, since there was no previous experience of joint projects in non-life insurance R&D functions. However, in an alliance consisting of business – university – research centre, it is important to pay attention to "cultural gaps" regarding, for example, the publication of results, long-term vs. short-term project benefits and ownership of Intellectual Property Rights (IPR).

Project Activities

eInsurance can be described as a development project, based on academic research, aiming at innovative service concepts in the electronic environment. Following from this, the operational team concentrated on carrying out research tasks first and the results of these guided the development of the service concepts.

Both eInsurance projects contained a number of research tasks. The eInsurance 1 project consisted of two questionnaire-based surveys targeted at private and corporate customers, international market analysis of the electronic insurance service offering, interviews to study the current technological state of insurance companies with regard to the utilization of technology within electronic services and the development of the electronic "insurance selector and cover evaluator" service. The eInsurance 2 project consisted of extensive consumer research related to risks and insurance products, research on the legal requirements related to insurance services on the web, research on utilization of log analysis and semantic web modeling techniques within the electronic insurance service context, research on insurance web service usability issues and development of the electronic "safety and insurance advisor" service. Research partners presented all their research results during the project management team meetings and thereafter the utilization of the results moved to the operational team.

The operational team carefully studied the results of each research item. It was the role of the management team to give permission to publish research reports, conference papers and articles. Examples of the main results that guided the development stage are presented below. Some of the results may look like minor details, but small issues can often have a strong effect on the outcome.

During the summer of 2006 a large questionnaire-based survey was targeted at a group of 800 consumers. The research results, concerning consumers' risk perceptions, revealed that 77 per cent of Finnish consumers value most the opportunity to compare different insurance types on the Internet (Peura-Kapanen et al., 2007). This kind of service, however, was not commonly available, although in Sweden, Estonia and the Netherlands there is an Internet portal which allows comparison of insurance prices. The other services that consumers valued on the Internet are examples of accepted and rejected claims (73%), price calculators (71%), electronic claims applications (58%) and the opportunity to check and update their personal insurance policies (52%) (Peura-Kapanen et al., 2007).

In addition, the above survey and another qualitative study by Peura-Kapanen and Järvinen (2006) confirmed that most consumers had visited insurance companies' web sites with the intention of seeking price details or other information on insurance types, but they discovered that prices were difficult to find and to compare. Because of this, many of them still prefer a personal service provided by insurance clerks working in branch offices. In addition, they value the interaction with insurance clerks since insurance policies are considered complicated. In fact, many consumers avoid insurance issues altogether because of their complex nature (see Järvinen & Heino, 2004). As a consequence of this, only 80 per cent of Finnish consumers have home insurance and the number of those with home insurance has decreased during recent years.

At the same time, other research work was also performed to help in development of different concepts. The lessons learned from the research tasks led the operational team into paying more attention to the design of web sites, and to take steps towards a more comprehensible and appealing operating environment for customers. At the early stage of the project the operational team discovered that many online insurance service providers, at least American, British and German insurance companies, have adopted a more lively and non-insurance-like approach in their electronic insurance service environments. These firms seem to prefer fresh and lively colors instead of dark and matter-of-fact ones, and use illustrative - in some cases even animated - pictures on their web sites. A more extensive discussion of the different types of electronic insurance service providers in different insurance markets is available in Ahonen and Windischhofer (2005) and Windischhofer and Ahonen (2004). Some members of the research parties even carried out the comparative analysis of the web pages of some international insurance companies.

The operational team decided that the utilization of visual elements is welcomed in the Finnish insurance world as well (see Ahonen, 2007). Since insurance services are often perceived as complex and confusing, visual elements operate as vehicles which help to familiarize customers with the electronic service environment. However, up to now, Finnish insurance companies have preferred the more conservative and matter-of-fact approach when offering electronic insurance services. More precisely, they have put a large amount of unstructured information on the web sites without the use of visual design, and not including colors and pictures, which would make the electronic service content more comprehensible to customers.

The operational team also realized that Internet services are often fairly standardized whereas the needs of customers are not uniform. Electronic insurance offerings should, therefore, at least be mass customized as suggested in the earlier study by Järvinen et al. (2003). One way to address this issue in the electronic service environment is to offer insurance cover consisting of various elements that customers can pick and choose according to their personal requirements. However, many customers are afraid of buying insurance on the Internet as they are afraid to choose the wrong insurance type or insufficient cover (Peura-Kapanen & Järvinen, 2006). Electronic insurance services therefore, have to take account of the customers' actual situation and life style, and automatically include this information in the minimum insurance cover offered.

Overall, research confirmed that electronic insurance services should be combined with a new and more customer-friendly perspective. This issue was the central principle in both eInsurance projects. The two project managers took responsibility for collecting and combining the results of each study and discussed them with project members in order to gather their opinions. As a result the project management team agreed that an electronic insurance service environment would need visible and easy-to-use features in order to respond better to the needs of customers using self-service logic. Without this, customers are not likely to use them, because they perceive them as complex and confusing. Thus, the operational team assumed as their guiding philosophy of design to create a more visually appealing and easy-to-use concept for the electronic insurance service environment. The operational team believes that this philosophy encourages customers to commit themselves.

The eInsurance project management team decided to emphasize visual illustration in the electronic insurance service environment, in spite of the fact that information is traditionally presented in the form of text (and lots of it!) explaining insurance cover and terms. This choice is aimed at making the electronic insurance service environment more appealing and comprehensible to the customers. After that decision, the operational team raised the question: "What does this philosophy mean in practice?" As a starting point for the development work, the project managers utilized the customer service life cycle model from Ives and Mason (1990) in developing the "insurance service life cycle" (see Figure 5). The model is depicted in Figure 1.

Throughout both the eInsurance projects, the main attention was aimed at the first phase (requirements) and the second phase (acquisition) of the life cycle. The first eInsurance project focused mainly on specifying the possible need for insurance cover for customers. In turn, the main focus of the eInsurance 2 project was on providing a tool for facilitating the acquisition of insurance cover by offering customized and visual information on safety and insurance-related issues for customers.

In the middle of the eInsurance 2 project, a team of three key members conducted interviews in all of the participating organizations in order to make a list of their needs and their ideas related to the service concept. In addition to the interviews, an internal workshop was organized in March 2006 for all project participants. The main objectives of the workshop were to disseminate information about the current project results and to collect information for the development of the forthcoming service concept. The initial idea behind the service concept was developed in mid-2006 on the basis of the feedback from the existing service and the project partners' needs that were gathered during the interviews and the internal workshop. The participants provided comments on the draft models of the service concept at specific meetings that the project managers organized monthly from September to the end of 2006.

Outcome of the Project: "Safety and Insurance Advisor"

The most crucial practical target for the eInsurance 1 project was to develop an "electronic service concept for consumers following a logic based on visual information." The target materialized in a service concept called "insurance cover evaluator" that was introduced in January 2005. The main objective of the eInsurance 2 project was to "support customers during the insurance transaction process by developing a comprehensive electronic insurance service environment that is combined with the insurance customer life cycle" and it produced a service concept called "safety advisor", which was introduced at the beginning of 2007. Both service concepts were combined into one entity called "safety and insurance advisor". It was first published internally at the project management team meeting and evaluated by the project partners. Before introducing the service concept to the public, external (invited) parties also evaluated it. The overall concept was published in March 2007 and it provided consumers with safety information related to their living environment and suggested various insurance cover alternatives. The overall service concept is an Adobe Shockwave (Adobe, 2007) application that was freely accessible via the project web site until the end of 2007. The application type selected enabled the development of a suitable graphical user interface and the use of an external database that provided easy-to-update storage for the information used by the "safety and insurance advisor".

The project team proudly presented the new innovative service concept at the closing seminar of the eInsurance 2 project on 31 March 2007. The project was also selected for presentation at the conference hosted by Berkeley University in April 2007. The presentations contained the following functions of the service concept:

Figure 1. Customer service life cycle (adapted from Ives & Mason, 1990, p. 59)

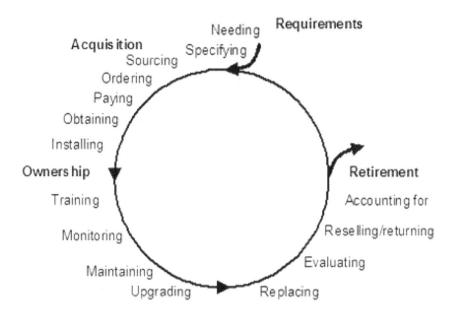

selector function, insurance cover evaluator function and safety advisor function. They are briefly described below in order to give an understanding of the innovativeness of the two novel concepts in the insurance sector.

The general idea behind the new concept was to keep it as simple as possible for the users. In order to maintain the level of simplicity, user interaction involves using the mouse in a graphical user interface, in which the customer either selects an object (e.g. choosing a housing type on the screen to describe his living conditions by clicking with the mouse) or uses drag and drop to combine objects with each other (e.g. choosing family members to describe his living situation by dragging appropriate family members to the selected house). In addition, the service also provides information in balloons that appear when the user moves the mouse cursor over certain objects (e.g. family members).

"Selector"

The first phase of the service concept is called a "selector" function. The "selector" function collects information about the customers' living environment in order to provide suggestions regarding suitable insurance products for them, together with tailored safety information. First, users have to provide information on the following topics:

- Accommodation (choices: apartment, terraced house, detached house).
- Family members (choices: male, female, teen, child, pet).
- Assets (choices: vehicles, valuables, summer cottage, forest, etc.).
- Activities (choices: travel, hobbies).

The user interface, as well as the overall appearance of the service concept, is illustrated in Figure 2. The other phases of the selector function follow the same graphical model in order to maintain understanding of the different process phases as well as for ease of use throughout the whole service concept.

"Insurance Cover Evaluator"

The second phase of the service comprises the "insurance cover evaluator" function that summarizes the selections made earlier by the user and combines them with insurance types suitable for each selected item (e.g. family member, asset). The insurance types are divided into the following two categories:

- **Primary Insurance Types:** The most common and therefore highly recommended types for the particular household (e.g. car, home and travel insurance).
- **Secondary Insurance Types:** Optional, but recommended types for the particular household (e.g. all-risk car insurance, health and sports insurance), especially for those who want full insurance cover against all risks.

By selecting an object from the summary of the user's selections, he or she is provided with information about the insurance type related to that specific (selected) item. The combination of customer selections and insurance types clarifies the relationship between them and provides a better understanding of household insurance cover as a whole. The information can also be printed out and used for reference when contacting the insurance company or an independent broker.

"Safety Advisor"

The third phase of the service consists of the "safety advisor" function. This function combines the earlier customer selections with examples of accidents and hazards which may occur within the customers' living environment. The customer can acquire safety information on four different topics within his or her living environ-

Figure 2. eInsurance service concept - selecting family members (adapted from Ahonen & Salonen, 2007, p.14)

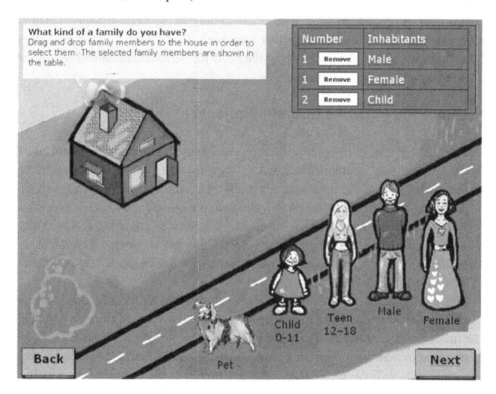

ment: home, vehicles, travel and hobbies. The graphical user interface provides several scenarios within each topic; for example a fire in the kitchen (Figure 3) or losing one's luggage during a trip abroad. The individual scenarios are illustrated both in written and graphical form, with some of them including animation, and they include the following information:

- What might happen? (a scenario of an accident or hazard that might happen).
- How to avoid damage? (how to prevent the accident and/or minimize the damage).
- In the case of damage (insurance cover and instructions for insurance claim applications).
- Did you know…? (statistical, instructional and/or other information related to the scenario).

The service concept provides customized information by adjusting itself according to users' earlier selections. In other words, a family with children receives a scenario and safety information appropriate to their living circumstances which is different from that of a single person or a couple with no children. This originates from the research results emphasizing the need for personalization and relevance of the insurance and safety information.

Practical Implications from the Projects

The results of the two eInsurance projects produced practical applications, developed by the participating insurance companies. A few months after the first eInsurance project ended, one of the insurance companies, If, published an insurance service of their own, with the objective of providing simple insurance-related information in a new way to the visitors to their web site. The service consisted of visual elements similar to those of the insurance selector, but it was considered more as an information providing web page than as an interactive service supporting customers in their specific needs.

IC1 published its own insurance cover evaluator service in 2006. The service used a similar structure to the insurance selector and cover evaluator developed in the first eInsurance project. The main improvements were that IC1's service was customized to their own insurance products and it used a professional design that was more suitable for a commercial product. In addition, the insurance cover evaluator service was seamlessly integrated into IC1's customer service processes. This made it possible for a member of the customer service team to call the potential customer almost immediately after they received a completed form from a new or existing customer, using the customer's insurance profile based on the cover evaluator service, and their contact information. The insurance cover evaluator service has been successful enough for it to be still available.

Furthermore, as a result of the second eInsurance project the safety advisor section of the insurance cover evaluator service has been developed into a non-commercial service. This service has been developed by the Federation of Finnish Financial Services as part of a campaign for reducing domestic accidents and can be accessed through their website (http://turvallinenkoti.net) though the service is only in Finnish. The service provides information about the different risks at home and provides useful hints on how to minimize these risks. These cases and the fact that research results from the project had been developed into concrete commercial services show the topicality of the both eInsurance project.

Figure 3. eInsurance service concept - a screenshot of the safety advisor (Ahonen et al., 2007, p. 15)

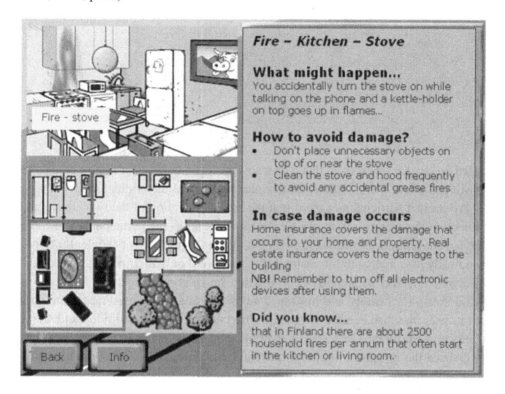

EVALUATING THE PROJECT AND ITS MANAGEMENT

Towards the end of the two eInsurance projects, the five members of the project team summarized the project structure and the different functions of the overall service concept as shown in Figure 4. They divided the figure into three horizontal sections describing (a) user information (input level), (b) service concept, consisting four different functions (functional level) and (c) output provided to the customer in each function (output level).

Thereafter, the key members of the management team evaluated the degree of innovation according to the five innovation categories by Garcia and Calantone (2002). First, *radical innovation* involves a new technology (or service: authors' comment) that changes the current market infrastructure. Second, new innovation changes either the technology or the market. Third, discontinuous innovation is radical or really new innovation depending on how much and how quickly the innovation changes the technology or the market. Fourth, incremental innovation is

Figure 4. Structure and phases of eInsurance service concept

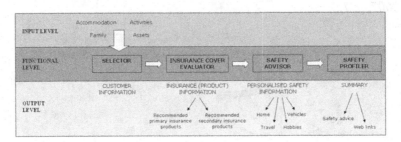

based on current technology that offers new features, benefits or improvements to existing markets. Fifth, imitative innovation challenges the original innovation.

All project participants agreed that the main innovation of the two eInsurance projects is the "safety and insurance advisor". As far as the participants knew, the service concept developed was new in the insurance market as a whole. It offered a radically new approach for customers to chart, not only their personal needs for insurance but also personalized information on safety management and how to avoid risks. The "safety and insurance advisor" is based on existing technology, but its user interface is more visual and entertaining than the traditional interfaces of electronic insurance services. In addition, the "safety and insurance advisor" has influenced the insurance market in general by opening up a new communication channel between customers and insurance companies. On that basis, the project management team suggested that the insurance selector can be considered as a truly new or even a radical innovation. On the other hand, the influence of the insurance selector on the insurance business has so far been marginal at a macro level, even though it is a radically new concept. From the insurance business point of view, the "safety and insurance advisor" can, so far, only be considered an incremental innovation, although in time it may develop into a major one if more insurance firms adopt the idea.

The Customer Service Life Cycle Model by Ives and Mason (Figure 1) provides a suitable approach to assessing the utility of the main results of the both eInsurance projects, e.g. "safety and insurance advisor". However, the project managers refined the model to the scope of electronic insurance services. The modified model is shown in Figure 5.

The first phase of the life cycle is called *requirements* (i.e. recognizing the need). The main purpose of the "insurance cover evaluator" concept was to make it easy for consumers to recognize their insurance needs. The main function of the "insurance cover evaluator" is to collect background information about the consumer's life situation (i.e. housing, family, property, hobbies, travelling etc.) and provide the consumer with an insurance cover solution suitable for his or her life situation. The

Figure 5. The "insurance service life cycle" and the new web services (adapted from Kivistö-Rahnasto et al., 2006, p. 8)

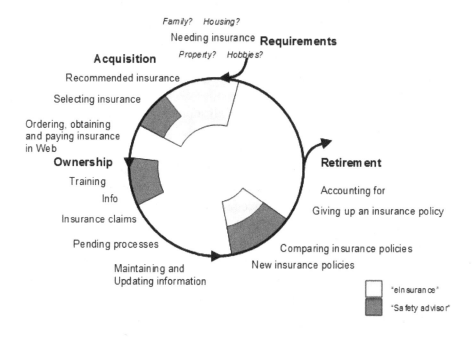

second phase of the life cycle is called *acquisition*. The "safety advisor" makes use of the information provided by the consumers on the "insurance cover evaluator" and provides them with customized information concerning risks and other safety-related issues as well as on how to protect themselves in their own environment. In addition, the "safety advisor" provides consumers with information on how insurance types relate to the previously mentioned risks and includes statistical data and/or other useful information on safety measures and products that can be found on the Internet.

As Figure 5 indicates, the overall service concept, "safety and insurance advisor", covers a major proportion of the customer service life cycle in the electronic insurance service context, especially in the "requirement" and "acquisition" phases. Hence, the "safety and insurance advisor" seems to be a valuable step in bringing electronic insurance services closer to the customer's mindset.

When evaluating the project management, several strengths and weaknesses are worth to pay attention to. The most important strength of the whole project organization was the ability to innovate. The atmosphere was utmost open to all kinds of new ideas that the members of the research parties usually started to create, and the members of the corporate partners continued to develop. The ideas were put on "clean table" and the members of the operational and management team decided to forget the existing systems and traditions. Strength was the combination of applied sciences from various disciplines that opened avenues for fresh thinking from many perspectives - and also the combinations of these perspectives. Finally, the common targets of the eInsurance projects, that project members described "do it more simple" and "easy and funny e-shopping" guided into connecting the world of net-playing to e-commerce.

From the organizational point of view, both eInsurance projects were successful. They were well organized and they started and ended on schedule. Even though the budget was strict, the project teams managed to keep approximately within its limits. In addition, both projects provided all the research items agreed in the R&D plan and developed promising pilot versions of the service concepts.

As pioneering projects, both eInsurance projects suffered from lack of existing theories and extensive amount of research publications. However, there are currently more research concerning R&D of financial services, but most of it relates to banking services and only a minor part to insurance services. At least in Finland there have been no followers for eInsurance projects. Therefore, the main weaknesses of the projects relate to the development work, that is somehow unfinished and the further development in this field is slowing down. There is a serious danger that insurance companies are left behind in all activities that take place on the internet.

The eInsurance projects did not follow general R&D process models in strict order starting from idea generations and ending to the successful launch of the service (see e.g., Edvardsson & Olsson, 1996; Goldstein et al., 2002). Instead, the various stages of the process were interwoven with each other. E.g., idea generation stages materialized at the beginning of the both projects, but also after conducting research items and receiving material of marketing analysis from the corporate members. Yet, in addition to idea generation, the other stages of the process can be identified as follows: Data gathering and analysis, developing the pilot concept of the service, concept test-marketing and launch of the service. The latter was executed after the project was closed and the test-marketing is discussed under the sub-title "Challenges facing the project organization".

CHALLENGES FACING THE PROJECT ORGANIZATION

The first eInsurance project provided a clear message that insurance companies are interested in developing their electronic services, although in their own quiet way. As concrete evidence of this, the two participating insurance companies launched their own modified versions of an electronic service for their private customers (i.e. consumers), which was based on the logic of the "insurance cover evaluator" service concept.

When closing the eInsurance 2 project, the operational team realized that challenges remain before the concepts are successfully launched and marketed to customers, and even more challenges will be faced before the concepts are accepted as common tools to evaluate risks and insurance cover by customers. The remaining challenges were identified as follows:

- Gaining acceptance for the novel concepts inside insurance companies,
- Concept testing, utilizing customer feedback,
- Information transfer from the project organization to participating companies,
- Challenge related to insurance products themselves.

Many innovative ideas never see the light of day because the working climate can set certain norms of behavior which hinder the creativeness of individuals and along time prevents novel concept development in the overall organization. The two eInsurance projects were intended to provide a new platform for innovative ideas that might otherwise have been rejected within the insurance company's own R&D department. Ordinary users tested the novel concepts in order to obtain information on the functionality of the novel service concept(s), before decisions regarding further development and commercialization of the concept(s) were made by the participating corporate partners.

In order to test the concept, the operational team agreed to collect feedback during the summer 2007. Data was gathered by a questionnaire survey completed by IC1 insurance company customers who had used its electronic services. The questionnaire design was similar to previous studies concerning the suitability of insurance services in the electronic context. The data was subject to a series of statistical analyses carried out using SPSS statistical software.

Table 1 shows that information searching, comparing insurance types and prices are the three main customer favorites when they use the Internet in connection with insurance business. Insurance companies should take this message seriously, as customer preferences of priorities drive their choices and acceptance of the Internet is dependent on their attitudes.

One of the major challenges concerning the case relates to further development of the concept within the corporate partner organizations. In order to commercialize the service concept successfully, the project organization transmitted information collected during the eInsurance projects to the R&D and marketing departments of the project partners. In this case departmental representatives were assigned to the project team, and the operational team interacted with them during the different phases of the project. Furthermore, one way to transfer information was to report

Table 1. Use of electronic insurance services (Nenonen et al., 2007)

	Used service in question (% of n)
Searched information on insurance (n=97)	90
Compared insurance costs (n=96)	84
Compared cover of various insurance types (n=95)	80
Worked out the insurances needed (n=92)	62
Sent an inquiry (n=92)	53
Submitted a claim report (n=93)	39
Purchased an insurance (n=90)	36
Submitted a claim application (n=93)	35
Updated personal insurance information or insurance cover (n=92)	34

the research results via publications during and after the project, including the summary report on the research results of the project. The report describes the most crucial results of both projects and lists corresponding reports and articles that provide further information. In addition to the information transfer described above, it is relevant to ask what else should be done to assist corporate partners in proceeding from the concept to a successful launch of a service.

One challenge arises from insurance products themselves as various academics consider insurance one of the most intangible of services (cf. Ahonen, 2007; Järvinen et al., 2009; Majaro, 1983). The intangible nature of services usually makes it easier to shift them to the Internet. On the other hand, the intangibility and the facelessness of electronic services may increase risk perception and distrust towards internet services (Beldad et al., 2010). However, the complexity (see Vroomen et al., 2005) of the insurance services may hinder the frequent use of electronic services. As a consequence, customers prefer individual and personal service provided by insurance experts. Following on from the previous comments, customers use the internet for gathering information, but for the next stage they still prefer discussion with an insurance clerk before making their decision (Järvinen & Heino, 2004). These habits pose great challenges for insurance services on the internet. Following from this, the new electronic insurance services should provide a new communication platform for customers and the insurance clerk, allowing them to share and combine customer needs and feasible insurance products.

At the very beginning, the preliminary guideline for planning the essential scope of the eInsurance projects took into account the fact that, since insurance is not easy for customers to comprehend, the electronic service environment should be designed in a way which makes it easy and appealing to use and thus, provides customers with opportunities to become more familiar with electronic insurance services. In order to increase customers' willingness to use electronic insurance services, a few critical issues need to be taken into consideration. First of all, customers usually need to contact the insurance company only once or at most a few times a year. Secondly, customers' operations are based on self-service logic, since the physical service contact is missing in the electronic service environment (e.g. Ahonen, 2007; Bolton & Saxena-Iyera, 2009; Meuter et al., 2000; Walsha et al., 2010). Instead, customers have to rely on their own know-how and skills in order to fulfill their service needs. For these reasons, it is more difficult for the customers to start operating in the electronic environment than in the physical environment. It is, therefore, of the utmost importance that there should be real benefit-providing services available for customers in the electronic service environment, and not just bits and pieces of additional information here and there in the content.

Finally, the project organization itself proved to be innovative in its nature, even though during the projects its working habits seemed to be natural for the purpose of that type of project. However, the project organization managed to combine academic and practical expertise in a fruitful way, that lead to the successful outcome of the projects. This case study article describes two eInsurance projects mainly from the project organization perspective, but it also pays attention to the outcomes of the research and development activities performed during the project. The "safety and insurance advisor" introduced a novel approach to offering electronic insurance services to customers, and thus, it is the main innovation of the two projects. The service content is made more appealing and comprehensible to customers by providing with better opportunities to use electronic services based on self-service logic. Thus, it is relevant to conclude, that the service concept developed brought electronic insurance services closer to the consumers' mindset when compared to existing services.

REFERENCES

Adobe. (2007). *Adobe Shockwave Player.* Retrieved from http://www.adobe.com/products/shockwaveplayer

Ahonen, A. (2007). *From complex to simple: Designing a customer-friendly electronic insurance service environment* (Academic Dissertation No. 1257). Tampere, Finland: University Press.

Ahonen, A., & Salonen, J. (2005). *eInsurance: Kohti asiakaslähtöisempää sähköistä vakuutuspalvelua [eInsurance. Towards a more customer-oriented electronic insurance service].* Tampere, Finland: VTT Industrial Systems.

Ahonen, A., Salonen, J., Kivistö-Rahnasto, J., Järvinen, R., & Silius, K. (2007, April 26-28). *eInsurance - Novel services in the electronic environment.* Paper presented at the Innovation in Services Conference, Berkeley, CA.

Ahonen, A., & Windischhofer, R. (2005). The Web performance of different types of online insurance providers - A wake up call to traditional insurance providers. In X. Zhao & B. Liu (Eds.), *Proceedings of the Fifth International Conference on Electronic Business (ICEB2005)* (pp. 245-252). Hong Kong: The Chinese University of Hong Kong.

Annique Un, C. (2010). An empirical multi-level analysis for achieving balance between incremental and radical innovations. *Journal of Engineering and Technology Management, 27*(1-2), 1–19. doi:10.1016/j.jengtecman.2010.03.001

Beldad, A., de Jong, M., & Steehouder, M. (2010). How shall I trust the faceless and the intangible? A literature review on the antecedents of online trust. *Computers in Human Behavior, 26*(5), 857–869. doi:10.1016/j.chb.2010.03.013

Bolton, R., & Saxena-Iyera, S. (2009). Interactive services: A framework, synthesis and research directions. *Journal of Interactive Marketing, 23*(1), 91–104. doi:10.1016/j.intmar.2008.11.002

Edvardsson, B., & Ollson, J. (1996). Key concepts for service development. *Service Industries Journal, 16*(2), 140–164. doi:10.1080/02642069600000019

Garcia, R., & Calantone, R. (2002). A critical look at technological innovation typology and innovativeness terminology: A literature review. *Journal of Product Innovation Management, 19*, 110–132. doi:10.1016/S0737-6782(01)00132-1

Goldstein Meyer, S., Johnston, J., Duffy, J., & Rao, J. (2002). The service concept: The missing link in service design research. *Journal of Operations Management, 20*, 121–134. doi:10.1016/S0272-6963(01)00090-0

Ives, B., & Mason, R. O. (1990). Can information technology revitalize your customer service? *The Academy of Management Executive, 4*(4), 52–69.

Järvinen, R., Eriksson, P., Saastamoinen, M., & Lystimäki, M. (2001). *Vakuutukset verkossa – Vakuutusyhtiöiden tarjonta ja kuluttajien odotukset* [Insurance on the Web – The offerings of the insurance companies and the expectations of consumers]. Helsinki, Finland: National Consumer Research Centre.

Järvinen, R., & Heino, H. (2004). *Kuluttajien palvelukokemuksia vakuutus- ja pankkisektorilta [Consumer experience from insurance and banking sectors].* Helsinki, Finland: National Consumer Research Centre (English summary).

Järvinen, R., Laitamäki, J., & Lehtinen, A.-R. (2009). Managing service encounter in knowledge intensive services – Mystery shoppers in financial markets. In N. Helander, M. Hannula, I. Ilvonen, & M. Seppä (Eds.), *EBRF 2008 Conference Proceedings.*

Järvinen, R., Lehtinen, U., & Vuorinen, I. (2003). Options of strategic decision making in services: Tech, touch and customisation in financial services. *European Journal of Marketing, 37*(5/6), 774–795. doi:10.1108/03090560310465143

Kivistö-Rahnasto, J., Ahonen, A., & Salonen, J. (2006, May 10-12). New service concepts for selecting and evaluating insurance cover within the electronic environment. In P. Mondelo, M. Mattila, W. Karwowski, & A. Hale (Eds.), *Proceeding of the 4th International Conference on Occupational Risk Prevention (ORP),* Seville, Spain. ISBN 84-933328-9-5

Majaro, S. (1983). Marketing insurance services: The main challenges. In Foxall, G. (Ed.), *Marketing in the service industries* (pp. 77–91). London, UK: Routledge.

McDermott, C. (1999). Managing radical product development in large manufacturing firms: A longitudinal study. *Journal of Operations Management, 17*, 631–644. doi:10.1016/S0272-6963(99)00018-2

Meuter, M. L., Ostrom, A. L., Roundtree, R. I., & Bitner, M. J. (2000). Self-service technologies: Understanding customer satisfaction with technology-based service encounters. *Journal of Marketing, 64*(3), 50–64. doi:10.1509/jmkg.64.3.50.18024

Nenonen, S., Salonen, J., Ahonen, A., Järvinen, R., & Kivistö-Rahnasto, J. (2007). How consumers react to electronic services in the insurance sector. In M. Hannula, M. Koiranen, M. Maula, M. Seppä, M. Suoranta, & J. Tommila (Eds.), *Proceedings of EBRF 2007.*

O'Connor, G., & McDermott, C. (2004). The human side of radical innovation. *Journal of Engineering and Technology Management, 21*, 11–30. doi:10.1016/j.jengtecman.2003.12.002

Peura-Kapanen, L., & Järvinen, R. (2006). *Kuluttajien käsityksiä riskeistä, niiden hallinnasta ja sähköisestä vakuuttamisesta* [Consumer perceptions of risk, risk management and electronic insurance]. Helsinki, Finland: National Consumer Research Centre.

Peura-Kapanen, L., Nenonen, S., Järvinen, R., & Kivistö-Rahnasto, J. (2007). *Kuluttajien arkipäivän riskit ja turvallisuus. Riskeihin liittyvät käsitykset, turvallisuuden edistäminen ja suhtautuminen sähköiseen asiointiin turvallisuuskontekstissa* [Consumers' everyday risks and safety – Risk-related views, promotion of safety and attitude towards electronic transactions in safety context]. Helsinki, Finland: National Consumer Research Centre.

Salonen, J., & Ahonen, A. (2007). *eInsurance project website*. Retrieved from http://www.einsurance.fi

Tödtlinga, F., Lehnera, P., & Kaufmann, A. (2009). Do different types of innovation rely on specific kinds of knowledge interactions? *Journal of Service Research, 8*(1), 37–47.

Vroomen, B., Donkers, B., Verhoef, P. C., & Franses, P. H. (2005). Selecting profitable customers for complex services on the internet. *Journal of Service Research, 8*(1), 37–47. doi:10.1177/1094670505276681

Walsha, G., Hennig-Thuraub, T., Sassenbergd, K., & Bornemanne, D. (2010). Does relationship quality matter in e-services? A comparison of online and offline retailing. *Journal of Retailing and Consumer Services, 17*(2), 130–142. doi:10.1016/j.jretconser.2009.11.003

Windischhofer, R., & Ahonen, A. (2004). The effect of physical distribution channels on online distribution channels in the insurance industry: An examination of electronic insurance services on the internet. In J. Chen (Ed.), *Service Systems and Service Management: Proceedings of ICSSSM'04* (Vol. 2, pp. 753-758). Beijing, China: International Academic Publishers/Beijing World Publishing Corporation.

This work was previously published in the Journal of Cases on Information Technology, Volume 12, Issue 4, edited by Mehdi Khosrow-Pour, pp. 35-49, copyright 2010 by IGI Publishing (an imprint of IGI Global).

Chapter 15
Paradigms, Science, and Technology:
The Case of E–Customs

Roman Boutellier
ETH Zurich, Switzerland

Mareike Heinzen
ETH Zurich, Switzerland

Marta Raus
ETH Zurich, Switzerland

EXECUTIVE SUMMARY

This chapter explores the concept of paradigms, science, and technology in the context of information technology (IT). Therefore, the linear model of Francis Bacon and Thomas Kuhn's notion of scientific paradigms are reviewed. This review reveals that the linear model has to be advanced, and supports the adoption of Kuhnian ideas from science to technology. As IT paradigms transform business processes, a five-level concept is introduced for deriving managerial implications and guidelines. Within the case of e-customs, a European-funded project tries to ease border security and control by adopting a common standardized e-customs solution across the public sector in Europe. The rise of the IT paradigm within customs and its effect on business operations will be explained. This chapter contributes to the research in diffusion and adoption of innovation using science progress and the interplay of science and technology as dominant concepts.

DOI: 10.4018/978-1-4666-2071-1.ch015

INTRODUCTION

Give a little boy a hammer and everything looks like a nail.
Abraham Harold Maslow (1908-1970), American psychologist

The quote of Abraham Harold Maslow (1908-1970), an American psychologist, guides the reader through each section. In analogy to the case of electronic-customs (e-customs), which will be presented in Section 4, the quote could be interpreted as giving Internet technology to a customs office, while that office's export processes remain paper-based.

The boy instinctively relates what he already knows about the hammer to new problems and challenges. Only if major problems cannot be solved by this method and more problems accumulate, we begin to ask ourselves if there are other ways of looking at the situation. In Thomas Kuhn's words, this is the heart of the scientific progress, which will be introduced in Section 3.

Thomas Kuhn's notion of scientific paradigms (Kuhn, 1962) that have been early adopted as technological paradigms (Dosi, 1982), can be described as the punctuated nature of technological change combined with path dependency of innovation processes in times of incremental progress (Peine, 2008). When analyzing the quote, the path dependency of the innovation process shows that the boy will use the hammer very efficiently for nails, whereas in times of radical technological change, he will scrutinize the one-sided use of the hammer. A paradigm sets out an array of expected solutions to accepted problems (Lakatos & Musgrave, 1970).

The description of an advanced model of Francis Bacon (Bacon, 1605) in Section 2 supports the transferability from science to technological paradigms, which are exemplified with IT paradigms. Examples are software and programming developments, as well as the technical progress from mainframe to personal computers, are currently finalized in a technological paradigm of virtual resources accessible through the Internet.

Internet technology is the underlying technology of e-customs as described in Section 4. Theories are applied to an e-customs project called Information Technology for Adoption and Intelligent Design for e-Government (ITAIDE), which has been launched for the adoption of standardized e-customs systems on an international level. A value assessment and a five level business transformation plan accompany the description of technical progress in IT.

SCIENCE AND TECHNOLOGY

While science is considered a knowledge base, technology is defined as the physical manifestation of that knowledge (Khalil, 1999). Some definitions of science and technology are:

- Science analyzes and looks for explanations in general terms. The benchmark is still the natural law and the periodic system for classification. Explanation is a natural law applied to specific boundary conditions. Technology is very much problem solving oriented, where problems come from practical considerations.
- Science lives on open questions – surprises. Every surprise is a potential candidate for a new research field and new results. Within a technology, side effects are objectionable; everything has to be controlled to avoid accidents and non-performance.
- Technology must have a goal to fix or build something, a reliable and sturdy bridge for example. The goal in science usually comes from within science. The goals of technology are defined by the needs of customers– short term solutions are better than solutions for the long term.

Indeed, science and technology are much closer today than in earlier times. A good example is computer technology. It developed in a logical path from Leibniz to Microsoft, yet only in hindsight. Another example is the X-ray technology invented by Konrad Röntgen in 1895.

Within one year after the detection of X-rays, more than 49 scientific books were on the market, including more than 1,000 scientific papers. X-ray technology spread with a speed that is amazing even for 21st century standards. Just two months after invention, it was used for forensic evidence in an American court. Thus, fact that both science and technology developed parallel to each other, is evident within a historical perspective.

LINEAR MODEL

In ancient times, technology was simply a tool to survive. In Galileo's times, around 1650, this changed. Telescope and microscope helped to improve our scientific understanding of the world. Technology became more and more a tool of improving conditions of life.

In order to explain the interaction between science and technology, a simple model was created in the 17th century: The linear model of Francis Bacon (Figure

1). Basic science leads to applied science which leads to technology, and with that to growth and welfare (Bacon, 1605).

Until the late 19th century, technology and science developed in parallel, but well separated from each other. There is some evidence that technology fertilized science more than the other way around. Galileo did not understand the optics of his telescope but used it to prove his theories. Stevenson, the inventor of the locomotive, was illiterate and his first machines contradicted accepted thermodynamic theories of his time. The middle of the 19th century brought the turning of the tide: Justus Liebig applied science to improve fertilizers and storage of meat. Scientific technology began its victorious campaign.

Today, most people are strong believers of Francis Bacon's linear model: Because in current times, we try to explain everything with as much science as possible. For example, even in management mathematical models predominate with all the risks involved: Black-Sholes equations are the fundament of all structured financial products.

Advanced Linear Model

While the linear model has useful explanatory value, its output, discovery, and innovation are much less deterministic. As history shows, most innovations derived from small improvements in technology and were surprisingly random products. Sometimes innovation developed through the application of unspecified research results, like the ABS, airbag, calculator, and telephone. As (Bygrave, 1989) stated, "We should avoid reductionism in entrepreneurship research. Instead, we should look at the whole."(p.20).

An alternative model to consider is the interdependence of science and technology which includes technology, basic and applied research, innovation, and wealth (Figure 2). Not only basic research, but applied research as well can lead to technology and vice versa, and thus, to economic wealth. Innovation plays a big role too, as it is the outcome of science and technology and the major driver for economic growth and important for the future wealth of nations (Easterly, 2001).

Figure 1. Linear model of Francis Bacon (1561 – 1626): 17th century and the scientists' optimism (Bacon, 1605)

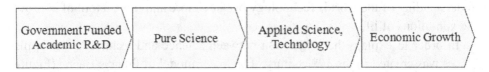

Figure 2. The multi-dimensional model of scientific progress: We have to look at the whole (Bacon, 1605 modified)

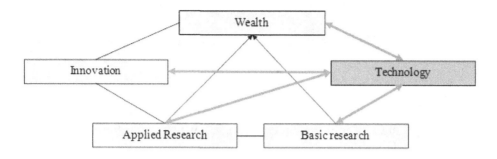

Technology is certainly one of the most important drivers in today's economy. Scientific results push frontiers forward, engineers improve existing technologies and introduce new ones, and society is as receptive for new technologies as never before. In the middle of the 19th century, technology became more and more driven by science. Hence, today's society is very much driven by technology - progress has become technical progress. Neill Postman, an American scholar of communication calls it "Technopoly", the submission of all forms of cultural life to the sovereignty of technique and technology (Postman, 1992).

That science can lead to technology is clear, but the reverse is as true as well: Without technology, no modern science could exist. Just think about CERN, the European organization for Nuclear Research, in Geneva or medical imaging technology like Computed Tomography Angiography (CTA) and Magnetic Resonance Imaging (MRI). Science tries to explain existing objects, technology and engineering want to create new objects, artifacts, and objects created by human beings.

The Sunniberg Bridge near Klosters, Switzerland, could be built only by an experienced engineer inspired by strong aesthetical thinking. The engineer behind it, Christian Menn from ETH Zurich, has succeeded in harmonizing technology, material functionality, environment, and usage. The bridge is a masterpiece of simplicity and functionality, just like Mario Botta's church on Monte Tamaro/Ticino (Figure 3). Mario Botta used only two local materials. An integral innovation; however social choices are driven by human values, aesthetics, which influence science and technology.

The fact that science, technology, and values are highly interwoven is the basis for the following Section 3 of scientific paradigms, with its underlying thesis that scientific problems influence technological problems and vice versa.

Figure 3. Mario Botta: The chapel of St. Mary of the Angel, Monte Tamaro

Such multi-dimensional models have greater explanatory value in the development and application of information technologies, which is illustrated in the case study following in Section 4.

THEORY OF PARADIGMS

One of the ways we solve problems is by instinctively applying what we already know to new problems and challenges. However, if over time major problems in a field cannot be solved by this method, more and more problems accumulate. We begin to ask ourselves if there are other ways to look at the situation—perhaps it is time to change the basic "paradigms" of our thinking.

The term "paradigm" refers to accepted practices. Paradigms are the way we perceive, think and value the world, based upon a particular vision of reality. They provide us with a valid set of expectations about what will most likely occur based on a shared set of assumptions. Paradigms establish boundaries and define how to succeed within the boundaries. When we are in the middle of a paradigm, it is difficult to imagine any other paradigm. Conditions are ripe for a "paradigm shift" when a sufficient number of people agree that the old ways no longer solve important problems and that new ways are needed.

Of course, not everyone in a field does change because a new paradigm comes on the scene. Some people are so committed to particular paradigms that they will never change. It is not always easy to know when to change and when to step around those who do not. According to Max Planck (1949), "A new scientific truth does not triumph by convincing its opponents and making them see the light, but rather because its opponents eventually die, and a new generation grows up that is familiar with it" (p.596).

Thomas Samuel Kuhn, a historian of science, gave the word "paradigm" its contemporary meaning when he adopted it to refer to the set of practices that define a scientific discipline during a particular period of time. According to Kuhn (1962), a scientific paradigm is as fundamental belief which is signified by a consensus on problems and methods within a field of research. From time to time, it is followed by systemic innovations, what Kuhn termed "paradigm shifts". Then, the period of the old paradigm is over and a new one begins.

Kuhn's model is one of the most often cited philosophical results of the 20th century. Historic examples are the struggle between the Ptolemaic systems and Copernicus' heliocentric system or the introduction of relativity through Einstein at the beginning of the 20th century. Even today, Newton's theory of mechanics is still in use concurrently to Einstein's theory. The system of Copernicus was more complicated than the old Ptolemaic system, since Copernicus stuck to circles. Numerical results predicting star positions were no better than results obtained in the Ptolemaic system. Only Kepler's ellipses brought the unification much sought after. An explanation in the sense of a law was given later by Newton. However, Newton had to introduce the notion of gravitational force working at infinite speed without any intermediaries. A notion perceived as an unacceptable setback by many contemporary scientists (Koestler, 1989).

Kuhn confirmed also the notion in Section 2 that science develops in a non-linear pattern and not within a linear model. Each generation solves its own problems - not because the problems have changed, but because the knowledge and mindsets of each generation evolve after each scientific revolution (Lakatos & Musgrave, 1970).

Therefore, science and technology are highly interacting, and thus, leading to innovation. Several authors adopted Kuhn's notion of scientific paradigms as technological paradigms (Dosi, 1982; Granberg & Stankiewicz, 1981; Johnston, 1972), using Kuhnian ideas describing technological progress. But also profound progress in medicine, transportation, the physical sciences, labor laws, social attitudes, and the way we work are taking place within a continuous strain, broken up by disruptive innovations from time to time (Christensen, 1997).

An example of management trend triggered by earlier paradigm shifts includes the Total Quality movement that began in Japan in the late 1950s, spreading to manufacturing all over the world. A technological paradigm shift was Sony's invention of the Walkman in the field of personal entertainment. The Walkman was the direct predecessor of the concept of mobile communications embodied by today's cellular telephones.

As Kuhn pointed out, changes in paradigms have a predictable pattern. Understanding this pattern improves our ability to use it for problem solving. Those who recognize that a paradigm shift is taking place will benefit from consequences of the shift. Many become leaders in their industry or field. For example, Albert Einstein was a youthful beginner in the field of science when he first defined his theory of relativity. The founders of FedEx and of Apple Computer were also new to their fields when they conceived new technical and business paradigms.

Applying Abraham Maslow's quote again, the boy who will not use only the hammer when he sees nails will create a new paradigm.

Thomas Kuhn's Scientific Paradigms

Diving deeper into Thomas Samuel Kuhn's work, he differentiates between 'normal science' and 'scientific revolutions' (Kuhn, 1962). Normal science is a process of puzzle-solving, where scientists work with proven methods to achieve expected solutions on accepted problems. The puzzles within these problems are perceived as scientifically interesting and attract an enduring group of adherents from competing modes of scientific activity. They also have to be open-ended leaving problems for their group of practitioners (and their students) to resolve. For example, in the Ptolemaic astronomical model, the earth was at the center of the universe. This scientific model gave unsatisfactory explanations to the retrograde motion of the outer planets until the Middle Ages, when Copernicus presented a heliocentric framework to explain planetary movement.

Students study these paradigms in order to become members of the specific scientific community in which they will later practice. Because students largely learn from and are mentored by researchers who learned the bases of their fields from the same models, there is seldom disagreement over fundamentals. Scientists, whose research is based on shared paradigms, are committed to the same basic rules and standards for their scientific practice. This way, the paradigm implicitly drives how scientists solve problems. Scientists automatically prefer problems that can be solved with these rules leading to a repetitive application of methods, tools, and routines through which scientists become efficient. The more positive results we get, the higher the acceptance of this theory – a self-reinforcing circle. This is Kuhn's second definition of a paradigm (Kuhn & Neurath, 1970), where paradigms embody tacit norms and rules. It even refers to the priority of paradigms: "Paradigms may be prior to, more binding and more complete than any set of rules for research that could be unequivocally abstracted from them" (p. 24).

According to Kuhn, scientists will apply the current paradigms' methods until anomalies or surprising discoveries emerge – the beginning of 'scientific revolutions' (Kuhn, 1962). The emergence of a new theory is generated by the persistent failure to solve puzzles within normal science. Failure of existing approaches is the prelude to a search for new ones. In early stages of a new paradigm, many alternatives are explored. Once a paradigm is entrenched (and the tools of the paradigm prove useful to solve the problems the paradigm defines), alternative theories are consolidated. Crises provide the opportunity to retool. Like one of the most intriguing aspects in Einstein's theory the Clock Paradox, this started a big discussion among scientists.

Technology Adoption Seen as Paradigm Change

Kuhn's scientific paradigm has been applied to technological progress (Dosi, 1982; Granberg & Stankiewicz, 1981; Johnston, 1972). Johnston ascribed the punctuated nature of technological change to the internal structure of technology, meaning a "set guiding principles accepted by practitioners in a particular field of technology" (p. 122). With his definition, he focused especially on the paradigm shift. In contrast to Johnston, Granberg and Stankiewicz elaborated the activities of the community of technologists, such as technological research and functional analysis, in more detail (p. 216). Also, Dosi described that phases of incremental technological change are alternating with punctuated changes of radical shifts.

"In broad analogy with the Kuhnian definition of a 'scientific paradigm', we shall define a 'technological paradigm' as 'model' and a 'pattern' of solutions of selected technological problems, based on selected principles derived from natural sciences and on selected material technologies" (Dosi, 1982, p. 152). Further, Dosi defined two drivers of technological progress: (1) the material part of a technology, which is the exemplary artifact representing the function of a paradigm; and (2) the disembodied part of a technology containing expertise, experiences and practical knowledge.

Peine (2008) described the adoption of the Kuhnian framework of scientific paradigms to technological change as still underexposed, and Vincenti (1995) highlighted the instructive impact of Kuhn's work in understanding the "technical shape of technology."

Thus, this research applies Kuhn's idea of scientific paradigms to technological progress that moves also in revolutionary steps and long eras of small improvements. Both scientific and technological progress needs four steps in three phases (Figure 4) for the birth of a new paradigm: (1) puzzle solving within an existing paradigm, (2) anomalies, leading to disputes among scientists, (3) change of paradigm and change of culture, and (4) puzzle solving within a new accepted theory.

However, it is important that material and the disembodied part of a technology are considered separately (Dosi, 1982). Staying with the example of the Sony Walkman, the material technology of personalized entertainment had a different pace of progress than the expertise, experience and practical knowledge developing that technology.

TECHNOLOGICAL AND COMPUTING PARADIGMS

A big technological revolution was the development from analog to digital systems. At some point, analog signals were too limited in bandwidth, and hence, a better

Figure 4. Kuhn's scientific theory adapted to technological paradigms (based on Kuhn 1970)

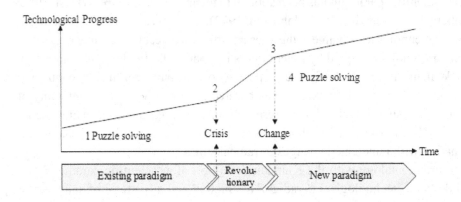

system had to be developed. The big advantages of a digital system are that operations can be conducted more frequently and are less error-prone, and therefore, copies can be made indefinitely. Without digital systems, computing paradigms would have developed differently.

A computing paradigm emerged due to modularization in software development. Until 1980, procedural programming was in place. After that time, three industry layers evolved: (1) a generic layer that is responsible for generic software components, (2) an application layer that is responsible for special industry applications, and (3) a customer layer that is responsible for customer requests. Such layer modules are applied by companies like SAP, Oracle, Sony and Ericsson. Further, procedural programming was redeemed by object-oriented programming, using "multiple inheritances" within the concept of classes and instances – a new programming paradigm. Object-oriented programming developed as the dominant programming methodology during the mid-1990s, largely due to the influence of C++.

Another big information technological progress has been reached through the development of personal computers. Before the introduction of the microprocessor in the early 1970s, computers were generally large, costly systems owned by large corporations, universities, government agencies, and similar-sized institutions. Until that time, none in the information technological community thought computer systems could be of interest for individuals. In 1977, Apple Computers introduced the Apple II as the world's first PC. From that time on, computers were developed for household use. A new paradigm had evolved, convincing the community of computer scientists that computers would be demanded by individuals. Since that time, computer scientists have kept working on processor performance, speed and miniaturization, resulting in ever smaller, highly productive PCs including laptops, net books, table PCs and Pocket PCs.

Another paradigm in IT-Management goes a little bit further: Cloud computing offers the customer virtualized resources provided as a service over the Internet. Cloud computing customers do not generally own the physical infrastructure. Instead, they avoid capital expenditure by renting usage from a third-party provider. They consume resources as a service and pay only for resources that they use. Some of the vendors providing cloud computing services are Google, Amazon, Microsoft and Yahoo. However, opinions of specialists about cloud computing differ. Some call it the biggest revolution since the Internet, others criticize cloud computing as being a regression in limiting both freedom and creativity of the user. Thus, cloud computing cannot be called a paradigm yet – the revolution is still up in the air.

The Paradigm Effect on Business Transformation: Managerial Guidelines

Because most business processes today are IT related, computing paradigms have had and will continue to have an impact on business transformation. IT has become a fundamental enabler in creating and maintaining flexible business networks. Thus, understanding these paradigms, together with the knowledge of Kuhnian non-linear concepts, provides guidance to managers.

Venkatraman (1994) breaks the IT-enabled business transformation into five levels with two dimensions: the range of IT's potential benefits and the degree of organizational transformation (Figure 5). The central underlying hypothesis is that benefits of IT progress are lower if organizational strategies, structure processes, and culture are not adapted to IT development.

The first level is called "Localized Exploitation". In this stage, managers often respond to an operational problem with a localized isolated system; for example, a customer order-entry system or a toll-free customer service system. Learning among managers is minimal and thus limits potential benefits. Competitors can easily imitate these standard technical applications.

The second level, "Integral Integration", is characterized by two types of integration: (1) technical interconnectivity through a common IT platform; and (2) business process interdependence across different functions within the organization. Venkatraman (1994) observed that managers allocate their interest more to technical interconnectivity than to business process interdependence.

The first two levels are called "evolutionary" because only small changes to the business processes are required; whereas, the subsequent three higher levels are "revolutionary", since they require fundamental changes in organizational routines.

Figure 5. Five levels of IT-enabled business transformation (Venkatraman, 1994, p. 74)

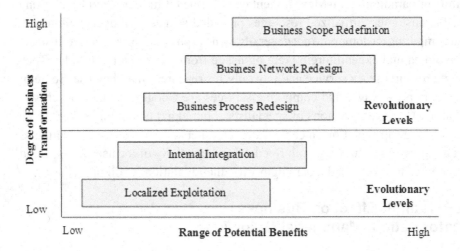

The higher the level of transformation, the greater the benefits of organizational routine changes.

With "Business Process Redesign", IT is fully integrated in the organization. However, benefits of IT functionality cannot be fully realized because general concepts of business processes are still valid, such as centralization vs. decentralization, functional specialization and administrative mechanisms.

The three lower levels focus only on a single organization, whereas the next higher level, "Business Network Redesign", expands interconnections to include external businesses, such as suppliers, buyers and other intermediaries with regard to IT deployment. Potential benefits, besides administrative and operational efficiency, are leveraging competencies due to IT-enabled strategic alliances and enhanced learning.

Within the top level "Business Scope Redefinition", IT deployment enables or facilitates the repositioning of a firms' business scope. Strategy concepts that led to increased emphasis on vertical integration would be replaced by newer concepts, such as joint ventures or virtual business networks.

Thus, an organization should first identify the transformational level that is appropriate for its situation. This evaluation will depend on managers' perception as to whether IT capabilities are seen as an opportunity or a threat to the status quo. It can be helpful to to assess where other leading companies are positioned in order to create organizational awareness of limitations and to get commitment.

In summary, we have shown that the linear model of Francis Bacon has to be enlarged; and also that Kuhn's notion of scientific paradigms, with its emphasis on progress in steps, can be applied not only on science, but also to technology and management. After presenting scientific and technological examples for theory clarification, we focused on computing paradigms. As IT paradigms enable business transformations, we introduced a five level framework for deriving managerial guidelines and implications. This theoretical background will be used to get a better understanding of the Case of e-customs.

THE CASE OF E-CUSTOMS

One of the interesting effects of information technology is that it changes organizational paradigms. As problems with an existing paradigm surface, technological solutions may be applied, resulting in a paradigm shift. This can be illustrated by a case concerning border control, where the old paradigm of government customs officers processing paperwork, as a way of ensuring border control and security, has been shown to be inadequate. With the application of information technologies under the auspices of e-customs, a new paradigm in border security has emerged. The technology for e-customs exists, using the Internet as a service-tool. However, business processes have not been aligned yet to the new technology available in Europe and worldwide.

Therefore, the EU currently funds the project called the Information Technology for Adoption and Intelligent Design (ITAIDE, IST-02789) involving stakeholders from academy, industry, and governmental institutions to support European member states with e-Custom solutions. Within that project, one initiative of the European Commission to create a simple and paperless environment for customs and trade is the Multi-Annual Strategic Plan (MASP) setting the framework for the following case. The main goal of MASP is to share vision, objectives, strategic framework, and milestones for an e-customs implementation.

The Advanced Linear Model within E-Customs

The boundaries of science and technology are hard to establish, as many computer scientists find their research in algorithms or programs immediately applicable as a technology. This is the case in e-customs, where progresses in scientific and technology interact with one another. Scientific progress started with the development and diffusion of information and communication technology (ICT). The invention of the Internet revolutionized ICT and enabled electronic business concepts, where individuals or groups do not deal face to face, but conduct business remotely, regardless of location and time.

In addition to traditional business-to-business (B2B) and business-to-consumer (B2C) technologies, business-to-government (B2G) technologies recently have incorporated transactions from public sectors. According to Wassenaar (2000), e-Government describes an information exchange which can be a transaction or a contract between companies, governments, customers, suppliers or other partners. E-customs is an innovation within e-Government and focuses mainly on border control and security. Its underlying technology is ICT using electronic data networks, such as provided by the Internet. With the diffusion and adoption of a common standardized e-customs solution across Europe, EU hopes to mainly reduce administrative burden and strengthen the European economy. As the application of ICT in customs transforms business processes, a new field of research about organizational change has evolved. This is demonstrated by the vast research literature put forth by authors, such as, Baida, Liu, & Tan (2007), Baida, Rukanova, Wigand, & Tan (2007); Bjørn-Andersen, Razmerita, & Henriksen (2007), Boyd, Hobbs, & Kerr (2003), Henriksen & Rukanova (2008), Henriksen, Rukanova, & Tan (2008), Kuiper (2007), and Raus, Kipp, & Boutellier (2008).

As scientific results push frontiers forward, engineers continue to improve existing technologies and introduce new ones. Society is unprecedently receptive to the introduction of new technologies. As such, the project of ITAIDE is a perfect example of Francis Bacon's advanced model (Figure 6), as explained in the following paragraph.

In modern research, engineers and industry are both involved in research projects from the beginning. This is the case with the ITAIDE project. These types of research projects, funded by the EU, may be considered as partnerships between research universities and industries. Pure Science, applied science and technology go hand in hand, working in workshops, projects and at universities together. This is unlike Bacon's linear model where one typically follows the other. Even though science and technology have different objectives and methods, they can enrich each other, which leads to innovation and thus, to economic growth.

An intensive integration of distinct research disciplines: social sciences, information technology, and political science lead to balanced solutions, higher efficiency and hopefully wealth in the future.

The Technological Paradigm of E-Customs

As basis for studying the application of the theory of technological paradigms to the case of e-customs, this section will focus on the export of goods from EU countries to non-EU countries. This is a pilot project within ITAIDE concentrating on a food

Figure 6. The e-customs EU-funded project ITAIDE is a good example of an advanced model of Francis Bacon

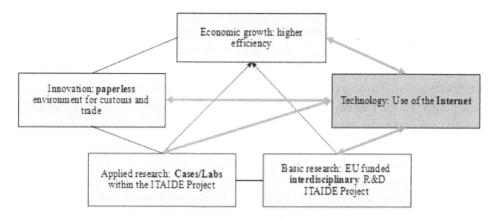

industry company, exporting from Denmark to Russia (ITAIDE 2009). Important in this regard is that Denmark already has a national e-customs system in use, which in comparison is different from Germany or Italy whereby ERP-systems such as Atlas or Aida are used.

The following sections will describe the adoption of e-customs as a technological paradigm by means of Kuhn's four steps: (1) the old paradigm of customs, (2) issues, questions and problems with the old paradigm, (3) technological opportunities, and (4) the new paradigm.

The Old Paradigm of Customs

E-customs focuses on international trade, where "International trade is characterized not only by the physical movement of goods across national boundaries but by voluminous paperwork that captures information pertinent to identification, delivery, and government control of transported goods"(Teo, Tan, & Wei, 1997). Although today's information technology offers modern e-Solutions, e-customs management is still associated with administrative processes, filling documents, multiple data entry on paper, and electronically processed forms. It is not seen as innovative as product design or manufacturing automation (Raus, Flügge, & Boutellier, 2008). The customs authorities still have a bureaucratic, administrative, and old-fashioned image – a paradigm that sets the rules of the game: At present, EU customs offices communicate by telephone, emails, and fax, or by periodic meetings. Data, despite being virtually identical, are processed via separate IT systems. Personnel still feel they are more efficient with their old tools in comparison to applying and learning new ones. Metaphorically speaking, *they still use the hammer for fixing the nail.*

The case of the exporting food company in Denmark confirms the old paradigm described above. The export procedure from Denmark to Russia is currently paper based. This has been examined by an as-is analysis with the help of interviews and a value modeling tool, where all communication, transportation and transaction paths are documented. Throughout the export process, several value exchanges have to be arranged by the Danish food company, such as getting money from the importing Russian company, paying the logistics or shipping costs, and obtaining various certificates for export to Russia. For these value exchanges, various documents are required. An example is the GOST certificate, which is an acronym for state standards of Russia and is obligatory for export to Russia and has to be submitted in original form along with 20 to 30 copies. It takes at least two months to get a GOST certificate and costs about 2000 Euro for the exporter. Another example is the packaging list, which is a Microsoft Excel spreadsheet created manually. More than 12 other documents are required, most of them paper-based, with mandatory stamps and signatures.

Obviously, the technological paradigm of a common Internet-based customs solution is not sufficiently interesting to attract market entry by the customs community in the competing paper-based customs process. Therefore, EU has set up an EU-Directive that makes the implementation of a standardized common e-customs system mandatory by 2013. In spite of this directive, the old paradigm is still ruling. Kuhn (1970) said that paradigms can be more binding than any rules.

Although information and Internet technologies are developing rapidly, basic e-customs solutions are currently available, and Internet usage is growing worldwide, there is an international resistance to the adoption of e-customs. Kuhn's explanation to such resistance is the loss of efficiency by implementing new technologies.

Issues, Questions, and Problems with the Old Paradigm

The first big change in thinking about the traditional paper-based border control and security came with the September 11th terrorist attacks in the United States as well as subsequent attacks in other places. These events led to higher legal standards and safety regulations in trade and customs. With this crisis, the necessity of new global standards and transparency evolved. As Internet technologies in general reduce corruption through transparency and harmonization of rules, e-customs received a new wave of attention: The perception became that the globalized world trade is to be treated with corresponding techniques – IT solutions. Metaphorically speaking, "nails changed and they cannot be treated with a hammer anymore. The old paradigm runs into difficulties."

That political developments can have a big influence on scientific or technological developments has been stressed by Kuhn (1970) in the section entitled, "The nature and necessity of scientific revolutions" where he states, "This genetic aspect of the parallel between political and scientific developments should no longer be open to doubt." (p. 93) and also, "One aspect of parallelism must already be apparent … that existing institutions have ceased adequately to meet the problems posed by an environment they have in part created." (p. 92).

After the September 11th terrorist attacks, the US customs wanted to increase safety regulations by requiring one common and standardized European e-customs system. Then, the US would have a universal European customs partner instead of several national trading partners with different systems.

A big issue within the Danish Russian export example is the co-existence of trade infrastructure, which makes the different actors dependent on one another. The reason is that data sets are not standardized, multiple authorities have to be approached for one and the same commercial transaction, and economic zones have different certification programs.

In the European Union, national e-customs declaration systems are already used in many countries (e.g., Atlas in Germany, Aida in Italy or Sagitta Entry in the Netherlands). However, the European member states are self-reliant on how to adopt an individual e-customs system, hampering trade and transactions on the European market when compared to American, Asian or Pacific businesses.

Technological Opportunities

The technological opportunities for an e-customs system have been in existence since the Internet started a vigorous campaign that lead to e-Business solutions. This is the first dimension in our transformation model, shown in Figure 5. As previously mentioned, some EU members are taking advantage of these opportunities. Although countries, such as Denmark, already use e-customs, a common standardized electronic customs system is still missing. For this reason, the EU is funding the project ITAIDE for trade facilitation as well as securing import and export by the use of an e-customs system to be implemented no later than 2013.

Two e-customs concepts of the ITAIDE project will simplify the adoption of a new standardized e-customs system in Europe: (1) the Single Window Access (SWA) and (2) the Authorized Economic Operator (AEO). Both topics are addressed by the EU initiative to reduce the administrative burden of trade transactions and increase security and control mechanisms. A single window is "a facility that allows parties involved in trade and transport to lodge standardized information and documents with a single entry point to fulfill all import, export, and transit-related regulatory requirements. If information is electronic, then individual data elements should only be submitted once" (Dedrick & West, 2003; United Nations Economic Commission for Europe, 2005). This common solution would harmonize differences in both systems and regulations. In addition, the automation would help to accelerate the export execution process and decrease entry errors supporting both government and business companies in a faster, more efficient collaboration. With the AEO status, reliable operators can be certified, including those that are also compliant in respect of security and safety standards, and thus, can be considered secure traders.

A redesign of the Danish-Russian export example would incorporate the idea of a common European customs coordinator, which is implemented as a web service. The scenario builds on an elimination of papers in the customs process and harmonization of European customs processes through the introduction of a common data model (ITAIDE, 2009).

Several authors have summarized facilitators for the diffusion of e-customs solutions (Henriksen & Rukanova, 2008; Raus, Flügge, & Boutellier, 2009), which will support the paradigm shift:

1. E-customs leads to time and financial savings, as well as higher accuracy in data processing. Time savings have been realized due to executing procedures faster and diminishing multiple manual data entries. Financial savings were the result of streamlining operations and the computerization of repetitive tasks. New puzzles can be solved.
2. The implementation of precertification of organizations and accessing data prior to the arrival of the shipment helped to eliminate irrelevant process steps and the redesign of processes, so that tasks can be carried out in parallel.
3. The formulation of new laws or changing current ones are a key requirement to stimulate environment for the development of e-customs in the countries.
4. E-customs will define common process patterns. Considering the variety of stakeholders involved in the export process, the standardization of the process steps, such as ordering, export declaration, and delivery, would ease the supply chain flow.

In Kuhn's words, these enablers represent a typical paradigm shift: If the technology of e-customs is established, processes get more and more standardized, efficient and routine. The access of registration-related information worldwide will broaden the scientific community and will support the paradigm shift, as rules are visible for everybody. This is especially the case if IT standards are capable of spreading on a global basis. In order to reach a large community, the determination, definition, and specification of standard characteristics are key factors.

The New Paradigm

As globalization, statutory provisions, IT modernization of public authorities and growth of world trade continue to increase, IT standards in the field of customs management will expand worldwide. The vision of e-customs is a paperless environment for customs and trade. Internet technology in customs has changed practices and regulations and leads to new ways of working between government and businesses.

On the European path to this new paradigm, EU has introduced a strategic action plan to connect IT-systems and procedures of business units with e-customs systems of all European member states. Due to business networks or statistical specifications, non-EU members are affected by this plan as well. At an international level, the Kyoto ICT Guidelines[1] demand to apply common standards for imports, exports and documentation worldwide.

According to Kuhn, these treaties are the first step to a paradigm shift, as they set new rules for the environment. (2004) confirm: "regulation is the intentional activity of attempting to control, order or influence the behavior of others" (p.332). The definition outlines a common understanding of regulation as a steering mechanism in society.

As international e-customs solutions are not in use yet, the paradigm has not shifted completely. However, some approaches have been made in the last years to stimulate common e-customs system worldwide. For instance, the case project ITAIDE in which e-custom solutions are being tested includes actual business scenarios. The development phase is conducted in so-called living laboratories that are characterized by pre-defined industry specific or cross-industrial trade scenarios with one exporting country and one importing country. Resolutions take place in specific places and move on much later, like the pilot project of using a national e-customs system in Denmark and the exemplary Danish Russian export case.

Denmark, Sweden and Switzerland are examples of successful implementation of parts of e-customs solutions fostering the paradigm's diffusion.

Denmark reported in 2009 almost all export declarations electronically. As there is no standardization across Europe, Denmark had to directly computerize the previous manual and paper-based system. Thus, it is still possible to have paper equivalents for electronic messages in situations where companies do not want to submit export data electronically (such as in the case of an export to Russia).

In the Danish-Russian export case, an information bridge between Danish and Russian customs will be linked by extra information, the "e-Import" information, which is directly derived from the "e-Export" information achieved from the Danish customs. With this linking between the two customs offices, Russian customs will know about the status of the goods before the goods actually arrive. Import tax fraud with double invoicing can be minimized. The same is true regarding certificate han-

341

dling. An "e-Certificate" will replace the current paper and stamp based certificate. No posting and human handling will be necessary, and all the certificates will be verified electronically by certification authorities and sent directly to the Russian customs. Risk of certification fraud is thus minimized (ITAIDE 2009). This is a typical example of loss of efficiency during a Kuhnian revolution.

On a conceptual level, export processes from Sweden and Denmark are very similar and follow the same steps. For example, Sweden introduced digital signatures in their customs procedures and replaced paper-based and stamped document checks. Consequently, they can comply with the requirement of the four eye-principle[2] by requesting visible control checkpoints across organizations (Tullverket, 2006).

Switzerland is a special example in demonstrating the importance of facilitated legislations and e-customs systems as a small non-EU country inside the EU. It needs specific customs regulations for every single trade within Europe. For being compliant with EU regulations and especially with the e-customs initiative, the Swiss Federal Customs Administration launched in June 2007 a project called IDEE (Ideale elektronische Exporteurlösung, ideal solution for exporters). The goal of this project is the replacement of its old, paper-based VAR system (VAR = Vereinfachte Ausfuhrregelung, a simplified set of export rules), originated from the 1970's, with a new e-customs system called e-dec[3] (electronic declaration), which will be binding from July 1, 2009. After that date, Swiss companies can declare their exports electronically. Consequently, approximately 900 Swiss companies using VAR today have to adapt their export procedures to electronic ones.

That e-customs indeed drives value in the public sector shows value assessment in a Danish food company, belonging to the ITAIDE project (Raus, 2009). Four major goals with an e-customs adoption have been identified: (1) security, (2) reduction of administrative burden, (3) compliance and (4) communication.

In the Danish food company case, the common e-customs system reduced monthly safety irregularities by 50-75%. This accelerated the order execution and reduced personnel cost by 25-50%. Due to the reduction of administrative burden, export process cycles increased about 25-50%. Even though the company is already compliant with current regulations, e-customs directives, like Single Window, make it easier to be compliant to all regulations being processed and tested electronically. It is now easier to move to higher levels of business transformations: New puzzles may be solved like business network redesign.

Figure 7 summarizes this study. The figure concentrates on the diffusion of e-customs in general using Kuhn's notion of scientific progress with the mentioned four steps of: (1) puzzle solving, (2) crisis, (3) change and (4) new puzzle solving. The paradigm shift from a paper-based customs administration to electronic customs can be confirmed to a certain degree given e-customs is viewed as mandatory in international trade. EU has a committed time schedule for 2013 e-customs implementation.. Thus, the paradigm shift to a common e-customs solution may be considered predetermined.

Globalization and the complexity of trade and political events such as terror attacks, led to stronger regulations that supported the necessity of a transparent and safe international trading system. With the technological opportunity of the Internet and IT modernization this could be realized by IT standards. Consequently, most of the rules of the paradigm are set through treaties, guidelines, and technical standards. In spite of these rules, there is still resistance within the customs community.

Problems, Issues, and Questions within the New Paradigm of Border Control

The diffusion of a standardized common e-customs system across European countries turns out to be difficult, as the procurement of information and technology and the implementation of e-customs solutions is not specified across countries (Raus, Flügge, & Boutellier, 2009). Rules and guidelines mandated by governments and EU are still unclear and unspecified for some members of the customs community, such as companies and Custom authorities. This uncertainty leads to a resistance within the "old scientific community" to switch to the new paradigm.

The three major barriers of the adoption of e-customs are (Henriksen & Rukanova, 2008; Raus, Flügge, & Boutellier, 2009):

Figure 7. E-customs is currently still on the edge between invention and adoption due to barriers like unclear regulations and missing cultural change

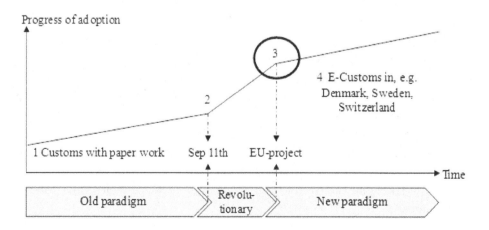

1. Regulations can be a powerful instrument on a national level for e-customs implementation, the power of regulation fades to recommendations and soft laws on an international level. If customs aim to fulfill the principle Pacta Sunt Servanda (agreements must be kept), one of the oldest principles in international law (Henriksen, Rukanova, & Tan, 2008), they have to stick to their old instruments, as the new one is missing procedural details and direction.

2. Speaking in Kuhn's words, regulations of an international e-customs system do not involve the whole customs community, as not all standards are applicable to all industries. SMEs have difficulties in implementing and maintaining different standards or systems. Even though the EU aims for establishing one common e-customs system for all, countries still have to adopt the systems individually. Thus, some countries might not deploy the outlined roadmap to its full extent (Raus, Flügge, & Boutellier, 2009).

3. While e-customs support citizens and businesses through more convenient and accessible services (Burn & Robins, 2003), governmental activities might change or become obsolete. This leads to an intermediate loss of efficiency. The fear of losing jobs or not having the right skill-set to cope with the new technical environment constitutes a crucial issue. The risk of resistance within organizations is still big, due to cultural diversity across the European member states. The theory of e-customs is still not valid enough to even take away their fears of adopting a new theory.

Jeyaraj, Rottman, and Lacity (Jeyaraj, Rottman, & Lacity, 2004) support these findings affirming that the relative advantage will be perceived if the innovation can be adapted to the individual situation of the adopters. In addition, the authors explain that the behavior of individual adopters to accept a new solution is very much linked to the social network the adopter is embedded in. This leads back to Kuhn's concept of the scientific community. The community will only accept a new paradigm if its members are strong believers and involved in the process. (Henriksen, Rukanova, & Tan, 2008) state that "an interesting trend is the tendency to emphasize that regulation is created by technocrats but it is the practitioners which have to deal with regulation. Thus, the need to manage change is one of the major outcomes of the analysis in the case of diffusion and adoption of e-customs system innovations."(p. 17).

A change in e-Government initiatives was developed by Guha, Grover, Kettinger, and Teng (1997), and later modified by Burn and Robins (2003) based on the statement of Kalakota, Oliva, and Donath (1999), "top management support is essential" in taking an "active role organizationally to shape their firms' policies and standards.".

Although the paradigm has changed, the culture has not. As the barriers showed, some involved parties still fear new technology and change. Nevertheless, an information technological paradigm shift from customs to e-customs is irrevocable.

Implications for Business Processes and Customs Officials

Shifting from paper-based to paperless processes does not necessarily involve significant changes in the processes. However, in order to make full use of the optimizations incurred by the reduction of paper, a process redesign can yield further significant optimizations in time, complexity and money. New puzzles may be solved in a different way.

According to Venkatraman's (1994) five-level model (shown in Figure 8), the EU has already defined the transformational level that would be appropriate in 2013: Business Network Redesign where interconnections are expanded to external businesses, like suppliers, buyers or other intermediaries with regard to IT deployment. This is the goal the EU is trying to achieve with ITAIDE, not for competitive reasons like a company, but for facilitating trade and transactions worldwide and enhancing operational and financial efficiency in the public sector.

Currently, the adoption of e-customs appears to be located in levels two or three. In some countries, such as, Denmark, Sweden and Switzerland, IT is fully integrated in the customs area. This places these countries in level three "Business

Figure 8. Different countries are on different levels and seek level four (according to Venkatraman, 1994, p. 74)

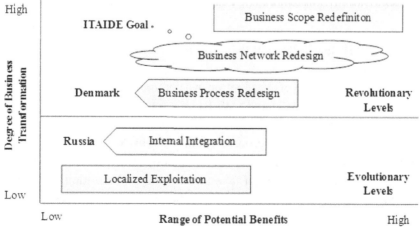

Process Redesign". General business principles in these countries avoid optimized IT integration in their e-customs systems. Countries, such as Russia, relying on paper-based importing and exporting, may be located in level two "Internal integration", where technical interconnectivity surely takes place due to IT modernization. However, the export processes have not been adapted to the new technology.

Thus, one managerial implication for customs officers is to continuously develop their country's e-customs systems. As such, they further push for a common standardized e-customs system. The formal paradigm shift will occur with the EU-Directive saying that the 27 member states have to adopt the system by 2013. As such, the customs community, including all exporting companies, customs officials and customs workers, has to be convinced entirely to adopt the e-customs system. The revolution will be over in 2013. Thereafter, companies may differentiate themselves with business process redesign, network redesign and business scope redefinitions.

CONCLUSION

History has shown that the linear model of Francis Bacon had to be advanced with feedback mechanisms that include organizational issues. This led to the notion of technological paradigms associated with Thomas Kuhn's concept of scientific paradigms and proved that Kuhnian ideas could also describe technological progress. Here, Kuhn's idea of a community forming a paradigm is still valid: If a majority of engineers working on one technology are convinced of a need for change, paradigms shifts will occur.

Historical examples of information technological (IT) progress are the modularization of software development, the move from mainframe to personal computers, and currently finalized in a technological paradigm of virtual resources accessible through the Internet.

The underlying technology in the Case of e-customs is the Internet, starting with e-Business (B2B and B2C) and then also reaching the public sector with e-Government solutions.

The technological progress of the adoption of a common standardized e-customs system in Europe has been explained with Kuhn's four steps of a paradigm: (1) puzzle solving, (2) crisis, (3) change and (4) new puzzle solving.

About 30 years ago, an export process within customs was fully paper-based and required approximately 200 documents. Even though the Internet evolved, the adoption of e-customs system did not take place. With globalization, increasing trading complexity and political events, such as the terrorist attacks that occurred in the US on September 11th, new legal standards and safety regulations in trade and customs are required. As the Internet in general reduces corruption through transparency and harmonization of rules, e-customs got a new wave of attention:

The US required one common and standardized European e-customs system with the intention of having a universal European customs partner instead of several national trading partners with different systems. As a result, the EU currently funds the project ITAIDE for achieving trade facilitation as well as to secure import and export with a common European e-customs system to be implemented by 2013. With this EU-Directive and an implemented strategic action plan, the technological paradigm shift to a common use of e-customs system is predetermined. Some pilot projects have already taken place in Denmark, Sweden and Switzerland. The Danish example shows that an e-customs adoption would significantly increase financial and security values in the public sector.

However, there is still resistance in adopting e-customs, since the EU-Directive only dictates the time schedule and not the way of implementation on a national level. Thus, countries are missing procedural details and direction and some standards do not involve the whole customs community, e.g. Small and Medium Enterprises (SMEs). Like always with the introduction of Internet technology, people fear losing jobs and are concerned about the usefulness of their skill-sets to cope with the new technical environment. Although the paradigm has changed, the culture has not. Nevertheless, an information technological paradigm shift from customs to e-customs is irrevocable.

The EU has set its managerial goals with its EU-Directive, aiming at a "Business Network Redesign" where interconnections are expanded to external businesses, like suppliers, buyers or other intermediaries with regard to IT deployment. However, with countries being still at the level of "Internal Integration" regarding their process transformation, like Russia, the EU has to find the commitment of the whole customs community in giving them clear and standardized directions for e-customs implementation. Propositions are to introduce one common European customs coordinator and to strengthen the value added due to e-customs adoption. For customs officers it means to further develop the e-customs system to convince the whole customs community.

ACKNOWLEDGMENT

The presented case study is based on the integrated project ITAIDE (Nr.027829), funded by the 6th Framework IST Programme of the European Commission (see www.itaide.org). The ideas and opinions expressed by the authors do not necessarily reflect the views/insights/interests of all ITAIDE partners.

REFERENCES

Bacon, F. (1605). *The advancement of learning*. Adamant Media Corporation.

Baida, Z., Liu, J., & Tan, Y.-H. (2007). Towards a methodology for designing e-government control procedures. In *Electronic Government, 4646*, 56-67. Berlin, Germany: Springer.

Baida, Z., Rukanova, B., Wigand, R., & Tan, Y. H. (2007). Heineken shows benefits of customs collaboration. *Supply Chain Management Review, 11*(7), 11–12.

Bjørn-Andersen, N., Razmerita, L. V., & Henriksen, H. Z. (2007). The streamlining of cross-border taxation using IT: The Danish eExport solution. In Makolm, J., & Orthofer, G. (Eds.), *E-taxation: State & perspectives: E-government in the field of taxation: Scientific basis, implementation strategies, good practice examples* (pp. 195–206). Linz, Austria: Trauner Verlag.

Boyd, S. L., Hobbs, J. E., & Kerr, W. A. (2003). The impact of customs procedures on business to consumer e-commerce in food products. *Supply Chain Management: An International Journal, 8*(3), 195–200. doi:10.1108/13598540310484591

Burn, J., & Robins, G. (2003). Moving towards e-government: A case study of organisational change process. *Logistics Information Management, 16*(1), 25–35. doi:10.1108/09576050310453714

Bygrave, W. D. (1989). The entrepreneurship paradigm (I): A philosophical look at its research methodologies. *Entrepreneurship Theory and Practice, 14*(1), 7–26.

Christensen, C. (1997). *The innovator's dilemma: When new technologies cause great firms to fail*. Harvard Business School Press.

Dedrick, J., & West, J. (2003). Why firms adopt open source platforms: A grounded theory of innovation and standards adoption. In J. L. King & K. Lyytinen (Eds.), *Proceedings of the Workshop on Standard Making: A Critical Research Frontier for Information Systems*, (pp. 236-257). Seattle, WA, USA.

Dosi, G. (1982). Technological paradigms and technological trajectories. *Research Policy, 11*(3), 147–162. doi:10.1016/0048-7333(82)90016-6

Easterly, W. (2001). *The elusive quest for economic growth: Economists' adventures and misadventures in the tropics*. Cambridge: MIT Press.

Granberg, A., & Stankiewicz, R. (1981). The development of generic technologies - The cognitive aspects. In Grandstrand, O., & Sigurdson, J. (Eds.), *Technological and industrial policy in China and Europe* (pp. 196–224). Lund, Sweden: Research Policy Institute.

Guha, S., Grover, V., Kettinger, W. J., & Teng, J. T. C. (1997). Business process change and organizational performance: exploring an antecendent model. *Journal of Management Information Systems, 14*(1), 119–154.

Henriksen, H. Z., & Rukanova, B. (2008, April 23-25). *Barriers and drivers of ecustoms implementation: Never mind IT.* Paper presented at the 6th Eastern European eGovernment Days, Prague, Czech Republic.

Henriksen, H. Z., Rukanova, B., & Tan, Y.-H. (2008). Pacta Sunt Servanda but where is the agreement? The complicated case of e-customs. In Wimmer, M. A., Scholl, H. J., & Ferro, E. (Eds.), *EGOV 2008* (pp. 13–24). Berlin, Germany: Springer-Verlag.

ITAIDE. (2009). *Report on redesign of administrative processes, interoperability and standardization.* Retrieved from http://www.itaide.org

Jeyaraj, A., Rottman, J. W., & Lacity, M. C. (2004, December). *Understanding the relationship between organizational and individual adoption of IT innovations: Literature review and analysis.* Paper presented at the Diffusion Interest Group in Information Technology, Washington DC, USA.

Johnston, R. (1972). The internal structure of technology. In Halmos, P., & Albrow, M. (Eds.), *The Sociological Review Monograph 18 - The Sociaology of Sciences* (pp. 117–130). Keele, UK: J.H. Brookes Printers Limited.

Kalakota, R., Oliva, R. A., & Donath, B. (1999). Move over, e-commerce. *Marketing Munagement, 8*(3), 22–32.

Khalil, T. M. (1999). *Management of technology.* McGraw-Hill Science/Engineering/Math.

Koestler, A. (1989). *The sleepwalkers.* Arkana/Penguin.

Kuhn, T. S. (1962). *The structure of scientific revolutions.* Chicago, IL: University of Chicago Press.

Kuhn, T. S., & Neurath, O. (1970). *The structure of scientific revolutions: International encyclopedia of unified science.* Chicago, IL: University of Chicago Press.

Kuiper, E. J. (2007). *Convergence by cooperation in IT – The EU's customs and fiscalis programmes.* Delft, The Netherlands: Delft University of Technology.

Lakatos, I., & Musgrave, A. (1970). *Criticism and the growth of knowledge*. Cambridge University Press.

Parker, C., Scott, C., Lacey, N., & Braithwaite, J. (2004). *Regulating law*. Oxford University Press. doi:10.1093/acprof:oso/9780199264070.001.0001

Peine, A. (2008). Technological paradigms and complex technical systems—The case of smart homes. *Research Policy, 37*(3), 508–529. doi:10.1016/j.respol.2007.11.009

Planck, M. (1949). A scientific biography. In *The Oxford dictionary* (2004 ed., p. 596).

Postman, N. (1992). *Technopoly: The surrender of culture to technology*. New York, NY: Knopf.

Raus, M. (2009). *Value assessment of business-to-government IT innovations: A case study. 22nd Bled eConference eEnablement: Facilitating an Open, Effective and Representative eSociety*. Slovenia: Bled.

Raus, M., Flügge, B., & Boutellier, R. (2008). Innovation steps in the diffusion of e-customs solutions. In S. A. Chun, M. Janssen, & J. R. Gil-Garcia (Eds.), *ACM International Conference Proceeding Series* (Vol. 289, pp. 315-324). Montréal, Canada: Digital Government Society of North America.

Raus, M., Flügge, B., & Boutellier, R. (2009). Electronic customs innovation: An improvement of governmental infrastructure. *Government Information Quarterly, 26*(2). doi:10.1016/j.giq.2008.11.008

Raus, M., Kipp, A., & Boutellier, R. (2008). Diffusion of e-government IT innovation: A case of failure? In Cunningham, P., & Cunningham, M. (Eds.), *Collaboration and the knowledge economy: Issues, applications, case studies*. Amsterdam, The Netherlands: IOS Press.

Teo, H. H., Tan, B. C. Y., & Wei, K. K. (1997). Organizational transformation using electronic data interchange: The case of TradeNet in Singapore. *Journal of Management Information Systems, 13*(4), 139–165.

The Economist. (2000, May 27). Growth is good. *The Economist, 82.*

(2006). *Tullverket* (1st ed., pp. 1–9). Säkerhetsfragor I Tullverkets EDI-System.

United Nations Economic Commission for Europe. (2005). *Recommendation and guidelines on establishing a single window - Recommendation No. 33*. Geneva: UN/CEFACT.

Venkatraman, N. (1994). IT enabled business transformation. *Sloan Management Review, 35*(2), 73–78.

Vincenti, W. (1995). The technical shaping of technology: Real-world constraints and technical logic in Edison's electrical lighting system. *Social Studies of Science*, *25*(3), 553–574. doi:10.1177/030631295025003006

Wassenaar, A. (2000). *E-governmental value chain models-E-government from a business (modelling) perspective.*

ADDITIONAL READING

Drews, J. (1998). *Die verspielte Zukunft - Wohin geht die Arzneimittelforschung?* Basel, Switzerland: Birkhäuser.

Fukuyama, F. (2003). *Our posthuman future*. New York, NY: Picador.

Kealey, T. (1997). *The economic laws of scientific research*. Palgrave Macmillan.

Kuhn, T. (1996, July 13). The nature of science. *The Economist*.

Lightman, A. (2005). *The best American science writing* (p. 76). Harper.

Snow, C. P. (1964). *The two cultures*. Cambridge University Press.

Wilson, E. O. (1998). *Consilience: The unity of knowledge*. New York, NY: Knopf.

Yoshikawa, H. (1995). President Tokyo University. In *Technology's New Horizon* (p. 123). Oxford.

ENDNOTES

[1] The Kyoto ICT Guidelines suggest that Customs should review their current procedures and processes prior to adopting any IC technology tools (www.wcoomd.org – World Customs Organization).

[2] For assuring integrity of information and communication, the four-eye principle guarantees that all communications should generally be checked and countersigned by a person who was not involved in drafting it.

3 E-dec designates a cargo processing IT product, developed by the Swiss federal customs administration, which is to standardize existing IT-supported (cargo processing) procedures (www.ezv.admin.ch).

This work was previously published in Cases on Technology Innovation: Entrepreneurial Successes and Pitfalls, edited by S. Ann Becker and Robert E. Niebuhr, pp. 134-155, copyright 2010 by Business Science Reference (an imprint of IGI Global).

Chapter 16
GIS:
A New Tool for Criminology and Victimology's Studies

Elena Bianchini
"lAma Mater Studiorum," University of Bologna, Italy

Sandra Sicurella
"lAma Mater Studiorum," University of Bologna, Italy

EXECUTIVE SUMMARY

The advent of the GIS technology has revolutionized the traditional field of information and cartographic production. The GIS, indeed, enables the management of much more numerous and more complex data and it is able to overcome the static and the traditional two-dimensional cartography. The Geographic Information Systems (GIS), which is used in various fields and disciplines, also represents a valuable tool for investigation in the university research. In criminology in particular, it has facilitated, regarding the city of Bologna, a kind of crime mapping on the nature of the so called "petty crimes" within the jurisdiction of the criminal Justice of the Peace, and the creation of a city's map on which have been identified support centers for victims operating in them. The use of GIS software is the basis in order to realize and put into practice not only operational measures designed to combat and to prevent crime, but it is also of help to social control measures, to public policy and to security. To the end of ensuring public safety, nowadays, it is essential to have a clear, spatial, and graphic representation of the high concentrations of crime areas and of the degraded ones, in which there is a greater likelihood that some type of crime is committed.

DOI: 10.4018/978-1-4666-2071-1.ch016

ORIGINS

The history of cartography has very ancient origins; the first evidences, even still elementary, in fact, date back to primitive civilizations: their tendency to nomadism seems to have refined the ability to draw maps on stone or wood. The production of maps was already known among Egyptians and Babylonians (III millennium BC) who built rudimentary maps of property and territorial representations of the known world, with decorative or religious function. Between the VII and VIII BC among Persian, Phoenician and Chinese developed the use of trace land and sea routes as a guide for commercial routes. In classical times were the Greeks to give a scientific basis to the cartography applying mathematical and geometric notions to the geographic representations. The first map of the known world is to be traced back to the philosopher Anassimandro (VI century BC) and Eratosthenes of Cyrene (III century BC) calculated with great approximation the circumference of the globe and created maps marked by a perpendicular grid of lines to measure distances. In the second century AD Claudius Ptolemy brought changes to the cartographic system introducing a network of meridians and parallels. The roman cartography, instead, pursued administrative and military purposes (http://digilander.libero.it/ diogenes99/Cartografia/Cartografia01.htm). These first cartographic representations used methods based on perception and subjective reconstruction and the surveying of the earth could vary depending on the point of observation of the cartographer.

During modern times occurred the problem of representing the spherical Earth's surface on a flat surface that was resolved, initially, using geometric solutions and, subsequently, using analytical performances, which the principles of modern projections maps are based on. To represent a three-dimensional space on a two dimension's map, is necessary to recall the concept of map projection; it refers to a series of geometric, mathematical and empirical transformations of geographical points expressed in geographical and Cartesian coordinates. Through the projections or representations we can approximately represent the spherical surface of the Earth on a plane surface, managing to maintain some geometric properties such as isogony, equivalence and equidistance (http://digilander.libero.it/diogenes99/ Cartografia/Cartografia02.htm).

Over the last century the aerial photos, the ortho-photos (Image solution system) and satellite images later, made it possible to achieve real representation of the earth, before unknown. Today the most widespread cartography is no longer representing only places, spaces and geographical distances, but, it is also representing data and information of all sorts, associated with many different disciplines. Among the many uses of thematic maps we can include agriculture, services to citizens, environment, statistics, tourism, transport, cultural assets and university research.

THE USE OF GEOGRAPHICAL MAPPING IN CRIMINOLOGY

Within the criminological research, geographical mapping has ancient origins. Already Quételet and Guerry, after a careful consultation of official data, had prepared a "paper crime" and Guerry in particular, in 1833, created a "social cartography" of relative crime on analyzing the socio-structural data belonging to different French departments (Melossi, 2002). However it is with The Chicago School of Sociology, in the first half of 1900, that are carried out systematic studies on the city, as an organic whole, making use of maps.

One of the recurring themes of this School is that of development and change of human behavior induced by the physical and social environment. According to the thought of Matza, The Chicago School of Sociology thought to individuals as complex creatures, able to adapt very different lifestyles and it considered the community as the main element of influence on the individuals' behavior. The community was to be regarded as the natural human environment and it was the main factor of influence on the behavior of individuals. The natural human environment was to be considered the city, a microcosm of the human universe (Williams & McShane, 2002). The Chicago School of Sociology had to face with a social-historical context characterized by many social phenomena until that time unpublished, such as the development of large cities, rapid industrialization, mass immigration, the effects of the First World War, the prohibition, the great depression.

The theorists of The Chicago School of Sociology developed an attempt of scientific approach to the study of deviant behavior. These scientists, in addition to data obtained from the life stories and the ecological studies, made use of official data on crime, of the results of the census and of data on housing accommodations. This type of information was collected and analyzed for each different areas and districts of the city. They realized in this way a crime mapping that allowed the identification of areas of social disadvantage. The geographical statistic descriptions of social phenomena, repeated several times, showed stability, which revolutionized the explanation of the causes of crime: it underlined that certain areas of the city were prone to crime despite repeated changes of their social and ethnic composition (Williams & McShane, 2002).

These researchers, inspired by the idea of the study of plants and animals in their natural environment, tried to rebuild a human ecology, to study people from how they naturally behave over time and space. It is for this reason that The Chicago School of Sociology is also commonly defined as the Ecological School: because it studies the correlation of organism between them and the environment.

The most important contribution of The Chicago School of Sociology was certainly the organic approach to the life of the community, led by Robert Park who, together with his collaborator E. Burgess, arrived at the conception of the city as a set of separate concentric circles, which radiate from the central business district.

Park and Burgess located three areas: a central businness area (characterized by few residents, but a lot of factories and offices); the second area was called "transitional area" because of the presence of immigrants (it was the cheaper one); and then the "worker area," without urban decay.

The mapping of the city allowed to show how the incidence of social problems and crime was inversely proportional to the distance from the center. The basic idea was that the growth of the city, but also the location of areas and different social problems, do not occur by chance but obey to a specific model; the theory established that there are dominant land uses within each zone. The concept of growth of cities according to a model with concentric zones provided, later, The Chicago School of Sociology, of the groundwork for explaining crime and delinquency (Melossi, 2002).

A few years later C. Shaw and H.D. McKay, on the basis of these premises, put in relation the spatial structure of the city of Chicago and its various types of settlement both with particular demographic characteristics, such as the composition of the immigrant population, and indicators of various social diseases, for example the crime rate and the rate of mental illness considered area by area. The comments of researchers described the city as a place where social life were superficial, the people were anonymous, the relations were transitional, the friendship and parental ties weak. The Chicago School of Sociology read the weakness of social relations as a primary process of social disintegration: if there is a social disruption within a community or a neighborhood, for example a low economic status, a mix of ethnic groups, a high mobility of residents inside and outside the district, disadvantaged or broken families, then it is possible a correlation with the distribution of crime's rates and delinquency (Williams & McShane, 2002).

Shaw and McKay subdivided the city of Chicago in five concentric zones, which radiated from a commercial business center (central), then there are transition areas, the workers' houses area, the residential area and the area of commuters.

They considered the study of an individual only as an approach to the study of crime. The authors, so, developed an analysis of "delinquent areas" as special type of natural area and found that the incidence of crime was significantly higher in certain areas, precisely defined delinquent (Berzano & Prina, 2004).

The method used was to locate the criminal acts marking on a map of Chicago the place of residence of the offender or the place where the crime took place, the resulting paper was subsequently corrected in relation to the population's density of the area.

Thanks to this method, they formulated the "law of the gradient," reaching the same conclusions of Park and Burgess: the delinquency rate is inversely proportional to the distance from the city center, that is more increased the distance from the center more decreased crime rates; furthermore, areas with high crime rate have other symptoms of social disorganization (for example high number of attended, suicides): according to the ecological point of view, the forms of "social pathology" does not arise so much from the individuals proper qualities, but from attributes of the socio-cultural context they live in. So, the inhabitants of the central region of Chicago had higher rates of social pathology since resided in an area where turnover, mobility and anonymity were higher (Balloni, 1983).

A further contribution of Shaw and McKay is the explanation of the process through which the disintegration influence young people and lead them to delinquency. This conceptual elaboration is defined as theory of cultural transmission: deviant behavior is determined by a subsystem of knowledge, beliefs that make possible, permit or require special types of deviant behavior in specific situations. Those knowledges and beliefs must exist first and foremost in the actor's social contest and are taken and incorporated into the personality in the same way as the other elements of local culture Balloni, 1983, p.104).

The two experts put in evidence how the youths who lived in socially disrupted areas were more likely to come into contact with individuals who embraced criminals and delinquents values, and how in these areas developed a delinquent tradition, through which deviant values were transmitted. They focused that most delinquent acts take place in small groups, that the crime and deviance were aspects that in neighborhoods with high crime rates, had become, more or less, a traditional part of the social life. These traditions of delinquency were transmitted through personal or group's contacts. Shaw and McKay provided an important contribution on the process by which the social disintegration influences young people and leads them to delinquency (Williams & McShane, 2002).

The experts researches of The Chicago School of Sociology have, over the years, maintained their influence. Exhaustive it is to say that some police departments take over from the tradition of The Chicago School of Sociology, the use of a geographical map of the city (spot map) over which they put in evidence the criminals streets. The more recent approaches are no longer referring to the spot map, but to the analysis of the so-called hot spots ("hot spots" describe urban areas characterized by criminality and degrade), which are defined, empirically identifying on a map, their geographic centers and then tracing their borders (Williams & McShane, 2002, p.195).

The interpretative and methodological implications of this school have had special influence on the development of that part of the "crime analysis" known as "crime mapping." The crime mapping can be defined as an investigative technique that allows to graphically display on a map a set of data, a technique certainly valid to provide a detailed imagine of the urban areas most affected by crime or degradation.

The use of maps, as known, was experienced for some time (according to the police department of New York it dates back to early 1900), however, over the years, numerous limits have been exceeded, thanks to the development of tools ever more advanced. The first crime maps used in the United States, representing the various jurisdictions, as well as presenting logistic difficulties and resulting hardly manageable due to their extension, they were static, presenting difficulties to store unless they had been photographed, and when containing many data, they were not easy to read. In addition, from the logistical point of view, the old maps occupied much space on the wall, for all these reasons they had a limited duration. In the first maps used by U.S. police departments, the information from various sources regarding the crimes (for example, where was the crime committed, the place of residence of the author and the victim of crime) were placed manually, using the pins in different colors. The technique of maps "on pins" has taken, in recent decades, to computerized mapping: the computers' elaboration was certainly faster and mapping became a common activity in the police districts (Harries, www.ncjrs.gov).

A transformation in qualitative terms revealed itself with the advent of the technological instrument of GIS (Geographic Information System), which allows not only to overcome the typical two-dimensional display of maps and provide a space temporal dynamic framework, but also allows to enter different data in connection with crimes that occur in a certain place. The American tradition, in fact, shows that the use of GIS by creating maps of reality under study enables to show when and where the crime occurred, what kind of weapon was used, whether there was a victim, if the victim was a man or woman and so on (www.ojp.usdoj.gov/ovc/publications/infores/geoinfosys2003/191877.pdf), so, the union between crime mapping and GIS tools should allow professionals to obtain a number of valuable information that they can use in a preventive viewpoint, providing a clear interpretation of reality and of the problems closely related to it.

THE GEOGRAPHIC INFORMATION SYSTEM

The Geographic Information Systems (GIS) have led to a revolution in the field of information and cartographic production. These systems are based on the merging of two programs: computerized design systems (CAD) and relational database (DBMS - Database Management System-), which are also among the first creations of computing. The first system has fostered the computerized geographical entity design, the second to storage data and information related to these entities. The merging of these two systems in GIS has enabled the overcoming of the compromise inherent in any cartography: in fact, every representation of geographical entity is always somewhat symbolic and in scale, or rather it is based on paradigms of representation according to which a particular symbol (for example a small rectangle) in the paper is a real object with certain geometric properties (for example a house). (...) With these new systems, the applications of cartographies are proliferating: each Figure can be represented in a map through its geographical position, defined by the coordinate system adopted and together with all the information concerning it, which are stored in a database. In this way the analysis of the geometric properties of the entities represented on a map (for example their exact physical dimensions), could be combined with the general properties of other cartographic entities (for example the reciprocal distance between houses, residences, between schools and hospitals, etc.), and of any chosen entity it will be possible to analyze in detail all the information concerning it (http://www.geotecnologie.unisi.it/Geotecnologie/gis.php).

According to Burrough's definition (1986), GIS is composed of a series of software tools for capturing, storing, extracting, processing and displaying spatial data from the real world (p.194); Mogorovich (Mogorovich & Mussio, 1988) instead defines it as the complex of men, tools and procedures (often informal) allowing the acquisition and distribution of data within the organization and making them available when they are required to those who need to carry out any activities (p.503).

The GIS technology allows the integration of the typical operations of databases, such as data's storage, research and statistical analysis, with the specific advantages of geographic visualization and analysis provided by the cartographic tools. These innovative capabilities make it an indispensable tool for a wide range of public and private users who need to view and analyze information, to plan events, to foresee scenarios, to define strategies. The GIS provides wide opportunity for interaction with the user and a set of tools that facilitate its customization and adaptation to specific issues.

A GIS system, contrary to a purely geometric representation of reality, must be able to handle information concerning the spatial relationships between different elements, while defining the topology.

The characteristic of GIS, as well as geometric and topological dimension, is entering data on its internal, defined as attributes that describe the individual real objects.

Another key aspect of this software is its ability to geo-reference data; or rather to assign to each element its real space's coordinates. This means that the coordinates of an object are stored in their concrete size (not to scale) and following the coordinates of the reference system in which the object is actually located and thus, the information is not recorded in relation to an arbitrary reference system.

In the GIS system, there are three types of information, which are managed in a relational database:

- **Geometric:** on the mapping of the objects represented, such as shape (point, line, polygon), the size and location;
- **Topological:** referring to relations between objects (connection, adjacency, inclusion etc ...);
- **Information:** about the data (numeric, text and so on ...) associated with each object.

GIS is characterized by geometric features: it stores the position of data using a real projection system that defines the actual location of the object.

The real world is represented in a geographic information system through two main types of data: the vector data and the raster data.

The vector data consists of simple elements such as points, lines and polygons, encoded and stored on the basis of their coordinates. To each element is joined a record of information database that contains all the attributes of the represented object. A vector is a system of storing graphic data according to which the objects are stored in conformity with Cartesian coordinates of points and lines used.

The raster consists of a set of identical small areas (pixels), ranked according to lines and columns, such as to constitute a matrix. The values associated to each cell in the matrix can express both graphic information (color, gray tone, etc.) and descriptive ones (temperature, slope, etc.). It therefore allows to represent the real world through an array of cells called pixels, which is a contraction of picture elements and it is the primary component of a raster characterized by an associated value containing the relevant information to what it represents in the territory (http://it.wikipedia.org/wiki/Sistema_informativo_territoriale).

GIS have functionalities that allow us to transform and develop geographical elements of attributes. Some examples might include: topological overlay consisting of a spatial analysis procedure which allows to overlap and intersect the information layers (layer) joining, thus, the associated information with each of them, to the purpose of producing a new layer of synthesis; the buffering: it is a process of analysis belonging to the topological overlay that allows to create polygons within predefined elements.

USE OF ArcGIS

ESRI's ArcGIS (Environmental System Research Institute, world's market leader for GIS, of which it is the Italian official distributor) is an integrated collection of software for creating a complete geographic information system (GIS).

The ArcGis, thanks to a comprehensive set of tools, processes geographic data on three different approaches:

1.   The Geo-database through a specialized data model allows the management of vector elements (features), raster images, topologies, networks and so on.

This approach is represented by the Arc-Catalog, a whole of geographic dataset, synthesized in a number of shape-file (a popular vector format, developed and regulated by ESRI. "Shape-file" usually refers to a set of files with an extension .shp,. dbf, .shx., often, with shape-file is indicated only the ." shp." The shape-files describe spatially points, polygons, usable poly -lines, for example, to represent respectively institutions, buildings and roads. To Each item may be associated additional attributes that describe the items (for example name or address).

In a geo-database there are some fundamental components:

- The geographic representation, which specifies with what kind of geometry the real elements are represented; for example, territorial portions are represented as polygons, lines as roads, trees as points;
- Descriptive attributes are included in tables relating to specific geographic objects describing their characteristics;
- The spatial relationships affect the topology and networks. The topology is a set of rules to define clearly the relations, reports of connection and continuity between the spacecraft and to connect those details to the relevant descriptions (attributes). In a topological data model, for example, it is possible to recognize contiguous areas and identify lines that surround each area (borders). A network is generally described by a graph, namely a set of interconnected arches (linear elements in vector format);
- Thematic layer: the layer is the whole of homogeneous elements that make up a map, such as roads, rivers, forests, etc..

2.   The Geo-visualization, achievable thanks to the assistance of ArcMap, enables to draw up complete and complex maps that show the elements (features) and their spatial relationships on the hearth's surface.

Such maps can be stored and reused to support the question, the editing and the analysis of the data. "Geo-visualization" means the ability of a GIS to visualize geographic data in various ways, including: interactive maps, three-dimensional models, charts and tables, representation of temporal events and schematic views of relations within a network.

The maps are the main tools for presenting the geographic information to users and for allowing their interaction. The maps of a GIS system differ from those printed because these are dynamic and at the same time we can interact with them; this allow to exceed the limit of traditional maps which allowed the creation of static maps only.

An interactive map can be so explored, enlarged, cut and the information levels (layer), represented in it, can be "turned on" and "turned off" from the table of contents, according to the specific needs of the user. We can also select (click) any geographical object on the map and get more information about it or make search and spatial analysis. The maps are used to communicate geographic information, and at the same time, to perform several complex tasks, including the compilation of data, mapping, analysis and data collection.

3.   Geo-processing, corresponding, from an operational point of view, to ArcToolbox. The Geo-processing is another approach based on a set of operational tools for analyzing and processing data in a dataset.

A GIS software includes a rich set of tools for working and processing geographic information. The merging of features associated with geo-database and the use of tools, Geo-processing instruments, allows us to create new data from those already stored (http://www.esriitalia.it/gis/index.htm).

After a purely theoretical complaint of functionality and technical characteristics, we can deepen the operative contribute of the GIS software in the University of Bologna's research.

Among the researches included in the following paragraphs, in fact, one of the tools used is the ArcGis - ArcView 9.x. This tool has facilitated, on the one hand, a kind of crime mapping of the city of Bologna which refers to petty crimes under the responsibility of criminal Justice of the Peace, and the other, creating a reality map of the city of Bologna on which have been identified centers victim support that operate in that context.

The useful data for the creation of the city map, found at municipal offices, relate to different shape-files, such as roads, buildings, hydrography, urban furniture, street numbers, etc ... According to the purposes of the research, the shape-files were selected, framed on the program and moved into the contents, in order to obtain the graphical display on the main screen map.

In this way it was possible to obtain a representation of the city containing: the border, roads and street numbers with their labels, neighborhoods, buildings. Subsequently, have been created by the Arc Catalog, new shape-files matching to the points of interest for each search, i.e. crimes and support centers for victims of crime. New items can be placed spatially (obviously based on their position in the real world) on the map, thanks to the Editor that allows us to modify the map.

The new maps thus obtained, offer a representation of the reality under study: in fact, in the first search, the crimes were located exactly where they had been perpetrated, in the second, instead, the services to assist victims were identified and reported in the corresponding address.

The maps, to be more understandable, need a title, a legend that can interpret the information within, a scale and guidance (for example, a compass or a rose of the winds).

THE CRIME MAPPING UNDER THE JURISDICTION OF THE CRIMINAL JUSTICE OF THE PEACE IN BOLOGNA

As has been already noted, in many fields where GIS can be applied, crime mapping founds a privileged place, that is the description of the distribution of the facts of crimes that occur in a given reality in an interactive map. For example, we can put in connection the analysis and distribution of certain types of crimes to the presence of specific areas and urban elements, such as closed roads, crumbling buildings, public parks, unattended car parks.

A sort of Bologna's real crime mapping was performed thanks to a research conducted by the University of Bologna, Department of Sociology, on "Criminal Jurisdiction of the Justice of the Peace and author- victim crime interaction in a party law suit; a criminology and socio-victimology analysis."

The study was conducted at the Court of Justice of the Peace of Bologna and it is designed to analyze the data found in the archives of the tribunal related to all measures defined by storage decree or *judicata res* in criminal matters following the entering on force of Legislative Decree No. 274 of 2000 delegating powers precisely at the criminal Court of Peace.

The data found in the Court cover the period from 2002 (the first year it became operational on Legislative Decree No. 274/2000) to 2006. There are party law suit, and reports of crimes by security forces.

It is important to dwell briefly on the news introduced by the new legislation in the Italian legislative scene. From a substantive point of view, it offers a slenderness through the procedural process of redress for lawsuit proceedings crimes, in which is the person offended by the crime, assisted by a defender, to deliver the summons directly to trial before the Justice of the Peace (immediate claim to the Justice of the Peace), being that, a judicial response, quickly given to the person offended by the crime, by two institutions that fall under the so-called alternative definitions to the proceedings (the low degree of seriousness of the event and the crime's release as result of reparatory conducts), it offers also sanctions with a rehabilitation and not merely afflictive function (work of public interest and house arrest), and finally, give a chance of reconciliation between the parties and a renewed importance recognized to the victim.

As a result of the above mentioned decree, the Justice of the Peace is now responsible for a series of crimes that relate to the sphere of criminal law concerning a micro inter-individual conflict which, although it generally produces not particularly serious illegal behaviors, it ends with nourishing situations of significant social disadvantage (Vezzadini, 2006, p. 229). Indeed, in the case of conviction, the court applies the fine (not more than prison sentence) and, in more severe cases, the house arrest or work of public interest.

Moreover, precisely because of the petty crimes, the penalty is imposed only after the failure of the conflict reconstruction: so, a reconciled solution to the dispute becomes the basic principle of the proceedings before the Justice of the Peace (Marzaduri, 2002).

The widespread crimes, those of Justice of the Peace's competence and only in the most mild cases (the responsibility for aggravated hypothesis is included in the functions of the Court), concern the person's sphere (such as blows, bodily harms, failure to rescue), the honor (such as insult and slander), the property (such as damages and squating other people's property), the animals (such as hurting or killing someone else's animals).

From an operational point of view, the procedural files were reviewed taking into account: the lawsuit's date of filing and the date of reporting it, the decision of the Justice of the Peace, the motivation of the incident, the perpetrated crime, the place where the victim reported a complaint, the decision of the court (archiving, conviction or acquittal), some features regarding both the victim and the offender (such as sex, age, nationality, marital status, the municipality of residence, the profession and academic titles) on the basis of which a kind of identikit has been drawn, the exact location and address in which the crime occurred, any relationship and knowledge which exist between the two actors, finally, the presence or absence of witnesses.

The research has a double purpose: on the one hand the task is to investigate the relation between the author and the victim, to examine the different degrees of kinship (for example parents-children, brothers, cousins, father-in-law /daughter-in-law /son-in-law, brother-in-law, grandparents-grandchildren), the acquaintance (for example friendly, co-workers, employee-employer, neighbors, buyer-dealer), affective-sentimental relations (for example spouses, cohabitants, partners, separated, divorced) or situations with no type of relationship between the two actors of a criminal scene. With only a brief mention, it was found that with regard to the relationship, it moves from 3.2% in 2002 to 4.9% in 2003 to 7.6% in 2004 to 9.4% of 2005 up to 7.1% in 2006; besides, there is knowledge between author and victim of the crime of 28.4% in 2002, in 35% of cases in 2003, in 39.7% of cases of 2004,45, 6% of cases in 2005, in 33.3% of cases in 2006. So, while just over half of crimes within the jurisdiction of the magistrate was committed by people who did not have any relationship with the victim, on the other hand, almost half of crime is perpetrated by members of the same family or by people linked by a relationship of friendship and more or less close.

The second purpose of research, achieved thanks to the use of GIS software, is to put on an interactive map of the City of Bologna a crime (for example, non intentional bodily harm, a slander, threats, etc..) exactly in the location (road, building, public park) where it happened.

Indeed, the GIS program allows us to produce, only inputting on it data of the location where the crime occurred, computerized maps which give the chance to see real-world data. In this way have been highlighted the areas, the neighborhoods and the roads most affected by this crime under the responsibility of the Justice of Peace, called "petty crimes," which are certainly less serious than other types of crimes, but significantly and adversely affecting the perception of safety and quality of people's life.

Indeed, the criminal offences included in the so-called "petty crime" category, are the ones that generate fear, influencing the collective imaginary and causing those feelings of concern affecting the quality of life and connecting to the fear of crime (...) Hence the need of a relevant experimentation on an operating model that addresses to the better management of information and to the establishment of a data network to provide security to citizens, and especially to provide cooperation to all agencies of social control (Sette, 2003, p.80).

It was built, in this way, a sort of crime mapping of the city of Bologna's reality, divided in the five years under consideration (2002, 2003, 2004, 2005, 2006 - refer to Figures 1, 2, 3, 4 and 5), which provides a picture of areas, neighborhoods, and of the roads most affected by the crimes under the responsibility of the Justice of Peace.

Thus, only with a widespread and detailed knowledge of the territory, through awareness of offenses known, and with a proper management of the information will be possible to carry out prevention policies. Therefore, the crime is not a phenomenon neither isolated nor random and, due to this reason, it should be studied in relation to certain space-time conditions (Sette, 2003, pp.80-81).

The use of GIS software constitutes the basis to be able to realize and implement operational measures to combat crime; it has precisely the aim to prevent crime. Only through the knowledge of the territory and the areas at most risk, the local administrators can, for example, decide the location of police stations, the development of activities of Public Forces, or the creation of centers for victims' support; besides, it may be highlighted the presence or the absence of public institutions, and agencies responsible for social control.

Precisely for this reason, the identification of hot spots of the city of Bologna, in addition to providing detailed image of urban areas most affected by crime and delinquency, offers a solid basis both for the police to product a social control, and for those who formulate policies for the security in a city like Bologna that, in recent years, has seen an increase in crime and the emergence of troubling feelings of insecurity in the population. Finally, the mapping of areas with a high criminal

Figure 1. Map in 2002

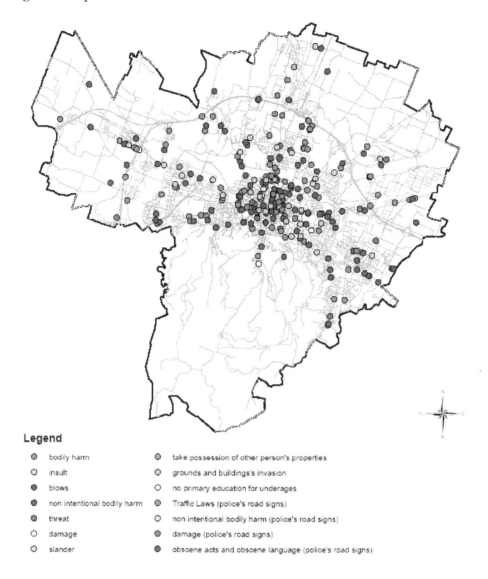

Legend

◉	bodily harm	◉	take possession of other person's properties
○	insult	○	grounds and buildings's invasion
●	blows	○	no primary education for underages
◉	non intentional bodily harm	◉	Traffic Laws (police's road signs)
◉	threat	○	non intentional bodily harm (police's road signs)
○	damage	◉	damage (police's road signs)
○	slander	●	obscene acts and obscene language (police's road signs)

concentration should allow the elaboration of strategies to minimize the risk of victimization of all citizens and, particularly, of certain categories of individuals most exposed, and should also help the decrease of the victimization impact of crime by encouraging the design of places for supporting the victims and their placement in the most disadvantaged areas (Vezzadini, 2006, pp. 93-94).

The use of crime mapping, and as in the Bologna research, the GIS software, can become a valuable aid for managers and staff working in centers, for local

Figure 2. Map in 2003

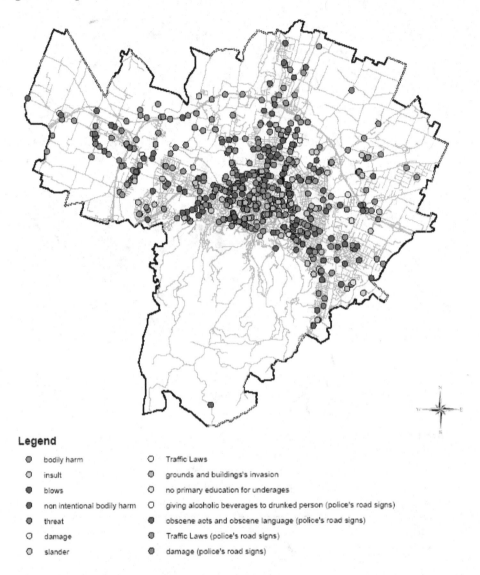

Legend

◕	bodily harm	○	Traffic Laws
◑	insult	◕	grounds and buildings's invasion
●	blows	○	no primary education for underages
◕	non intentional bodily harm	○	giving alcoholic beverages to drunked person (police's road signs)
◕	threat	◕	obscene acts and obscene language (police's road signs)
○	damage	◑	Traffic Laws (police's road signs)
◔	slander	◕	damage (police's road signs)

administrators, for criminologists, for psychologists. But above all, it becomes an instrument of high importance for the victims: it is also through the way of new technologies that they can find the right help, the right assistance, the right support.

Figure 3. Map in 2004

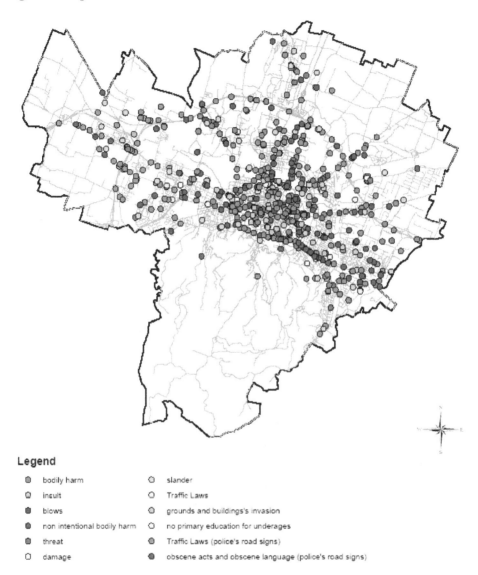

Legend

◐	bodily harm	○	slander
◔	insult	○	Traffic Laws
●	blows	○	grounds and buildings's invasion
◕	non intentional bodily harm	○	no primary education for underages
◑	threat	◐	Traffic Laws (police's road signs)
○	damage	●	obscene acts and obscene language (police's road signs)

THE MAPPING SERVICE IN BOLOGNA

As part of the research on mapping services, have been identified, in Bologna, the institutes involved in supporting the victims. They are, first of all, but not exclusively, victims of crime (such as terrorism, extortion, usury, rape, pedophilia, mobbing);

Figure 4. Map in 2005

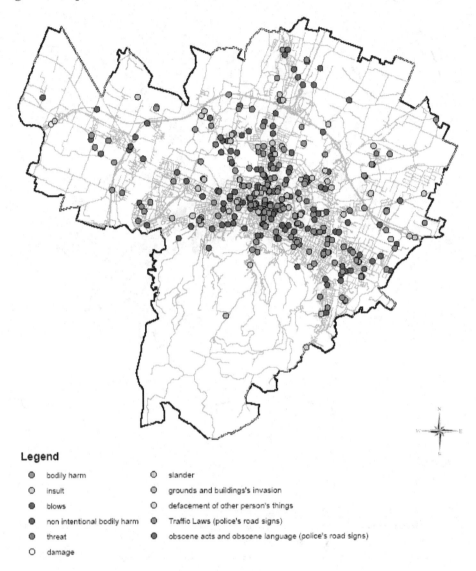

Legend

◉	bodily harm	○	slander
○	insult	◎	grounds and buildings's invasion
●	blows	○	defacement of other person's things
●	non intentional bodily harm	◎	Traffic Laws (police's road signs)
●	threat	◉	obscene acts and obscene language (police's road signs)
○	damage		

among the centers taken into consideration, in fact, are also included those which look after, for example, the victims of drug or prejudice.

After a necessary selection, given the numerous number, such centers were divided into two categories: institutional centers, referring, therefore, to the municipality, to the Province and to the Region and voluntary associations. Once selected the centers, their representatives were contacted by phone to ascertain their willingness to grant an interview and possibly set a appointment.

Figure 5. Map in 2006

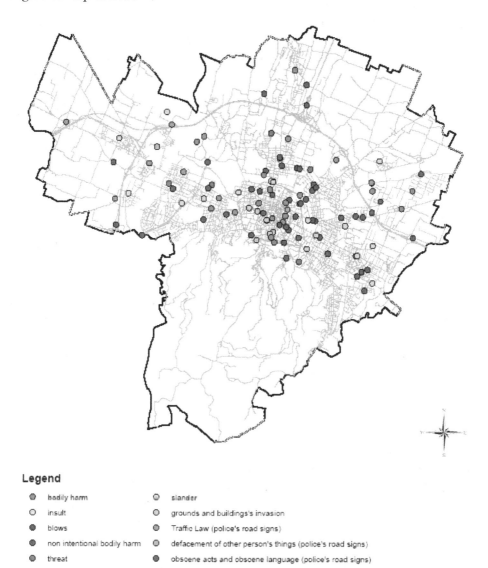

Legend

◒	badily harm	◔	slander
○	insult	◔	grounds and buildings's invasion
●	blows	◔	Traffic Law (police's road signs)
◕	non intentional bodily harm	○	defacement of other person's things (police's road signs)
◔	threat	●	obscene acts and obscene language (police's road signs)

Now we go on with a brief excursus to understand what the centers object of our research are dealing with.

1.   Public Services:
   a.   Fondazione Emiliano- Romagnola per le Vittime di Reato (the Emilia Romagna foundation for the victims of crime);
   b.   Il Faro (The Lighthouse, local center specialized in child abuse);

c. Servizi Sociali per Minori E Famiglie del Comune (Social Services for minors and local families);

d. Ufficio Sicurezza del Comune (Local security office);

e. Ufficio Vittime Dell'Usura e del Racket Presso la Prefettura – Ufficio Territoriale del Governo – (The office for victims of organized crime).

2. Private Services:

a. Associazione Familiari Vittime della Strage 2 Agosto 1980 (The Association for victims of terrorism);

b. Associazione Familiari Vittime uno Bianca (The Association for the victims of "The White Fiat Uno" – armed attacks in Italy in the 90's where the perpetrators used a white Fiat Uno);

c. Associazione Prima contro il mobbing e lo stress psicosociale (The First Association against physical and psychological harassment at work);

d. Casa Delle Donne per Non Subire Violenza (Refuge for women victims of domestic violence);

e. Codici Onlus: Contro L'usura e il Racket (for victims of organized crime);

f. Gruppo Giustizia UDI (Refuge for women victims of domestic violence);

g. Il Pettirosso: Per il Recupero della Tossicodipendenza (Drug rehabilitation center);

h. MIT, Movimento Italiano Transessuali: Contro la Stigmatizzazione della Diversità (Movement for Italian Transexuals: against the stigmatization of marginal groups).

Afterwards, the leaders of each center were submitted to a semi-structured interview focused on issues particularly relevant in terms of victimology, such as the difficulties encountered in setting up and managing the centers, the definition of victim, the types of harms observed, the applications received concerning the satisfaction of needs, the operators' training, the integration between public and private, the prevention of the risk of victimization, the criminal mediation, the contact with the other groups in their areas, etc.

The semi - structured interview, subjected to privileged and selected witnesses, had, in fact, the purpose of investigating and deepening, whenever possible, topics related not only to the life of the association and/or public service, thus, to the history, to the handled issues and to the types of services offered, but also related to the condition of victims in our country considering the European directives issued in this matter.

The interviews were subjected to particularly representative characters, which may be the presidents of voluntary associations and representatives of public institutions, who by choice or professionals, deal with the victims of crime (Sicurella, 2008, p.81).

Starting from the foreign experiences of the victims' supporting centers, and continuing with a careful consultation of the existing literature on the subject, the aim of the research is to analyze the reality of the region Emilia-Romagna, particularly of the city of Bologna and its province, to understand strengths and limitations of the first centers of support for victims on the national territory, and to describe the type of victims more represented in these centers.

But what are the centers of support for victims?

The supporting centers for victims have the purpose to provide material, legal and psychological assistance to who, unfortunately, has been object of a crime, remaining victim of the same.

In Great Britain, Country forerunner in this institution, the support to the victims dates back to 1974 in Bristol, and today it is primarily known as Victim Support.

The "Victim Support" (Sette, 2003) is a national non-profit service. It is an attending center and a place of first aid which works in close collaboration with the Ministry of Interior and Police.

The staff, which has received the necessary training, provides a psychological assistance, information and practical help to all the victims of crime.

The Victim Support of Britain has three main aims:

1. To provide support and assistance to the victims, to their relatives and to their friends;
2. To increase the public awareness about the effects of crime;
3. To promote the victims' rights.

Following the English example, the Italian centers for victims' support, could offer a range of services to the victims of crimes, that include not only the psychological support, but also the answer to other problems of various kinds (such as being followed during the trial, or to have the chance to ask for professionals and craftsmen, who are, following the provision of turnovers, always available, and for example, able to replace a forced lock or a broken glass) that the victims are suddenly forced to confront with, often, without having the right means.

The support to the victims and the possibility of their psychosocial treatments are not only useful to implement attempts which, with success, may have the effect to heal the wounds as a result of the self-pitying experience, but also are to be considered in order to prevent new victimization.

Supports of this kind for the victims of any crime are, undoubtedly, essential if we imagine the severe inequality of treatment between the offender, the guilty, and the one who suffers the criminal act (Sicurella, 2008, p.78).

We must emphasize here that the Italian situation is quite unique compared, for example, to what happen in United States. In our country, in fact, there are no real victims' supports and, anyhow, the initiatives that can be read in these terms are light years distant from the overseas experiences, using the creative realism, centers for the victims' assistance should be set up, along with centers for the youth social deviance and for the adults perpetrators of crime (Sette & Vezzadini, 2008, p.96).

Emilio Viano has recently underlined many changes that, over the time, have focused the scope of supporting and helping the victims. Compared to the '70s, in fact, the United States of America, although there remain serious weaknesses as, for example, the existence of a certain racial and ethnic barriers in providing assistance and services to some part of the population (Sette & Vezzadini, 2008), nowadays, they can boast a qualified professional training, financing more stable and secure, successful integration between the various sectors that operate differently in this field such as police, judges, doctors and psychiatrists; there are also significant changes within the judiciary contest. The police receives a greater awareness in terms of assistance and support to the victims of crime, and the logistical arrangements, then, allow greater protection to victims, such as the creation, in the courts, of separate waiting classrooms for defendant and witness, for family members or for the victims themselves. Information concerning the judiciary procedure, the reimbursement costs for the participation to the trial and the assistance to disadvantaged persons (Sette & Vezzadini, 2008) are all a series of conquests that Italy is not yet able to boast.

During the research, the technological instrument, named GIS, has given a spatial location to the structures in the area of Bologna, the leaders of which were interviewed.

In truth, it would be appropriate, to achieve a complete mapping of the present structures, considering each existing, but actually they are too numerous to be surveyed in this work and also, our aim was to have the perception, certainly realistic, of what happen in Bologna and what it was done specifically to help the victims.

The computerized mapping of the territory and areas with high criminal concentration, should allow the development of strategies act to minimize and to reduce the risk of victimization which all citizens suffer from, in particular, some groups of people exposed to more risk, it should help to decrease the self-pitying crime's impact, it should encourage the generation of centers for the victims' support, and their placement in the most disadvantaged areas, thus, trying to fill the gaps and to cover the absence, which are the result, in most cases, of this type of service on our territory.

In order to realize a map of Bologna (refer to Figure 6) on which to place spatially the support services, have been used, as mentioned above, the ESRI's ArcGIS software which consists of three main modules: ArcCatalog to manage data and display them in preview; ArcMap to create maps, to display geographic data and make some space operations and Arctoolbox to convert data and enable editing functions.

On the map of the city of Bologna were so created (edited) some points corresponding to the physical location of the structures object of our interviews.

Specifically, for example, have been identified centers relating to private services (refer to Figure 7) or public services (see Figure 8) and each of them has been identified with an icon, which, in some way, could visually bring to the history or to the activities of the association.

The use of GIS technology in this case can be considered experimental because it represents an attempt to graphically illustrate and spatially place on the map of the city of Bologna, the centers of support for victims involved in our interviews. The ultimate aim is, in fact, to obtain a complete, public and private services' mapping, of the territory of Bologna (illustrated in Figure 9).

Figure 6. Bologna

This work, as mentioned above, should be combined with a kind of crime mapping, namely a study on a crime's mapping, with its different types and its hot spots, which might find a useful feedback on social control, public policies and security. In this way, the institutions could intervene, having an accurate and not only mental representation, especially spatial and graphics, supported by appropriate and effective tools, of the areas with high concentrations of crime and of the degraded

Figure 7. Private services

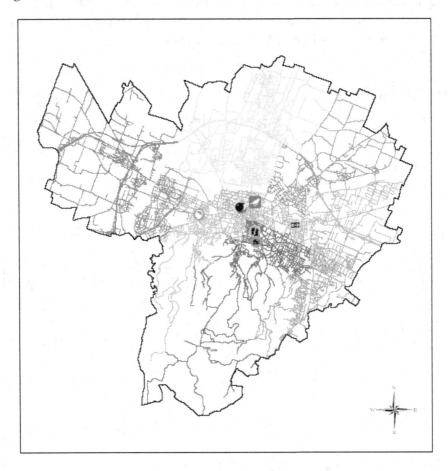

Legend

🔴	Women's refuge for victims of domestic violence	Associations for victims of organized crime
🔵	The First association against psychological bullying	MIT
🔴	The Association for victims of terrorist	Association for victims of domestic violence
🔸	The Association for the victims of "the White Fiat Uno"	Drug rihabilitation centre

Figure 8. Public services

Legend

P Public Services

ones, in which there is a greater probability that a certain crime is committed, not only in a timely, that is, making appropriate interventions in disreputable areas, or increasing surveillance by security forces in some districts. They could, at the same time, prepare, in strategic positions, for example where is more necessary, the creation and placement of support centers for victims, to intervene, if the victim so wishes, after the occurrence of a crime.

Figure 9. Public and private services

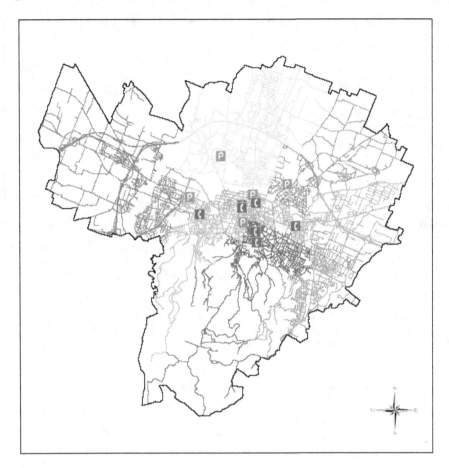

Legend

🄲 Private Services

🄿 Public Services

NOTE

This paper is a collaboration between the authors. In particular Elena Bianchini redacts the paragraphs "The use of geographical mapping in criminology," "Use of ArcGis" and "The crime mapping under the jurisdiction of the criminal Justice of the Peace in Bologna"; Sandra Sicurella redacts the paragraphs "Origins," "The Geographic Information System" and "The mapping service in Bologna."

REFERENCES

Aprile, E. (2007). *La competenza penale del Giudice di Pace*. Milano, Italy: Giuffrè.

Baldi, F. (2000). *Manuale del giudice di pace. Tutti i reati di competenza del giudice di pace, con ricchi richiami di dottrina e giurisprudenza; il nuovo processo ed il nuovo sistema sanzionatorio introdotti dal D.lgs. 28 agosto 2000, n. 274*. Milano, Italy: Giuffrè.

Balloni, A. (1983). *Criminologia in prospettiva*. Bologna, Italy: Clueb.

Balloni, A. (Ed.). (1989). *Vittime, crimine, difesa sociale*. Bologna, Italy: Clueb.

Balloni, A. (Ed.). (2006). *Cittadinanza responsabile e tutela della vittima*. Bologna, Italy: Clueb.

Balloni, A., & Bisi, R. (2004). *The evolution of victimology: A view over Italy and Europe through research. International Perspectives in Victimology, 1(1)*. Tokiwa International Victimology Institute Journal.

Balloni, A., & Bisi, R. (Eds.). (2008). *Processi di vittimizzazione e reti di sostegno alle vittime. Rivista "Salute e Società," 7(1)*. Milano, Italy: Franco Angeli.

Balloni, A., Mosconi, G., & Prina, F. (Eds.). (2004). *Cultura giuridica e attori della giustizia penale*. Milano, Italy: Franco Angeli.

Balloni, A., & Viano, E. (Eds.). (1989). *IV Congresso Mondiale di vittimologia. Atti della giornata bolognese*. Bologna, Italy: Clueb.

Berzano, L., & Prina, F. (2004). *Sociologia della devianza*. Roma, Italy: Carocci.

Bianchini, E. (2008). Processi di vittimizzazione e competenze penali del giudice di pace. In Balloni, A., & Bisi, R. (Eds.), *Processi di vittimizzazione e reti di sostegno alle vittime* (pp. 27–29). Milano, Italy: Franco Angeli.

Bisi, R. (1996). Vittime, vittimologia e società. In Bisi, R., & Faccioli, P. (Eds.), *Con gli occhi della vittima*. Milano, Italy: Franco Angeli.

Bisi, R. (Ed.). (2004). *Vittimologia. Dinamiche relazionali tra vittimizzazione e mediazione*. Milano, Italy: Franco Angeli.

Bisi, R. (Ed.). (2006). *Scena del crimine e profili investigativi. Quale tutela per le vittime?* Milano, Italy: Franco Angeli.

Bisi, R., & Faccioli, P. (Eds.). (1996). *Con gli occhi della vittima: Approccio inter-disciplinare alla vittimologia*. Milano, Italy: Franco Angeli.

Bisi, R., & Sette, R. (2002). Victimes de tragédies en Italie. Ombres et lumières d'une réalité oubliée. *Revue Francophone du Stress et du Trauma, 2*(1).

Burrough, P. A. (1986). *Principles of geographical information systems for land resource assessment.* Oxford, UK: Clarendon Press. doi:10.1080/10106048609354060

Cernetti, S., & Spriano, M. (2006). *La sentenza penale del giudice di pace.* Torino, Italy: G. Giappichelli.

Chiavario, M., & Marzaduri, E. (Eds.). (2002). *Giudice di pace e processo penale. Commento al D. lgs. 28 agosto 2000 n. 274 e alle successive modifiche.* Torino, Italy: UTET.

Cipolla, C. (Ed.). (2003). *Il ciclo metodologico della ricerca sociale.* Milano, Italy: Franco Angeli.

Corbetta, P. (1999). *Metodologia e tecniche della ricerca sociale.* Bologna, Italy: il Mulino.

Guidicini, P. (Ed.). (1991). *Nuovo manuale della ricerca sociologica.* Milano, Italy: Franco Angeli.

Guidicini, P. (1995). *Questionari, Interviste, Storie di vita: Come costruire gli strumenti, raccogliere le informazioni ed elaborare i dati.* Milano, Italy: Franco Angeli.

Gulotta, G. (1976). *La vittima.* Milano, Italy: Giuffré.

Lana, M. (2004). *Il testo nel computer.* Torino, Italy: Bollati Boringhieri.

Losito, G. (1993). *L'analisi del contenuto nella ricerca sociale.* Milano, Italy: Franco Angeli.

Marzaduri, E. (2002). L'attribuzione di competenze penali al giudice di pace: Un primo passo verso un sistema penale della conciliazione? In Chiavario, M., & Marzaduri, E. (Eds.), *Giudice di pace e processo penale. Commento al D. lgs. 28 agosto 2000 n. 274 e alle successive modifiche* (pp. 17–19). Torino, Italy: UTET.

Mattevi, E., Panizzo, F., & Pongiluppi, C. (2007). *I reati di competenza del giudice di pace. Il giudice di pace, Quaderni, 8.* Milano, Italy: Ipsoa.

Mazza, F. A., & Caruso, R. (2006). Giudice penale di pace protagonista fra conciliazione e giurisdizione. *Diritto e Giustizia, 1,* 58–76.

Melossi, D. (2002). *Stato, controllo sociale, devianza.* Milano, Italy: Bruno Mondatori.

Migani, M., & Salerno, G. (2008). *Manuale ArcGis.* Palermo, Italy: Dario Flaccovio editore.

Mogorovich, P., & Mussio, P. (1998). *Automazione del Sistema Informativo territo-riale. Elaborazione Automatica dei Dati Geografici (Vol. 2)*. Milano, Italy: Masson.

Nappi, A. (2004). *La procedura penale per il giudice di pace*. Milano, Italy: Giuffrè.

Pavone, M. (2005). *Le nuove competenze del Giudice di Pace*. Matelica, Italy: Halley.

Piccialli, P., & Aghina, E. (Eds.). (2001). *Il procedimento penale davanti al giudice di pace. Manuale teorico-pratico per gli operatori giudiziari*. Napoli, Italy: Edizioni Giuridiche Simone.

Saponaro, A. (2004). *Vittimologia*. Milano, Italy: Giuffrè.

Sette, R. (2003). Sicurezza urbana e centri di victim support. In Balloni, A. (Ed.), *Il vigile di quartiere a Milano* (pp. 80–81). Milano, Italy: Franco Angeli.

Sette, R. (2008). *Controllo sociale e prevenzione. Un approccio criminologico*. Bologna, Italy: Clueb.

Sette, R., & Vezzadini, S. (2008). Quale sostegno per quali vittime? Tavola rotonda con: Augusto Balloni, Gemma Marotta, Monica Raiteri, Raluca Simion, Emilio Viano. In A. Balloni A., & R. Bisi (Eds.), *Processi di vittimizzazione e reti di sostegno alle vittime* (pp. 89-118). Milano, Italy: Franco Angeli.

Sicurella, S. (2008). Processi di vittimizzazione e centri di ascolto alle vittime. In Balloni, A., & Bisi, R. (Eds.), *Processi di vittimizzazione e reti di sostegno alle vittime* (pp. 73–87). Milano, Italy: Franco Angeli.

Stella, F. (2003). *Giustizia e modernità. La protezione dell'innocente e la tutela delle vittime*. Milano, Italy: Giuffrè.

Taylor, I., Walton, P., & Young, J. (1975). *Criminologia sotto accusa*. Firenze, Italy: Guaraldi.

Turnaturi, G. (1991). *Associati per amore: L'etica degli affetti e delle relazioni quotidiane*. Milano, Italy: Feltrinelli.

Venafro, E., & Piemontese, C. (2004). *Ruolo e tutela della vittima in diritto penale*. Torino, Italy: Giappichelli Editore.

Vetere, E., & David, P. R. (2005). *Victims of crime and abuse of power (Bangkok, 18-25 April 2005): Festschrift in honour of Irene Melup*. New York, NY: United Nations.

Vezzadini, S. (2006). Profilo geografico e crime mapping. Il contributo della criminologia ambientale allo studio del delitto. In Bisi, R. (Ed.), *Scena del crimine e profili investigativi. Quale tutela per le vittime?* (pp. 83–94). Milano, Italy: Franco Angeli.

Vezzadini, S. (2006). *La vittima di reato tra negazione e riconoscimento*. Bologna, Italy: Clueb.

Viano, E. (1989). *Crime and its victims: International research and public policy issues*. New York, NY: Hemisphere Publishing Corporation.

Wertham, F. (1949). *The show of violence*. New York, NY: Doubleday.

Williams, F. P., & McShane, M. D. (2002). *Devianza e criminalità*. Bologna, Italy: Il Mulino.

This work was previously published in Cases on Technologies for Teaching Criminology and Victimology: Methodologies and Practices, edited by Raffaella Sette, pp. 87-110, copyright 2010 by Information Science Reference (an imprint of IGI Global).

Chapter 17

Towards a Customer Centric E-Government Application:
The Case of E-Filing in Malaysia

Santhanamery Thominathan
Universiti Teknologi MARA Malaysia, Malaysia

Ramayah Thurasamy
Universiti Sains Malaysia, Malaysia

EXECUTIVE SUMMARY

Information Communication Technology (ICT) has played an important role in today's global economy. Many countries have gained successful growth due to the implementation of ICT. In Malaysia, increased utilization of ICT has contributed significantly to the total factor productivity. One of the main contributing factors is the e-commerce and Internet based services. Therefore, this case study aims to examine the contribution of the newly introduced E-government application namely E-filing system. E-filing system is a newly developed online tax submission services offered by the government to the tax payers in the country where they are able to easily, quickly and safely file their tax returns. The primary discussion in this case study concerns on the Malaysian's ICT revolution, followed by the introduction of E-Filing system, the challenges and barriers faced by the government, concluding with the future trends in the implementation of this system.

DOI: 10.4018/978-1-4666-2071-1.ch017

INTRODUCTION

Role of ICT

The advances in information and communication technologies (ICT) have raised new opportunities for the implementation of novel applications and the provision of high quality services over global networks. The aim is to utilize this "information society era" for improving the quality of life of all citizens, disseminating knowledge, strengthening social cohesion, generating earnings and finally ensuring that organizations and public bodies remain competitive in the global electronic marketplace (Hesson & Al-Ameed, 2007).

Developed economies are identified with countries that properly use technology for the creation of wealth and less developed economies are identified with countries lacking technological know-how necessary to create wealth (Khalil, 2000). As such, a proper management of technology also includes low-tech to high-tech to super-high technologies. Khalil (1993) asserted that a proper management of low or medium level technologies can still create a certain competitive advantage and be effectively used for wealth creation. This is especially evident in newly industrialized countries (NICs) such as Taiwan, Korea, Singapore and Malaysia.

In Malaysia, ICT has assimilated into people's lives in many ways such as communication, logistics or in their working environment. Malaysia has invested enormously in ICT over the years. For example in the Ninth Malaysian Plan (2006-2010), a total of US$6 billion was allocated for enhancing ICT diffusion throughout the country. This shows the importance given by the country for ICT accelerate the economic competitiveness of Malaysia (Kuppusamy et al.2009).

Impact of ICT on Economic Growth

Solow (1957) through his famous seminal research on the contribution of technology on productivity growth in the US had sparked great interest among scholars on the relationship between technology and economic progress.

Since then, various firms, industries and countries have undertaken studies to find out more on the relationship between technology and economic growth.

Based on the study of Jalava and Pohjola (2002), both the production and use of ICT have been the factors behind the improved economic performance of the United States in the 1990s. A further research done by Jalava and Pohjola (2007) proves that the ICT's contribution to the economic growth of Finland was three times larger than the contribution of electricity industry.

In relation to the study done on Korea's economic development from 1996-2001, it is proven that Korea's economic development in the 20th century are mainly due to the growth of industries related to ICT and also the government's treatment of ICT as a strategic focus for future development (Lee, 2003)

Kuppusamy and Shanmugam (2007) examined the impact of ICT on Malaysia over the periods of 1983-2004 and reveals that ICT investment has statistically improved Malaysia's economic growth. Antonopoulos and Sakellaris (2009) investigated the impact of ICT on Greece and found that the ICT has increased the total factor productivity and also benefited the finance, real estate and business services industries and the wholesale and retail industries in Greece.

This case study sets out to describe the approach adopted by the Malaysian government in enhancing the usage of ICT in the country. In particular, this case study will focus on the success of the newly introduced E-government services in Malaysia that is the E-filing System.

Literature Review on Technology Adoption

Previous studies have proven the various reasons affecting the technology adoption. Survey done by Lai et al. (2004) on the tax practitioners and the electronic filing system in Malaysia founds that there is a strong relationship between technology readiness and intention to use E-Filing system. Technology readiness is the main motivation in using the particular system. However, the survey also reveals that perceived insecurity could be an obstacle in promoting the E-filing system.

This survey is supported by another survey done by Lai et al. (2005) which claims that tax practitioners are willing to accept a technology which is easily to be used and can enhance their job performance; however the fear of Internet security has stopped many of them on filing tax online. This is also supported by study done by Sena and Paul (2009) which finds that the main reason for the decrease in the usage of Internet banking (IB) in Turkey are due to perceived risk on security features of IB.

Ramayah et al. (2008) posit that apart from less knowledge on how to use the E-Filing system, the main reason less people engaged in the system is because they are sceptical over the security and privacy of data transmitted through the web.

Furthermore, based on a study done by Azleen et al. (2009) on taxpayers' attitude, they found that education background of taxpayers plays an important role in encouraging the attitude of taxpayers to use E-filing. Meanwhile the gender of the taxpayers does not contribute any significant differences in the usage.

Conversely, study done on the selected working women in Malaysia to identify the learning barriers in ICT adoption among them finds that ICT skills of Malaysian women are lower than expected compared to their male counterpart although they do not face any serious learning barriers. One of the possible reasons given was may be due to the attitude of the women. (Junaidah, 2008)

In addition, based on the study done by David (2008) on the adoption of e-recruitment services among job seekers in Malaysia, concluded that job seekers widely accepted the e-recruitment services despite its perceived risk due to its ease of use, usefulness, application posting speed and advantages over other job application methods.

Another study conducted by Md Nor and Pearson (2007), posit that trust is another factor that can significantly affect the attitude of users in the acceptance of Internet Banking in Malaysia. According to a survey done by Abdullatif and Philip (2009) finds that one of the criteria on winning the customers trust in adopting a particular technology is the web features particularly the utilitarian (usefulness) and hedonic (attractiveness) features. This finding is similar with the findings by Irani et al. (2008) which indicate that factors such as utilitarian outcomes, perceived resources, social influence, self-efficacy and behavioural intentions are the most important factors in determining the decision on technology adoption.

The above research findings are also supported by another group of researchers Astrid et al. (2008) whose findings reveals that hedonic features (perceived enjoyment) is more powerful determinant of intention to use a technology compared to perceived usefulness. However, according to Raman et al. (2008), their study finds that despite the attractiveness of Internet Banking (IB), the core factor for adoption of IB in Malaysia is the quality of the services provided mainly on the ease of use and reliability (less time to download).

As such we can conclude that, consumers are ever willing to adopt a technology that is useful, ease to use, has hedonic and utilitarian features, higher security or lower perceived risk, trust and quality.

BACKGROUND: INFORMATION COMMUNICATION TECHNOLOGIES (ICT) AND EMERGING TECHNOLOGIES

ICT Revolution in Malaysia

For the past thirty years, Malaysia has undertaken various initiatives to enhance the ICT diffusion and its' economy. The initiatives can be divided into two categories, macro level and micro level initiatives.

Macro Level ICT Initiatives: The Multimedia Super Corridor (MSC)

With the advent of the IT revolution and its positive impact on economic growth and competitiveness, many countries including Malaysia are developing their very own regional development strategies through the dynamic of a high-technology cluster. Guided by the *Vision 2020*, Malaysia has embarked on an ambitious plan by launching MSC in 1996 as the macro level initiative. *Vision 2020* is the blueprint strategy that stated that Malaysia must be a fully developed and knowledge-rich society by the year 2020, among other visions. MSC is one of the main initiatives to achieve this vision (Figure 1).

Basically, MSC is a technology park with a dedicated corridor (15 km wide and 50 km long) which stretches from the one of the world's tallest Petronas Twin Towers at the Kuala Lumpur City Centre (KLCC) in the north to the new Kuala Lumpur International Airport (KLIA) in the south.

The development of MSC is a necessity as the new engine of economic growth to ensure Malaysia is moving in the right direction in embracing the IT revolution. This huge technology park is considered as the nucleus for the concentric development of the ICT and multimedia driven industries in Malaysia. In brief, MSC is the vehicle for transforming Malaysia - social and economic development levels – in

Figure 1. Vision 2020 (Source NEAC)

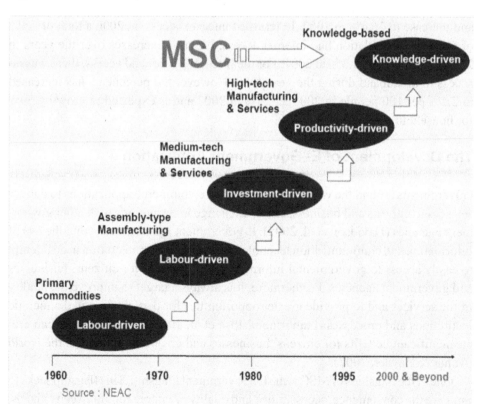

to a knowledge-based economy. There are seven key flagship applications being engineered to jumpstart in the development of MSC and also to create an ICT and multimedia utopia for producers and users of these technologies. These flagship applications are expected to expedite the diffusion of E-government and E-commerce activities in Malaysia. These applications are E-Government Flagship, Multi-Purpose card flagship, Tele-health Flagship, Smart School Flagship, R&D Cluster Flagship, E-Business flagship and Technopreneur Development Flagship.

Micro Level Initiatives: ICT Infrastructure

In order to support the ICT growth in Malaysia, the government also has concentrated on building the right and proper infrastructures to ensure speedy and efficient network of facilities and services for better transmission of ICT. During the 1980s, most of the ICT infrastructures investment went into provision of basic telephony services to rural and urban people. In the new millennium, Malaysia focused on increasing accessibility to Internet and its related services (Kuppusamy et al. 2009). As a result, there is a significant growth of the three ICT related services for the year 2000, 2005 and 2007. Based on the Figure 2, it can be seen that PC computers penetration rate per 100 populations was 9.4% in 2000, increased to 22.5% in 2005 and increase to 26.4% in 2007. In terms of internet access, in 2000 a total of 7.1% of every 100 population had internet access. Figure 3 increases over the years in 2005 to 13.9% and 14.3% in 2007. For the Internet Broadband access, there was no access to broadband during the year 2000. However the percentage has increased to 2.2% per 100 people in 2005 and 5% in 2007 and is expected to grow by 50% for household penetration by 2010.

The Development of E–Government Application

Governments around the world have developed e-commerce applications to deliver services to citizens and business, and to exchange in formations with other government agencies (Davidson et al. 2005). E-government is a term reflecting the use of information and communication technologies in public administration in an attempt to easily access to governmental information and services for citizens, businesses and government agencies. Furthermore, it is always a target to improve the quality of the services and to provide greater opportunities for participating in democratic institutions and processes (Lambrinoudakisa et al. 2003). E-Government can create significant benefits for citizens, businesses and governments around the world (Mihar & Hayder, 2007).

One of the flagships of MSC is the E- Government Flagship. This flagship seeks to improve the convenience, accessibility, and quality of interactions between citizens,

Figure 2. PC penetration rates (Adapted From The National ICT Association of Malaysia (PIKOM))

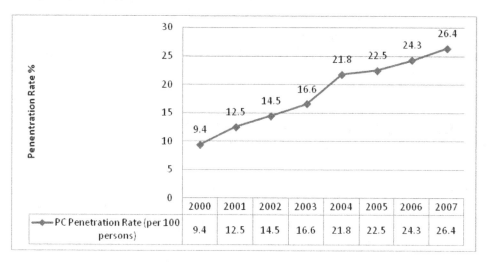

	2000	2001	2002	2003	2004	2005	2006	2007
PC Penetration Rate (per 100 persons)	9.4	12.5	14.5	16.6	21.8	22.5	24.3	26.4

the business and government sectors. It uses ICT and multimedia technologies to transform the way the government operates and improves the processes of policy development, coordination and enforcement. It includes Generic Office Environment (GOE), Electronic Procurement (eP), Project Monitoring System (SPP II), Human Resource Management System (HRMIS), Electronic delivery Services (E-services++), Electronic Labor Exchange (ELX) and E-Syariah.

Another prominent E-government application introduced in 2005 in Malaysia is the Electronic Tax- Filing (E-Filing) of income taxes. The electronic filing of

Figure 3. Internet and broadband penetration rates (Adapted From PIKOM 2008)

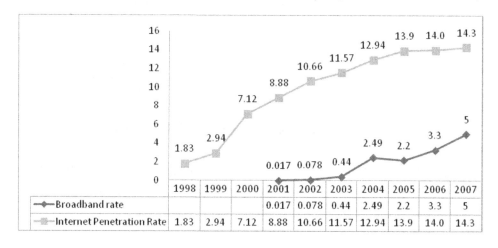

	1998	1999	2000	2001	2002	2003	2004	2005	2006	2007
Broadband rate				0.017	0.078	0.44	2.49	2.2	3.3	5
Internet Penetration Rate	1.83	2.94	7.12	8.88	10.66	11.57	12.94	13.9	14.0	14.3

income tax returns is an invaluable application that assists tax filers with the process of collecting their personal tax information and provides them the ability to electronically transmit their return. According to Fu et al. (2006) electronic filing of income taxes has the potential of improving the overall process of tax filing for the individual filer while at the same time reducing the cost to both taxpayers and tax collection agencies.

CASE DESCRIPTION: THE DEVELOPMENT OF E-FILING SYSTEM IN MALAYSIA

In Malaysia currently there are two major tax filing methods: manually and E-Filing (Internet filing). Since 2005 the Malaysian government has moved aggressively to promote the Internet filing (E-Filing) with the aim for paperless transaction, efficient process and faster refunds. Traditionally the tax payers in Malaysia have to file their tax returns manually by receiving the B (companies) or BE (individuals) forms from the Inland Revenue Board (IRB) department. Then they need to fill up the forms, do a self- calculation on their tax, attach together all the payment receipts and send it over in person or by mail to the IRB branches and later the IRB will send to them the confirmation on the tax payment amount.

However a new paradigm has taken place when the Inland Revenue Board introduces the E-Filing system. The E-Filing system developed in 2005 was one of the remarkable businesses to consumer (B2C) E-government services established by the Malaysian government. Via E-Filing and Public Key Infrastructure features, the individual tax payers in Malaysia are able to easily, quickly and safely file their tax returns.

According to Inland Revenue Board public relations officer Najlah Ishak, the electronic filing (E-Filing) of the income tax returns have increased by 30% to 1.25 million this year (2009). She stated that the number of taxpayers making E-Filing had increased gradually from 78,718 in 2006 to 538,558 (2007) and 881,387 (2008) (The Star, 01/05/2009).

Basically there are four main steps involve in filing tax electronically, refer to Figure 4.

The Advantages and Disadvantages of E- Filing System

E-filing provides many advantages to taxpayers. Among the advantages are: (http://www.mykad.com.my/Website/secureefiling.php)

Figure 4. How e-filing works (Adapted from: MSC Trustgate.com Sdn. Bhd)

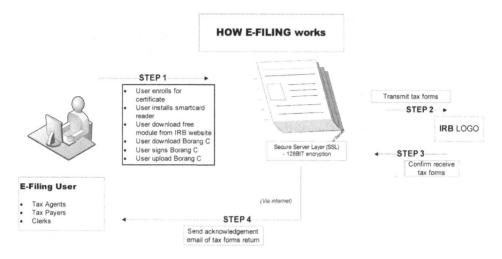

- **Immediate Acknowledgement:** The tax filers will get immediate acknowledgement from IRB after submission online
- **Round the Clock Availability and Convenience:** E-Filing is available round the clock daily. The submission work is not constrained by IRB' working hours. As long as the tax filers submit the tax forms before midnight on the due date, no late penalty will be payable.
- **Immediate Processing Time:** With E-filing submissions, the tax filers can enjoy the benefits of immediacy. There is no need to physically move tax forms or wait in queues for 20 minutes or more for manual processing.
- **Cost Savings:** There are net savings in using E-Filing system - no physical movement of tax forms, no waiting time, no transport cost and no risk of losing tax forms. Instead, tax filers enjoy convenience, 24-hour accessibility, and fast, secured and accurate tax computation.
- **User Friendly:** The look and feel of the E-Filing-system has been designed with a user-friendly interface to allow the tax filers to easily enter or amend any information before it is submitted to IRB.
- **Security:** The tax filers can be assured on the security features that can prevent the hacker from altering your data as the main key features in assessing to the system will be your password and tax file number

However, E-Filing has its disadvantages as well. Some of the disadvantages are:

- **Minimum Hardware and Software Requirement:** In order for the E-Filing system to be executed at the filer's convenience the main important device is personal computer (PC). It is then must be followed by Internet access and

Network configuration. The minimum requirement for the PC must also be installed with Windows XP or higher software and must have an Adobe reader application for the forms to be successfully downloaded. Failure to have all this features will enable the tax filers to access to the E-Filing website and perform the transactions.

- **Non-Modification:** Once the forms are sent to IRB, there will be no room for modification. If the tax filers have missed any information that are supposed to be included or excluded then they have to proceed with it manually by referring to the respective IRB branches.
- **Non-User Friendly:** There have been a lot of complaints from the tax payers that the time allowed to do the transaction is limited. Most of the time the key-in are stopped due to time elapsed and once the system is re-entered, all the data would have to be key in once again. This has created a problem for last minute filers. (http://thestar.com.my/news/story.asp?file=/2009/3/2/focus/3380923&sec=focus)

CURRENT CHALLENGES OF E -GOVERNMENT

Low Level of Personal Computer (PC), Internet and Broadband Penetration

It can be seen that the cellular phone growth is much more pronounced than PC or internet or broadband. This may be due to the ease of application, versatility, and convenience of anytime and everywhere usage and ongoing price reduction resulting from stiff competition among service providers. Various reasons such as poor access, lack of adequate local content, low level of awareness and motivation and lack of affordability have been cited for the low uptake of PC, Internet and Broadband (The National ICT Association of Malaysia (PIKOM), 2008)

Mandatory Usage

Based on survey done by Skillman (1998) in United States, the tax accountants asserted that the only way to make their tax clients to use the E-Filing is by making it a mandated usage. However, this is not the case for Malaysia where mandating electronic filing too early will attract mush resistance and criticism due to the inequality of Malaysian citizens in terms of the digital divide; income level and age factor (Lai et al. 2005). The survey also finds that the traditional channels will still need to be retained for the need of social ties, human contact and for personalization.

According to Paul and Kim (2003) quoting the articles of Wang et al., if a person is unable to use the technologies that E-government relies upon, for lack of education or limited ability, that person cannot be denied access to government information and services. "If less-advantaged segments of the population are less able to access government on the Web, their other channels to government must not be closed off or contracted."

Availability of IT Workforce

It is widely believed that with respect to IT manpower resources, the tax authority is generally suffering from a shortage IT workforce. According to IRB's Annual Report 2006, the percentage of workforce distributed for IT tasks were only 2.6%. This figure has not increased much from 2001 where the percentage of IT workforce distributed in 2001 was 2.1% (IRB Annual Report, 2001). This low distribution of workforce could dampen the effectiveness of the IT related services offered by the tax authority.

Digital Divide

Low ownership of PCs and disparities in internet access are among the most important challenges Malaysia faces today in implementing E-government services. Efforts to narrow the digital divide will be further intensified. For example, more Medan Info Desa and Pusat Internet Desa will continue to be built and upgraded. The government has set target to provide at least one telecentre for each mukim by 2010. (Mid Term Review, 9MP)

BARRIERS TO E-GOVERNMENT ADOPTION

ICT Infrastructure

In order for a technology to be adopted successfully, any E-government initiatives must ensure that it has sufficient resources, adequate infrastructure, management support, capable Information Technology (IT) staff and effective IT training and support. Although with the introduction of E-government services the cost will be reduced but adequate IT infrastructure still a key barrier to e- government adoption. The infrastructure is composed of hardware and software that will provide secure electronic services to citizens, businesses, and employees. For example, Local Area Network (LAN), reliable server, and internet connections are important to build a strong foundation for E-government infrastructures (Zakareya & Zahir, 2005).

Security Concerns

Another most significant barrier in implementing E-government applications is the security of the particular system. According to Lai et al. (2005), concerns over security of online tax transactions constitute a tremendous barrier to technology adoption. Sena and Paul (2009) agreed that the main reason for the decrease in the usage of Internet banking (IB) in Turkey is due to perceived risk on security features of IB. These findings is also supported by Mc Clure (2000) who finds that E-government will only succeed when all its participants including the government agencies, private business and individual citizens feel comfortable using electronic means to carry out private sensitive transactions. Stories about the hacker attack, page defacement makes the general public reluctant to do "real" business over the Internet.

Change Factor

As with E-government, public sector administrations are required to change and re-engineer their business process to adapt new strategies and culture of E-government. Government staff should be prepared for new ways of dealing with new technologies that emerge with E-government. For example, they are used in dealing with physical papers and forms, paper receipts, and traditional physical signatures, while E-government allows citizens access to the organization back-office remotely to complete the transaction processing, which emerged with new technology solutions such as electronic forms, digital signatures, electronic receipts and certificates. This reluctant to change from traditional way of doing work to a new paradigm is a major barrier to adoption (Zakareya & Zahir, 2005)

Low Confidence in the Electronic Administrative

According to Lai et al. (2005) one of the reasons for low usage of E-Filing system is due to low confidence in the electronic administrative capabilities of the tax authority in managing the E-Filing system successfully. The respondents perceived that the tax officers lack in the required skills, experience and competency as well as the ability in handling disaster recovery and technological crisis. Lai et al. also quoted Bird and Oldman's (2000) study which found that favourable attitude and trust in the tax authorities in managing electronic tax administration system has lead to high level of usage of E-Filing system in Singapore.

FUTURE TRENDS

Building a successful E-government adoption especially the E-Filing system may involve multiple approaches. There are general approaches and technical details. The general approaches will be first, bridging the digital divide. Government must always ensure that efforts are taken to bridge the difference in ICT supply and usage between the rural and the urban people. The Malaysian government in bridging the digital divide has constructed 108 Medan Info Desa in rural areas, 387 telecentres established, 42 Pusat Internet Desa was upgraded and targeted to provide at least one telecentre for each mukim by 2010 (PIKOM, 2008). Second approach is the IRB must create a long term marketing campaign strategy to convert reluctant taxpayers by tout that E-Filing is more convenient and less time consuming than sending paperwork via the mail, reduces preparation time, provide faster refunds, improves accuracy of returns and gives an acknowledgement-of-return receipt (Matthew, 2006). Third approach is by arranging programs such as Volunteer Income Tax Assistance and Tax Counselling for the Elderly in an effort to bring the elderly people to use the E-Filing system (Matthew, 2006). Fourth approach is on the security concerns; the normal procedure used to log in is the password and tax file number. This normal security codes are quite weak and passwords are often easy to guess, steal or crack.

In recent years, technical details approach is biometrics-based identification and authentication systems have become more widespread and have been considered for application in many application domains. Biometric techniques, such as fingerprint verification, iris or face recognition, retina analysis and hand-written signature verification, are increasingly becoming basic elements of authentication and identification systems (Zorkadis & Donos, 2004).

CONCLUSION

It is our tentative conclusion that the ICT industry in Malaysia is poised to grow positively in years to come. The role of the government in spearheading the deployment of ICT in major development corridors, continuing efforts to computerization of public services, globalization and market liberalization of financial and telecommunication verticals are among many other factors poised to contribute substantially to the economy (PIKOM 2008). The rate of increase in the number of tax filers using the E-Filing system shows the effectiveness and success of the system each year. However, for a better security, the third factor authentication process should be provided. The third authentication factor is the use of biometric such as iris or thumbprint recognition. As such, if passwords have been compromised, fraudsters need to get through another two levels of authentication to access a customer account. This would be difficult, if not, totally impossible.

REFERENCES

Abdullatif, I. A., & Philip, J. K. (2009). Rethinking models of technology adoption for internet banking: The role of website features. *Journal of Financial Services Marketing, 14*(1), 56–69. doi:10.1057/fsm.2009.4

Antonopoulos, C., & Sakellaris, P. (2009). The contribution of information and communication technology investments to Greek economic growth: An analytical growth accounting framework. *Information Economics and Policy, 21*, 171–191. doi:10.1016/j.infoecopol.2008.12.001

Astrid, D., Mitra, A., & David, M. (2008). The role of perceived enjoyment and social norm in the adoption of technology with network externalities. *European Journal of Information Systems, 17*, 4–11. doi:10.1057/palgrave.ejis.3000726

Azleen, I., Mohd Zulkeflee, A. R., & Mohd Rushdan, Y. (2009). Taxpayers' attitude in using e-filing system: Is there any significant difference among demographic factors? *Journal of Internet Banking and Commerce, 14*(1), 2–13.

David, Y. K. T. (2008). A study of e-recruitment technology adoption in Malaysia. *Industrial Management & Data Systems, 109*(2), 281–300.

Davidson, R. M., Wagner, C., & Ma, L. C. K. (2005). From government to e-government: A transitional model. *Information Technology & People, 18*(3), 280–299. doi:10.1108/09593840510615888

Economic Planning Unit (EPU). (2008). *The midterm review of the ninth Malaysian plan: 2006-2010.*

Fu, J. R., Farn, C. K., & Chao, W. P. (2006). Acceptance of electronic tax filing: A study of taxpayers' intention. *Information & Management, 43*, 109–126. doi:10.1016/j.im.2005.04.001

Hesson, M., & Al-Ameed, H. (2007). Online security evaluation process for new e-services. *Journal of Business Process Management, 13*(2), 223–245. doi:10.1108/14637150710740473

Irani, Z., Dwivedi, Y. K., & Williams, M. D. (2008). Understanding consumer adoption of broadband: An extension of the technology acceptance model. *The Journal of the Operational Research Society, 60*, 1322–1334. doi:10.1057/jors.2008.100

IRB. (2001). *Annual report 2001*. Malaysia: Inland Revenue Board.

IRB. (2006). *Annual report 2006*. Malaysia: Inland Revenue Board.

Jalava, J., & Pohjola, M. (2002). Economic growth in the new economy: Evidence from advanced economies. *Information Economics and Policy, 14*, 189–210. doi:10.1016/S0167-6245(01)00066-X

Jalava, J., & Pohjola, M. (2007). The role of electricity and ICT in economic growth: Case Finland. *Explorations in Economic History, 45*, 270–287. doi:10.1016/j.eeh.2007.11.001

Junaidah, H. (2008). Learning barriers in adopting ICT among selected working women in Malaysia. *Gender in Management: An International Journal, 23*(5), 317–336. doi:10.1108/17542410810887356

Khalil, T. M. (1993). Management of technology and the creation of wealth. *Industrial Engineering (American Institute of Industrial Engineers), 25*(9), 16–17.

Khalil, T. M. (2000). *Management of technology: The key to competitiveness and wealth creation*. Singapore: McGraw Hill.

Kuppusamy, M., Raman, M., & Lee, G. (2009). Whose ICT investment matters to economic growth: Private or public? The Malaysian perspective. *The Electronic Journal on Information Systems in Developing Countries, 37*(7), 1–19.

Kuppusamy, M., & Shanmugam, B. (2007). Information communication technology and economic growth in Malaysia. *Review of Islamic Economics, 11*(2), 87 100.

Lai, M. L., Siti, N. S. O., & Ahamed, K. M. (2004). Towards an electronic filing system: A Malaysian survey. *eJournal of Tax Research, 5*(2), 1-11.

Lai, M. L., Siti, N. S. O., & Ahamed, K. M. (2005). Tax practitioners and the electronic filing system: An empirical analysis. *Academy of Accounting and Financial Studies Journal, 9*(1), 93–109.

Lambrinoudakisa, C., Gritzalisa, S., Dridib, F., & Pernul, G. (2003). Security requirements for e-government services: A methodological approach for developing a common PKI-based security policy. *Computer Communications, 26*, 1873–1883. doi:10.1016/S0140-3664(03)00082-3

Lee, S. M. (2003). Korea: From the land of morning calm to ICT hotbed. *Journal of the Academy Management Executive (USA)*, *17*(2).

Matthew, W. (2006). *E-file goals too ambitious.* FWC.COM. Retrieved February 11, 2009, from http://fcw.com/articles/2006/02/27/efile-goal-too-ambitious.aspx

Mc Clure, D. L. (2000). *Federal initiatives are evolving rapidly but they face significant challenges.* Testimony, United States General Accounting Office, GAO/T-AIMD/GGD-00-179.

Md Nor, K., & Pearson, J. M. (2007). The influence of trust on internet banking acceptance. *Journal of Internet Banking and Commerce*, *12*(2), 2–10.

Mihyar, H., & Hayder, A. (2007). Online security evaluation process for new e-services. *Journal of Business Process Management*, *13*(2), 223–246. doi:10.1108/14637150710740473

Paul, T. J., & Kim, M. T. (2003). E-government around the world: Lessons, challenges and future directions. *Government Information Quarterly*, *20*, 389–394. doi:10.1016/j.giq.2003.08.001

Raman, M., Stephenaus, R., Alam, N., & Kuppusamy, M. (2008). Information technology in Malaysia: E-service quality and uptake of internet banking. *Journal of Internet Banking and Commerce*, *13*(2), 2–17.

Ramayah, T., Ramoo, V., & Ibrahim, A. (2008). Profiling online and manual tax filers: Results from an exploratory study in Penang, Malaysia. *Labuan e-Journal of Muamalat and Society*, *2*, 1-18.

Sena, O., & Paul, P. (2009). Exploring the adoption of a service innovation: A study of Internet banking adopters and non-adopters. *Journal of Financial Services Marketing*, *13*(4), 284–299. doi:10.105 //fsm.2008.25

Skillman, B. (1998). Fired up at the IRS. *Accounting Technology*, *14*, 12–20.

Solow, R. M. (1957). Technical change and the aggregate production function. *The Review of Economics and Statistics*, *39*(3), 312–320. doi:10.2307/1926047

The STAR. (2009, May 1). *Amount of Malaysian's choosing e-filing up by 30%.*

The, S. T. A. R. (2009). *It's time inland revenue board got real on e-filing.* Retrieved on June 19th, 2009, from http://thestar.com.my/news/story.asp?file=/2009/3/2/focus/3380923&sec=focus

The National ICT Association of Malaysia (PIKOM). (2008). *ICT strategies, societal and market touch*. Retrieved on June 24th, 2009, from http://www.witsa.org/news/2009-1/html_email_newsletter_jan09_b.html

Trustgate Sdn, M. S. C. Bhd. (2009). *Secure e-filing*. Retrieved on June 24th, 2009, from http://www.mykad.com.my/Website/secureefiling.php

Zakareya, E., & Zahir, I. (2005). E-government adoption: Architecture and barriers. *Business Process Management Journal, 11*(5), 589–611. doi:10.1108/14637150510619902

Zorkadis, V., & Donos, P. (2004). On biometrics-based authentication and identification from a privacy-protection perspective deriving privacy-enhancing requirements. *Information Management & Computer Security, 12*(1), 125–137. doi:10.1108/09685220410518883

KEY TERMS AND DEFINITIONS

Authentication: Is the process through which an Internet merchant can be established via a trusted third party that guarantees that the merchant is indeed whom he is.

E-Filing System: E-Filing system in Malaysia which is recently launched in 2006 is the way to submit the tax documents to the Inland Revenue Board through internet or online without the need to submit any paper documents. This system has provided an easy, faster and safer way of submitting the tax documents by the tax filers.

E-Government: E-government refers to electronic government which means governments in a particular country use ICT or internet base to provide their services. This is done in order to improve the quality of their services, interactions and transactions with customers and businesses mainly.

Economic Growth: Growth is the increase in the country's profit in terms of goods and services produced, monetary profits earned and increased in total productivity. Normally, economic growth is calculated based on the increase in Gross Domestic Product of the particular country.

Information Communication Technologies: ICT covers the use of advanced technologies in private and public sectors in order to give a better service to the customers. It includes the technologies such as broadcasting information and wireless mobile telecommunications.

Security: In the context of E-Filing System threats can be made either through network and data filing attacks or through unauthorized access to the tax file by means of false or defective authentication.

Technology Adoption: Technology Adoption refers to the rate of usage a particular technology by the consumers when it is introduced in the country either by the government or the private sectors. There are various reasons has been outline that can affect the usage or adoption of the particular system such as readiness, security concerns and level of education.

Chapter 18
Road Safety 2.0:
A Case of Transforming Government's Approach to Road Safety by Engaging Citizens through Web 2.0

Dieter Fink
Edith Cowan University, Australia

EXECUTIVE SUMMARY

The aim of this case study is first, to determine the extent to which web 2.0 can be the technology that would enable a strong relationship between government and its citizens to develop in managing road safety, and second, to examine the endeavours of the WA Office of Road Safety (ORS) in fostering the relationship. It shows that in ORS' road safety strategy for 2008-2020, community engagement is strongly advocated for the successful development and execution of its road safety plan, but the potential of web 2.0 approaches in achieving it is not recognised. This would involve the use of blogs and RSSes as suitable push strategies to get road safety information to the public. Online civic engagement would harness collective intelligence (the wisdom of crowds) and, by enabling the public to annotate information on wikis, layers of value could be added so that the public become co-developers of road safety strategy and policy. The case identifies three major challenges confronting the ORS to become Road Safety 2.0 ready: how to gain the publics' attention in competition with other government agencies, how to respond internally to online citizen engagement, and how to manage governmental politics.

DOI: 10.4018/978-1-4666-2071-1.ch018

BACKGROUND

Government's responsibility for road safety is widely accepted since the public expects government to provide the infrastructure and regulatory environment in which the road user can have confidence that his or her safety is protected. It is now commonly expected that roads are well constructed and road behaviour is controlled by effective legislation. However, as the volume of traffic increases so have road deaths and injury, thereby focusing the publics' attention on the role that government is performing in ensuring road safety. In Western Australia (WA), where this case is situated, the publicity given to the road toll is reflected in prominent newspaper headlines. The following are two such examples.

On July 17, 2009, the daily "The West Australian" newspaper contained an article with the headline "Road deaths, injuries costing State billions" in which the social cost of deaths and injuries was estimated at $Australian 2.4 billion. A possible remedy was identified in the same newspaper on July 24, 2009 under the title "Money can halve road toll in WA, says expert." The expert quoted in the article advocated safety measures such as big roundabouts to slow vehicles, incorporating electronic stability controls into cars, fixed speed cameras at known blackspots and reducing speed limits. However, the expert quoted in the article speculated that motorists would "laugh at" any moves that would drop regional speed limits below the current 110 km/hr. This shows the need to better understand the attitudes of the public towards road safety.

The WA government has long recognised the concern of the public for safer roads and regards safety as an important governmental responsibility. This and the unique characteristics of the state of WA are succinctly stated on the Office of Road Safety website (ORS, 2010).

Western Australia (WA) is the largest State in Australia. It covers 2,525,500 square kilometres (i.e., over four times the area of France). However its population is only approximately 10 per cent (2.1 million) of the country's total population, with the majority of people living in the state capital city of Perth. With over 50,000 kilometres of sealed and 127,000 kilometres of unsealed roads, WA relies extensively on its road network for transporting both people and freight.

Since the 1970s as Western Australia developed as a State and population increased, road safety issues emerged as a major concern. In 1970, 351 people were killed on Western Australian roads - about 35 deaths per 100,000 people. By 1996, we experienced 14 deaths per 100,000 after major changes such as random breath-testing and compulsory seatbelts were introduced. During this time the responsibility for road safety largely rested with the Police whose role was centred on enforcement and education.

In 1996 a parliamentary review of road safety recommended an independent body would provide the coordination required to work with multiple stakeholders and develop a state-wide strategy and response to road safety. The council would comprise members from government, local government and the community and would also include an independent chair drawn from the community.

The independent body referred to above is the Council of Road Safety (CRS) which is supported by the Office of Road Safety (ORS), a WA government department.

SETTING THE STAGE

During the late 2000, the CRS formulated a strategic plan for road safety, based on the work carried out by the ORS, which was adopted by the WA government in 2009. "Towards Zero: Getting there together 2008-2020" contains strategies that aim to reduce road deaths and serious injuries on WA roads. The road map to achieving community participation (i.e., getting there together) is provided by another body within the WA government, namely the Office of e-Government (OEG). This body requires each agency to transform its approach to one that is citizen centric. It laid out a staged-approach which guides the agency to move from a mere static web presence to one that offers online access of services and transactions and then to reach a transformation stage in which strong relationships are developed between itself and the public.

The Council and Office of Road Safety

The WA government manages its approach to road safety through the CRS supported by the ORS. Representatives from various government agencies and motoring bodies constitute the Council. They are charged with providing advice to government on matters pertaining to road safety as well as seeking input from academics and experts on latest research findings and developments. The Council's role is to make policy recommendations to the WA State Government which has the final say on strategic directions for road safety in the state.

According to its organisation chart, CRS's long term vision "is of a road transport system where crashes resulting in death or serious injury are virtually eliminated in WA" (ORS, 2010). The coordinating mechanism adopted by CRS shows that it operates at 2 levels. At the top is the Ministerial Council which is chaired by the Minster for Police and Road Safety and is made up of the ministers for Health, Education, Local Government, Planning, and Regional Development. At the supporting level, the Council has representatives from a range of government agencies and is chaired by an independent person. The government agencies represented are Police, Health, Road Safety, Main Roads, Education, Transport and Planning. The remaining members represent The Insurance Commission of WA, the Local Government Association, and The Royal Automobile Club (RAC) of WA on behalf of road use representatives.

Council members have specific responsibilities for road safety as shown in the Appendix (Figure 3). Responsibilities can be classified as active and passive. Active roles include the education of road users (Education and Training, RAC), designing, building, operating and maintaining the road network (Main Roads, Local Government) and enforcing road use behaviour (Police). More passive roles include collecting data on road fatalities and injuries (Health, Insurance Commission, Main Roads, Police) and being an advocate for safer roads (Planning and Infrastructure, ORS, RAC, Local Government). The role of ORS is critical since it is charged with the responsibility to provide leadership among the agencies in the co-ordination of road safety activities as well as reporting progress on the reduction of road fatalities and injuries.

ORS is a small government department and it supports the CRS by gathering and assessing research, preparing community education campaigns and giving advice and making recommendations to the Council. An important function it fulfilled was the development of a comprehensive road safety strategy titled "Towards Zero: Getting there together 2008-2020" (ORS, 2009). This document was endorsed by the WA government in March 2009 on the recommendation of the Road Safety Council.

Towards Zero: Getting there Together 2008-2020

The above report succeeded the earlier 2003-2007 one titled "Arriving Safely" and builds on the experiences gained with the earlier strategy. The plan makes recommendations for achieving a significant improvement in road safety over the next 12 years by focusing on four cornerstones as shown in the extract (Figure 1).

As seen in Figure 1, the recommended strategy aims to save lives of or serious injuries to, 11,000 people over twelve years in four ways; first, by safe road use. This implies affecting behaviour change on the part of road users, such as reducing the incidence of impaired driving (caused by excessive alcohol consumption for example), enforcing restraint use (e.g., wearing seatbelts), implementing graduating licensing (e.g., probationary driving) and deciding on speed choice (50 km/hr speed limit in suburban areas). Second, safe roads and roadsides seek to improve current infrastructure through larger road verges and more roundabouts. Third, safe speeds will be achieved through speed enforcement measures such as increasing the number of speed cameras. Lastly, the uptake of safer vehicles should also reduce death and injury and this is where government can take a lead through appropriate purchasing for its vehicle fleet.

Figure 1. Road safety strategy recommendations (Office of Road Safety, 2009)

STRATEGY RECOMMENDATIONS

Towards Zero incorporates the Safe System, which aims to improve road safety through four cornerstones: Safe Road Use; Safe Roads and Roadsides; Safe Speeds; and Safe Vehicles.

If all cornerstones of the **Towards Zero** strategy are fully implemented we have the potential to save **11,000 people** from being killed or seriously injured between 2008 and 2020. That is a reduction of around 40 percent on present day levels.

The ambition to "save 11,000 people being killed or seriously injured," as targeted in the plan, should be compared with the progress made towards reducing the road toll over the past 30 years (ORS, 2009) as seen in the Appendix (Figure 4). It shows the road toll in WA from 1960 to 2007 and key road safety initiatives adopted by the WA government at various times. As can be seen the CRS was formed in 1987 when the road toll was on the increase. It subsequently fell for the period 1998-2001 but rose again after that. It peaked around 2005 but declined in later years. Some of the key road safety measures adopted were the introduction of random breath testing and speed cameras in 1998 and, more recently, the reduction of speed limits in suburban neighbourhoods to 50 km/hr as well as the doubling of demerit points during public holidays.

Measuring the road toll in terms of deaths and serious injury suffers from the problem of how injuries are captured and measured. This requires data capturing methods and processes of a sophistication that are unlikely to exist. Instead, the Australian Government publishes more reliable statistics on road deaths only and provides comparisons between the Australian states. For Australia, road deaths per year per 100,000 population have decreased from about 9.5 to 6.4 for the 10 years ending July 2010 as seen in the Appendix (Figure 5). A comparison of road deaths indicates that WA experiences the second highest deaths among the Australian states and territories as shown in Table 1.

The road toll becomes even more significant when the impact of road traffic crashes is estimated in economic terms. On a global scale, it is estimated to cost high-income countries, such as Australia, more than 2% of their Gross National Product. In dollar terms the annual cost across Australian states and jurisdictions is

Table 1. Comparative road deaths per 100,000 population as at July 2010 (adapted from Australian Government, 2010)

New South Wales	**6.3**
Victoria	5.6
Queensland	5.8
South Australia	7.3
Western Australia	8.2
Tasmania	6.3
Northern Territory	18.4
Australian Capital Territory	5.9
National	6.4

costed at $A17.85 billion, equivalent to Australia's defence budget and three times Australia's higher education budget (Rodwell, 2010).

The "Towards Zero" strategy was submitted to the Legislative Assembly on 19 March 2009 by the Minister for Road Safety. When tabling the document, the minister acknowledged the challenges facing government and the community and appealed for a joint effort in achieving the envisioned reduction in the road toll. The minster opened his submission of the strategic plan with the following words.

Much is asked of Western Australia in this new road safety strategy. The work ahead is demanding and requires community and political support. I am asking you all to join me in confronting the great challenges before us. Towards Zero is an ambitious target but its expected outcomes are achievable if we work together (ORS, 2009, p. 3).

According to the plan, development of the strategy for 2008-2020 involved a greater degree of community and stakeholder engagement than had been the case with the preceding 2003-2007 strategy. It was stated that this allowed the community to see, and debate, the best evidence about the options available to improve road safety. The mode of community consultation was a mix of public forums and online surveys as discussed in a later section.

The Office of E-Government

Adopting a whole-of-government perspective, the Office of e-Government (OEG) is charged with the responsibility of developing e-government strategies for the WA Public Sector. According to its website (OEG, 2004) its e-Government strategy seeks to establish a roadmap for how WA will progress to a transformational model of government. The vision for e-government conveyed in the strategy is "a more efficient public sector that delivers integrated services and improved opportunities for community participation" (p. 24). There are three goals that support the e-government vision.

- **Service delivery:** provide more personalised and accessible services that are easy for the community to use.
- **Internal efficiency:** improve processes within and between agencies leading to lower costs and improved services.
- **Community participation:** ensure easier interaction so that people can understand and contribute to government.

The strategy document identifies the stages of development that agencies will need to move through to achieve full e-government transformation. The four phases of e-government are identified as web presence, interaction, transaction and transformation. Each phase has different activities that seek to achieve the three goals of e-government (service delivery, internal efficiency, community participation). The stages and ORS' progress towards achieving transformation will be discussed in a later section.

For community participation, which is a key goal of the transformation process, "Online engagement will be the preferred choice of interaction with government by citizens. The machinery of government processes will be adapted to better fit the technological environment" (OEG, 2004). In other words, the strategy proposed by OEG takes a citizen's view of what e-government transformation will look like and recommends the adoption of technology to enhance government-citizen interaction. According to OEG (2004), transformation should occur in 2010, facilitated by the following key enablers:

1. Leadership,
2. Culture change – thinking 'corporate WA',
3. Governance mechanisms,
4. Citizen-centric approach,
5. Collaborative relationships – looking for synergies,
6. Policy and legislative framework,
7. Technology architecture and interoperability,
8. Information management.

For each of the above enablers, OEG identified its role and that of a government agency. OEG provides leadership for the e-government agenda in WA and expects senior executives in agencies to show commitment to, and understanding of, the concept. The move to e-government requires a change away from the silo or agency-centric approach to government to one that views the WA government as a coordinated entity offering a one-stop frontage to the public. Instead of searching for services on various agency websites, citizens would enter a common access point from which they gain access to government information or services wherever they may reside. This is recognised as a big challenge for agencies and requires the introduction of workplace learning and knowledge sharing networks of staff across agencies. A new approach to governance should emerge in the form of a whole-of-government understanding of how to maximise government resources, transparency and accountability. Flexibility and willingness to accommodate the needs of each other should result in agencies opening their systems to embrace collaborative opportunities.

A citizen-centric approach is viewed as core to e-government; it is "the first principle of e-government (in that) services and information will be designed and focused on the needs of Western Australians" (OEG, 2004, p. 36, parentheses added). Information and Communications Technology (ICT) is seen as a vital tool to build this community of interest and sustain it. For agencies this means creating an environment that supports and encourages citizens to engage with them. Agencies will have to identify the needs of their customer base and develop multiple channels for service delivery and consultation.

The above objective can best be achieved by developing collaborative relationships and synergies. According to OEG (2004), traditional government agencies are known for not looking outside their own resources for knowledge, ideas or best practice. Since agencies essentially service the same customer base (the Western Australian public); synergies would result from agencies partnering with each other to reduce duplication and costs. Agency executives have the responsibility to open dialogue between agencies and focus on outcomes that achieve these benefits. A key facilitator of collaboration is a whole-of-government ICT infrastructure that uses processes that span agencies in order to deliver more integrated services to the public. It is also recognised that information management should focus on sharing data and information among agencies and with the public in a secure and timely manner.

The way such projects should be valued by OEG is not clear. Essentially, e-Government projects should be assessed according to the value they provide to the public. Various evaluation approaches currently exist with no agreement as to which is best. An excellent review of current frameworks is provided by Liu et al. (2008) who came to the conclusion that the approach should take into consideration "multiple value dimensions (financial, social, political/strategic and operational) and multiple stakeholders for the e-government project valuation" (p. 95). Public sector value differs from that of the private sector in that it is more than purely economic value. Such values can include Moore's social value, the U.S. Federal

Value Measurement Methodology (VMM) that seeks to balance value, cost and risks, and the U.K. government framework that focuses on services, outcomes and trust (Liu et al., 2008).

CASE DESCRIPTION

This case is about the progress of the ORS to transform itself with the aim of achieving citizen engagement on road safety. A number of drivers can be identified from the preceding material. First, the road safety strategy document, outlining the planned approach to reducing the WA road toll, raises the expectation of "getting there together." In other words, ORS can only fulfill its mission with the co-operation of other government bodies, such as policing and main roads, and the public taking ownership of road safety. The Minister responsible for road safety himself appealed, when tabling the road safety strategy, for community and political support. These requirements are recognised by the OEG when seeking to transform WA government agencies; key enablers are adopting a citizen-centric approach and collaborative relationships with other agencies.

Community Engagement

As outlined above, the OEG provides the broad guidelines for WA government agencies to follow in their transformation to a citizen-centric model of operations. It views citizen engagement as one in which citizens actively contribute to government decision-making. More specifically, citizens most directly affected and interested in a specific issue are identified and consulted so that their views can be considered in the decision-making process. An assessment of the current modes of operation within the agency is required to ensure that an environment is created that supports and encourages citizens to engage with government. While OEG provides the overarching framework, the ORS strategic plan and website provides details on its progress towards achieving the transformation.

The ORS sees the objective of engaging the public on road safety as highly desirable. It demonstrated this by conducting an extensive consultation programme during the two years preceding the release of its most recent strategy in 2009. All up 4,170 people (ORS, 2009) provided input for the development of the new strategy in a number of ways. Initially, 39 forums were conducted in 19 locations, spread throughout the state, to which community members were invited. Subsequently 8 forums, targeted at stakeholders (defined by ORS as those directly involved and concerned about road safety) in major population centres, were held at which 807 people provided feedback at forums or when submitted online. Subsequently, specific groups and organisations were targeted to meet at the Perth Convention Centre where 200 people attended. Finally, more people provided input via a questionnaire available online or being emailed in response to press advertisement (1,188) or by being contacted telephonically (649).

Consultation of the public during strategy development appears extensive by the number of people approached. However, interaction between government and citizens was restricted by the mode used to engage. The public responded to invitations from ORS to meet at specific locations (public forums) or to complete a questionnaire available online, by email or by telephone. In other words, citizens responded to ORS initiated contact and engagement with individuals was once off rather than ongoing. This appears to be a constraint on enabling citizens to gain a deep understanding of road safety and being able to develop their contribution to strategy and policy over time as they gained greater insights.

As far as future community engagement is concerned, a search of "Towards Zero: Getting there together 2008-2020" found the term had been used three times (no results were found for citizen engagement). In the document's introduction, a brief section is provided titled "Build relationships with the community." The section outlines the range of consultations that took place to develop the strategic plan through community forums and surveys as outlined above. Recognition is then given to the need for ongoing engagement. "Community engagement has now evolved into an ongoing relationship. The community owns the strategy as much as the Government. The continued support and involvement of the community is essential for effective implementation and ambitious gains" (ORS, 2009, p. 11). Community engagement is again mentioned in respect of accepting government's safe roads and roadside initiatives. It is argued that as the community becomes accustomed to accepting the changes, they will demand more changes for safer roads.

The Potential of Web 2.0

The emergence of web 2.0, or so-called social software, offers an opportunity to achieve more effective community engagement with the topic of road safety. What appears to be missing in the current strategy is the recognition of this online technology, one that does not rely on physical contact (e.g., public forums) and is able to reach many more citizens than before through the web. According to Smith et al. (2005), there are three 'meta categories' that describe online civic engagement enabled by web 2.0.

- **Collaboration:** many people working together on a single activity, effort or project through wikis and discussion boards.
- **Communications:** talking with and among constituents through email, chat rooms, listservs, text messaging and instant messaging.
- **Content development:** generating and disseminating original news through websites, web logs (weblogs), newsletters, RSS (Really Simple Syndication) and podcasting.

Key technologies among the above are wikis, weblogs, RSS and podcasting. A wiki is a website on which a document is created and to which the initial author allows access to others via a common web browser. Users can add, remove, or otherwise edit and change the document's content. By attracting a large number of authors the document is potentially enriched through a collective, collaborative effort. Weblogs on the other hand serve the purpose of delivering and/or sharing information by capturing reactions and comments from its readers. They are web pages that contain user created entries updated at regular intervals. Weblogs complement traditional media since they may consist of text, images, audio, video or combination of them. As such they are replacing the static nature of websites with a more dynamic exchange of ideas and ever-changing content. RSS is a different type of technology, one that is termed an "aggregator technology" (Cong & Du, 2007) that can be used to pull pieces of information together and feeds to subscribers frequently updated digital content such as blogs and podcasts. For this reason, the term 'live web' is used since a RSS feed provides notification to the subscriber every time the website page changes. Content can be delivered as part of a podcast which is a multimedia file distributed over the web to be played back on mobile devices and personal computers.

There are many potential benefits associated with involving those interested in road safety through the approaches identified above. Increasing public involvement leads to greater networks of people interested (and committed) to road safety. The use of blogs, podcasting and RSS are suitable push strategies to get road safety information to the public. By enabling the public to annotate information on wikis, collective intelligence ('the wisdom of crowds') is harnessed so that the public become co-developers of road safety strategy and policy. Overall, web 2.0 approaches would enable the ORS to inform the public about road safety as well as gaining a better understanding of what the community is willing to accept in respect of road safety. Consequently the development of new strategies and policies would reflect better the expectations of the public and provide an indication of their willingness to take ownership of road safety.

Web 2.0 Abilities and Expectations

To establish the readiness of the public to engage with road safety issues, the author (Fink, 2010) conducted a survey of young people, generally acknowledged as being over-represented in road accident statistics. They were students at the author's university and hence it was assumed that they had some familiarity with web 2.0 tools and applications. From a group of 108 students, 103 satisfactory questionnaire responses were obtained, with a roughly equal mix of under- and post-graduate students. Most participants (57%) were under 25 years of age and possessed a driver's license between 1 and 4 years.

Participants indicated their overall understanding of web 2.0 as 3.30 and using web 2.0 as 3.51, both on a 5-point scale where 1=very poor and 5=very high. More specifically, their abilities with web 2.0 approaches were rated above the scale midpoint (3.0) as shown in Table 2.

High levels of understanding as well as using web 2.0 are promising indicators that young drivers by ready to use web 2.0 should it be available to them. Their expectations to engage with road safety as a citizen via a web 2.0 based website are reflected in Table 3.

Again responses were above the scale midpoint of 3 indicating the potential of electronic engagement with government if available. Rated relatively highly by participants were sharing opinions with the broader community (akin to the 'wisdom of the crowd'), and making a contribution to the community (i.e., possibly indicating taking responsibility for road safety).

The survey also captured participants' experience with the ORS website (Table 4), both what they expected from it and what they perceived it was providing.

Statistical analysis revealed that for 4 of the variables above, expectations exceeded experiences in a significant way (Sig.<.001); the exception being 'emphasis on road safety' for which expectations and experiences with the website were not

Table 2. Ability with Web 2.0 tools (adapted from Fink, 2010)

I am able to engage with a website on road safety issues through being familiar with	Mean	St dev
1. sending text messages through email	3.60	1.32
2. engaging with others on electronic forums	3.57	1.14
3. generating content material through weblogs	3.33	1.15
4. generating content material through wikis	3.21	1.10
5. controlling how data is displayed	3.32	1.13
6. RSS that feed information to me	3.21	1.15

(1=strongly disagree 5=strongly agree, N=101)

Table 3. Expectations for citizen engagement (adapted from Fink, 2010)

The use of a road safety website should enable me	Mean	St dev
1. to be engaged with developing road safety policy	3.91	0.97
2. to share opinions with the broader community on road safety	4.00	1.01
3. to contribute to my community on road safety	3.98	1.00
4. to edit road safety information provided on the website	3.21	1.25
5. to be treated as a co-developer of road safety information	3.44	1.18
6. to be part of the collective intelligence of the public on road safety	3.82	1.04

(1=strongly disagree 5=strongly agree, N=102)

significantly different (t=.207, df=24, Sig.=.207). All expectations were rated high (all over 4.00) while all experiences were rated low (all under 3.00). By improving website features, the gap between expectations and actual website experience on road safety would be narrowed.

Citizen engagement with government has been researched in various other settings. For example, Sommer and Cullen (2009) studied the "ParticipativeNZ wiki" that was set up to foster dialogue and collaboration in creating content for the New Zealand government. For two New Zealand agencies (bioethics and policing) engagement could be observed but e-empowerment of the public had not yet been fully achieved. In the case of bioethics, engagement was sought on the cultural, ethical and spiritual aspects of biotechnology. However, the project indicated lack of clarity about the type of input being desired and required a new mix of skills to drive the project including subject experts, facilitators, marketers, communicators and writers. Furthermore, because of the complex nature of bioethics, hardened positions were encountered that were found difficult to reconcile. The Police Act wiki invited the public to engage on the future of policing in New Zealand. While

Table 4. Expectations of and experience with road safety website (adapted from Fink, 2010)

To me, the government road safety website, **should/does**	Expectation		Experience	
	Mean	St dev	Mean	St Dev
1. Emphasise road safety as an important issue	4.34	0.97	3.92	1.12
2. Demonstrate that knowledge exists to make roads safer	4.26	0.95	3.50	1.03
3. Raise the public's awareness about road safety	4.31	0.99	3.58	0.98
4. Engage the public on road safety	4.25	1.02	3.31	1.01
5. Be a major information source on road safety	4.15	1.12	3.35	1.09

(1=strongly disagree 5=strongly agree, Expectations N=102, Experiences N=26)

the approach was seen as empowering the public, it was recognised that it could also lead to disempowerment because of the digital divide excluding those with no or limited access to the new technology. It became clear that an approach using multiple channels (e.g., emails, forums, workshops), and not relying on the wiki only, proved the most effective way to generate ideas and discussions.

That technology alone was not sufficient to encourage engagement with government was confirmed by Tan et al. (2008); their research found that websites that deliver e-government services need "human-like traits" to convey service competency, benevolence and integrity. This was endorsed by Barnes and Vidgen (2007) who found that "interactors" (as opposed to information seekers) rated website quality much lower for the UK Inland Revenue because they expected empathy and personalisation for their individual needs. What the findings indicate is that technology is viewed by the public as a social actor with whom it interacts. To be adopted by the public government needs to ensure that it addresses technologically- and sociologically-oriented issues. These challenges also confront the ORS as will be argued later.

Perceived Progress towards Transformation at ORS

According to the OEG (2004), the four phases of e-government are identified as web presence, interaction, transaction and transformation. Each phase has different activities that seek to achieve the three goals of e-government (service delivery, internal efficiency, community participation) outlined earlier. The last phase, transformation, was scheduled for 2010 according to the OEG strategy. Diagrammatically, the three goals of transformation for ORS within an e-government approach can be viewed as Figure 2.

For service delivery in the transformation stage, there should be increasing levels of "push" services tailored to meet citizens' individual needs with a corresponding decreased reliance on traditional service delivery channels. For the latter, the public would contact a government agency by phone or mail with the request for information to be mailed to them. This is not only expensive but also time consuming. Obtaining material directly from a website is far more cost effective and convenient. Currently, much road safety information is available from the ORS website in the form of online directories of road safety topics, research facts and statistics, and links to other road safety sides. However, no RSS feature exists that would conveniently notify interested subscribers of changes that have occurred on the website for information the subscriber is interested in.

The aim of achieving internal efficiencies is to increase cross-agency collaboration and integration for improved information and cost sharing. This is critical to road safety because of the wide range of stakeholders represented on the CRS.

Figure 2. The goals of road safety within an e-government approach

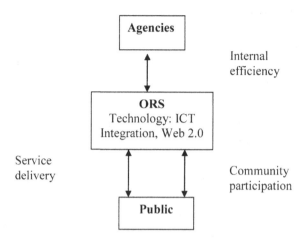

Council members representing various agencies have specific responsibilities for road safety as shown in Appendix A (Figure A1) that are of an active (e.g., education) and/or passive (e.g., collecting data) nature as discussed in an earlier section. As ICT systems become more integrated, an efficient flow of information between agencies themselves and with the ORS results. Only through effective systems integration would ORS meet its key responsibility, as determined by the CRS, of providing leadership among key agencies by coordinating road safety activities.

According to OEG (2004), community participation would have been achieved when online engagement is the preferred choice of interaction with government by citizens. It is during this stage that the "machinery of government processes will be adapted to better fit the technological environment" (p. 35). Appropriate technology (i.e., web 2.0) would enable the public to easily and conveniently engage with ORS who in turn would collect more and richer information on the publics' perceptions of, and attitudes to, road safety. A search of the ORS website and strategy document, however, did not reveal the use of web 2.0 or social software.

CURRENT CHALLENGES

While extensive public consultations took place during the development of the road safety strategy for the period 2008-2020, they largely took place at physical locations and were once-off when questionnaires were completed online, by email or by telephone. The challenge for ORS is to maintain ongoing contact with the public as to maximise the 'wisdom of the crowd' that resides outside its boundaries. The availability of web 2.0 approaches provides the opportunity to intensify government-citizen engagement and to sustain it. There was no evidence that could be observed on the ORS website or its publications that the web 2.0 approach was being considered. Yet the survey of young drivers conducted by the author indicated relatively high abilities with web 2.0 approaches and high expectations for a web 2.0 based road safety website. For the ORS to become Road Safety 2.0 ready it will have to evaluate the following issues.

Can ORS Gain Eyeball Time?

From an external perspective, it is suggested that ORS raises the publics' awareness of, and encourage it to give attention to, the topic of road safety. As observed by Marche and McNiven (2003) "in terms of the 'attention economy', the expansion of media, especially in terms of television and the web, means that government will have to work harder to acquire 'eyeball time' or 'mind sharing'" (p. 80). Road safety is only one among many government activities competing for the publics' attention. Other government departments, particularly those of education, health and policing, are actively seeking the publics' support for their activities to promote their existence. The traditional approach of allocating ministerial responsibility for separate government agencies entrenches the stove-pipe approach to service delivery and hence competition for resources among agencies.

Furthermore, citizens may not be satisfied with the information provided by what they perceive to be functional, insular departments structured as silos. Marche and McNiven (2003) refer to an increasingly reflexive society, defined as "the tendency of citizens and customers to react concretely to events on a basis of their own choosing, rather than just accept the explanation of authorities" (p. 77). In the case of road safety, citizens may, for example, want to access information on road safety related topics such as health, policing and road construction to form their own opinion on the topic rather than accepting information that is currently provided. For the ORS this means that it has to achieve ICT integration with diverse road safety stakeholders represented on the CRS.

Literature, however, indicates that government inward-looking systems tend to be generally much less funded than the outward-looking ones. Marche and McNiven (2003) provide the example of the Canadian Federal government which spend $780 million on citizen-facing e-government compared to $2.2 million on a government-wide intranet portal. The concern is that, as observed in the Canadian example, the ORS will give less attention, and hence less funding, to inward-looking systems integration than outward-looking website systems.

How Will ORS Respond to Online Engagement?

With increasing electronic citizen engagement, the impact of this on ORS' internal systems and processes will be significant. An analysis of the success or otherwise of web 2.0 technologies led Short (2008) to conclude "Regardless of which specific technologies are used, it is how web 2.0 is implemented and how the associated risk are managed that will be most important" (p. 30). The interactive nature of applications requires new and immediate organisational responses. For example, technological security measures have to be implemented to overcome new vulnerabilities (e.g., hacker attacks) and social risks (e.g., an employee's response is taken to imply formal policy). Furthermore, new types of costs are emerging. The nature of social software implies a greater involvement of a public with varying levels of interest in road safety. The ORS will have to be capable to process far greater volumes of feedback than they would have experienced before. The sources of input will also change such as those associated with the emergence of pressure groups. ORS staff and management will have to become more politically savvy in interacting with the public. These are skills that have to be acquired through training and/or brought into the agency at additional costs.

The overarching 'disruptive' impact of web 2.0 (increased collaboration, communication, etc.) requires a broad organisational response. Mintz (2008) refers to this as "turning inside out the classical approach to organizational structures and business relationships" (p. 24). He argues that organisations, including government, have to be agile or they will fail in meeting the demands of the marketplace. For the ORS this means that it will have to develop internal structures that are best suited to realising the opportunities presented by web 2.0. For example, young employees, already familiar with web 2.0 approaches, will demand from senior management that they are capable of embracing the new technology and make it visible or they will be tempted to leave the organisation. A rigid organisational hierarchy that controls the information flow as opposed to making information freely available to staff and community will be seen by them as being unresponsive to their and the publics' needs.

Garnett and Ecclesfield (2008) termed the new environment, where the technology-enhanced organisation and public value are aligned, an "organisational architecture of participation." They identified the key organisational characteristic required as leveraging constituent knowledge through adopting a team-oriented approach that recognises the knowledge of its people and creating a sociable, trusting and collaborative culture. The ORS will have to review its current organisational strengths and weaknesses and develop strategies that would bring about an internal culture of collaboration that translates into the delivery of better services and enhanced citizen participation. Public value would be created by using web-based networks in which ORS staff and the public have the confidence to actively communicate and collaborate with each other. The question of what constitutes public value should be resolved as there exists various approaches to evaluating the value projects provide to the public (Liu et al., 2008).

Barbagallo et al. (2010) provide some guidance on how to approach this emerging environment by suggesting developing e-Government ontologies that are based on participative and social processes. They make the point, however, that it is necessary for each government department to develop its own ontology to reflect its domain specific nature. Their Social Ontology Building and Evolution (SOBE) methodology requires extensive participation of citizens for the ontology to be built and evolve as it is progresses through different stages: the construction of intermediate structures, seeking consensus, validating outcomes and concept development. By following this process, ORS should be able to derive a Road Safety 2.0 ontology that models actors (e.g., road users, agencies, politicians), processes (e.g., laws and regulations, road safety projects), and citizens' needs (e.g., safer roads, reduced speeds).

Will ORS Manage Governmental Politics?

While the leaders in the use of web 2.0 practices have been Google, eBay, Amazon and others, Tapscott and Williams (2006) concluded that government still struggles with cultural inertia, complex legislation and political wrangling in coming to grips with web 2.0. Government agencies are among the largest sources of data but still only "a small number of government agencies are getting on the API bandwagon. This is an opportunity whose time is long overdue" (Tapscott & Williams, 2006, p. 199). The progress to fully exploit the opportunities offered by web 2.0 in the public sector is an uncertain one and the conclusion formed by Mintz (2008) appears to capture the current state of concern very well.

By its varied nature, these new Internet enabled technologies allow unpredictable interactions between unexpected stakeholders producing unplanned results, none of which offer comfort to the typical government agency. To participate, government agencies will need to define small pilot projects and give staff flexibility to experiment. In our current 'blame first, ask questions later' environment, it will take strong leadership for this to occur (p. 24).

Yet, despite these hindrances, the overriding benefit of a citizen-centric approach to ORS lies in the potential increase in social capital, defined and perceived as follows. "It is the 'grease' that enables people to set aside self-interests and personal priorities to help one another. A huge opportunity exists to take a quantum leap forward for social good with a new form of social capital bred and sustained through online engagement" (Smith et al., 2005, p. 28). Performance towards achieving this goal could be judged by how successfully the ORS will, in future, engage citizens in taking a stake in the responsibility of managing road safety. In the final event, by adopting a citizen-centric approach, the ORS has the opportunity to significantly benefit its constituency. Through the use of web 2.0 it can potentially transform citizens' perceptions on an important issue and enhance its reputation for effectively meeting the expectations of the public for safer roads.

The Lessons Learned

The case introduces the concept of stages of growth in respect of transforming a government agency to become online citizen-centric. The stages through which the approaches of an agency would evolve are laid out by a central policy unit (the OEG) and provide the theoretical framework to be adopted by the WA public sector. It was estimated by OEG that transformation would occur in 2010. However, as shown in the case discussion, the ORS has not achieved the full potential of having online citizen engagement supported by up-to-date technology. This technology is web 2.0 which has the potential to significantly improve collaboration, communication and content development.

A key reason for not having adopted the web 2.0 approach may lie in the challenges this poses for the ORS. As observed in literature, there are few instances of successful web 2.0 adoption by government. Web 2.0 is a paradigm shift from the implementing previous types of ICT and requires a new set of management techniques and organisational structures for its success. At the micro level, the case identified a range of these in areas that include risk, cost and benefit management. At the macro level, a new approach to information processing has to be designed to cater for large volumes of data provided by the public. Unless the ORS adopts an organisational architecture of participation, the transformation to a citizen-centric agency will not be achieved.

The concept of interacting with the public in strategy and policy development in a major way, when enabled by web 2.0, requires political resolve by government itself. First, it requires an acceptance by current domain experts within government agencies that potentially valuable knowledge as well as web 2.0 abilities exist among the public. The public knows best what it is willing to accept in terms of road regulations and so on. Second, government has to get used to taking risks. Mintz (2008) points to unpredictable interactions between unexpected stakeholders producing unplanned results and recommends the approach of conducting small pilot projects and giving staff flexibility to experiment. For the ORS the journey to adopting web 2.0 approaches promises much but also provides major challenges.

NOTE

The case study of the Western Australian Council of Road Safety, Office of Road Safety and Office of e-Government was developed from material available in the public domain on the Western Australian Government websites referenced in the paper. The interpretation and discussion of the material obtained from these websites are entirely those of the author.

REFERENCES

Australian Government, Department of Infrastructure, Transport, Regional Development and Local Government. (2010). *Road deaths Australia*. Retrieved from http://www.bitre.gov.au/publications/72/Files/RDA_July.pdf

Barbagallo, A., De Nicola, A., & Missikoff, M. (2010). eGovernment ontologies: Social participation in building and evolution. In *Proceedings of the 43rd Hawaii International Conference on System Sciences*, Honolulu, Hawaii (pp. 1-10).

Barnes, S. J., & Vidgen, R. (2007). Interactive e-government: Evaluating the web site of the UK inland revenue. *International Journal of Electronic Government Research*, *3*(1), 19–37. doi:10.4018/jegr.2007010102

Cong, Y., & Du, H. (2007). Welcome to the world of Web 2.0. *The CPA Journal*, *77*(5), 6–10.

Coplin, W. D., Merget, A. E., & Bourdeaux, C. (2002). The professional researcher as change agent in the government-performance movement. *Public Administration Review*, *62*(6), 699–711. doi:10.1111/1540-6210.00252

Fink, D. (2010). Road safety 2.0: Insights and implications for government. In *Proceedings of the 23rd Bled eConference*, Bled, Slovenia.

Garnett, F., & Ecclesfield, N. (2008). Developing an organisational architecture of participation. *British Journal of Educational Technology*, *39*(3), 468–474. doi:10.1111/j.1467-8535.2008.00839.x

Liu, J., Derzsi, Z., Raus, M., & Kipp, A. (2008). eGovernment project evaluation: An integrated framework. In M. A. Wimmer, H. J. Scholl, & E. Ferro (Eds.), *Proceedings of the 7th International Conference on Electronic Government* (LNCS 5184, pp. 85-97).

Marche, S., & McNiven, J. D. (2003). E-Government and e-governance: The future isn't what it used to be. *Canadian Journal of Administrative Sciences, 20*(1), 74–86. doi:10.1111/j.1936-4490.2003.tb00306.x

Mintz, D. (2008). Government 2.0 – Fact or fiction? *Public Management, 36*(4), 21–24.

Office of e-Government (ORS). (2004). *E-government strategy for the Western Australian public sector*. Retrieved from http://www.egov.dpc.wa.gov.au

Office of Road Safety (ORS). (2009). *Towards zero - Road safety strategy*. Retrieved from http://ors.wa.gov.au/

Office of Road Safety (ORS). (2010). *Welcome*. Retrieved from http://www.ors.wa.gov.au/Search.aspx?searchtext=welcome&searchmode=anyword

Rodwell, L. (2010). Roadside safety assessment. In *Proceedings of the Insurance Commission of Western Australia Road Safety Forum*, Perth, Australia.

Short, J. (2008). Risks in a Web 2.0 world. *Risk Management, 55*(10), 28–31.

Smith, J., Kearns, M., & Fine, A. (2005). *Power to the edges: Trends and opportunities in online civic engagement*. Retrieved from http://www.pacefunders.org/pdf/42705%20Version%201.0.pdf

Sommer, L., & Cullen, R. (2009). Participation 2.0: A case study of e-participation within the New Zealand government. In *Proceedings of the 42nd Hawaii International Conference on System Sciences*, Big Island, Hawaii (pp. 1-10).

Tan, C., Benbasat, I., & Cenfetelli, R. T. (2008). Building citizen trust towards e-government services: Do high quality websites matter. In *Proceedings of the 41st Hawaii International Conference on System Sciences* (p. 217).

Tapscott, D., & Williams, A. D. (2006). *Wikinomics*. London, UK: Penguin Books.

APPENDIX

Figure 3. Road Safety Council members' responsibilities (Office of Road Safety, 2010)

ROAD SAFETY COUNCIL MEMBERS
IMPLEMENTING TOWARDS ZERO

The following table lists each member of the Road Safety Council as at March 2009 and highlights road safety responsibilities.

Road Safety Council Agency	Areas of Authority
Department of Education and Training	Educates young road users through school and TAFE systems
Department of Health	Treats those injured in road crashes Collects and analyses road crash injury data
Insurance Commission of Western Australia	Manages motor vehicle injury claims Collects and analyses road crash injury data Provides supplementary funding to support agreed road safety initiatives
Main Roads Western Australia	Designs, builds, operates and maintains the state road network Sets speed limits Collects and analyses road crash injury data
Department for Planning and Infrastructure	Sets standards for the licensing of drivers, riders and vehicles Licenses drivers, riders and vehicles Supports and encourages the use of alternative forms of transport Encourages urban design and planning that enhances road safety
Department of the Premier and Cabinet (Office of Road Safety)	Provides leadership among key agencies in the co-ordination of road safety activities Undertakes community education, research, policy development and data analysis Monitors and reports on progress
Royal Automobile Club of WA Inc.	Represents all road users on the Road Safety Council Educates the community (particularly in relation to safe roads and safe vehicles) Advocates for road safety improvement
Western Australian Local Government Association	Represents local government on the Road Safety Council Provides leadership to, and advocacy for, local government (which designs, builds and maintains the local road network) Educates the community Advocates for road safety improvement
Western Australia Police	Enforces road user behaviour Collects and analyses information about road crashes

Figure 4. The road toll in WA over 30 years (Office of Road Safety, 2009)

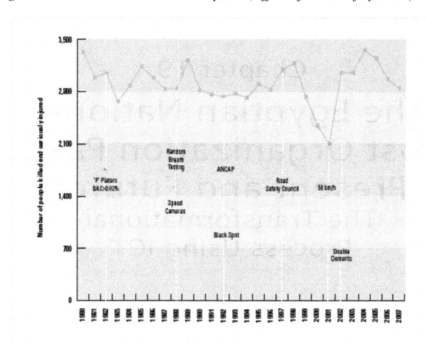

Figure 5. Australian road deaths per year per 100,000 population (Australian Government, 2010)

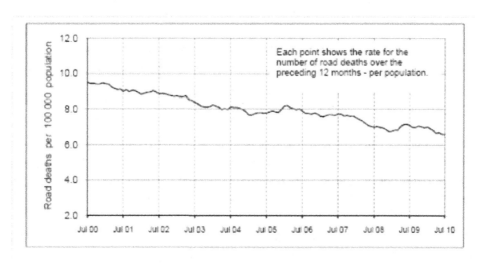

Chapter 19
The Egyptian National Post Organization Past, Present and Future:
The Transformational Process Using ICT

Sherif Kamel
The American University in Cairo, Egypt

EXECUTIVE SUMMARY

Over the last 20 years, the international postal sector has changed drastically due to several forces, including globalization, changing technology, greater demands for efficient services and market liberalization. For Egypt, keeping up with the changing atmosphere in the global market meant investing in information and communication technology. The Ministry of Communication and Information Technology (ICT), as part of its efforts to transforming government performance using ICT, chose the Egyptian National Post Organization (ENPO) as a model for ICT integrated government portal. The selection was due to ENPO's extensive network, the public's confidence and its trust in the organization. The case of ENPO, capitalizing on public-private partnership models, proved successful when reflecting ICT deployment for organizational transformation within the context of an emerging economy. In addition to its importance in providing e-Government services to citizens, ENPO is evolving as a critical medium for effectively developing Egypt's e-Commerce. This case study takes an in-depth look at how ICT has improved the quality and range of services offered by ENPO, while asserting the magnitude of its impact on the country's emergence as a competitor in today's global postal market.

DOI: 10.4018/978-1-4666-2071-1.ch019

INTRODUCTION

As Amr Badr Eldin, ENPO vice chairman for Information Technology (IT), and responsible for IT strategy, infrastructure deployment and utilization, approached his office at the headquarters of ENPO, which is ironically Egypt's oldest museum, located in Ataba square, one of the busiest squares in down town Cairo; the first object that immediately grabbed his attention was the 1865 automatic stamp vending machine. In a country like Egypt, where automatic vending machines were scarcely found and were still considered innovative, one immediately realized the great role that this place once had in the establishment of modern Egypt. The postal sector, on an international level, had changed drastically in the last 20 years. Several key forces had driven this evolution in the postal market including but not limited to changes in the volume of supply and demand of postal services, globalization effects, market liberalization, changing technology, dynamic communications shift, and regulatory progress, amongst other factors.

One other primary reason was the ever-growing competition from the private sector threatening the comfortable monopoly enjoyed by public operators for centuries. The level of services offered by the private sector had grown dramatically forcing public operators to change to meet the demand of the globally and growingly integrated mail market. Postal organizations across the world had started to transform their business and use Information and Communication Technology (ICT) in order to compete with the change in market trends. There were various successful models of services offered by various postal organizations. This included the United States Postal Service (USPS) offering email and eCommerce services; the South African Post Office offering hybrid mail services; and, Korea Post offering a synchronized information network (mobile, radio communication and RFID) whereby consumers have access to mail services and track the whereabouts of mail or packages anytime, anywhere. ENPO was determined to join that league in offering new services beyond the traditional mail services it used to over for decades.

Since 1999, Egypt had been implementing an aggressive ICT strategy as part of its national development plan; and ENPO was perceived as an integral part of such strategy. ENPO has been leveraging its capability to serve millions of consumers and trust to regain lost ground and compete, offering a plethora of services similar to those of other national postal organizations and pursuing further developments; thus turning it into a highly competitive organization. With images of newspaper titles racing in Badr Eldin's mind, celebrating ENPO's latest achievement in succeeding to become the only governmental institution to be part of Egypt's third mobile operator, he started to wonder where this organization once was, where it currently is and, most importantly, where it is going. The question immediately presented itself; was Egypt's National Post Organization rediscovering itself once again? The development of ENPO using ICT comes as an integral factor in the overall ICT development in Egypt. Table 1 demonstrates the evolution of ICT in Egypt.

BACKGROUND

ENPO volume and diversity of service had reached more than 18 million local customers and led to a long lasting trust between the national post and the local population from different segments and backgrounds. Such trust led to increasing the number of customers who took part in the financial services of ENPO to 2 million last year. A trust that has resulted in having *"Daftar Tawfeer"* (Arabic translation for a savings account) becoming the generic name for a saving account used by literally all segments of the society from all ages and from different social and economic segments and groups. ENPO was the main pillar for connecting Egypt with the outside world. This unmatched penetration within the Egyptian culture was made possible by the organization's large and extensive distribution network of more than 3,700 post offices located in every province and across the nation's 4,000 villages making ENPOs' distribution network the largest in Egypt coming in second to the network of national schools. One of the major characteristics of such a huge organization was the exceptionally large number of employees working in it; whereas, ENPO employed over 45,000 people of which 50% are located in remote offices in order to secure the quality and rate of the services provided to clients and enabling the same service on a nationwide scale.

Table 1. Development of the information society in Egypt

Programs	Year
Open Door Policy	1974
Economic Reform Program	1985
Information Project Cabinet of Ministers (IPCOM)	1985
Information and Decision Support Program (IDSC)	1986
National Information and Administrative Reform Initiative	1989
Egypt Information Highway	1994
Ministry of Communications and Information Technology (MCIT)	1999
National Information and Communications Technology Master Plan	2000
Egypt Information Society Initiative (EISI)	2003
Egypt ICT Strategy 2007-2010	2007

SETTING THE STAGE

Organizational History

ENPO was established on January 2, 1865. Located in the heart of Cairo, it is thought to be one of the oldest and most prestigious governmental organizations in Egypt. Since its inception, Egypt post was united with the ministry of occupation, under the British rule, which lasted from 1882 to 1954. Later on, its association was transferred to a number of ministries until 1965, when Egypt post was under the umbrella of the ministry of finance, which issued a regulation specifying that the transfer of letters and issuance of stamps is exclusive to the government of Egypt. In March 1876, all employees working for the post were required to wear a uniform. In 1899, services that were offered since the posts' inception were cancelled including salt and soda stamps, steamboat tickets and telegram and telephone services.

In 1919, the ministry of transportation was established and was given control of the post authority. Later on that year, law number 9 was issued to set all postage fees; and the post authority headquarters was moved from Alexandria to Cairo in Ataba Square. In 1934, the 10th conference of the International Post was held in Cairo, coinciding with the 70th anniversary of the established Egypt post. After the 1952 revolution, Egypt post was transformed into a cost center using revenue surplus to improve its services to the community. In 1957, Egypt post was replaced by the Egyptian Post Authority (EPA), and in 1966, EPA was replaced by the General Post Authority (GPA). In order to regulate Egypt, post law number 16 was passed in 1970. In 1982, the name was changed again to the National Post Authority (NPA) under law number 19. Finally, in 1999, the Ministry of Communications and Information Technology (MCIT) was established and became in charge of supervising the National Post Authority (NPA), Telecom Egypt (TE) and the National Telecommunication Institute (NTI). In 2008, Egypt Prime Minister, Ahmed Nazif, inaugurated the new headquarters of ENPO in the Smart Village. Table 2 demonstrates the development timeline of ENPO. This was perceived as a new phase in Egypt post evolution where its role was being repositioned as a tool to avail eGovernment and as a platform for services provision that can reach all segments of the community.

ENPO TRADITIONAL SERVICES

Since its redesigned services and repositioning under MCIT in 1999, ENPO has been focusing its services on three main areas: postal services, financial services and social services. In the Appendix, Figure 1 demonstrates details of the services offered.

Table 2. ENPO timeline

Time Line	Evolution Phase
1865	Egypt Post Established (associated with ministry of occupation under British rule)
1919	Egypt Post was associated with ministry of transportation
1952	Egypt Post was transformed into a cost center
1954-1964	Egypt Post was associated with a number of ministries
1957	Egypt Post was replaced by the Egyptian Post Authority (EPA)
1965	EPA associated with ministry of finance
1966	EPA was replaced by the General Post Authority (GPA)
1982	GPA name was changed to National Post Authority (NPA)
1999	NPA was transformed to ENPA and became associated with MCIT

Postal Services

The postal services are considered one of the oldest and cheapest methods of communication between individuals provided by ENPO and they include:

- Regular post, which has enjoyed price stability over the years that is not available by any other service offered.
- Fast/express mail, which is the fastest means of sending parcels and documents, within 24 hours in Egypt, and 48-75 hours outside Egypt to over 215 countries. The service is totally insured with door-to-door delivery and confirmation provided to ensure efficiency.
- Postal parcels, which is a service that allows the transfer of parcels, luggage, and gifts that weigh more than 2 kilograms with fees fixed by the authority according to the weight, distance, kind and value of contents.
- Public postal services, which includes private post boxes, postal cards and stamps

Financial Services

Despite some minor unreliability in its postal services, ENPO's financial services have always enjoyed a good reputation as a reliable financial institution, owing to the fact that it has never defaulted in payment of interest to the depositors. This has allowed it to earn the trust of all segments of the society for more than 100 years. ENPO started its financial services in 1905 by issuing saving booklets (Postal Saving PassBook), which is one of the oldest financial services offered in Egypt. In addition to the benefits of privacy, flexibility of depositing and monthly awards, the saving booklet's main advantage lies in the fact that the government guarantees its balances as well as the interests. Additionally, ENPO offers individuals, companies and organizations safe money transfer from one post office to another. With the number of depositors reaching 14.4 million and an enormous amount of deposits reaching 6.3 billion US dollars, it was becoming obvious that ENPO was a hidden treasure waiting to be discovered, or more accurately, waiting to be correctly invested. Other services include GiroNil, which has been introduced as result of cooperation between ENPO, Misr bank and Commercial International Bank, a private bank operating in Egypt. The GiroNil Company specializes in utility payments, allowing customers to pay their bills to large corporations and multinationals via ENPO offices. Customers also have the option of simply signing a document that allows ENPO to pay utility bills on their behalf, thus avoiding the risk of forgetting bills or queuing long hours to pay.

Social Services

ENPO's social service initiatives began in 1963 based on its conviction with its role in Egypt's socioeconomic development. For instance, the organization started paying pensions to around 3 million citizens with a total pension of 1.6 billion US dollars per year (www.egyptpost.org). The service has allowed pensioners to receive their pensions from 3,600 national post offices distributed all over the country, thus facilitating the process. This is part of the new services offered by ENPO to the government and a disbursing agent. It is important to note that this service has also removed the pensioner's burden of commuting from different areas in Egypt and queuing for long hours. Moreover, for customer convenience, some pensions are delivered directly to the customer's homes free-of-charge. More than 300 thousand pensioners (many over the age of 70, ill, and people with special needs) benefit from this service. ENPO also manages to deliver parcels to customer's homes through post offices nationwide. Another social service is the housing project where customers through the post office can benefit by buying application forms and making housing reservations provided by the state to young graduates. Finally, there is the fourth social service known as "lost property", which involves ENPO's cooperation with police forces to return lost property to the original owners.

ENPO on the National ICT Agenda

The main drive of the eGovernment initiative is to modernize the citizen's experience of public services and to improve the functionality of the government. (Tarek Kamel, Minister of Communications and Information Technology)

ICT Sector Reform

In 1999, MCIT announced the formulation of the first national ICT plan. The plan was focused on upgrading the existing infrastructure in terms of information and technology and availing an ecosystem that can help diffuse ICT in Egypt in terms of laws and regulations. The success of this plan was intended to create more business opportunities through ICT-empowered products and services that can benefit all stakeholders. The convergence between information, media and telecommunications was one of the most important developments. Based on a number of amendments in 2000, 2004, and 2007, a new ICT strategy was developed focusing on three main pillars: (a) ICT sector restructuring, (b) ICT for development; and, (c) Innovation and ICT industry development. The strategy was formulated by MCIT in collaboration with leading expertise in the ICT sector. The aim is to continue the development of the ICT infrastructure to maximize its benefits, leverage public-private partnerships, create more community involvement and link Egypt globally.

ICT Sector Restructuring

MCIT stated that the ICT sector restructuring would be realized through the development of state-of-the-art telecommunications infrastructure and export of services, reform of the postal sector, and enhancing the framework governing the use of ICT networks and services.

ICT for Development

The use of ICT for economic development could be achieved through ensuring easy, affordable access to ICT for all citizens, diffusing education and lifelong learning through the Egyptian Education Initiative (EEI), integrating ICT in health services, supporting the production, use and distribution of Arabic digital content (eContent) and providing the necessary ICT support for the government. It is important to note that ICT for development is a collective effort by different government entities in collaboration with the private sector in an attempt to create industry-related opportunities using ICT.

Innovation and ICT Industry Development

Innovation and creativity using ICT is integral in the development process and MCIT formulated a plan to realize this objective through developing export-oriented IT-enabled services, developing the ICT capacity of Egypt, formulating strategic plans for research and innovation and promoting local and foreign direct investments in the ICT sector.

CASE DESCRIPTION

The Beginning

Since the inception of the eGovernment program, the government of Egypt was determined to deliver high quality government services to the public where they are and in the format that suits them. The vision was guided by three main principles:

- **Citizen Centric Service Delivery:** The program slogan is "government now delivers" reflecting government intention to develop a one stop shop eSer-*vices* approach focused at citizen's needs.
- **Community Participation:** E-Government is a project with nationwide impact, thus community participation is necessary. Citizens' demands are constantly being analyzed and reflected, and private/public sector companies are active participants in project's implementation and management.
- **Efficient Allocation of Government Resources:** The emphasis was focusing on techniques to improve the level of efficiency, increase productivity, work on cost reduction, as well as the efficient allocation of resources.

When Egypt first launched its eGovernment initiative in 2001 in partnership with Microsoft Corporation to design and implement a web portal that would serve as a gateway to government services, the project was faced with much criticism for its low usage levels. According to the literature, the eGovernment initiative faced several challenges, illiteracy being the biggest challenge along with an Internet penetration rate of 20%, which endorsed the idea that eGovernment services are just for the rich educated segment of the society instead of being a nationwide targeting tool to improve the way governmental services are offered. There was a need for providing enabling technologies, products and services to underpin the development of Egypt as a knowledge economy in the global market. The initiative, which also aimed at crossing the boundaries between ministries by offering joint services, has been accused of being an unrealistic step towards improving governmental services, the reason being the low acceptance of the newly introduced eServices. Low acceptance is a problem, which, according to the minister of state for administrative development, Ahmed Darwish, lies in the word trust or more accurately, lack of it. According to Darwish, "the process of gaining people's trust will take time, but we are working on building that trust by providing tangible results". This is where the role of ENPO emerges.

Moreover, the emphasis of the role of ENPO was clearly highlighted in a speech by Tarek Kamel concerning Egypt's national ICT agenda, which included three objectives. First, developing and modernizing ENPO infrastructure; second, transforming ENPO as a delivery arm for financial and eGovernment services; and third, building on the trust with the citizens in maximizing the utilization of their postal savings. The positioning of ENPO was invaluable due to its constant interaction with different clusters of the community irrespective of the social or economic segment.

Reform of the Postal Sector

MCIT's investigation of ENPO showed that it was performing below potential. The services offered to both individuals and businesses were inefficient. The reform program was aimed at resolving these issues, achieving national development objectives and increasing national competitiveness. The following objectives were identified: (a) to develop a worldclass postal service in terms of quality, innovation and accessibility; (b) to increase overall levels of private sector investment in the postal market through open and fair competition and progressive regulation; and, (c) to create a new export-oriented postal industry in Egypt. It is important to note that all these objectives were formulated with a platform that reflects the notion that ICT is an enabler for service improvement, government efficiency and economic development.

Development of a State-of-the-Art Postal Network

A fundamental component of the MCIT strategy for developing the postal sector is modernizing Egypt Post by availing state-of-the-art ICT. MCIT is working tediously with ENPO to facilitate the development of services and systems that support eGovernment and eCommerce. Moreover, MCIT encourages ENPO to form partnerships with businesses and the private sector through outsourcing business models, bringing innovative products and services to customers by making use of the ICT industry. By restructuring ENPO through ICT, citizens have greater accessibility to information and government services. This is especially true for citizens who reside in rural areas and underprivileged communities in Egypt allowing them to easily register with the government, apply for licenses and obtain tax documents by simply visiting their nearest postal retail office. MCIT works with ENPO to develop new and innovative products that combine digital and physical communications systems, such as "*hybrid mail*". This will eventually result in the development of systems for sorting, tracing, addressing and customer care. An additional area of interest for MCIT is eCommerce, which can benefit by utilizing postal networks and ICT to manage global supply chains and enhance delivery. It is important to note that since the inception of MCIT and the leadership at the helm of ENPO selected was long-time ICT professionals and experts with extensive experience in diffusing ICT, which clearly indicates the intention of transforming ENPO to be ICT-enabled in terms of services offered.

Regulating the Postal Market

Creating an open and competitive postal market has been met with some success, but has also been accompanied with complications. Given the fact that ENPO is the entity that is granted the sole authority for issuing licenses to postal operators, it could easily utilize its power to monopolize the postal market. However, this has not been the case. On the contrary, ENPO has a high level of competition with 12 operators providing various forms of postal services. ENPO actually promotes private sector participation in the market by forming partnerships with a number of private sector individuals and businesses to expand services and products in the market. This has been very promising and indicated vast potentials in a fast growing and competitive marketplace.

It is important to note that increasing private sector investments has been a more difficult process for a number of regulatory reasons. This is problematic because, as the Egyptian economy grows and mail-heavy industries such as financial services and utilities expand, there will always be an increasing need for an efficient postal network to handle advertising, bill delivery and payment, and goods and cash transfers. In order to meet this anticipated increase in demand, the level of partnerships and private sector investment must increase and keep pace with the developments taking place. However, in order to increase private sector participation in the market, reform of the postal sector and effective policies was necessary. MCIT is brainstorming incentives to encourage private sector participation in projects that could stimulate further market progress. The biggest barrier hindering private sector investment in the postal market has been the lack of an effective regulatory oversight. A study carried out by the Universal Postal Union (UPU) concluded that the "postal market in Egypt is performing below capacity and that there is room for expansion and additional private sector investment". This has been the ENPO focus over the last few years while assessing what emerging ICT tools and techniques can bring in to the postal services.

However, lack of transparency concerning ENPO's dual role as a regulator and an operator in the market, as well as legitimate regulations of the sector, have affected the willingness of the private sector to invest. Respectively, a number of measures were taken by MCIT, postal operators and other stakeholders between 2007 and 2008 to develop effective postal regulatory policies, laws and regulations; in addition to establishing a neutral regulatory mechanism responsible for monitoring ongoing growth and innovation in the Egyptian postal market and benchmarking the sector's progress against international standards. It is hoped that, with proper regulation and market definition, private sector participation will significantly increase in the postal market.

Creating an Export-Oriented Industry

Faced with opportunities for global expansion, ENPO has been adapting itself to new international postal regulations. International regulatory advances, such as WTO's General Agreement for Trade in Services, are rapidly reducing or eliminating trade barriers, creating new opportunities for Egypt Post's penetration into the global market. Egypt Post envisions itself as a "*hub*" in the region, managing supply chains on a regional level. Egypt's geographic position, in conjunction with its growing ICT infrastructure, puts the country in a favorable position for regional expansion. When postal networks work with customs counterparts, import and export channels are strengthened, supporting the growth of Small and Medium Enterprises (SMEs) and other businesses.

MCIT continues to build on its successful experience with multinational telecom and IT companies to generate international appeal for its candidacy as a regional "*hub*". Working on a national level to create the first postal free zone in the Middle East, MCIT is mediating with governmental agencies responsible for transport and trade including aviation, transport, finance and investment, the Customs Authority, Egypt Post, private operators and other stakeholders. The establishment of the postal free zone will require that the current regulatory frameworks being developed will parallel those in prominent regional and international free zones. New infrastructure and supply systems are being created to connect the zone to global and regional markets, while appropriate regulatory processes and inspection mechanisms being developed to facilitate transactions and promote business. To promote Egypt's free trade zone as a regional hub and logistics center on an international level, MCIT is cooperating with the General Authority for Investment and Free Zones (GAFI), as well as other international postal and supply-chain operators. However, despite the developments in its ICT infrastructure, MCIT recognizes the postal sector's need to develop the regulatory laws necessary for liberalize services and complying with international trade regimes. Regulatory reforms will need to be introduced to prepare the postal sector for future changes in international postal regulatory systems, allowing it to succeed as a global market player.

Modernizing ENPO

Starting his position as ENPO Chairman, Alaa Fahmy knew that his job was going to be anything but easy. As Chairman, he is mainly responsible for providing strategic directions, explore business opportunities and promote ENPO in different market, business and industry circles. ENPO's history of being the oldest, most widely used and trusted governmental organization in Egypt simply represented the missing link between the government and the people. Fahmy knew that ENPO was desperately in need of a restructuring process, whether organizational or ICT-related. Moreover, he knew the burden of being the executing arm of Egypt's new eGovernment initiative that was being placed as part of ENPO's agenda. During Aly Moselhy tenure, the former ENPO chair, and current member of government, he realized that there was a potential for ENPO to do more for its customers and most importantly, for Egypt. He had a vision that with a comprehensive ICT infrastructure coupled with availing easy-to-use services by the community, ENPO could be the gateway for an eService-oriented society in Egypt.

During this time, the seeds of a new business model began to be planted. The former team started the first phase of creating an image that would turn this ever regarded, highly trusted governmental institution into an institution with a corporate image, objective and most importantly organizational infrastructure that enables service provision in a smooth and easy way. ENPO's new business model had to capitalize on the new, healthy investment atmosphere in Egypt and the ICT infrastructure made available by MCIT, and integrating the new offerings with the former products in order to create a better value proposition for ENPO customers. Based on this plan, and under the current chair, Fahmy, the image of ENPO started to manifest itself into a reality. In the early phase, some 920 post offices were modernized beginning with the main traffic offices located in Ramses, Alexandria, Tanta and Cairo international exchange centers at the Cairo airport.

The modernization process was done in three phases based to the location of the office. Many of the offices located in small alleys or villages, ironically, did not need to look too polished or else the regular customer would have started to have doubts and would have reconsidered dealing with ENPO, directly shattering the concept of trust, which is the edge that ENPO enjoys and intended to capitalize upon. However, in order to implement this business model and introduce a profit making culture to a governmental organization of more than 45,000 employees a lot had to be changed, and with an organization as old as ENPO, this was definitely a challenge.

ICT and Postal Services

A strong postal network reaches all residents, many of whom have no other means of communicating with the outside world. By providing this universal level of communication, posts can also provide the increased access to information that is essential to poverty reduction in the information age. But postal services do much more: they connect people and raise their level of social development and cohesion. (Nemat Shakif, Vice-President, Private Sector Development and Infrastructure, The World Bank Group)

Although the core of the postal business would remain paper-based for years to come, ICT had created a new realization to the world's postal services. By applying ICT-based infrastructure, postal services could improve the quality of their "traditional" services and introduce new, reliable, affordable products and rapid services to meet the growing needs of the community. New ICT offers enormous potential to post offices that are reinventing themselves to remain the primary means of communication and continue playing a significant role in the world's economy and information society. Merging ICT and the post was a big challenge waiting to be transformed into an opportunity that would effectively lead to a powerful entity, which provides accessibility, trustworthiness, security and privacy.

Accessibility

Combining around 700,000 worldwide postal outlets with ICT facilitate Internet access to people in remote areas. Posts are often seen as attractive partners in the provision of eGovernment services.

Trust and Security

The post office has always been trusted with people's mail. As people start to send messages through new communication networks they expect to deal with a trusted party who can securely and confidentially deliver information. Through ICT, post offices can provide innovative and secure services and products to continue honoring their role.

Privacy

Direct or advertising mail delivered physically to consumers could be converted electronically to customers who specifically request to receive such information.

ICT Back Then, ICT Now

The coming era will witness an expansion in the use of ICTs in developing Egypt's postal organization and providing the citizens with better services in a more efficient way.

Badr Eldin, ENPO Vice Chairman for IT, sat in his office reviewing his IT infrastructure development plan as he realized the long way they had come, and the longer way they were yet to go. The deadlines were strict and tangible benefits were awaited. Prior to the new developments, the concept of using IT as a tool to improve the quality and efficiency of the services offered by ENPO was simply non-existent. All services, such as opening accounts, invoices and payments were offered using paper. This was unfavorable to customers due to the time wasted. The lack of communication between offices made the process inefficient and costly in terms of paper and time wasted. Moreover, there were no networks, PC's or application software present in any of the offices.

During the period 2001-2005, the mission was to connect all offices through the postal network. However, this was easier said than done. Starting from scratch, the former ENPO team managed to connect 640 offices because of the threat ICT posed to the employees especially in poor and underprivileged communities where these offices were located, and the lack of the infrastructure needed to support it. Sometimes offices had to be connected through satellite, which involved high costs. The 640 offices being connected on a network marked the introduction of a new culture to the staff and to operations of ENPO in general.

In February 2006, Fahmy urgently continued to build on what was previously accomplished. Respectively, the total number of branches reached 3,688 at the end of the second quarter in 2009. With more advanced ICT came an even greater responsibly. Now the ICT team has to make sure that the four pillars of ICT in ENPO were present and functioning in a reliable way. The pillars could be demonstrates as follows:

- With respect to networks, reliability needs to reach 5-nine (99.999%) availability as a target. Currently, availability stands at 75% with backups for emergencies.
- With respect to application rings, there need to avail databases and applications working in parallel and reliably.
- With respect to PC penetration and PC support, the target is to reach 24 hours a day, 7 days a week reliability.
- With respect to servers and database center, the objective is that if any of the servers fail, backups should be ready for replacement. However, the cur-

rent problem is that some companies offer services using the NPO network, which sometimes causes confusion when a company's server fails and people think it is ENPO's server.

Establishing the ICT Platform

In his plan, Badr Eldin decided that his department's main mission was to provide quality IT products and services to help ENPO reach its goals. Consequently, the organizational structure and strategic goals of the IT department should pave the way towards achieving the objectives of ENPO as a whole *"by transforming itself into a quality focused, highly productive, responsive organization supporting a market driven system"*. Realizing the importance of having a complete and up-to-date ICT infrastructure, major changes to the IT department's organizational structure had to be taken. Figure 2, in the Appendix, demonstrates the former organization structure of the IT department. Depicted in the chart is a strategic business unit structure in which each department has IT as a complimentary tool integrated within the function itself. The functions, which are divided into finance, communication, human resources, security and IT sourcing all reported to the chief information officer (CIO) after passing through the steering committee. The vice chair for IT realized that several disadvantages were associated with such a structure, which would directly hinder the role of IT in the progress of ENPO. These disadvantages could be summarized as follows.

ICT Core Business

The structure is not placing IT as a core business behind the whole organization, which is the case in real life. Combining functions like communications, human resources and finance, which are not directly linked to ICT presents ICT as a tool rather than the main driver for the whole organization.

ICT Operational Methodology

Badr Eldin specifically objected to the idea of dividing the structure into small business units. In his own defense, he asserted that in a newly transforming giant organization like ENPO, a business unit structure (as demonstrated in Figure 2 in the Appendix) is not suitable. It is only suitable for large multinationals where business units are set up like separate companies, with full profit and loss responsibility invested in the top management of the unit and the units are at a level to compete with each other. Such condition was neither present, nor currently requested within ENPO's ICT organization structure. Other disadvantages included the minimal strategy coordination that occurs across business units and the performance recognition, which is often very blurred. Making his point, the vice chair for IT suggested that the new organization structure would consolidate the role of ICT as the core business of ENPO. The structure mainly focused on creating six functions that are directly related to ICT including information centers, technical support, operations, services, infrastructure, and design and planning. Figure 3, in the Appendix, demonstrates the new ICT structure. Each function has a vice president responsible for the subordinate sub-functions and eventually all departments report to the CIO, passing by the executive committee and reporting secondly to the financial services and human resources departments. The functions are further grouped into three phases, which represent the IT life cycle, beginning with design then implementation and lastly, technical support.

According to Robert Dailey, Organizational Behavior Professor at Drake University, there are numerous advantages to this structure. Firstly, the structure is based on specialization, which allows employees within each function to speak a common language. It also minimizes the extent of duplication and facilitates tight control. Badr Eldin was extremely convinced with the need to introduce a double reporting system in the ICT structure to ensure that the system will always function effectively. The department's manager will not only be reporting to financial services and human resources, but he/she will also be reporting to the main office, which ensures that each department is functioning as expected and that work is evaluated objectively. The new structure takes into consideration the maximum number of people that can report to the CIO which, in this case, are seven people reporting on behalf of their functions. Although the suggested changes were approved by senior management, there were a number of challenges that still faced the IT department including:

- ENPO is the largest organization (number of employees).
- Increased business dependency on ICT.
- Growth in business applications and storage requirements.
- National and international coordination.
- Increasingly remote workforce.
- Technology obsolescence cycles, which related to the employees' changing attitudes toward ICT requiring regular attempts to channel them from the inherited manual systems to the newly digital ones.

In an effort to instill this new concept in the minds of staff, and also to aid its transformation process, Fahmy had decided to take advantage of Egypt's new high-tech business district, the Smart Village, by relocating the Ataba office to relocate into a consolidated premises at the Smart Village. Often referred to as Egypt's Silicon Valley, the Smart Village hosts 54 buildings, providing 336 square meters of office space over 300 acres of land. The Village hosts 55,000 jobs, and is built using state-of-the art ICT infrastructure and high speed connectivity for integrated services, (whether data, audio or video) making it an ideal location for most of Egypt's ICT based companies both national and international. In conjunction with the move, ENPO planned to eliminate paper entirely within the organization in order to transform it into a digital workplace. Knowing the difficultly in implementing such a decision, the management decided to undertake dual operations during the phased implementation of the relocation. The management needed to develop an electronic file management system, including support and an operational system in order to process ENPO applications electronically allowing automated enterprise operations. In addition to this, a reliable IT infrastructure was needed to connect the main office in Ataba square with the Smart Village premises requiring the design, development, installation and testing of fiber connections, cable plants, data switches and telecommunications. The telecommunication services covered meeting room capabilities, electronic building directories, a facility help desk and a full-fledged security control system.

HUMAN CAPITAL: INVESTING IN WHAT MATTERS MOST

With over 45,000 employees working at ENPO, the human factor was an essential part in the transformation process, if not the most important one. With such a huge number of employees, having a well-constructed organization structure was a necessity in order to manage and administer effectively, while also adding value to their development process. Unfortunately, that was not the case until the new transformations were introduced. In the former organizational structure, all functions reported to a single vice president who in turn reported directly to the CEO. According to El-Labban, director of international relations, *"how can anything be done effectively when you have 45,000 employees reporting to one person? It can never work"*. Based on this, the organizational structure itself was transformed in order to achieve decentralization; with six vice presidents, each concerned with a certain function/area.

Moreover, the new management team has tried to introduce the idea of having a human resources department, which was not common in most governmental organizations and the customary approach was to deploy a personnel department that mainly handled employee files as a storage room. However, the new human resource department could manage the appraisals and elevate the HR function as a whole by managing employee performance and most importantly concerning itself with the training necessary in the coming transformational period. In an attempt to introduce a market oriented and customer-focused culture, the marketing campaign began functioning instantly, with new marketing material announcing ENPO's services, as well as its new image and entrance into the market. Marketing material included pens, mouse pads, newspaper announcements and advertisements highlighting the new services offered by ENPO in Egypt's most wide spread daily newspapers like Al-Ahram and Al-Akhbar.

Public and Private Partnerships

The post is based on the concept of connecting two parties together which is the same concept on which communication is based, so if any organization should be part of the new operator it should be ENPO, the oldest supplier of the service (Amr Badr El Din, Vice Chairman, IT)

Etisalat

Outside the ICT Minister's office at the Smart Village, Fahmy and Badr Eldin were anxiously waiting to know the results for the long bidding process. The Minister came out and congratulated them, "You took it" he said, "ENPO won the bid". They were thrilled. According to Badr Eldin, "The feeling was indescribable, everyone was congratulating us and that is the moment when I felt that my post was most fulfilling". The next day the news was all over Egypt that ENPO would become the first governmental organization to be part of a huge corporation like Etisalat, UAE's number one operator and currently Egypt's third. The consortium included Etisalat, Egypt Post, National Bank of Egypt and Commercial International Bank; they won the bid for over 3 billion US dollars and a 6% of the annual revenues to be paid to the National Telecommunications Regulatory Authority (NTRA). Figure 4, in the Appendix, demonstrates the public-private partnership model and the shareholders in this consortium. This step was one of Fahmy's major strategies to transform ENPO into a profit-making organization by diversifying their offerings and introducing some major public private partnerships that could capitalize on ENPO's competitive advantage, manifested in its distribution network and credibility within the society. According to Badr Eldin, "Public Private Partnerships are arrangements between the government and private sector entities for the purpose of improving public infrastructure and community facilities. Although these partnerships entail sharing investment, risk and responsibility, this long term partnership is very rewarding in many ways".

Referring to his partnership with Etisalat, Badr Eldin knew that ENPO's capabilities would be important for the company to penetrate successfully the local market. Some of the partnership benefits include: (a) using ENPO's network of offices that extends all over Egypt as a distributor of the company for selling their prepaid charging cards and accessories; and, (b) using ENPO office buildings to install the company's antenna instead of using resident buildings and paying hefty amounts of money in return. Another similar agreement was made with Vodafone, Egypt's second mobile operator, according to which ENPO would provide prepaid charging cards for Vodafone consumers in its offices.

Egypt Air

ENPO Chairman Fahmy and Egypt Air Chairman Galal signed a memorandum of understanding (MoU) to utilize the post office for booking airline tickets. According to the Minister of ICT, *"The MoU reflects the collaboration between different stakeholders and Egypt Post to facilitate the service delivered to the community"*. This MoU is part of ENPO's bigger strategy to turn their post offices into full-fledged service centers.

Jordan Post Company

After studying, the executive and legislative framework of Jordan Post Company in cooperation with EFG Hermes and Jordanian Riyada Ventures, Egypt decided to bid for a share in the Jordanian postal service. Egypt Post is competing with La Poste France, Aramex Jordan and British Consultative Post Services over acquiring a share in this company. This was another strategic move through alliances in order to develop the investment volume of Egypt Post and derive revenues with limited risks. These different steps indicated the intention of the government of Egypt to transform the role played by ENPO in providing a diversified portfolio of digital services while being one of the tools and platforms to diffuse eGovernment services.

International Agreements

ENPO extended their activities to regional levels. In February 2007, ENPO signed off 1.8 million US dollars *"Institutional Twining Program"* with the French National Post Organization, *"La Poste"*. It was aimed at developing the various departments at ENPO in order to match European and international standards applied. The program allows exchange of expertise, allowing ENPO to capitalize on La Poste expertise in marketing, service monitoring and quality assurance. Furthering boosting their bilateral economic and technical relations, they signed a cooperation agreement. The agreement that went into effect in 2008 would aid in developing postal and financial services and marketing tools for these services. This was another step in the integrated plan to utilize international expertise to upgrade the Egyptian post. Moreover, another agreement between ENPO and the Italian Post (Poste Italiane) was concluded in order to develop the sector in both countries. The minister indicated that the postal sector is a key economic and service driver to Egypt's modernization system. It is important to note that the agreement involved training human resources and raising the value of its assets.

Moreover, Fahmy signed an agreement with 7 Arab countries to exchange the financial remittances through the congress postal conference which was held in July 2008 in Geneva. The seven countries included Egypt, UAE, Syria, Yemen, Morocco, Tunisia, and Qatar. Just recently, Fahmy signed a pact to run electronic remittances between both Egyptian and Jordanian postal services, which started functioning in January 2009. This new agreement will enable Egyptian citizens working in Jordan, around 1 million, to transmit their money through the post offices at extremely competitive prices.

SERVICES OFFERED BY ENPO

A plethora of ICT-powered services was added to the "traditional" list of services after restructuring the ICT sector.

Government Services

With about 5 million Egyptians using the Internet, the adoption of eGovernment services is a far-fetched idea. However, as previously mentioned, being a delivery arm to the government concerning these services and having an integral role in servicing its community became one of Fahmy's priorities. Capitalizing on its intensive distribution network, ENPO currently offers 3 million citizens their pensions with a total sum that exceeds 1.6 billion US dollars through its 3600 offices, which are geographically dispersed across Egypt. Additionally, the service has also extended to reach citizens who are ill or having special circumstances and those aging 70 years and above, who ca not make it to any of the offices by offering them a delivery of their pension to their doorstep.

The "Tamween" card is another practical application of ICT that is utilized to help provide better services to the citizens. Previously, everything regarding food subsidies, which citizens were entitled to receive was documented on paper, which made the system more liable to fraud and human error. However, in this project and after installing the electronic platform, citizens are given smart cards; a person passes his card through the point of sale (POS) that is connected to the post network. This in turn, is connected to the network of the ministry of social solidarity, which holds the files of all citizens who are entitled to receive monthly nutrition subsidies. These records show the utilization of every item supplied based on the needs of citizens. This provides feedback that helps the ministry to decide, which items to increase depending on consumption. According to Badr Eldin, this was just a prototype that was tested in the Suez province, because of the limited geographical coverage making it more controlled and possible to monitor. Moreover, the limited population was a very important determining factor making Suez an ideal place to test the new electronic platform. If proven successful, the *"Tamween"* card will be implemented in all of Egypt's 28 provinces.

Financial Services

During 2007, as demonstrated in the Appendix, Figure 5 showing the postal financial services, there was witnessed the launch of a new postal savings account based on investment in the stock market. Minister Kamel stated that the new service aims to facilitate changeable high revenues through long-term investments. The new savings account requires a minimum of 18 US dollars with no ceiling while enabling citizens to invest in the Cairo-Alexandria Stock Exchange (CASE) and raises their investment awareness. The service has proven to be a success collecting 2 billion US dollars of small savings in less than a week. During the Cairo ICT 2009 Trade Fair and Forum several new financial services were launched which continue to meet the needs of the post's wide spectrum of customers. The services included a variety of offerings including current accounts in US dollars and Euros and earning daily variable revenues for companies and individuals; *Hadiyati* (Arabic translation for *"My Gift"*), a prepaid electronic gift card that can be charged with up to 181 US dollars. It also include *Mahfazti* (Arabic translation for *"My Wallet"*), a prepaid rechargeable card that can be used for purchasing goods and services and to withdraw cash from ATM machines.

To complement the above, Egypt Post will launch Universal Windows in 600 post offices in June 2009 in order to offer a diversified portfolio of financial services that meets the needs of the citizens including different types of money orders. More than 20,000 employees have been trained to aid in the dissemination of these financial services nationwide. In order to keep pace with the introduction of these financial services, ENPO signed a cooperation agreement with SAP who will provide business software applications to speed up the implementation of postal and financial services offered. In addition

Misr Mail

Now that our ENPO is entering the new era of ICT, certain applications cannot be ignored. E-mail is the new version of what we have always offered. Delivering mail is now done electronically, and we are doing it as well as anyone else. (Amr Badr El Din, Vice Chairman, IT)

ENPO introduced *"Misr Mail"*, which offers a list of services that include 2GB capacity mail, a portal with exclusive news from Egypt and high security that ensures privacy. Moreover, Misr Mail offers career and training opportunities for all those registered on it. Misr Mail is complemented by another service called *"hybrid mail"*. The service makes use of the new electronic signature to track and confirm the delivery, acceptance and delivery date of emails sent, which is an essential step along the way to governing and encouraging eCommerce activities in Egypt. Furthermore, they extended to reach other services like EPEM service, which is crucial for eCommerce. The service allows electronic checking of all electronic documents involved in any electronic transaction by verifying and validating the signatures on the documents, as well as the date and time of signature and automatically stores this information for future reference. This helps eliminate fraud in business transactions taking place over the Internet, and thus encourages the citizen use of these services by establishing trust. With these security measures, eCommerce has a greater chance of flourishing in Egypt. Finally, Egypt Post has recently introduced the International Post Service (IPS) system allowing the sender to *"track and trace"* their message from the time it leaves their home until it is delivered to the addressee.

Table 3. ENPO critical success factors

Critical Success Factors	Definition
Completing ENPO ICT infrastructure build-up	Design, develop and implement a nationwide infrastructure connecting all ENPO offices across Egypt's 28 provinces
Availing value-added services	Availing connectivity and develop value-added information networks between ENPO and the community of organizations and users
Linking Egypt globally-digitally	Link Egypt to the growing information and postal networks across continents capitalizing on the outreach of ICT
Investing in human capital	Invest in human capacities across different ENPO departments and units to be able to transform the organization and promote eServices
Building an online society	Build an online electronically ready community that can appreciate and use ENPO services

CURRENT CHALLENGES/PROBLEMS
FACING THE ORGANIZATION

Egypt has been gradually building its information society since the mid 1980s, adapting its strategy and approaches to the evolution of the global ICT sector. The steps taken included supplying accurate and timely information, encouraging private investment, formulating effective economic reforms, improving productivity, providing programs for lifelong learning, making public services more efficient, improving health care, optimizing the use of natural resources and protecting competition. Despite the major progress in IT deployment, policy and regulatory frameworks and implementation levels, many milestones must still be achieved to reach the critical mass of ICT users and critical level of ICT utilization that can enable organizational such as ENPO that are transforming themselves to become ICT-enabled to be successful. There needs to be an overall strategy that promotes electronic readiness and help create a critical mass of ICT-literate users that can appreciate and use the type of services that ENPO is offering. Table 3 demonstrates the critical success factors for ENPO.

REFERENCES

Badr, E. A. (2007, April 1). *ENPO Vice President for IT interview*.

Cairo ICT. (2009). Retrieved March 20, 2009, from, www.cairoict.com.

Egypt Post. (2009). Retrieved March 25, 2009, http://egyptianpost.net/en/index.asp.

El-Labban, D. N. (2007, April 1). *ENPO Director for International Relations interview*.

Gillingham, A. (n.d.). *Bulk mail takes notes and goes hi-tech*.

Roger, W. (1999). *Postal service getting wired*. Retrieved May 31, 2009, from www.interactive-week.com

Si-Young, H. (2007, June 11). Korea post utilizes cutting-edge IT. *The Korea Herald*.

Universal Postal Union. (2003). *The role of postal services*. Bern: WSIS Summit.

World Summit on Information Society. (2009). Retrieved February 10, 2009, from www.wsis-egypt.gov.eg

Zekri, N. (2006, April 16). Transformation of the post organization. *Al-Ahram Newspaper.*

ADDITIONAL READING

Editorial. (2006, April 16). Marketing and electronic signature as latest services offered. *Etisalat Al Mostaqbal.*

Editorial. (2006). *Egypt's third mobile license to benefit from the Egypt National Post Offices distribution network.* Retrieved July 7, 2009, from, www.dailystaregypt.com

Editorial. (2007). *Egyptian-european postal institutional twinning program under way.* Retrieved May 3, 2009, from, www.mcit.gov.eg

Information and Decision Support Center. (2008). http://www.idsc.gov.eg

Kamel, S. (1999). Information technology transfer to Egypt. In *Proceedings of the Portland International Conference on Management of Engineering and Technology (PICMET). Technology and Innovation Management: Setting the Pace for the Third Millennium,* Portland, Oregon, United States, 25-29 July (pp. 567-571).

Kamel, S. (2008). The use of ICT for social development in underprivileged communities in Egypt. In *Proceedings of the International Conference on Information Resources Management (Conf-IRM) on Information Resources Management in the Digital Economy*, Niagara Falls, Ontario, Canada, May 18-20.

Ministry of Communications and Information Technology. (2005). *Egypt information society initiative* (4th ed.).

Ministry of Communications and Information Technology. (2009). *Egypt post launches new financial services at Cairo ICT 2009.* Retrieved April 22, 2009, from, www.mcit.gov.eg.

Ministry of Communications and Information Technology. (2009). Retrieved May 5, 2009, from, www.mcit gov.eg

Ministry of State for Administrative Development. (2008). Retrieved September 3, 2009, from, http://www.ad.gov.eg.

APPENDIX

Figure 1. Detailed list of ENPO services offered

Postal Services		Financial Services		
Letters	Registered Mail	Electronic Payment		ATM Cards
	Ordinary Mail			Visa
	Net Courier			Mastercard
	Banking letters	GiroNil		
	Direct Mail	Postal Savings Passbook		
	Cassette Post	Daily interest account		Golden Account >10000
	Fax Post			Silver Account <10000
	E-document exchange	Postal Investment Book		
	Publications	Postal Remittances		Internal remittances
Express Mail (EMS)				Governmental Remittances
Parcel Services	Domestic			Electronic remittances
	International			Cashed external remittances
Public Postal Services	Postal Cards	Postal Proxy		
	Private Post Box			
	Clearance Tools			
Social Services				
Home Delivery	Delivery of Pensions			
	Delivery of Parcels			
	Delivery of Remittance			
Housing Projects	Youth Housing Project			
	Miscellaneous			
Lost Property				

Figure 2. Former ICT structure

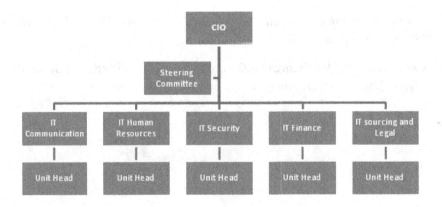

Figure 3. Current ICT structure

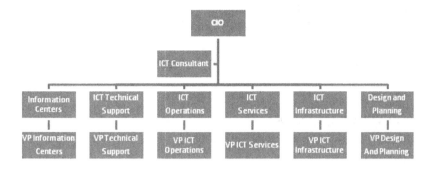

Figure 4. Public private partnerships

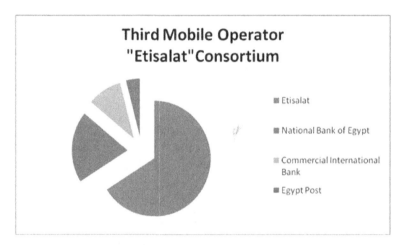

- Planning, designing, deploying, and managing ENPO IP network.
- Full responsibility of IP Network and voice services operation activities.
- Services will include network operations center, service desk, field operations, onsite support, customer care, third party support.

ACTION TIMELINE (2007)

Telecommunication:

- Fiber cable, WiMax and Co-location (Q2)
- 640 Branch SDSL and ISDN (Running)
- Upgrade 512K (Q2)

- 450 Branch ADSL, VSAT and VPDN (Q3)
- Co-Location 40 TE POP (Q3 and Q4)
- 1000 Branch VPDN (Q4-2006/2007 and Q1-2007/2008)

Data Centers-Op & Mo:

- Ramses (Q3 and Q4)
- Smart Village (Q3 and Q4)
- Alex (Q1-2007/2008 and Q2-2007/2008)
- Assiout (TBD)

Peripherals:

- 3500 PCs + 450 LANs (Running)
- 1500 PCs + Printers (Q3)
- 3000 PCs (Q4)

Figure 5. Postal financial services

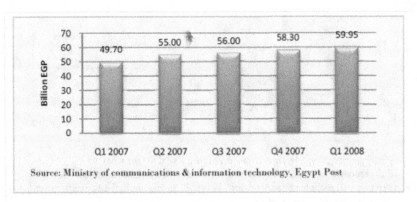

The total number of postal investment accounts invested in the Egyptian Stock exchange reached 33 thousand accounts since November 2007 with a total balance of 55.4 million US dollars until February 2008.

Chapter 20
Vision Impairment and Electronic Government

Reima Suomi
Turku School of Economics, Finland

Irene Krebs
Brandenburgische Technische Universität, Germany

EXECUTIVE SUMMARY

Visually impaired people are in a distinctive disadvantage when using computer screens based on visual presentation of data. Their situation becomes increasingly critical, as most society services, including issues such as e-Commerce, e-Business, e-Health, and e-Government go online. Yet modern technologies can also offer solutions to their problems, both at hardware and software level, and often with reasonable cost. Effective ICT can open up new communication channels and functionalities for say totally blind people, which would not have been available for them otherwise. General sensitivity for this issue, and especially sensitivity among designers of governmental e-services, must be developed. E-Government is an especially demanding activity area as it comes to all sorts of imparities (not just vision impairment), as governmental services are often in a monopoly service delivery situation: citizen have to use them, and there is often no other alternative. The issue binds it to the wider discussion on digital divide, where vision impairment is one cause for digital divide, and often very devastating, especially if still combined with other sources of digital divide.

DOI: 10.4018/978-1-4666-2071-1.ch020

ORGANIZATION BACKGROUND

Vision impairment is vision loss (of a person) to such a degree as to qualify as a handicap through a significant limitation of visual capability (Arditi & Rosenthal, 1998). It is a form of disability. Countries around the globe are acting to promote e-governance, so that people with disability are increasingly able to get access to information on the Internet. However, it is always a difficult commitment for many countries to reach the whole community (AHRC, 2009), and majority of the websites in the education, cultural and business sectors are still inaccessible to people with vision impairment. (HKBU, 2006).

Currently, there is less than 6% percent of printed material that is accessible for those citizens who are vision impaired or have other print disabilities. Moreover, people with vision impairment report frustration that they must continually request that government documents are presented online in multiple formats apart from PDF such as RTF, MS Word, and HTML (ACCAN, 2009; BSI, 2006). The system should be able to consider the needs of people with disabilities, such as providing alternative keyboard navigation, animated displays, color and contrast setting, and other means of making the system usable to people with vision impairment (Govt. of US, 2007). In addition to these blind, deafblind and vision-impaired people have particular needs. Skill development programmes must not be designed solely for people who can see and read standard print, and who can use software without altering its on-screen appearance or using adaptive technology. (NZ Foundation, 2009; EATT Project, 2003). Foremost, there sould be studies to identify factors accounting for why some states or countries are more responsive than other states or countries to the needs of people with disabilities in their use of e-government (Rubaii-Barrett & Wise, 2008).

In this context, digital divide could be termed as the inequality in assessing services of the information society (Drodic, Flournoy et al. 2000; Compaine 2001; Norris 2001; Siochrú, Girard et al. 2002; Akhter 2003), and one form of digital divide is caused by vision impairment, that can take several forms from total blindness to minor shortcomings say in colour recognition. The number of people with visual impairment worldwide in 2002 was in excess of 161 million, of whom about 37 million were blind (Resnikoff, Pascolini et al. 2004).

The case is discussing governmental support for vision impairment in two well-developed countries, Germany and Finland. It is well clear that the problems might be totally different in less-developed countries, in which vision impairment can too be even more a severe problem; especially the area of e-Government is looking at. By e-Government this research means the delivery of governmental services to citizen through electronic means, mainly the Internet. In this perspective, parts of the government activities are; providing the needed regulation and legislation for both public and private organizations to deliver good services for vision impaired through electronic means; and delivering robust and well-designed government services to citizen with vision impairment. If the government fails in providing these services, pressure to serve citizen with vision impairment materializes strongly in other service channels.

SETTING OF THE STAGE

Vision Impairment

Equality of citizen is a central value in modern societies. In reality, the equality is of course eroded by many factors. Most permeating factors causing inequality are of course permanent physical capabilities of individuals. Alongside conditions such as deafness, dumbness, inability to move normally because of missing limbs etc. or failures in the neural system, vision impairment, at its worst form totally blindness, is a key source of inequality. The term often used in this connection is vision impairment.

In worldwide statistics vision impairment officially touches upon 160 million people (Resnikoff et al., 2004), but in reality the figure is most likely much bigger. The amount of totally blind people is expected to be around 37 million (Resnikoff et al., 2004).

The most common causes of blindness around the world are (World Health Organisation, 2009):

- Cataracts (47.8%),
- Glaucoma (12.3%),
- Uveitis (10.2%),
- Age-related macular degeneration (AMD) (8.7%),
- Trachoma (3.6%),
- Corneal opacity (5.1%), and
- Diabetic retinopathy (4.8%).

In this chapter, authors discuss the activities public authorities need to take when assisting vision impaired people, especially in the field of eGovernment. In Table 1 they have provided some basic vision impairment statistics from those two case countries, Finland and Germany. These countries were selected to be the sample countries in this research of piloting character, as the authors are from these countries and have access to documentation at the local language. Of course it must be noted that the two countries are very much alike, and drawing conclusions based on this discussion to less developed countries is not possible.

One form of visual impairment is that of colour blindness. Colour blindness can for example harm the interpretation of maps and other visual information sources. There is nowadays a tool called vizcheck (http://www.vischeck.com), which can be used to study the colour schemes of web portals. The study by showed that there were no major shortcomings as it comes to colour use in the studied governmental www-pages (Choudrie, Ghinea, & Weerakkody, 2004). Other automated tools to evaluate the user friendliness of www-sites as it comes to visual impairment are Dottie and Usability Enforcer (Becker, 2004).

E-Government

E-Government is usually presented as using IT to (Grönlund, 2002):

- Provide easy access to government information and services for citizens and businesses
- Increase the quality of services, by such things as increased speed, completeness and process efficiency
- Give citizens opportunities to participate in the democratic process.

E-Government is a generic term meaning all electronic contacts between citizens and their government. It is divided into two main areas: first, e-Democracy, catering for democratic processes in government, and secondly, e-Administration, containing many applications such as health care (eHealth), taxation, public procurement and police operations.

Silcock (2001) defines eGovernment as follows: "...the use of technology to enhance the access to delivery of government services to benefit citizens, business partners and employees." Banerjee & Chau (Banerjee & Chau, 2004) provide the following illustration of the fast development of eGovernment: in 1996, less than

Table 1. Vision impairment in Germany and Finland, some statistics from 2007 (combined from (Ojamo, 2008) and (Bertram, 2005)

Aspect	Germany	Finland
Total population	82,3 Mio	5,3 Mio
Vision impaired people total*, percent of total population	1.000 000; 1,34	80 000; 1,5
Totally blind people*, percent of total population	160 000; 0,2	10 000; 0,19

50 official government homepages could be found on the World Wide Web. In 2001, it was estimated that globally there were well over 50 000 official government websites. Of the 190 UN Member States, 169 were providing some degree of information and services on-line.

In the US, the State eGovernment strategy delivers the following summary of proceedings in the field: "Federal information technology spending in the United States will exceed $48 billion in 2002 and $52 billion in 2003... a good portion of current federal IT spending is devoted to Internet Initiatives, yielding over 35 million web pages online at over 22,000 web sites."

Goverment and thus eGovernment activities take place at different levels: munipality, area, state/nation, federal and international. Yet the national level is often a natural level to study, as many important decisions, such as most of regulation and legislation. Different public-private partnerships are easily blurring the boundaries of eGoverment, as well as the tendency of public administration to work increasingly in a business way, approaching practices of eBusiness. The third sector adopting different responsibilies from the public authorities if further mixing the cards. A national government cannot always take the lead in eGovernment. As (Jarvenpaa, Tiller, & Simons, 2003) put it: "The role of government varies, and at times it reverses from its typical stance in public choice as a supplier of regulation to being a customer of regulation."

SUPPORT FOR VISUALLY IMPAIRED PEOPLE

In this section we study what the Finnish and German authorities have made to support vision impaired people.

Finland

In Finland a person is entitled to help equipments based on vision impairment, when the vision of his/her better eye is after best available glass correction less than 0,3, or the total vision scope of both eyes is less than 60 grades, or the total invalidated defined in her/his case is at least 50% because of blindness.

As other health care services too, health care services are organized by individual municipalities. The government sets the regulation and laws for handicapped people. There is little disease-specific legislation, but rather general government guidance. This leads to a situation in which the real services individual get can vary a lot between different municipalities.

By law services without co-payment from vision impaired people are definition of the need for help equipment, tuning of the needed equipment, use education, follow-up and needed maintenance. Devices are given to the vision impaired either for use of for ownership, depending on the case and policy of the municipality.

Eyeglasses are of course the basic device for most vision impaired. Being as standard and wide-scale service, it is covered with a complicated and detailed legislation. We do not dwell into the details of providing eyeglasses for vision impaired people in Finland.

Help equipment is provided at two levels: Municipal health centers provide standard devices, such as white sticks, audio devices and audio enhancements to mobile phones. Luckily, such programs most often nowadays are a standard part of mobile phone operating and user interface systems. Municipal health centers are not allowed to refund any acquisitions vision impaired people have made themselves.

Central hospitals cater for expensive and non-standard devices for vision impaired people. These items might be special devices for reading normal paper-based text or extra lenses that are attached to normal televisions. Many of these devices however have to do with normal personal computers, to which non-standard extensions for vision impaired people can be given. These are items such as:

- Scanner
- Speech synthesizer
- Braille displays
- Special software for helping reading the screen contents

An expensive item decided upon by the central hospital is the need for a guide dog. In Finland, 10 special journals distributed in point writing are provided.

Germany

Hardly for any other group the paradigm shift in Germany in institutions and authorities for social care is so important than for people with disabilities. Not any action of the authoritarian state as well as a patronized and super coordinated care by institutions shall determine the everyday life, but self-determination, participation and equality must be focused more and more. This can be a step toward greater transparency and openness in dealing with disabled people, especially with visually impaired and blind people. Dignity, equality and participating are key concepts of human living together in Germany.

About ten percent of the German population has a handicap which complicates the access to computer and Internet. These include blind, impaired, deaf / hard of hearing, physically and motor-driven disabled persons, mentally and psychically disabled persons as well as intellectually disabled and people with learning difficulties. But also elder people and people with a temporary handicap often find barriers on the Internet which complicate the use for them. Just for these target groups the Internet illustrates an ideal platform to take part in the modern information society. And, however, not only differs the availability of technical preconditions for each of these persons as a user (e. g. browser versions or input devices), but there are also individual needs that should be taken into consideration with the programming of a web page.

A big part of the barriers towards the access to the Internet can be overcome thanks to modern technology and program-technical capabilities. However, the implementation often fails according to the fact, that this is widely unknown. The German Act on Equality for People with Disabilities here refers in § 4 as following: "Free of barriers are (…) systems of the data processing, acoustic and visual sources of information and communication facilities as well as other living spaces if they are accessible and usable to handicapped people in the general usual way, without special difficulty and basically without foreign help and support" (ibid.) At present, many cities and municipalities work at the launching of "Guiding Principles and Participation Action Plans" as well as resulting legal recommendations in this sense.

The use of e-health and information and communication technologies (ITK) in the public health sector has been recognized and particularly great hope regarding process optimization and saving is set on the voluntary application of the electronic health card.

The use of the electronic health card (obligatory applications "Transfer of insurance data" as well as "Electronic prescription transport") is highly appreciated in the study on health economy and e-health in Germany. The highest benefit is seen in the storage of emergency data and medicine documentation (Wegweiser GmbH Berlin, 2007).

The German National Ministry of Research has announced a major funding program for ambient assisted living (AAL). There are 16 million people in Germany now who are older than 65. In the year 2050 there will be 23 million. This means that with increasing age people's eye sight will continuously deteriorate. For this reason, €125m will be invested in 17 AAL projects over the next year. The goal is to develop IT-solutions that help elderly and chronically ill people to stay in their own flat or house as long as possible.

In Germany develop a lot of towns and villages, policy guidelines and local strategies, and out of it resultant list of recommendations in this spirit.

In Germany, some special journals distributed in point writing are provided, e.g. Electronic Journal of e-Government, eGovernment computing, Sonderpädagogik, eHealth International.

CURRENT CHALLENGES FACING THE ORGANIZATION

Governmental service provision is increasingly turning into electronic channels, under the phenomenon of eGovernment. This means that services have to be well designed and state-of-the art in the way that they are self-explaining without or with minimal human intervention. This creates challenges as such, but especially for services meant for impaired – say vision impaired – people. Governmental agencies are in a big pressure, as they should be good examples even for other actors in cyberspace – such as private companies.

SOLUTIONS AND RECOMMENDATIONS

Technical means to provide eGovernment and other services through the web to vision impaired are already on the market, and the selection of tools is increasing all the time. Yet market scan necessitates resources, and some tools might need financial resources in an amount becoming critical even for big organizations. A mostly important issue is in government as well as in private sector sensitivity to the needs of impaired people. Services can be well designed for vision impaired people, but first the wake-up to this issue must take place, and then the organizations must strengthen their service orientation even towards the vision impaired citizen.

Overcoming the handicap and digital divide caused by vision impairment necessitates actions at many levels, so even in the case of eGovernment. Many technological solutions are already there, and they are so powerful that they can crucially help even totally blind people However, technology is yet not used to its full extend, and awareness and availability of different solutions can vary considerably between different population groups.

Designers of eGovernment services have to be especially sensitive to different impairment, including vision impairment, as their services affect everyone in the society, and are often obligatory for citizen to use. Making these services available through well-designed web-interfaces is at their own interest too, because ignoring the design on good web-services will manifest itself in pressure in other, often more expensive and inefficient, delivery channels.

REFERENCES

AAL Ambient Assisted Living Programme. (2009). Retrieved March 23, 2009, from http://www.aal-europe.eu/about-aal

ACCAN. (2009). *Submission to government 2.0 taskforce secretariat, Australian Communications Consumer Action Network*. Australia: ACCAN.

AHRC. (2009). *Web accessibility and government 2.0 Australian Human Rights Commission submission to the Government 2.0 Taskforce – Towards Government 2.0 an issues paper*. Retrieved from www.humanrights.gov.au

Akhter, S. H. (2003). Digital divide and purchase intention: Why demographic psychology matters. *Journal of Economic Psychology, 24*(3), 321–327. doi:10.1016/S0167-4870(02)00171-X

Arditi, A., & Rosenthal, B. (1998). Developing an objective definition of visual impairment. In *Vision '96: Proceedings of the International Low Vision Conference* (pp. 331-334). Madrid, Spain: ONCE

Banerjee, P., & Chau, P. Y. K. (2004). An evaluative framework for analysing e-government convergence capability in developing countries. *Electronic Government, 1*(1), 29–48. doi:10.1504/EG.2004.004135

Becker, S. A. (2004). E-Government visual accessibility for older adult users. *Social Science Computer Review, 22*(1), 11–23. doi:10.1177/0894439303259876

Bertram, B. (2005). *Blindheit und Sehbehinderung in Deutschland: Ursachen und Häufigkeiten. Der Augenarzt, 6*. Dezember.

Brodie, M., & Flournoy, R. E. (2000). Health information, the Internet, and the digital divide. *Health Affairs, 19*(6), 255–265. doi:10.1377/hlthaff.19.6.255

BSI. (2006). *Guide to good practice in commissioning accessible websites. British Standards Institution*. UK: BSI.

Choudrie, J., Ghinea, G., & Weerakkody, V. (2004). Evaluating Global e-government sites: A View using web diagnostic tools. *Electronic Journal of E-Government, 2*(2), 105–114.

Compaine, B. M. (Ed.). (2001). *The digital divide: Facing a crisis or creating a myth?* Cambridge, MA: MIT Press.

EATT Project. (2003). *Equal access to technology training: UK literature review*. UK: Royal National Institute of the Blind.

Foundation, N. Z. (2009). *Digital strategy 2.0 submission*. Auckland, New Zealand: Royal New Zealand Foundation of the Blind.

Govt. of US. (2007). *FY 2007 report to Congress on implementation of the E-Government Act of 2002*. Office of Management and Budget, Government of the USA.

Grönlund, Å. (2002). Electronic government - Efficiency, service quality, and democracy. In Grönlund, Å. (Ed.), *Electronic government: Design, applications and management* (p. 62). Hershey, PA: Idea Group Publishing. doi:10.4018/978-1-930708-19-8.ch002

HKBU. (2006). *HKBU's views & comment on the digital 21 strategy 2007.* Hong Kong: The Hong Kong Blind Union.

Jarvenpaa, S., Tiller, E. H., & Simons, R. (2003). Regulation and the internet: Public choice insights for business organizations. *California Management Review, 46*(1), 72–85.

Norris, P. (2001). *Digital divide: Civic engagement, information poverty, and the internet wordwide.* Cambridge, UK: Cambridge University Press. doi:10.1017/CBO9781139164887

Ojamo, M. (2008). *The Finnish register of visual impairment. Annual statistics 2007.* National Research and Development Centre for Welfare and Health in Finland and the Finnish Federation of the Visually Impaired.

Resnikoff, S., Pascolini, D., Etya'ale, D., Kocur, I., Pararajasegaram, R., & Pokharel, G. P. (2004). Global data on visual impairment in the year 2002. *Bulletin of the World Health Organization, 82*, 844–851.

Rubaii-Barrett, N., & Wise, L. R. (2008). Disability access and e-government: An empirical analysis of state practices. *Journal of Disability Policy Studies, 19*(1), 52–64. doi:10.1177/1044207307311533

Silcock, R. (2001). What is e-government. *Parliamentary Affairs, 54*, 88–91. doi:10.1093/pa/54.1.88

Siochrú, S. Ó., & Girard, B. (2002). *Global media governance. A beginner's guide.* Lanham, MD: Rowman & Littlefield Publishers.

Wegweiser GmbH Berlin. (2007). *Monitoring eHealth & Gesundheitswirtschaft 2007/2008.*

World Health Organisation. (2009). *Causes of blindness and visual impairment.* Retrieved April 14, 2009, from http://www.who.int/blindness/causes/en/

ADDITIONAL READING

Becker, S. (2005). E-government usability for older adults. *Communications of the ACM, 48*(2), 104. doi:10.1145/1042091.1042127

Buch, H., Vinding, T., la Cour, M., Appleyard, M., Jensen, G., & Vesti Nielsen, N. (2004). Prevalence and causes of visual impairment and blindness among 9980 Scandinavian adults The Copenhagen City Eye Study. *Ophthalmology, 111*(1), 53–61. doi:10.1016/j.ophtha.2003.05.010

Bundrick, M., Goette, T., Humphries, S., & Young, D. (2006). An examination of web site accessibility issues. *Communications of the IIMA, 6*(2), 9–18.

Choudrie, J., Ghinea, G., & Weerakkody, V. (2004). Evaluating global e-government sites: A view using web diagnostic tools. *Electronic Journal of E-Government, 2*(2), 105–114.

Congdon, N., Friedman, D., & Lietman, T. (2003). Important causes of visual impairment in the world today. *Journal of the American Medical Association, 290*(15), 2057. doi:10.1001/jama.290.15.2057

D'Allura, T. (2002). Enhancing the social interaction skills of preschoolers with visual impairments. [JVIB]. *Journal of Visual Impairment & Blindness, 96*(08).

Dandona, L., & Dandona, R. (2006). What is the global burden of visual impairment. *BMC Medicine, 4*(6), 1741–7015.

Jackson, W., Taylor, R., Palmatier, A., Elliott, T., & Elliott, J. (1998). Negotiating the reality of visual impairment: Hope, coping, and functional ability. *Journal of Clinical Psychology in Medical Settings, 5*(2), 173–185. doi:10.1023/A:1026259115029

Kocur, I., & Resnikoff, S. (2002). Visual impairment and blindness in Europe and their prevention. *The British Journal of Ophthalmology, 86*(7), 716. doi:10.1136/bjo.86.7.716

Rahmat, L., Yaakop, S., Mara, U., Tamil, E., & Idna, M. (2006). *The experiences of blind & visually impaired users with the Malaysian Government Ministries Website.* Paper presented at the Conference on Social Science and ICT.

Reinhardt, J. (1996). The importance of friendship and family support in adaptation to chronic vision impairment. *Journals of Gerontology Series B, 51*, 268–278. doi:10.1093/geronb/51B.5.P268

Rubaii-Barrett, N., & Wise, L. (2008). Disability access and e-government: An empirical analysis of state practices. *Journal of Disability Policy Studies, 19*(1), 52. doi:10.1177/1044207307311533

Šimonová, S. (2005). *E-government and approaches of e-inclusion.* Paper presented at the 5th WSEAS International Conference on Applied Informatics and Communications table of contents.

Šimonová, S. (2006). E-inclusion and disabled-people-friendly web. *Scientific Papers of the University of Pardubice Series D,* 164–168.

Tielsch, J., Sommer, A., Katz, J., Quigley, H., & Ezrine, S. (1991). Socioeconomic status and visual impairment among urban Americans. *Archives of Ophthalmology, 109*(5), 637. doi:10.1001/archopht.1991.01080050051027

Wang, J., Mitchell, P., Smith, W., Cumming, R., & Attebo, K. (1999). Impact of visual impairment on use of community support services by elderly persons: The Blue Mountains Eye Study. *Investigative Ophthalmology & Visual Science, 40*(1), 12.

Weih, L., Hassell, J., & Keeffe, J. (2002). Assessment of the impact of vision impairment. *Investigative Ophthalmology & Visual Science, 43*(4), 927.

West, S., Rubin, G., Broman, A., Munoz, B., Bandeen-Roche, K., & Turano, K. (2002). How does visual impairment affect performance on tasks of everyday life?: The SEE Project. *Archives of Ophthalmology, 120*(6), 774. doi:10.1001/archopht.120.6.774

Wood, J., & Troutbeck, R. (1994). Effect of visual impairment on driving. *Human Factors: The Journal of the Human Factors and Ergonomics Society, 36*(3), 476–487.

KEY TERMS AND DEFINITIONS

Act on Equality for People with Disabilities: In German Behindertengleichstellungsgesetz (BGG), is a German Federal law from year 2006. The purpose of this law is to abolish and prevent any discrimination against persons with disabilities, to ensure their equal participation in social activities and to enable them to lead a normal life.

Ambient Assisted Living (known as AAL): Includes methods, concepts, (electronic) systems, devices as well as services that are providing unobtrusive support for daily life based on context and the situation of the assisted person.

Braille Display: A computer input/output device supporting the Braille system. The Braille system is a leading method used by blind people to read and write.

Colour Blindness: Limited capability to differentiate between different colours, as to what can be expected from a similar individual or cohort.

E-Government: Refers to the usage of modern information and communication technologies to enhance the scope of communication and to make it more efficient between authorities and citizens, for mutual benefit.

Speech Synthesizer: A software component that turns written text in digital form into speech. Typical user options are for example male/female voice. Speech synthesizers should too be adapted to different languages.

Vision Impairment: Refers to a condition of an individual or group, where the individual's or groups seeing capability is less than what can be expected from a similar individual or cohort.

Compilation of References

AAL Ambient Assisted Living Programme. (2009). Retrieved March 23, 2009, from http://www.aal-europe.eu/about-aal

Abdullatif, I. A., & Philip, J. K. (2009). Rethinking models of technology adoption for internet banking: The role of website features. *Journal of Financial Services Marketing, 14*(1), 56–69. doi:10.1057/fsm.2009.4

Abissath, M. K. A. (2007). *E-government: The Singapore experience.* Retrieved November 26, 2007, from http://abissathfeatures-mawu.blogspot.com/2007/10/e-government-singapore-experience2.html

ACCAN. (2009). *Submission to government 2.0 taskforce secretariat, Australian Communications Consumer Action Network.* Australia: ACCAN.

Accascina, G. (1999). *Keynote presentation, APDIP Regional Information technology Conference.* March 24-27, 1999, Kuala Lumpur, Malaysia.

Ad hoc Committee on E-Democracy of the Council of Europe (CAHDE). (2006). *Introduction to the Ad Hoc Committee on E-democracy (CAHDE).* Retrieved from http://www.coe.int/t/e/integrated_projects/democracy/02_activities/002_e-democracy/00%20Intro%20CAHDE_en.asp

Adobe. (2007). *Adobe Shockwave Player.* Retrieved from http://www.adobe.com/products/shockwaveplayer

Ahmed, R., Haggblade, S., & Elahi Chowdhury, T. (Eds.). (2000). *Out of the shadow of famine: Evolving food markets and food policy in Bangladesh.* Baltimore, MD: John Hopkins University Press.

Ahonen, A. (2007). *From complex to simple: Designing a customer-friendly electronic insurance service environment* (Academic Dissertation No. 1257). Tampere, Finland: University Press.

Ahonen, A., & Salonen, J. (2005). *eInsurance: Kohti asiakaslähtöisempää sähköistä vakuutuspalvelua [eInsurance. Towards a more customer-oriented electronic insurance service].* Tampere, Finland: V I I Industrial Systems.

Ahonen, A., & Windischhofer, R. (2005). The Web performance of different types of online insurance providers - A wake up call to traditional insurance providers. In X. Zhao & B. Liu (Eds.), *Proceedings of the Fifth International Conference on Electronic Business (ICEB2005)* (pp. 245-252). Hong Kong: The Chinese University of Hong Kong.

Compilation of References

Ahonen, A., Salonen, J., Kivistö-Rahnasto, J., Järvinen, R., & Silius, K. (2007, April 26-28). *eInsurance - Novel services in the electronic environment.* Paper presented at the Innovation in Services Conference, Berkeley, CA.

AHRC. (2009). *Web accessibility and government 2.0 Australian Human Rights Commission submission to the Government 2.0 Taskforce – Towards Government 2.0 an issues paper.* Retrieved from www.humanrights.gov.au

Akerlof, G. A., & Shiller, R. J. (2009). *Animal spirits: How human psychology drives the economy, and why it matters for global capitalism.* Princeton, NJ: Princeton University Press.

Akhter, S. H. (2003). Digital divide and purchase intention: Why demographic psychology matters. *Journal of Economic Psychology, 24*(3), 321–327. doi:10.1016/S0167-4870(02)00171-X

Anderson, C. (2006). *The long tail: Why the future of business is selling less of more.* New York, NY: Hyperion.

Anderson, R. (2004). *Removing barriers, not creating them: Submission to the senate inquiry on the progress and future direction of life-long learning.* Canberra, Australia: Adult Learning Australia.

Annamalai, K., & Rao, S. (2003). *ITC's e-Choupal and profitable rural transformation: Web-based information and procurement tools for Indian farmers.* Technical report, World Resource Institute Case Study.

Annique Un, C. (2010). An empirical multi-level analysis for achieving balance between incremental and radical innovations. *Journal of Engineering and Technology Management, 27*(1-2), 1–19. doi:10.1016/j.jengtecman.2010.03.001

Antonopoulos, C., & Sakellaris, P. (2009). The contribution of information and communication technology investments to Greek economic growth: An analytical growth accounting framework. *Information Economics and Policy, 21,* 171–191. doi:10.1016/j.infoecopol.2008.12.001

Anttiroiko, A.-V. (2003). Building strong e-democracy: the role of technology in developing democracy for the information age. *Communications of the ACM, 46*(9).

Aprile, E. (2007). *La competenza penale del Giudice di Pace.* Milano, Italy: Giuffrè.

Archmann, S., & Kudlacek, I. (2008). Interoperability and the exchange of good practice cases. *European Journal of ePractice, 2.*

Arditi, A., & Rosenthal, B. (1998). Developing an objective definition of visual impairment. In *Vision '96: Proceedings of the International Low Vision Conference* (pp. 331-334). Madrid, Spain: ONCE

Ashley, C., & Maxwell, S. (2001). Rethinking rural development. *Development Policy Review, 19*(4), 395–425. doi:10.1111/1467-7679.00141

Astrid, D., Mitra, A., & David, M. (2008). The role of perceived enjoyment and social norm in the adoption of technology with network externalities. *European Journal of Information Systems, 17,* 4–11. doi:10.1057/palgrave.ejis.3000726

Australian Government, Department of Infrastructure, Transport, Regional Development and Local Government. (2010). *Road deaths Australia*. Retrieved from http://www.bitre.gov.au/publications/72/Files/RDA_July.pdf

Azleen, I., Mohd Zulkeflee, A. R., & Mohd Rushdan, Y. (2009). Taxpayers' attitude in using e-filing system: Is there any significant difference among demographic factors? *Journal of Internet Banking and Commerce, 14*(1), 2–13.

Bacon, F. (1605). *The advancement of learning*. Adamant Media Corporation.

Badr, E. A. (2007, April 1). *ENPO Vice President for IT interview*.

Baida, Z., Liu, J., & Tan, Y.-H. (2007). Towards a methodology for designing e-government control procedures. In *Electronic Government, 4646*, 56-67. Berlin, Germany: Springer.

Baida, Z., Rukanova, B., Wigand, R., & Tan, Y. H. (2007). Heineken shows benefits of customs collaboration. *Supply Chain Management Review, 11*(7), 11–12.

Balaji, P., & Keniston, K. (2005, July). Tentative conclusions. *Information and communications technologies for development: A comparative analysis of impacts and costs*. Department of Information Technology, Government of India. Retrieved from http://www.iiitb.ac.in/Complete_report.pdf.

Baldi, F. (2000). *Manuale del giudice di pace. Tutti i reati di competenza del giudice di pace, con ricchi richiami di dottrina e giurisprudenza; il nuovo processo ed il nuovo sistema sanzionatorio introdotti dal D.lgs. 28 agosto 2000, n. 274*. Milano, Italy: Giuffrè.

Baliamoune-Lutz, M. (2003). An analysis of the determinants and effects of ICT diffusion in developing countries. *Information Technology for Development, 10*, 151–169. doi:10.1002/itdj.1590100303

Balloni, A., & Viano, E. (Eds.). (1989). *IV Congresso Mondiale di vittimologia. Atti della giornata bolognese*. Bologna, Italy: Clueb.

Balloni, A. (1983). *Criminologia in prospettiva*. Bologna, Italy: Clueb.

Balloni, A. (Ed.). (1989). *Vittime, crimine, difesa sociale*. Bologna, Italy: Clueb.

Balloni, A. (Ed.). (2006). *Cittadinanza responsabile e tutela della vittima*. Bologna, Italy: Clueb.

Balloni, A., & Bisi, R. (2004). *The evolution of victimology: A view over Italy and Europe through research. International Perspectives in Victimology, 1(1)*. Tokiwa International Victimology Institute Journal.

Balloni, A., & Bisi, R. (Eds.). (2008). *Processi di vittimizzazione e reti di sostegno alle vittime. Rivista "Salute e Società," 7(1)*. Milano, Italy: Franco Angeli.

Balloni, A., Mosconi, G., & Prina, F. (Eds.). (2004). *Cultura giuridica e attori della giustizia penale*. Milano, Italy: Franco Angeli

Banerjee, P., & Chau, P. Y. K. (2004). An evaluative framework for analysing e-government convergence capability in developing countries. *Electronic Government, 1*(1), 29–48. doi:10.1504/EG.2004.004135

Barbagallo, A., De Nicola, A., & Missikoff, M. (2010). eGovernment ontologies: Social participation in building and evolution. In *Proceedings of the 43rd Hawaii International Conference on System Sciences*, Honolulu, Hawaii (pp. 1-10).

Compilation of References

Barnes, S. J., & Vidgen, R. (2007). Interactive e-government: Evaluating the web site of the UK inland revenue. *International Journal of Electronic Government Research, 3*(1), 19–37. doi:10.4018/jegr.2007010102

Barton, C., & Bear, M. (1999). *Information and communication technologies: Are they the key to viable business development services for micro and small enterprises?* Report for USAID as part of the Micro enterprises Best Practices Project. March 1999 by Development Alternatives Inc, MD, USA.

Bassanini, A. (2002). Growth, technology change, and ICT diffusion: Recent evidence from OECD countries. *Oxford Review of Economic Policy, 18*(3), 324–344. doi:10.1093/oxrep/18.3.324

Baumol, W. J., & Solow, R. (1998, Fall). Comments. *Issues in Science and Technology, 15*(1), 8–10.

Beck, R., Wigand, R. T., & König, W. (2003). Beyond the electronic commerce diffusion race: Efficiency prevails. *Proceedings of the 11th European Conference on Information Systems (ECIS) on ICT standardization,* 14 December 2003. Sheraton Seattle WA.

Becker, S. A. (2004). E-Government visual accessibility for older adult users. *Social Science Computer Review, 22*(1), 11–23. doi:10.1177/0894439303259876

Beldad, A., de Jong, M., & Steehouder, M. (2010). How shall I trust the faceless and the intangible? A literature review on the antecedents of online trust. *Computers in Human Behavior, 26*(5), 857–869. doi:10.1016/j.chb.2010.03.013

Benjamin, P. (2000). *Telecentres in South Africa.* Retrieved August 13, 2009, from http://ip.cais.cornell.edu/commdev/documents/jdc-benjamin.doc/

Benjamin, P. (1999). Community development and democratization through Information Technology: Building the new South Africa. In Heeks, R. (Ed.), *Reinventing government in the information age. International practice in ICT-enabled public sector reform* (pp. 194–210). London, UK: Rutledge.

Berman, A. (n.d.). *ICT in the dairy farming system.* Retrieved on June 6, 2009, from http://departments.agri.huji.ac.il/economics/gelb-farming-6.pdf

Bertram, B. (2005). *Blindheit und Sehbehinderung in Deutschland: Ursachen und Häufigkeiten. Der Augenarzt, 6.* Dezember.

Berzano, L., & Prina, F. (2004). *Sociologia della devianza.* Roma, Italy: Carocci.

Beukes, L. (2007). *Managing director, Capricorn Investment holdings: Botswana Financial service conference presentation slides.* Wednesday 8th May 2007. Retrieved 15 June, 2011, from http://www.google.co.bw/search?q=Beukes+L.+(2007).+Managing+Director.+Capricorn+HOLDINGS&hl=tn&ei=KB7iTITeDJHzsgaq24XwCw&start=20&sa=N

Beyene, B., Möller, P. F., & Wittmann, J. (2007). *Introducing ICT supported education for sustainable rural development in Ethiopia.* 2007 Summer Computer Simulation International Conference. San Diego, CA: International Society for Computer Simulation.

Bhaduri, A. (1983). *The economic structure of backward agriculture.* London, UK: Academic Press.

Bharadwaj, K. (1985). Agricultural market reforms in South Asia. *A View on Commercialization in Indian Agriculture and the Development of Capitalism, 13*, 82-89.

Bharadwaj, K. (1974). *Production conditions in Indian agriculture*. Cambridge, UK: Cambridge University Press.

Bhatnagar, S. (2000). Social implications of information and communication technology in developing countries: Lessons from Asian success stories. *The Electronic Journal on Information Systems in Developing Countries* [Electronic version]. Retrieved from http://www.unimas.my/fit/roger/EJISDC/EJISDC.htm

Bhatnagar, S. (2006). *Paving the road towards pro poor e-governance*. UNDP, APDIP, UN-CRD Workshop Report, 26-27, Bangkok.

Bianchini, E. (2008). Processi di vittimizzazione e competenze penali del giudice di pace. In Balloni, A., & Bisi, R. (Eds.), *Processi di vittimizzazione e reti di sostegno alle vittime* (pp. 27–29). Milano, Italy: Franco Angeli.

Bisi, R. (1996). Vittime, vittimologia e società. In Bisi, R., & Faccioli, P. (Eds.), *Con gli occhi della vittima*. Milano, Italy: Franco Angeli.

Bisi, R. (Ed.). (2004). *Vittimologia Dinamiche relazionali tra vittimizzazione e mediazione*. Milano, Italy: Franco Angeli.

Bisi, R. (Ed.). (2006). *Scena del crimine e profili investigativi. Quale tutela per le vittime?* Milano, Italy: Franco Angeli.

Bisi, R., & Faccioli, P. (Eds.). (1996). *Con gli occhi della vittima: Approccio interdisciplinare alla vittimologia*. Milano, Italy: Franco Angeli.

Bisi, R., & Sette, R. (2002). Victimes de tragédies en Italie. Ombres et lumières d'une réalité oubliée. *Revue Francophone du Stress et du Trauma, 2*(1).

Bjørn-Andersen, N., Razmerita, L. V., & Henriksen, H. Z. (2007). The streamlining of cross-border taxation using IT: The Danish eExport solution. In Makolm, J., & Orthofer, G. (Eds.), *E-taxation: State & perspectives: E-government in the field of taxation: Scientific basis, implementation strategies, good practice examples* (pp. 195–206). Linz, Austria: Trauner Verlag.

Blair's Commission for Africa. (2005). *Our common interest*. London: Blair's Commission for Africa Report.

Bloch, M., Robert, B., & Beoku-Betts, J. (1998). *Women and education in Sub-Saharan Africa: Power, opportunities, and constraints*. New York, NY: L. Reinner Publishers.

Blomstrom, M., & Kokko, A. (1998). In G. B. Navaretti Foreign investment as a vehicle for international technology transfer. In G. Barba Navaretti, P. Dasgupta, K-G. Maler, & D. Siniscalco (Eds.), *Creation and transfer of knowledge: Institutions and incentives*. New York, NY: Springer Verlag.

Bolton, R., & Saxena-Iyrea, S. (2009). Interactive services: A framework, synthesis and research directions. *Journal of Interactive Marketing, 23*(1), 91–104. doi:10.1016/j.intmar.2008.11.002

Borgatti, S. P., Everett, M. G., & Freeman, L. C. (2002). *UCINET for Windows: Software for social network analysis*. Analytic Technologies, Harvard.

Compilation of References

Bouguettaya, A., Ouzzani, M., Medjahead, B., & Cameron, J. (2001). Helping citizens of Indiana: Ontological approach to managing state and local government databases. *IEEE Computer,* February.

Bovet, D., & Martha, J. (2000). Value nets: Reinventing the rusty supply chain for competitive advantage. *Strategy and Leadership, 28*(4), 21–26. doi:10.1108/10878570010378654

boyd, d., & Ellison, N. B. (2007). *Social network sites: Definition, history, and scholarship.*

Boyd, S. L., Hobbs, J. E., & Kerr, W. A. (2003). The impact of customs procedures on business to consumer e-commerce in food products. *Supply Chain Management: An International Journal, 8*(3), 195–200. doi:10.1108/13598540310484591

Bridges. (2004). *The real access/real impact framework for improving the way that ICT is used in development,* November 2004.

Bridges.org. (2001). *Comparison of e-readiness assessment models: Final draft.* Retrieved July 16, 2003, from http://www.bridges.org/eredainess/tools.html

Brodie, M., & Flournoy, R. E. (2000). Health information, the Internet, and the digital divide. *Health Affairs, 19*(6), 255–265. doi:10.1377/hlthaff.19.6.255

BSI. (2006). *Guide to good practice in commissioning accessible websites. British Standards Institution.* UK: BSI.

Budhiraja, R., & Sameer, S. (2009). *E-readiness assessment (India).* Retrieved March 2, 2009, from http://www.unpan1.un.org/intradoc/groups/public/documentsAPCITY/UNPAN014673.pdf

Bunnell, T. (2002, March). Multimedia utopia? A geographical critique of high-tech development in Malaysia's multimedia super corridor. *Antipode, 34*(2), 265. doi:10.1111/1467-8330.00238

Burger, R. (2005). What we have learnt from post-1994 innovations in pro-poor service delivery in South Africa: A case study-based analysis. *Development Southern Africa, 22*(4), 483–500. doi:10.1080/03768350500322966

Burn, J., & Robins, G. (2003). Moving towards e-government: A case study of organisational change process. *Logistics Information Management, 16*(1), 25–35. doi:10.1108/09576050310453714

Burrough, P. A. (1986). *Principles of geographical information systems for land resource assessment.* Oxford, UK: Clarendon Press. doi:10.1080/10106048609354060

Burt, R. (1984). Network items and the general social survey. *Social Networks, 6*(4), 293–339. doi:10.1016/0378-8733(84)90007-8

Bygrave, W. D. (1989). The entrepreneurship paradigm (I): A philosophical look at its research methodologies. *Entrepreneurship Theory and Practice, 14*(1), 7–26.

Caine, K., Hargrove, W., & Sun, M. (2007). Information and communication needs of Rwandan coffee stakeholders. In Best, M. (Ed.), *Last mile initiative innovations: Research findings from Georgia Institute of Technology.* Washington, DC: AED.

Cairo ICT. (2009). Retrieved March 20, 2009, from, www.cairoict.com.

Cardoso, J., & Sheth, A. P. (Eds.). (2006). *Semantic Web services: Processes and applications.* Springer. doi:10.1007/978-0-387-34685-4

Casale, M., & Whiteside, A. (March 2006). *IDRC working papers on globalization, growth and poverty. The impact of HIV/AIDS on poverty: Inequality and economic growth.* Health Economics and HIV/AIDS Research Division (HEARD) University of KwaZulu Natal, South Africa. Retrieved 15 June, 2011, from http://www.idrc.ca/uploads/user-S/122157487911438239471GGPWP3-AIDS.pdf

Central Intelligence Agency. (n.d.) *CIA - The World Factbook country comparison: Distribution of family income Gini index.* Retrieved from https://www.cia.gov/library/publications/the-world-factbook/rankorder/2172rank.html

Cernetti, S., & Spriano, M. (2006). *La sentenza penale del giudice di pace.* Torino, Italy: G. Giappichelli.

Chademana- Munodawafa. K. E. (2009). *An analysis of livelihood strategies of HIV/AIDS affected households receiving support from Catholic Relief Services (CRS) in Chegutu, Zimbabwe.* Unpublished dissertation, University of Kwazulu-Natal.

Chadwick, B. P. (2005). Information technology revolution in the Republic of Korea: Socio-economic development issues and policymaking challenges. In Mansourov, A. Y. (Ed.), *Bytes and bullets: Information technology revolution and national security on the Korean peninsula* (pp. 52–69). Honolulu, Hawaii: Asia-Pacific Center for Security Studies.

Chapman, R., & Slaymaker, T. (2002). *ICTs and rural development: Review of the literature, current interventions and opportunities for action.* Overseas Development Institute, Working Paper No. 192.

Chiavario, M., & Marzaduri, E. (Eds.). (2002). *Giudice di pace e processo penale. Commento al D. lgs. 28 agosto 2000 n. 274 e alle successive modifiche.* Torino, Italy: UTET.

Choudrie, J., Ghinea, G., & Weerakkody, V. (2004). Evaluating Global e-government sites: A View using web diagnostic tools. *Electronic. Journal of E-Government, 2*(2), 105–114.

Chowdhury, N., Farid, N., & Roy, D. (2006). *Food policy liberalization in Bangladesh: How the governments and the markets delivered.* MTID Discussion Paper No. 92. Washington, DC: International Food Policy Research Institute

Chowdhury, N. (1992). *Rice markets in Bangladesh: A study in structure, conduct and performance. Bangladesh Food Policy Project Manuscript 22.* Washington, DC: International Food Policy Research Institute.

Chowdhury, N. (1994). *Credit and Bangladesh's food grain market: New evidence on commercialization, credit relations, and effect of credit access. Bangladesh Food Policy Project Manuscript 64.* Dhaka: International Food Policy Research Institute.

Chowdhury, N., & Haggblade, S. (2000). Evolving rice and wheat markets. In Ahmed, R., Haggblade, S., & Elahi Chowdhury, T. E. (Eds.), *Out of the shadow of famine: Evolving food markets and food policy in Bangladesh.* Baltimore, MD: John Hopkins University Press.

Chrissafis, T. (2005). *eDemocracy: Challenges and actions in the EU.* TED Conference on e-Government Electronic Democracy: The Challenge Ahead, Bolzano, Italy.

Compilation of References

Christensen, C. (1997). *The innovator's dilemma: When new technologies cause great firms to fail*. Harvard Business School Press.

CIAT. (2007). What is Tradenet? *The Highlights Series, 38*. Retrieved from www.ciat.cgiar.org

Cipolla, C. (Ed.). (2003). *Il ciclo metodologico della ricerca sociale*. Milano, Italy: Franco Angeli.

Cloate, F. (2007). *Knowledge management and trust in government: Lessons from South Africa*. Global Forum on Reinventing Government: Building Trust in Government, 26 – 29 June 2007 Vienna, Austria.

COA. (2001). *COA's standards and self-study manual,* 7th edition, for Public Organizations. Council on Accreditation of Services for Children and Families.

Cohen-Blankshtain, G., & Nijkamp, P. (2003, August). Still not there, but on our way: Thinking of urban ICT policies in European cities. *Tijdschrift voor Economische en Sociale Geografie, 94*(3), 390–400. doi:10.1111/1467-9663.00265

Commonwealth Telecommunications Organisation. (2004). *Regional roundup: Libraries help bridge the digital divide*. IFLA Submission to WSIS Process. Retrieved July 22, 2009, from http://www.ictdevagenda.org/frame.php?dir=07&sd=10&sid=1&id=441

Compaine, B. M. (Ed.). (2001). *The digital divide: Facing a crisis or creating a myth?* Cambridge, MA: MIT Press.

Cong, Y., & Du, H. (2007). Welcome to the world of Web 2.0. *The CPA Journal, 77*(5), 6–10.

Coplin, W. D., Merget, A. E., & Bourdeaux, C. (2002). The professional researcher as change agent in the government-performance movement. *Public Administration Review, 62*(6), 699–711. doi:10.1111/1540-6210.00252

Corbetta, P. (1999). *Metodologia e tecniche della ricerca sociale*. Bologna, Italy: il Mulino.

Creswell, J. W. (1998). *Qualitative inquiry and research design: Choosing among five traditions*. Thousand Oaks, CA: Sage Publications.

Creswell, J. W., & Plano Clark, V. L. (2011). *Designing and conducting mixed methods research* (2nd ed.). Thousand Oaks, CA: Sage Publications.

Crow, B. (2001). *Markets, class and rural change in Bangladesh*. London, UK: Palgrave.

David, P. A. (1997). Rethinking technology transfers: Incentives, institutions and knowledge-based industrial development. In Feinstein, C., & Howe, C. (Eds.), *Chinese technology transfer in the 1990s: Current experience, historical problems and international perspectives*. Cheltenham, UK: Elgar.

Davidrajuh, R. (2004). Planning e-government start-up: A case study on e-Sri Lanka. *Electronic Government, 1*(1), 92–106. doi:10.1504/EG.2004.004139

Davidson, R. M., Wagner, C., & Ma, L. C. K. (2005). From government to e-government: A transitional model. *Information Technology & People, 18*(3), 280–299. doi:10.1108/09593840510615888

David, Y. K. T. (2008). A study of e-recruitment technology adoption in Malaysia. *Industrial Management & Data Systems, 109*(2), 281–300.

Dede, C. (2000). Emerging influences of information technology on school

Dedrick, J., & West, J. (2003). Why firms adopt open source platforms: A grounded theory of innovation and standards adoption. In J. L. King & K. Lyytinen (Eds.), *Proceedings of the Workshop on Standard Making: A Critical Research Frontier for Information Systems,* (pp. 236-257). Seattle, WA, USA.

Department of Communications. (2008). *South African yearbook.* Retrieved July 30, 2009, from http://www.gcis.gov.za/docs/publications/yearbook/2008/chapter5.pdf

Department of IT e-technology Group (India). (2003). *Assessment of central ministries and departments: E-governance readiness assessment 2003.* Draft Report 48.

Department of Public Service and Administration. (1996). *Green paper transforming public service delivery.* Pretoria, South Africa: GCIS.

DFID. (2001). *Sustainable livelihoods guidance sheets.* Department for Informational Development, 2001.

Digital Dividend. (2003). Retrieved June 08, 2003 from www.digitaldividend.org.

Docktor, R. (2004). *Successful global ICT initiatives: Measuring results through an analysis of achieved goals, planning and readiness efforts, and stakeholder involvement.* Presentation to the Council for Excellence in Government.

Dosi, G. (1982). Technological paradigms and technological trajectories. *Research Policy, 11*(3), 147–162. doi:10.1016/0048-7333(82)90016-6

DRAP. (2003-2004). *Digital review of Asia Pacific2003/2004.* Orbicom, IDRC, UNDP-APDIP.

DRAP. (2005-2006). *Digital review of Asia Pacific2005/2006.* Orbicom, IDRC, UNDP-APDIP.

DRAP. (2007-2008). *Digital review of Asia Pacific 2007-2008.* Orbicom and the International Development Research Centre. SAGE Publications India Pvt., Ltd.

DRAP. (2009-2010). *Digital review of Asia Pacific 2009-2010.* Orbicom and the International Development Research Centre. SAGE Publications India Pvt Ltd.

Dutta, S., Lopez-Claros, A., & Mia, I. (2008). *The global information technology report. INSEAD.* New York, NY: Oxford University Press.

Easterly, W. (2001). *The elusive quest for economic growth: Economists' adventures and misadventures in the tropics.* Cambridge: MIT Press.

EATT Project. (2003). *Equal access to technology training: UK literature review.* UK: Royal National Institute of the Blind.

Economic Commission for Africa. (2006). *Per capita electricity use in Africa is less than 2 percent, says new report by ECA's NEPAD Unit.* Retrieved April 2, 2007, from http://www.uneca.org/nepad/Story070326.htm

Economic Planning Unit (EPU). (2008). *The midterm review of the ninth Malaysian plan: 2006-2010.*

Economist Intelligence Unit. (2006). Digital divide narrows. *The Economist.* Retrieved May 28, 2007, from http://www.ibm.com/news/be/en/2006/04/2601.html

Edvardsson, B., & Ollson, J. (1996). Key concepts for service development. *Service Industries Journal, 16*(2), 140–164. doi:10.1080/02642069600000019

Compilation of References

Egypt Post. (2009). Retrieved March 25, 2009, http://egyptianpost.net/en/index.asp.

Eisenstein, E. (1983). *The printing revolution in early modern Europe.* Cambridge, UK: Cambridge University Press.

EIU. (2009). *E-readiness ranking 2009: The usage imperative.* A report from the Economist Intelligent Unit, The Economist Intelligence Unit Limited, UK.

Ekong, E. E. (2003). *Introduction to rural sociology* (2nd ed.). Uyo, Nigeria: Dove Educational Publishers.

El-Labban, D. N. (2007, April 1). *ENPO Director for International Relations interview.*

Engström, Y. (1995). Innovative organisational learning in medical and legal settings. In Martin, L., Nelson, K., & Tobach, E. (Eds.), *Theory and practice of doing and knowing.* Cambridge, UK: Cambridge University Press. doi:10.1017/CBO9780511896828.016

Escudero-Pascual, A. (2008). *Tools and technologies for equitable access.* Association for Progressive Communication (APC) issue paper. Retrieved from www.apc.org

EU. (2007). *Inclusive e-government: Survey of status and baseline activities.* European Commission, DG Information Society and Media, e-Government unit, December.

European Commission. (2005). *EU report on millennium development goals 2000-2004.* Brussels, Belgium: Directorate-General Development.

European Commission. (2005). *Transforming public services.* Report of the Ministerial eGovernment Conference, Manchester, UK. Retrieved December 12, 2008, from http://www.egov2005conference.gov.uk/documents/pdfs/eGovConference05_Summary.pdf

FAO. (1997). *FAO and socio-economic impact of HIV/AIDS on agriculture. World Food Summit Report.* Rome, Italy: Food and Agriculture Organisation.

FAO. (2008). *Expert meeting on climate-related transboundary pests and diseases*

FAO. (2009). *Mobile phones in sustainable fisheries livelihoods programme.* Retrieved from http://www.e-agriculture.org/ict_project.html?&L=tisihaiufsjqrvj&tx_ictproject_pi1[showUid]=10&cHash=d8b6dd2a31

FAO. (2009). *Pilot fishnet initiative.* Retrieved from http://www.e-agriculture.org/ict_project.html?&L=tisihaiufsjqrvj&tx_ictproject_pi1[showUid]=35&cHash=df4f74bfa2

Farelo, M., & Morris, C. (2006). *The working group on e-government in the developing world: Roadmap for e-government in the developing world, 10 questions e-government leaders should ask themselves.* Retrieved December 24, 2008, from http://researchspace.csir.co.za/dspace/bitstream/10204/1060/1/Morris_2006_D.pdf

Feinson, S. (2003, June). National innovation systems overview and country cases. Knowledge flows and knowledge collectives: Understanding the role of science and technology policies in development. In Bozeman, B. (Eds.), *Synthesis report on the findings of a project for the global inclusion program of the Rockefeller Foundation.*

Fink, D. (2010). Road safety 2.0: Insights and implications for government. In *Proceedings of the 23rd Bled eConference*, Bled, Slovenia.

Finnegan, R. (1988). *Literacy and orality: Studies in the technology of communication.* Oxford, UK: Basil Blackwell.

Food and Agricultural Organization/ World Bank. (2000). *Agricultural knowledge and information systems: Strategic vision and principles.* Rome, Italy: FAO/ World Bank.

Fouche, B. (1999). *A Web-based agricultural system for South Africa. Feasibility study - Part 1.* National Department of Agriculture March 1999. Unpublished document.

Foundation, N. Z. (2009). *Digital strategy 2.0 submission.* Auckland, New Zealand: Royal New Zealand Foundation of the Blind.

Free Daily Newsletter. (2007). Is SEACOM racing past EASSy? *MyBroadband.* Retrieved September 12, 2008, from http://mybroadband.co.za/news/Telecoms/563.html

Frieden, R. (2005). Lessons from broadband development in Canada, Japan, Korea and the United States. *Telecommunications Policy, 29*, 595–613. doi:10.1016/j.telpol.2005.06.002

Fu, J. R., Farn, C. K., & Chao, W. P. (2006). Acceptance of electronic tax filing: A study of taxpayers' intention. *Information & Management, 43*, 109–126. doi:10.1016/j.im.2005.04.001

G8DOT Force. (2001). *Digital opportunities for all.* Meeting the Challenge Report of the Digital Opportunity Task Force (DOT Force) including a proposal for a Genoa Plan of Action, May 2001.

Garcia, R., & Calantone, R. (2002). A critical look at technological innovation typology and innovativeness terminology: A literature review. *Journal of Product Innovation Management, 19*, 110–132. doi:10.1016/S0737-6782(01)00132-1

Garegae, K. G. (2005). Mathematics in different cultures and societies: The case of Botswana. In Sica, G. (Ed.), *What mathematics from Africa?* Monza, Italy: Polimentrica International Scientific Publisher.

Garegae, K. G., & Moalosi, S. S. (2010). Botswana ICT policy and curriculum concerns: Does school connectivity guarantee technology integration into mathematics curriculum? In Adomi, E. E. (Ed.), *Handbook of research on information communication technology: Trends, issues and advancements* (*Vol. 1*, pp. 15–32). Hershey, PA: IGI Global. doi:10.4018/978-1-61520-847-0.ch002

Garnett, F., & Ecclesfield, N. (2008). Developing an organisational architecture of participation. *British Journal of Educational Technology, 39*(3), 468–474. doi:10.1111/j.1467-8535.2008.00839.x

Gaspereni, L., & Mclean, S. (2001). *Education for agriculture and rural development in low-income countries: Implications of the digital divide.* A paper presented at the Global Junior Challenge, Rome, Italy, December 3-4.

Geness, S. (2004). *E-government, the South African experience.* Paper presented at SADC E-government Workshop, Gaborone 14-16 April 2004.

Gerhan, D., & Mutula, S. M. (2005). Bandwidth bottlenecks at the University of Botswana: Complications for library, campus, and national development. *Library Hi Tech, 23*(1), 102–117. doi:10.1108/07378830510586748

Ghyasi, A. F., & Kushchu, I. (2004). *M-government: Cases of developing countries.* Mobile Government lab report. Retrieved from http://www.mgovernment.org/resurces/mgovlab_afgik.pdf

Gillingham, A. (n.d.). *Bulk mail takes notes and goes hi-tech.*

Gilmore, J. H., & Pine, B. J. (2000). *Markets of one: Creating customer-unique value through mass customization.* Boston, MA: Harvard Business School Press.

GITR. (2005). *Global information technology report* (2004-2005). World Economic Forum. Retrieved March 12, 2005, from www.weforum.org

GITR. (2006). *Global information technology report* (2005-2006). World Economic Forum. Retrieved January 12, 2009, from www.weforum.org

GITR. (2007). *Global information technology report* (2006-2007). World Economic Forum. Retrieved January 12, 2009, from www.weforum.org

Global facts and figures. (2008). *UN-AIDS: Report on the global AIDS epidemic 2008.* Retrieved 15 November, 2010, from http://data.unaids.org/pub/globalreport/2008/20080715_fs_global_en.pdf

Goldstein Meyer, S., Johnston, J., Duffy, J., & Rao, J. (2002). The service concept: The missing link in service design research. *Journal of Operations Management, 20*, 121–134. doi:10.1016/S0272-6963(01)00090-0

Government Gazette. (2008). *Broadband Infraco Act 2007.* Retrieved June 14, 2009, from http://llnw.creamermedia.co.za/articles/attachments/10610_broadinfraact33.pdf

Government of Canada. (2006). *Online forms and services.* Retrieved May 13, 2007, from http://canada.gc.ca/form/e-services_e.html

Government of Singapore. (2004). *E-citizen: Your gateway to all government services.* Retrieved May 14, 2007, from http://www.ecitizen.gov.sg/

Govt. of Korea, (2007). The best practice, UNI-PASS Korea customs service. *Korea e-Government Webzine, 6*. Ministry of Government Administration and Home Affairs (MOGAHA), Government of the Republic of Korea. Retrieved September 30, 2009, from http://www.idrc.ca/en/ev-140957-201-1-DO_TOPIC.html

Govt. of Korea. (2002). *e-Korea Vision 2006: The third master plan for informatization promotion* (2002-2006). Ministry of Information and Communication, Government of the Republic of Korea Govt. of Korea. (2003). *To enhance efficiency and transparency in the public procurement sector by utilizing the government electronic procurement system (GePS).* Government Procurement Experts Group, Phuket, Thailand, 15-16 August 2003, 2003/SOMIII/GPEG/009 Agenda Item:7a, Asia-Pacific Economic Cooperation (APEC).

Govt. of US. (2007). *FY 2007 report to Congress on implementation of the E-Government Act of 2002.* Office of Management and Budget, Government of the USA.

Graham, S. (2000, March). Symposium on cities and infrastructure networks: Constructing premium network spaces: Reflections on infrastructure networks and contemporary urban development. *International Journal of Urban and Regional Research, 24*(1), 183. doi:10.1111/1468-2427.00242

Granberg, A., & Stankiewicz, R. (1981). The development of generic technologies - The cognitive aspects. In Grandstrand, O., & Sigurdson, J. (Eds.), *Technological and industrial policy in China and Europe* (pp. 196–224). Lund, Sweden: Research Policy Institute.

Gray, H., & Sanzogni, L. (2004). Technology leapfrogging in Thailand: Issues for the support of ecommerce infrastructure. *Electronic Journal on Information Systems in Developing Countries, 16*(3), 1–26.

Grimes, S. (1992). Exploiting information and communication technologies for rural development. *Journal of Rural Studies, 8*(3), 269–278. doi:10.1016/0743-0167(92)90004-P

Grönlund, Å. (2002). Electronic government - Efficiency, service quality, and democracy. In Grönlund, Å. (Ed.), *Electronic government: Design, applications and management* (p. 62). Hershey, PA: Idea Group Publishing. doi:10.4018/978-1-930708-19-8.ch002

Grönroos, C. (2000). Service management: A management focus for service competition. *International Journal of Service Industry Management, 1*(1), 6–14.

Grubesic, T. H., & Murray, A. T. (2004, Spring). Waiting for broadband: Local competition and the spatial distribution of advanced telecommunication services in the United States. *Growth and Change, 35*(2), 139–165. doi:10.1111/j.0017-4815.2004.00243.x

Guha, S., Grover, V., Kettinger, W. J., & Teng, J. T. C. (1997). Business process change and organizational performance: exploring an antecendent model. *Journal of Management Information Systems, 14*(1), 119–154.

Guidicini, P. (1995). *Questionari, Interviste, Storie di vita: Come costruire gli strumenti, raccogliere le informazioni ed elaborare i dati*. Milano, Italy: Franco Angeli.

Guidicini, P. (Ed.). (1991). *Nuovo manuale della ricerca sociologica*. Milano, Italy: Franco Angeli.

Gulotta, G. (1976). *La vittima*. Milano, Italy: Giuffré.

Gunatunge, R. S., & Karunanayake, M. M. (2004). *Information and communication technologies for enhancing socio-economic development at the local level in Sri Lanka: Issues, challenges and strategies*. A research report for Sida/SAREC Research Cooperation Project on Overcoming Regional Imbalances and Poverty, 2004.

Gunawardana, N., & Wattegama, C. (2004). Sri Lanka. In *Digital Review of Asia Pacific*. GKP.

Gurstein, M. (2000). *Community informatics: Enabling communities with communication technologies*. Hershey, PA: Idea Group Publishing.

Gurstein, M. (2003). Effective use: A community informatics strategy beyond the digital divide. *First Monday, 8*(12).

Hamlyn, M. (2008, September 4). *UhuruNet broadband cable, INet-Bridge*. Retrieved July 12, 2009, from http://mybroadband.co.za/news/Telecoms/5094.html

Harrison, D. D. (1995). Community development. In Edwards, R. L. (Ed.), *Encyclopedia of social work* (19th ed., Vol. 1, pp. 555–562). Washington, DC: NASW Press.

Harriss-White, B. (2007). *Rural commercial capital: Agricultural markets in West Bengal*. New Delhi, India: Oxford University Press.

Compilation of References

Heeks, R. (1999). *Information and communication technologies, poverty and development.* Development Informatics: Working paper Series. Paper No 5, June 1995 Institute of Development Policy and Management. Retrieved from www: http://www.man.ac.uk/idpm

Heeks, R. (2006a). *Most e-government projects-for-development fail: How can risk be reduced?* Working Paper 14, IDPM, University of Manchester, UK.

Heeks, R. (2009). *The ICT4D 2.0 manifesto: Where next for ICTs and international development?* Working Paper Series for Development Informatics Group, Institute for Development Policy and Management. University of Manchester, Manchester, UK

Heeks, R., & Alemayehu, M. (2009b). *Impact assessment of ICT-for-development projects: A compendium of approaches.* Working Paper 36, IDPM, University of Manchester, UK.

Heeks, R. (2002). *E-government in Africa: Promise and practice.* Manchester, UK: Institute for Development Policy and Management University of Manchester.

Heeks, R. (2002). Information systems and developing countries: Failure, success and local improvisations. *The Information Society, 18*(2), 101–112. doi:10.1080/01972240290075039

Henriksen, H. Z., & Rukanova, B. (2008, April 23-25). *Barriers and drivers of ecustoms implementation: Never mind IT.* Paper presented at the 6th Eastern European eGovernment Days, Prague, Czech Republic.

Henriksen, H. Z., Rukanova, B., & Tan, Y.-H. (2008). Pacta Sunt Servanda but where is the agreement? The complicated case of e-customs. In Wimmer, M. A., Scholl, H. J., & Ferro, E. (Eds.), *EGOV 2008* (pp. 13–24). Berlin, Germany: Springer-Verlag.

Herselman, M., & Britton, K. (2002). Analyzing the role of ICT in bridging the digital divide amongst learners. *South African Journal of Education, 22*(4), 270–274.

Hesson, M., & Al-Ameed, H. (2007). Online security evaluation process for new e-services. *Journal of Business Process Management, 13*(2), 223–245. doi:10.1108/14637150710740473

HKBU. (2006). *HKBU's views & comment on the digital 21 strategy 2007.* Hong Kong: The Hong Kong Blind Union.

Hobday, M., & Howard, R. (2007). Upgrading the technological capabilities of foreign transnational subsidiaries in developing countries: The case of electronics in Thailand. *Research Policy, 36*(9), 1335–1356. doi:10.1016/j.respol.2007.05.004

Holmes, R. (2004). *Advancing rural women's empowerment: Information and communication technologies (ICTs) in the service of good governance, democratic practice and development for rural women in Africa.* Women's Net Resource Paper. Retrieved from http://womensnet.org.za/dimitra_conference/papers.shtml

Holmes, D. (2001). *E-gov: E-business strategies for government.* London, UK: Nicholas Brealey.

Holzer, M., & Kim, S. T. (2005). *Digital governance in municipalities worldwide: A longitudinal assessment of municipal websites across the world.* Retrieved February 15, 2007, from http://unpan1.un.org/intradoc/groups/public/documents/ASPA/UNPAN022839.pdf

Hornik, R. C. (1988). *Development communication: Information, agriculture, and nutrition in the third world.* White Plains, NY: Longman Inc.

Hsiao, F. S. T., & Hsiao, M.-Ch. W. (2003, February). Miracle growth in the twentieth century – International comparisons of East Asian development. *World Development*, 227–257. doi:10.1016/S0305-750X(02)00188-2

Iansiti, M., & Levien, R. (2004). *The keystone advantage: What the New dynamics of business ecosystems mean for strategy, innovation and sustainability*. Boston, MA: Harvard Business School Press.

ICTA. (2005). *Draft ICT policy for the government*. Colombo, Sri Lanka: Information and Communication Technology Agency of Sri Lanka (ICTA).

ICTA. (2009). *Information and Communication Technology Agency of Sri Lanka*. Retrieved November 05, 2009 from http://www.icta.lk/index.php/en/icta/739-e-sri-lanka-transforming-a-nation-through-ict

IGF. (2006). *First IGF Meeting*, Athens, Greece. Retrieved December 5, 2009, from http://www.intgovforum.org/cms/index.php/athensmeeting

IGF. (2007). *Second IGF Meeting*, Rio de Janeiro, Brazil. Retrieved December 5, 2009, from http://www.intgovforum.org/cms/index.php/secondmeeting

IGF. (2008). *3rd Annual Internet Governance Forum (IGF)*, Hyderabad, India. Retrieved December 5, 2009, from http://www.intgovforum.org/cms/index.php/2008-igf-hyderabad

IGF. (2009). *Fourth Annual IGF Meeting*, in Sharm El Sheikh, Egypt. Retrieved December 5, 2009, from http://www.intgovforum.org/cms/index.php/the-meeting

including relevant aquatic species. Food and Agriculture Organization of the United Nations, 25-27 February 2008, Options for Decision Makers.

Intarakumnerd, P. (2004, April). Thailand's national innovation system in transition. *First ASIALICS International Conference on Innovation Systems and Clusters in Asia: Challenges and Regional Integration*. National Science and Technology Development Agency, Bangkok Thailand.

Interactive Policy Making Online Consultations website. (2007). *Report on interactive policy making*. Retrieved from http://ec.europa.eu/yourvoice/ipm/index_en.htm

International Telecommunication Union. (2003). *ITU report*, 2003.

Internet World Stats. (2009). *World internet users and population stats*. Miniwatts Marketing Group. Retrieved from http://internetworldstats.com/

Irani, Z., Dwivedi, Y. K., & Williams, M. D. (2008). Understanding consumer adoption of broadband: An extension of the technology acceptance model. *The Journal of the Operational Research Society*, 60, 1322–1334. doi:10.1057/jors.2008.100

IRB. (2001). *Annual report 2001*. Malaysia: Inland Revenue Board.

IRB. (2006). *Annual report 2006*. Malaysia: Inland Revenue Board.

Islam, M. A., Murelli, E., Noronha, F., & Rahman, H. (2006). Capacity development initiatives for marginal communities: A few case studies. In Rahman, H. (Ed.), *Empowering marginal communities with information networking* (pp. 318–353). Hershey, PA: Idea Group Inc. doi:10.4018/978-1-59140-699-0.ch013

Compilation of References

Ismail, R., & Yussof, I. (2003). Labour market competitiveness and foreign direct investment: The case of Malaysia, Thailand and the Philippines. *Papers in Regional Science, 82*, 389–402. doi:10.1007/s10110-003-0170-2

IST policy on the objective of ICT research for innovative Government website. (2004). Retrieved from http://cordis.europa.eu/ist/so/govt/home.html

IST-507767 – QUALEG. (2004). *Deliverable 4.1: Marketing research.*

ITAIDE. (2009). *Report on redesign of administrative processes, interoperability and standardization.* Retrieved from http://www.itaide.org

Itano, N. (August, 26, 2005). Africa's cellphone boom creates a base for low-cost banking. *The Christian Monitor* (p. 2). Johannesburg, South Africa.

Ito, M., & Okabe, D. (2005). Technosocial situations: Emergent structurings of mobile email use. In Ito, M., Okabe, D., & Matsuda, M. (Eds.), *Personal, portable, pedestrian: Mobile phones in Japanese life.* Cambridge, MA: MIT Press.

ITU. (2006a). *World telecommunication/ICT development report 2006.*

ITU. (2007b). *World information society report, beyond WSIS. Ministry of Information Technology.* (2009). Retrieved March 3, 2009, from http://www.mit.gov.in/default.aspx?id=832

Ives, B., & Mason, R. O. (1990). Can information technology revitalize your customer service? *The Academy of Management Executive, 4*(4), 52–69.

Jalava, J., & Pohjola, M. (2002). Economic growth in the new economy: Evidence from advanced economies. *Information Economics and Policy, 14*, 189–210. doi:10.1016/S0167-6245(01)00066-X

Jalava, J., & Pohjola, M. (2007). The role of electricity and ICT in economic growth: Case Finland. *Explorations in Economic History, 45*, 270–287. doi:10.1016/j.eeh.2007.11.001

Jansen, K. (1995). The macroeconomic effects of direct foreign investment: The case of Thailand. *World Development, 23*(2), 193–210. doi:10.1016/0305-750X(94)00125-I

Jarillo, J. C. (1988). On strategic networks. *Strategic Management Journal, 9*(1), 31–41. doi:10.1002/smj.4250090104

Jarvenpaa, S., Tiller, E. H., & Simons, R. (2003). Regulation and the internet: Public choice insights for business organizations. *California Management Review, 46*(1), 72–85.

Järvinen, R., & Heino, H. (2004*). Kuluttajien palvelukokemuksia vakuutus- ja pankkisektorilta [Consumer experience from insurance and banking sectors].* Helsinki, Finland: National Consumer Research Centre (English summary).

Järvinen, R., Laitamäki, J., & Lehtinen, A.-R. (2009). Managing service encounter in knowledge intensive services – Mystery shoppers in financial markets. In N. Helander, M. Hannula, I. Ilvonen, & M. Seppä (Eds.), *EBRF 2008 Conference Proceedings.*

Järvinen, R., Eriksson, P., Saastamoinen, M., & Lystimäki, M. (2001). *Vakuutukset verkossa – Vakuutusyhtiöiden tarjonta ja kuluttajien odotukset* [Insurance on the Web – The offerings of the insurance companies and the expectations of consumers]. Helsinki, Finland: National Consumer Research Centre.

Järvinen, R., Lehtinen, U., & Vuorinen, I. (2003). Options of strategic decision making in services: Tech, touch and customisation in financial services. *European Journal of Marketing*, *37*(5/6), 774–795. doi:10.1108/03090560310465143

Javary, M., & Mansell, R. (2002). Emerging internet oligopolies: A political economy analysis. In Miller, E. S., & Samuels, W. J. (Eds.), *An institutionalist approach to public utilities regulation* (pp. 162–201). East Lansing, MI: Michigan State University Press.

Jensen, R. (2007). The digital provide: Information (Technology), market performance, and welfare in the South Indian fisheries sector. *The Quarterly Journal of Economics*, *122*(3), 879–924. doi:10.1162/qjec.122.3.879

Jeyaraj, A., Rottman, J. W., & Lacity, M. C. (2004, December). *Understanding the relationship between organizational and individual adoption of IT innovations: Literature review and analysis.* Paper presented at the Diffusion Interest Group in Information Technology, Washington DC, USA.

Johnston, R. (1972). The internal structure of technology. In Halmos, P., & Albrow, M. (Eds.), *The Sociological Review Monograph 18 - The Sociaology of Sciences* (pp. 117–130). Keele, UK: J.H. Brookes Printers Limited.

Jomo, K. S. (2003). Growth and vulnerability before and after the Asian crisis: The fallacy of the universal model. In Martin, A., & Gunnarsson, C. (Eds.), *Development and structural change in Asia-Pacific: Globalising miracles or end of a model?* (pp. 171–197). London, UK: RoutledgeCurzon.

Jomo, K. S., Chung, C. Y., Folk, B. C., Ul-Haque, I., Phongpaichit, P., Simatupang, B., & Tateishi, M. (1997). *Southeast Asia's misunderstood miracle: Industrial policy and economic development in Thailand, Malaysia, and Indonesia*. Boulder, CO: Westview.

Jomo, K. S., Rasiah, R., Alavi, R., & Gopal, J. (2003). Industrial policy and the emergence of internationally competitive manufacturing firms in Malaysia. In Jomo, K. S. (Ed.), *Manufacturing competitiveness in Asia: How international competitive national firms and industries developed in East Asia* (pp. 106–172). London, UK: RoutledgeCurzon.

Jonassen, D. H. (2000). *Computers as mindtools for schools: Engaging critical thinking*. Ohio: Prentice Hall.

Junaidah, H. (2008). Learning barriers in adopting ICT among selected working women in Malaysia. *Gender in Management: An International Journal*, *23*(5), 317–336. doi:10.1108/17542410810887356

Kalakota, R., Oliva, R. A., & Donath, B. (1999). Move over, e-commerce. *Marketing Management*, *8*(3), 22–32.

Kam, W. P. (1999). Technological capability development by firms from East Asian NIEs: Possible lessons for Malaysia. In Jomo, K. S., & Felker, G. (Eds.), *Technology, competitiveness, and the state: Malaysia's industrial technology policies* (pp. 53–64). London, UK: Routledge. doi:10.4324/9780203031179.ch3

Compilation of References

Kang, K. J. (2002). A study on the status and the direction of agricultural information technology workforce development in Korea. *Journal of Korean Agricultural Education, 34*(2), 87–98.

Kekana, M., & Heeks, R. (2008). *Design-reality gap case no. 3: Computerised integration of two pension funds in Southern Africa.* Retrieved August 20, 2009, from http://www.egov4dev.org/success/case/twinpension.shtml

Keniston, K., & Kumar, D. (Eds.). (2004). *Bridging the digital divide: Experience in India.* London, UK: Sage Publications.

Khalil, T. M. (1993). Management of technology and the creation of wealth. *Industrial Engineering (American Institute of Industrial Engineers), 25*(9), 16–17.

Khalil, T. M. (2000). *Management of technology: The key to competitiveness and wealth creation.* Singapore: McGraw Hill.

Kiangi, G. E., & Tjipangandjara. (1996). Opportunities for information technology in enhancing socio-economic development of a developing country. In M. Odedra-Straub (Ed.), *global information technology and socio-economic development,* (pp. 73-81). Nashua, NH: Ivy League Publishing.

Kivistö-Rahnasto, J., Ahonen, A., & Salonen, J. (2006, May 10-12). New service concepts for selecting and evaluating insurance cover within the electronic environment. In P. Mondelo, M. Mattila, W. Karwowski, & A. Hale (Eds.), *Proceeding of the 4th International Conference on Occupational Risk Prevention (ORP),* Seville, Spain. ISBN 84-933328-9-5

Koestler, A. (1989). *The sleepwalkers.* Arkana/Penguin.

Kohpaiboon, A. (2006). Foreign direct investment and technology spillover: A cross-industry analysis of Thai manufacturing. *World Development, 34*(3), 541–556. doi:10.1016/j.worlddev.2005.08.006

Koh, W. T. H. (2006). Singapore's transition to innovation-based economic growth: Infrastructure, institutions and government's role. *R & D Management, 36*(2), 143–160. doi:10.1111/j.1467-9310.2006.00422.x

Kuhn, T. S. (1962). *The structure of scientific revolutions.* Chicago, IL: University of Chicago Press.

Kuhn, T. S., & Neurath, O. (1970). *The structure of scientific revolutions: International encyclopedia of unified science.* Chicago, IL: University of Chicago Press.

Kuiper, E. J. (2007). *Convergence by cooperation in IT – The EU's customs and fiscalis programmes.* Delft, The Netherlands: Delft University of Technology.

Kuppusamy, M., Raman, M., & Lee, G. (2009). Whose ICT investment matters to economic growth: Private or public? The Malaysian perspective. *The Electronic Journal on Information Systems in Developing Countries, 37*(7), 1–19.

Kuppusamy, M., & Shanmugam, B. (2007). Information communication technology and economic growth in Malaysia. *Review of Islamic Economics, 11*(2), 87–100.

Kwapong, O. A. (2007). Problems of policy formulation and implementation: The case of ICT use in rural women's empowerment in Ghana. *International Journal of Educational Development, 3*(2). Retrieved from http://ijedict.dec.uwi.edu/viewarticle.php?id=324&layout=html

Lai, M. L., Siti, N. S. O., & Ahamed, K. M. (2004). Towards an electronic filing system: A Malaysian survey. *eJournal of Tax Research, 5*(2), 1-11.

Lai, M. L., Siti, N. S. O., & Ahamed, K. M. (2005). Tax practitioners and the electronic filing system: An empirical analysis. *Academy of Accounting and Financial Studies Journal, 9*(1), 93–109.

Lakatos, I., & Musgrave, A. (1970). *Criticism and the growth of knowledge*. Cambridge University Press.

Lal, R. (1999). *Mission report: SDNP Bangladesh*. Retrieved from http://www.sdnbd.org/mission_report.htm

Lallana, E. (2004). *E-government for development, m-government definitions and models*. Retrieved from http://www.egov4dev.org/mgovdefn.htm

Lall, S. (1999). Technology policy and competitiveness in Malaysia. In Jomo, K. S., & Felker, G. (Eds.), *Technology, competitiveness, and the state: Malaysia's industrial technology policies* (pp. 148–179). London, UK: Routledge. doi:10.4324/9780203031179.ch6

Lambrinoudakisa, C., Gritzalisa, S., Dridib, F., & Pernul, G. (2003). Security requirements for e-government services: A methodological approach for developing a common PKI-based security policy. *Computer Communications, 26*, 1873–1883. doi:10.1016/S0140-3664(03)00082-3

Lana, M. (2004). *Il testo nel computer*. Torino, Italy: Bollati Boringhieri.

Laumann, E. O. (1966). *Prestige and association in an urban community*. Indianapolis, IN: Bobbs-Merrill.

Lauriat, S. M. (2007). *AJAX- Advanced Ajax: Architecture and best practices* (1st ed.). Upper Saddle River, NJ: Prentice Hall PTR.

Lave, J., & Wenger, E. (1991). *Situated learning: Legitimate peripheral participation*. Cambridge, UK: Cambridge University Press. doi:10.1017/CBO9780511815355

Lee, S. M. (2003). Korea: From the land of morning calm to ICT hotbed. *Journal of the Academy Management Executive (USA), 17*(2).

Lekoko, R. N., & Garegae, K. G. (2006). Intuitive mathematical knowledge as an essential aspect of contemporary adult learning: A case of women street vendors in the city of Gaborone. *Literacy & Numeracy Studies, 15*(1), 61–77.

Lenhart, A., Horrigan, J., Rainie, L., Allen, K., Boyce, A., Madden, M., & O'Grady, E. (2003). *The ever–shifting Internet population: A new look at internet access and the digital divide*. Retrieved May 11, 2003, from http://www.Pewinternet.org/

Levin, A. (2008). *E-government for development: Success and failure in e-government projects*. Retrieved August 21, 2009, from http://www.egov4dev.org/success/case/golaganang.shtm

Levy, B., & Spiller, P. T. (1994). The institutional foundations of regulatory commitment: A comparative analysis of telecommunications regulation. *Journal of Law Economics and Organization, 10*(2), 201–246.

Liefner, I., & Schiller, D. (2008). Academic capabilities in developing countries – A conceptual framework with empirical illustrations from Thailand. *Research Policy, 37*, 276–293. doi:10.1016/j.respol.2007.08.007

Compilation of References

Lisbon Strategy. (2000). *Lisbon European Council 23 and 24 March 2000 presidency conclusions.* Retrieved from http://www.europarl.europa.eu/summits/lis1_en.htm

Liu, J., Derzsi, Z., Raus, M., & Kipp, A. (2008). eGovernment project evaluation: An integrated framework. In M. A. Wimmer, H. J. Scholl, & E. Ferro (Eds.), *Proceedings of the 7th International Conference on Electronic Government* (LNCS 5184, pp. 85-97).

Lonergan, B. (1971). *Method in theology.* Toronto, ON: University of Toronto Press.

Losito, G. (1993). *L'analisi del contenuto nella ricerca sociale.* Milano, Italy: Franco Angeli.

Madu, I. A. (2009). The structure and pattern of rurality in Nigeria. *GeoJournal, 75*(2), 175–184. doi:10.1007/s10708-009-9282-9

Maglio, P., & Spohrer, J. (2008). Fundamentals of service science. *Journal of the Academy of Marketing Science, 36,* 18–20. doi:10.1007/s11747-007-0058-9

Mail and Guardian Online. (2008, August 20). DA points to service-delivery problems. *Mail and Guardian.* Retrieved August 18, 2009, from http://www.mg.co.za/

Majaro, S. (1983). Marketing insurance services: The main challenges. In Foxall, G. (Ed.), *Marketing in the service industries* (pp. 77–91). London, UK: Routledge.

Malaysian Communications and Multimedia Commission and Ministry of Energy, Water and Communications. (2006). *The national broadband plan: Enabling high speed broadband under MyICMS 886.* Cyberjaya, Malaysia: Malaysian Communications and Multimedia Commission. Retrieved from http://www.mcmc.gov.my

Marche, S., & McNiven, J. D. (2003). E-Government and e-governance: The future isn't what it used to be. *Canadian Journal of Administrative Sciences, 20*(1), 74–86. doi:10.1111/j.1936-4490.2003.tb00306.x

Marsden, P. V. (1987). Core discussion networks of Americans. *American Sociological Review, 52,* 122–131. doi:10.2307/2095397

Marzaduri, E. (2002). L'attribuzione di competenze penali al giudice di pace: Un primo passo verso un sistema penale della conciliazione? In Chiavario, M., & Marzaduri, E. (Eds.), *Giudice di pace e processo penale. Commento al D. lgs. 28 agosto 2000 n. 274 e alle successive modifiche* (pp. 17–19). Torino, Italy: UTET.

Matsepe-Casaburri, I. (2008). *Budget vote speech by minister of communications Dr. Ivy Matsepe-Casaburri.* Cape Town, South Africa: National Assembly.

Mattevi, E., Panizzo, F., & Pongiluppi, C. (2007). *I reati di competenza del giudice di pace. Il giudice di pace, Quaderni, 8.* Milano, Italy: Ipsoa.

Matthew, W. (2006). *E-file goals too ambitious.* FWC.COM. Retrieved February 11, 2009, from http://fcw.com/articles/2006/02/27/efile-goal-too-ambitious.aspx

Mawar, N., Sahay, S., Pandit, A., & Mahajan, U. (2005). The third phase of HIV pandemic: Social consequences of HIV/AIDS stigma & discrimination & future needs. *The Indian Journal of Medical Research, 122,* 471–484.

Mazza, F. A., & Caruso, R. (2006). Giudice penale di pace protagonista fra conciliazione e giurisdizione. *Diritto e Giustizia, 1,* 58–76.

Mbeki, T. (2005). *Address of the President of South Africa. Second Joint Sitting of the Third Democratic Parliament, Cape Town 11 February 2005*. Cape Town, South Africa: The Presidency.

Mbuende, K. (1986). *Namibia the broken shield: Anatomy of imperialism*. Malmo, Sweden: Liber.

Mc Clure, D. L. (2000). *Federal initiatives are evolving rapidly but they face significant challenges*. Testimony, United States General Accounting Office, GAO/T-AIMD/GGD-00-179.

McCallister, L., & Fischer, C. S. (1978). A procedure for surveying personal networks. *Sociological Methods & Research, 7*, 131–148. doi:10.1177/004912417800700202

McDermott, C. (1999). Managing radical product development in large manufacturing firms: A longitudinal study. *Journal of Operations Management, 17*, 631–644. doi:10.1016/S0272-6963(99)00018-2

McDowell, C. L., Nagel, A., Williams, S. M., & Canepa, C. (2005). Building knowledge from the practice of local communities. *Knowledge Management for Development, 1*(3), 30–40.

McGuckin, R., & Stiroh, K. (1998, Summer). Computers can accelerate productivity growth. *Issues in Science and Technology, 14*(4), 41–48.

McIntyre, J. (2005). *Adult learning and Australia's ageing population: A policy briefing paper*. Canberra, Australia: Adult Learning Australia. Retrieved June 15, 2009, from http://www.artpages.com.au/johnmac/Age_learn_report.pdf

Md Nor, K., & Pearson, J. M. (2007). The influence of trust on internet banking acceptance. *Journal of Internet Banking and Commerce, 12*(2), 2–10.

Melossi, D. (2002). *Stato, controllo sociale, devianza*. Milano, Italy: Bruno Mondatori.

Mephokee, C., & Ruengsrichaiya, K. (2005, December). *Information and communication technology (ICT) for development of small and medium-sized exporters in East Asia: Thailand*. United Nations Publication, Comisión Económica para América Latina y el Caribe (CEPAL), Project Document.

Meuter, M. L., Ostrom, A. L., Roundtree, R. I., & Bitner, M. J. (2000). Self-service technologies: Understanding customer satisfaction with technology-based service encounters. *Journal of Marketing, 64*(3), 50–64. doi:10.1509/jmkg.64.3.50.18024

Meyer, J. A. (2007). *E-governance in South Africa: Making the populace aware: An Eastern Cape perspective, communities and action*. Johannesburg, South Africa: Prato CIRN Conference.

Mezirow, J. (1991). *Transformative dimensions of adult learning*. San Francisco, CA: Jossy-Bass.

Michael, N., & Margaret, R. (2007). Creating older adults technology training policies: Lessons from community practices. *Australian Journal of Adult Learning, 47*(2), 308–324.

Migani, M., & Salerno, G. (2008). *Manuale ArcGis*. Palermo, Italy: Dario Flaccovio editore.

Mihyar, H., & Hayder, A. (2007). Online security evaluation process for new e-services. *Journal of Business Process Management, 13*(2), 223–246. doi:10.1108/14637150710740473

Compilation of References

Ministry for Food. Agriculture, Forest, and Fisheries. (2008). *The 2009 master plan for agricultural ICT education*. Retrieved from http://jinlae.com/Jinlae/area_04.php?ptype=view&code=area_04&idx=1254

Mintz, D. (2008). Government 2.0 – Fact or fiction? *Public Management, 36*(4), 21–24.

Mishra, D. C. (2007). *Sixty years of development of e-governance in India (1947-2007). Are there lessons for developing countries?* ICEGOV2007, December 10-13, Macao, ACM. 978-1-59593-822-0/07/12

Misra, H. K. (2009). Managing rural citizen interfaces in e-governance systems: A study in Indian context. *Proceedings of ACM ICE-GOV2009*, November 10-13, 2009, Bogota, Colombia, (pp. 155-162).

Misra, H. K., & Hiremath, B. N. (2009). *Livelihood perspective of rural information infrastructure and e-governance readiness in India: A case based study*. IRMA Working Paper Series 215, IRMA, Anand, India.

Misra, H. K. (2009). *Governance of rural information and communication technology: Opportunities and challenges*. New Delhi, India: Academic Foundation.

Misra, H. K., & Hiremath, B. N. (2006). Citizen-led participatory e-governance initiatives: An architectural perspective. IIM Lucknow. *Metamorphosis, 5*(2), 133–148.

Mogorovich, P., & Mussio, P. (1998). *Automazione del Sistema Informativo territoriale. Elaborazione Automatica dei Dati Geografici (Vol. 2)*. Milano, Italy: Masson.

Moore, J. F. (1996). *The death of competition: Leadership and strategy in the age of business ecosystems*. Winchester, UK: J. Wiley & Sons.

Murty, S. A. (2005). The future of rural social work. *Administration in Social Work, 6*(1), 132–144.

Mwilima, F. J. (2008). Practical reality of media freedom: An examination of the challenges facing the Namibian media. *Global Media Journal, 2*(2). Retrieved from http://sun025.sun.ac.za/portal/page/portal/Arts/Departemente1/Joernalistiek/Global%20Media%20Journal/Global%20Media%20Journal%20-%20Files/8C98544F010C4CCDE04400144F47F004

Naidoo, S. (2007, April 8). Telkom has lost its head. *Business Times*. Retrieved April 18, 2008, from http://www.mybroadband.co.za/nephp/?m=show&id=6099

Nappi, A. (2004). *La procedura penale per il giudice di pace*. Milano, Italy: Giuffrè.

NASW. (2006a). *National Association of Social Workers policy statements: 2006-2009*. Washington, DC: NASW Press.

NASW. (2006b). *Social work speaks*. Washington, DC: NASW Press.

NASW. (2006c). *Community development: The community development policy statement* (pp. 56–60). Washington, DC: National Association of Social Workers.

National Traffic Information System. (2008). *eNATIS*. Retrieved August 12, 2009, from http://www.enatis.com/

NCA. (2003). *Informatization: White paper*. Seoul, Rep. of Korea: National Computerization Agency (NCA).

NECTEC. (2003). *Thailand: Information and communication technology master plan (2002-2006)*. Bangkok, Malaysia: National Electronics and Computer Technology Center.

Nenonen, S., Salonen, J., Ahonen, A., Järvinen, R., & Kivistö-Rahnasto, J. (2007). How consumers react to electronic services in the insurance sector. In M. Hannula, M. Koiranen, M. Maula, M. Seppä, M. Suoranta, & J. Tommila (Eds.), *Proceedings of EBRF 2007*.

NESSI. (2006). *Strategic research agenda: Framing the future of the service,* Vol. 1.

Net 1 U.E.P.S presentation. (2007). *Smartcard to smartcard: Distribution of social*

Ngulube, P. (2007). The nature and accessibility of e-government in sub Saharan Africa. *International Review of Information Ethics, 7*. Retrieved November 25, 2007, from http://www.i-r-i-e.net/inhalt/007/16-ngulube.pdf

Normann, R., & Ramirez, R. (1993). From value chain to value constellation: Designing interactive strategy. *Harvard Business Review, 71*(4), 65–77.

Norris, P. (2001). *Digital divide: Civic engagement, information poverty, and the internet wordwide.* Cambridge, UK: Cambridge University Press. doi:10.1017/CBO9781139164887

NUA. (2004). *Internet surveys.* Retrieved from http://www.nua.ie/surveys/how_many_online

Nyasato, R., & Kathuri, B. (2007). High phone charges hamper region's growth, says W Bank. *The Standard.* Retrieved April 10, 2007, from http://www.eastandard.net/hm_news/news.php?articleid=1143967136

O'Connor, G., & McDermott, C. (2004). The human side of radical innovation. *Journal of Engineering and Technology Management, 21*, 11–30. doi:10.1016/j.jengtecman.2003.12.002

OASIS. (2006). *Reference model for service oriented architecture 1.0.* Retrieved from http://www.oasis-open.org/committees/tc_home.php?wg_abbrev=soa-rm

OASIS. (2009). Business process execution language v 2.0. Retrieved October 22, 2009, from http://docs.oasis-open.org/wsbpel/2.0/OS/wsbpel-v2.0-OS.html

OASIS. (2009). *Security assertion markup language* (SAML). Retrieved September 22, 2009, from http://www.oasis-open.org/committees/tc_home.php?wg_abbrev=security

OASIS. (2009). *Web services atomic transaction* (WS-AtomicTransaction). Retrieved October 22, 2009, from http://docs.oasis-open.org/ws-tx/wsat/2006/06

O'Donnell, S. (2000, October 9). Closing the digital divide. *The Irish Times,* (p. 8).

OECD. (2001a). *Cities for citizens: Improving metropolitan governance* (pp. 39–43). Paris, France: OECD Publications.

OECD. (2001b). *Citizens as partners: Information, communication and public participation in policy making* (pp. 20–22). Paris, France: OECD Publications.

OECD. (2004). *Organisation for Economic Co-operation and Development annual report*, 2004.

Office of e-Government (ORS). (2004). *E-government strategy for the Western Australian public sector.* Retrieved from http://www.egov.dpc.wa.gov.au

Office of Road Safety (ORS). (2009). *Towards zero - Road safety strategy.* Retrieved from http://ors.wa.gov.au/

Compilation of References

Office of Road Safety (ORS). (2010). *Welcome*. Retrieved from http://www.ors.wa.gov.au/Search.aspx?searchtext=welcome&searchmode=anyword

Ohanga, M. (2005). *Ministry of Economic Development*. Retrieved on June 6, 2009, from http://www.med.govt.nz/templates/Multipage DocumentPage_1085.aspx

O'Hear, S. (2006, June 20). Web's second phase puts users in control. *The Guardian, Education*. Retrieved November 21, 2009, from http://education.guardian.co.uk/elearning/story/0,1801086,00.html

Ojamo, M. (2008). *The Finnish register of visual impairment. Annual statistics 2007*. National Research and Development Centre for Welfare and Health in Finland and the Finnish Federation of the Visually Impaired.

Ong, W. J. (1982). *Orality and literacy: The technologizing of the word*. New York, NY: Routledge. doi:10.4324/9780203328064

Ozowa, V. N. (1995). Information needs of small scale farmers in Africa: The Nigerian example. *Quarterly Bulletin of the International Association of Agricultural Information Specialists, 40*(1).

Pacific Council on International Policy. (2002). *Roadmap for e-government in the developing world: 10 questions e-government leaders should ask themselves*. CA, USA: Pacific Council on International Policy.

Painter, M., & Wong, S.-F. (2007). The telecommunications regulatory regimes in Hong Kong and Singapore: When direct state intervention meets indirect policy instruments. *The Pacific Review, 20*(2), 173–195. doi:10.1080/09512740701306832

Parker, C., Scott, C., Lacey, N., & Braithwaite, J. (2004). *Regulating law*. Oxford University Press. doi:10.1093/acprof:oso/9780199264070.001.0001

Parker, E. (2000). *Closing the digital divide in rural America*. Elsevier. doi:10.1016/S0308-5961(00)00018-5

Pascual, P. J. (2003). *e-Government*. e-ASEAN Task Force, UNDP-APDIP, Malaysia.

Paul, T. J., & Kim, M. T. (2003). E-government around the world: Lessons, challenges and future directions. *Government Information Quarterly, 20*, 389–394. doi:10.1016/j.giq.2003.08.001

Pavone, M. (2005). *Le nuove competenze del Giudice di Pace*. Matelica, Italy: Halley.

PCU. (2009). *Nigeria agricultural market information service* (NAMIS). Retrieved from www.pcuagric.org

Peine, A. (2008). Technological paradigms and complex technical systems—The case of smart homes. *Research Policy, 37*(3), 508–529. doi:10.1016/j.respol.2007.11.009

Perry, S. (2008, June 8). E-governance in Africa goes backwards. *ITweb*. Johannesburg.

Petter, J., Byrnes, P., & Choi, D. (2002). *Social work speaks: Community development* (pp. 56-60). Policy statement approved by the NASW Delegate Assembly. Washington, DC: NASW Press.

Peura-Kapanen, L., & Järvinen, R. (2006). *Kuluttajien käsityksiä riskeistä, niiden hallinnasta ja sähköisestä vakuuttamisesta* [Consumer perceptions of risk, risk management and electronic insurance]. Helsinki, Finland: National Consumer Research Centre.

Peura-Kapanen, L., Nenonen, S., Järvinen, R., & Kivistö-Rahnasto, J. (2007). *Kuluttajien arkipäivän riskit ja turvallisuus. Riskeihin liittyvät käsitykset, turvallisuuden edistäminen ja suhtautuminen sähköiseen asiointiin turvallisuuskontekstissa* [Consumers' everyday risks and safety – Risk-related views, promotion of safety and attitude towards electronic transactions in safety context]. Helsinki, Finland: National Consumer Research Centre.

Piccialli, P., & Aghina, E. (Eds.). (2001). *Il procedimento penale davanti al giudice di pace. Manuale teorico-pratico per gli operatori giudiziari.* Napoli, Italy: Edizioni Giuridiche Simone.

Pistore, M., Traverso, P., Paolucci, M., & Wagner, M. (2009). From software services to a future internet of services. In Tselentis, G. (Eds.), *Towards the future internet*. IOS Press.

Planck, M. (1949). A scientific biography. In *The Oxford dictionary* (2004 ed., p. 596).

Planning Commission. (2001). *Government of India, report of The Working Group on Convergence and E-Governance for tenth five year plan* (2002-2007), (pp. 6-25). New Delhi, November.

PNC-ISAD. (2005). *Towards an inclusive information society for South Africa*. A country report to Government, November 2005.

Polak, P. (2008). *Out of poverty: What works when traditional approaches fail*. San Francisco, CA: Berrett Koehler.

Population Division of the Department of Economic and Social Affairs of the United Nations Secretariat. (n.d.). *Population prospects: The 2008 revision*. Retrieved from http://esa.un.org/unpp

Postman, N. (1992). *Technopoly: The surrender of culture to technology*. New York, NY: Knopf.

Prahalad, C. K. (2006). *The fortune at the bottom of the pyramid: Eradicating poverty through profits*. Upper Saddle River, NJ: Wharton School Publishing.

Prahalad, C. K., & Ramaswamy, V. (2000). Co-opting customer competence. *Harvard Business Review, 78*(1), 79–87.

Prahalad, C. K., & Ramaswamy, V. (2003). The new frontier of experience innovation. In Rosenberg, J., & Remy, D. (Eds.), *Securing Web services with WS-Security: Demystifying WS-Security, WS-Policy, SAML, XML Signature, and XML Encryption*. Pearson Higher Education.

Prahalad, C. K., & Ramaswamy, V. (2004). *The future of competition: Co-creating unique value with customers*. New York, NY: Harvard Business School Press.

Rahman, H. (2004). *Empowering marginal communities with interactive education systems, Commonwealth Open Learning* (COL). 3rd Pan-Commonwealth Forum on Open Learning (PCF3), Dunedin, New Zealand, July 4-8, 2004.

Rahman, H. (2006). Empowerment of marginal communities through information driven learning. In Rahman, H. (Ed.), *Empowering marginal communities with information networking* (pp. 16–43). Hershey, PA: IDEA Group Publishing. doi:10.4018/978-1-59140-699-0.ch002

Rahman, H. (2007). Role of ICT in socioeconomic development and poverty reduction. In *Data mining applications for empowering knowledge societies* (pp. 180–219). Hershey, PA: IGI Global.

Compilation of References

Rahman, H. (2008). An overview on strategic ICT implementations toward developing knowledge societies. In *Developing successful ICT strategies: Competitive advantages in a global knowledge-driven society* (pp. 1–39). Hershey, PA: Information Science Reference.

Rahman, H. (2009). Local e-government management: A wider window of e-governance. In *Handbook of research on e-government readiness for information and service exchange: Utilizing progressive information communication technologies* (pp. 295–323). Hershey, PA: Information Science Reference. doi:10.4018/978-1-60566-671-6.ch015

Rainford, S. (2006). *e-Sri Lanka: An integrated approach to e-government case study.* Bangkok, Thailand: Asia Pacific Development Information Programme (APDIP).

Raman, M., Stephenaus, R., Alam, N., & Kuppusamy, M. (2008). Information technology in Malaysia: E-service quality and uptake of internet banking. *Journal of Internet Banking and Commerce, 13*(2), 2–17.

Ramasamy, B., Chakrabarty, A., & Cheah, M. (2004). Malaysia's leap into the future: An evaluation of the multimedia super corridor. *Technovation, 24*, 871–883. doi:10.1016/S0166-4972(03)00049-X

Ramayah, T., Ramoo, V., & Ibrahim, A. (2008). Profiling online and manual tax filers: Results from an exploratory study in Penang, Malaysia. *Labuan e-Journal of Muamalat and Society, 2*, 1-18.

Rasiah, R. (2003). Foreign ownership, technology and electronics exports from Malaysia and Thailand. *Journal of Asian Economics, 14*, 785–811. doi:10.1016/j.asieco.2003.10.006

Raus, M., Flügge, B., & Boutellier, R. (2008). Innovation steps in the diffusion of e-customs solutions. In S. A. Chun, M. Janssen, & J. R. Gil-Garcia (Eds.), *ACM International Conference Proceeding Series* (Vol. 289, pp. 315-324). Montréal, Canada: Digital Government Society of North America.

Raus, M. (2009). *Value assessment of business-to-government IT innovations: A case study. 22nd Bled eConference eEnablement: Facilitating an Open, Effective and Representative eSociety.* Slovenia: Bled.

Raus, M., Flügge, B., & Boutellier, R. (2009). Electronic customs innovation: An improvement of governmental infrastructure. *Government Information Quarterly, 26*(2). doi:10.1016/j.giq.2008.11.008

Raus, M., Kipp, A., & Boutellier, R. (2008). Diffusion of e-government IT innovation: A case of failure? In Cunningham, P., & Cunningham, M. (Eds.), *Collaboration and the knowledge economy: Issues, applications, case studies.* Amsterdam, The Netherlands: IOS Press.

Remmen, A. (2003). *Images of e-government – Experiences from the digital north.* Aaolborg, Denmark: Department of Development and Planning, Aalborg University.

Republic of Botswana. (1997). *Vision 2016: Towards prosperity for all.* Gaborone, Botswana: Government Printers.

Republic of Botswana. (2007). *Maitlamo: Botswana ICT policy.* Gaborone, Botswana: Government Printers.

Resnikoff, S., Pascolini, D., Etya'ale, D., Kocur, I., Pararajasegaram, R., & Pokharel, G. P. (2004). Global data on visual impairment in the year 2002. *Bulletin of the World Health Organization, 82*, 844–851.

Riga Declaration. (2006). *Internet for all: EU ministers commit to an inclusive and barrier-free information society.* Press release of June, IP/06/769.

Rijsenbrij, D. B. B. (1997). *The design, development and deployment of ICT systems in the 21st century.* Retrieved from http://www.cs.vu.nl/~daan/progx/eng/contents.htm

Robinson, S. (1998). *Telecentres in Mexico: The first phase.* Paper presented to the UN-RISD Conference.

Rodwell, L. (2010). Roadside safety assessment. In *Proceedings of the Insurance Commission of Western Australia Road Safety Forum*, Perth, Australia.

Roger, W. (1999). *Postal service getting wired.* Retrieved May 31, 2009, from www.interactive-week.com

Rostow, W. W. (1960). *The stages of economic growth.* Cambridge, UK: Cambridge University Press.

Rubaii-Barrett, N., & Wise, L. R. (2008). Disability access and e-government: An empirical analysis of state practices. *Journal of Disability Policy Studies*, *19*(1), 52–64. doi:10.1177/1044207307311533

Rudra, A. (1984). Local power and farm level decision making. In Desai, R., & Rudra, A. (Eds.), *Agrarian power and agricultural productivity in South Asia.* New Delhi, India: Oxford University Press.

Rushid, M. M., Roy, B. C., Asaduzzaman, M., & Alam, M. M. (2007). Study of the dairy cattle management systems at farmer's level in Jessore District of Bangladesh. *Pakistan Journal of Nutrition*, *6*(2), 155–158. doi:10.3923/pjn.2007.155.158

Rust, R. T., & Kannan, P. K. (2003). E-service: A new paradigm for business in the electronic environment. *Communications of the ACM*, *46*(6), 37–42. doi:10.1145/777313.777336

Rust, R. T., & Lemon, K. N. (2001). E-service and the consumer. *International Journal of Electronic Commerce*, *5*(3), 85–101.

Sachs, J. (2005). *The end of poverty: Economic possibilities of our time.* New York, NY: Penguin Books. doi:10.1111/j.1600-0579.2007.00476.x

SADC E-readiness Task Force. (2002). *SADC e-readiness review and strategy.* Johannesburg, South Africa: SADC.

Saelee, K. (2002). *Sustainable use of biological resources: Indigenous peoples' contributions to COP-8 of the CBD,* (pp. 227-243).

Salonen, J., & Ahonen, A. (2007). *eInsurance project website.* Retrieved from http://www.einsurance.fi

Saponaro, A. (2004). *Vittimologia.* Milano, Italy: Giuffrè.

Sarkar, S. (1979). *Marketing of foodgrains and patterns of exploitation.* Department of Economics, Occasional Paper No.1, Visva Bharti, Santiniketan, WB, India.

Saunders, R. J., Warford, J. J., & Wellenius, B. (1994). *Telecommunications and economic development* (2nd ed.). Baltimore, MD: Published for the World Bank by the Johns Hopkins University Press.

Sawhney, M., Balasubramanian, S., & Krishnan, V. V. (2003). Creating growth with services. *Sloan Management Review*, *45*(2), 34–44.

Sawhney, M., & Parikh, D. (2001). Where value lives in a networked world. *Harvard Business Review*, *79*(1), 79–86.

Scopes, P. G. (1973). *Mathematics in secondary schools: A teaching approach.* New York, NY: Cambridge University Press.

SDNP. (2001). *Project implementation plan: Sustainable development networking programme, Bangladesh, Version-D, 2001.* Retrieved from www.sdnbd.org

SDNP. (2003). *Status report of sustainable development networking programme (SDNP): Bangladesh Institute of Development Studies.* September 30, 2003. Retrieved from www.sdnbd.org

SDNP. (2004) *Sustainable development networking programme: Final assessment.* Report of an independent external assessment, February, 2004. Retrieved from www.sdnbd.org

Segar, S. (2008, June 11). eNATIS working well now. *The Witness.* Retrieved August 12, 2009, from http://www.enatis.com/Media-coverage-2008/eNaTIS-working-well-now-The-Witness-11-June-2008.html

Segrave, R. (2004). Communication technologies and knowledge building in agriculture. *Australian Journal of Adult Learning, 44*(1), 27–43.

Sen, A. (1999). *Development as freedom.* New York, NY: Alfred P. Knopf.

Sena, O., & Paul, P. (2009). Exploring the adoption of a service innovation: A study of Internet banking adopters and non-adopters. *Journal of Financial Services Marketing, 13*(4), 284–299. doi:10.1057/fsm.2008.25

Servaes, J. (Ed.). (2008). *Communication for development and social change.* New Delhi, India: Sage Publications.

Sette, R., & Vezzadini, S. (2008). Quale sostegno per quali vittime? Tavola rotonda con: Augusto Balloni, Gemma Marotta, Monica Raiteri, Raluca Simion, Emilio Viano. In A. Balloni A., & R. Bisi (Eds.), *Processi di vittimizzazione e reti di sostegno alle vittime* (pp. 89-118). Milano, Italy: Franco Angeli.

Sette, R. (2003). Sicurezza urbana e centri di victim support. In Balloni, A. (Ed.), *Il vigile di quartiere a Milano* (pp. 80–81). Milano, Italy: Franco Angeli.

Sette, R. (2008). *Controllo sociale e prevenzione. Un approccio criminologico.* Bologna, Italy: Clueb.

Shaffer, C. R., & Anundsen, K. (1993). *Creating community anywhere.* New York, NY: Tarcher/Perigree.

Shapira, P., Youtie, J., Yogeesvaran, K., & Zakiah J. (2005, May). *Knowledge economy measurement: Methods, results and insights from the Malaysian knowledge content study.* Triple Helix 5 Conference - Panel Session on New Indicators for the Knowledge Economy, Turin, Italy.

Shari, I. (2003). Economic growth and social development in Malaysia, 1971-98: Does the state still matter in an era of economic globalisation? In Andersson, M., & Gunnarsson, C. (Eds.), *Development and structural change in Asia-Pacific: globalising miracles or end of a model?* (pp. 109–124). London, UK: RoutledgeCurzon.

Sheridan, W., & Riley, T. B. (2006). *Comparing e-government and e-governance.* Retrieved December 12, 2008, from http://www.electronicgov.net/pubs/research_papers/SheridanRileyComparEgov.d

Shirky, C. (2003). Social software: A new generation of tools. *Esther Dyson's Monthly Report, 10.*

Short, J. (2008). Risks in a Web 2.0 world. *Risk Management, 55*(10), 28–31.

Sicurella, S. (2008). Processi di vittimizzazione e centri di ascolto alle vittime. In Balloni, A., & Bisi, R. (Eds.), *Processi di vittimizzazione e reti di sostegno alle vittime* (pp. 73–87). Milano, Italy: Franco Angeli.

Silcock, R. (2001). What is e-government. *Parliamentary Affairs, 54,* 88–91. doi:10.1093/pa/54.1.88

Siochrú, S. Ó. (2002*). Sustainable development networking programme, Bangladesh: Final report.* December 2002. Retrieved from www.sdnbd.org

Siochrú, S. Ó., & Girard, B. (2002). *Global media governance. A beginner's guide.* Lanham, MD: Rowman & Littlefield Publishers.

SITA. (2002). *Government to government initiatives.* Retrieved July 26, 2009, from http://www.sita.co.za

SITA. (2002b). *E-government experience in South Africa.* Retrieved May 21, 2007, from http://www.sita.co.za

Si-Young, H. (2007, June 11). Korea post utilizes cutting-edge IT. *The Korea Herald.*

Skillman, B. (1998). Fired up at the IRS. *Accounting Technology, 14,* 12–20.

Slim, H., & Thompson, P. (1993). *Listening for a change: Oral history and development.* London, UK: Panos Publications.

Smartswitch Botswna. (2007). Special report on e-banking. Smartswitch Nigeria—E-payment for all Nigerians. *Smartswitch, 12*(4500). Retrieved from http://www.smartswitch.co.bw/news/release070817 retrieved on 2009/08/07

Smith, J., Kearns, M., & Fine, A. (2005). *Power to the edges: Trends and opportunities in online civic engagement.* Retrieved from http://www.pacefunders.org/pdf/42705%20Version%201.0.pdf

Smith, S. (2005). *Ending global poverty.* New York, NY: Palgrave Macmillan.

SMS of the Day. (2008, November 24). *The Namibian.* Retrieved from http://www.namibian.com.na/smses/full-story/archive/2008/november/article/smses-for-monday-24-nov-08/

SMS of the Day. (2008, November 26). *The Namibian.* Retrieved from http://www.namibian.com.na/smses/full-story/archive/2008/november/article/smses-for-wednesday-26-nov-08/

SMS of the Day. (2009, March 16). *The Namibian.* Retrieved from http://www.namibian.com.na/smses/full-story/archive/2009/march/article/smses-for-mon-16-mar-09/

SMS of the Day. (2009, March 17). *The Namibian.* Retrieved from http://www.namibian.com.na/smses/full-story/archive/2009/march/article/smses-for-tue-17-mar-09/

SMS of the Day. (2009, March 20). *The Namibian.* Retrieved from http://www.namibian.com.na/smses/full-story/archive/2009/march/article/sms-of-fri-20-mar-09/

SMS of the Day. (2009, November 23). *The Namibian*. Retrieved from http://www.namibian.com.na/smses/full-story/archive/2009/november/article/smses-of-monday-23-november-2009/

SMS of the Day. (2010, March 17). *The Namibian*. Retrieved from http://www.namibian.com.na/smses/full-story/archive/2010/march/article/sms-of-the-day-17-march-2010/

Solow, R. M. (1957). Technical change and the aggregate production function. *The Review of Economics and Statistics, 39*(3), 312–320. doi:10.2307/1926047

Sommer, L., & Cullen, R. (2009). Participation 2.0: A case study of e-participation within the New Zealand government. In *Proceedings of the 42nd Hawaii International Conference on System Sciences*, Big Island, Hawaii (pp. 1-10).

Songan, P., Hamid, K. A., Yeo, A., Gnaniah, J., & Zen, H. (2004). Community informatics: Challenges in bridging the digital divide. In Khalid, H. M., Helander, M. G., & Yeo, A. W. (Eds.), *Work with computing systems 2004* (pp. 267–270). Kuala Lumpur, Malaysia: Damai Sciences.

Sorel, E., & Padoan, P. C. (Eds.). (2008). *The Marshall Plan: Lessons learned for the 21st century*. OECD Publishing.

Southwood, R. (2005). E-government special – Does it exist in Africa and what can it do? *Balancing Act, 93*.

Spergel, I. A. (1987). Community development. In Minahan, A. (Ed.), *Encyclopedia of social work* (18th ed., *Vol. 1*, pp. 299–308). Silver Spring, MD: NASW Press.

Steinmueller, W. E. (2001). ICTs and the possibilities for leapfrogging by developing countries. *International Labour Review, 120*(2), 193–210. doi:10.1111/j.1564-913X.2001.tb00220.x

Stella, F. (2003). *Giustizia e modernità. La protezione dell'innocente e la tutela delle vittime*. Milano, Italy: Giuffrè.

Stigler, G. J. (1961). The economics of information. *The Journal of Political Economy, 69*, 213–225. doi:10.1086/258464

Stillitoe, P. (1998). The development of indigenous knowledge: A new applied anthropology. *Current Anthropology, 49*(2), 223–253. doi:10.1086/204722

Stork, C., & Aocahmub, A. (2003). *Namibia in the information age*. (NEPRU Research Report No. 25). Windhoek, Namibia: Namibian Economic Policy Research Unit. Retrieved from http://www.nepru.org.na/index.php?id=159&no_cache=1&file=155&uid=227

Storm, S., & Naastepad, C. W. M. (2005). Strategic factors in economic development: East Asian industrialization 1950–2003. *Development and Change, 36*(6), 1059–1094. doi:10.1111/j.0012-155X.2005.00450.x

Strover, S., & Berquist, L. (1999, November 22-24). *Telecommunications infrastructure development: The evolving state and city role in the United States*. Cities in the Global Information Society Conference, Newcastle upon Tyne.

Sturges, P., Katjihingua, M., & Mchombu, K. (2005). Information in the national liberation struggle: Modelling the case of Namibia (1966-1990). *The Journal of Documentation, 61*(6), 735–750. doi:10.1108/00220410510632068

Suarez, P., Givah, P., Storey, K., & Lotsch, A. (2009). *HIV/AIDS, climate change and disaster management: Challenges for institutions in Malawi*. The World Bank Development Research Group Sustainable Rural and Urban Development Team (May 2008) WPS4634.

Suh, J., & Chen, D. H. C. (Eds.). (2007). *Korea as a knowledge economy: Evolutionary process and lessons learned*. Washington, DC: The World Bank. doi:10.1596/978-0-8213-7201-2

Swelyn, N. (2006). ICT in adult education: Defining the territory. In OECD (Ed.), *ICT and learning: Supporting out-of-school youth and adults* (pp. 13–42). Paris, France: OECD.

Tamang, N. B., & Perkins, J. M. (2005). Cattle management systems in humid subtropical areas of Western Bhutan. *Journal of Bhutan Studies*, *13*, 105–117.

Tan, C., Benbasat, I., & Cenfetelli, R. T. (2008). Building citizen trust towards e-government services: Do high quality websites matter. In *Proceedings of the 41st Hawaii International Conference on System Sciences* (p. 217).

Tandon, S. D. (2007). *Progress in community health partnerships: Research, education, and action* (pp. 11–30). The Johns Hopkins University Press.

Tapscott, D., & Williams, A. D. (2006). *Wikinomics*. London, UK: Penguin Books.

Taylor, I., Walton, P., & Young, J. (1975). *Criminologia sotto accusa*. Firenze, Italy: Guaraldi.

Taylor, R. T. (1969). *Cultural ways: A compact introduction to cultural anthropology*. Boston, MA: Allyn and Bacon, Inc.

Telkom. (2007). *Telkom corporate profile*. Pretoria, South Africa: Corporate Communications.

Tella, A. (2007). An assessment of secondary school teachers uses of ICTs: Implications for the further development of ICT's use in Nigerian secondary schools. [Disclosur]. *The Turkish Online Journal of Educational Technology*, *6*(3), lic.

Tellis, W. (1997). Introduction to case study. *Qualitative Report*, *3*(2). Retrieved from http://www.nova.edu/ssss/QR/QR3-2/tellis1.html

Tenywa, M. T., Fungo, B., Tumusiime, F., Bekunda, M., Niuitengeka, M., Nakanyike-Musisi, B., et al. (2008). *ICT in agricultural education, research, and outreach in Uganda*. Presented at World Conference on Agricultural Information and IT, Tokyo University of Agriculture, Tokyo, Japan.

Teo, H. H., Tan, B. C. Y., & Wei, K. K. (1997). Organizational transformation using electronic data interchange: The case of TradeNet in Singapore. *Journal of Management Information Systems*, *13*(4), 139–165.

The Bank of Korea. (2008). *Quarterly national accounts*. Retrieved on November, 2009 from http://www.kosis.kr/search/totalSearch2.jsp

The Bridges Network. (2001). *Spanning the digital divide: Understanding and tackling the issues*. Retrieved from www.bridges.org/spanning/report.html

The Economist Newspaper and the Economist Group. (2005). *Behind the digital divide*. Retrieved April 10, 2009, from http://www.economist.com/printedition/PrinterFriendly.cfm?Story_ID=3714058

Compilation of References

The Economist. (2000, May 27). Growth is good. *The Economist, 82.*

The Helsinki Manifesto. (2006). Retrieved from http://elivinglab.org/files/Helsinki_Manifesto_201106.pdf

The National ICT Association of Malaysia (PIKOM). (2008). *ICT strategies, societal and market touch.* Retrieved on June 24th, 2009, from http://www.witsa.org/news/2009-1/html_email_newsletter_jan09_b.html

The STAR. (2009, May 1). *Amount of Malaysian's choosing e-filing up by 30%.*

The, S. T. A. R. (2009). *It's time inland revenue board got real on e-filing.* Retrieved on June 19th, 2009, from http://thestar.com.my/news/story.asp?file=/2009/3/2/focus/3380923&sec=focus

Tödtlinga, F., Lehnera, P., & Kaufmann, A. (2009). Do different types of innovation rely on specific kinds of knowledge interactions? *Journal of Service Research, 8*(1), 37–47.

Traunmuller, R., & Lenk, K. (1996). *New public management and enabling technologies: Advanced IT tools.* London, UK: Chapman and Hall.

Trustgate Sdn, M. S. C. Bhd. (2009). *Secure a-filing.* Retrieved on June 24th, 2009, from http://www.mykad.com.my/Website/secureefiling.php

Turnaturi, G. (1991). *Associati per amore: L'etica degli affetti e delle relazioni quotidiane.* Milano, Italy: Feltrinelli.

Tyagi, S. (2006). *RESTful Web services.* Retrieved October 22, 2009, from http://java.sun.com/developer/technicalArticles/WebServices/restful/

UN. (2006). *E-procurement, a joint publication of Economic and Social Commission for Asia and the Pacific* (UNESCAP). Asian Development Bank (ADB) Institute, and Public Procurement Service of the Republic of Korea, United Nations publication.

UN. (2008). *UN e-government survey: From e-government to connected e-governance.* New York, NY: UN.

UNDESA. (2006). *E-government readiness assessment methodology.* Retrieved July 14, 2009, from http://www.unpan.org/dpepa-kmb-eg-egovranda-ready.asp

UNDP. (1991). *Human development report. United Nations Development Programme (UNDP).* Oxford University Press.

UNDP. (1998). *Human development report.* UNDP, Rosemberg & Seller.

UNDP. (2001). *Human development report: Making new technologies work for human development.* UNDP.

UNDP. (2003). *South Africa human development report (2003): The challenges of sustainable development- Unlocking people's creativity.* Pretoria, South Africa: Oxford University Press.

UNDP. (2005). *Promoting ICT for human development in Asia: Realizing the millennium development goals. Regional Human Development Report.* Elsevier.

UNDP. (2007). *E-government interoperability: Guide.* Bangkok, Thailand: UNDP.

UNESCO. (2004). *E-governance.* Retrieved June 15, 2008, from http://portal.unesco.org/ci/en/ev.php-url_id=3038&url_do=do_topic&url_sec

UNICEF. (May 2007). *Rapid assessment of cell phones for development*. Women's Net,

UNICEF. Retrieved 16 November, 2010, from http://www.unicef.org/southafrica/SAF_resources_cellphones4dev.pdf

United Nations Development Program, and UNESCO. (1976). *The experimental world literacy program: A critical assessment.* Paris, France: UNESCO Press.

United Nations Development Program. (2001). *Making technologies work for human development. Human Development Report 2001.* Washington, DC: Author.

United Nations Economic Commission for Europe. (2005). *Recommendation and guidelines on establishing a single window - Recommendation No. 33.* Geneva: UN/CEFACT.

United Nations. (2000). *Report of the high-level panel on information and communication technology.* New York, 17-20 April, 2000, United Nations.

United Nations. (2005). *Global e-government readiness report: From e-government to e-inclusion.* Retrieved November 16, 2006, from http://unpan1.un.org/intradoc/groups/public/documents/un/unpan021888.pdf

United Nations. (2005). *The millennium development goals report.* New York, NY: United Nations.

United Nations. (2008). *UN e-government survey 2008: From e-government to connected government.* Retrieved June 29, 2009, from http://unpan1.un.org/intradoc/groups/public/documents/UN/UNPAN028607.pdf

Universal Postal Union. (2003). *The role of postal services.* Bern: WSIS Summit.

Unwin, T. (2004). ICT & education in Africa: Partnership, practice & knowledge sharing. *Review of African Political Economy, 31*(99), 150–160.

van den Berg, L., van der Meer, A., van Winden, W., & Woets, P. (2006). *E-governance in European and South African cities: The cases of Barcelona, Cape Town, Eindhoven, Johannesburg, Manchester, Tampere, The Hague and Venice.* Rotterdam, The Netherlands: Ashgate.

Venafro, E., & Piemontese, C. (2004). *Ruolo e tutela della vittima in diritto penale.* Torino, Italy: Giappichelli Editore.

Venkatraman, N. (1994). IT enabled business transformation. *Sloan Management Review, 35*(2), 73–78.

Vetere, E., & David, P. R. (2005). *Victims of crime and abuse of power (Bangkok, 18-25 April 2005): Festschrift in honour of Irene Melup.* New York, NY: United Nations.

Vezzadini, S. (2006). *La vittima di reato tra negazione e riconoscimento.* Bologna, Italy: Clueb.

Vezzadini, S. (2006). Profilo geografico e crime mapping. Il contributo della criminologia ambientale allo studio del delitto. In Bisi, R. (Ed.), *Scena del crimine e profili investigativi. Quale tutela per le vittime?* (pp. 83–94). Milano, Italy: Franco Angeli.

Viano, E. (1989). *Crime and its victims: International research and public policy issues.* New York, NY: Hemisphere Publishing Corporation.

Vincenti, W. (1995). The technical shaping of technology: Real-world constraints and technical logic in Edison's electrical lighting system. *Social Studies of Science, 25*(3), 553–574. doi:10.1177/030631295025003006

Vroomen, B., Donkers, B., Verhoef, P. C., & Franses, P. H. (2005). Selecting profitable customers for complex services on the internet. *Journal of Service Research, 8*(1), 37–47. doi:10.1177/1094670505276681

W3C. (2009). *Resource description framework (RDF).* Retrieved October 22, 2009, from http://www.w3.org/RDF/

W3C. (2009). *Simple object access protocol (SOAP).* Retrieved October 22, 2009, from http://www.w3.org/TR/soap/

Wah, L. Y., & Narayanan, S. (1999). Technology utilization level and choice: The electronics and electrical sector in Penang, Malaysia. In Jomo, K. S., Felker, G., & Rasiah, R. (Eds.), *Industrial technology development in Malaysia* (pp. 107–124). London, UK: Routledge.

Walsha, G., Hennig-Thuraub, T., Sassenbergd, K., & Bornemanne, D. (2010). Does relationship quality matter in e-services? A comparison of online and offline retailing. *Journal of Retailing and Consumer Services, 17*(2), 130–142. doi:10.1016/j.jretconser.2009.11.003

Walters, D., & Lancaster, G. (1999). Value and information: concepts and issues for management. *Management Decision, 37*(8), 643–656. doi:10.1108/00251749910291613

Wankel, C. (Ed.). (2008). *Alleviating poverty through business strategy.* London, UK: Palgrave Macmillan. doi:10.1057/9780230612068

Wassenaar, A. (2000). *E-governmental value chain models-E-government from a business (modelling) perspective.*

Wasserman, S., & Faust, F. (2007). *Social network analysis: Methods and applications.* London, UK: Cambridge University Press.

Wasserman, S., & Faust, K. (1994). *Social network analysis.* Cambridge, UK: Cambridge University Press.

Watson, D. (2006). Understanding the relationship between ICT and education means exploring innovation and change. *Education and Information Technologies, 11*(3), 199–216. doi:10.1007/s10639-006-9016-2

Waverman, L. (2010). *Connectivity scorecard.* Calgary, Canada: University of Calgary.

Wee, V. (2001, June). Imperatives for the k-economy: Challenges ahead. *InfoSoc Malaysia Conference,* Penang, Malaysia.

Wegweiser GmbH Berlin. (2007). *Monitoring eHealth & Gesundheitswirtschaft 2007/2008.*

Weil, M. O., & Gamble, D. N. (1995). Community practice models. In Edwards, R. L. (Ed.), *Encyclopedia of social work* (19th ed., *Vol. 1*, pp. 577–594). Washington, DC: NASW Press.

welfare grants through smart card food coupons for destitute persons, orphans and community home based care patients.

Wellenius, B. (2003). *Sustainable telecenters: Private sector and infrastructure network.* World Bank, Note number 251, January 2003.

Wellman, B. (1979). The community question: The intimate networks of East Yorkers. *American Journal of Sociology, 84,* 1201–1231. doi:10.1086/226906

Wertham, F. (1949). *The show of violence.* New York, NY: Doubleday.

Williams, F. P., & McShane, M. D. (2002). *Devianza e criminalità*. Bologna, Italy: Il Mulino.

Wilson, E. J. III, & Wong, K. (2003). African information revolution: A balance sheet. *Telecommunications Policy, 27*, 155–177. doi:10.1016/S0308-5961(02)00097-6

Windischhofer, R., & Ahonen, A. (2004). The effect of physical distribution channels on online distribution channels in the insurance industry: An examination of electronic insurance services on the internet. In J. Chen (Ed.), *Service Systems and Service Management: Proceedings of ICSSSM'04* (Vol. 2, pp. 753-758). Beijing, China: International Academic Publishers/Beijing World Publishing Corporation.

Wong, P. (1999). *National innovation systems for rapid technological catch-up: An analytical framework and a comparative analysis of Korea, Taiwan, and Singapore*. Paper presented at the DRUID's Summer Conference, Rebild, Denmark.

World Bank. (1988). *Agricultural research and extension: An evaluation of the World Bank experience*.

World Bank. (1999). *Knowledge for development: World Development Report 1998-99*. Oxford, UK: Oxford University Press.

World Bank. (2000). *World development report 1999/2000*. Washington, DC: World Bank.

World Bank. (2008). *World Bank development indicators data base 2006*. Washington, DC: World Bank.

World Bank. (n.d.). *Namibia data*. Retrieved from http://data.worldbank.org/country/namibia

World Health Organisation. (2009). *Causes of blindness and visual impairment*. Retrieved April 14, 2009, from http://www.who.int/blindness/causes/en/

World Health Organization. (2009). *WHO, UNODC, UNAIDS technical guide for countries to set targets for universal access to HIV prevention, treatment and care for injecting drug users*. Retrieved 16 November, 2010, from http://www.unodc.org/documents/hiv-aids/idu_target_setting_guide.pdf

World Information Society Report. (2006). *Digital opportunity index 2005*. Retrieved February 13, 2007, from http://www.itu.int/osg/spu/publications/worldinformationsociety/2006/World.pf

World Summit of the Information Society. (2003). *Background note. High-level panel on women in the information society: Building a gender balanced knowledge-based economy*.

World Summit on Information Society. (2003). *Document WSIS-03/GENEVA/DOC5-E, December 2003*. Geneva, Switzerland: WSIS.

World Summit on Information Society. (2009). Retrieved February 10, 2009, from www.wsis-egypt.gov.eg

Yin, R. (2009). *Case study research: Design and methods* (4th ed.). Thousand Oak, CA: Sage Publishing.

Zakareya, E., & Zahir, I. (2005). E-government adoption: Architecture and barriers. *Business Process Management Journal, 11*(5), 589–611. doi:10.1108/14637150510619902

Compilation of References

Zambrano, R. (2003). *Mission report: SDNP Bangladesh*. 22–27 February 2003. Retrieved from www.sdnbd.org

Zekri, N. (2006, April 16). Transformation of the post organization. *Al-Ahram Newspaper.*

Zorkadis, V., & Donos, P. (2004). On biometrics-based authentication and identification from a privacy-protection perspective deriving privacy-enhancing requirements. *Information Management & Computer Security, 12*(1), 125–137. doi:10.1108/09685220410518883

About the Contributors

Hakikur Rahman, PhD, is Founder-Principal of Institute of Computer Management & Science (ICMS), and President of ICMS Foundation Bangladesh. He is currently serving as a Post-Doctoral researcher at the University of Minho, Portugal. He is an Adjunct Faculty of the Bangabandhu Sheikh Mujibur Rahman Agricultural University (BSMRAU), and a former faculty of the International University of Business Agriculture and Technology (IUBAT), Bangladesh. He served Sustainable Development Networking Foundation (SDNF) as its Executive Director (CEO) from January 2007 to December 2007, the transformed entity of the Sustainable Development Networking Programme (SDNP) in Bangladesh where he was working as the National Project Coordinator since December 1999 (1999-2006). SDNP is a global initiative of UNDP and it completed its activity in Bangladesh on December 31, 2006. Before joining SDNP he worked as the Director, Computer Division, Bangladesh Open University. He also served the South Asia Foundation Bangladesh Chapter as Secretary-Coordinator (2001-2008) and Head Examiner, Computer, Bangladesh Technical Education Board (1996-2008). Graduating from the Bangladesh University of Engineering and Technology (BUET) in 1981, he has done his Master's of Engineering from the American University of Beirut (AUB) in 1986 and completed his PhD in Computer Engineering from the Ansted University, UK in 2001.

* * *

Aki Ahonen, PhD (Econ.) is working as Business Development Manager at a leading Finnish financial service provider OP-Pohjola Group. In collaboration with Jarno, Aki was another project manager of the eInsurance project, and at the time, he was also working as a researher at the University of Tampere. Aki defended his doctoral thesis on 2007. His area of research was on service management, especially developing new customer-friendly electronic insurance services. After gaining the doctroral degree he started working at OP-Pohjola Group, specializing on developing electronic banking services. Currently he is responsible for consulting the independent banks of OP-Pohjola Group on developing their customer and sales strategies as well as the integration of banking and insurance services.

Tutaleni I. Asino is currently a Dual Title PhD candidate in Instructional Systems and in Comparative International Education at Penn State University. He has over ten years of instructional design and training experience and consulting with organization ions on integrating new media into their communication strategy. Tutaleni's work experience includes: student affairs; web design; teaching in face-to-face and online classes in information technology and instructional design at both the graduate and undergraduate level. He has conducted cross-cultural research on the use mobile devices for learning and training. His research interests include mobile learning, instructional design for mobile devices, contextually appropriate learning technologies, indigenous knowledge, and the role of culture in the development and evaluation of learning technologies. Tutaleni holds a BA in Political Science and Media Studies, a MS in Multimedia Technologies, a MA in Corporate Communication, and a MS in Instructional Systems.

Sandeep Bhaskar is currently pursuing his Doctoral studies in Economics at Temple University, Philadelphia, USA where he also teaches International Trade, International Monetary Economics, Macroeconomics, and Microeconomics. He has a graduate degree in Information Technology and a strong believe that ICT has the potential to bring the fruits of development to millions in the developing world. Having grown with the transformation of the Indian economy over the last two decades and having seen the impact of ICT on day-to-day basis, he developed unwavering interest to continue to learn what technologies can do for the third world, hence his chapter in this book.

Elena Bianchini has a degree in Political Sciences (curriculum: Social Sciences), obtained on the 20.01.2006 at the faculty of Political Sciences at the University of Bologna "Alma Mater Studiorum" (Italy). The title of her thesis in criminology was: "Conflicts and Justice of the Peace: A victimological and criminological analysis." On the 1st November 2006 she had one year contract at the University of Bologna "Alma Mater Studiorum," that consists of a research in criminology named: "Justice of the Peace, Criminal Jurisdiction and relationship between author and victim: a criminological and social-victimological analysis." On the 1st November 2007 she had resigned one year contract at the University of Bologna "Alma Mater Studiorum." Now she is enrolled for the 1st year of PhD in Sociology at the University of Bologna "Alma Mater Studiorum."

Roman Boutellier is since October 1, 2008, Vice President Human Resources and Infrastructure of ETH Zurich. He is professor and leads the Chair for Technology and Innovation Management at the Department of Management, Technology, and Economics (D-MTEC) at ETH Zurich since 2004. Since 1999 Prof. Dr. Boutellier is titular Professor at the University of St. Gallen (HSG). His works appeared in R&D Management, Harvard Business Manager, ZFO and Drug Discovery Today. Roman Boutellier has held several leading positions in the industry, e.g. he was member of the management of Leica, Heerbrugg as well as CEO and delegate of the board of directors of the SIG Holding AG, Neuhausen. He is member of the board of directors of several Swiss large-scale enterprises. The focus of his research is the management of technology driven enterprises with a specific focus on innovation.

Sharmila Pixy Ferris (PhD Penn State) is Professor in the department of Communication at the William Paterson University in New Jersey, where she recently completed a six year term as Director of the Center for Teaching Excellence. She teaches undergraduate and graduate courses in the areas of interpersonal, organizational and communication theory. Her research brings an interdisciplinary focus to computer-mediated communication, in which she has published in a variety of print and electronic journals. Previous books with IGI Global include "Virtual and Collaborative Teams: Theories, Process and Practice" (2004, with Sue Godar), "Teaching and Learning with Virtual and Collaborative Teams" (2006, with Sue Godar), and "Online Instructional Modeling" (2007, with Robert Zheng).

Dieter Fink is an Associate Professor in the School of Management at Edith Cowan University in Perth, Western Australia. Prior to joining academe he worked as a Systems Engineer for IBM and as Manager, Information Technology (IT) Consulting for Arthur Young (now Ernst & Young). He has been a visiting academic at a number of universities including Australian National University, University of Cape Town, Canterbury University, and Free University of Berlin. His primary interest is in IT Governance which includes the management of information and knowledge, as well as the adoption of IT systems.

Kgomotso Gertrude Garegae has a PhD in Mathematics Education from the University of Manitoba, Canada. She is currently with the University of Botswana in the Department of Mathematics and Science Education. The focus of her teaching, research, and publication has been on contemporary issues including equity, language, ethnomathematics, ICT in education, and also on teacher education. Dr. Garegae reviews for both national and international journals of education, particularly mathematics education. She subscribes to various associations and research groups both in and outside Africa.

Mareike Heinzen, Dipl.-Wi.-Ing., works as Research Associate at the Chair of Technology and Innovation Management at the Department of Management, Technology, and Economics (D-MTEC) at ETH Zurich and at the Swiss CAR

Group since 2008. She is PhD candidate in Management with focus on product development and innovation. Her research focuses on efficiency in the back-end of product development regarding routine innovation and continuous product improvement. Mareike Heinzen gained her MSc in Industrial Engineering at the Technical University of Karlsruhe, Germany and several years work experience with Daimler AG in Thailand, USA and Germany.

Keba Hulela is a Lecturer in the Botswana College of Agriculture, Botswana.

Raija Järvinen, PhD, has been a Professor of Insurance for four years at the University of Tampere and a Professor of Marketing for one year at Turku School of Economics, Pori unit. She is appointed to head of research in National Consumer Research Centre since 2001 (on leave 2001-2005 and 2008-2010 because of university appointments). Originally she is focused on various fields in services marketing, such as service channels, e-services and service innovations, but also retailing, safety and security management and financial investments are the topics of her interests. Her publications amount to over 90 pieces among which around 30 are scientifically refereed. She is currently member in the editorial board of one international journal.

K.P. Joo is a Doctoral student studying Adult Education and Comparative International Education in the Department of Learning and Performance Systems at the Pennsylvania State University. He is also an online Instruction Coordinator at Penn State Great Valley, School of Graduate Professional Studies. Previously, he was Instructor at the Department of Education, Korea National Open University and an online Program Coordinator at Korea Unification Education. He has published in *Journal of Adult and Continuing Education* and *Journal of Vocational Education and Training*.

Sherif H. Kamel is Dean of the School of Business and Professor of MIS at the American University in Cairo. Previously, he was Associate Dean for executive education. He was director of the Management Center (2002-2008). Prior to joining the university, he was director of the Regional IT Institute (1992-2001) and co-established and managed the training department of the Cabinet of Egypt Information and Decision Support Centre (1987-1992). In 1996, he was a co-founding member of the Internet Society of Egypt. His research and teaching interests include management of information technology, information technology transfer to developing nations, electronic business, human resources development, and decision support systems. Kamel is the author of many publications in IS and management books and journals. Kamel serves on the editorial and advisory board of a number of IS journals and is the associate editor of the Journal of Cases on Information Technology, Journal of IT for Development and the Electronic Journal of IS in Developing Countries. He served as VP for communications in the Executive Council of the Information Resources Management Association (2000-2007). He was appointed as member of the board of trustees of the Information Technology Institute since 2005 and the Sadat Academy for Management Sciences (2006-2007). He was the Chairman of the Chevening Association in Egypt (2004-2009). He is an Eisenhower Fellow (2005) and a member of the Eisenhower Fellowships Alumni Advisory Council since 2008. He serves as the co-chair of the ICT core committee of the American Chamber of Commerce in Egypt since 2008. He holds a PhD from London School of Economics and Political Science, an MBA and a BA in Business Administration from The American University in Cairo.

Jouni Kivistö-Rahnasto, Dr. Tech., is a Professor at Tampere University of Technology in the Department of Industrial Management. Currently he is also Vice Dean of the Faculty of Business and Technology. Professor Kivistö-Rahnasto is focused on risk management of human-technology systems and organizations and he has around 30 scientifically refereed publications. In addition to the risk management expertise, he has considerable experience in product development methods and processes.

Adamantios Koumpis heads the Research Programmes Division of ALTEC S.A., which he founded at 1996 (then as independent division of Unisoft S.A.). His previous job position was at the Institute of Computer Science, FORTH, at Heraklio, Crete, where he worked at the Rehabilitation Tele-Informatics and Human-Computer Interaction Group in several EC RTD projects (RACE, ACTS and TAP). He is author of research papers, technical reports and Project deliverables and has successfully lead many industrial and European research projects in the areas of E-Commerce, public sector and business enterprise re-organisation and information logistics, concerning linking of data/information repositories with knowledge management and business engineering models. Adamantios holds a PhD degree from the University of Kingston, UK and a Bachelor degree from the University of Crete, Greece.

Irene Krebs has been Graduate engineer (Diploma), Specialist Translator, Dr.-Ing., Honorary Professor; since 1989 a Research Associate at the Brandenburg University of Technology Cottbus (BTU) at the Chair for Industrial Information Technology; Honorary Professor at the University of Potsdam, Human-scientific Faculty, Institute for Business and Employment Studies; since 1989 research associate at the BTU Cottbus; 1989 – 1994 at the Chair for Automation Technology (fields of activity: teaching: automata theory, mathematical methods of simulation, SPS programming, petri networks, research: modeling and development of information systems in industry); since September 1994 at the Chair for Industrial Information Technology (fields of activity: teaching: information systems in administration, ERP systems, business process modeling, data bases, data base management systems, interfaces, research: modeling and development of information systems for both production and near-production and administrative areas, among others eGovernment, eParticipation); doctoral thesis in 2001 (topic "Production-oriented Information Systems in Administration"); since 2002 lectureship at the University of Potsdam, Institute for Business and Employment Studies/Technology: "eBusiness – Systems and Application"; in 2004 conferment of degree of Honorary Professor at the University of Potsdam; member of Association of Computer Science (GI), technical committee for computer science in administration; member of management of degree course "eBusiness"; coeditor, author and coauthor of approx. 50 publications.

Nicholas C. Maynard is a Policy Researcher at the RAND Corporation where he focuses on information technology, S&T policy, and economic development. His current projects include technology acquisition, economic development policies, and best practices for R&D management. Dr. Maynard has led research teams to develop strategic plans for technology development initiatives as well as performed several national case studies, and developed a plan for cross-border technology centers. Dr. Maynard also led a multi-year effort to benchmark the US national innovation system for European Commission, comparing the US system against its peers in Europe and the Americas. Dr. Maynard received his BA and MA from the University of Chicago in Political Science and he completed a Public Policy PhD at University of North Carolina at Chapel Hill. His dissertation research on national technology strategies was supported through a National Science Foundation grant.

Harekrishna Misra is a Professor in the area of IT & Information Systems Group at the Institute of Rural Management Anand. He is an Electronics and Communication Engineer, has Post-graduate Diploma in Business Management degree in Systems and Operations Management from XIM-Bhubaneswar and has Masters Degree in Software Systems from BITS-Pilani. He also holds a doctorate degree from Utkal University, Bhubaneswar, in the area of Information Systems Management. He has around 28 years of experience in industry and academia in the fields of IT infrastructure management, communication, and networks. His current research interests include software engineering (process modelling), e-governance, information systems management in development organisations, e-Business for rural enterprises and ICT enabled value chain in rural enterprises. His current interests include information systems modelling related to business and development processes with citizen participation. He is a life member of Institution of Engineers (India), member of IEEE, Association of Computing Machinery (ACM) and Association of Information Systems, USA. He is in the reviewers' panel of the Computing Reviews-ACM. He has widely published in national and international reputed and refereed Journals. He has also participated in technical as well as programme committees and presented papers in national and international refereed academic conferences.

Francesco Molinari holds a MA in Public Management (Siena University, 2005) and a degree in Social and Economic Disciplines (Milan "L. Bocconi" University, 1990). Independent consultant for several public and private organisations, including ALTEC SA, for which account he leaded the TELL-ME consortium. Since 1995 he has been Economic & Financial Manager at a Development Agency with 800+ associated industrial SMEs. Since 2002, he has been a Manager at local Chamber of Commerce and until now member of Massa City Mayor Administrative Staff. Since 2003, he has been a contract Professor at Pisa University, he has been advisor of the Steering Committee of the e-Government module at the Political Science Faculty. ISince 2003 he has been designer of the e-Government module at the Pisa Faculty of Political Science and more recently, the "animator" of Servizi per la Politica (www.serviziperlapolitica.it), a professional virtual community born in the year 2005 to provide services to policy makers.

Vasiliki Moumtzi is a member of the Research Programmes Division of Altec S.A. in Thessaloniki. She is a graduate Informatics and Communication Engineer from the Informatics and Communications department of Technological Educational Institute of Serres, Greece. She also worked as a researcher at the reactor of Institut fór Festkφrperforschung Forschungszentrum Jólich at Germany and at the accelerator of ISIS Rutherford Appleton Laboratory at England for the demand of her diplomacy program AMphOrEAs(Archaeometric multiphase of ornament & element analysis), approved by the European union. Vasiliki is MSc dedicated at the University of Kingston, UK.

Stephen M. Mutula is an Associate Professor in the Department of Library and Information Studies, University of Botswana where he serves as the head of department. He holds a PhD in Information Science, University of Johannesburg, South Africa. He has published extensively in international refereed journals and books. He is a first co-author of a book titled: "Web Information Management: A Cross Disciplinary Textbook" published by Chandos Publishing, London, 2007. He is also the author of "Digital Economies: SMEs and E-readiness," published in 2009 by IGI Global. He is an honorary research fellow of the University of Zululand, South. He has won several international excellence awards for his extinguished research work from various academic societies and such as the Emerald Literati Club (UK).

O.I Oladele is a Senior Lecturer in the Department of Agricultural Economics Education and Extension, Botswana College of Agriculture, University of Botswana. As a specialist in Technology Transfer and Extension Education he has worked in different countries of West Africa and South East Asia to understand socio-economic variables influencing technology transfer and their impact on livelihoods

Marta Raus, Dipl.-Ing., works as Research Associate at the Chair of Technology and Innovation Management at the Department of Management, Technology, and Economics (D-MTEC) at ETH Zurich and at SAP Research Lab Zurich since 2006. She is PhD candidate in Management with focus on Business Innovation at the University of St. Gallen (HSG). Her research focuses on diffusion of IT innovations and value assessment models in the field of e-government at European level. Marta Raus gained her MSc in Managerial and Production Sciences at ETH Zurich with emphasis on integrated product development and technology and innovation management.

Jarno Salonen, BSc (Eng.), is a Research Engineer at VTT Technical Research Centre of Finland specialized in electronic services, information security, and different identification technologies. Jarno was the project manager of the eInsurance project with the objective of developing novel, innovative electronic insurance services. He was also responsible for the security and privacy work package in the SmartTouch project, which was the largest effort on piloting Near Field Communication (NFC) technology in the EU. He has also been the primary representative of VTT in several working groups of the NFC Forum. Currently Jarno is the project manager of VTT in the Role-ID project, planning to develop an organization-oriented identity extension based on a role-centric vision.

Ladislaus M. Semali is Professor of Education at the Pennsylvania State University, in the Department of Learning and Performance Systems. Academically, he specializes in adult literacy education, comparative and international education and non-Western place-based educational epistemologies. He has published extensively and with renowned sources such as *International Review of Education, Journal of Social Anthropology,* and *Comparative Education Review.* He is author of Literacy in Multimedia America (Routledge/Falmer), Postliteracy in the Age of Democracy (Austin & Winfield), and editor of What is Indigenous Knowledge? Voices from the Academy with Joe Kincheloe (Garland).

Sandra Sicurella has a Bachelor's degree in Sociology, obtained at the faculty of Sociology at the University of Urbino "Carlo Bo" (Italy), on the 2.07.2003. Thesis in cultural anthropology: "Outside the borders. The foreigner' s role in setting–up social identities." She has M.A in applied Criminology for investigations and security (Capis), obtained at the Faculty of Political Sciences "Roberto Ruffilli" in Forlì (Italy), on the 20.09.2005. Thesis in applied criminology a: "Proximity police and centres for victims' assistance: case study of the situation in Forlì." She has finished her 3rd year of PhD in Criminology at the University "Alma Mater Studiorum" in Bologna (thesis in criminology: "Victimization and walk of life: a challenge for the institutions") and she has obtained one year contract research at the University of Bologna "Alma Mater Studiorum," Department of Sociology.

Reima Suomi is a Professor of Information Systems Science at Turku School of Economics and Business Administration, Finland since 1994. He is a docent for the universities of Turku and Oulu, Finland. Years 1992-93 he spent as a "Vollamtlicher Dozent" in the University of St. Gallen, Switzerland, where he led a research project on business process re-engineering. Currently he concentrates on topics around management of telecommunications, including issues such as management of networks, electronic and mobile commerce, virtual organizations, telework, and competitive advantage through telecommunication-based information systems. Different governance structures applied to the management of IS and are enabled by IS belong too to his research agenda, as well as application of information systems in healthcare. Reima Suomi has together over 300 publications, and has published in journals such as *Information & Management, Information Services & Use, Technology Analysis & Strategic Management, The Journal of Strategic Information Systems, Behaviour & Information Technology, Journal of Management History,* and *Information Resources Management Journal.* For the academic year 2001-2002 he was a senior researcher "varttunut tutkija" for the academy of Finland. With Paul Jackson he has published the book "Virtual Organization and workplace development with Routhledge, London.

Santhanamery Thominathan is a Lecturer at Universiti Teknologi Mara, Malaysia.

Ramayah Thurasamy has an MBA from Universiti Sains Malaysia (USM). Currently he is an Associate Professor at the School of Management in USM. He is an avid researcher, especially in the areas of technology management and adoption in business and education. His publications have appeared in *Computers in Human Behavior, Direct Marketing: An International Journal, Information Development, Journal of Project Management* (JoPM), *Management Research News* (MRN), *International Journal of Services and Operations Management* (IJSOM), *Engineering, Construction and Architectural Management* (ECAM), and *North American Journal of Psychology.* He also serves on the editorial boards and program committees of many international journals and conferences of repute. In 2006 he was awarded the "AGBA Distinguished ASEAN Scholar" for his contribution to research and publication in the ASEAN region. He was a Visiting Professor at the National Taiwan University for a month in 2007.

Hilary Wilder, EdD, is an Associate Professor in the Educational Leadership and Professional Studies department in the College of Education at William Paterson University of New Jersey in the United States. She teaches undergraduate and graduate courses in Educational Technology and also directs a M.Ed. program in Learning Technologies. Her research includes the use of online and as well as low-cost cell phone-based social networking technologies to promote writing literacies and afford effective written communication skills. She is especially interested in the use of these technologies to promote writing in disadvantaged and/or previously marginalized student populations.

Index